COOKERY ILLUSTRATED AND
HOUSEHOLD MANAGEMENT

A NURSERY BREAKFAST—Young children should have milk at every meal, fresh fruit and vegetables such as raw carrot—preferably grated—every day, and two or three eggs a week.

COOKERY
ILLUSTRATED
and
HOUSEHOLD
MANAGEMENT

Edited by
ELIZABETH CRAIG

ODHAMS PRESS LIMITED
LONG ACRE LONDON W.C.2

Copyright

FOREWORD

MANY cookery books fail in taking for granted that the housewife knows more than she does about cookery. Special care has been taken in this book to describe the recipes as clearly as possible. It has been written to appeal equally to the experienced and inexperienced housewife, and even a novice in cookery should be able to follow the recipes without any difficulty.

All directions are given in the order in which they are to be carried out, and the time required for cooking each dish is clearly indicated. The number of persons for whom the dish is designed is shown at the beginning of the recipes, and the quantities can be increased or decreased proportionately for larger or smaller families. Remember that although a list of household utensils has been given with each recipe in order to simplify the preparation of food, the dishes can sometimes be prepared without many of them. On the other hand, cooking in a kitchen with up-to-date equipment usually takes less time than when makeshifts are used.

I am glad to be able to present to housewives not only a large number of modern recipes, but also a large number of old favourites, which I have often been asked for and which I have found very few books carry. There is one thing husbands won't be able to say any more if their wives use this cookery book, and that is that they can't get the dishes mother used to make.

ELIZABETH CRAIG

CONTENTS

ILLUSTRATIONS

PLATES IN FULL COLOUR

PLATES IN BLACK AND WHITE

TECHNIQUE OF COOKING

TO be a successful cook, one must practise methods. A good cook serves meals punctually. This means, first of all, that she has to rise early so as to get forward with her general household work. *For it is impossible to cook well and do other household work at the same time.* Then she should learn to assemble her ingredients and utensils before starting to prepare food. For example, if she has partly mixed a cake before assembling all the ingredients, she may find that while she is, say, stoning raisins or blanching almonds, the ingredients already mixed are spoiling.

Before making a cake, prepare the tin. Before mixing a steamed pudding, grease the basin, and have water almost boiling in the saucepan. Before baking anything, have the oven at the required temperature. Before making a jam sandwich or a Swiss roll, have a cloth sprinkled with castor sugar lying smoothly on your table or pastry board, to take the sandwich or roll when turned out. If you require eggs, have both basin and beater handy.

In a word, *be sure to assemble all the utensils and all the ingredients before you start to prepare food. If you do not, your food will take longer to prepare.*

How you cook your food depends to a certain extent on your cooker, and the number of courses required. Also on whether you work single-handed or not. If short of burners, you could make soup in advance and keep it warm. Sauces can also be prepared and kept hot in the top of a double boiler. Salads, cold sweets, and cold savouries, may be made in advance, and kept fresh either in the larder or in the refrigerator. Any garnishes you require can be prepared beforehand, such as minced parsley, butterflies or fingers of lemon, strips of pimento, slices of olives, mustard and cress, minced nuts, crushed macaroons, etc. When sandwiches are wanted, prepare plates by covering with lace paper d'oyleys, write the varieties on flags, and mix fillings required before buttering and slicing the bread.

The one point to remember in cooking, is *to prepare everything in advance that will not spoil, before starting to cook any meal.*

Methods of Cooking

Whether you cook by gas, electricity, the more old-fashioned coal range, or even on oil stoves, you have quite a large choice of different cooking methods, including boiling, steaming, baking, frying, pot-roasting, etc., while there are several modern inventions such as table cookers and toasters, pressure cookers and fuelless cookers designed to save time, labour or fuel.

Some methods of cooking render the food more indigestible than others. Some foods are made more digestible by cooking—most vegetables, for instance—while others, such as meat, are definitely more digestible in the raw state.

BOILING

Boiling and simmering are methods which can be used for the majority of foodstuffs. Boiling is probably the simplest of all fundamental cooking methods provided that, in certain cases, the heat can be regulated so as not to cook the food too violently. Most foods that are being boiled, however, require little attention, beyond an occasional glance to see that there is still sufficient water in the pan.

VEGETABLES which require cooking at all can all be boiled, and this is the most usual way of cooking them in this country. It is always important, however, not to overcook them, or they lose their colour and flavour and their vitamins are destroyed. Root vegetables should be cooked in just sufficient water to cover, and a few green vegetables, such as spinach, require only enough water to cover the bottom of the saucepan. Directions for cooking the different vegetables will be found in the vegetable section.

MEAT should be plunged in sufficient fast-boiling water to cover, and boiled fast for 5 minutes in order to harden the proteins on the outside. The heat must then be reduced, and cooking continued at simmering point only, or the meat will become tough and indigestible.

FISH, like meat, requires very slow boiling, but should not first be plunged into fast-boiling water or it may fall to pieces. Most cuts of fish are better steamed than boiled, as this is a more suitable method for delicate foods and helps them to retain their flavour. The water which has been used for cooking meat, fish and vegetables should always be kept to add to stock, soups, etc.

PUDDINGS.—Many puddings are designed for boiling, and these will be found under " Puddings, Hot."

STEAMING

You can safely steam any foods that you can boil excepting large joints of meat, which would be difficult to cook thoroughly in this way. A much longer time must be given to the process, however, but it has the advantage of conserving more of the natural flavour, and preventing waste and spoiling. Steamers of all sizes can be bought quite cheaply, and consist of a saucepan with one or more separate upper divisions which are placed over the saucepan and covered with a closely fitting lid. The upper vessel either has a well-perforated floor through which the steam rises from the boiling water below, or, if there are several upper divisions, there is a small chimney at the side allowing some of the steam to enter each container. In this way the odour of the fish in the lower division cannot ascend to taint the pudding or vegetable above.

STEWING

This is a method of cooking at a moderate temperature with a little liquid only. Meat, vegetables, fruit, cereal puddings, fish, cheese and egg dishes, etc., can be placed in a covered saucepan over a low flame, or in a casserole in a slow oven. The cooking is slow and gentle, and is therefore suitable for cheap cuts of meat, as it does not toughen. The liquid in which the food is cooked is served as part of the dish.

You can cook green vegetables in this way if you first boil them quickly for 5 minutes to conserve their colour, then pour off the water, chop them slightly, and cook slowly in their own moisture.

HAY-BOX COOKERY is a modification of stewing. The contents of the casserole are brought to the boil, cooked for a short time, then left to simmer, tightly packed away in the hay-box—a slow method, but one involving great saving of fuel. Modern adaptations of the hay-box, known as fuelless cookers, are special boxes lined with some non-conducting material such as asbestos.

BRAISING

By this method, meat and vegetables are first fried, after being dusted in flour, and are then slowly simmered in water or stock in a covered saucepan at the side of the stove, or in a casserole in the oven. It is an economical way of cooking, and makes tough meat appetising and digestible.

BAKING

Baking, as applied to meats, is the modern equivalent of roasting, by which joints, birds, etc., were hung on a spit in front of or over a clear fire, and were turned from time to time during the cooking. Baking is not quite so savoury a method, but is more convenient with our modern equipment. Meat, fish, vegetables, eggs, and a large variety of made-up dishes can be baked in the oven, and for bread, cakes and some kinds of puddings this has always been the accepted method.

All foods of the meat class should first be subjected to great heat, from about 400 to 450 degrees Fahr., to harden the protein on the outside. The oven temperature should then be reduced to between 360 and 380 degrees Fahr., so as not to scorch or toughen the joint. The secret of successful baking is to baste the joint or bird very frequently with the boiling fat which surrounds it ; the flesh will then be juicy and tender and cooked evenly throughout, and the process, which can be a very wasteful one, will then have been carried out as economically as possible.

If desired, meats can be cooked in a self-basting pan. This has a cover to prevent evaporation, scorching, and splashing the oven with fat, and it does away with the need of hand-basting. The joint, however, is not so crisp or tasty when cooked in this kind of baking tin, though if the lid is removed during the last 10 minutes or so, the appearance and flavour will be improved.

FRYING

There are two methods of frying—shallow and deep. The latter is the quicker and the more digestible, but is not suitable for large pieces of food which require thorough cooking. It is a good way of treating fillets of fish, croquettes, etc., and of heating up food which is already cooked. The pan should contain sufficient boiling fat—at a temperature of about 380 degrees Fahr.—to cover the fish, etc., which should be plunged in and fried for only a few minutes.

In SHALLOW FRYING the fat must be smoking hot—with a blue vapour rising from it—and the food must be turned over when half done so as to cook the other side. The fat should be just deep enough to come half-way up the side of the eggs, steak, sausages, etc., in the pan.

The real secret of frying is to have the fat sufficiently hot before putting in the food—smoking hot, not just beginning to bubble. If not, the fat penetrates into the food and makes it sodden and indigestible. However well done, this is a somewhat extravagant method of cooking, and one of the least digestible.

GRILLING

This is a quick process, and so is unsuitable for very thick pieces of food, just as is the case with deep frying. Steak, kidneys, ham, fish, etc., can be cooked by this method, which retains their full flavour as in old-fashioned spit roasting. They can be placed on an oiled gridiron over a clear fire, or beneath a gas or electric grill, and cooked quickly, first on one side, then on the other. Food for grilling must be of good quality or the fibres will become tough and hard.

POT-ROASTING

This is a good method for inexpensive cuts of meat, and fowls and game that are not of the best quality. Choose an iron saucepan with a tightly-fitting lid. Melt in it 2 or 3 tablespoonfuls of dripping, and fry the meat, turning it frequently, till it is brown all over. Add pepper and salt, put on the cover, and cook slowly by the side of the fire. A little stock or water can be added, if the meat is inclined to burn. Cuts will take about 1 hour to the pound.

HIGH PRESSURE AND WATERLESS COOKERY

No modern kitchen is complete without a high pressure and waterless cooker. Given a HIGH PRESSURE COOKER, a single course or a three-course meal can be prepared in record time. With most cookers, you place the food inside, adjust the lid, bring to the boil after setting the indicator, and when the whistle blows, remove the cooker from the stove, and let it stand for the same length of time it had been over the heat before removing the lid and dishing up, It is good for making soup, making split peas, lentils, haricot beans into purées, for roasting, etc. However, full directions are always supplied with each different make, so there is no need to go into details here.

As for a WATERLESS COOKER, it can be used over a single flame like a steamer. Fitted with half moon containers, it can be used for cooking a three-course meal, or its containers can be removed, and a large joint can be cooked in it. You can bake, fry, stew, and even boil in a waterless cooker, although you should not use it as a boiler, unless necessary. Use it without the base on an electric stove, and always be sure to grease the inside before placing it on any stove. However, there are full directions given with each make of cooker, and it is better to follow them each time.

Chemistry in the Kitchen

Food, properly cooked, must be appetising, digestible, and nourishing. To obtain this result, you must not only know the different methods of cookery, but the proper way to cook each foodstuff. Better still if you know what food factors compose each different foodstuff, and what mission each food factor has to perform in the human body.

PROTEINS, which include eggs, fish, meat, milk, nuts and vegetables, need slow cooking. If cooked at a high temperature they are made indigestible.

STARCHES, which include all cereals and puddings made from cereals, as well as all breads, biscuits, cakes, etc., must be thoroughly cooked in order that starch may be converted into a sweet substance like sugar. If the foods mentioned are only half-cooked, such as doughy bread or scones, or half-raw cereals, they cause indigestion.

FATS, which include butter, lard, margarine, and oil, should not be over-cooked.

To take the guesswork out of cooking, you need either a gas stove with an automatic oven heat controller, or any cooking range fitted with an oven thermometer, as well as a frying and a sugar thermometer.

TEMPERATURE TABLE FOR BAKING

Very hot oven	.	.	375–425 degrees Fahr.	
Quick oven	.	.	375	,, ,,
Fairly hot oven	.	.	350–375	,, ,,
Moderate oven	.	.	350	,, ,,
Slow oven	.	.	325–350	,, ,,
Very slow oven	.	.	250-325	,, ,,

TO SAVE TIME IN COOKING

Keep your store cupboard well-stocked, plan meals carefully, at least two days ahead, and buy ahead in quantity foodstuffs that keep in good condition. If your kitchen is conveniently arranged so that the cooker, preparation table, and the sink are close together, you will save steps and, therefore, time. You can also save time in the kitchen by preparing part of the next meal while cleaning up.

You can also plan to make full use of each cooking operation. When you require to use the oven for one cake, make something else at the same time, so that the same amount of fuel will suffice.

No kitchen is complete without two measuring cups, two sets of measuring spoons, and weights and measures. Given these, you should tack up this table of weights and measures on a level with your eyes above your kitchen table.

Tables of Weights and Measures

1 Cupful	= 1 Average teacupful.
½ Pint	= 1 Cupful and a quarter.
1 Wineglassful	= ½ Gill.

LIQUID MEASURES

15 drops	1 saltspoonful.
1 saltspoonful	¼ teaspoonful.
4 saltspoonfuls	1 teaspoonful.
4 teaspoonfuls	1 tablespoonful.
8 tablespoonfuls	1 gill.
2 gills	½ pint.
4 gills	1 pint.
2 pints	1 quart.
4 quarts	1 gallon.

SOLID MEASURES

2½ cupfuls castor sugar	1 pound.
3½ cupfuls icing sugar	1 pound.
2⅔ cupfuls brown sugar	1 pound.
2½ cupfuls fats	1 pound.
1 cupful currants	6 ounces.
1 cupful raisins	6 ounces.
⅓ cupful chopped nuts	1 ounce.
4 cupfuls flour	1 pound.
2 cupfuls rice	1 pound.

3 cupfuls (about) oatmeal . . .	1 pound.
4¼ cupfuls ground coffee . . .	1 pound.
2½ cupfuls (packed) meat . . .	1 pound.
1 cupful stale crumbs . . .	2 ounces.
1 square of chocolate . . .	1 ounce.
9 or 10 eggs	1 pound.
1 heaped tablespoonful fat . .	1 ounce.
2 heaped tablespoonfuls coffee . .	1 ounce.
2 heaped tablespoonfuls flour . .	1 ounce.
1 heaped tablespoonful castor sugar .	1 ounce.
2 heaped tablespoonfuls icing sugar .	1 ounce.
8 lumps sugar	1 ounce.

When measuring ingredients with a cup or a spoon, remember that all quantities mentioned in the recipes should be measured level. To measure any dry ingredient accurately, fill the cup or spoon and level it with a straight knife blade. When measuring ingredients which are not liquid, such as butter, flour, sugar, etc., a heaped spoonful equals 2 level or liquid spoonfuls.

PROCESSES USED IN COOKERY

In this section, detailed instructions are given for carrying out the various culinary processes referred to now and again throughout the book. The instructions are not, therefore, repeated in the recipes themselves, but reference is made in them to the appropriate pages of this chapter. The "processes" are chiefly concerned with the preparation of food, and describe methods with which every cook should be familiar.

Using a Forcing-Bag, for Éclairs, etc.

Put the paste into a forcing-bag having a large plain pipe, but do not fill the bag full. Twist the top of the bag round. Hold it firmly in the right hand, and gently squeeze out the paste in straight rows on the tin. With the left hand take a knife, and cut the paste off sharply when the desired length has been forced out. The length for éclairs is about three inches and a half.

Tammying

Lay the tammy-cloth over a dish, and pour the mixture to be tammied on to the centre of the cloth, gather up the two ends firmly, always keeping the edges of the cloth tight ; then insert two large wooden spoons, with the hollow of the bowl of each spoon towards the person holding it. Then each, at the same moment, rub the spoons backwards and forwards firmly, and keep pressing the point of one spoon against the other. As the mixture is rubbed through, stretch the cloth tight and scrape with a palette knife.

Wringing Through a Tammy-Cloth

Lay the cloth over a basin, and pour the sauce into the cloth. Gather up the ends firmly, and twist them in opposite directions until the sauce begins to run through. One person must then stop twisting and hold the cloth firmly as near the sauce as possible. The other goes on twisting, and also pulls hard all the time. Keep the cloth scraped (with a palette knife) as the sauce wrings through.

Rubbing a Purée Through a Sieve

Stand the sieve upside down over a plate or basin and put the mixture which is to be rubbed on to the sieve. Only a little should be done at a time, say a breakfastcupful. Take a wooden spoon and hold it firmly just above the bowl, then put two fingers in the bowl so that pressure can be put on it as required. Rub the mixture until it goes through, keeping it scraped off from the underside of the sieve.

NOTE.—It is a mistake to attempt to do too much at once, for a little goes through much more easily, and all is more quickly done in the end.

Turning and Shaping Vegetables

Pare the vegetables, which are to be turned, very evenly, and trim them all to an equal size for olive-shaped pieces. Then, with the fluted part of the knife, make incisions from one end of the vegetable in the direction of the other end, but keep turning the vegetable round as you go on so that the flutings go in a spiral direction.

To USE A VEGETABLE SCOOP, pare the vegetable evenly, hold it firmly in the left hand, and take the scoop in the right ; with the thumb of the left hand press the bowl of the scoop well into the vegetable. Now twist the scoop right round, and draw it out. If the scoop is not well pressed in first, the piece scooped out will not be round, but will have one flat side.

Filleting Fish

Lay the fish on a slab, with the tail towards you. Make an incision in the skin all round the outer edge by the fins, also straight down the centre of the fish along each side of the backbone. Then, with a sharp knife, commence raising the fillet from the head to the tail, keeping the knife pressed flat on the bones. Take hold of the fillet with a cloth if it is too slippery to hold firmly with the fingers.

When the first fillet is removed, turn the fish round and commence raising the other fillet from the tail. Afterwards turn the fish over and take the third fillet commencing from the head, and the fourth from the tail.

One fish yields four fillets, two from each side, and these can, of course, be cut into as many pieces as required, and according to the size of the fish.

TO FILLET A SOLE

Lay the fish on the board with the dark side upwards. With a sharp-pointed knife cut along the edge, just by the fins, and round the tail. Raise the skin at the tail with the point of the knife, then put your thumb underneath, and loosen the skin all along the edge on the right-hand side, then the left-hand side.

Now, with a cloth, take a firm hold of the skin at the tail end, and with the other hand hold the tail down firmly on the table. Then draw the skin off sharply towards the head. The other side may be done in the same way, but, as a rule, the white skin is left on.

Cut down the backbone straight from head to tail. Then with a sharp knife begin to raise the flesh off the bone, keeping the blade of the knife flat against the bone and working from the backbone to the right-hand edge. Turn the fish round, and take off the other fillet. Turn the fish over and repeat the process. A fish thus yields four fillets, and they are ready for use. If very large, they can be cut in two or even three pieces.

Boning Fish

First of all clean and wash the fish well, then lay it flat on the table. Cut through the skin along the back from tail to head. Scrape the flesh carefully from the bone on one side, keeping the blade of the knife as flat against the bone as possible. When one side is done begin on the other, without turning the fish over, passing the knife under the bone, and raising it off the fish. This leaves the flesh of the fish lying on the table. Pull out any small bones that you can feel. It is a mistake to try to bone small fish, or any that have very small bones, for it is impossible to get them all out, and it is much easier to remove them when the fish is cooked.

Boning Birds and Joints

Break the legs of the bird just above the feet, and cut the skin around where they are broken. Hold the bird firmly with one hand and with the other twist round one of the feet and pull it off. When it comes away most of the sinews of the leg should come with it. Do the other foot in the same way. Now take the legs and twist them right back so as to dislocate the joints, but be careful not to break the skin. Then treat the wings in the same way. Cut a slit in the skin at the back of the neck, and twist the neck right off quite close to the carcase.

Now begin to separate the flesh from the carcase at the neck end. Scrape the bones with a sharp knife as clean as possible, folding back the flesh as you go along. When the wing bones are reached sever them from the carcase. Then go on to the breast, but care must be taken not to cut the skin at the breast-bone. Now turn the bird over and proceed with the back. When the leg bones are reached, sever them too.

When all the flesh is off the carcase, remove the bones from the legs and wings, scraping the bones with a knife as you go along. It depends on what it is proposed to do with the bird as to what extent the leg and wing bones are removed.

IN BONING FOR A GALANTINE the wings are chopped off at the first pinion, then boned and the flesh turned inside the bird. The legs are boned entirely, the flesh of them also being turned in.

IF THE BONED BIRD IS TO BE TRUSSED INTO ITS NATURAL SHAPE AGAIN, bone only to the first joints of both legs and wings, then when the body is filled with forcemeat the trussing can be easily done.

IN BONING A SMALL BIRD FOR CUTLETS, the feet are left on, and only the bones from the thighs removed. The flesh is loosened from the drumsticks, but these bones are left in to give a support to the cutlet.

IN BONING JOINTS, the flesh is worked off the bones in the same way, the chief thing to be remembered being not to cut the flesh more than is possible. Keep the knife very close to the bone and fold the flesh back as the work proceeds, so that you can see what you are doing.

Trussing Fish

WHITING are first skinned and the tail drawn through the mouth. Pin the fish in this position by a skewer passed first through the top of the head, then through the tail and out through the lower jaw. After the fish is cooked, the skewer may be carefully removed, and the fish will retain its shape.

HADDOCKS for boiling, if large, are trussed in the shape of the letter S by passing a long stout skewer through the side of the head in the centre, then through the middle of the body, then through again just above the tail. Tie a piece of tape round the skewer just above the head, then again at the end of the skewer just below the tail of the fish. This helps to keep the fish a good shape.

If it is a small haddock, make a hole in the head through the cavities from which the eyes were removed. Draw the tail through this hole. It is hardly necessary to skewer it, but if liked a small skewer can be passed through the head and tail just to keep it firm.

Trussing Poultry and Game

This is a subject in which country readers may require copious and minute instruction, as the birds, etc., seldom come from a poulterer's and the trussing has therefore to be done in the kitchen. In London and large towns the poultry and game come from the shops ready dressed, and therefore many cooks do not make quite such a study of the subject of trussing as they should.

Apart from the fact that country houses have to rely on the cook in this respect, there are not a few people who prefer that the process be conducted in the kitchen, for the poulterer's trussing is often done to hide defects and blemishes. There is also the fact that birds are not always drawn as nicely as they might be, and the professional trussing covers this also.

DRAWING AND TRUSSING A FOWL

First pluck the fowl, then hold it by the neck in the left hand, and in the right hand hold a piece of lighted paper. Singe the fowl all over quickly, taking care to singe those parts that will be covered up in trussing, as they will not be reached in the second singeing. Be careful not to scorch the bird in any way, and previous to singeing it should be looked over to see that it is well plucked. Singeing is only resorted to for removing any down or hairs that it is impossible to pull out.

Next, lay the bird on its back on the table, cut a slit in the skin at the back of the neck, and draw the skinned neck out through it, then chop off the neck at the base, close to the body. Cut off the skin of the neck, leaving about two inches to fold under. Turn back the skin and insert the fingers through the opening to loosen the entrails as much as possible. Cut a small slit just above the vent; insert two fingers and as carefully as possible draw out the entrails. Be particularly careful not to break the gall-bladder, as this would probably spoil the bird, making it bitter. When all the entrails are removed, cut off the vent, carefully wipe out the inside of the fowl with a clean cloth, also the flap of the neck.

Do not wash the inside of the bird unless you have broken any part of the entrail when cleaning it. If, unfortunately, you have done so, then it may be washed inside, but must be thoroughly dried afterwards. Chop off the ends of the claws and the points of the pinions.

Having cleaned the fowl thoroughly, it is now ready for trussing. Have ready some suitable skewers and string, or if it is not intended to use skewers, have the trussing needle at hand. Lay the fowl on the table with the tail towards you, and twist the ends of the wings under the back. Take a skewer, long enough to go through the bird, in your right hand, and secure the pinions by passing it through the first joint of the wing on the right side. Push the leg well up close to the side, then pass the skewer through it also. Now let the skewer go through the body, and as it comes out on the other side, let it pass through the leg and pinion on the left side. Next, to fasten the legs, pass a skewer through a piece of the loose skin of the back, then through the first joints of the legs, then through a piece of the loose skin on the other side. Fold the loose skin of the neck neatly over the back, and fasten with a small skewer. Now take a lighted taper and give the bird a final singeing so that there may be no stray hairs left.

Some people like the liver and gizzard put in the wings, but nowadays it is not usual to do so, as the liver is so useful for making up into many savoury dishes. If the liver and gizzard are required with the fowl, cleanse them thoroughly and split the gizzard in half. Make a slit in the skin on the inside of the wings and put the liver in one and the gizzard in the other. This is done before twisting the pinions under the back.

THE TRUSSING NEEDLE

The trussing needle is used instead of skewers. Fold the wings under the bird as for trussing with skewers, then thread the needle with strong white twine. Take hold of both the thighs firmly with one hand and push the needle through the thighs and body ; draw the string through, and then arrange the legs straight by the sides of the fowl.

Next pass the needle under the joint of the wing nearest to where it came out of the leg, then through the thick part of the wing. Draw the flap of the neck tightly down and put a stitch through to secure it to the back. Then pass the needle through the thick part of the other wing and out through the joint. Press all the joints down neatly into their places and draw the string tight. Tie the two ends firmly together.

Fix the legs in position by passing the needle through a leg, just below the first joint (the joint where the claw joins the leg), then through the loose skin just above the vent, then through the loose skin on the other side, and through the other leg. Finally pass it through the back, bringing the needle out and then into the back again. Draw the string tight, tie the ends firmly and see that both the bows are on the same side of the fowl, as that makes it so much easier when they come to be removed.

FOWLS FOR BOILING, also PIGEONS, are trussed with needle and string.

TRUSSING A FOWL FOR BOILING

Twist the wings under the back in the same way as for roasting. Cut the legs off at the knee, and, with the finger, loosen the skin from the legs thoroughly. When the skin is quite free push the legs right back into the body, and tuck the ends quite out of sight under the skin apron, then make a slit in the flap, and pass the tail through.

Secure the wings in their place by passing a trussing needle and string through the wing and leg on one side, then out at the other. Then pass it back again through to the other side, the strings about one inch apart. Tie the two ends of the string firmly. Fasten the flap of the neck on the back with a stitch, and tie it. Livers and gizzards are never put into the wings of poultry for boiling.

Make the bird look as plump and smooth as possible, and always try to get a white fleshed fowl for boiling, as the darker coloured ones do not look nearly so nice.

TRUSSING A TURKEY

This is done in the same way as with fowls, only that the legs are broken just above the feet, and the sinews must be drawn, otherwise the legs will be uneatable. To draw the sinews, pass a hook through the leg (where it is broken), between the sinews and the bone, then pull the bird firmly with all your strength. It is best to choose a hook rather high up on the wall, as the sinews are sometimes very hard to draw, and it is easier if you can bring your weight to bear as well.

Chop off the feet, leaving about two inches and a half of the dark part of the leg on. Scald and skin the latter. Clean the liver and gizzard, cut a slit in the skin of the wings, and put them in. Twist the wings under the back of the bird, press them well in, and skewer firmly. Press the legs firmly in also, and skewer these through at the first joint, right through the body, then skewer the legs again at the last joint. Three large and strong skewers are required for these processes.

Now put the stuffing in the breast (through the neck opening), and afterwards draw the skin over on to the back, and fasten it with a small skewer. Take a long piece of stout string, and wind it across the back, from skewer to skewer, so as to keep the trussing thoroughly firm.

TRUSSING A GOOSE

Pluck, singe and draw the goose, then chop off the neck close to the body, leaving a good piece of skin to fold under. Chop off the two end pinions of the wings, so that there is only one joint left on each. Cut off the legs at the first joint. Pass a skewer through one wing, then through the body, and out through the other wing. Pass a second skewer through the end of the wing joint, through the thick part of the leg, and out on the other side in the same way.

To fasten the legs, pass a skewer through a piece of the loose flap of skin, then under the first joint of the leg, through the body, under the other leg, lastly, through the flap skin of the other side.

Cut off the end of the vent, and make a hole in the skin large enough for the tail to be passed through, and fasten with a small skewer. This latter is done after the seasoning is put in. Then string the bird to keep all secure.

TRUSSING A DUCK

Cut off the two joints of the wings, and skewer the wings, as described with geese. Next, scald and skin the feet, press the legs close into the sides, and fasten them with a skewer. Twist the feet round, and spread them out over the back. Stuff the duck, and finish off as described with geese, but only one string is required to keep the pinions secure.

TRUSSING GROUSE

Pluck the birds, and draw them, then cut off the first two joints of the wings, leaving but one joint on each. Press the legs down firmly to the sides, between the side bone and the breast. Pass a skewer through the wing, then through the thigh, through the body, and through the other thigh and wing. Pass a piece of string round each end of the skewer, cross it over the back, bring it up, and tie the two legs together with it. Tie a piece of bacon or buttered paper over the breast.

TRUSSING SNIPE

Pluck the birds as gently as possible, that the skin may not be broken, and do not draw them. Skin the neck and head, and wipe the bird well with a damp cloth. Twist the legs right round, so that the feet come close in to the body. Bring the head round, and tuck the beak under a wing. Skewer the wings, and be very careful to truss the heads all one way.

WOODCOCK are trussed in the same way, though, if preferred, the beaks may be passed through the thighs, right through the body. Lay them on slices of well-buttered toast before roasting, so that the trail may drip on to it. It is also best to tie a strip of fat bacon over the breast to keep it moist.

TRUSSING PIGEONS

Pigeons should, if possible, be plucked and drawn as soon as they are killed. Then wash them thoroughly, and wipe perfectly dry. Cut off the head and neck close to the body, and chop off the toes at the first joint.

Cross the legs by cutting a slit in the skin of one and passing the other through it. Pass a trussing needle and string through the pinions and legs, and bring it out at the other side. Pass it back again, and bring it out near where it first entered, then tie the two ends of the string firmly. Put buttered paper or bacon on the breast. This should be done with most small birds to keep them moist.

TRUSSING A PARTRIDGE

Pluck and singe the bird, and draw it. Then wipe it well, inside and out. Press the legs as much as possible in under the breast, between it and the side bones, in order to make a nice plump breast. Pass a skewer through the pinions and legs, to keep them in place, and tie the legs together, but do not cross them. Cut a square of fat bacon, large enough to cover the breast of the bird, and lay it on the breast ; take a piece of tape, pass it round the point and the head of the skewer, bring both ends up on top of the bacon, and tie them firmly to keep the bacon in place. Melt about three table-spoonfuls of dripping and pour it over. This will prevent the bird getting too dry in the cooking.

TRUSSING A HARE

Cut a small slit in one of the hind legs, just above the foot, then hang the hare on a nail by it. Cut the skin round the leg, by the foot, and begin to pull it off gently, easing it with a sharp knife where necessary. Do the other leg in the same way. As the skin comes off be careful not to pull the tail off also, as this is to be skinned, and left on. Now pull the skin gently down, until it leaves the body, down to the forelegs. Draw the forelegs out, and continue skinning until you come to the head.

Care must be used in skinning the head, and the skin may be eased off with a sharp knife. Be sure not to cut the ears off, but skin them, and leave them on the head.

When the skin is all off, take down the hare, chop off the feet, and remove the eyes. Next lay it on the table, cut a slit in the flap, paunch it, and wash the body thoroughly in luke-warm water. Dry it in a clean cloth. Now stuff it, and sew up the flap. Cut the sinews of the hind legs, and bring the forelegs towards the back, flat against the sides, and skewer them. Now bring the hind legs forward, flat against the front ones, and skewer them. Take the head, press it well back between the shoulders, and run a skewer down the mouth and into the back, to keep the head in position. Take a small skewer, curl the tail up on to the back of the hare, and fasten it there. Pass a piece of string round the end of each skewer, and tie on top of the back, so as to keep the legs well pressed to the body. Butter a piece of paper and tie it over the head of the hare, like a hood, to protect the ears from burning.

TRUSSING A RABBIT

Rabbits should be paunched as soon as they are killed. Skin them in the same way as a hare, and wash well in several waters.

If for roasting, a rabbit is trussed in the same way as a hare, only, if preferred, the ears may be cut off. For boiling, cut the first joints off the legs, then split the rabbit on the inside by the tail, so that it opens out flat. Bring the hind legs forward and the forelegs back, and bring the head round to one side. Run a skewer through the head, through a fore-leg and a hind leg (one laid over the other), through the body, and out through the two legs on the other side.

To Prepare Saddle of Mutton or Lamb

Trim the saddle from any superfluous fat, but leave in the kidneys if possible. Take off the skin if it has not already been removed. Turn in the flaps to cover the kidneys and keep them moist in cooking. Cut four pieces of tape long enough to go round the saddle, then bind it round and tie the tapes on the top. Curl the tail round on to the top of the joint and fix it with a small skewer.

If desired, the flaps can be cut off. It is more economical as they are not usually eaten when roasted. If cut off before roasting, they can be used for various dishes. The saddle has a handsomer appearance with the flaps left on.

To Roll Ribs of Beef

Take out the bones carefully, keeping the meat as whole as possible. Lay the meat out flat on a board, trim it neatly, then roll it up tightly. Pass a long skewer right through the roll. Take a piece of broad tape, and bind it round twice to keep the joint nice and firm. After the joint is cooked and the tapes removed ready for the table, the wood skewer should, if possible, be replaced by a silver one.

Larding

All that is required for this is a larding-needle and some fat bacon. The bacon should have been cured without saltpetre, as this reddens the meat, and it should be quite firm. Lay it on the table, rind downward, and cut it in slices parallel with the rind, rather more than one-eighth of an inch thick. Then cut the slices again, so as to form strips rather more than one-eighth of an inch thick both ways. These strips can be cut into pieces a little over two inches long.

This is the general size for larding fillets or sweetbreads. Larger joints, or large birds, should have rather larger lardons, while smaller ones should be used for small birds. If the bacon is not firm, lay the lardons on ice to stiffen.

Take the fillet, or whatever is to be larded, and hold it in a cloth. Put a piece of the bacon fat (a lardon) into the larding-needle, as far as it will go. With a skewer, draw a line across the top of the fillet. Insert the needle into the meat about a quarter of an inch on one side of the line and push it out again a quarter of an inch on the other side of the line. Draw the needle through, and the lardon which follows it, until there is about half an inch of bacon exposed on each side of the line, then release the lardon from the needle. Put in the next lardon half an inch further on, and so continue until right across the meat. When that line is finished, draw another, leaving an inch between the lines, and lard this in the same way, only that the lardons must be brought out just at the side of where the others go in. Keep the lines as neat and as even as possible. After all is finished, trim the ends of the lardons neatly with a pair of scissors, so that all are the same length.

It is not necessary always to use bacon fat. Sometimes strips of lean ham or tongue are used as well. If the larding is to go right through the meat, larger needles and longer strips of bacon must be used. Never have the bacon too large for the needle, as it may break or pull out before it is through the meat.

Icing a Cake

See that the cake is free from crumbs, then stand it on a reversed plate, so that the bottom edge of the cake can easily be got at. Spread it over with a thin layer of royal icing (see Index for Royal Icing), smoothing it with a broad, flat palette knife, which must be frequently dipped into boiling water. When all the cake is covered let the icing set quite hard.

Now spread it with another layer in the same way, and let this harden also. Have ready two or three icing-bags, with different designs of pipes in them, and different coloured icings. Mark the centre of the cake, and arrange the icing in any design you may like. Let the icings set quite hard before the cake is touched.

Glazing a Joint, etc.

Let the joint, bird, tongue, etc., become thoroughly cold and set, then wipe it with a cloth wrung out of hot water. Have the glaze ready, and brush it on thickly and evenly with a soft brush. Glaze can be made by boiling down stock from about 2 quarts to 1 gill, keeping it well skimmed all the time ; or a mixture of gelatine, water and meat extract can be used.

KEEPING DOWN THE HOUSEHOLD BILLS

To economise on your housekeeping bills and keep them down to a minimum, you must shop carefully and buy the foods that are most plentiful on the day you shop, during the week you shop, and according to the season. You should also plan meals beforehand very carefully, so that when you come to shop you do not buy more than is necessary. Remember, too, that it is more economical to shop daily than to give weekly orders, that large joints are often more economical than small ones, and that it is sometimes cheaper to buy whole fish such as brill or turbot, and use it for two dishes, than to buy it by the pound—but only if you have refrigeration. It is a short-sighted policy to buy perishables in quantity unless you have some means of keeping the food fresh.

HINTS ON SHOPPING

(1) Shop personally, when you can.

(2) Remember that a bargain is not a bargain when you do not need it.

(3) Buy in quantity goods that store well.

(4) Watch the newspapers and food bulletins for cheap offers.

(5) Cheap food is not necessarily inferior.

If you cannot shop personally, and have to depend on the telephone, or on giving orders at the door to tradesmen's representatives, do not make up your mind what you want until you find out what is cheap and plentiful, and in every way " a good buy," then inspect purchases as soon as they arrive, and immediately return anything that does not meet with your approval. If you shop personally, try to pay cash, and carry home your purchases with you. Particularly does this apply to perishables. If you adopt this system, you will be sure of receiving what you have chosen, and there will be no discrepancies in your bills.

To Store Food

You may buy well and economically, but if you do not store the food you buy as carefully as you should, you may lose in the end what you saved in the beginning. This means that you must have refrigeration or some method of cold storage.

HINTS ON STORING FOOD

(1) Remove all dry purchases from paper bags, and place them in their own containers. This applies to sugar, tea, coffee, cereals, etc.

(2) Remove any wrappings from fish, meat, game or poultry. Place the purchases in either your larder or refrigerator, depending upon the weather. If in the larder, place a gauze meat cover on top, unless you have a meat safe, to prevent tainting by flies.

(3) See that all milk containers and cream containers are scalded, and cooled before use, and that milk and cream are kept covered. On no account store dairy products near fish or strong smelling food.

(4) Keep greens and salads wrapped up in a cool, dark cellar or larder.

Foolproof Cookery

Even so, you will not keep your household bills low, after shopping carefully and storing carefully, unless you cook scientifically. It is quite time that every one gave up cooking by guess-work. More money is usually wasted in cooking by guessing than by careless shopping and storing, for not only is the food wasted if dishes are spoilt, or cakes are burnt, but fuel and time are wasted as well.

EQUIPMENT TO ENSURE FOOLPROOF COOKERY

(1) A gas cooker fitted with an automatic oven heat controller, as well as boiling and simmering burners, or

An electric cooker, fitted with an oven thermometer, and with high, low and medium switches, or

An oil cooker with an oven thermometer.

(2) A set of measuring spoons and a standard measuring cup.

(3) A quart and a gill measure.

(4) A set of weights and scales.
(5) Lipped bowls, and jugs.
(6) A palette knife.
(7) A mincing machine.
(8) A waterless and a high-pressure cooker.
(9) Steamers.
(10) Half-moon saucepans.

The measuring spoons enable you to measure exactly. The measuring cup, as it is marked with quarters and thirds as well as a half, will prevent any mistakes in measuring liquids or solids. Measuring by the $\frac{1}{4}$ gill is more exact than by any kind of cup. Using lipped bowls for liquids prevents any waste when pouring out. When making cakes or puddings or any other dish in which the basis is a batter, a palette knife will enable you to scrape up every particle of the mixture. With a food mincer, no scraps of meat need be wasted. If you use a waterless or a high-pressure cooker, or both, you will save not only in fuel but in the washing up of saucepans, and your food will retain vitamins often thrown down the sink with the water in which they are cooked in a saucepan. The same can be said of steamers. As for half-moon saucepans, you can cook with two on one burner or hot plate ; you can even obtain a set of four saucepans which, when put together, form a circle, and can all be kept hot on one burner or hot plate.

MAKING THE MOST OF LEFT-OVERS

WHITES OF EGGS

Use these up for making macaroons, meringues, lemon sponge, white cakes such as snow cake and angel cake, for adding to cream to make it go farther, making into fruit whips, etc.

Almond Macaroons

3 Whites of Eggs.	6 oz. Ground Almonds.
1 cupful Icing Sugar.	$\frac{1}{2}$ saltspoonful Salt.

UTENSILS—Three basins, sieve, wire whisk, wooden spoon, teaspoon, saltspoon, cup, baking sheet, waxed paper, pastry board, pastry brush, wire cake rack.

Place the ground almond in a basin, then sift the icing sugar and stir it gradually into the almonds. Beat the egg whites to a stiff froth, and gradually stir them into the sugar and almonds. Add the salt, and mix until perfectly smooth. Drop the mixture from the tip of a teaspoon on to a baking pan covered with waxed paper, taking care that the macaroons are fully an inch apart. Bake in a slow oven, about 325 degrees Fahr., from 20 to 30 minutes. When baked, turn the macaroons upside down on a pastry board and moisten the paper with a pastry brush dipped in water, then the cakes can be easily removed from the paper. Cool on a wire cake rack.

Cocoanut Macaroons

3 Whites of Eggs.   1½ cupfuls Desiccated Cocoanut.
1 cupful Icing Sugar.   A pinch of Salt.

UTENSILS—Two basins, sieve, wire whisk, cup, wooden spoon, teaspoon, baking sheet, waxed paper, pastry board, pastry brush, wire cake rack.

Sift the sugar into a basin. Beat the whites of eggs to a stiff froth. Stir in the sugar, then beat in the cocoanut and salt. Bake as in Almond Macaroons, above.

Lemon Sponge

Rind of 1 Lemon.   1½ tablespoonfuls Gelatine
Juice of 2 Lemons.   White of 1 Egg.
1 cupful Castor Sugar.   3 cupfuls boiling Water
2 tablespoonfuls cold Water.

UTENSILS—Three basins, saucepan, knife, lemon squeezer, wire whisk, strainer, wooden spoon, tablespoon, cup, jelly mould.

Place the gelatine in a basin, and cover it with cold water. Stand it aside for 10 minutes. Measure the sugar into a saucepan, then add the thinly-peeled lemon rind, and the boiling water, then stir this mixture into the gelatine. Leave till cool, then add the strained lemon juice and stiffly-frothed egg white. Leave till about to set, in a cold larder or refrigerator, then whip until spongy and white. Turn the sponge into a jelly mould rinsed out with cold water. Leave till set and chilled, then unmould into a glass dish. Serve with cream or custard.

USING UP HARD-BOILED EGGS—Tomatoes and apple are two of the ingredients for Curried Eggs, which also should be sweetened with a little brown sugar (p. 29).

USING UP COLD FISH—Mashed potato and left-over fish form the basis of fish cakes which can be made in any shape you like (p. 45).

Orange Sponge

3 Sweet Oranges.	1 breakfastcupful cold Water.
2 Bitter Oranges.	1 oz. Leaf Gelatine.
3 Whites of Eggs.	12 oz. Lump Sugar.

UTENSILS—Three basins, wooden spoon, breakfast cup, saucepan, lemon squeezer, strainer, wire whisk, mould.

Place the gelatine in cold water, then stand it near a gentle heat and stir till the gelatine is dissolved, but on no account allow the water to boil. Add the sugar and allow it to melt, then stir in the strained orange juice and leave till cool. Lastly, add the stiffly-frothed egg whites, and continue whisking with an egg-beater till well mixed, then pour into a mould rinsed out of cold water. When required, and well chilled, turn on to a glass dish. Serve with cream or custard.

MANDARIN SPONGE can be made in the same way, substituting 4 or 5 mandarin oranges for the sweet oranges

Meringue for Puddings or Tarts

| 2 Whites of Eggs. | 3 tablespoonfuls Icing Sugar. |
| A pinch of Salt. | 2 or 3 drops Vanilla Essence. |

UTENSILS—Basin, wire whisk, tablespoon, sieve.

Beat the egg whites in a large basin till very stiff, using an egg whisk for the beating, as it makes them more spongy than a rotary beater. Sift in the sugar and salt, then stir in the flavouring, and beat till glossy. Pile up on top of an open pie, or on a cooked, baked pudding. Bake in a cool oven, 275 degrees Fahr. for 10 minutes, when the meringue should be quite set and shaded with gold.

Kokernut Kisses

| 2 Whites of Eggs. | $\frac{1}{4}$ lb. Icing Sugar. |
| $\frac{1}{4}$ lb. Desiccated Cocoanut. | |

UTENSILS—Basin, wire whisk, sieve, metal spoon, baking tins.

Beat the egg whites until stiff. Gradually stir in 3 oz. of the sifted sugar. Continue to beat until the mixture holds its shape, then lightly fold in the remainder of the sugar and cocoanut. Drop the mixture from the point of a spoon in small heaps half an inch apart on baking tins. Bake till pale gold, from 45 to 50 minutes in a slow oven, starting at 275 and reducing to 250 degrees Fahr.

C.I.O.   B

Tutti Fruttis

3 Whites of Eggs.
1 cupful Castor Sugar.
2 oz. Glacé Pineapple.
2 oz. Glacé Cherries.
½ cupful blanched Almonds.

UTENSILS—Two basins, nut grinder, wire whisk, cup, knife, large spoon, teaspoon, baking tins.

Put the almonds twice through a mincer, or use ground almonds, then mix them to a paste with the sugar and beaten egg whites. Stir in half the chopped cherries, and all the chopped pineapple. Mix well, then drop the mixture in little rounds from a teaspoon on to buttered baking tins. Cut the remainder of the cherries each into three, and place one piece on top of each cake. Bake in a moderate oven, about 350 degrees Fahr. till firm and crisp.

(Another recipe for TUTTI FRUTTI KISSES will be found on page 746).

Plain White Cake

2 Whites of Eggs.
6 oz. Castor Sugar.
6 oz. Flour.
1 teaspoonful Vanilla Essence.
¼ teaspoonful Salt.
½ cupful cold Water or Milk.
2½ oz. Butter.
2 teaspoonfuls Baking Powder.

UTENSILS—Two basins, cup, teaspoon, sieve or flour sifter, wooden spoon, cake tin, knife.

Sift the flour once, then measure it. Sift the flour again, with the salt, baking powder, and sugar, four times. Turn this into a basin. Place the whites of eggs in a cup—either a standard measuring cup or a teacup. Add the butter, softened but not melted, till the cup is half full, then fill it up with cold water. Make a hollow in the centre of the flour mixture, add the liquid and the vanilla, and beat hard until very smooth. Turn into a small, ungreased cake tin, preferably one with a tube in the centre—otherwise bake in a baking tin. Place in a slow oven, 325 to 350 degrees Fahr. When the cake rises to the top of the tin, increase the heat gradually to 375 degrees, and bake till firm. Turn the tin upside down to cool, then cut the cake out.

Banana Whip

2 Whites of Eggs.
½ pint Banana Purée.
3 tablespoonfuls Castor Sugar.
1 tablespoonful Lemon Juice.
2 tablespoonfuls Fruit Syrup.
Maraschino Cherries. Pistachios.

UTENSILS—Basin, wire whisk, tablespoon, knife, lemon squeezer, pint or gill measure, sieve, sundae glasses. *Enough for 3 or 4 persons*.

Beat the egg whites till dry and stiff. Stir in the sugar, lemon juice and syrup by degrees, then mix in the banana purée, made by rubbing ripe bananas through a sieve. Pile the mixture up in sundae glasses. Decorate each with a chopped maraschino cherry and a chopped pistachio nut. Serve chilled.

Prune Fluff

3 Whites of Eggs.
½ pint stewed, stoned Prunes.

1 teaspoonful Lemon Juice.
2½ tablespoonfuls Castor Sugar.

UTENSILS—Two basins, pint or gill measure, measuring spoons, wire whisk, wooden spoon, knife, baking tin. *Enough for 2 or 3 persons*.

Drain the prunes and chop them finely, then stir in the sugar and lemon juice. Beat the egg whites to a stiff, dry froth, then fold in the prune mixture. Turn into a buttered baking dish, and bake in a slow oven, 325 to 350 degrees Fahr., from 20 to 25 minutes.

YOLKS OF EGGS

Use them for making mayonnaise, salad cream, custard, gold cake, for adding to eggs to be scrambled or to be made into an omelet, for almond paste when a yellow one is wanted, for enriching milk puddings, etc. Beat well before adding to either almond paste or puddings, and dilute them with milk before adding to a pudding.

Salad Cream

2 Yolks of Eggs.
1 cupful Salad Oil.
1 cupful boiling Water.

1 teaspoonful Salt.
2 tablespoonfuls Flour.
3 tablespoonfuls Vinegar.

A pinch of Pepper.

UTENSILS—Two basins, wooden spoon, measuring spoons, cup, saucepan, wire whisk.

Mix the flour with 3 tablespoonfuls of the oil. Turn the vinegar and water into a saucepan, bring to the boil and when boiling stir the mixture quickly and gently into the flour and oil. Season to taste with salt and pepper, return to the saucepan and boil till thick for about 5 minutes. Beat the egg yolks slightly in a basin. Pour in the boiling sauce, beating constantly, then stand till cool when add the remainder of the oil. Chill, and when required, thin with any left-over whipped cream or with stiffly-frothed egg white.

Egg Custard

3 Yolks of Eggs.	1 pint Milk.
2 oz. Castor Sugar.	A pinch of Salt.

½ teaspoonful Vanilla Essence.

UTENSILS—Saucepan or double boiler, gill or pint measure, teaspoon, wooden spoon, basin, egg-beater, jug or bowl. *Enough for 3 or 4 persons.*

Bring the milk to boiling point in a saucepan or in the top of a double boiler. Beat the egg yolks slightly in a basin. Stir in the sugar and salt, then pour a tablespoon or two of the milk into the yolks, stirring quickly. Pour the diluted yolks into the milk, stirring constantly, and keep stirring until the mixture thickens and coats the back of a spoon. Pour into a jug or shallow bowl. Flavour to taste, and stand till chilled. Serve with stewed or tinned fruit.

Gold Cake

3 Yolks of Eggs.	5 oz. Castor Sugar.
6 oz. Flour.	2 tablespoonfuls Butter.
½ cupful Milk.	2 teaspoonfuls Baking Powder.

1 teaspoonful Vanilla Essence.

UTENSILS—Two basins, wooden spoon, measuring spoons, cup, egg-beater, sieve, cake tin.

Beat the butter to a cream, stir in the sugar, beat again, then add the well-beaten yolks. Add the flavouring and a little of the milk. Beat for a moment or two, then stir in the milk alternately with the flour, sifted with the baking powder. Beat well again. Place in a well-buttered and floured cake tin, or in two layer cake tins. Bake in a moderate oven, from 350 to 375 degrees Fahr., from 35 to 45 minutes, depending on whether the cake is baked in a loaf or in a slab.

LEFT-OVER BOILED EGGS

If any boiled eggs are left over from breakfast, boil them till hard, shell them, and use them in any of the following ways :

(1) Slice or quarter the eggs, and serve them in a glass dish masked with mayonnaise and sprinkled with minced parsley or chives, as an hors d'œuvre.

(2) Halve the eggs crosswise or lengthwise, and beat the yolks to a paste with a little mayonnaise. Season to taste with tomato ketchup, Yorkshire relish, Worcester sauce, or anchovy sauce, and stuff the egg whites with the mixture. Sprinkle with minced parsley or chives, and one or two shrimps can be planted on top. Serve on a dish lined with mustard and cress, watercress, or heart of lettuce leaves, as a first course at lunch or dinner.

(3) Add the eggs, sliced, to pie fillings such as veal and ham or rabbit pie, when they are to be eaten cold.

(4) Place the eggs, end to end, down the middle of a meat or chicken galantine before rolling it up.

(5) Dip each egg in seasoned flour, and cover with either sausage meat or a savoury minced meat mixture, then roll in egg and breadcrumbs and fry in deep, smoking hot fat. Serve hot for breakfast, with halved grilled tomatoes, or cold for lunch with heart of lettuce salad, or with tomato and onion salad.

(6) Add the eggs, sliced, to fish when a fish pie is wanted.

(7) Use them sliced for garnishing brawn, tongue, any cold meat salad, or for garnishing mixed vegetable salad to be served with cold meat.

(8) Serve them masked with onion sauce, and garnished with boiled rice as a luncheon dish.

(9) Serve the eggs curried.

Curried Eggs

3 Hard-boiled Eggs.	$\frac{1}{2}$ tablespoonful Flour.
1 tablespoonful Butter.	$\frac{1}{4}$ teaspoonful Salt.
$\frac{1}{2}$ teaspoonful Curry Powder.	$\frac{3}{4}$ cupful Stock.
1 teaspoonful minced Onion.	$\frac{1}{2}$ teaspoonful Lemon Juice.

UTENSILS—Stewpan, knife, cup, measuring spoons, wooden spoon, saucepan, colander. *Enough for 2 or 3 persons.*

Cook the onion in butter till it begins to turn colour. Stir in the flour, curry powder and salt. When smoothly mixed, stir in the stock, and keep stirring until boiling. Simmer for 10 minutes. Add the quartered eggs, and when they are hot, stir in the lemon juice. Serve in a hot dish surrounded with boiled rice.

LEFT-OVER FRIED EGGS

If only lightly fried, eggs can be fried again till the yolks are set, cut into squares, placed on anchovy toast, sprinkled with grated cheese, held under the grill till the cheese is melted, and served as a savoury. Here are two other ideas :

(1) Line a fireproof baking dish with spinach, boiled, mashed, seasoned and moistened with butter. Place left-over fried eggs on top. Cover with cheese sauce, allowing 2 tablespoonfuls for each egg. Bake in the top of the oven till the sauce is pale brown.

(2) Make into sandwiches for lunch or Sunday night supper. Use bread toasted only on one side, and butter the untoasted side. Spread one slice of toast per person with minced ham moistened with mayonnaise, and mixed with a little shredded lettuce or celery. Cover with fried egg, then with the other slice of toast. Allow one per person.

LEFT-OVER BACON

If fried, bacon can be chopped and added to an omelet or to buttered green peas or French beans, or to a potato salad, to make them more satisfying. It can also be added to scrambled eggs, or used in company with the fat, heated up, for pouring over boiled or steamed dumplings, when an inexpensive dish is wanted for the nursery. It can also be added to batter for savoury pancakes, or mixed with a thick batter and cooked like fritters.

If undercooked, it can be heated again in a frying pan or under the grill and served with eggs or tomatoes for breakfast the following day. Here are some other ideas.

(1) Add the bacon to the mixture for meat pies or rissoles.

(2) Add the bacon to spaghetti or macaroni dishes.

(3) Add it to a tomato sauce to enhance its flavour, but strain the sauce before serving.

(4) Add it to cooked broad beans that are to be served with melted butter or a little white sauce.

(5) Add chopped bacon to stewed mushrooms, when a mushroom toast is wanted.

(6) Re-heat the bacon, chop it and sprinkle it over fried herrings' roes.

CORNER OF COLD BACON OR END OF HAM

(1) Mince the ham or bacon and serve it piled on toast with a grilled tomato on top.

(2) Add it chopped to omelets, rissoles, or scrambled eggs.

(3) Serve cold ham chopped and heated up in a well-seasoned and onion-flavoured white sauce, adding a few left-over cooked or tinned peas, or a little chopped pimento, or a few chopped, cooked mushrooms as a flavouring.

(4) Mince the ham and set it with a few cooked or tinned peas in a lemon jelly dissolved according to the instructions on the packet. Serve with an egg mayonnaise as a Sunday night supper dish.

(5) Chop the ham, moisten it with mayonnaise, and mix it with a third of its quantity of celery. Serve in a dish lined with lettuce leaves.

(6) Mix $\frac{3}{4}$ cupful of finely diced ham with $\frac{1}{4}$ cupful of minced celery, and use the mixture as a filling for buttered brown bread sandwiches.

SOUR MILK

Sour milk can be made into sour milk cheese, and can be used for making scones, cakes, etc.

Sour Milk Cheese

2 quarts Sour Milk. | 3 tablespoonfuls Cream.
1 teaspoonful Salt. | Pepper, to taste.

UTENSILS—Double boiler, two basins, cheese cloth or sieve, measuring spoons, large spoon, quart measure.

Turn the milk into the top part of a double boiler, and cook it over hot water till it separates into curds and whey, then strain through a double cheese cloth or a fine sieve into a dish, until all the whey is through. Place the curd in a basin, mix it well, and stir in the seasonings and cream. Cool, and serve in a pat on a dish lined with lettuce leaves.

Sour Milk Scones

$\frac{3}{4}$ cupful Sour Milk. | 1 teaspoonful Castor Sugar.
$\frac{1}{2}$ lb. Flour. | 1 teaspoonful Baking Soda.
2 oz. Butter or Margarine. | $\frac{1}{2}$ teaspoonful Salt.

UTENSILS—Sieve, basin, teaspoon, wooden spoon, cup, pastry board, rolling pin, round cutter, baking sheet.

Sieve the dry ingredients into a basin. Rub in the butter

with the tips of the fingers, and stir in enough sour milk to make a stiff dough. Roll out on a lightly floured pastry board and cut into rounds. Bake for about ¼ hour in a hot oven.

Sour Milk Girdle Scones

½ pint Sour Milk.	1 Egg.
10 oz. Flour.	1¼ teaspoonfuls Baking Soda.
½ teaspoonful Salt.	2 tablespoonfuls melted Butter.

UTENSILS—Sieve, two basins, egg-beater, wooden spoon, measuring spoons, tablespoon, pint or gill measure, saucepan, girdle, knife or palette knife.

Mix and sift the dry ingredients into a basin. Stir in the sour milk, melted butter, and well-beaten egg. Beat well, then drop the mixture in tablespoonfuls on a hot, greased girdle. When the scones are full of blisters on top, and cooked on the edges, turn them carefully and cook on the other side. As they are cooked, pile them up on a hot dish lined with a folded napkin. Serve buttered, with honey or strawberry jam.

Sour Milk Gingerbread

½ cupful Sour Milk.	¼ teaspoonful Allspice.
1 Egg. ½ lb. Flour.	1 teaspoonful Ground Ginger.
3 oz. Castor Sugar.	¼ teaspoonful Ground Cinnamon.
½ cupful Treacle. 4 oz. Butter.	¼ teaspoonful Salt.
2 teaspoonfuls Cocoa Powder.	¾ teaspoonful Baking Soda.

UTENSILS—Three basins, wooden spoon, teaspoon, cup, sieve, egg-beater, shallow baking tin, cake rack, knife.

Beat the butter to a cream in a basin, then stir in the sugar, treacle, beaten egg and milk, then the dry sifted ingredients. Beat well. Bake in a shallow, buttered baking tin in a moderate oven for about ½ hour. Remove from the oven, stand one minute, then cool on a cake rack. Serve cut in squares.

Spiced Raisin Cake

¾ cupful Sour Milk.	2 cupfuls stoned Raisins.
1 lb. Flour. 3 Eggs	½ teaspoonful Ground Cloves.
1 cupful Brown Sugar.	1 teaspoonful Baking Soda.
1 cupful Treacle or Syrup.	½ teaspoonful Salt.
¾ cupful Butter or Margarine.	2 teaspoonfuls Ground Cinnamon.

½ teaspoonful Ground Mace.

UTENSILS—Three basins, wooden spoon, teaspoon, cup, egg-beater, knife, sieve, shallow baking tin, cake rack.

Beat the butter or margarine in a basin till creamy. Stir in the sugar and the syrup or treacle. Beat well, then add the beaten eggs, and when well mixed, stir in the sour milk in which the soda has been dissolved. Add the chopped, stoned raisins to the flour sifted with the salt and spices, and then mix all the ingredients together. Turn the mixture into a shallow, buttered baking tin, and bake in a moderate oven, 350 degrees Fahr., for about ¾ hour. Remove from the oven, stand for a moment or two, then turn out and cool on a cake rack. Serve cut into squares.

ROOT VEGETABLES

There are many ways in which cold boiled root vegetables can be used. They can be chopped into dice and mixed with mayonnaise or salad cream, then used as a salad with any cold meat. They can be mashed and put through a sieve, and used as a basis for a cream soup. They can be added to a curry, or made into a vegetable curry.

COLD BOILED POTATOES

(1) Add one part of diced celery or cucumber to every two parts of diced potato. Sprinkle with minced onion to taste, and moisten with salad cream or mayonnaise, then serve with cold meat.

(2) Mash the potatoes till smooth, add pepper and salt to taste and enough milk to moisten. A pat or two of butter can also be added, if liked. Use with flaked tinned salmon or flaked left-over fish, for making into fish cakes, or use as a crust for cottage pie, or shape into small flat cakes, dip in flour, fry, and serve with cold meat.

(3) Slice the potatoes and fry them in smoking hot dripping or bacon fat, and flavour with minced onion, if liked. Serve with cold meat, or with grilled or fried steak or chops. A little minced parsley can be added to the potatoes just before serving, if wanted.

Potato Croquettes

1 pint mashed Cold Potatoes.	1 Yolk of Egg.
2 tablespoonfuls Butter.	½ teaspoonful Salt.

UTENSILS—Two basins, wooden spoon, measuring spoon, sieve, knife, 2 plates, frying pan.

Mix all the ingredients together except the egg, and beat till light. Stir in the egg yolk, and when well mixed rub through a sieve, and add, if liked, 1 teaspoonful of minced parsley, and pepper to taste. Shape into balls, then into corks, roll in breadcrumbs and egg, then in crumbs again. Fry in deep, smoking hot fat till crisp and brown. Drain well before serving on a hot dish lined with a lace paper d'oyley.

Potato Soup

1½ lb. Boiled Potatoes.   ½ pint Milk.
4 small Onions.   1 oz. Butter.   Parsley.
1½ quarts Water or Stock.   Pepper and Salt, to taste.

UTENSILS—Knife, 2 saucepans, basin, wooden spoon, gill and quart measures, sieve, chopping board.

Peel the onions and place them in a saucepan with water, and pepper and salt to taste. Cover and boil for 2 hours, then add the sliced potatoes and rub through a sieve. Return the soup to the saucepan, add the butter, bring to the boil, and stir in the milk which has been brought to boiling point. Add a little minced parsley to taste, and serve at once.

COLD GREENS

Cold boiled cabbage, Brussels sprouts, and other green vegetables can be made into soup or into bubble and squeak.

Green Vegetable Cream Soup

1 pint minced, Cooked Greens.   1 teaspoonful minced Parsley.
1½ pints Milk.   2 oz. Flour.   2 slices minced Onion.
2 oz. Butter or Bacon Fat.   Salt and Pepper, to taste.
     1 pint Water, Potato Water, or Chicken or Veal Stock.

UTENSILS—Knife, saucepan, wooden spoon, teaspoon, basin, pint measure, sieve.

Put the parsley and onion into the potato water or stock, cover and cook for 20 minutes. Stir in the milk and greens, and season to taste. Bring to boiling point. Mix the butter and flour to a cream, and stir them into the soup. The soup can be sieved or not, as preferred, before serving.

Bubble and Squeak

1½ pints Left-over Cabbage.   Pepper, to taste.
Slices of cold Corned Beef.   4 tablespoonfuls Butter, Dripping
1 tablespoonful Vinegar.   or Bacon Fat.

UTENSILS—Knife, stewpan, pint measure, tablespoon. *Enough for about 6 persons.*

Slice the meat thinly, and fry it in hot dripping or butter till golden. Remove it to a hot dish. Heat the chopped cabbage in the fat, season to taste, and stir in the vinegar. Arrange the cabbage in the centre of the dish in a pile and have the slices of meat overlapping round.

TOMATOES

Left-over fried tomatoes can be added to casseroles of meat, stews, or to stock. Tinned tomatoes can be used for tomato sauce to accompany grilled or fried steak, or boiled spaghetti or macaroni. They can also be used for tomato soup, purée, or cream of tomato, or can be made into scalloped tomatoes.

Scalloped Tomatoes

½ tin Peeled Tomatoes.
1 small Onion.
Breadcrumbs.
½ teaspoonful Castor Sugar.
Pepper and Salt, to taste.
Butter.

UTENSILS—Basin, large spoon, teaspoon, gill measure, knife, grater, fireproof dish. *Enough for 2 or 3 persons.*

Drain a little liquor from the tomatoes and add it to the stock pot. Season with sugar, pepper, salt, and finely-minced onion, to taste. Cover the bottom of a thickly-buttered fireproof dish with breadcrumbs, and place the tomatoes with the remainder of the liquor on top. Sprinkle thickly with stale breadcrumbs, dab with tiny bits of butter or margarine, and bake till the crumbs are brown. If liked, the breadcrumbs can be sprinkled with an equal quantity of grated cheese before using.

Spaghetti Italienne

½ pint tinned Peeled Tomatoes.
1 gill grated Cheese.
Breadcrumbs.
1 pint cooked Spaghetti.
Salt and Pepper, to taste.
Butter or Margarine.

UTENSILS—Large spoon, pint or gill measure, grater, saucepan, fireproof dish, knife, teaspoon. *Enough for 2 or 3 persons.*

Place the spaghetti in a layer in a buttered fireproof dish. Cover with half the grated cheese, then with half the tomatoes, seasoned with salt, pepper, and ¼ teaspoonful of sugar. Repeat the layers, and cover with stale breadcrumbs. Dab here and there with tiny bits of butter or margarine, and bake for ¾ hour in a moderate oven.

VEGETABLE MARROW

Left-over vegetable marrow can be turned into a savoury custard ; made into cream of marrow soup with 2 cupfuls of chicken or veal stock and 3 cupfuls of white sauce to 2 cupfuls of sieved marrow ; or baked in the oven. To bake in the oven, cut the marrow into dice, place it in a buttered fireproof dish, and moisten with fried bacon and fat, allowing two rashers of bacon, cooked and diced, to 1½ cupfuls of diced marrow. Bake until thoroughly heated through.

Mashed Marrow

3 cupfuls sieved, Boiled Marrow. | 3 tablespoonfuls Butter.
Pepper and Salt, to taste.

UTENSILS—Saucepan, basin, wooden spoon, tablespoon, cup, sieve. *Enough for 4 persons.*

Melt the butter in a saucepan, add the marrow, season to taste, and beat over the fire till light. Serve with cold meats in place of potatoes.

Marrow Custard

3 gills sieved Marrow. | 2 Eggs.
1½ pints Milk. | Pepper and Salt, to taste.

UTENSILS—Saucepan, 2 basins, egg-beater, wooden spoon, gill or pint measure, sieve, pie-dish or ramekins, baking tin. *Enough for about 4 persons.*

Scald the milk, and stir it into the sieved marrow in a basin. Season to taste, then stir in the beaten eggs. Cook at once in a shallow buttered pie-dish or in ramekins, placed in a baking tin containing a little hot water, in a rather slow oven, till the custard is set. The mixture must never boil.

BEANS AND PEAS

(1) Make peas into a cream soup, using the same liquids and the same quantities as given under vegetable marrow, above.

(2) Use in any recipe that calls for either cooked string beans or peas.

(3) Re-heat in the top of a double boiler containing a little melted butter, and season with pepper, salt, minced chives, parsley or onion.

(4) Add to any casserole of meat.

(5) Add to scrambled eggs wanted for supper.

(6) Make into a salad.

Bean Salad

1 pint sliced String Beans.	1 medium-sized Onion.
1 tablespoonful Bacon Fat.	½ pint Bean Liquor.
2 tablespoonfuls Vinegar.	Salt, Pepper and Paprika.

UTENSILS—Saucepan, basin, knife, tablespoon, wooden spoon, pint measure, colander, cup.

Throw the beans into boiling salted water, and boil till tender, unless sufficient cooked beans are left over. Drain the beans well, and reserve a cupful of the liquid. Stir into the beans the vinegar, bacon fat, salt, pepper and paprika to taste, and 2 tablespoonfuls of peeled and minced onion. Stir in the hot bean liquor, and leave till cold. Serve with cold boiled ham or tongue.

LEFT-OVER GRAVY

(1) Add left-over gravy to any brown soup, or to broth made with meat stock.

(2) Use it as the basis of tomato sauce, when this is required to accompany chicken cutlets, croquettes or rissoles.

(3) Thin the gravy with stock, add a little rice or vermicelli, re-season, and cook until the cereal is tender. The addition of a few peas improves this soup.

(4) Add to hot pots and use in savoury pies in addition to stock.

(5) Re-heat beef gravy and serve it with grilled steak. Serve lamb or mutton gravy, re-heated, with lamb or mutton chops.

FISH SAUCES

CHEESE, TOMATO OR WHITE SAUCE—Add to scalloped fish or fish cakes, or when making a fish curry use any left-over tomato or white sauce as part of the curry sauce.

MAYONNAISE OR TARTARE SAUCE—Moisten left-over boiled fish with the sauce, after flaking the fish lightly. Serve it in a dish lined with green salad, and garnish with slices of hard-boiled egg, or any other fish garnish that is handy.

MEAT SAUCES

A brown sauce can be added to any brown soup, to the filling for any meat pie, or to any meat casserole, stew or hot pot. If an elaborate sauce, such as Espagnol, is left over, it can be stirred into a curry.

SWEET SAUCES

JAM SAUCE—Re-heat, and use as originally intended with sponge or batter pudding or with a plain blancmange ; or moisten a plain sweet dumpling or sponge pudding with it, thinned as required with milk, and cook as usual.

WHITE SAUCE—(1) Add black coffee, or sugar melted with a little butter till brown, and use with sponge pudding or railway pudding. (2) Stir in a cupful of chocolate to taste, bring it to the boil, and serve hot with vanilla ice cream.

CUSTARD SAUCE—(1) Serve cold with any stewed or tinned fruit. (2) Mix with an equal quantity of fruit purée, and serve chilled in a shallow bowl or in sundae glasses, as a fool. (3) Use in place of fresh custard in making a trifle or tipsy cake. (4) Add to a melted jelly, to make it go further. (5) Re-heat, and serve with any boiled or steamed pudding.

LEFT-OVER PUDDINGS

Hot fancy puddings cannot be treated like either boiled, steamed, or baked puddings, but should be re-heated with a cover on top and served as they are. Some hot baked fancy puddings can be covered with meringue and put in the oven till warm through and golden on top. Cold fancy puddings, such as trifles or other sweets decorated with whipped cream, can be re-decorated and served again. A good decoration for fruit cream or blancmange is a half-used jelly, chopped up. Left-over blancmange may be used in the same way for decorating a fresh jelly.

BOILED OR STEAMED PUDDINGS—(1) Slice the left-over pudding and fry it in a little hot butter. Serve dredged with sugar. (2) Arrange slices of pudding in a buttered baking tin, dab each with a tiny piece of butter, and bake for 10 minutes. (3) Place in the top of a double boiler after buttering the container well, cover and re-heat over boiling water. Serve with sweet white or custard sauce.

BAKED MILK PUDDINGS—(1) A pudding made without eggs can be simply turned into a fresh pie-dish, and a beaten egg, diluted with 2 or 3 tablespoonfuls of milk, according to the thickness of the mixture, can be added to it before re-baking for a short time in a moderate oven. (2) Another method of using up left-over milk pudding is to turn it into a saucepan, cook it till thicker, and set it in a wet mould. Serve it, when chilled, turned out and accompanied by stewed or tinned fruit, jam, or fruit juice. Left-over rice, semolina and ground rice make the best moulds of this kind.

ODD PIECES OF PASTRY—These can be made into cheese straws, into a few cheesecakes, pastry cases, tartlet cases, sausage rolls or a pie case. What is done with them depends on the quantity left over, and what is required at the time.

TO MAKE PASTRY CASES, ETC.

SHORTCRUST—Roll the paste out thinly and line with it a pie-plate or tartlet tins. Prick the bottom well all over with a fork, and bake in a quick oven—375 degrees Fahr.

FLAKY OR ROUGH PUFF PASTRY—Roll the paste to an eighth of an inch in thickness, line a pie-plate or tartlet tins with it, and bake. Do not prick the bottom of the case to prevent it rising, as this makes puff pastry heavy. A little of the centre can be scooped out, when cooked, before the case is filled.

FILLINGS FOR PASTRY CASES—(1) Creamed chicken, veal, pheasant or guinea-fowl, with peas or chopped mushrooms. (2) Welsh rarebit, piping hot. (3) Jam or lemon or orange cheese, decorated with whipped cream or meringue. (4) Tinned or stewed fruit, moistened with the juice which has been drained off and cooked to a syrup.

TO MAKE TURNOVERS—Cut the pastry, rolled to an eighth of an inch thick, into rounds about four inches in diameter. Brush the edges with a pastry brush dipped in cold water. Place a spoonful of jam, lemon cheese, or fruit marmalade, or fresh or left-over minced meat, well seasoned, on one half near the centre. Fold in two. Press the edges together, and ornament. Make a cross with a knife in the centre, brush with milk or egg and milk, and bake in a hot oven—375 degrees Fahr.

TO MAKE CHEESE STRAWS—Roll the pastry to $\frac{1}{4}$ inch in thickness. Sprinkle thickly with strongly flavoured, grated yellow cheese. Fold over, and roll out once again. Cut in strips ½ inch wide and 4 inches long. Dust with paprika. Bake in a hot oven—375 degrees Fahr.

To MAKE JAM TARTLETS—Either fill cooked pastry cases with jam, or line tartlet tins with rounds of pastry, thinly rolled, place a teaspoonful or more of jam in each, cover with a thin cross of pastry, and bake in a hot oven—375 degrees Fahr.

STEWED FRUIT

Make left-over stewed fruit into a compôte by draining off the syrup, and cooking this with a little more syrup if thin, then cooling it a little before pouring it over any stewed fruit to which you have added a little fresh, such as one or two sliced bananas, pears, or peaches, or some of each. You can also use up left-over stewed fruit in the following ways :

(1) Put it through a sieve and mix it with an equal quantity of thick custard or sweetened whipped cream to form a fool. If very juicy, you may need to drain off part of the juice, but do not throw it away. Pour it over a blancmange or a sponge or batter pudding, or use it as the basis of a fruit drink.

(2) Place the fruit in the bottom of a pie-dish, make a Swiss roll or sponge sandwich mixture, pour it over the fruit, and bake in a quick oven at once till the sponge is risen, firm and golden.

(3) Either make a pastry case, and fill it up with the remainder of the stewed fruit, drained from a little of the juice if necessary, and top with whipped sweetened cream flavoured with vanilla, or cover with meringue and bake in a slow oven till set.

(4) Melt a fruit jelly according to the instructions on the packet, using the stewed fruit and its juice as part of the liquid. Set in a wet mould. Serve with custard or cream.

STALE BREAD

(1) Dip the bread in milk or water, and leave it on the rack of a baking tin in the oven till dry, then use it hot in place of rolls. If preferred, tear the bread with the fingers into small, ragged, roll shapes before treating in this way.

(2) Make it into breadcrumbs and fry them in butter, allowing ½ oz. of butter to each ounce of crumbs. Serve with roast game or chicken.

HAM JELLIES—Tempting dishes such as Ham Jellies (p. 31) for supper and high tea can often be prepared from small quantities of meat and vegetables left over from the main meal.

Peel and slice the apples into a saucepan. Add 2 tablespoonfuls of brown sugar and the water. Cover, and stew gently till the apples are tender. Mix the crumbs, suet, sugar and cinnamon together. Place a layer of the dry mixture in the bottom of a buttered pie-dish. Pour the apples on top, cover with the remainder of the dry mixture, fork neatly over so that the top is even, and bake from $\frac{1}{2}$ to $\frac{3}{4}$ hour in a moderate oven. Butter can be substituted for the suet if preferred, or left-over stewed rhubarb can be used instead of apples.

BREAD AND BUTTER

(1) Arrange slices of bread and butter, with crusts removed, neatly in a buttered pie-dish till the dish is half full. Sprinkle with a few cleaned currants, sultanas or raisins. Pour over enough milk to fill up the pie-dish, enriched with one or two beaten eggs. Bake in a slow oven till the custard is set. Left-over custard sauce can be used instead of the fresh custard.

Marmalade Pudding

$\frac{3}{4}$ lb. Bread and Butter, weighed without crust.	1 small cupful Marmalade.
$\frac{1}{4}$ lb. Suet. 2 Eggs.	$\frac{1}{2}$ teaspoonful Baking Soda.
	$\frac{1}{2}$ teaspoonful Mixed Spice.

Milk to moisten.

UTENSILS—Two basins, knife, fork, cup, measuring spoons, gill measure, wooden spoon, egg-beater, pudding basin, 2 saucepans. *Enough for 4 persons.*

Place the bread in a basin and pour over 1 gill of hot milk, then break it down with a fork. Stir in the beaten eggs, and rinse out the basin with two or three tablespoonfuls of milk. Stir in the suet, the marmalade, the soda dissolved in a tablespoon of milk, and spice. Beat well with a fork for a moment or two. Steam in a buttered, covered basin for $2\frac{1}{2}$ hours.

NOTE.—Any kind of marmalade can be used, or jam or honey can be substituted.

STALE CAKE

SPONGE CAKE—(1) Cut it into fingers and put these together with apricot or raspberry jam, and use as a basis or tipsy cake or a trifle.

(3) Use it for bread sauce.

(4) Use it to lighten suet puddings, allowing an equal quantity of breadcrumbs and flour.

(5) Make it into hot boiled, baked, or steamed bread puddings.

(6) Make it into cold summer pudding.

Cold Summer Pudding

UTENSILS—Two basins, knife, sieve, wooden spoon, saucepan.

Line a buttered basin with layers of thin slices of bread. Fill the centre with layers of bread. Rub 1 lb. of raspberries and red currants through a sieve and pour this purée into the basin. Stand it in a cold place until all the juice is absorbed by the bread, then turn into a glass dish. Stew ½ lb. red currants and ½ lb. raspberries with enough sugar to sweeten, until the sugar is dissolved. Rub this through a sieve, or strain it over the pudding. Serve with cream or chilled custard.

Brown Bread Pudding

6 oz. Brown Breadcrumbs.
2½ oz. Butter.
2 oz. Glacé Cherries.
3 Eggs.

¼ lb. Castor Sugar.
1 cupful Milk.
2 tablespoonfuls Cream.
½ teaspoonful Vanilla Essence.

UTENSILS—Three basins, wooden spoon, measuring spoon cup, knife, wire whisk, mould or pudding basin, sie saucepan. *Enough for 3 or 4 persons.*

Beat the butter and sugar to a cream. Stir in 1 w egg and 2 egg yolks, then the cream, milk, crumbs, cho cherries, and vanilla. Mix well and fold in 2 stiffly fr egg whites. Place in a greased pudding basin or Cover and steam slowly till set—in about 1 hour. turned out with hot custard sauce.

Swiss Pudding

1 pint Breadcrumbs.
2 oz. minced Suet.
2 tablespoonfuls Water.

2 oz. Brown Sugar.
1 lb. Apples.
Cinnamon, to taste

UTENSILS—Knife, tablespoon, pint measure wooden spoon, basin, pie-dish, fork, sieve or gra *for 4 to 6 persons.*

(2) Arrange in individual pieces in a glass dish, cover with custard sauce, spike with blanched almonds, and cover with tinned or stewed fruit.

(3) Use the sponge cake in place of breadcrumbs for putting on top of an apple or rhubarb Charlotte.

(4) Use it in place of breadcrumbs in a steamed pudding where breadcrumbs are suggested.

FRUIT CAKE—Crumble fruit cake into a basin, moisten it with egg and milk, allowing 1 egg to $\frac{1}{2}$ pint of milk—the mixture should be the same thickness as the original cake mixture. Pack into a buttered basin, cover, and steam for 1 hour till the pudding is set. Serve turned out on a hot dish with custard sauce, or with white sauce flavoured with vanilla or lemon.

Ratafia Pudding

$\frac{1}{4}$ lb. left-over Sponge Cake.	1 oz. Castor Sugar.
$2\frac{1}{2}$ gills Milk.	1 oz. Glacé Cherries.
2 Eggs. 1 Yolk of Egg.	8 Ratafias. Vanilla Essence.

UTENSILS—Mould, 2 basins, knife, egg-beater, gill measure, saucepan. *Enough for about 4 persons.*

Break the sponge cake into small pieces, and crumble the ratafias. Mix the ratafias together with any crumbs that come from the sponge cake. Halve the cherries, butter a round mould and use the cherries to decorate it. Fill up the mould with the crumbs. Beat the eggs and egg yolk in a basin with the sugar, then stir in the milk and $\frac{1}{2}$ teaspoon of vanilla essence. Pour gently over the cake and stand for 30 minutes. Cover, and steam slowly from $\frac{1}{2}$ to $\frac{3}{4}$ hour till the pudding is set. Remove from the saucepan (or from the tin if cooked in the oven with the mould standing in a baking tin containing a little hot water). Stand for a moment or two, then turn gently into a hot dish. Serve with cream or custard sauce.

TO USE UP FRUIT RINDS

If your favourite recipe for marmalade calls for the juice of a certain number of oranges but the peel only of a few of them, either candy the remaining peel and use it for cakes, puddings, etc., or make it, after candying, into balls as the Californians do, and serve them at dessert or as a sweetmeat.

To CANDY ORANGE PEEL—Wash, dry, and cut the peel into

¼ inch wide strips. Place them in a saucepan, cover with cold water, and bring slowly to boiling point. Drain off the water, add fresh water, and repeat the boiling up, draining and adding fresh water process. Then measure the rind, return it to a saucepan, add an equal quantity of sugar, and just enough boiling water to cover. Simmer till the rind is clear and tender, then cool it, drain it from the syrup, and roll it in castor sugar. Spread the strips on wax paper to dry overnight, then next day roll again in castor sugar.

Any lemon rind not required can be candied after squeezing out the juice, and all grapefruit rind from the breakfast grapefruit can be used in the same way, but both should be soaked in cold water overnight to extract some of their bitterness, and well drained before putting them to boil in fresh water. Candied grapefruit and lemon rinds are as delicious as the orange for using in cakes, puddings, and mincemeat.

To MAKE ORANGE BALLS—Soak any washed orange peel in cold water for 3 days, draining off the water and adding fresh each day. Then place the peel in a saucepan of hot water, bring to the boil, and boil till soft. Now turn the peel into a colander, squeeze out all the water, dry it, and mince it finely. Weigh the minced peel, then take the same weight of sugar. Turn the sugar into a saucepan, add a little water, just enough to dissolve the sugar ; when the sugar is dissolved, and not before, bring it to the boil, and boil until the syrup " hairs," when you shake a spoon dipped in it. Then stir in the chopped peel, boil it for a moment or two, remove the pan from the fire, cool, then turn the contents on to a pastry board, thickly sprinkled with castor sugar, and with your hands roll small portions of the sugar and peel into small balls, about the size of marbles. Roll the balls in sugar, and leave them well apart, on a plate sprinkled with sugar, to dry.

You can make grapefruit and lemon balls in the same way, only soak them for 5 or 6 days instead of for 3.

COLD FISH

Left-over fish is always useful. Sometimes it can be made into kedgeree for breakfast or supper, sometimes into fish cakes, a pie or pudding, sometimes into a soufflé, occasionally into a salad. The following are some short-cuts to using up cooked fish.

1. CREAMED FISH—Make 1 pint of white sauce, season it well, add 1 pint of flaked cooked fish, 1½ teaspoonfuls of minced parsley, and 1 tablespoonful of cooked peas or minced pimento Serve on rounds of buttered toast.

2. KEDGEREE—Melt 3 tablespoonfuls of butter in a saucepan. Add 1½ cupfuls of cooked flaked fish, 2 cupfuls of cooked rice, 2 hard-boiled eggs (diced whites, and sieved yolks), and paprika and grated nutmeg to taste. Serve piping hot.

3. FISH PIE—Flake enough cooked fish to give you 3 cupfuls. Mash and season enough potatoes to give you 3 cupfuls. Line a buttered casserole with the potato. Place the fish in the centre. Cover with more potato and rough this up with the prongs of a fork. Brush with melted butter, and bake in a moderate oven till brown.

Fish Cakes

¾ pint flaked Cooked Fish.	1½ pints mashed **Potato.**
1 teaspoonful minced Parsley.	½ teaspoonful Salt.
1 Egg. 1 oz. Butter.	Pepper, to taste.

UTENSILS—Two basins, wooden spoon, teaspoon, pint measure, pastry board or plate, knife, frying pan. *Enough for 4 to 6 persons.*

Mix the fish in a basin with the potato, salt, parsley, pepper, and melted butter. Stir in as much of the egg as needed to moisten the mixture. Divide it into twelve, and shape it into balls with lightly floured hands, flatten the tops and bottoms, then roll the balls lightly in flour again, and fry in a little bacon or ham fat. The cakes can be egged and crumbed after flouring, if preferred, before frying in deep smoking hot fat. Serve garnished with slices of lemon and sprigs of parsley.

Curried Fish

1 pint flaked Cooked Fish.	2 oz. Butter.
1 oz. Flour.	3 gills Milk **or Stock.**
1 tablespoonful Lemon Juice.	1 teaspoonful Curry Powder.
Boiled Rice.	Salt, to taste.

UTENSILS—Two saucepans, fork, wooden spoon, measuring spoons, lemon squeezer, gill or pint measure. *Enough for about 4 persons.*

Melt the butter in a saucepan. Add the flour, and stir

gently over a slow heat till smooth. Stir in the curry powder and salt, then milk or stock as preferred. Stir till boiling then simmer for 5 minutes. Add the fish, heat it through, stir in the lemon juice, and serve on a hot dish surrounded with a border of boiled rice.

Fish Salad

1 pint flaked Cooked Fish.	3 tablespoonfuls French Dressing.
¾ cupful diced Celery.	Cucumber.
1½ tablespoonfuls Lemon Juice.	Mayonnaise, to taste.

UTENSILS—Shallow dish, lemon squeezer, cup, tablespoon, wooden spoon, pint measure, knife. *Enough for about 4 persons.*

Place the fish in a shallow dish and sprinkle it with the French dressing mixed with the lemon juice. Chill well, then stir in the celery, and diced cucumber to taste. Drain the mixture and place it in a salad bowl lined with any green salad, spread it with mayonnaise, and decorate it to taste with any fish salad garnish.

NOTE.—For other dishes made from left-over fish, see section on FISH.

LEFT-OVER MEAT

REMAINS OF JOINTS AND STEAKS—There is no end to the ways in which cold meat can be used up. It can be curried ; heated in a casserole with gravy ; sliced and re-heated in a white sauce enriched with egg yolks at the last moment ; made into croquettes, rissoles, shepherd's pie, toad-in-the-hole, or hash ; and used in stuffings for tomatoes, aubergines, and vegetable marrows. If there is not enough meat left over to provide a course for lunch or dinner, it goes farthest when curried, or made into shepherd's pie or toad-in-the-hole. Sometimes when short of meat, balls of sausage meat can be added to a hot pot or casserole, or toad-in-the-hole. Here are some other ways in which you can use up left-over meat :—

(1) Put it through a mincer and mince it to a paste with butter. Season to taste, and use for sandwiches or on toast, or for high tea with toast.

(2) Chop the meat and add it to cooked rice when risotto is wanted, or spaghetti when spaghetti and tomato sauce is wanted for lunch or supper.

(3) Chop it, season it to taste with grated onion moistened with gravy, and use it as a filling for savoury pancakes.

(4) Prepare the meat as for pancakes, and use it as a filling for little rounds of mashed potatoes hollowed in the centre.

(5) Make it into a salad, first soaking it for ½ hour in a little French dressing, then draining, chopping, and moistening it with mayonnaise or a salad cream. Serve on a dish lined with lettuce leaves.

(6) Roll out suet crust and spread it with savoury mince (see No. 3). Roll up and steam like a roly-poly.

Blanquette of Meat

1 lb. left-over Roast Meat.	2 oz. Butter.
1 oz. Flour. Minced Parsley.	2 Yolks of Eggs.

UTENSILS—Knife, wooden spoon, saucepan, basin, egg-beater, chopping board. *Enough for 4 persons.*

Cut the meat into wafer slices. Melt the butter in a saucepan, stir in the flour till smooth, then stir in enough hot water, stock or gravy to make a thick sauce. Season to taste with salt and pepper. Cook for 2 minutes, then draw the pan to the side of the fire and add the meat. Simmer for 10 minutes.

Remove the meat to a hot dish and keep it warm while you stir the beaten egg yolks into the gravy, and re-heat the gravy, stirring constantly until thick. Add parsley to taste, and pour the gravy over the meat. Serve with mashed potatoes. This dish is best made with cold meat or pork.

Miroton of Beef

1½ lb. cold Roast Beef.	1 lb. Onions, chopped.
3 rashers of Bacon.	Pepper, Salt and minced Parsley
1½ tablespoonfuls Vinegar.	to taste.

1½ gills Gravy.

UTENSILS—Knife, tablespoon, gill measure, frying pan, baking dish, saucepan. *Enough for 5 or 6 persons.*

Cut the meat into wafers. Remove the rind from the rashers, then chop the bacon and fry it with ½ oz. butter and the chopped onions for 5 minutes. Then add parsley and pepper and salt to taste. Put a layer of meat in a greased baking dish, cover it with onion and bacon, repeat the layers, then pour the vinegar and gravy, heated together, over the meat. Cover, and bake for 20 minutes. Serve with riced or creamed potatoes.

Indian Cutlets

4 cooked Mutton Cutlets.
1 gill Curry Sauce.

¼ oz. Gelatine.
¾ oz. Butter.
1 Tomato.

UTENSILS—Saucepan, wooden spoon, knife, basin, wire rack. *Enough for 4 persons.*

Use instantaneous gelatine. Heat the sauce, add the gelatine, and when melted stir it into a basin and leave till cold. Mask one side of the cutlets with the sauce. Place them on a wire rack, and when set decorate them with a little chopped aspic jelly, then put a cutlet frill on each bone. Garnish with chopped jelly, sprigs of parsley, and crescents of beetroot. The cutlets can also be arranged round a mound of potato salad or Russian salad.

Scalloped Mutton

Left-over Chops or Cutlets.
1 oz. Breadcrumbs.
1 tablespoonful minced Parsley.

3 oz. Butter.
1 oz. grated Parmesan Cheese.
Gravy, or White Sauce.

Pepper and Salt, to taste.

UTENSILS—Knife, chopping board, basin, wooden spoon, tablespoon, grater, scallop shells. *Enough for 4 or 5 persons.*

Remove all the lamb or mutton from the chops or cutlets, or from any joint. Cut the meat into dice, taking away all fat and gristle. Mix it in a basin with the chopped parsley, pepper and salt, and add enough white sauce or gravy to moisten. Rub 4 or 5 scallop shells well with butter, and divide the meat between them. Sprinkle over the remainder of the butter and the cheese, mixed with an equal quantity of breadcrumbs. Brown in a hot oven for 15 minutes.

OTHER RECIPES FOR CHOPS AND CUTLETS—Cut the meat into dice, and either curry it or heat it up in a savoury white sauce, or in a cheese sauce, and serve either in hot pastry cases or on rounds or squares of buttered toast or fried bread. To vary creamed meat, you can add a few cooked or tinned peas, or a little minced pimento.

Mutton Pilau

12 oz. Left-over Mutton.
6 oz. Rice.   3 oz. Butter.
2 rashers of Bacon.

2 Spanish Onions.
1 quart Stock.
Chopped Parsley.

UTENSILS—Saucepan, frying pan, knife, wooden spoon, quart measure, plate, chopping board. *Enough for 4 persons.*

Melt 2 oz. of butter in a saucepan. Add the rice, and stir it over the fire till pale brown. Moisten with stock, and stir again until the rice is tender, and the stock nearly all absorbed. Season to taste with pepper and salt. Melt $\frac{1}{2}$ oz. butter in a frying pan. Slice in the mutton, and fry lightly, then remove a layer of the rice. Place the meat in its place, and cover with the rice that was removed. Cover, and cook gently for 20 minutes. When ready to serve, fry the bacon cut in strips, and fry the onions peeled and cut into rings, in the bacon fat and the remainder of the butter. Pile the rice up in a hot dish. Arrange the slices of mutton, overlapping round it. Garnish alternately with onion and bacon, sprinkle with parsley and serve at once.

CALF'S HEAD

Make left-over calf's head into brawn, or re-heat it in white sauce flavoured with onion and sharpened with a little vinegar, or in brown sauce. Serve brawn with salad and the other dishes with a border of mashed potatoes.

Calf's Head Brawn

The remains of a Calf's Head.
Cold Ham or Bacon.
1 grated Lemon Rind.
$\frac{1}{2}$ pint Stock.
$\frac{1}{4}$ teaspoonful Ground Mace.

2 hard-boiled Eggs.
1 teaspoonful minced Parsley.
$\frac{1}{8}$ teaspoonful Ground Nutmeg.
$\frac{1}{8}$ teaspoonful Ground Cloves.
Salt and Pepper, to taste.

UTENSILS—Saucepan, mould, knife, teaspoon, pint or gill measure, grater, basin, wooden spoon.

To every pound of calf's head meat allow $\frac{1}{2}$ lb. cold ham or bacon. Cut the meat into dice, and slice the hard-boiled eggs. Butter a large mould, and arrange some of the slices of egg in the bottom. Mix together the parsley, lemon rind, and all the seasonings. Cover the bottom of the mould with a layer of diced meat, then arrange a few slices of egg on top. Cover with another layer of meat, and so on till the mould is full. Heat the jellied stock, which should consist of the liquor from the calf's head reduced to a thick jelly, pour over the mould until full. Cover with a buttered paper, and bake in a slow oven for about 2 hours. Add a little more hot stock, as soon as you take the mould from the oven. Leave till cold and set. When required, turn the brawn out, and garnish it with parsley or chervil, and serve with potato or Russian salad.

CALF'S TONGUE—The tongue should be boiled with the head, then remove it from the pan, skin it, and trim away any fat or gristle. Squeeze it round into a small mould, cover with some of the liquid in which it has been boiled, and press down with a weight till set. You can set a few peas in the stock if you wish. Serve with salad.

TONGUE SALAD—To make a tongue salad of pressed calf's tongue, allow 3 cupfuls of diced calf's tongue, ½ pint of mayonnaise, and 1 tin of baked beans. Mix the beans and tongue together. Mix the mayonnaise with the bean sauce. Line a salad bowl with lettuce or endive leaves, and place the beans and tongue in the centre. Pour over the mayonnaise.

TO USE UP LEFT-OVER LIQUOR—To use up the liquid in which the calf's head has been boiled : Strain, bring it to the boil, season if necessary (but it should not be necessary if the head has been properly seasoned to begin with), and serve hot as a soup. Add 1 tablespoonful of tinned, well-drained peas to each portion. A steamed egg can be slipped into each portion of soup, after the cups or plates have been filled. On the other hand, if the weather is hot, the egg can stand in the soup till it gets cold and jellies, and then be served jellied.

LEFT-OVER LIVER

The simplest way to use up scraps of liver is to put them through a mincer, then mix them to a paste with melted butter. Season to taste, and use as a paste for sandwiches, or as a toast or a savoury at dinner. Here are some other recipes for larger quantities :

Calf's Liver Pâté

1½ cupfuls Cooked Calf's Liver.
2 tablespoonfuls minced Lean Ham.
2 Eggs. Breadcrumbs.

3 or 4 slices of Fat Bacon.
2 teaspoonfuls minced Parsley.
A dash of Ground Mace.
1 small Onion.

Salt, Pepper and Paprika, to taste.

UTENSILS—Mincing machine, knife, measuring spoons, cup, 2 basins, egg-beater, large mixing spoon, mould.

Put the liver, uncooked bacon and ham twice or three times through a mincer. Add the parsley, mace, salt, pepper, paprika, and onion finely minced. Beat the eggs, and stir them into the mixture. Mix thoroughly, then turn into a mould or baking dish, well greased with butter or oil, and thickly sprinkled with breadcrumbs. Bake in a slow oven for 1 hour. Cool, unmould, and serve cut in thin slices.

Liver Terrapin

2 cupfuls cold Cooked Liver, cut into dice.	1¼ cupfuls Stock.
	2 hard-boiled Eggs.
2 tablespoonfuls Butter or Margarine.	1 tablespoonful Flour.
	1 tablespoonful Worcester Sauce.
1 teaspoonful dry Mustard.	Salt, Pepper and Paprika, to taste.

UTENSILS—Saucepan, wooden spoon, measuring spoons, cup, knife, sieve, 2 plates, toasting fork or toaster. *Enough for 4 to 6 persons.*

Melt the butter in a saucepan. Add the mustard, flour, salt, and paprika, and when well mixed add the stock and sauce. Cook for 5 minutes after the mixture comes to the boil. Add the diced liver, the chopped whites of eggs, and the sieved yolks. Re-heat, then serve on rounds or squares of buttered toast, or with rice or macaroni.

Liver Curry

2 cupfuls cold Cooked Liver.	3 tablespoonfuls Fat.
1 minced Onion.	2 tablespoonfuls Flour.
1 teaspoonful Curry Powder.	2 cupfuls Stock or Water.
½ diced Apple, or 1 tablespoonful Lemon Juice.	Boiled Rice.
	Salt, to taste.

UTENSILS—Frying pan, wooden spoon, measuring spoons, knife, cup, saucepan. *Enough for 6 persons.*

Melt the fat in a frying pan, add the onion, and cook until golden brown. Add the flour, salt, and curry powder, and mix to a smooth paste with the fat. Pour in the stock or water gradually, and bring to the boil, stirring constantly. Add the diced meat and apple, bring again to the boil, and simmer for 10 minutes. Serve with boiled rice.

Left-over Tripe and Onions

1½ pints Tripe and Onions.	1 oz. Butter or Margarine.
1 pint mashed Potatoes.	Pepper and Salt, to taste.

UTENSILS—Pie-dish, fork or potato masher, pint measure, basin, wooden spoon, knife, saucepan. *Enough for 5 or 6 persons.*

Turn the tripe into a buttered pie-dish. Mash the potatoes, and when quite free from lumps, add a little hot milk, seasoning to taste, and a third of the butter or margarine. Beat well till light and fluffy, then spread evenly over the tripe. Dab here and there with the remainder of the butter or margarine, and decorate with the prongs of a fork. Bake until pale brown in a fairly hot oven.

TO USE UP DRIPPING

(1) Keep beef, mutton and bacon dripping apart. Use bacon dripping for frying fish, chicken, vegetables, and for making fried croûtons for soup, etc.

(2) Use beef dripping in any recipe in which dripping is required, but clarify it first.

(3) If a very inexpensive spiced fruit cake is wanted, you can substitute dripping for butter, or use half dripping and half butter.

(4) Dripping can also be used in place of any other fat when making a meat pie.

(5) Children usually prefer mashed potatoes with dripping added instead of butter.

(6) Some people prefer beef dripping on toast to butter.

(7) Clarify any superfluous dripping and sell it to the butcher.

Dripping and Potato Cake

½ oz. Dripping.	1 oz. Flour.
¼ lb. mashed Potatoes.	A pinch of Salt.

UTENSILS—Basin, fork, wooden spoon, pastry board, knife, baking tin or girdle.

Place the potatoes in a basin. Stir in the melted dripping, then the flour and salt. Knead till smooth, then turn on to a floured pastry board, flatten into a cake or cakes, and bake in a moderate oven or on a hot girdle for 10 minutes. Serve with butter.

BONES, SCRAPS OF GAME, ETC.

(1) Place the bones or fragments in the stock pot when a brown stock is wanted.

(2) Add them to any brown soup in preparation.

(3) Make them into gravy.

(4) Put scraps of meat or game through a mincer, pound them to a paste with enough melted butter to moisten. Use with bread or with fried bread as a savoury.

DODGES TO PREVENT WASTE

To Preserve Food in Hot Weather

MILK

(1) Scald milk as soon as it arrives, and place it in a container scalded and rinsed out with cold water.

(2) Store it in an ice box, or if you have not got one, stand the milk bottle in a basin containing ice.

(3) Store milk away from all foods with a strong odour, such as cabbage, onion or fish.

(4) Never wipe a milk container with a towel used for other dishes. It is enough to rinse the vessel in cold water, then wash and scald it, and rinse it with cold water before using.

(5) If you have an ice-making refrigerator, store the milk bottle close to the freezing coil.

(6) A simple way of preventing milk going sour is to buy a milk bottle cooler. Moisten the flannel bag, which is drawn over the perforated zinc container, with cold water, then stand the cooler, with the milk bottle inside, in a basin or soup plate of water. By natural evaporation the milk cooler will keep your milk sweet and fresh for use in the hottest weather.

FISH AND MEAT, WITH NO REFRIGERATOR

(1) Place the food on a dish, protect it with a perforated cover, and stand it on ice.

(2) Place the fish or meat or other perishable articles of food in a dish, and stand this in a basin of cold water. Cover with a piece of butter muslin long enough to allow the ends to touch the water. The evaporation from the damp cloth keeps the food cool. When a small quantity is to be kept fresh, you can cover it with a clean flower pot.

TO PRESERVE BUTTER

Buy an iceless butter cooler. Place the butter in a dish, cover it, and fill it with cold water through the hole provided in the top. Place the cooler in a current of air.

TO KEEP COLD FOOD CHILLED

Use a "cold plate cover." It is especially good for placing over butter, mayonnaise, or whipped cream.

TO PREVENT SPOILAGE BY FLIES OR WASPS

Spray floors, and the inside of doors and windows, taking care to let none of the spray fall on the food, with an insecticide lotion sold with the spray.

Simple Cooking Dodges

TO PREVENT SPOILING OF FOOD OR UTENSILS

(1) To prevent custards curdling, or delicate baked puddings or savoury dishes burning, stand the dish in a baking tin containing a little hot water before placing it in the oven.

(2) Use an asbestos mat under a casserole or " saucepan " made of fireproof ware, etc.

(3) Boil your water in a whistling kettle to prevent water boiling over, to save fuel, and to secure a good cup of tea. Water long boiled is tea spoiled.

(4) Cook all sauces with a milk basis, all custards, creams, fish, meat, poultry, etc., cheese mixtures, cereals, etc., in the top of a double boiler with water boiling below. By using a double boiler, slow cooking without burning or boiling over is ensured.

(5) Add a tablespoonful or two of water to the fat in a dripping tin before roasting, to prevent the fat burning.

(6) Have an automatic oven heat controller attached to your gas oven to save waste of food and fuel.

(7) Place fish to be boiled on a rack to avoid breaking when removing from pan.

(8) Add a small pat of butter to jam when boiling to prevent it boiling over.

(9) Place a pie funnel in the centre of each pie-dish to prevent the pastry from falling into the filling.

(10) To keep the juice from running out of fruit pies, bind the edges with an inch-wide strip of cotton dipped in milk.

(11) Test a cake with a skewer before removing it from the oven, to see if it is dry.

(12) Use a palette knife when frying fish or meat cakes to prevent breaking.

Soap in the Kitchen Sink

(1) Keep a good supply of household soap always by you. Cut it as soon as it arrives from the shop with a piece of string or steel wire, and place on the top shelf of your store cupboard to dry before using. Dry soap lasts much longer than moist soap.

(2) Never leave soap lying in the bottom of a sink or basin. Place it in a soap dish with perforated holes in the bottom.

(3) Buy a soap saver, or make one at home by punching holes in a small tin and giving it a handle of string. Throw odds and ends of soap into this container, and swirl it about in the water when you want soapy water for washing up.

(4) Keep soap suds left over after washing clothes for washing floors, steps or verandah, or for watering roses.

Uses for Old Linen

SHEETS—Turn worn sheets sides to middle. Join them and hem the sides. If too thin or too worn, make pillow cases from the sound parts. If too worn for bedroom use, turn into small dust sheets.

PILLOW SLIPS AND FACE TOWELS—Make into lavatory cloths.

WORN BATH TOWELS—Make into face towels.

To Guard Against Pests

VERMIN—Remove all food from paper bags, and store it in suitable containers as soon as it is received from the shops. If you leave food lying about in paper wrappings you are simply courting mice and other pests. Destroy all refuse after every meal. Wash doors and window frames weekly with water containing a little disinfectant.

Take care not to feed any animals on the floor, nor to leave any pets' food in vessels on the floor where vermin can touch it. As soon as you know that vermin is about, take steps to get rid of it.

TO GUARD AGAINST MOTHS—After airing and brushing clothing to be stored away, wrap it in newspaper, and store it tightly in boxes sealed with gummed paper. If moths should appear, squirt paraffin in all cracks around floors and walls, and around the skirting boards.

To WARD OFF MOSQUITOES—Keep open drains flushed weekly with a strong disinfectant. Wash out all flower vases to be stored away very carefully, and if mosquitoes should appear near the house, wipe the window frames and doors with paraffin.

NOTE.—A clean house always kept free from crumbs, and where no food is exposed, does not attract vermin.

Methods of Saving Fuel

If you want to keep your fuel bill as low as possible, you must plan ahead. Haphazard cooking makes fuel bills soar. Here are some methods of saving fuel :

(1) Use waterless cookers, and cook a whole meal in them at one time.

(2) Use a high pressure cooker, which is the greatest fuel saver of all.

(3) When you want a baked dish or a cake, have a baked dinner or lunch that day.

(4) Carefully follow instructions given for cooking by gas, electricity, etc., for you will often find that many dishes cook after the gas or the electric current has been turned off.

(5) Use semi-circular pans, two of which can be placed on one hot plate or burner. Use a set of four triangular saucepans which can also all be used on one burner or hot plate.

(6) Use a steamer for cooking a whole meal.

(7) When cooking by gas, use a simmering burner when you want to cook at a slow pace. When cooking by electricity, switch to the heat desired. It is foolish to keep the switch at " high " when you want to stew or cook by any other gentle method. You are only wasting current.

Just as you can have an oven meal one day, and so make the most of your fuel, you can have a boiled or steamed meal or waterless cooked meal another day. Here is a sample of two boiled menus :

(1) Boiled salt beef, dumplings, carrots and turnips and potatoes. Boiled marmalade pudding with custard sauce.

(2) Boiled salmon or turbot with egg sauce and boiled potatoes. Stewed fruit and custard or cream

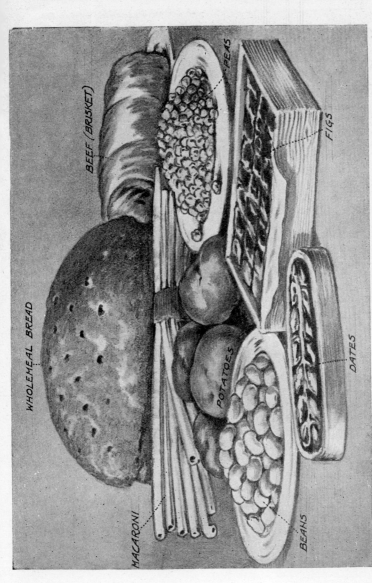

The FAMILY BUDGET (1)—Energy producing foods which give adequate food value cheaply.

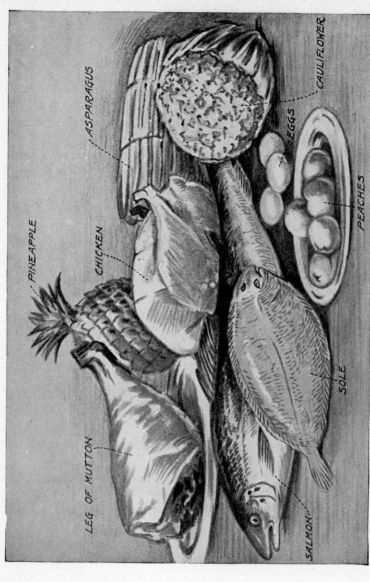

PINEAPPLE

ASPARAGUS

CAULIFLOWER

EGGS

CHICKEN

PEACHES

LEG OF MUTTON

SOLE

SALMON

THE FAMILY BUDGET (2)—These are expensive foods with no more energy value than the cheaper ones on the previous page.

Saving on Home-made Things

PRESERVE YOUR OWN EGGS—Preserve eggs, while they are most plentiful, with waterglass, according to the instructions on the tin. Reserve them for winter use when eggs are dear.

LEMONADE AND ORANGEADE—Make lemonade and orangeade at home with fresh fruit or with crystals. It is cheaper than buying bottled lemon and orangeade.

MARMALADE AND JAM—Make your own when fruits are cheapest, or make from your own fruit. If made with pectin, your fuel bill will be less, and the fruit and sugar will go farther than if made by old-fashioned methods.

PICKLES—Pickle, or make into a relish such as chutney or ketchup, all superfluous vegetables that can be treated in this way. You will find it much cheaper to pickle shallots and walnuts at home than to buy them.

CAKES, PIES AND TARTS—Make them at home, then you know that all the ingredients are pure, and that the cakes or pies are what they pretend to be.

BREAD—If your household consumes a large quantity of bread it pays to make it at home. If you are small bread eaters, it is cheaper to buy bread.

MAYONNAISE AND SALAD DRESSING—Both can be made easily and quickly at home, and it is more economical to make them when eggs and cream are cheap than to buy them.

BOTTLED FRUIT AND VEGETABLES—Bottle surplus fruit and vegetables or buy and bottle when they are cheapest.

SAVOURY PASTES—Mince any left-over fish, meat, poultry or game, mixed with a little softened butter, then rubbed through a sieve. Season highly to taste. Pot and cover with a layer of clarified butter. Serve at breakfast or high tea, or as a savoury at dinner, with toast.

CHRISTMAS FARE—Make your own mincemeat and plum puddings in October. Store mincemeat in tightly covered jars as you would jam and suspend puddings from a nail in a cool, dry, airy cupboard.

HERBS—Grow and dry your own herbs, then bottle them and tightly cork bottles before storing.

COOKING IN EMERGENCIES

To speed up work in the kitchen, to provide emergency meals, and to save labour in every-day catering as well as when an emergency occurs, you must learn to take short cuts to meals. You must also save labour wherever you can. This really means that you must plan ahead not only your work, but your shopping and your menus.

SHORT-CUTS FROM KITCHEN TO TABLE

(1) Buy non-perishables in quantity, if your store cupboard will accommodate them.

(2) Buy semi-perishables twice a week if you have refrigeration.

(3) Plan meals always two days ahead of the time.

(4) Keep a seasoning tray near the cooker.

(5) When a meal is wanted in an emergency, choose dishes that can be cooked quickly, and augment them from the store cupboard, so as to make an attractive menu.

(6) Memorise standard recipes for standard dishes.

(7) While cleaning up after one meal, prepare part of the next meal, or let part of the next meal cook.

(8) Use a high-pressure cooker.

(9) Work with stainless knives and on a porcelain-topped table.

(10) Specialise in half-hour meals.

(11) Arrange short menus. When working against time it is usually easier to serve one course with several accompaniments, such as a meat dish with two vegetables and a salad, and then a sweet, than to have a three-course meal, for you only have to serve and wash up for two courses.

(12) Cook and serve in fireproof ware.

(13) Cook at table when possible.

(14) When a meal is wanted in 5 minutes, fly to the nearest delicatessen shop and titivate what you buy at home before serving it.

Foods that can be Prepared Quickly

LIGHT SAVOURY DISHES—Scrambled eggs; baked eggs with cheese sauce; steamed eggs and cheese sauce; grilled sausages and mushrooms or tomatoes, and potato crisps; Welsh rarebit; savoury omelets; grilled fish; mixed grill; fish, meat, game or poultry cream with sliced, bottled mushrooms, or tinned peas, served on fried bread, buttered toast or in pastry cases which can be bought and kept in a tightly-closed tin.

VEGETABLES—Tinned peas drained and heated in melted butter or moistened with mayonnaise and made into a salad. Tinned beetroot, sliced thinly and sprinkled with equal quantities of minced parsley and onion—$\frac{1}{2}$ teaspoonful of each to a tin—and moistened with equal quantities of oil and vinegar. Serve with any cold meat.

HORS D'OEUVRES—Select from olives, tunny, and liver pâté, slices of cooked sausage, smoked ham, fillets of smoked herring, anchovies, sardines, and smoked mackerel, potato salad, Russian salad, green pea salad, etc. You should always have a cooked vegetable salad, a little fish and a little sausage, and some appetiser like olives, radishes, or salted nuts. Bismarck herring are a nice change from sardines.

SOUPS—Heat according to the directions on the tin, using stock in place of water or in place of part of it.

DESSERTS—Tinned fruit, served plain with cream or with custard made from custard powder; or made into a fool with an equal quantity of whipped cream or custard sauce; or made into fruit salad with the addition of sliced bananas, or one or two sliced fresh pears or peaches.

ICE CREAM—Serve alone to make stewed fruit go farther; or with hot tinned raspberries or strawberries poured over; or in sundae glasses with a tablespoonful of black coffee poured over, and sprinkled with chopped walnuts; or with a tablespoonful of tinned raspberries or strawberries poured over, and with whipped sweetened cream. Serve between slices of Swiss roll, or use as a filling for meringue cases.

WHAT TO KEEP IN YOUR STORE CUPBOARD

BOTTLED OR TINNED GOODS—All tinned vegetables and fruits; olives and anchovies (for hors d'œuvres or garnishing); cream; soups; liver pâté; fish, (tunny, salmon, mackerel, brislings, sardines, rollmops, etc.); grated or flaked cheese; cheese biscuits and ice cream wafers; fruit syrups; tomato juice; lemonade crystals; fruit juices; cup chocolate, etc., etc.

PACKET FOODS—Cereals (for breakfast); cereals (for milk puddings); jellies; custard powder and blancmange powder; sponge sandwich powder, etc.

MISCELLANEOUS STORES—Maraschino cherries for cocktails; pastry cases, meringue cases; ratafias and macaroons for trifles; packets of potato crisps; plain and self-raising flour, baking powder, yeast cakes; paper cases for soufflés and little cakes; soup squares; mincemeat; sauces, such as tomato and piquant sauce for steak, grated horseradish; junket powder; gelatine; jams, jellies and marmalades; lemon cheese and orange honey, etc.

MEAT CUBES AND EXTRACTS—If you always have a small stock of meat cubes and meat extract in your store cupboard, you will never be in want of soup stock or gravy. You can keep a small supply of both meat and turtle soup cubes, as well as extracts, then when any one wants a cup of hot soup in a hurry, it takes only a minute or two to prepare if you have no fresh stock handy.

These cubes or extracts are also useful for making stock when it is wanted in an emergency, and there is no time to make stock from meat and bones. An easy recipe is as follows : Put a quart of cold water in the stock-pot. Prepare and slice one carrot, half a head of celery, one onion and half a turnip, and add them to the cold water together with a bunch of herbs. Boil for $1\frac{1}{2}$ hours, then strain in half a cupful of hot water, in which you have dissolved two meat cubes, and season to taste with pepper and salt.

QUICKLY-MADE RECIPES
Salmon Ramekins

1 tin Middle-cut Salmon.	2 Eggs.
1 cupful fine Breadcrumbs.	1 cupful Milk.
1½ teaspoonfuls Parsley.	Pepper and Salt.

UTENSILS—Two basins, knife, fork, wooden spoon, teaspoon, cup, sieve or grater, chopping board, egg-beater, 6 ramekins. *Enough for 6 persons.*

Remove all skin and bone from the salmon. Flake it into a basin, then stir in the crumbs, minced parsley, eggs beaten and mixed with the milk, and pepper and salt to taste. Divide between buttered ramekins. Bake till set and pale gold on top, from 8 to 15 minutes, or the mixture can be steamed for 1 hour.

Tomato Purée

To continue with savoury dishes which you can provide at short notice so long as you have a well-stocked store cupboard, remember that a small tin of tomato purée can be added to boiled rice, just enough to moisten, then flavoured with grated cheese and shaped into croquettes, and you have a delicious substitute for potatoes if you fry them in the usual way.

There is so much you can do with tomato purée or sauce or pulp. Sliced, hard-boiled eggs can be served masked with one or other for lunch ; mayonnaise can be flavoured with it ; or it can be made into a sauté, together with a little bacon and onion, and served with boiled spaghetti, sprinkled thickly with grated cheese. Again, it can form the basis of cream of tomato soup with the assistance of well-seasoned white sauce.

Tinned Peas

The simplest way to serve tinned peas is to heat them in their own liquor in a tin, then drain them, season to taste with pepper and salt, and moisten with butter. Serve on a hot vegetable dish.

Carrots and Peas

1 tin of Carrots.	1 cupful Stock.
2 tablespoonfuls Butter.	1 tin of Peas.
2 tablespoonfuls Flour.	

UTENSILS—Tin-opener, cup, tablespoon, saucepan.

Mix the carrots well with the peas. Sprinkle them with flour, salt, sugar, and pepper to taste. Add the butter and stock, and boil for a short time, then serve hot.

Corn Fritters

1 tin of Corn.	1 cupful Flour.
1 teaspoonful Baking Powder.	2 teaspoonfuls Salt.
¼ teaspoonful Paprika.	2 Eggs.

UTENSILS—Three basins, knife, teaspoon, wooden spoon, cup, sieve, egg-beater, frying pan.

Chop the corn, drain it and add to it the dry ingredients mixed and sifted. Add the yolks of eggs beaten until thick, and fold in the whites of eggs beaten stiff. Cook in a frying pan in fresh hot lard. Drain on paper before serving.

To Prepare Tinned Asparagus

Open one end of the tin, as indicated on the wrapper, so that the tips will be at the opening. Pour off the liquid and allow cold water to run gently over the asparagus and to rinse it. Drain again, then pour boiling water over, and set the tin in a hot oven to heat thoroughly. When ready to serve, drain the stalks and arrange them carefully on a hot plate, and serve like fresh asparagus, hot with melted butter, or cold with salad dressing. If liked, Hollandaise sauce can be poured over.

Stewed Tomatoes

1 quart tin of Tomatoes.	1 small Onion.
1 tablespoonful Sugar.	1 tablespoonful Butter.

Pepper and Salt.

UTENSILS—Knife, tablespoon, plate, stewpan. *Enough for 6 persons.*

Drain the tomatoes, add the finely chopped onion, the sugar, and salt and pepper to taste, then simmer for 10 minutes. Add the butter just before serving.

TINNED FRUIT RECIPES

No matter what else you have in your store cupboard, you should always have a plentiful supply of tinned fruit. There is so much that you can do with a tin of fruit, especially if called upon to provide an emergency meal. You can, if it is fruit salad, serve it in a glass dish accompanied by thick cream or almond or vanilla custard sauce, or, if you have time to cook, a baked custard or a blancmange. If you want it for a party, you can cut it up into small pieces, and serve it in tall glasses, each decorated with a bottled cherry. You can make it into fritters, into a trifle, or into a fool by putting it through a sieve and stirring slowly into it an equal quantity of whipped cream or vanilla custard. You can make it into shortcake by slicing it and spreading it between two rounds of shortcake, and heaping it on top with whipped cream.

When it is served in a dish or in tall glasses with cream, sponge fingers or thin triangles of jam sandwich can be passed with it. When it is made into a trifle, place the sponge cakes, split and spread with jam, in the bottom of the dish, using half apricot and half raspberry jam, then pour over the cake the juice from the tin of fruit, and when the cake has absorbed all the juice, lay a layer of the fruit on the top. Cover this with a thin layer of vanilla custard, and when cold, pile it up with whipped cream. When cream is scarce, it can be eked out by the addition of two stiffly whipped whites of egg, but if you do this, you must serve the trifle immediately it is prepared. Decorate with grated chocolate, chopped candied fruits, silver balls or hundreds and thousands.

The following are other recipes for using up tinned fruits :

Pineapple Pudding

1 cupful Pineapple Juice.	2 tablespoonfuls Cornflour.
1 cupful Pineapple Cubes.	2 Eggs, separated.
1 cupful Water.	Whipped Cream.
Juice of 1 Lemon.	½ cupful Sugar.

UTENSILS—Double boiler, wooden spoon, tablespoon, cup, lemon squeezer, 2 basins, wire whisk, baking dish. *Enough for 4 persons.*

Mix the sugar and cornflour together, place them in the top of a double boiler, stir in the pineapple juice, water and lemon, and cook until smooth. Pour this mixture on to the beaten yolks, fold in the beaten whites, and then add the pineapple cubes. Pour into a buttered baking dish, set in a slow oven, and bake for 20 minutes. When cool, top with whipped cream and serve.

Loganberry Pudding

¾ cupful Tinned Loganberries.	Butter.
6 slices of stale Bread.	Loganberry Juice.

UTENSILS—Mould, knife, cup. *Enough for 3 persons.*

Spread 6 slices of stale bread with butter, place one half in the bottom of a well-greased mould, put ¾ cupful of tinned loganberries in a layer over this, and place the remainder of the bread on top. Pour 1 cupful of the syrup over all, place a weight on top, and stand in a cold place for 12 hours. Turn out of the mould and serve with cream, if desired.

Cherry Mould

1 cupful Cherry Juice.	1 Egg. ½ Lemon.
1 cupful Cherries.	1 tablespoonful Cooking Oil or
1 cupful fine, dry Breadcrumbs.	melted Fat.
2 teaspoonfuls Baking Powder.	1 cupful Rolled Oats.

1 teaspoonful Cornflour.

UTENSILS—Two basins, measuring spoons, cup, wooden spoon, egg-beater, lemon squeezer, grater, knife, mould, saucepan. *Enough for 3 or 4 persons.*

Mix 1 cupful of fine dry breadcrumbs with 1 cupful of rolled oats, add the baking powder and cornflour, and mix thoroughly. Beat the egg, add a cupful of syrup from the tinned cherries, and the grated rind and juice of half a lemon, and mix them with the dry ingredients. Add a cupful of tinned cherries, stoned, and 1 tablespoonful of cooking oil or melted fat. Pack in a greased mould and steam for 2 hours. Serve with Cherry Mould sauce.

CHERRY MOULD SAUCE

½ cupful Syrup from Cherries.	½ cupful Brown Sugar.
1 tablespoonful Cornflour.	3 tablespoonfuls cold Water.

1 Orange.

UTENSILS—Saucepan, basin, wooden spoon, tablespoon, cup, orange squeezer.

Bring ½ cupful of syrup from tinned cherries, and the brown sugar, to the boiling point. Add the cornflour, moistened with 3 tablespoonfuls of cold water. Boil for 5 minutes, add the juice of an orange, and serve.

Peach Betty

1½ cupfuls Tinned, Sliced Peaches.	1 cupful Breadcrumbs.
Sugar.	Cinnamon.
2 tablespoonfuls Butter.	¾ cupful Water.

UTENSILS—Baking dish, tablespoon, cup, sieve or grater, knife. *Enough for 3 or 4 persons.*

Arrange the breadcrumbs and tinned sliced peaches, which have been drained, in alternate layers in a greased baking dish. Sprinkle each layer of peaches with sugar and a little cinnamon, dot with 2 tablespoonfuls of butter, pour the water over all, and bake for 35 minutes in a moderate oven.

Baked Pears

6 halved Tinned Pears.	½ Lemon. Soft Crumbs.
¼ cupful Pear Syrup.	Cinnamon. Butter.
Brown Sugar.	½ cupful Seedless Raisins.

UTENSILS—Baking dish, lemon squeezer, cup, knife, metal spoon, grater. *Enough for 3 persons.*

Arrange the halved tinned pears in a shallow greased baking dish. Pour over them the lemon juice and ½ cupful of syrup from the pears. Cover with soft crumbs, sprinkle lightly with brown sugar, cinnamon, and the seedless raisins. Dot with a little butter, and bake until the crumbs are brown.

Scalloped Plums

1 cupful Tinned Plums.	1½ cupfuls Breadcrumbs.
¼ cupful Plum Syrup.	Hot Water.

UTENSILS—Knife, basin, grater or sieve, cup, spoon, baking dish. *Enough for 3 persons.*

Mix a cupful of tinned plums, stoned and cut in pieces, with the breadcrumbs. Put in a greased baking dish, pour over ¼ cup each of syrup from the plums and hot water, and bake in a moderate oven for 25 minutes. Serve with Lemon Sauce or Plum Sauce.

PLUM SAUCE

1 cupful Syrup from Tinned Plums.	**1** tablespoonful **Cornflour.**
	3 tablespoonfuls Sugar.
2 tablespoonfuls cold Water.	

UTENSILS—Saucepan, tablespoon, cup, basin, wooden spoon.

Heat 1 cupful of syrup from the tinned plums, add the sugar and the cornflour moistened with the cold water. Boil for 10 minutes and serve hot.

Loganberry Bavaroise

1½ cups Tinned Loganberries.	¼ cupful Castor Sugar.
1 tablespoonful Lemon Juice.	¼ tablespoonful Gelatine.
3 gills whipped Cream.	

UTENSILS—Two basins, double boiler, cup, tablespoon, gill measure, wooden spoon, sieve, lemon squeezer, wire whisk, mould. *Enough for 3 or 4 persons.*

Rub the loganberries through a sieve. Then pour just

enough cold water over the gelatine to cover it. Stir the gelatine over hot water till melted. Now add the melted gelatine to the lemon juice and the loganberry purée, and keep beating till the mixture begins to thicken, when fold in the whipped cream, sweetened with castor sugar. Pour into a mould, and turn out when cold and set. Garnish with blobs of whipped, sweetened cream flavoured with lemon and with whole loganberries.

Amber Soufflés

Tinned Peaches.	1 gill Cream.
2 tablespoonfuls Peach Syrup.	1 tablespoonful Gelatine.
2 tablespoonfuls Castor Sugar.	1 teaspoonful Lemon Juice.

3 Whites of Eggs.

UTENSILS—Three basins, sieve, wooden spoon, measuring spoons, gill measure, strainer, wire whisk. *Enough for 3 or 4 persons.*

Rub enough tinned peaches through a sieve to give you ½ pint of peach purée. Then dissolve the gelatine in peach syrup, and strain it into the purée. Now add the strained lemon juice, sugar, the stiffly beaten whites of eggs, and the cream. If very thick, quickly stir in a little more peach syrup. Pile up in champagne glasses, and when cold and set place half a peach on top of each.

READY-MADE ICE CREAM

If you are unable to buy ice in quantity, you can still have various ice cream dishes if you can obtain ice bricks of ready-made ice cream. These bricks can be served as they are, or in the form of sundaes, or with stewed fruit or crushed sweetened berries.

TO MAKE SUNDAES

Allow a quart of ice cream for 9 persons.

Put a scoop of ice cream on each plate, or in each glass, and finish in any of the following ways :

(1) Pour over each a tablespoonful of coffee butterscotch sauce and sprinkle with crushed meringue or with home-made praline powder. This is made by cooking 2 cupfuls of castor sugar till it turns into caramel, then adding a cupful of blanched almonds, and stirring them into the caramel for a few moments before cooling and rolling into powder.

(2) Pour a tablespoonful of honey over each portion of ice cream, then sprinkle with chopped nuts.

(3) Pour 2 tablespoonfuls of hot coffee over each portion of vanilla ice cream.

(4) Melt $\frac{1}{2}$ lb. marshmallows in a double boiler, add 2 cupfuls of icing sugar, and $\frac{1}{2}$ cupful of water. Stir till smooth, then bring to the boil, and pour over chocolate or coffee ice cream.

(5) Boil $\frac{3}{4}$ cupful of castor sugar and $\frac{1}{2}$ cupful of water for 10 minutes. Cool, and stir the syrup into 1 pint of crushed berries. Use with lemon or vanilla ice cream.

(6) Peel and slice 4 bananas, and place them in the bottom of 9 sundae glasses. Put a spoonful of pineapple juice over each, and divide the ice cream between the glasses. Decorate with a ring of angelica.

HINTS ON MAKING SIMPLER SUNDAES

Place a scoop of vanilla ice cream in the bottom of each sundae glass, and cover with the following :

(1) Crushed pineapple, then whipped cream, and top with a berry or cherry.

(2) Two tablespoonfuls of maple or chocolate syrup, then whipped cream, and sprinkle with chopped nuts.

(3) Two tablespoonfuls of crushed berries, then grated cocoanut or crushed meringue.

(4) Chopped dates, nuts and figs in equal quantities, moistened with maple syrup, then with cream, and decorated with chopped marshmallows.

CAKE IN EMERGENCIES

LAYERS OF SPONGE CAKE

If you always keep several rounds of sponge cake or cake made with Victoria sandwich mixture, in a tightly closed cake tin, you will never be short of either cakes for tea or Sunday night's supper, or cold sweets for lunch or dinner. It is a good idea to have four layers always in hand. They need not go to waste, because they can be used up in a trifle or in custard, and in several other cold sweets.

If you have these rounds, you can put two together with any jam, or with lemon curd or a thick custard, and either ice the top and decorate with glacé fruits, or simply dust it with powdered sugar, and you have a delicious cake for tea.

The following are some recipes for easily-made fillings for making layers into attractive cakes, as well as some simple sponge mixtures.

Nut Filling

2 cupfuls Icing Sugar.
1 tablespoonful finely-minced Pecans or Walnuts.

½ tablespoonful Cocoa Powder.
½ cupful fresh Butter.
4 tablespoonfuls strong Coffee.

UTENSILS—Basin, cup, tablespoon, wooden spoon, coffee percolator or pot, knife.

Beat the butter and sugar to a cream. Add the cocoa, coffee, and the nuts, finely crushed, then use.

Whipped Fruit Filling

1½ cupfuls grated Apple, mashed Berries or Pears.

1½ cupfuls Sugar.
2 Whites of Eggs.

Grated Rind of 1 Lemon.

UTENSILS—Basin, cup, grater, fork, wire whisk.

Mix all the ingredients together and beat with a wire egg-beater until very stiff, then use.

Whipped Cream Filling

¾ cupful thick Cream.
¼ cupful Powdered Sugar.

1 White of Egg.
½ teaspoonful Vanilla.

UTENSILS—Two basins, wire whisk, cup, teaspoon, pan.

Set a medium-sized bowl in a pan of crushed ice to which water has been added. Place the cream in the bowl and beat it until stiff with a wire whisk, or, if possible, use a patent cream whipper. Whip up well, so that the air bubbles may not be too large. Add the sugar, the white of egg beaten stiff, and the vanilla. Keep cool until ready to serve.

Any layer cake may be filled with crushed stewed berries thickened with syrup or gelatine.

Sponge Mixture

You can make sponge sandwiches with eggs, sugar and flour, or with butter, eggs, sugar and flour in the spring when eggs are very plentiful, but when prices rise, and you think twice before using three or four or more eggs in a cake, a packet of sponge mixture comes in very handy.

A packet of sponge mixture is also very useful when friends turn up unexpectedly to tea, and the cake tin is empty. The following are simple recipes for using with sponge mixture, which can be bought in three or four different flavours—standard, lemon, vanilla, or almond.

Sponge Sandwich

2 Eggs.
1 packet of Sponge Mixture.

1 teaspoonful Butter.
Raspberry Jam.

UTENSILS—Two basins, egg-beater, wooden spoon, teaspoon, 2 sandwich tins, palette knife, knife, cloth.

Turn the sponge mixture into a basin. Beat the eggs thoroughly, and stir them into the mixture and add the teaspoonful of butter, slightly melted. Beat to a smooth paste. Well grease two round sandwich tins, and pour the mixture half into one and half into the other. Spread evenly with a palette knife. Bake in a hot oven for about 5 minutes. Turn out on to a cloth sprinkled with castor sugar, and when cold spread one half with raspberry jam.

To Make a Swiss Roll

Follow exactly the method for making a sponge cake, but pour the mixture into a well-buttered, oblong tin. When baked, turn out quickly, and trim the edges just as quickly with a sharp knife. Spread with warm jam, heated before the cake comes out of the oven. Roll up as fast as you can.

Economical Sponge Sandwich, or Roll

Follow the directions for making the above sandwich, but use only 1 egg. Add sufficient milk to make up for the second egg, and beat all together thoroughly.

To vary sponge sandwiches and Swiss rolls, you can use lemon cheese, pineapple jam, honey, or orange honey as a filling. If the whole sandwich is baked in one tin, it can be split into three instead of two, and two layers can be put together with raspberry jam, and the third with apricot jam.

BREAKFAST DISHES

Grilled Bacon

UTENSILS—Knife, double gridiron, frying pan.

Choose nice, firm, streaky bacon for grilling. With a sharp knife cut off the rind, and any bones there may be. Cut the bacon into very thin slices, unless it is bought in rashers—the slices should be longer for grilling than for frying. Lay the slices on a double gridiron, and grill them, turning them once during the cooking. Arrange the bacon on a hot dish, and garnish with tippets of fried bread.

Rice Cakes and Bacon

2 cupfuls Cooked Rice.	½ teaspoonful Salt.
2 tablespoonfuls Milk.	Rashers of Wiltshire Bacon.
1 beaten Egg.	½ teaspoonful Baking Powder.
½ cupful Flour.	

UTENSILS—Two basins, sieve or flour dredger, egg-beater, measuring cup and spoons, wooden spoon, frying pan, fork. *Enough for 3 or 4 persons.*

Sift the flour, salt and baking powder into a basin, then stir in the egg, mixed with the milk, and then the rice. Have the bacon ready to serve, and arrange it in a circle on a round dish, while the rice batter is frying in tablespoonfuls in the fat from the bacon. Fry the cakes on both sides till brown, turning them only once. Pile them up in the centre of the bacon, and serve.

French Toast

4 thick slices of Bread.	½ pint Milk.
1 Egg.	Pepper and Salt.
4 rashers of Bacon.	

UTENSILS—Egg-beater, basin, spoon, baking tin, fork, knife. *Enough for 2 persons.*

Beat the egg and gradually stir in the milk, and season to taste. Dip the slices of bread in the mixture and arrange them on a greased tin. On each slice place a thin, rolled rasher of fat bacon. Place the tin in a hot oven or under the gas griller. Serve when nicely browned—in about 10 minutes' time.

Fried Cod's Roe with Scrambled Eggs

1 tin Smoked Cod's Roe.	1½ oz. Butter.
6 rashers Bacon, halved.	1 teacupful Milk.
1 tablespoonful Fat.	Minced Parsley.
4 Eggs.	Pepper and Salt.

UTENSILS—Frying pan, knife, basin, egg-beater, teacup, tablespoon, fork. *Enough for 3 persons.*

Turn out a tin of cod's roe. Melt the fat in a frying pan, when smoking hot fry the roe, cut up into suitable pieces, until pale brown on each side.

Serve on a hot dish, arranged round a heap of well-seasoned scrambled eggs, made with the eggs, butter, milk and pepper and salt, and sprinkled with minced parsley. Arrange fried rashers of bacon round each roe.

Eggs on the Dish

6 Eggs.	3 tablespoonfuls Cream.
1 oz. Butter.	Pepper and Salt.

UTENSILS—Fireproof baking dish, larger baking dish, measuring spoon, knife. *Enough for 6 persons.*

Butter a shallow fireproof china dish. Break the eggs carefully into it, one by one, being careful not to break the yolks. Sprinkle a little salt and white pepper over the eggs, pour the cream on them, and put in the remainder of the butter.

Stand the dish in another, containing water, and put into a moderate oven for 4 or 5 minutes. Take out, and brown the eggs under the grill. Serve in the dish in which the eggs were cooked, placed in another.

Egg and Sausage Scramble

8 Midget Pork Sausages.	3 tablespoonfuls Milk.
1 Egg.	½ teaspoonful chopped Parsley.
2 extra Yolks	Pinch of Herbs.
2 oz. Butter.	Salt and Pepper.

UTENSILS — Knife, fork, egg-beater, 2 basins, measuring spoons, saucepan. *Enough for 4 persons.*

Skin and mash par-boiled sausages, moisten them with the beaten egg and yolks, and add the milk, parsley, crushed herbs, pepper and salt. Place the mixture in a saucepan and cook till tender. Serve piled up on squares of hot buttered toast.

Mushroom Omelet [1]

| 4 Eggs. | 1½ oz. Butter. |
| ¼ lb. Mushrooms. | A dust of Cayenne. |

Salt to Taste.

UTENSILS—Knife, frying pan, omelet pan (measuring 6 inches across), basin, egg-beater, palette knife. *Enough for 2 persons.*

Peel the mushrooms and chop them rather finely. Melt half an ounce of butter in a frying pan, put in the mushrooms, season slightly with pepper and salt, and fry gently.

Melt one ounce of butter in the omelet pan. Beat the eggs slightly, and season them with cayenne pepper and salt. Mix well together, and when the butter is boiling in the omelet pan, pour in the eggs.

Keep the egg well stirred from the sides and bottom of the pan to prevent it from sticking ; a broad palette knife is the most convenient for this purpose. Keep raising the mixture from the bottom of the pan, letting that which is uncooked run underneath. When it is nearly all set, put the fried mushrooms on one half of it, and tilt the pan, so that the other half folds over the mushrooms. See that the mixture is quite free from the pan everywhere, then turn it quickly on to a hot dish and serve at once.

NOTE.—Many kinds of cooked vegetables, such as asparagus points, peas, tomatoes, etc., or minced kidneys, prawns warmed in white sauce, lobster, and other savoury foods may be used in place of the mushrooms.

Grilled Dried Haddock

| 1 Haddock. | Pepper. | 3 oz. Butter. |

UTENSILS—Knife, brush for melted butter, dish, gridiron, saucepan. *Enough for 2 to 4 persons, according to size of fish.*

Trim off the fins and tail of the haddock, and lay it on a dish. Melt two ounces of butter. Brush this over the haddock, then sprinkle the fish with white pepper. Let it stand for ½ hour, or longer. Grease the bars of a fish gridiron, and lay the fish on it. Broil over a clear fire or under a gas flame for 10 or 12 minutes, according to size.

Melt the remainder of the butter, and when the fish is done lay it on a hot dish and pour this melted butter over it. Sprinkle with a little coralline pepper. Now lay the fish on

[1] See INDEX for other OMELETS.

another hot dish with a fish-paper under it, and garnish with a few sprigs of parsley. Serve very hot.

Fried Fresh Herrings

| 3 Herrings. | Frying Fat. |
| Flour. | Pepper and Salt. |

UTENSILS—Large basin, drying cloth, knife, frying pan, fish-slice. *Enough for 3 persons.*

Wash the herrings well in salt water and dry them thoroughly on a clean cloth. Cut off the heads, tails and fins. Make three incisions (cut with a knife, but not deep) down each side of the fish. Sprinkle them with pepper and salt, seeing that it goes well into the cuts. Then roll the fish in flour so that they get well coated with it. Put them into boiling fat, but draw the pan to one side so that it just continues to boil, but not fast. This will prevent the herrings from becoming too brown before they are cooked through. Fry for 10 minutes, or rather less according to size, and take up when they are a nice golden brown.

Place on a dish lined with a fish-paper, and garnish with fresh green parsley. Send to the table at once.

Kedgeree

2 teacupfuls Boiled Fish.	1 oz. Butter.
1 teacupful Boiled Rice.	2 teaspoonfuls Milk.
2 hard-boiled Eggs.	Cayenne. Salt.

UTENSILS—Knife, fork, saucepans, wooden spoon, teacup, teaspoon. *Enough for 2 persons.*

Almost any boiled fish will do for this dish, but fresh or smoked haddock is best. Before the fish is quite cold, free it from skin and bone, and divide it into flakes. Melt the butter in a saucepan. Add the milk and a seasoning of cayenne, then boil up. When the milk is boiling, stir in the flaked fish and mix well.

Now add the boiled rice, eggs (coarsely chopped), and salt to taste. Let all get thoroughly hot, then turn it out on to a hot dish, in a neat pile. Garnish with slices of hard-boiled egg and sprigs of parsley. If liked, a tablespoonful of chutney may be added.

Grilled Kidneys

6 Kidneys.
6 rashers of Bacon.
Buttered Toast.

Maître d'Hôtel Butter.
Pepper and Salt.
A few Mushrooms.

UTENSILS—Knife, skewers, grill, toasting fork or toaster. *Enough for 3 persons.*

Split the kidneys in two lengthways, then skin and thread them on skewers. Pass the skewer first through one end of a rasher of bacon, then through one edge of a kidney, with the cut side of the kidney towards the bacon. Then through the other edge of the kidney, then the other end of the rasher. Do all in the same manner, then lay the skewered kidneys and bacon on a hot grill, with the bacon side next the fire. Cook on this side for 3 or 4 minutes, then turn over. Cook the other side for the same time, then sprinkle with pepper and salt.

Have ready three slices of hot buttered toast. Slip the kidneys off the skewers on to the toast, two on each. Put a small piece of maître d'hôtel butter quickly into each one. If the bacon is not cooked too much, serve it with the kidneys. Send to table at once, very hot, garnished with fried mushrooms.

NOTE.—If wanted for luncheon, serve with potato straws, garnished with watercress.

Fried Kippers

UTENSILS—Shallow dish, cloth, frying pan, fork.

Place the kippers, allowing one for each person, in a shallow dish. Cover them with hot water, and stand for 1 minute, then wipe them quite dry. Melt a spoonful of butter in a frying pan, and arrange as many kippers as the pan will hold, skin downwards, in the smoking-hot butter. Fry slowly, and when brown, turn the kippers and brown them on the other side. Serve at once with toast and butter.

NOTE.—If kippers are dry or too strongly smoked, steep them for an hour instead of a minute before drying and frying.

LUNCHEON AND SUPPER DISHES[1]

Egg and Tomato Toast

3 Eggs.	Onion.
2 medium-sized Tomatoes.	2 oz. Butter.
¼ teaspoonful Shallot.	Pepper and Salt.

UTENSILS—Knife, saucepan, basin, egg-beater, kitchen spoon, teaspoon, toasting fork or toaster. *Enough for 3 persons.*

Skin the tomatoes (dip them first in boiling water), and slice them, after removing the seeds. Melt one ounce of butter in a saucepan, put in the shallots, finely chopped (or onion will do), and the slices of tomato, and cook these gently for 10 minutes. Beat the eggs, and season with pepper and salt. Stir them into the saucepan, with the tomato, and keep constantly stirred until the mixture thickens.

Have ready some neat squares of buttered toast, and spread the mixture thickly on these. Arrange them on a hot dish, and garnish with sprigs of parsley, and serve.

Eggs in Cases

5 Eggs. 1 oz. Butter.	3 tablespoons Béchamel Sauce.
2 tablespoons chopped Ham.	2 tablespoons grated Cheese.
Pepper and Salt.	1 teaspoonful chopped Parsley.

UTENSILS—China egg dishes, knife, measuring spoons, grater, saucepan, deep baking tin, wooden spoon. *Enough for 3 to 5 persons.*

Take five little china cases, and butter them well. Sprinkle chopped ham in the bottom of each. Then break an egg into each one. Mix the grated cheese with the sauce. Sprinkle pepper and salt on the eggs, then put a tablespoonful of the sauce on top of each one. Stand the china cases in a tin of water, the water reaching three-fourths the way up the cases. Stand them in a moderate oven, near the top, so that they may brown when cooking. They will cook in 8 to 10 minutes.

Take them out, stand the cases on a dish, with a fancy

[1] See also ENTREES, page 216.

dish-paper beneath. Sprinkle a little finely chopped parsley on each, and serve.

Curried Eggs

4 Eggs. 1 Onion.	1 dessertspoonful Flour.
1 oz. Butter. Rice.	¼ pint Milk. Salt.
1 dessertspoonful Curry Powder.	1 dessertspoonful Desiccated
1 teaspoonful Curry Paste.	Cocoanut.

UTENSILS—Knife, stewpan, wooden spoon, measuring spoons, gill or pint measure, strainer, saucepan. *Enough for 4 persons.*

Peel the onion, and chop it finely. Melt the butter in a stewpan, add the onion, and fry together gently for 10 minutes, without browning. Then mix in the curry powder and paste, and cook them together gently for another 5 minutes. Now stir in the flour, and add the milk by degrees, stirring all the time, then add the cocoanut. Let all simmer gently for ½ hour, then strain, and add salt to taste.

Boil four eggs quite hard, and cut them in halves, lengthways. Lay them in the curry sauce, and let them remain in it for an hour or two. Then gently heat them thoroughly in the sauce.

Make a border of rice down each side of a hot dish, lay the eggs carefully down the centre, pour the sauce over them, and serve. If liked, the yolk of a hard-boiled egg can be rubbed through a sieve, and the rice sprinkled with this.

Egg Cutlets

4 Eggs.	1 teaspoonful chopped Parsley.
1 tablespoonful cooked Lean Ham	Breadcrumbs.
or Tongue, finely chopped.	Frying Fat.
1 oz. Flour.	Seasoning of Salt and Cayenne
1 oz. Butter.	Pepper.
¼ pint Milk.	A few pieces of Macaroni or
4 Mushrooms.	Spaghetti.

UTENSILS—2 saucepans, basin, knife, measuring spoons, pastry board, wooden spoon, plate, egg-beater, grater, frying pan, frying basket. *Enough for 4 persons.*

Boil three eggs for 10 minutes in sufficient water to cover them well. Take them up, and put into cold water to keep them a good colour. When cold, shell, and chop them up rather coarsely. Now melt butter in a saucepan, add the flour, and fry together for a minute without browning. Add the milk by degrees. Cook sauce gently for 7 minutes, then add the raw yolk of the fourth egg, and after this the finely chopped ham, parsley, the mushrooms finely chopped, seasoning, and the chopped eggs. Mix all well together, and put on a plate to cool.

When cool, dust some dry flour on a board, put a table-spoonful of the mixture on it, flour your hands, and roll the material into a ball. Flatten the ball slightly and, with the flat side of a broad knife, form into cutlet shape. Keep the thumb of the left hand at the side of the cutlet and work the mixture down it, so that you make the curve of the cutlet, working the knife with the right hand. With a little practice the cutlets can be formed perfectly, but do not make them too flat. Dip each cutlet into beaten egg, then into finely-made white breadcrumbs.

Put in a frying-basket, and fry a nice golden brown. Stick a piece of macaroni or spaghetti, about one inch and a half long, in the narrow end of each cutlet, and dish on a paper on a circle, resting one on the other. Put a cutlet frill on each piece of macaroni, and a bunch of parsley should be placed in the centre of the dish as a garnish.

Scotch Eggs

5 Eggs.	6 oz. Cold Meat.	1 teaspoonful chopped Parsley.	
2 oz. stale Bread.		½ teaspoonful nutmeg.	
Breadcrumbs.		¼ teaspoonful Pepper.	
1 teaspoonful chopped Onion.		½ teaspoonful Salt.	

UTENSILS—Saucepan, 2 basins, mincing machine, knife, stewpan, teaspoon, cloth, wooden spoon, egg-beater, grater, 2 plates, chopping board. *Enough for 4 persons.*

Put 4 eggs into a saucepan, cover them with cold water, bring them to the boil and boil for 7 minutes, then pour off the boiling water and stand the eggs in cold water. Weigh 6 oz. of any cold meat, without skin or gristle, and if you have them, include slices of ham or bacon in the 6 oz. Soak the stale bread—crusts will do—in cold water, and pass the meat through the mincing machine. Add to the meat the finely chopped parsley and onion, a grate of nutmeg, the pepper, salt according to taste, not forgetting the saltness of the bacon. Wring the bread quite dry in a cloth, break it up well, and add it to the other ingredients, then mix with a whole raw egg.

Shell the hard-boiled eggs and cut them in half length-ways. Take a piece of the minced meat mixture, flatten it out, put the half of an egg in the centre, and fold the meat all round. Roll it in flour, then in whole beaten-up egg, then in fine white breadcrumbs. Drop the eggs into boiling fat and fry till golden. Drain from fat and serve.

NOTE.—Any bought sausage meat can be substituted for the prepared cold meat.

Stewed Kidneys

6 Sheep's Kidneys.	1 small teaspoonful Salt.
1 teaspoonful finely chopped Parsley.	2 tablespoonfuls Flour.
	1 oz. Butter.
½ teaspoonful Pepper.	12 slices of Bacon.

UTENSILS—Knife, plate, frying pan, measuring spoons, fork, saucepan, toasting fork or toaster, coarse strainer, skewer. *Enough for 6 persons.*

When the kidneys are obtained from the butcher, see that they are perfectly thawed and soft, if they are imported. To thaw them, stand them in the warm kitchen, but not near the fire. They may take several hours to thaw properly. When quite soft, like an ordinary English kidney, skin them, cut them in halves lengthwise, and remove as much of the kernel as possible. Dip each half-kidney in flour mixed with the parsley and pepper and salt, on a plate.

Melt the butter in a frying-pan, and lay the kidneys in it with the cut side downward, only covering the pan with one layer. If the pan will not hold all the kidneys at once, they must be cooked in two batches. Cook very gently at the side of the range for 10 minutes, but *be sure not to cook them fast or they will become hard.* Turn them once only in the frying, and do this when the red gravy is seen to come to the surface of the kidney.

When the kidneys are thus sautéd, put them into a saucepan with a liquid made up as follows :

Pour ½ pint of water or weak stock into the frying pan, and boil it up with the gravy left by the kidneys. Pour this sauce into the saucepan with the kidneys, simmer gently, in fact, barely simmer, for 1 hour.

Lay six half-slices of buttered toast on a dish, put two half-kidneys on each half-slice, and garnish with small rolls of bacon placed round. Boil the gravy up, strain it through a coarse strainer, and pour it round the kidneys. Serve with mashed potatoes.

TO PREPARE THE BACON

Cut twelve slices of bacon about 2½ inches long. Roll the slices, then run them on a skewer, and either grill them or cook them in the oven. If the oven is nice and hot, 3 minutes will be long enough. Remove the rolls from the skewer, place them round the kidneys, and serve at once.

Devilled Kidneys

6 Sheep's Kidneys.
1 oz. Butter.
1 dessertspoonful Worcester
    Sauce.

2 teaspoonfuls Mustard.
1 small teaspoonful Salt.
½ teaspoonful Black Pepper.
Maître d'Hôtel Butter.

UTENSILS—Knife, skewers, gridiron, measuring spoons, 2 plates. *Enough for 6 persons.*

Skin the kidneys, split them open, and take out the cores, then thread them on skewers, as directed for GRILLED KIDNEYS (see Index), but without the bacon. Dip them into oiled butter or salad oil. Broil them over a clear fire, or under the gas grill, for a minute.

Have ready, well mixed on a plate, the mustard, Worcester sauce, pepper and salt. Roll the kidneys in this, then again in the oiled butter or salad oil. Finish broiling them, giving 3 or 4 minutes on each side. Slip them off the skewers, on to a very hot dish, put a small piece of maître d'hôtel butter (see Index) on each, and serve quickly.

Brains on Toast

2 sets of Brains.
White Stock.
1 Egg.   Vinegar.
8 rolled slices of Bacon.

4 croûtons of Fried Bread.
Breadcrumbs.
Lemon.   Parsley.
Frying Fat.

UTENSILS—Basins, knife, saucepan, frying pan, skewers, grater, egg-beater, baking tin, fork. *Enough for 4 persons.*

Always be careful that the brains are quite fresh. Let them lie for an hour in a basin of cold water, to which a teaspoonful of vinegar has been added. Remove the skins, and put the brains into a saucepan, with sufficient well-flavoured cold white stock to cover. Bring to the boil, simmer gently for 10 minutes, then lift the brains out, and let them get cold.

Cut four croûtons of bread, the same size round as the brains, and fry them a pale gold colour.

When the brains are cold, dip them into whole beaten-up

egg, and then into fine white breadcrumbs. Fry them a nice brown. Roll and thread the bacon on skewers, and while the brains are frying, put it in a tin, into a hot oven, and cook for two or three minutes. Drain the brains, and stand each one on a croûton of bread, on a dish. Put the rolled bacon in the centre, and garnish with a few sprigs of either fried or fresh parsley and slices of lemon.

Fish and Tomato Scallops

Any left-over White Fish.   **Some mashed Potatoes.**
½ lb. Tomatoes.   **½ pint White Sauce.**

UTENSILS—Basin, spoon, pint measure, fork, scallop shells, knife. *Enough for 4 persons.*

Mix boned fish with white sauce and fill scallop shells with same. Cover with mashed potato, and place on each scallop two halves of tomato and a piece of butter. Bake in the oven until the tomato is cooked.

Sausage Rolls

½ lb. Sausages.   **1 Egg.** | **½ lb. Puff Paste.**

UTENSILS—Two basins, knife, pastry board, rolling pin, pastry brush, saucepan, wooden spoon, egg-beater, baking sheet. *Enough for 3 or 4 persons.*

Boil the sausages for 5 minutes, then skin them, and when cold, cut them in half, lengthways. Prepare half a pound of puff paste, and roll it out to about an eighth of an inch in thickness. (For PUFF PASTE, see Index.) Cut it into squares, about four inches and a half across. Brush along the two side edges of these with cold water. Lay a piece of sausage on the side nearest you, seeing that the paste reaches half an inch beyond each end of the sausage. Now roll it over, until the far edge of the paste is reached, and brush this edge over with cold water, to make it stick. Press the ends of the paste gently together, and brush the tops of the rolls over with whole beaten-up egg.

Lay the rolls on a wet baking sheet, and bake in a moderately quick oven for 20 to 30 minutes. Stand them on a fold of paper to drain when taken from the oven. Arrange them on a fancy dish-paper, garnish with fresh parsley, and serve, either hot or cold.

It is best to boil the sausages before making them into

rolls, in order to extract some of the fat. If this is not done the puff paste is apt to be sodden.

NOTE.—Home-made forcemeats can be used instead of sausage meat, if liked; either raw or cooked meat, moistened with a little sauce, and seasoned.

Baked Sausages

1 lb. Sausages.	Potato Purée.
1 oz. Bacon Fat or Dripping.	Grated Cheese.
Tomato Sauce or Gravy.	

UTENSILS—Fork, baking tin, grater, saucepan, knife, basting spoon, forcing-bag. *Enough for 3 or 4 persons.*

Separate and prick one pound of pork sausages. Put them in a greased baking dish, and bake for 12 to 15 minutes, in a moderate oven, until nicely browned, basting them occasionally with their own liquor.

Make about one pound of potato pureé, and mix into it two ounces of grated cheese.

Put this into a forcing-bag with a large rose-pipe, and force it into two rows, down the centre of a dish. Lay the sausages, side by side, across the rows of purée, forcing out a strip of potato between each. Pour tomato sauce, or a good brown gravy, round, and serve.

Rice Pilau

¾ lb. Rice.	1 teaspoonful White Pepper.
¼ lb. Butter.	½ small teaspoonful Ground
1 quart White Stock.	Cinnamon.
4 oz. Sultana Raisins.	½ teaspoonful Salt.
1 Onion stuck with 4 or 5 Cloves.	Garnish of Fried Onions.

UTENSILS—Saucepan, wooden spoon, strainer, frying pan. *Enough for 4 persons.*

Put the rice into a saucepan, with sufficient cold water to cover it. Bring to the boil, then strain, and rinse the rice in cold water. Put it into a saucepan, with the butter, white stock made from chicken bones, the onion stuck with cloves, the sultanas, cleaned and freed from stalks, the cinnamon, pepper and a little salt. Cook this over a moderate heat, until the rice is quite tender and has absorbed all the stock, stirring it constantly during this time with a wooden spoon, to prevent it sticking. When cooked, remove the onion and cloves, turn the rice on to a hot dish, garnish with fried onion rings, and serve.

If a meat dish is desired, cut the meat from a cold boiled fowl, say half a pound, cut into dice shapes. Also cut two ounces of bacon into dice shapes. Fry these for a few minutes in a little butter, until they get thoroughly hot. Season with pepper, and a little salt. Make a circle of the rice, pile the fowl and bacon in the centre, and serve.

Chicken Pilau

1 Chicken.	A few Raisins.
1½ cupfuls Rice.	1½ cupfuls of Stock.
A few Almonds.	Onions. Salt.

UTENSILS—Knife, steamer, frying pan, measuring cup, sieve or colander for rice. *Enough for 6 persons.*

Take the chicken, cut it up into suitable portions, and steam it until tender. Lightly fry some raisins, until plump and golden brown ; remove from pan.

Blanch and slit some almonds, fry a golden brown and remove from pan. Slice and fry some onions a golden brown ; remove them from pan. Wash the rice, and gently fry it for 15 minutes. Add the stock and the raisins.

Simmer gently for 25 minutes, when the rice will have absorbed the stock and become soft and dry. Salt according to taste, and serve on a hot dish, with chicken piled up one end, rice the other, and almonds and onions scattered on top.

Chicken Croquettes

½ lb. cooked Chicken.	1½ gills Milk.
1 oz. Butter.	2 Eggs.
1 oz. Flour.	Breadcrumbs.
Pepper and Salt.	

UTENSILS — Knife, saucepan, tablespoon, egg-beater, basin, dish, wooden spoon, grater, stewpan, frying basket, sieve. *Enough for 2 to 4 persons.*

Free the chicken from all skin and gristle, and mince it finely. If a slice of tongue or ham can be added and minced with it, it is a great improvement. Season well with pepper and salt, and the smallest pinch of powdered mace or a very small grating of nutmeg. Melt the butter in a saucepan, stir in the flour, and fry together without browning them. Add the milk gradually, and stir till it boils. Put in the minced meat, and when the ingredients are thoroughly mixed remove from the fire, and then stir in the yolk of an egg.

Turn the preparation out on to a dish, and leave until cold. To form the croquettes, flour your hands slightly, take a tablespoonful of the mixture, roll it in flour, only using just enough to prevent it from sticking to the hands. Form into the shape of a pear. Roll each in some well-beaten egg, then in fine white breadcrumbs, and lay in a frying basket.

Have a stewpan half-full of frying fat, and when it is quite boiling (with a slight blue vapour rising from it) plunge in the croquettes. As soon as they are a nice golden colour, lift them from the fat and stand them on a sieve lined with paper to drain. Stick a parsley stalk into the narrow end of each to represent the stalk of the pear. Serve in a ring round the dish, with the stalk ends uppermost, and garnish with fried parsley.

Chicken Curry

1 small Chicken.	2 tablespoonfuls **Desiccated** Cocoanut.
2½ oz. Butter, **or good Beef Dripping.**	½ lb. plainly boiled Rice.
1 pint White Stock.	2 teaspoonfuls Crème-de-riz.
1 tablespoonful Curry Powder.	1 tablespoonful chopped **Chutney.**
1 tablespoonful Curry Paste.	Lemon Juice.
3 oz. Shallots or Onion.	Salt.

UTENSILS—Knife, cloth, breakfast cup, measuring spoons, stewpan, wooden spoon, frying pan, saucepan. *Enough for 4 persons.*

Choose a nice young chicken, and cut it into neat joints. Wash these well, then dry them in a clean cloth. Chop the onion, or shallot, quite finely. Put the cocoanut into a breakfast cup, pour boiling water on it, and let it infuse while making the curry.

Melt an ounce and a half of butter in a stewpan. Put in the minced onion, or shallot, and fry gently over a slow fire, until it is a pale gold colour. Now add the curry powder and paste, and cook for another 10 minutes. Stir in the crème de riz, and gently moisten the whole with one pint of white stock. This stock, or broth, can be made from the trimmings of the chicken. Bring to the boil gently, then simmer slowly.

Now take the pieces of chicken, and flour them. Melt the remainder of the butter in a pan, put in the chicken, and fry until lightly coloured. Then put the chicken into the curry sauce, and let it all stand by the side of the stove for about ½ hour. Strain the liquid from the cocoanut, squeezing out as much moisture as possible. Add this, also the chutney, to the curry. Bring all to the boil, then let it simmer gently for ½ hour. By this time the chicken, if young, should be quite cooked ; if not, it must cook longer. Lastly, add about a teaspoonful of strained lemon juice.

Arrange the pieces of chicken in the centre of a dish, pour the sauce round, and, if liked, garnish with a few slices of lemon. Put the plainly-boiled rice in a separate dish, and serve. Or the rice may be dished round the curry, but this is not considered best, although it adds to the appearance of the dish.

VEAL or RABBIT may be cooked in the same way.

NOTE.—Curry powders vary considerably, as there are no less than nine different recipes, chiefly of Oriental origin. The following are ingredients most commonly used in the preparation of the curry powders usually met with : turmeric, coriander seeds, cumin, ginger, cardamoms, caraway seeds, black pepper, cayenne, cinnamon, mace, pimento, mustard, and fenugreek. The ingredients are ground to fine powder and put into stoppered bottles or tins.

Brown Curry

1 lb. fresh Meat.	1 large tablespoonful Curry Powder
1 teaspoonful Meat Extract.	1 dessertspoonful Curry Paste.
½ pint Brown Stock.	½ pint Cocoanut Milk.
½ lb. plainly boiled Rice.	1 Cooking Apple.
6 oz. Onion.	1 tablespoonful Sweet Chutney.
2 oz. Butter, or Clarified Dripping.	Flour. Salt.

UTENSILS—Knife, stewpan, kitchen spoon, saucepan, strainer to wash rice, measuring spoons, pint measure. *Enough for 4 persons.*

Cut the meat into dice shapes and flour it well, and chop the onions finely. Slice the apple thinly.

Melt the butter in a stewpan, fry the meat in it until it is a nice gold colour, then take it out. Next fry the vegetables, adding a little more butter or dripping, if necessary. Mix the curry powder and paste in with the vegetables, and fry these as well. When the vegetables are nicely browned, put the meat back again. Add the brown stock, by degrees, also the meat extract, and salt to taste. Simmer all gently for ½ hour. adding more stock, if necessary.

Now add the chutney and the cocoanut milk, and simmer for another ½ hour. It must simmer very gently indeed. When cooked, turn the curry out into a very hot dish, and sprinkle a little cocoanut over the top. Put the rice in a separate dish, sprinkle a little coralline pepper, or hard-boiled yolk of egg, over it, and serve.

NOTE.—This curry can also be made with cooked meat, but in that case cook the sauce first, and only put the meat in about 20 minutes before it is ready. If possible, it is even better to let the cooked meat stand in the sauce off the fire for ½ hour or so, in order to get it thoroughly seasoned with the curry.

Stewed Ox-Tail

1 Ox-tail. Flour.	1 tablespoonful Mushroom Ketchup.
1 pint Stock.	6 Peppercorns.
1 oz. Dripping.	3 Cloves. 3 Allspice.
1 Onion. 1 Carrot.	A bunch of Herbs (Bayleaf, Thyme
½ a Turnip.	and Parsley).

Garnish of Croûtons.

UTENSILS—Knife, stewpan, cloth, strainer, piece of muslin, plate, frying pan. *Enough for 4 or 5 persons.*

Divide the ox-tail at the joints. Put it into a stewpan, with sufficient cold water to cover, bring to the boil, then strain. Wash it well in cold water, and dry it in a cloth.

Wash and prepare the vegetables, cutting them into slices. If the carrot and turnip are large, split them down the centre before slicing. Dredge the pieces of tail with flour. Melt the dripping in a stewpan, and fry the tail in it, until it is a nice golden brown. Take out the tail, flour the vegetables, and put them in. Fry these also, using a little more dripping, if necessary. Tie the spices and herbs in a piece of muslin. Now put the fried tail, vegetables, and bag of herbs and spices into a stewpan, with the stock. Add the ketchup, then bring to the boil. Cover the pan closely, and simmer very gently until tender. This will take about 2 hours. Add a little salt, if needed, but do not overdo it, as the ketchup is in it. If ketchup is not procurable, it can be omitted, and more salt used.

When all is cooked, remove the bag of herbs, arrange the pieces of tail neatly on a hot dish, and pour the gravy and vegetables round. Garnish with fried croûtons of bread, and serve.

Tripe

| 2 lb. Tripe.   2 Onions. | 1 pint Onion or Tomato Sauce. |
| Milk and Water. | Garnish of Croûtons. |

UTENSILS—Knife, stewpan, large strainer or colander, pint measure, brush, frying pan. *Enough for 4 to 6 persons.*

Choose freshly prepared thick tripe, trim off the coarsest fat, and cut the tripe into neat pieces. Put it into a stewpan, with two onions, peeled, and well cover with equal proportions of milk and water. Bring to the boil, and simmer gently for quite an hour, or a little longer if the tripe is under-dressed.

When cooked, strain the tripe, and rinse it in hot water. Drain it thoroughly, then put it into a saucepan with a pint of onion or tomato sauce. (For these SAUCES, see Index.) Bring to the boil, then turn it out into a hot deep dish. Garnish with heart-shaped croûtons of bread, fried a pale golden brown, brushed over with white of egg, and sprinkled with coralline pepper and finely chopped parsley.

Shrimped Tomatoes

| 2 large British Tomatoes. | 1 oz. Breadcrumbs. |
| ½ pint Shrimps. | 1 Egg. |

UTENSILS—Knife, grater, egg-beater, basin, kitchen spoon, baking tin. *Enough for 2 persons.*

Cut the tomatoes in half and remove some pulp. Add the breadcrumbs and shrimps to the beaten egg, then place the mixture on each half tomato. Cook in a moderate oven until the tomatoes are soft.

Pork Cutlets

2½ lb. Loin of Pork.	Pepper. Salt.
2 teaspoonfuls finely minced Sage.	Mashed Potato.
Egg and Breadcrumbs.	Tomato Sauce, or Sauce Robert.

UTENSILS—Knife, grater, basin, egg-beater, frying pan, saucepan, fork or potato masher. *Enough for 4 or 5 persons.*

Choose a nice loin of young pork, cut it into neat chops, pare off part of the fat, if necessary, and trim neatly. Season the breadcrumbs highly with pepper, salt, and the minced sage leaves. Dip the cutlets into whole beaten-up egg, then into the crumbs. Put the cutlets into a frying pan, with plenty of boiling lard, or good dripping. Fry for 15 minutes turning them once or twice during cooking, for pork must always be thoroughly well cooked.

Have ready a pyramid of mashed potato, on a hot dish, and stand the cutlets up round it. Put a bunch of parsley in the centre, pour either tomato sauce or Robert sauce, or any suitable sharp sauce, round, and serve. (For SAUCES, see Index.)

Ham, to Boil

| Ham. | Browned Breadcrumbs. |

UTENSILS—Boiler or ham-kettle, cloth, knife, skimmer,

The length of time a ham should be soaked before boiling depends on its age and the manner in which it has been cured. Some require no soaking whatever, while, on the other hand, if old and highly salted, they may require to be soaked a whole day and night, or even longer. The usual time, however, for ordinary highly salted ham is 12 hours.

Before boiling, trim the ham lightly of any discoloured parts, then wash it well. Put it in a boiler, or ham-kettle, large enough to hold it easily, and cover with cold water. Bring very slowly to the boil, and carefully skim off any scum that may rise. As soon as the water comes to the boil, draw the pan slowly to one side, so that it may simmer gently until cooked ; be careful not to let it boil fast.

When done, take the ham out of the pot. Take hold of the skin with a cloth, and strip it off. Sprinkle the top of the skinned ham freely with browned breadcrumbs. Put a ham-frill round the knuckle, garnish with parsley, and serve.

NOTE.—A ham weighing 10 lb. will take 4 hours.

Fricassee of Rabbit

1 Rabbit.	1 teaspoonful Pepper.
1 oz. Butter.	Lemon Peel.
1 pint White Stock or Water.	1 small Onion.
1 Yolk of Egg.	A bunch of Herbs (Parsley, Thyme
1 gill Cream.	and Marjoram).
½ blade of Mace.	Garnish of rolls of Bacon and
1 dessertspoonful Flour.	Lemon.
1 teaspoonful Salt.	

UTENSILS—Knife, stewpan, strainer, fork, wooden spoon, measuring spoons, basin, egg-beater, plate, frying pan. *Enough for 4 persons.*

Take a young rabbit, cut it into neat joints, and wash these well in warm water. Put the head and trimmings into the stock made from mutton, veal, or chicken, or water will do, if no stock is available. Add the onion, mace, a strip of lemon peel, salt, pepper and bunch of herbs. Simmer gently for 1 hour, then strain.

Return the stock to the saucepan, add the joints of rabbit, and simmer very gently for ¾ to 1 hour. Lift out the pieces of rabbit, and strain the broth into a basin. Rinse out the saucepan, put in the butter and melt it, then stir in the flour and mix smoothly together. Add the stock by degrees, stirring all the time, and bring to the boil. Put the rabbit in, and when it again boils remove the saucepan and stir in the yolk of an egg, well beaten in the cream. Do not let this sauce boil after the egg is added, or it will curdle. Add a little more salt if needed. Place the joints of rabbit on a very hot dish, pour the sauce over and garnish with thin slices of rolled bacon and slices of lemon.

Rabbit Pie

2 Rabbits.	Parsley. Nutmeg.
3 or 4 slices boiled Pickled Pork.	Pepper and Salt.
3 hard-boiled Eggs.	Puff Paste.

UTENSILS—Three basins, saucepan, knife, pastry board, rolling pin, grater, pastry brush, egg-beater, pie-dish. *Enough for 6 to 8 persons.*

Choose young rabbits. Soak them in warm water for an hour, then rinse well. Put them into a saucepan with sufficient cold water to cover. Bring to the boil, then take them out and rinse in cold water. Put them into a saucepan again, with sufficient cold water to cover, and seasoned with pepper and salt. If liked, an onion may be added. Bring to the boil, and simmer for ½ hour.

Take the rabbits out, cut all the meat from the bones, and put the bones back into the liquor in the saucepan.

Cut up the boiled pork into small pieces, and slice the hard-boiled eggs. Put the liquor with the bones in it to boil, and while this stock is boiling make some good puff paste.

Place a layer of the rabbit meat in the bottom of a pie-dish, then a layer of the bacon and egg. Season with finely chopped parsley, pepper, salt and a grate of nutmeg. Then put in more layers of rabbit, bacon, egg and seasoning until the dish is filled. Add a half-pint of the stock, or rather more.

Roll the pastry out to about a quarter of an inch in thickness. Wet the edges of the pie-dish, cut a strip of the paste, and put it round the edge. Wet the top of this edging of paste, then put a cover of paste on the pie. Trim the edges, make a hole in the centre, then brush over the top with whole beaten-up egg. Ornament round the centre hole with a few leaves of paste, and make an ornamental pattern round the edge.

Stand the pie in a moderate oven, and bake for $\frac{3}{4}$ of an hour. When the puff-paste has well risen, put the pie in the bottom of the oven. When cooked, fill the pie with the stock through the hole in the centre of the crust, stand it on a dish, put a frill round, garnish with parsley, and serve.

Spaghetti and Tomatoes

$\frac{1}{2}$ lb. Spaghetti.	2 oz. Butter.
1 lb. Tomatoes.	$\frac{1}{4}$ lb. grated Cheese.

Pepper and Salt.

UTENSILS—Saucepan, pie-dish, knife, grater. *Enough for 4 persons.*

Cook the spaghetti in boiling, salted water for 20 minutes, drain, and pour into a pie-dish. Season with pepper and salt, and dot with small pieces of butter. Cover all over with sliced tomatoes and a thick layer of grated cheese. Put into a fairly brisk oven, and bake until the cheese is brown and crisp.

A Simple Hot Pot

Neck of Mutton.	Potatoes.
Onion.	Pepper and Salt.

UTENSILS—Knife, casserole or deep pie-dish.

Cut some chops from the best end of a neck of mutton ; trim them neatly, removing most of the fat, then lay them at the bottom of a deep dish or pot, and season with pepper and salt. Lay a few slices of onion on the chops, if the flavour is liked, then a layer of sliced potatoes on top of these. Now lay more chops in and season these, then cover with a layer of potatoes. Pour half a pint of water over, and place in a moderate oven to bake for $1\frac{1}{2}$ to 2 hours, according to the size of the dish.

NOTE.—Dishes of fireproof glass or earthenware made specially for hot-pot, can be procured.

C.I.O₁   D

Macaroni à la Reine

¼ lb. Macaroni.	1½ oz. Butter.
4 tablespoonfuls grated Cheese.	2 Eggs. Cayenne.
½ pint new Milk.	1 blade of Mace.

1 teaspoonful Salt.

UTENSILS—Saucepan, double saucepan, grater, measuring spoons, wooden spoon, basin for egg whites. *Enough for 3 or 4 persons.*

This is a delicious way of preparing macaroni, but it requires care. Put the macaroni into plenty of fast-boiling water, to cover it well, with half an ounce of butter, the mace and salt, and boil until tender ; some kinds of macaroni take but 20 minutes, others an hour, so the time taken is uncertain. If the water boils away add more.

When the macaroni is quite tender, drain thoroughly, then put it gently into a well-warmed double saucepan, in the underneath part of which is boiling water. Stir into the macaroni the grated cheese, the remaining ounce of butter, a dust of cayenne, a bare half pint of warmed milk, and the yolks of eggs. Stir all gently together, and simmer for half an hour. It must nearly boil, but not quite. If allowed to boil it will be spoiled. Turn it into a hot dish, and serve.

Macaroni Soufflé

¼ lb. Macaroni.	1 oz. Flour.
½ pint Milk.	2 oz. grated Cheese.
White Stock.	A blade of Mace.
½ oz. Butter.	White Pepper.
3 Eggs. 1 Onion.	Cayenne. Salt.

UTENSILS—2 saucepans, knife, wooden spoon, basin, grater, egg-beater, mould or soufflé case, buttered paper. *Enough for 3 or 4 persons.*

Put the macaroni into plenty of fast-boiling, slightly salted water. Boil fast for 5 minutes, then strain. Now put it on to boil in white stock (made from veal, rabbit or chicken bones), with the onion and mace, and boil until the macaroni is tender. Strain as dry as possible, then cut the macaroni up into small pieces.

Melt the butter in a saucepan, and stir in the flour. Add the milk, by degrees, stir until it boils, then boil for 10 minutes. Remove the saucepan from the fire, add the yolks of eggs and grated cheese, also salt, cayenne, and white pepper, to taste, and beat well. Lastly, beat the whites of eggs to a stiff froth, with a tiny pinch of salt, and stir them lightly into the mixture. Fix a well-buttered paper round the outside of a buttered mould, or soufflé case, and put in the mixture. Bake for ½ hour in a moderate oven, and sprinkle a few browned breadcrumbs on top.

Remove the paper quickly, and, if the mixture is in a tin, pin a napkin neatly round, stand it on a dish, and serve quickly, or it will soon fall. This mixture may be baked in small soufflé cases, if liked, but then it would only require 15 to 20 minutes in the oven.

Vol-au-vent of Veal

6 tablespoonfuls cold Veal, cut into dice. 1 Egg.
2 tablespoonfuls Ham.
2 tablespoonfuls Tongue.

2 tablespoonfuls Button Mushrooms.
½ lb. Puff Paste.
¾ pint Veloute Sauce.

UTENSILS—Basins, wooden spoon, pastry board, rolling pin, cutters, pastry brush, egg-beater, baking sheet, measuring spoons, pint measure, knife, double saucepan. *Enough for 4 to 6 persons.*

Roll the paste out, three-quarters of an inch thick. Stamp or cut it out, oval shape, about eight inches long. With another cutter, about five inches long, cut the centre of the paste oval, but only about two-thirds through it. Brush the paste over with whole beaten-up egg. Lay it on a wetted baking sheet, and bake until it is done. Take it from the oven, lift out the centre piece (marked out with the five-inch cutter) and lay it carefully on one side. Scoop out the soft middle of the paste, then fill this centre space with the mixture described below.

For the mixture, make three-quarters of a pint of veloute sauce. Stir into it the sliced button mushrooms, the same amount of lean cooked ham, cut into dice shapes, and the same of tongue, cut into dice. Add also the veal, cut into dice. Heat all thoroughly in a double saucepan.

Have the pastry case quite hot, and fill the centre with the mixture. Lay the lid gently on, stand it on a hot dish, with dish-paper beneath, and garnish with a few sprigs of parsley. Serve at once.

NOTE.—1. Almost any good meat can be used if veal is not liked. The pastry case can also be filled with lobster and sauce, oysters, sweetbreads, etc.

2. If the case is to be decorated, whip the whites of four eggs to a stiff froth, with a pinch of salt, and put this into a forcing-bag with large rose-pipe. Force it out up the sides and round the top ; set it in a cool oven, and bake until tinged with a pale golden colour.

3. The pastry case can also be filled with a compôte of fruits, but in this case the paste lid, or centre, is left off, and whipped cream used instead.

Galantine of Veal

| A breast of Veal. | ½ lb. Ham.   3 Eggs. |
| 2 lb. Sausage Meat. | ¼ lb. Tongue. |

Pepper and Salt.

UTENSILS—Knife, chopping board, saucepan, cloth, stewpan, 2 dishes, brush. *Enough for 8 to 10 persons.*

Bone a breast of veal and beat it flat. Lay it on a board, and sprinkle the inside with pepper and salt. Cut off a little of the meat at each side and at the end furthest from you, so that the skin projects a little, then spread the breast with a layer of sausage meat. Boil the eggs hard, remove the whites, and lay the three yolks along the centre of the sausage meat, alternately with the ham (cut into strips about the thickness of dice) and the tongue.

Roll the breast up carefully, fold the skin over the ends, and wrap it tightly in a cloth. Tie the ends of the cloth firmly, then bind the whole round with broad tape, to keep it firm. Put it into a stewpan, with sufficient stock to cover, and boil very gently for 3 to 3½ hours.

When cooked, take the galantine out, drain it, place it on a flat dish with another on top, and some heavy weights on top of that. When cold, cut the tape, take off the cloth, and wipe the meat quite free from fat. It is a good plan to pour a little hot water quickly over, and then wipe the galantine. Brush over with liquid glaze, and, if liked, a thin coat of aspic jelly can be poured over that, when it is cold. Stand the galantine on a dish, garnish either with aspic jelly cut into fancy shapes or with sprigs of fresh parsley, then serve.

Minced Veal

1 lb. Veal.	1 oz. Flour. 1 Onion.
1 pint Milk.	3 or 4 thin rashers of Bacon.
1 strip of Lemon Peel.	Cayenne Pepper and Salt.
1 blade of Mace.	Potato Purée, as described.

UTENSILS—Two saucepans, 2 basins, wooden spoon, strainer, knife, 2 baking dishes, skewer, sieve, forcing-bag. *Enough for 3 or 4 persons.*

Boil the onion in nearly all the milk, with the lemon peel, mace and a dust of cayenne pepper, for 15 minutes. Mix the flour quite smoothly with the rest of the cold milk. Strain the boiled milk, return it to the saucepan, and when it boils again, stir in the mixed flour, and season with salt, to taste. If not quite smooth, strain it through a pointed strainer.

Free the veal from all gristle and brown skin, and chop it very finely with a sharp knife. Do not pass the veal through a mincing machine; no doubt the machine is quicker, but it spoils the veal. Put the veal into the saucepan with the milk and flour, and bring it slowly to boiling-point, but do not let it boil. Then stand it on one side to keep hot; or, better still, stand the saucepan in a small baking dish with boiling water in it, so as to ensure the mince not boiling. Just before serving, add a few drops of lemon juice.

Cut the bacon into very thin rashers, roll them into neat rolls, and run them on a skewer. Cook them, either in a brisk oven or in front of the fire, for a few minutes. Make a border of potato purée on a dish, pour the mince in the centre, and serve.

THE BORDER OF POTATO PURÉE

Take one pound of boiled potatoes, and rub them through a sieve whilst hot. To these add half an ounce of butter, two tablespoonfuls of milk, pepper and salt, to taste, and make all thoroughly hot. Now take a forcing-bag, with a large rose-pipe in it, and put the potato in. Force it out into roses, to form a border round the dish. Pour the mince in the centre, and arrange the rolls of bacon neatly on the mince. On the tops of the potato roses sprinkle a little coralline pepper or a little fine parsley.

Galantine of Sheeps' Tongues

6 Fresh or Salt Tongues.	Coralline Pepper.
3 hard-boiled Eggs.	¾ pint Stock.
½ oz. Gelatine.	Pepper and Salt.
1 teaspoonful chopped Parsley.	Garnish.

UTENSILS—Saucepan, knife, mould. *Enough for 6 persons.*
If fresh tongues are to be used, cook them for about 4

hours, until the skins come off quite easily ; skin, and cut them in half lengthways. Then melt the gelatine in the white stock (either chicken, rabbit or veal stock is the best). Season it nicely with pepper and salt. If the stock is very weak, use an ounce of gelatine.

Wet a mould with cold water, ornament the bottom with a slice of hard-boiled egg, sprinkle a ring of parsley round it, then one of coralline pepper, then put four more rings of hard-boiled eggs, and so on. Lay in the tongues, cut in halves, and the rest of the egg, sliced. Lastly, pour over the stock, with the gelatine melted in it. When quite set, turn out, and garnish round the bottom with shredded lettuce and slices of tomato. If tinned tongues are used, they only require to be made warm, then skinned and sliced, and prepared in the same way.

Devilled Slices of Mutton

6 or 8 slices of underdone Mutton.	½ teaspoonful Salt.
1 tablespoonful dry Mustard.	A small dust of Pepper.
1 tablespoonful Chutney.	¼ teaspoonful Sugar.
1 tablespoonful Salad Oil or Oiled Butter.	Worcester or Tomato Sauce.

UTENSILS—Knife, basin, kitchen spoon, gridiron or baking tin, measuring spoons. *Enough for 3 to 4 persons.*

Cut slices of underdone mutton, half an inch thick, in as neat pieces as the joint will allow. Put the mustard, chutney, salad oil, sugar, salt and pepper into a basin. Mix into a soft paste with Worcester or tomato sauce. If Worcester sauce is used, only put a few drops, using water or sherry as well. Spread the slices over with the mixture, and let them stand for about 3 hours to absorb the flavour.

When required, grill for about 5 minutes over a slow fire, on an oiled gridiron. If it is not convenient to grill, put a small piece of butter, about the size of a walnut, into a baking tin, melt it, lay in the slices, and bake in a hot oven for from 7 to 10 minutes. Serve very hot, with riced potatoes and spinach or buttered greens, or the slices can be served cold, garnished with watercress.

Hashed Lamb or Mutton with Bacon

Cold Lamb or Mutton.	Red Currant Jelly.
Fried Bread.	Mushrooms or Ketchup.
Bacon. 1 Onion.	A bunch of Herbs.

6 Peppercorns.

UTENSILS—Knife, flour dredger, saucepan, strainer, tea-spoon, wooden spoon, basin, pie-dish, double boiler.

Take as many slices of cold lamb or mutton as are required, trim them free from all skin and superfluous fat, and dredge over with flour.

Make a nice rich gravy from the bones and trimmings (but no fat) by putting them into a saucepan with a bunch of herbs, parsley and thyme, half a dozen black peppercorns, one small onion, and the trimmings of half a dozen mushrooms, if you have them. Just cover with cold water, and boil till all the goodness is out of the bones. Strain the gravy, return it to the saucepan, and thicken with about one teaspoonful of flour mixed to a smooth paste with cold water, to every half-pint of gravy. Add half a dozen mushrooms, cut in half if large, one teaspoonful of red currant jelly, and half a teaspoonful of salt. Simmer sufficiently long to cook the mushrooms, then add the slices of mutton, and simmer for 5 minutes. If you have no fresh mushrooms, add a dessertspoonful of ketchup, in which case omit the salt from the gravy.

Lay the slices of mutton in a pie-dish, pour the sauce over them, and leave for some hours. Then re-heat thoroughly in the top of a double boiler over boiling water. On no account must the hash boil, therefore this method of heating is best, although it takes longer than in a plain saucepan. Serve in a hot dish with tiny rolls of hot bacon and sippets of fried bread.

Mutton Cutlets with Tomato Butter

2 lb. best end Neck of Mutton.	Pepper and Salt.
Breadcrumbs.	Potato Border, as described.
1 Egg. Frying Fat.	Tomato Butter, as described.

UTENSILS—Knife, meat chopper, brush for melted butter, basin, tablespoon, egg-beater, grater, stewpan, frying basket or wire sieve, 2 saucepans, 2 fine sieves, wooden spoon, forcing-bag. *Enough for 5 or 6 persons.*

Cut the mutton into well-shaped cutlets, and flatten them out with a meat chopper, dipped in cold water. Trim them into neat shapes, leaving about an inch and a half of bone projecting beyond the meat, and scrape this bone free from any skin or fat. Brush the cutlets over with melted butter, and sprinkle them with pepper and salt, but be careful to keep the bone clean. Dip the cutlets well into whole beaten-up egg, and then into finely made white breadcrumbs, coating them well with the crumbs.

Have ready a stewpan, with plenty of boiling fat. If you have a frying basket, put the cutlets into it, and then plunge them into the fat. Cook for about 7 minutes, until they are a nice golden brown. If you have no frying basket, put the cutlets into the fat without it, and, when cooked, drain them on a wire sieve. Dish on a border of mashed potatoes, and pour tomato butter round.

THE POTATO BORDER

1½ lb. cooked Potatoes.	3 teaspoonfuls Milk or Cream.
1 oz. Butter.	Pepper and Salt to taste.

Boil the potatoes very dry, then steam, and rub them through a fine sieve. Melt the butter in a saucepan, and add the potato, milk, pepper and salt. Make all thoroughly hot, and put it into a forcing-bag with a large rose-pipe. Force the potato out of the pipe, in rows down the centre of the dish, so as to form a border about two inches and a half wide and two inches deep. Keep some of the potato back in the bag, to finish off the cutlets with.

Put small cutlet frills on each of the bones of the cutlets, and arrange them all along the central potato border, one just resting on the other. Now force out roses of potato between each cutlet, one on each side, to keep them in their place. Pour tomato butter round, and serve. All this must be done very quickly, so that the cutlets do not get cold.

THE TOMATO BUTTER

6 Tomatoes.	4 drops Carmine.
1 Shallot.	Seasoning of Salt and Pepper.
1 oz. Butter.	A pinch of Castor Sugar.

Chop the shallot, and put it into a saucepan with the butter. Fry gently, without browning, for 10 minutes, then add the tomatoes, sliced; also the carmine, sugar and seasoning. Let all cook slowly, at the side of the stove, till tender. When cooked, rub all through a hair sieve. Put it back into the saucepan to re-warm, and, when quite hot, pour down each side of the potato border, and serve.

Tomato Sausage Cakes

| 1 Medium Tomato. | 1 small Pork Sausage for each |
| Scrambled Eggs. | Person. |

UTENSILS—Knife, frying pan, fireproof dish, basin, egg-beater, spoon, saucepan.

Halve each tomato and skin each sausage, then shape the sausage meat into cakes, the size of tomatoes, and flour very lightly. Fry on both sides in a little hot bacon fat, and place one on each half tomato, covering with the other half of tomato. Place on a buttered fireproof dish, bake till soft but unbroken, in a moderate oven. Serve each on a hot plate, surrounded by a ring of scrambled egg.

Creams of Grouse

6 oz. Grouse.	1 oz. Butter.
2 well-beaten Eggs.	3 oz. fresh Breadcrumbs.
1 gill Milk.	Tomato Sauce.
1 gill whipped Cream.	Pepper and Salt.

UTENSILS—Mincing machine, grater, saucepan, wooden spoon, gill measure, egg-beater, 2 basins, dariole moulds, string, steamer. *Enough for 2 or 3 persons.*

Pass the meat through a mincer, mix it with the crumbs and add the butter. Bring the milk to boiling point, and pour it over the meat and crumbs. Stir in the eggs, season to taste, and add the cream. Fill into buttered dariole moulds, cover with buttered paper, and tie down with string. Steam the moulds from 10 to 15 minutes, and serve with either tomato or cream sauce.

Sausage and Potato Roll

1 lb. cold mashed Potatoes.	2 hard-boiled Eggs.
¾ lb. Sausage Meat.	1 beaten Egg.
Breadcrumbs.	Chopped Parsley.

UTENSILS—Dish, egg-beater, basin, grater, knife, pie-dish, brush. *Enough for 3 persons.*

Mix the potatoes, parsley and sausage meat evenly together on a large dish, then shape into a thick roll, enclosing the two eggs. Brush over with one well-beaten egg, sprinkle with breadcrumbs, and place in a suitable pie-dish with a small quantity of dripping. Bake for ¾ hour in a moderate oven. If the potatoes are very floury, it will be found advisable to mix them with an egg to hold the roll in shape.

Lobster Patties

4 tablespoonfuls Lobster.		A blade of Mace.	
½ lb. Flour.	½ lb. Butter.	½ lb. Puff Paste.	
½ Lemon.	Salt.	A dust of Cayenne.	
4 tablespoonfuls of Sauce.		Milk and Cream.	

UTENSILS—Pint measure, 2 saucepans, wooden spoon, tablespoon, lemon squeezer, 2 basins, pastry board, rolling pin, plate, knife, cloth, round cutters, brush, egg-beater, strainer, baking sheet. *Enough for 4 persons.*

Put ¼ pint of milk and cream on to boil, with a dust of cayenne, a blade of mace and a small strip of lemon peel. Let this infuse for 10 minutes, then strain. Melt an ounce of butter in a pan, and add an ounce of flour. Stir well together, and add the flavoured milk by degrees, stirring all the time. Boil for 2 or 3 minutes, and add 4 tablespoonfuls of chopped lobster and six drops of anchovy sauce. Set aside to cool.

To make the patties, roll out the pastry to a quarter of an inch thickness. Take a plain round cutter, two inches and a half across, also a cutter once inch across. Cut out sixteen rounds with the large cutter; then, with the small cutter, cut the centres out of eight of the large rounds. Brush over the eight rings with cold water on one side, and then lay them evenly, wet side down, on the eight large rounds.

Wet a baking sheet with cold water, lay the patty cases on the tin, also the little tops, and bake in a moderate oven, opening the door as little as possible. The tops will be done before the cases. When the pastry is baked sufficiently, take it out, and fill the cases with the lobster mixture. Put the tops on. The patties can be served hot or cold.

APPETISERS

OYSTERS, prawns, smoked salmon, egg mayonnaise, and a lobster, oyster, shrimp or prawn cocktail, as well as mixed hors d'œuvres, salami, potato salad, sardines, smoked herring, etc., all come under the heading of appetisers. They can be served in place of soup, or before soup if you like, or in place of grapefruit, melon or a fruit cocktail, at lunch or dinner.

Under the heading of appetisers also come stuffed olives ; salted or devilled almonds or other nuts ; celery stalks stuffed with cheese which has been moistened with cream, and sharpened with chopped pimento and flavoured with onion juice ; and dishes of spring onions and radishes. These are usually arranged in dainty dishes and left on the table until dessert arrives.

Oysters

Serve in their half shells on dishes lined with cracked ice, and accompanied by thin brown bread and butter, and fingers of lemon.

Oyster Cocktail

24 Oysters.	3 tablespoonfuls Lemon Juice.
2 tablespoonfuls Tomato Ketchup.	1 tablespoonful minced Onion.
½ teaspoonful grated Horseradish.	12 drops Tobasco.
1 saltspoonful minced Parsley.	1 saltspoonful French Mustard.

Salt to taste.

UTENSILS—Measuring spoons, basin, kitchen spoon. *Enough for 4 persons.*

Leave the oysters in the deep halves of their shells. Arrange half a dozen of them in a circle on plates of crushed ice, with the small ends of the shells towards the centre. Place a lemon basket, or a tiny fancy bowl, used in Chinese restaurants for soy sauce, in the centre of each plate. Mix the other ingredients well together and divide the mixture between each basket.

Lobster Cocktail

1 cupful Lobster Meat.	¼ cupful Lemon Juice.
½ cupful Tomato Ketchup.	2 teaspoonfuls Worcester Sauce.
½ teaspoonful chopped Chives.	½ teaspoonful Tobasco.

Salt and Paprika to taste.

UTENSILS—Basin, knife, kitchen spoon, measuring spoons, measuring cup. *Enough for 2 or 3 persons.*

Flake the lobster meat into a basin, and add other ingredients. Mix lightly together, and serve in sundae glasses.

Cucumber Rings

1 Cucumber.	3 Tomatoes.
2 tablespoonfuls Salmon Mayonnaise.	Minced Capers.

UTENSILS—Knife, cutter, tablespoon. *Enough for 6 persons.*

Peel and cut a cucumber into thick slices. Scoop out centre with a cutter. Place each ring on a thick slice of peeled tomato and fill centres with mayonnaise. Decorate with minced capers.

Canape à l'Espagnole

Croûtes of Toast.	Anchovy Paste.
1 Egg Yolk. Paprika.	Creamed Cheese. **Mayonnaise.**
2 teaspoonfuls chopped Pimento.	

UTENSILS—Toasting fork or toaster, knife, forcing-bag, teaspoon, saucepan.

Pipe mayonnaise, flavoured with paprika, round the edge of the croûtes, spread thinly with creamed cheese. Decorate each in the centre with a tiny heap of minced pimento.

Or, spread the croûtes with anchovy paste creamed with butter, and decorate each with a little heap of minced hard-boiled egg in the centre. Serve the croûtes on separate dishes, or make both varieties and serve them arranged alternately on a silver dish, lined with lace paper.

Smoked Salmon in Swedish Style

Smoked Salmon.	2 eggs. ½ oz. Butter.
½ teaspoonful minced Parsley.	2 teaspoonfuls minced **Pimento.**
Pepper and Salt. Capers.	1 tablespoonful Milk.

UTENSILS—Knife, saucepan, measuring spoons, wooden spoon. *Enough for 4 persons.*

Cut smoked salmon into small fingers about 2 inches wide, and 4 inches long. Roll each finger up and arrange round a serving dish. Break the eggs into a saucepan, add the butter, and 1 tablespoon of milk. Season to taste with pepper and salt, then stir until beginning to thicken. Add at once the parsley and pimento, and pile up in the centre of the salmon. Sprinkle with minced capers, and serve very cold.

Indian Eggs

2 hard-boiled Eggs.	2 Tomatoes. Mayonnaise.
4 stuffed Olives.	Buttered Toast.

UTENSILS—Saucepan, knife, basin, fork, spoon, toasting fork or toaster. *Enough for 4 persons.*

Halve the eggs, remove the yolks, and mash with a little well-seasoned mayonnaise, and return to the whites. Remove a small slice from the bottom of each white. Serve on little rounds of buttered toast, each one covered with a slice of tomato, and plant a stuffed olive in the centre of each filling.

Shrimp Cocktail

½ tablespoonful Tomato Ketchup.	2 drops Tobasco Sauce.
½ tablespoonful Lemon Juice.	3 drops Worcester Sauce.
¼ teaspoonful Celery Salt.	⅓ cupful Shrimps.

UTENSILS—Basin, tablespoon, teaspoon, cup. *Enough for 1 person.*

Mix the ingredients in the order given.

Caviare Croûtes

Caviare.	Minced Onion.
Rounds of Toast.	Baked Almonds.

UTENSILS—Toasting fork or toaster, forcing-bag, knife.

Make small rounds of toast ½ an inch thick. Heap them with caviare. Pipe tiny roses of maître d'hôtel butter round, and sprinkle with minced onion and stab with almonds.

Prawns and Watercress

Order a sufficient number of cooked prawns, allowing about six to each person. Remove the shells from the body only, leaving on the heads and tails. Half fill finger bowls with broken ice, and arrange the prawns round the edges, the tails hanging over the outside, and the heads on the inside. Wash some watercress and arrange a bunch neatly in the centre of each bowl, and place a butterfly of lemon in the centre. Serve with thin brown bread and butter.

Olives Stuffed with Anchovies

12 Olives.	Lemon Juice.
12 Croûtons of Bread.	Cayenne Pepper.
6 Anchovies.	Sprigs of Tarragon.
Butter.	Montpelier Butter, as described.

UTENSILS—Knife, pestle and mortar, hair sieve, plain cutter, frying pan, saucepan, forcing-bag, wooden spoon, basin. *Enough for* 12 *persons.*

Wash and bone the anchovies, and pound their flesh in a mortar with a few drops of lemon juice and a dust of cayene pepper. When quite smooth, rub the paste through a fine hair sieve. Cut three or four slices from a stale tin loaf, about one-eighth of an inch thick. Cut them into rounds with a plain cutter one and a half inches across. Fry these a very pale golden colour in clarified butter.

Turn the olives. Put the anchovy purée into a small forcing-bag, with a small rose-pipe, and force it out into the centres of the turned olives. Stand a stuffed olive in the centre of each croûton. Fill a small icing-bag, having a small rose-pipe, with Montpelier butter. Force out small roses of this round the base of each olive, to keep it in place, and force out a small rose on top of each. Stick a very small sprig of tarragon in the centre of each olive. Place these on small glass, silver, or china hors d'œuvre plates, the olive standing on a very small round lace paper. Serve one to each person.

THE MONTPELIER BUTTER

1 sprig Tarragon.	1 hard-boiled Yolk of Egg.
1 sprig Chervil.	3 oz. Butter. 1 Anchovy.
2 sprigs Watercress.	Coralline Pepper.

Blanch the tarragon, chervil, and watercress, and strain and dry them thoroughly. Put all into a mortar with the other ingredients, including the anchovy, which should be filleted first. Pound all well together and season with coralline pepper. Rub through a hair sieve, and then set in a cool place until required for use. If the mixture is not a good green colour, add a very little green colouring during the pounding. (Another recipe for MONTPELIER BUTTER will be found on page 146).

Croûtes à la Campagne

4 oz. Tongue.	1 hard-boiled Yolk of Egg.
1½ oz. Butter. 1 gill Cream.	A dust of Cayenne.
Croûtons of Bread.	A few drops of Carmine.

UTENSILS—Pestle and mortar, knife, hair sieve, forcing-bag, saucepan, frying pan, wooden spoon, cutter, basin, wire whisk. *Enough for about 8 persons.*

Chop the tongue finely, but keep back half an ounce for garnishing. Put the remainder into a mortar with the hard-boiled yolk of egg, a dust of cayenne pepper, a few drops of carmine and the butter. Pound them well, and then rub them through a fine hair sieve. Fry about eight croûtons of bread, one inch and a half in diameter. When cool, spread them with the tongue purée.

Whip the cream stiffly and put it into a forcing-bag with a second size rose-pipe. Force a rose out on the top of each croûton. Sprinkle with a little finely chopped tongue. Arrange either on hors d'œuvre plates or on one dish. Keep on ice, if possible, until required.

Hints on Serving Hors d'Œuvres

PRAWNS.—Serve suspended round a pretty glass bowl filled with cracked ice, decorated with fingers of lemon, and accompanied by thin brown bread and butter.

EGG MAYONNAISE.—Serve hard-boiled eggs, cut in slices lengthways, masked with mayonnaise and sprinkled with minced parsley, in an oval dish.

Serve sliced TOMATO sprinkled with minced parsley, and moistened with French dressing.

Serve BEETROOT sprinkled with minced onion and moistened with French dressing.

Serve slices of assorted SAUSAGES arranged alternately in a dish garnished with parsley.

SARDINES can be smoked, or the ordinary sardines in oil.

OLIVES also figure among appetising or palate-stimulating trifles. They should be arranged in pretty little dishes, with small French radishes.

Either serve hors d'œuvres in a proper hors d'œuvre dish, consisting of different compartments, and available in china and glass, or in separate dishes.

Toast, bread, bretzels and oatcakes can all be served with hors d'œuvres. Serve butter balls in hot weather, arranged on a dish with an inner compartment containing ice.

NOTE.—Several of the recipes given under SAVOURIES can be used as hors d'œuvres.

STOCKS AND SOUPS

General Rules for Stock Making

1. Boil stock up every day in summer, and twice in every 24 hours in very hot weather.
2. As vegetables will very quickly sour stock in hot weather, it is wiser to make stock without them during the summer months.
3. Boil stock up every day in the winter.
4. Meat and bones can be boiled up to make first, second and third stock, but fresh vegetables should be added each time.
5. Be careful about the amount of turnip used. A little bit of turnip goes a long way in flavouring.

If you keep a stock pot, you will find it is seldom necessary to obtain materials to make soup for an every-day dinner. There are many scraps of meats, vegetables, etc., which would probably be wasted if they were not used for making stock. Given a stock pot, you can add to it any trimmings of fresh or cold meat, such as cutlet trimmings, a knuckle bone, the carcase of a roast fowl, etc., and once the stock is made with these, plus vegetables and seasonings, all that is required to turn it into a savoury broth, is the addition of rice, vermicelli, sago, or spaghetti, and some chopped parsley.

The foundation of all meat soups is stock, either brown or white. Fish stock forms the basis of all fish soups.

TO MAKE STOCK

Break the bones up quite small and remove any fat. Always put the meat or bones on in cold water to bring out the goodness. Bring to the boil gently, skimming as soon as the scum rises. To facilitate this, add a cup of cold water when the stock comes to the boil. When the scum is removed, allow the stock just to boil again, then add the vegetables and seasoning. Draw the pan to the side of the fire or stove, or place it on a low flame and simmer gently for 5 or 6 hours. Always put stock through a fine sieve as soon as it is made.

The exact quantities of seasoning cannot well be given,

but it is always better to under-season than to overdo it. It is decidedly easier to add than to take away, and soup over-flavoured with either pepper or salt is quite uneatable.

The fat from the top of stock can always be clarified and used for frying. If the meat intended for stock is fat it is well to boil it first, just in plain water, then the fat that is taken off when cold is excellent for pastry or plain cakes. When the fat has been removed, vegetables and seasoning can be added and all boiled up in the usual way.

Never throw away the water in which poultry, meat, bacon, onions, carrots or parsnips have been boiled. It all comes in for flavouring stocks. Even the water that fish has been boiled in can be used for any kind of fish soup.

As previously stated, a hair sieve answers quite well for straining every-day dinner soups, but for clear soups for a dinner party a special cloth should be kept, an inexpensive dinner napkin being a very good thing.

There are practically four kinds of stocks :

(1) Clear stock, which is generally made from beef and veal.

(2) White stock, which is usually made from veal, chicken or rabbit bones.

(3) Brown stock, made from cooked meat, bones and trimmings.

(4) Fish stock, made from the trimmings and bones of fish.

There are also meat boilings and second stocks which do very well for any soups where there are plenty of good vegetables, etc., pea, potato, or artichoke soup being excellent made with this.

NOTE.—Never leave stock in a saucepan at night. Strain it up, otherwise it will be unwholesome and of bad flavour.

Good Stock for Clear Soups
(*The basis of all Consommés*)

6 lb. Shin of Beef.	A bunch of Herbs (Bayleaf, Thyme and Parsley).
2 Carrots. 1 Turnip.	
1 stick of Celery.	1 dessertspoonful of Salt.
3 Onions. 2 Tomatoes.	Any roast Game or Poultry Bones.
5 quarts Water. 4 Cloves.	
10 Peppercorns.	A piece of Bacon rind.

UTENSILS—Stockpot, knife, dessertspoon, piece of muslin, hair sieve, large metal spoon, basin.

Wash the vegetables well. Peel the onions, carrots and turnip and cut them all up into pieces about one inch and a half square. Tie the herbs and spices in a piece of muslin, and cut the meat up into quite small pieces, keeping back any of the fat. Put the meat into a large stewpan, with the cold water, and if possible, let it stand for about ½ hour. Then add the bones, bacon rind, vegetables, herbs, seasoning, etc., and put the stewpan on the stove and bring it to the boil. Directly it comes to the boil, add half a cup of cold water to make the scum rise. Skim well, simmer gently for 5 or 6 hours, and remove the scum as it rises while simmering.

When done, strain through a hair sieve and leave until the next day. When quite cold, remove every particle of fat, and clarify. This is the basis of all consommés.

If preferred, you can use only 4 lb. of shin of beef and 2 lb. of knuckle of veal. The method of clarifying this stock is described on page 108.

White Stock
(*The basis of White Soups*)

4 lb. White Meat (such as Veal, Rabbit or Chicken).
3 Onions.   ½ stick of Celery.
2 Blades of Mace.
6 White Peppercorns.

1 teaspoonful Salt.
A sprig of Lemon Thyme.
A small strip of Lemon Peel, pared very thinly.
A pinch of Cayenne Pepper.

UTENSILS—Stockpot, knife, large metal spoon, hair sieve, basin.

An old fowl does very well for this stock. Cut the meat up in small pieces, and then cut the vegetables. Put all the ingredients into a saucepan and cover well with cold water. Bring to the boil and skim well. Simmer gently for several hours, not omitting to skim as required. Strain, and when cold remove the fat.

Brown Stock, from Cooked Meat
(*May be used as the basis of thick Brown Soups*)

4 lb. cooked Meat Bones, Trimmings.
1 large Carrot.
2 Onions. 6 Cloves.
1 Leek. 1 Turnip.
2 oz. clarified Fat.
1 stick of Celery.

½ lb. Mushrooms.
12 Black Peppercorns.
1 dessertspoonful Salt.
2 blades of Mace.
1 bunch of Savoury Herbs (Parsley, Bayleaf and Thyme).

UTENSILS—Knife, stewpan, large metal spoon, hair sieve, basin, meat chopper.

Wash and dry the vegetables well, then slice them and put them in a stewpan with the clarified fat and any trimmings of meat. Fry till a nice brown. Add the bones (broken up quite small), the mushrooms (stalks and skins only will do equally well if washed in slightly salted water), the herbs, salt and spices. Cover with cold water and bring to the boil. Skim well and simmer gently for several hours. Strain through a hair sieve, and when cold, remove every particle of fat.

Fish Stock
(*The basis of Fish Soups*)

2 lb. raw Fish Bones or Trimmings.	A small strip of Lemon Peel, very thinly pared.
1 Onion. A blade of Mace.	2 quarts Water.
6 White Peppercorns.	A pinch of Herbs.
1 teaspoonful Salt.	A pinch of Cayenne.

UTENSILS—Knife, stewpan, large metal spoon, hair sieve, basin, pint measure.

The lemon peel must be pared very thinly. If there is any white left on the peel, it will give the stock a bitter taste. Chop up the fish bones and skin and put them with all the other ingredients into a stewpan, with the cold water, and bring to the boil. Skim well and simmer gently for several hours. Strain and set aside till wanted.

Economical Stock
(*For general purposes*)

Any Meat Bones and Trimmings.	A blade of Mace.
2 Onions. 3 Cloves.	1 dessertspoonful Salt.
1 Carrot. 1 Leek.	Cold Water.
1 stick of Celery.	A bunch of Parsley and Thyme.
1 teaspoonful Black Pepper.	

UTENSILS—Knife, stockpot, hair sieve, basin.

Chop up the bones and put them with any trimmings of meat, either raw or roast, into a saucepan, together with the vegetables, herbs, etc. A leg of mutton bone, or the bone of any joint, the trimmings of cutlets, a bone from bacon or a piece of bacon rind, all give a nice flavour to the soup. Add the water that any vegetables have been boiled in, such as carrots, onions, celery, potatoes, etc., if you have it. Cover the bones well with water and simmer for several hours. Strain through a hair sieve. When cold, remove the fat.

NOTE.—Do not use potato water if the stock will be required for clear soup.

Second Stock

(A foundation for Vegetable Soups)

This is made by re-boiling the materials from which the previous stocks have been made. The materials are not quite exhausted of their goodness and nourishing qualities in making the first stock, although it is not intended to leave much goodness in them. They should have a little pepper and salt added and then be re-boiled for some hours. Second stock is also used for gravies and sauces.

To Clarify Stock for Clear Soups

½ lb. raw lean Beef. | 1 quart Stock.
2 Whites and Shells of Eggs.

UTENSILS—Knife, basin, fork or egg-beater, stockpot, kitchen spoon, soup cloth, pint measure.

To every quart of stock allow half a pound of raw lean beef and the whites and shells of two eggs. Mince the meat very finely, slightly beat up the whites and shells of the eggs. Put the meat and the eggs into a perfectly clean stewpan. Add the stock and mix up well together. Bring to the boil gently, giving the mixture an occasional stir to prevent it from sticking. Simmer gently for a quarter of an hour. Stand the stewpan at the side of the stove and then strain the contents through a perfectly clean soup cloth which has been dipped in scalding water and wrung dry.

This clarified stock is now ready for use and should be a pale straw colour. It is used as a foundation for all clear soups or consommés. The soup cloth mentioned can be an inexpensive table napkin, kept entirely for soup and perfectly clean, otherwise the soup will be cloudy.

SOUPS[1]

Allow 1¾ pints of soup for 4 persons.

There are three distinct classes of soups, viz., clear, thick, and a purée. The term Consommé always applies to clear soups, and these have various names according to the different

[1] See also INVALID DIET, page 561.

garnishes used. Thick Soups are those that are thickened in some artificial way, either with yolks of eggs, rice flour or such like. A Purée is a soup which is thickened by rubbing the vegetables, such as peas, artichokes, etc., through a sieve. A purée can also be thickened in this way with meat, hare soup being an example, and there are many others.

The following recipes commence with soups of an inexpensive character, suited for every-day dinners, and end with more expensive soups.

Carrot Soup

2 quarts weak Stock.	½ oz. Butter. ½ oz. Flour.
3 large Carrots.	Salt and Pepper, if required.
1 Onion. ½ a Turnip.	1 saltspoonful Castor Sugar.

UTENSILS—Knife, stockpot, hair sieve, plate, kitchen spoon, basin, pint measure.

Wash and scrape the carrots and pare the turnip. Cut the carrots, turnip, and the onion into thin slices. For the stock, the liquor that a leg of mutton or any piece of fresh meat has been boiled in, will do. Put the cut vegetables into this and bring to the boil.

Simmer for 2½ to 3 hours or until the carrots are quite tender. (Old carrots take much longer than young ones.) Then rub all through a hair sieve. Mix the flour and butter together on a plate, with a knife, until they are quite smooth. Put the soup on to re-boil and add the flour and butter, and seasoning, if required. Just before sending to table stir in a saltspoonful of castor sugar.

Pea Soup

1 quart weak Stock.	A crust of Bread, about 2 oz.
½ pint Split Peas.	Croûtons of fried Bread.
1 Onion. 1 Carrot.	Dried Mint (sieved).

UTENSILS—Basin, stockpot, knife, kitchen spoon, hair sieve, frying pan, pint measure.

Put the split peas to soak in enough cold water to cover them, and let them remain all night. Put the soaked peas on to boil in one quart of stock, with one onion, a carrot, and the crust of bread. For the stock, the liquor that salt pork or salt beef has been boiled in is suitable (if not too salt) in fact, it is best. If you have no liquor of this kind then use ordinary weak stock and add some bacon bones or a ham bone, as pea soup is always improved by the flavour of salted pork.

Bring to the boil, and keep it well stirred, as it is very apt to stick. Simmer gently for 2 or 3 hours until the peas are quite tender, then rub all through a hair sieve. Re-heat, and serve with croûtons of fried bread.

THE CROÛTONS OF BREAD

Cut some crumb of bread into small squares about the size of dice. Fry them in butter or boiling dripping until they are a pale golden colour, then drain them on a piece of paper so that they are quite free from fat. Serve the croûtons sprinkled well with dried mint rubbed through a sieve to free it from stalks, arranged on a hot dish lined with a lace paper d'oyley.

Potato Soup

1 lb. Potatoes.	A teaspoonful Milk or Cream.
1 large Onion.	Pepper and Salt.
1 oz. Butter. 1 oz. Flour.	1 dessertspoonful finely chopped
3 pints weak Stock.	Parsley.

UTENSILS—Knife, stewpan, large kitchen spoon, hair sieve, 2 basins, wooden spoon, pint measure.

Slice one large onion finely and put it into a saucepan with the butter. Cover, and fry without browning for 15 minutes, stirring constantly. Add to this the potatoes, pared and cut into slices, also the weak stock. Stir well until soup boils, skim well and continue boiling till tender.

Rub all through a sieve, add pepper and salt to taste, and put back into the saucepan to re-boil. Mix the flour with milk or cream and stir into the soup. Just before serving, add the finely chopped parsley.

Brussels Sprouts Soup

1 lb. Brussels Sprouts.	½ pint Milk.
3 oz. Butter.	White Pepper.
1 oz. Flour.	½ teaspoonful Castor Sugar.
1 quart White Stock.	Salt. Soda.

UTENSILS—Two basins, knife, 3 saucepans, pestle and mortar, hair sieve, toasting fork or toaster, kitchen spoon, teaspoon, pint measure.

Trim off all the outside or discoloured leaves of the sprouts, wash them well, and let them stand in a basin of cold salted water for about an hour, then drain them. Have ready a saucepan three-parts full of fast-boiling water. Put in a small dessertspoonful of salt to each quart of water. Throw in the sprouts and boil fast for 15 to 20 minutes, but be careful not to overcook them or their colour will be spoiled. Drain well and squeeze out as much moisture as possible.

Now put the sprouts into a mortar, and pound them until they are quite smooth, then rub them through a hair sieve. Put this purée into a clean saucepan, stir in the stock gradually and season to taste with white pepper, salt, and half a teaspoonful of castor sugar. Bring it to the boil.

Rub the butter well into the flour and stir this into the soup until quite dissolved. Boil the milk in a separate saucepan, and just before serving the soup, add the boiling milk to it. Serve with small croûtons of toasted bread.

NOTE.—If it is not convenient to pound the sprouts, they can be merely rubbed through a sieve, but it adds to the smoothness of the soup if they are pounded first.

Spring Soup

1 quart Stock.	1 tablespoonful each shredded
½ teaspoonful Castor Sugar.	Lettuce, Carrot and Turnip.
1 tablespoonful Rice.	Pepper and Salt, if required.

UTENSILS—Knife, stockpot, measuring spoons, pint measure.

The Economical Stock on page 107 will do perfectly well for this, but any better stock can be used if liked.

Wash the vegetables well, then pare the turnip and scrape the carrot. Cut the turnip into thin ribands, as an apple is pared, only keep paring round and round until you have sufficient. The carrot can be cut lengthways into thin slices. Then cut both these into two-inch lengths, and then lengthways again into fine shreds about as thick as worsted. Cut the lettuce into shreds the same length. Add the rice and carrots to the stock and boil for 15 minutes, then add the lettuce, the turnip, the sugar, and the flavouring, if required, and simmer till tender.

Artichoke Soup

2 lb. Jerusalem Artichokes.
1 oz. Butter.
1 pint Second Stock.
1½ oz. Flour.
2 tablespoonfuls Cream (optional).

1 small Onion.
1 pint Milk.
1 blade of Mace.
¼ teaspoonful Cayenne.
1 teaspoonful Salt.

UTENSILS—Knife, basin, 3 saucepans, strainer, fine sieve, wooden spoon, frying pan, measuring spoons, pint measure.

Wash and pare the artichokes, keeping them under the water as much as possible while being pared. As each one is done throw it into a basin of fresh cold water. When all are pared, put them into a saucepan with sufficient cold water just to cover them, and add a little salt, also the onion, sliced. Bring to the boil, then strain them. Put on again in cold water and re-boil, then let them cook until tender. Now strain, and rub the artichokes through a fine sieve, using a wooden spoon for the purpose.

Boil the milk with a blade of mace and a quarter-teaspoonful of cayenne pepper. Melt one ounce of butter in a saucepan large enough to contain all the soup. Mix the flour in with the butter until quite smooth. Then add, by degrees, the stock, milk and seasoning, and lastly, the artichoke purée. Bring to the boil, and it is then ready to serve.

If a richer soup is required, add two tablespoonfuls of cream after it is taken off the fire. Small croûtons of fried bread, about the size of dice, should be handed with this soup.

Vegetable Marrow Soup

1 Vegetable Marrow.
1 small Onion.
2 oz. Butter.
½ small teaspoonful White Pepper.
1 pint Milk.

1 blade of Mace.
A dust of Cayenne.
1 pint White Stock.
1 small tablespoonful Crème-de-Riz.

1 teaspoonful Salt.

UTENSILS—Knife, measuring spoons, stewpan, hair sieve, milk saucepan, basin, spoon, frying pan, pint measure.

Scrape a nice young vegetable marrow, and remove the seeds, then cut it into pieces about three inches square. Peel one small onion and slice it thinly. Melt the butter in a stewpan, put in the vegetable marrow, onion, white pepper and salt. Put the lid on the stewpan, and let the contents cook gently at the side of the stove until quite tender, but do not let them brown at all. When cooked, rub through a hair sieve.

Put one pint of milk on to boil with a blade of mace and a dust of cayenne pepper, then let it infuse for 10 minutes. Put the marrow purée back into a saucepan, add the white stock, and bring to the boil, then strain the milk into it, stirring all the time.

Mix the rice flour in a little cold milk or stock, and stir it into the boiling soup. If too thick, reduce it with a little more milk or stock. The stock can be omitted altogether, and only milk used, if preferred. Add a little more salt if necessary. Serve with croûtons of fried bread.

Pumpkin Soup

3 lb. Pumpkin.	A grate of Nutmeg.
2 oz. Butter.	1 quart Milk.
Pepper and Salt.	1 tablespoonful Flour.

UTENSILS—Knife, 2 stewpans, hair sieve, milk saucepan, wooden spoon, basin.

Peel the pumpkin and cut it into small squares, throw it into plenty of boiling, salted water and boil until it is quite tender. Strain, and rub the pumpkin through a hair sieve.

Boil about a quart of milk. Melt the butter in a saucepan, and stir in the flour until smooth. Add a very little grated nutmeg and a small teaspoonful of white pepper. Pour in half the boiling milk by degrees, stirring all the time, then add the pumpkin pulp and mix well. Add sufficient milk to make all the consistency of single cream. Lastly, add salt to taste, and more seasoning if required.

Cabbage Soup

1 large Cabbage.	2 large Potatoes.
2 oz. Butter. 1 quart Milk.	Pepper and Salt.

UTENSILS—Basin, knife, stewpan, fork.

Wash a nice white cabbage well and let it remain in salted water for an hour. Then rinse it, and afterwards shred it finely. Melt the butter in the stewpan, put in the cabbage and stir until the cabbage has absorbed all the butter. Add enough water to cook it, and stew till done.

Pare the potatoes, slice them thinly and add them to the soup. When they are done, smash them up in the soup to thicken it. Season, add the milk, boil up and serve.

Rice Soup

½ teaspoonful Patna Rice.	1 Yolk of Egg.
1½ pints Chicken or Rabbit Stock.	A small blade of Mace.
½ pint Milk.　2 Shallots.	1 dessertspoonful chopped Parsley.
	Pepper and Salt.

UTENSILS—Two saucepans, knife, hair sieve, 2 basins, egg-beater, kitchen spoon, pint measure.

Wash the rice and put it in a saucepan with sufficient cold water to cover it, bring it to the boil and then strain it, wash it well in cold water, and put it back into the saucepan. Add the stock, sliced shallots, a little salt and pepper and boil until the rice is tender, then rub all through a hair sieve.

Boil the milk with the blade of mace in it. Rinse out the saucepan that the rice was boiled in, and put the rice purée back into it. Take out the blade of mace from the boiling milk, and pour the milk on the rice purée. Beat up the yolk of egg with a little cold milk, stir it into the soup just before sending it to the table, and at the same time add the finely chopped parsley.

NOTE.—On no account let the soup boil after the egg is in, or the egg will curdle.

Scotch Broth

2 lb. neck of Mutton.	1 tablespoonful Pearl Barley.
1 quart Water.	½ tablespoonful chopped Parsley.
1 Onion.　1 Carrot.	About ¼ teaspoonful Pepper.
½ Turnip.	1 teaspoonful Salt.

UTENSILS—Basin, knife, stewpan, large kitchen spoon, measuring spoons, pint measure.

The scrag end of the neck of mutton will do if it is first soaked in warm water to draw out the blood.

Cut the meat into pieces about two inches square. If the butcher has not cut it in small joints, chop the bones in half. Put the pieces into a clean saucepan with the cold water. Well wash the carrot, onion and half turnip, and cut them into small dice about the size of a pea. Put these into the saucepan with the stock, also the pearl barley, the pepper and the salt. Bring very gently to the boil and skim well. Draw to the side of the stove and simmer very gently for 2½ hours. On no account let the soup boil hard or the meat will be tough.

About a quarter of an hour before sending to the table, add half a tablespoonful of finely chopped parsley. Serve the soup with the meat in the tureen, or let the neck of mutton be the next course.

Mulligatawny Soup

1 Onion. 1½ oz. Butter.	1 small tablespoon Curry Powder.
1 large Cooking Apple.	1 teaspoonful Curry Paste.
1 tablespoonful Desiccated Cocoa-nut.	1 tablespoonful Chutney.
	1½ pints Stock.
1 large tablespoonful Crème-de-riz.	1 saltspoonful Salt.

UTENSILS—Knife, stewpan, basin, hair sieve, saucepan, wooden spoon, measuring spoons, pint measure.

Peel the onion and the apple, and chop them finely. Melt the butter in a saucepan, add the chopped onion and apple, and fry until they are a golden brown. Mix the crème-de-riz, the curry powder, and curry paste with a little cold stock. Add these to the onion and apple, and cook together for another 10 minutes. Then add the remainder of the stock, also the chutney, the desiccated cocoanut and the salt. Bring to the boil, and continue boiling for ½ hour. Then rub it all through a fine hair sieve.

Rinse out the saucepan, pour the soup back into it, and return to the fire until it boils. It is then ready to serve. Plainly boiled rice, dished on a hot plate lined with a lace paper d'oyley, and sprinkled with coralline pepper, can be handed with the soup.

Barley Cream Soup

1 large teacupful Pearl Barley.	2 oz. Butter.
1 large Onion.	½ blade of Mace.
¾ pint Milk.	2 Yolks of Eggs.
3 pints White Stock.	Pepper and Salt.

UTENSILS—Stewpan, hair sieve, 2 basins, knife, milk saucepan, egg-beater, teacup, wooden spoon, frying pan, pint measure.

Well wash the barley, and put it into a saucepan with sufficient cold water to cover it. Just bring to the boil, then strain it and wash well in cold water, and put it back into the saucepan with the peeled onion, mace and white stock. When it boils, reduce the heat beneath the saucepan, and let it simmer gently for about 5 hours. Then rub all through a hair sieve. Rinse out the saucepan and put the soup back into it.

Boil half a pint of milk separately and dissolve the butter in it. Add this to the soup, and season with salt and pepper to taste. It is impossible to say the amount of seasoning that should be used, as there is probably more or less seasoning already in the stock that is used. Beat the yolks of eggs with the remaining quarter-pint of milk, and stir this into the soup, which must be nearly boiling. Stir it at the side of the fire for a minute of two, just to cook the eggs, but do not let it boil or the eggs will curdle.

Pour into the soup tureen and serve. Hand with it dice-shaped pieces of bread, fried a pale golden colour in clarified butter.

Rosalind Soup

1 quart Brown Stock.	8 Button Onions.
8 spring Carrots.	Salt and Pepper.
8 spring Turnips.	A bunch of Herbs (Bayleaf, Thyme
16 Brussels Sprouts.	and Parsley).

UTENSILS—Knife, stewpan, kitchen spoon, frying pan, grater, pint measure.

Take small French carrots about one inch long, and wash and scrape them well. Take turnips, about the size of large marbles, and wash them. They should not be peeled, and about half an inch of the green leaf stalks should be left on them. Skin the onions and trim the Brussels sprouts neatly.

Put the good, brown, well-seasoned stock into a saucepan. Add the vegetables and herbs, and simmer until the carrots, onions and turnips are quite tender. The sprouts will have been boiled to pieces by this time. Lift the vegetables out carefully into the soup-tureen, which must have been previously heated. Boil up the soup, and, if necessary, add a little salt and pepper. Lift out the herbs, then pour the soup over the vegetables in the tureen. Hand little croûtons of fried bread, garnished with grated cheese, with this soup, if liked, but this is not necessary.

Fish Soup

2 lb. Fish. ½ pint Shrimps.	A bunch of Herbs (Bayleaf,
2 oz. Butter. 1 pint Milk.	Thyme and Parsley).
2 oz. Flour. 3 pints Water.	A blade of Mace.
2 Carrots. 1 Leek.	1 tablespoonful chopped Parsley.
½ stick of Celery.	Pepper and Salt.

UTENSILS—Knife, basin, stewpan, large kitchen spoon, wire sieve, 2 muslin bags, wooden spoon, milk saucepan, pint measure.

Any white fish answers for this soup, such as haddock, whiting, plaice, cod, etc. Take two pounds in all, but half of this may be trimmings. Wash them well, cut them into small pieces, and chop the bones. Put all into a saucepan with three pints of cold water. Add the vegetables, which must be well washed, and thinly sliced. Pick the shrimps, tie the shells in a piece of muslin and put them into the soup— the shrimps are kept for garnishing. Also put in the herbs and mace, but not the chopped parsley. Bring to the boil and skim well. Add the seasoning, and boil for 2 hours, until the vegetables are quite tender.

Strain the soup through a fine wire sieve into a basin. Remove the two muslin bags containing the herbs and shrimp shells. With a wooden spoon rub as much of the fish and vegetables as possible through the sieve, but be careful that no bones go through.

Melt the butter in a saucepan. Mix in the flour, then gradually stir in the milk. Stir all the time until it boils. Rinse out the soup saucepan, return the soup to it, and add the thickened milk, stirring until it almost boils. Just before serving add the finely chopped parsley, and the picked shrimps. If required, add a little more seasoning.

Tomato Soup

2 lb. Tomatoes.	2 oz. lean cooked **Ham**.
1 large Onion	1 tablespoonful **Sago**.
½ oz. Butter.	Salt and Pepper.
1 quart Stock.	½ teaspoonful **Sugar**.

UTENSILS—Knife, frying pan, hair sieve, stewpan, measuring spoons, wooden spoon, basin, pint measure.

Take the tomatoes, onion, and finely chopped, lean, cooked ham. Slice the tomatoes and onion and fry them with the ham in the butter for 20 minutes, then rub all through a hair sieve. Add to this purée one quart of weak stock (or even water will do), also the sago, sugar, and salt and pepper to taste. Bring to the boil and simmer until the sago is clear.

Chestnut Soup

1 lb. Chestnuts.	¼ teaspoonful **White Pepper**.
1 quart White Stock.	½ teaspoonful **Salt**.
4 tablespoonfuls Cream.	½ teaspoonful **Castor Sugar**.
1 oz. Butter.	A blade of Mace.

Toasted Bread.

UTENSILS—Knife, stewpan, wire sieve, basin, wooden spoon, measuring spoons, pint measure, toaster.

Cut the ends off a pound of chestnuts, and roast them in a moderate oven for about 20 minutes, until the outer and inner skins will peel off easily. Remove all the skins and then put the chestnuts in a saucepan with the white stock, white pepper, salt, and castor sugar. Part of the seasoning can be reduced or omitted if the stock is already highly seasoned. Simmer all together for 1 hour or longer, until the chestnuts are quite tender.

When they are cooked, take out the blade of mace, and rub the chestnuts through a fine sieve, moistening them with a little of the stock. Rinse out the saucepan, and return the chestnut purée and stock to it. Add the cream, and stir well until it boils, adding more seasoning if required. Simmer gently for 20 minutes until it is quite smooth, and it should then be of the consistency of thin cream, but if too thick, add a little milk or stock. If cream is not procurable, milk can be used in the place of it, but cream is much the best.

Cut two slices of thin bread from a stale tin loaf. Toast them quickly, and cut them into strips one inch and a half long and half an inch broad. Arrange these prettily on a plate, and hand them with the soup.

Pot-au-Feu

2 lb. lean Beef.	A bunch of Herbs (Bayleaf,
2 Carrots. 2 Leeks.	Thyme and Parsley).
1 Turnip. 1 Parsnip.	20 Black Peppercorns.
1 Onion. 15 Cloves.	1 large teaspoonful Salt.
1 small Cabbage.	3 quarts Water.

1 Stale French Roll.

UTENSILS—Knife, stockpot, pint measure, piece of tape, piece of muslin, kitchen spoon.

Tie the beef in shape with a piece of tape. Put it into an earthenware stockpot, with three quarts of water. Cleanse the vegetables well, and cut them into convenient sized pieces, with the exception of the cabbage, which is just cut into four. Tie the seasoning of spices up in a piece of muslin, and the herbs into a bundle. Put all into the pot with the salt, and let it simmer gently for about 4 hours.

Take out the bunch of herbs and the bag of spice. Cut a stale French roll into slices, and put it into the soup tureen. Lift the vegetables out carefully, and lay them on the bread. Put the meat on to a separate dish, and pour the soup into the tureen, and serve. The meat should be dished up separately, and, if liked, tomato sauce may be poured round it.

Imitation Mock-Turtle Soup

1 quart good Cooked Meat Stock.	1 tablespoonful chopped **Parsley**
1½ oz. Butter.	and Lemon Thyme mixed.
1 oz. Flour.	1 Egg. Frying Fat.
2 oz. Breadcrumbs.	1 teaspoonful **Castor Sugar.**
1 tablespoonful Sherry.	A pinch of Salt.
½ teaspoonful Tarragon Vinegar.	A dust of Coralline **Pepper.**

UTENSILS—Stewpan, grater, knife, basin, egg-beater, frying pan, measuring spoons, wooden spoon, pint measure.

Fry together in a saucepan, half an ounce of butter, and one ounce of flour, until they are a nice rich brown. Then stir in the cooked-meat stock, sherry, tarragon vinegar and castor sugar. Bring to the boil, and keep it boiling for 10 minutes.

Make some forcemeat balls with the breadcrumbs, one ounce of butter, the chopped parsley and lemon thyme mixed, a pinch of salt and a dust of coralline pepper. Rub all these ingredients together, and mix well with one whole beaten-up egg, then make into balls about the size of small marbles. Fry in boiling fat for about a minute, then drain well on paper. Put these forcemeat balls into the soup tureen and pour the soup on to them just before sending to table.

Chicken Broth

1 Fowl. 1 Onion.	1 blade of Mace.
2 quarts Water.	12 Peppercorns.

1 teaspoonful Salt.

UTENSILS—Knife, stewpan, large kitchen spoon, strainer.

Draw the fowl and save all the giblets, then chop the fowl up into small joints. Scald and skin the feet, and well clean the giblets. Put them all into a saucepan with the joints of fowl, and sufficient cold water just to cover them. Bring to the boil.

Strain off that water, then add two quarts of cold water, the peeled and sliced onion and the seasoning. Simmer gently for 4 hours, skimming well whenever necessary. Strain and let it cool before removing the fat. Skim off all the fat and re-heat. If any particles of fat remain, take them off with a piece of white paper.

Kidney Soup

1 lb. Ox Kidney.	3 oz. Butter.
4 pints Brown Stock.	1 small blade of Mace.
1 teaspoonful Peppercorns.	1 teaspoonful Worcester Sauce.
1 sprig of Thyme.	1 wineglassful Sherry.
1 Onion. 1 Shallot.	1 teaspoonful Vinegar.
2 small sticks of Celery.	Croûtons of fried Bread, as
1½ oz. Flour.	described.

UTENSILS—Two basins, knife, 2 saucepans, fine wire sieve, coarse sieve, large kitchen spoon, teaspoon, wineglass, fork or egg-beater, brush, frying pan, pint measure, small cutter.

Wash the kidney well in cold water with 1 teaspoonful of common brown vinegar in it. Dry it thoroughly, then cut it into small squares. Melt the butter in a saucepan. Roll the pieces of kidney in a little flour, then fry them in the butter for a few minutes.

Wash and dry the vegetables, and cut them into small pieces. Sprinkle the remainder of the flour on to these, add them to the kidney, and fry all together until they are a nice brown. Pour in the stock, and stir well for a few minutes, then add the thyme, spices and seasoning. Continue stirring the soup until it is boiling, then draw aside and simmer gently for 3 or 4 hours. Skim well during the cooking.

When the kidney is quite tender, strain the soup through a fine wire sieve. Take out about half of the pieces of kidney, and put them into the tureen. Skim off any fat that there may be on the soup. Rub the remaining pieces of kidney, and the vegetables, through a sieve, and add this purée to the soup in the saucepan and bring it almost to the boil. Add the wine and more seasoning if required, then pour the soup on to the pieces of kidney in the tureen, and serve with croûtons.

THE CROÛTONS OF BREAD

Cut two or three slices from a stale tin loaf and stamp them out into rounds with a small cutter about the size of a sixpence. Fry in plenty of boiling fat, until they are a very pale golden colour. Drain, and then brush them over on one side with either thin glaze or slightly beaten white of egg.

Have ready two hard-boiled yolks of eggs, rubbed through a fine wire sieve. Dip the brushed sides of the croûtons into this, and arrange them on a plate with a fancy paper. Hand them with the soup.

Green Pea Soup

1½ pints shelled Green Peas.	1 quart White Stock.
2 oz. Butter. ½ oz. Flour.	A few leaves of Spinach.
A small sprig of Mint.	A small teaspoon Castor Sugar.

UTENSILS—Stewpan, hair sieve, basin, saucepan, spoon, pint measure.

Put one and a quarter pints of green peas into a stewpan with one ounce of butter, a small sprig of mint and a few leaves of spinach. Cover, and let them steam well without browning, at the side of the stove, or on a low gas flame, for 15 minutes. Then add the white stock and castor sugar, bring to the boil and simmer until the peas are quite tender. Now rub all through a hair sieve. Melt the remaining ounce of butter in a saucepan and add half an ounce of flour and mix well together. Stir into this the purée of peas by degrees, and bring to the boil. Just before serving, add the remaining quarter-pint of peas which have just been plainly boiled.

Italian Cauliflower Soup (Clear)

2 quarts Clear Stock.	Parmesan Cheese.
1 small Cauliflower.	Coralline Pepper.
Chopped Parsley.	

UTENSILS—Knife, 2 saucepans, basin, colander.

Take a small young cauliflower. Pour about a quart of boiling water over it, then plunge it into cold water. Cut it up into small pieces, and boil in salted water till tender. When done, strain and put it into the soup tureen.

Bring about two quarts of well-flavoured clear stock to the boil and pour it over the cauliflower in the tureen. Serve with grated Parmesan cheese (on a plate separately) sprinkled over with coralline pepper and finely chopped parsley.

Alexandra Soup

1 quart Veal Stock.	A bunch of Herbs (Bayleaf,
1 oz. Butter.	Thyme and Parsley).
2 Onions or Leeks.	Seasoning to taste.
2 Lettuces.	A little Milk or Cream.
1 oz. Creme-de-riz.	Fried Croutons, as described.

UTENSILS—Stewpan, knife, piece of muslin, pint measure, basin, wooden spoon, frying pan, frying basket, brush, egg-beater.

C.I.O.   E

Melt the butter in a stewpan. Shred the hearts of the lettuces finely, also the onions or leeks. Add these to the butter, put on the lid, and cook gently at the side of the stove or on a low gas flame for about 20 minutes without browning. Add the stock to the vegetables, and put in the herbs, tied in muslin, then cook all together gently for about ½ hour, until the vegetables are quite tender. Remove the herbs and add the seasoning to taste. Mix the rice flour with a little milk or cream, pour it into the soup, and stir until it re-boils. Serve with fried croûtons.

TO MAKE THE FRIED CROÛTONS

Cut some stale bread into three-quarter inch squares. Put them in a frying basket and fry in plenty of boiling fat until they are a pale golden colour. When cold brush over with beaten-up egg, and dip one side in grated Parmesan cheese, and the other side in finely chopped parsley ; the parsley having been first wrung quite dry in a cloth.

Gamekeeper's Soup

The remains of any cold Game.	Veal or Poultry Stock.
1 large Onion.	2 Eggs. 6 Cloves.
1 Carrot.	2 oz. finely chopped Liver or
A bunch of Herbs (Bayleaf,	raw Beef.
Thyme and Parsley).	1 wineglassful Sherry and 1
A blade of Mace.	teaspoonful Arrowroot to
A dust of Sugar.	every quart of Stock.

UTENSILS—Stewpan, strainer, 2 basins, knife, egg-beater, soup-cloth, wooden spoon, pint measure.

Take the remains of any cold game that is not high, and put it into a saucepan with the onion, carrot, herbs, cloves, peppercorns, and sugar. Cover with veal or poultry stock and bring to the boil. Simmer for 3 or 4 hours, then strain. When cold add the shells and whites of the eggs, slightly beaten, also the finely chopped liver or raw beef, and nearly a wineglassful of sherry to every quart of stock.

Whisk all well, place it on the stove and bring to the boil. Let it stand for a few minutes, then strain through a soup-cloth which has been dipped in hot water and wrung out. Put the soup back into a clean saucepan. Thicken it with a teaspoonful of arrowroot mixed in a tablespoonful of the sherry to every pint of soup. A few of the best pieces of the game should be saved to be shredded and added to the soup just before serving.

Clear Sévigné Soup

2 quarts good Clear Stock   1 Lettuce.
   (clarified).   Tarragon.   Chervil.
           Savoury Custard, as described.

UTENSILS—Knife, 2 saucepans, pint measure, fork, 4 basins, cup, strainer, small round cutter.

Stamp the lettuce into rounds with a plain cutter about the size of a sixpenny piece. Put it into a small saucepan of cold water with a very small pinch of soda. Bring to the boil, and let it stand for a few minutes. Then strain and put into cold water till wanted. Pick the chervil into very small sprigs, and the tarragon into very small leaves, and treat each separately in the same way as the lettuce. Take two quarts of good clear stock which has been clarified, and bring it to the boil. Garnish with the prepared lettuce, chervil, and tarragon, also with savoury custard in small rounds about the size of a pea.

TO MAKE THE SAVOURY CUSTARD

1 whole raw Egg.   A dust of Cayenne Pepper.
1 tablespoonful Milk.   A pinch of Salt.

Beat the egg slightly, not enough to make it frothy, and add the milk and seasoning, then strain into a well-buttered cup. Stand the cup on a fold of paper in a saucepan, with water reaching half-way up the cup. Place a buttered paper on the top of the cup. Steam till firm, but on no account allow the water to boil, or the custard will be perforated.

Turn the custard out, and allow it to cool. When cold, cut it in thin slices and stamp out with a very small round cutter. Wash well in several warm waters, until the water remains quite clear. Then strain and put into cold water till wanted.

NOTE.—If the custard is not well washed, as described, the soup will be clouded.

Clear Toledo Soup

1 quart clear Brown Stock.   1 tablespoonful Yellow and White
1 cooked Carrot.   Egg Custard, as described.

UTENSILS—Stewpan, pint measure, vegetable cutters, 2 basins, egg-beater, 2 cups, saucepan, measuring spoons, knife.

Bring the clear brown stock to the boil, and garnish with cooked carrot cut into small stars, and with small half-moons of yellow and white custard. The custards must be well washed, first in hot then in cold water, and then left standing in cold water till required.

TO MAKE THE YELLOW CUSTARD

2 Yolks of Eggs.	1 dessertspoonful Milk.
A pinch of Salt.	A dust of Coralline Pepper.

Beat the yolks of eggs, add the milk and seasoning, and pour into a well-buttered cup. Stand on a fold of paper in a saucepan with water reaching half-way up the cup. Lay a piece of buttered paper on the top. Bring the water just to the boil, then draw the saucepan to one side, or lower the gas flame, and poach until the egg mixture is firm. Turn out and allow the shape to cool.

When cold, cut into thin slices with a wet knife on a wet paper, and stamp into small half-moons or other fancy shapes (with vegetable cutters). Wash well in several hot waters, then put in cold water until wanted. The cooked vegetable custard is cut into thin slices and stamped out in the same way.

TO MAKE THE WHITE CUSTARD

2 Whites of Eggs.	A tablespoonful Cream or Milk.
	A pinch of Salt.

Beat the whites of eggs slightly. Add the cream and a pinch of salt, mix well together, then pour into a buttered cup. Place the cup on a fold of paper in a saucepan, with water to reach half-way up the cup. Lay a piece of buttered paper on the top. Bring to the boil, then poach and finish in the same way as with yellow custard just described.

Clear Brunoise Soup

2 quarts Clear Stock.	¼ teacupful each of Celery, Leek,
¼ teacupful Italian Paste.	Onion, Turnip and Carrot.

UTENSILS—Vegetable cutter, 3 saucepans, strainer, tea-cup, pint measure.

Wash the vegetables, and cut them into dice shapes, using only the red part of the carrot. Put them into a saucepan with cold water and a little salt, and bring to the boil. Strain them, and then wash all in cold water. Put them on again in slightly salted cold water, and cook till tender. Treat the Italian paste in the same way in a separate saucepan. Put on the clear stock in another saucepan and bring to the boil. Just before serving strain the garnishes, and add to the soup.

Ox-Tail Soup

1 Ox-tail.	½ wineglassful Port Wine.
2 quarts weak Stock.	2 oz. Flour.
1 stick of Celery.	3 oz. Butter.
1 Onion. 1 Carrot.	Salt. 6 Cloves.
20 Peppercorns.	A bunch of Herbs (Bayleaf,
1 tablespoonful Ketchup.	Thyme and Parsley).

UTENSILS—Knife, stewpan, cloth, large kitchen spoon, fine hair sieve, 2 basins, wineglass, pint measure.

Divide the ox-tail into small joints, wash them well, and trim them from any superfluous fat. Put them in a stewpan with cold water, and bring to the boil. Strain, and rinse the pieces in cold water. This blanches the meat, and prevents such a quantity of scum from rising on the soup. Wash and dry the vegetables, also dry the pieces of tail. Rinse out the saucepan, and dry this as well. Melt the butter in the saucepan, roll the pieces of tail in the flour, and when the butter is smoking put them in and fry a deep brown. Add two quarts of weak stock and bring it to the boil, removing all scum as it rises. Now put in the vegetables (sliced up small), the seasoning, spices and herbs. Simmer gently for about 4 hours, until the pieces of tail are quite tender.

Then take the pieces of tail out of the soup and keep them hot. Strain the soup through a fine hair sieve into a basin. Skim off all the fat, then return the soup to the saucepan. Put the pieces of tail into it again, and almost bring to the boil. Add the wine, also more seasoning if needed. A few of the best pieces of carrot, turnip and onion must be taken out as soon as they are cooked, and cut into fancy shapes. Add to the soup, with the wine, last thing.

Cream of Celery

2 or 3 sticks of Celery.	½ pint Cream or Milk.
Well-flavoured Light Stock.	2 Eggs.
1 small Onion.	1 teaspoonful Lemon Juice.

UTENSILS—Knife, 2 saucepans, hair sieve, 2 basins, egg-beater, kitchen spoon.

Well wash celery, and cut off all the green. Prepare the

onion. Boil these together until quite tender in slightly salted water with a teaspoonful of lemon juice. When cooked, drain well, and then rub through a fine hair sieve. Put these back in the saucepan, and add sufficient well-flavoured light stock to make it rather thin. Boil up quickly. Just before serving, add two well-beaten yolks of eggs, and boiling cream or milk. When finished, this soup ought to be of the consistency of thin cream.

Mushroom Soup

2 pints White Stock.	A little Milk.
1 lb. Mushrooms.	A little Cream.
2 Eggs.	Salt and Pepper.
1 Spanish Onion.	Croûtons of Fried Bread, as
1 dessertspoonful Flour.	described.

UTENSILS—Knife, stewpan, hair sieve or tammy, basin, wooden spoon, egg-beater or fork, small cutter, brush, frying pan.

Wash the mushrooms, and chop them up. Chop up the onion finely, then bring the stock to the boil, and add the mushrooms and onion, then boil for ½ hour. Next pass all through a tammy or a fine hair sieve. Add a dessertspoonful of flour mixed into a smooth paste with a little milk, and salt and pepper to taste.

Boil up again, and just before serving remove the soup from the fire and add the yolks of two eggs beaten up in a little cream. Do not let the soup boil after adding the eggs. They only want to be cooked just enough to thicken the soup. Serve with small round croûtons of fried bread about the size of a sixpence.

THE CROÛTONS

Cut out some small rounds of bread about the size of a sixpence. Fry these and brush them over with white of egg. Dip one side in finely chopped tongue or truffles. Dish the croûtons in a circle on a round dish-paper.

Shrimp Soup

1½ pints Shrimps.	1 teaspoonful Lemon Juice.
4 oz. Butter.	A grate of Nutmeg.
1 penny Roll.	¼ saltspoonful Cayenne.
2 Yolks of Eggs.	Salt to taste.
1 gill Cream.	1 quart Fish Stock.

UTENSILS—Two saucepans, pestle and mortar, kitchen spoon, strainer, hair sieve, basin, egg-beater, toaster.

Shell the shrimps and put the shells on to boil in a break-fastcupful of water, and the lemon juice. Pound the picked shrimps in a mortar, with the butter, until they are a smooth paste. Soak the penny roll in some of the cold stock, and then pound it with the shrimps. Put the paste into a saucepan, and add the remainder of the quart of stock. Strain the shells and add the liquor to the soup, also the nutmeg, cayenne and salt to taste. Stir well, and simmer gently at the side of the stove for 1 hour.

Then rub the soup through a fine hair sieve. Return it to the saucepan, and bring it to boiling point. Then beat up the yolks of eggs in the cream, take the soup off the fire, and stir in the beaten yolks and cream. Pour it into the tureen and serve with small pieces of toasted bread floating on the top.

Hare Soup

1 Hare. 1 Leek.	1 Carrot. 1 Onion.
1 lb. Gravy Beef.	12 Black Peppercorns.
½ lb. lean Ham.	1 blade of Mace.
¼ pint Port Wine.	¼ teaspoonful Cayenne Pepper.
2 oz. Dripping.	2 tablespoonfuls Flour.
A bunch of Herbs (Bayleaf,	Seasoning of Salt.
Thyme and Parsley).	Forcemeat Balls, as described.

UTENSILS—Knife, cloth, sieve or flour sifter, stewpan, measuring spoons, large kitchen spoon, muslin bag, hair sieve, pestle and mortar, 3 basins, egg-beater, small saucepan or frying pan.

Skin and paunch the hare, and save the liver. Wash the hare, dry it, and cut it up into small joints. Wash and prepare the vegetables, and dry them thoroughly in a cloth. Cut the beef and ham into small pieces. Slice the vegetables finely. Then sift the flour over the ham, beef, hare and vegetables.

Melt the dripping in a stewpan, and put the hare, ham and vegetables in. Fry until they are a nice rich golden brown, which will take about 15 minutes. Add sufficient water to cover the ingredients, bring to the boil, then skim off all the fat. Tie the herbs and spices in a muslin bag, and put them in the soup. Add the cayenne and a little salt and simmer gently for 4 to 5 hours, skimming off all the fat as it rises.

When cooked, strain the soup through a hair sieve. Take

the best pieces of the hare, pound them in a mortar, then rub through a hair sieve. Moisten with a little stock during the process. Return the stock to the saucepan, add the hare purée, and stir until boiling. It should be of the consistency of single cream, but if not it can be thickened with a little crème-de-riz, mixed with a little cold stock. Or a little plain flour will do if smoothly mixed. Just before serving add the port wine, and small forcemeat balls. Small croûtons of bread, garnished with finely chopped ham, can also be served with a d'oyley under them. They would be handed round with the soup.

THE FORCEMEAT BALLS

Flour.
1 oz. Suet.   1 Egg.
2 oz. Breadcrumbs.
1 teaspoonful finely chopped Parsley.

¼ teaspoonful finely chopped Lemon Peel.
¼ teaspoonful mixed Herbs.
½ teaspoonful Salt.
1 saltspoonful Pepper.

The Liver of the Hare.

Chop the suet very finely. Put it in a basin with the parsley, lemon peel, seasoning, etc., also the liver of the hare. The liver must be previously cooked in a little stock and finely chopped. Add enough whole beaten-up egg to bind the forcemeat.

Take small portions of the forcemeat, and form it into balls the size of marbles, using a little flour, just enough to prevent the mixture sticking to your hands. Poach the balls in salted water for about 7 minutes, or else fry them a pale golden brown in clarified butter. Add them to the soup just before serving.

Clear Tomato Soup

2 quarts Clear Stock.
8 large ripe Tomatoes (or tinned ones will do).
1 teaspoonful Sugar.
A strip of Bacon Rind or Bone.
4 Eggs to each quart of Stock.
A few drops of Carmine.

½ gill White Wine to each quart of Stock.
A few drops of Tarragon Vinegar.
1 teaspoonful strained Lemon Juice.
1 teaspoonful Beef Extract.
Arrowroot.

Tomato Custard, as described.

UTENSILS—Stewpan, 3 basins, egg-beater or fork, soup-cloth, vegetable cutters, measuring spoons, hair sieve, cup, strainer, saucepan, wooden spoon.

Take two quarts of clear stock, eight ripe tomatoes (or

tinned tomatoes will do), sugar, a strip of bacon rind or bone, carmine, tarragon vinegar, strained lemon juice and beef extract. Put all in a stewpan together, bring to the boil, and simmer for 1 hour, then strain and remove the fat.

Now to each quart of soup add the shells and whites of four eggs, slightly beaten, a few drops of carmine, and the white wine. Bring to the boil and simmer gently for 15 minutes. Strain through a soup-cloth, previously dipped in hot water and wrung out. Put back into a clean saucepan, and add to each quart of soup a teaspoonful of arrowroot mixed with a little cold water. Garnish with tomato custard cut into fancy shapes.

THE TOMATO CUSTARD

The pulp of one medium-sized Tomato. | 2 Eggs.   A pinch of Salt.
A pinch of Coralline Pepper.
A few drops of Carmine.

Beat the eggs slightly, just sufficient to mix the whites and yolks. Add the other ingredients to them. Rub all through a hair sieve. Then pour into a well-buttered cup, and poach till firm. When cold, turn out, wash well, and cut into any fancy shapes. Leave in cold water until the soup is ready, then heat in hot water, strain, and add to the soup just before serving.

Bisque of Lobster

1 Lobster.   1 Onion.
A small stick of Celery.
1 Carrot.   1 Leek.
A bunch of Herbs (Bayleaf,
    Thyme and Parsley).
1 quart Water.

½ saltspoonful Cayenne.
1 quart Milk.
2 oz. Butter.
2 oz. Flour.
Salt to taste.
Lobster Coral or Carmine.

UTENSILS—Knife, stewpan, pestle and mortar, strainer, milk saucepan, basins, wooden spoon, fine sieve, double boiler, frying pan, brush.

Pick the meat from the lobster. Break up the shells and put them into a saucepan with the vegetables (cleaned and sliced), the herbs, salt, cayenne and lobster coral. The lobster coral must be previously pounded in a mortar, or if the coral is not procurable, use a few drops of liquid carmine instead. Add water, and simmer gently for ¾ hour.

Pound the flesh of the lobster in a mortar to a smooth paste. Strain the stock and take out the best of the vegetables and pound these also. Put the pounded lobster and vegetables into a clean saucepan with the stock, and bring to the boil. Add the butter.

Boil nearly all the milk. Mix the flour with the remainder of the milk, and thicken the boiling milk with it, then turn all into the soup. Stir well, then rub the whole through a very fine sieve. Re-heat, and, if required, add a little more seasoning, and enough colouring to make it a pale pink.

Stand the saucepan containing the soup in a double boiler or in a tin of boiling water to keep hot, but so that it does not boil. If wanted richer, use a pint of warm single cream instead of the milk. Hand with the soup small croûtons of fried bread, brushed on one side with warmed glaze, and dipped into grated Parmesan cheese. Arrange the croûtons on a plate with a fancy paper.

Oyster Soup

1 quart White Stock.	1 oz. Butter.
1½ dozen Oysters.	1 oz. Flour.
1 pint Milk.	A blade of Mace.
½ pint Cream.	A strip of Lemon Peel.

A dust of Cayenne Pepper

UTENSILS—Stewpan, saucepan, knife, strainer, basins, kitchen spoon.

Put the stock on to boil. Put the milk into a saucepan with the mace, pepper, and lemon peel (very thinly pared), and bring them to the boil. Draw to one side and let it infuse for 15 minutes. Beard the oysters and wash them free from grit in their own liquor. Put the beards in the stock to boil. When the stock boils, strain it, and put it on to re-boil. Then add the milk which must also first be strained.

Rub the flour well into the butter and add this to the soup. Stir till it thickens, but do not let it boil. Lastly, add the cream. The oysters are put in the soup just before serving and, if large, can be cut in two or even into three pieces.

GRAVIES, STUFFINGS, FORCEMEATS, Etc.

GRAVIES

Allow ½ pint of gravy for 6 persons

If you remember to save all your trimmings of meat, shank bones of mutton, and beef skirt, as well as all meat essence found at the bottom of a roasting pan when the fat has been drained off, or if you always have a supply of stock on hand, you should never be short of gravy. A little gravy added to soup stock or to dishes made from cooked meat, always improves their flavour.

When you wish to darken your gravies or sauces, add a little browning, but if short of browning, dissolve a lump of sugar until dark brown and stir this caramel into the gravy. One tablespoonful of flour, fried till dark brown in one tablespoonful of smoking hot fat or butter, can also be used for darkening the colour of gravies and sauces.

Always be sure that the flavour of the gravy is suitable to the dish for which it is intended. Some dishes require a much more highly flavoured gravy than others. The trimmings and peelings of mushrooms (well washed in salt and water), a slice of uncooked ham, a bacon bone (unsmoked), and tomato skins, when suitable, are all good additions to the gravy stock-pot.

Two important points to remember are that gravies must always be free from fat, and must always come to the table very hot. Gravies should, if possible, be re-heated in a bain-marie, or in a saucepan standing in another containing hot water. Always save the gravy from roast meat, as a good gravy for the table can be quickly made from it, and it also greatly improves hashes, ragoûts, etc.

Heat the gravy tureen thoroughly, and, even after the gravy is poured into it, it should be stood on the rack, or in an oven with the door open, until required for the table.

Gravy Stock

3 lb. cooked or raw Meat Bones;
 also the Necks, skinned Feet,
 Gizzards and Livers of Poultry,
 if you have them.
2 Onions.   1 Leek.
1 Carrot.   Salt.

1 Turnip, or a stick of fresh Celery.
1 teaspoonful Celery Seed.
1 slice of raw Ham, or Bacon, or
 Bones of either.
A bunch of Savoury Herbs (Bayleaf, Thyme and Parsley).

UTENSILS—Knife, meat chopper, stewpan, large kitchen spoon, strainer, basin.

Chop up the bones, and slice the vegetables. Put a table-spoonful of dripping into a stewpan, and melt it. Then put in all the ingredients except the salt. Put on the lid, and let the contents fry until they are brown. Now add sufficient cold water to cover, and bring to the boil.

Skim well and add salt. Simmer gently for 2 or 3 hours, but do not let it boil hard. When done, strain the gravy, let it get cold, then skim off all the fat. This gravy should always be kept ready, and in summer time must be boiled up every day.

Roast Meat Gravy

4 tablespoonfuls Fat.
1½ cupfuls boiling Water.

4 tablespoonfuls Flour.
Salt and Pepper to taste.

UTENSILS—Baking tin, large kitchen spoon, strainer, cup.

Drain off all the fat from the pan after the meat is removed except the quantity required. Place pan on top of the flame, and stir in flour until well browned. Add gradually the water, and cook, stirring constantly, for 5 minutes. Season to taste and strain into a hot sauce-boat.

NOTE.—Sometimes gravy is preferred when made simply by draining off the fat and adding boiling water to the essence that remains in the pan. Stir constantly, season with pepper and salt, and strain into a hot sauce-boat.

Brown Gravy for Game

1 lb. Giblets.
½ lb. Gravy Beef.
1 oz. good Dripping or Butter.
1 small Carrot.
3 Peppercorns.

½ an Onion.
A sprig of Thyme.
1 Bayleaf.   2 Cloves.
A dust of Mignonette Pepper.
1 small teaspoonful Salt.

Cold Water.

UTENSILS—Knife, stewpan, strainer, basin, large spoon, teaspoon, pint measure.

Wash, scald, and dry chicken giblets, also the giblets of the game that the gravy is to be served with. Chop them up into small pieces, cut up the beef into dice-shapes, and slice the onion and carrot. Put the onion, carrot and herbs into the bottom of a stewpan, with the butter, or dripping. On top of these lay the giblets and raw beef, and add the spices and salt.

Cover the pan and let these ingredients fry gently for about 20 minutes, until they are a light brown. Add rather less than a quarter of a pint of cold water. Cook this very gently until it forms a light glaze at the bottom of the pan, then add a pint of water. Bring to the boil, draw to the side of the stove, and simmer gently for 1 hour.

Strain carefully, and put on one side until the fat is cold, and the sediment has settled. Take off the fat, pour the gravy gently off the sediment, and it is ready for use. It only re-requires to be heated when wanted for use.

Gravy for Inexpensive Dishes

Bones and Trimmings of a cooked Joint.
1 oz. Dripping.
½ head of Celery.
1 Onion. Flour.

A bunch of Savoury Herbs.
1 teaspoonful Mushroom Ketchup or Sauce.
¼ teaspoonful Pepper.
¼ teaspoonful Salt.

¼ teaspoonful Allspice.

UTENSILS—Knife, meat chopper, basin, 2 stewpans, strainer, teaspoon.

Chop the bones and trimmings of the joint which is to be hashed into small pieces. Put them into a saucepan with the celery (cleaned and cut up small), the herbs, spices, pepper and salt, and cover with cold water. Bring to the boil, then draw to one side and simmer for an hour or longer. Strain this stock.

In another stewpan melt the dripping, and put in the onion, cut into small dice. Fry until the onion is a golden brown. Then add flour to this, in the proportion of one tea-spoonful to every half-pint of stock that you are going to add. Add the stock and simmer all together for 20 minutes. Flavour with ketchup, walnut pickle, or any sauce that may be suitable and convenient. Strain, and the gravy is ready for use.

Veal Gravy

1 lb. Giblets of Fowl.	1 blade of Mace.
1 lb. lean Veal.	A small sprig of Parsley.
1 slice of lean Ham.	A pinch of Cayenne.
1 Onion. 1 quart Water.	Salt to taste.

FOR WHITE SAUCE, FRICASSEES, ETC.

UTENSILS—Knife, stewpan, large kitchen spoon, strainer, basin, pint measure.

Cut up the giblets and meat into small pieces, put them into a stewpan with the water, and bring to the boil. Skim well, then add the onion, parsley and other ingredients. Re-boil, draw to the side, and simmer very slowly for 2 or 3 hours, keeping it constantly skimmed. Now strain off the gravy, and when cold remove all fat. This gravy may be used for Veloute and many other white sauces.

Chestnut Gravy

UTENSILS—Saucepan, knife, fork, cup.

Add ¾ cupful of cooked and mashed chestnuts to 2 cupfuls of unthickened pork, chicken, or turkey gravy.

STUFFINGS

To make successful stuffings, no matter what they are, you must prepare the ingredients very carefully—breadcrumbs must be sifted very finely ; parsley should be washed, scalded and thoroughly dried before chopping finely ; all fresh herbs should also be finely chopped. If dried herbs are used, crush them to a powder. If suet is used, it should be freed from all gristle and skin and finely chopped.

It is quite unnecessary to moisten stuffings with eggs ; milk, stock or water will do instead. The par-boiled minced liver of a chicken or duck can be added to the stuffing required for those birds. Stuffings are also improved by the addition of chopped ham, bacon, cooked mushrooms, tongue, an oyster or two, and, if possible, a truffle.

Sausage meat can be used in place of bread stuffing. It is a good practice to put a leek or a lump of butter inside a fowl or chicken before roasting, to improve the flavour.

Stuffing for Turkey, Veal, Hare, Rabbit, etc.

6 oz. Breadcrumbs.	2 dessertspoons chopped Parsley.
3 oz. Beef Suet.	2 Eggs.
1 dessertspoonful chopped Thyme.	2 oz. lean Ham.
1 dessertspoonful chopped Mar-	Peel of half a Lemon.
joram.	Salt and Cayenne to taste.

UTENSILS—Grater, fine wire sieve, knife, 2 basins, wooden spoon, egg-beater, dessertspoon.

Rub the breadcrumbs through a fine wire sieve, shred and mince the ham and suet finely, and chop the herbs and lemon peel very carefully. Mix all with the breadcrumbs, and add cayenne and salt to taste. Beat the eggs well, and mix them into the dry ingredients. Work all up well, and the stuffing is then ready for use.

NOTE.—1. If a very delicate stuffing or forcemeat is required, the ingredients should be pounded before they are moistened with the egg, but this is quite unnecessary for ordinary cookery.

2. For hares, the liver is sometimes added, but in that case the liver must be boiled for 5 minutes before mincing. It is, however, better reserved for making liver sauce to serve with the hare.

Stuffing for Duck, Goose, or Pork

4 Onions. 1 Egg.	2 oz. Butter.
6 oz. Breadcrumbs.	10 Sage Leaves.
Pepper and Salt to taste.	

UTENSILS—Basin, saucepan, knife, chopping board, wire sieve, fork, wooden spoon.

Blanch the onions in scalding water for 5 minutes, then strain and rinse them in cold water. Refill the saucepan with boiling water, then put in the onions and cook till tender. While the onions are cooking, pull the stalks off the sage leaves, then dip them in scalding water for 5 minutes. Dry the leaves and chop them very finely.

Drain the onions, squeezing out all the moisture. Turn them on to a board, and mince finely, then add the minced sage, and put both into a basin. Add the breadcrumbs, the butter, and seasoning, and mix well until all the ingredients are thoroughly incorporated. Now add the egg, work all well together, and the stuffing is ready for use.

NOTE.—The great mistakes many cooks make with this stuffing are omitting to blanch the onions, also boiling them insufficiently, and not scalding the sage leaves. The stuffing then has a strong and raw taste which is most unpleasant.

Chestnut Stuffing for Boiled Turkey

1 lb. Chestnuts.
3 oz. boiled Bacon.
1 oz. Butter.

White Stock.
Lemon Peel.
Pepper and Salt.

UTENSILS—Knife, saucepan, hair sieve, basin, wooden spoon, grater.

Cut the ends off the chestnuts, and roast them in the oven for 15 minutes, then peel off both the outer and inner skins. Put the peeled chestnuts into a saucepan, with the butter, and enough white stock to cover them. Cover them tightly, and cook gently for about 1 hour, until they are quite tender and all the moisture is absorbed.

Now rub them through a hair sieve. Put this purée into a basin, and season with pepper and salt. Add the boiled fat bacon, very finely minced, and a quarter-teaspoonful of grated lemon rind. Work all well together, and if required moisten with a little more stock. The stuffing is then ready for use.

Stuffing for Rabbit

1 large Onion.
1 breakfastcupful Breadcrumbs.
¼ lb. cooked Pickled Pork.

1 Egg.
1 teaspoonful Mixed Herbs.
Pepper and Salt.

UTENSILS—Saucepan, knife, 2 basins, egg-beater, wooden spoon, teaspoon, breakfast cup, sieve.

Blanch the onion in scalding water for 5 minutes, then strain and rinse it in cold water. Then put it in boiling water and cook till tender. Mince the onion finely, also the cooked pickled pork, and mixed herbs. Put all into a basin with the breadcrumbs, season with pepper and a very little salt. Mix all the ingredients well together, and bind the whole with one well-beaten egg.

FORCEMEATS

The chief points to note with regard to the preparation of forcemeats are (1) that all meat used for them must be perfectly fresh; (2) that it must be chopped very fine, or passed once or twice through a mincing machine; (3) that all the ingredients must be thoroughly pounded together, and sometimes rubbed afterwards through a fine wire sieve when required particularly smooth. They must be kept in a very cool place, and used as soon as possible.

Forcemeats are often used in making galantines, quenelles, for garnishing soups, large dishes, etc. They are also used in the making of entrées of various kinds.

Panard

(*The basis of most Forcemeats*)

4 large tablespoonfuls Flour. | 1 oz. Butter.
½ pint Water. | A pinch of Salt.

UTENSILS—Saucepan, pint measure, tablespoon, wooden spoon.

Put the water on to boil with the butter and salt in it. When boiling hard, stir in the flour quickly, beating well all the time. Beat until it leaves the sides of the pan quite clean, then cook gently for 10 minutes. Allow it to cool, and it is ready for use.

Bread Panard

(*Also used in Forcemeats*)

Stale Bread. | Stock or Milk.
Water.

UTENSILS—Basin, cloth, saucepan, wooden spoon.

Soak the required quantity of stale crumb of bread in cold water. When thoroughly soaked turn the pulp into a clean cloth and wring it thoroughly dry. Put it into a saucepan and gradually moisten it, over a moderate heat, with either stock, milk, or water, working it well with a wooden spoon until it leaves the sides of the saucepan. When cool, it is ready for use.

Veal or Rabbit Forcemeat

5 oz. Veal or Rabbit. | 2½ Yolks of Eggs.
5 oz. Panard. | A pinch of pounded Mace.
Pepper and Salt.

UTENSILS—Knife, mincing machine, pestle and mortar, basin, wooden spoon, hair sieve.

First entirely free the meat from skin and gristle. Pass it once or twice through a mincing machine if you have one, then pound it well in a mortar. The meat must weigh five ounces after being pounded. When the meat is well pounded, add the panard and pound both thoroughly well together. Add the yolks of eggs, mace, and seasoning. Work all thoroughly together, then pass all through a sieve. Now add a tablespoonful of Veloute sauce if necessary.

NOTE.—It is best, if for quenelles, to test the force by poaching a small quantity to ascertain if it is the right consistency. It should be just firm to the touch when cooked; if too stiff a little sauce may be added.

Oyster Forcemeat

1 dozen Oysters.	A pinch of Cayenne.
2 oz. Butter.	Seasoning of Salt.
¼ teaspoonful grated Lemon Peel.	1 Yolk of Egg.
A pinch of pounded Mace.	4 oz. Bread Panard.

1 teaspoonful chopped Parsley.

UTENSILS—Knife, 2 basins, pestle and mortar, teaspoon, wooden spoon, grater.

Open the oysters and save the liquor, trim off the beards, and rinse the oysters in the liquor. Make four ounces of bread panard, using the strained liquor of the oysters instead of stock or milk. Mince the oysters, and mix them with the panard and all the other ingredients. Pound all well together in a mortar till quite smooth.

This forcemeat may now be formed into quenelles and poached for garnishing soups; or fried in balls for garnishing various dishes; or used for masking fillets of fowl, etc. It can also be used for stuffing a boiled turkey.

Forcemeat for Boned Fowl

6 oz. raw Ham.	2 oz. Breadcrumbs.
1 lb. Fresh Pork.	2 teaspoonfuls chopped Parsley.
½ lb. Veal.	A pinch of chopped Thyme.
2 whole raw Eggs.	1 chopped Shallot.
5 hard-boiled Egg Yolks.	½ teaspoonful Pepper.

1 small teaspoonful Salt.

UTENSILS—Mincing machine, wire sieve, grater, pestle and mortar, knife, basin, wooden spoon, saucepan.

Pass the veal, pork, and ham twice through the mincing

machine, then rub it through a wire sieve. If the time can be spared, put it into a mortar with the hard-boiled yolks of eggs (previously rubbed through a sieve), the finely chopped parsley, thyme, shallot, seasoning, breadcrumbs, and two whole raw eggs, and pound all well together. The forcemeat will then be ready for use.

NOTE.—If there is not time to pound the mixture, then thoroughly mix the minced meats with the other ingredients, but pounding greatly improves the forcemeat.

PURÉES

This is a short description of purées for garnishing purposes, such as peas, potatoes, turnips, spinach, etc. They can also be served as vegetables to accompany meats, etc.

Potato Purée

1½ lb. Potatoes.	2 tablespoonfuls Cream or Milk.
1 oz. Butter.	Pepper and Salt.

UTENSILS—Knife, 2 saucepans, wire sieve, wooden spoon, tablespoon.

Peel and plainly boil the potatoes. When cooked and thoroughly dry, rub them through a wire sieve. Put the rubbed potatoes into a clean saucepan, an enamelled one if possible, and mix in the butter, pepper, salt and cream. Make thoroughly hot and use.

Purée of Peas

½ lb. cooked Peas.	1 tablespoonful Cream.
1 tablespoonful Flour.	1 teaspoonful Castor Sugar.
½ oz. Butter.	Pepper and Salt.

UTENSILS—Saucepan, hair sieve, basin or plate, wooden spoon, measuring spoons.

Old peas do quite well for this purée. Boil them till tender with a dessertspoonful of salt, and a teaspoonful of sugar. When cooked drain thoroughly, and rub them through a hair sieve. Weigh half a pound of the pulp, and put it into a saucepan with half an ounce of butter, the cream, flour, and seasoning of salt and pepper as required. Add a very little green colouring, and it is ready for use.

Purée of Turnips

3 lb. of Turnip.	1 oz. Butter.
1 tablespoonful Flour.	2 tablespoonfuls thick Cream.
White Pepper.	Salt.

UTENSILS—Knife, saucepan, basin, cloth, wire sieve, wooden spoon.

Wash and peel the turnips and cut each one into eight pieces. Put them into a saucepan with cold water and a pinch of salt. Bring them to the boil, then remove, and rinse them in cold water.

Now put them on in boiling salted water, and cook until tender. Drain well, then put them in a clean strong cloth and wring out all the moisture. Rub them through a fine wire sieve, and put the pulp back into a saucepan with the cream, butter, flour and seasoning. Bring to the boil, stirring all the time, and it is then ready for use. This purée is nice served with cutlets, and with many meat dishes.

Purée of Spinach

2 lb. Spinach Leaves.	2 tablespoonfuls Cream or Milk.
¾ oz. Flour.	A pinch of Sugar.
2 oz. Butter.	Pepper and Salt.

UTENSILS—Enamelled saucepan, wooden spoon, colander, chopping board, knife, stewpan, measuring spoons.

Take sufficient fresh young spinach to make two pounds of leaves after carefully removing all stalks. Wash the leaves well. Blanch them by putting the leaves into an enamelled saucepan with sufficient cold water to cover them, adding half a teaspoonful of salt and a very small piece of soda, then bringing them quickly to the boil. The leaves should be carefully pushed down under the water with a wooden spoon while the water is coming to the boil. Directly the water boils, strain off the leaves and rinse them thoroughly in cold water.

Press out every drop of moisture, then turn them out on to a board and chop very finely. Put one ounce of butter, the flour, a pinch of salt, a pinch of pepper, and a pinch of castor sugar into a stewpan. Melt together, then add the chopped spinach and stir well. Add the cream or milk ; stir till the mixture boils. Then add the remainder of the butter, and it is ready for use.

NOTE.—If the spinach is old it is best to rub it through a sieve before adding it to the butter, etc., in the stewpan.

Purée of Chestnuts

2 lb. Chestnuts.	White Stock.
2 oz. Butter.	A few drops of **Carmine.**
½ gill Milk.	Castor Sugar.

Pepper and Salt.

UTENSILS—Knife, baking tin, stewpan, wire sieve, wooden spoon, basin.

Cut the tops off two pounds of chestnuts. Roast them in the oven for 20 minutes, then remove the outer and inner skins, and put the chestnuts into a stewpan with one ounce of butter and enough white stock to cover them. Lay a buttered paper over the top, put on the lid, and cook gently for ¾ hour or longer, until the chestnuts are quite tender. The chestnuts should absorb all the stock in the cooking.

When cooked, rub all through a fine wire sieve. Thoroughly mix this purée with the remaining ounce of butter and the milk. They may not require all the milk, depending on how the stock has been absorbed. Season with pepper, a very little salt, and a pinch of castor sugar. Colour with a few drops of liquid carmine so as to give the purée a pale salmon tint. Re-warm and use for garnishing.

HARMLESS COLOURS AND FLAVOURINGS

By John Campbell, Ph.D.

Artificial colouring and flavouring of basic food is not necessary from the nutritive or dietetic standpoint, but foods can be rendered more attractive with the aid of colouring ; and more appetising with the aid of flavouring. Many kinds of stewed fruit, for example, are improved in appearance by a touch of red, and some vegetables are freshened up by the use of a green. Jellies and blancmanges, suitably tinted, confer a distinctive artistic note to the sweet course and help to brighten the appearance of the table.

The pleasing effects on the eye of harmonious colour, gleaming glass and spotless napery—the appetising odour and flavour of freshly cooked food on the olfactory nerves, and the palate—have a notable effect conducive to a mental condition most favourable to secretion, and have a distinct influence for good on the digestive processes.

There are numerous harmless natural colours, both vegetable and animal, which may be used for tinting purposes in the kitchen.

REDS.—The following may be used : Cochineal and its derivative carmine, obtained from the insect Coccus cacti.

Logwood derived from logwood chips.

Beetroot juice from expressed cooked beetroot.

YELLOWS.—Saffron extract from the dried stigmas and styles of the Crocus sativus.

Turmeric prepared from the root of the Curcuma longa.

ORANGE.—Annatto obtained from the seeds of the Bixa orellana gives a light orange.

Safflower prepared from the flowers of the Carthamus tinctorius gives a deep orange.

GREENS.—This colour is conferred generally by chlorophyll, the green colouring matter of plants.

Spinach extract or liquor gives a general green. Parsley a light bright green.

BLUE.—Litmus or orchil derived from lichens, chiefly Roccella tinctoria and Lecanora tinctoria, may be used when the foods are not acid.

Indigo.

BROWN.—Caramel from burnt sugar.

Alkanet prepared chiefly from the roots of the Anchusa tinctoria.

VIOLET.—Litmus at a certain degree of acidity produces violet.

Cochineal prepared with lime water.

These colours are non-poisonous and may be used with every confidence. In addition, natural fruit juices impart their specific colour to the foods to which they are added.

Essences and Flavours

These are derived mainly from fruit, flowers, seeds, nuts, barks, roots, and beans. The aromatic and flavouring constituents consist mainly of volatile ethers, aldehydes, and essential oils usually derived from nuts and fruit peel.

Fresh fruit juices are the safest sources of flavours for jellies and starch moulds, but fruit essences may be used if prepared from fresh fruit. These are usually alcoholic extracts holding in solution the flavouring ethers and aldehydes in a concentrated form from various fruits, (raspberry, strawberry, cherry, etc.). In a different class are the flavouring essential oils derived from rinds and nuts. These are safe and handy to use, and obviate the necessity of using peel. They include lemon, orange, almond and peppermint. Other harmless natural essences are vanilla and coumarin (tonka bean).

Many fruit flavouring essences can now be synthesised by the chemist and resemble the natural flavours very closely in their general characters. For example, apple essence is amyl-valerianiate dissolved in alcohol, pineapple essence is butyric ether in alcohol, and pear essence consists of amyl-acetate in alcohol.

It is not advisable to use these artificial essences, because for household purposes natural flavouring constituents are usually available. In lieu of the freshly expressed juice of the fresh lemon, or orange, one of the bottled preparations may be used. These are very convenient and represent the natural fruit juice in a preserved concentrated form.

In addition to the essences, many spices and herbs are used in more or less their natural state for improving the gustatory and digestive properties of food. Omitting the stimulating condiments (like mustard and pepper), paprika, cloves, cinnamon, ginger, mace, nutmeg, caraway seeds, coriander, aniseed, cassia, cardamom, thyme, sage, mint, fennel, parsley and majoram impart specific and pleasing flavours and aroma to food. Some of them also serve as harmless stimulants to salivary and gastric secretion, and others, like mint, act as antiseptics and counteract the tendency of certain foods to produce flatulency.

SAUCES

Allow ½ pint of sauce for 6 persons

There are two classes of sauces, white and brown, but it is possible to make many varieties of both kinds. The ingredients which go to make the foundation of nearly all savoury sauces are stock (white or brown), butter, milk, eggs, flour, water, seasonings, etc.

A common mistake is made in preparing too much sauce for the number of persons to be served. Half a pint for six persons is a fair allowance, and it is best to have just sufficient and of good quality. It is a great mistake to add flour after the liquid has been added. The secret of making a good brown sauce is to have the butter and flour well browned before the liquid is put in. First of all make a roux, or thickening, by melting the butter, adding the flour and frying them together either with or without browning. This would depend on whether the sauce is intended to be a white or brown one. If the sauce has to be thickened afterwards, it is better either to reduce it by fast boiling, or (for a yellow sauce) add the yolk of an egg, but the latter must be done after it is taken off the fire. Crème-de-riz, potato flour, or arrowroot are all good thickenings for sauces, and may all be added after the sauce boils, provided they are first slaked in a little cold liquid.

Another point is to have sauces of the right consistency, neither too thick nor too thin. They should just nicely coat the spoon if required for masking anything, or be a little thinner if for pouring round or serving in a sauce-boat. As a rule, one ounce of butter and one ounce of flour to a pint of liquid is the proper quantity, but flours vary much, and it is sometimes necessary to use a little more, or a little less. Another way of measuring is to allow, for an average thick sauce, 2 tablespoonfuls of butter and of flour to each cupful of liquid.

It is quite a mistake to think that white sauces must be made with milk. A white stock made from veal, rabbit or chicken, or even vegetables, is often preferable. It is best to avoid using plain water. Use stock, or even the water that peas, onions, celery or any other suitable vegetable has been boiled in. There are standard sauces, such as Béchamel,

Veloute (white) and Espagnol (brown) which are used as the foundations of many more elaborate sauces ; but in ordinary kitchens elaborate sauces are only required on special occasions.

The first step towards making a success of all sauces is to learn to make simple sauces, which lend themselves to many variations. Melted butter sauce is one of the commonest we have, yet this requires to be properly made, otherwise it will resemble thin flour and water paste.

The secret in making sauces of the melted butter class is to melt part of the butter first, then add the flour ; cook both together, then add the liquid ; lastly, add the remainder of the butter just before serving.

NOTE.—Cooking the flour and butter first, before adding the liquid, prevents that raw, floury taste appearing in the sauce ; whilst adding some of the butter at the finish gives that delicious fresh butter flavour which is so desirable, and which quite obviates the suggestion of thin paste that the sauce has when badly made.

PREPARATIONS OF BUTTER

Melted Butter Sauce

1 oz. Butter.	½ pint warm Water.
½ oz. Flour.	Salt to taste.

UTENSILS—Small saucepan, wooden spoon, pint measure, pointed strainer, knife.

Melt half the butter in a small saucepan. Add the flour, mixing it thoroughly with a wooden spoon until it is quite a smooth paste. Reduce the heat under the saucepan, and cook the flour and butter together for 2 or 3 minutes, but without letting it turn colour. Now stir in the warm water very gently, with a seasoning of salt. Increase the heat until it boils, stirring all the time.

It should now be soft and creamy. Pour it through a pointed strainer into a hot sauce-boat. Just before serving, add the remainder of the butter cut up into small pieces. A few drops of lemon juice is a great improvement.

NOTE.—Flours differ so greatly in their thickening qualities that it may be necessary to reduce the sauce by fast boiling ; or to add a little more liquid if too thick.

Melted Butter

¼ lb. Butter. | 1 teaspoonful Lemon Juice.
Salt and Pepper.

UTENSILS—Enamelled saucepan, teaspoon.

Put the butter into an enamelled saucepan, with a pinch of salt and pepper. Melt it slowly over the fire, but do not let it burn or even turn colour. Add the lemon juice and serve in a hot sauce-boat.

NOTE.—This is often served with asparagus, etc., in place of melted butter sauce.

Clarified Butter

UTENSILS—Basin, kitchen spoon.

To clarify butter, put the required quantity into a basin and stand it on the plate rack, or in front of the fire, until it is quite melted. Stir it round once or twice, then let it stand so as to allow the buttermilk to settle. Pour the butter gently off into the jars, leaving the sediment behind. The clear butter is used for pouring over potted meats, shrimps, etc., to exclude the air.

Black Butter

4 oz. Butter. | 2 tablespoonfuls French Vinegar.
Coralline Pepper. | 2 tablespoonfuls Parsley.

UTENSILS—Frying pan, cloth, tablespoon.

Put the butter into a frying pan, and let it gradually become a nice pale brown. When it smokes throw in the parsley which has been picked quite small, well washed and thoroughly dried. Shake the pan, and directly the parsley is crisp take it off the fire. Pour it all into a hot sauce-boat, or over the dish it is required for. Pour the vinegar into the pan, boil it up, then pour it over the butter. Sprinkle with pepper, coralline preferred, as it looks prettier. This butter is very good for serving with skate.

Montpelier Butter

2 sprigs of Tarragon. | 6 Chives, or 1 teaspoonful Shallot.
2 sprigs of Parsley. | 4 Anchovies.
2 sprigs of Chervil. | 2 Gherkins.
2 Eggs. Cayenne. | 2 teaspoonfuls Capers.
¼ lb. Butter. | Green Colouring.

UTENSILS—Saucepan, pestle and mortar, knife, hair sieve, teaspoon, wooden spoon, plate.

Blanch the tarragon, parsley, chervil and chives (in the manner described with GREEN SAUCE, page 158). Press all the moisture out, then pound them in a mortar with the anchovies (previously filleted), the butter, hard-boiled yolks of eggs, chopped gherkins, the capers, a dust of cayenne and sufficient green colouring to make the whole a pale green. When all is thoroughly pounded, rub it through a fine hair sieve. This is used for garnishing cold salmon, trout, etc.

Anchovy Butter

2 oz. Butter.	Lemon Juice.
1 teaspoonful Anchovy Sauce.	Cayenne.

A few drops Carmine or Cochineal.

UTENSILS—Basin, wooden spoon, teaspoon.

Put the butter into a small basin. Work it up with a wooden spoon. Add the anchovy sauce, carmine or cochineal, a few drops of lemon juice, and a small pinch of cayenne pepper. Mix all thoroughly well together. Keep in a cool place until wanted.

Maître d'Hôtel Butter

2 oz. Fresh Butter.	1 tablespoonful chopped Parsley.
Juice of a Lemon.	White Pepper. Salt.

UTENSILS—Knife, strainer, wooden spoon, tablespoon, dish, lemon squeezer, cloth, chopping board, butter pats.

Mix the butter with very finely chopped parsley, wrung quite free from moisture. Add the strained lemon juice, a dust of white pepper, and a little salt, and work together until thoroughly well mixed. Make into a nice shape with butter pats. If possible, stand on ice until required. If not, keep it in a very cool place.

NOTE.—This can be used as a garnish, or can be served in small lumps with meat or fish. In the latter case, the dish must be served quickly, if it is warm, so that the butter does not melt.

Brandy Butter

4 oz. Fresh Butter.	2 oz. Icing Sugar.

1 tablespoonful Brandy.

UTENSILS—Basin, wooden spoon, tablespoon, butter pats.

Work the butter and sugar to a cream, then add the brandy and mix well. Form it into a block with the pats. Stand it on ice until required ; or keep it in a very cool place. Cut it into any desired shapes just before serving.

RUM BUTTER is made in the same way, but rum is substituted for the brandy.

SAVOURY SAUCES

Anchovy Sauce (1)

1 oz. Butter.	A few drops of Carmine.
4 Anchovies.	½ pint Fish Stock, or Milk and
½ oz. Flour.	Water.

Cayenne.

UTENSILS—Saucepan, wooden spoon, pestle and mortar, pint or gill measure.

Melt half an ounce of butter in a saucepan. Add the flour, and fry together without browning. Stir in gradually the stock, or milk and water, and bring to the boil. Take the boned anchovies and pound them in a mortar until quite smooth. Add a very small dust of cayenne.

Mix this paste thoroughly in with the melted butter, and colour it with a few drops of carmine. Simmer for 3 or 4 minutes, add the remaining butter, and it is ready for use. Some consider a few drops of lemon juice should be added.

Anchovy Sauce (2)

1 teaspoonful Anchovy Essence.	1 large teaspoonful Flour.
½ oz. Butter.	¼ pint Milk.

UTENSILS—Saucepan, wooden spoon, teaspoon, pint or gill measure.

Melt the butter in a saucepan, and add the flour. Mix well together, then stir in the milk gradually until it boils. Add the anchovy essence, and serve.

Apple Sauce

1 lb. Apples.	2 tablespoonfuls Water.
½ oz. Butter.	1 teaspoonful Sugar, if required.

UTENSILS—Knife, saucepan, wooden spoon, measuring spoons.

Good cooking apples are required for this. Pare the apples, take out the cores, and slice them thinly. Put them into a saucepan with the water, and cover closely with a lid. Cook gently until they are quite a pulp.

Beat the pulp with a wooden spoon, and add the butter and sugar. Omit the sugar if the apples are found to be sweet enough. With some apples the sugar is not only best omitted, but a few drops of lemon juice are an improvement. Serve in a sauce-boat.

Aspic Jelly

1 dessertspoonful Meat Extract.	½ a Carrot.
2 oz. Gelatine.	1 small Onion stuck with Cloves.
1 Lemon. 2 Eggs.	6 Peppercorns.
1 Shallot. 1 Bayleaf.	1 dessertspoonful Salt.
Tarragon Vinegar.	Chilli Vinegar.

UTENSILS—Saucepan, knife, pint measure, 3 basins, egg-beater or fork, dessertspoon, lemon squeezer, jelly-bag.

Take the meat extract and put it in a pan with one quart of water, one shallot, one bayleaf, half a carrot, one small onion stuck with cloves, the peppercorns and salt. Simmer these ingredients well together, then add the gelatine, the juice of one lemon, the whites and shells of two eggs, slightly beaten, a few drops of chilli vinegar and a dessertspoonful of tarragon vinegar. Bring all to the boil.

Have the jelly-bag ready (by pouring two quarts of boiling water through it, to warm and clear it), then pour the jelly through. Have two basins for it, so that it can be poured through the bag again, until it is quite clear. Set aside to cool, and use it just before it sets.

Béchamel Sauce (Creamy)

1 oz. Flour.	2 tablespoonfuls thick Cream.
1½ oz. Butter.	A blade of Mace.
1 Shallot. ¾ pint Milk.	Cayenne. Salt.

UTENSILS—Two saucepans, wooden spoon, strainer, tammy-cloth, tablespoon, gill or pint measure.

Boil the milk with the shallot, mace and cayenne. Melt the butter in a saucepan, and stir in the flour. Strain the milk, add it by degrees to the butter and flour. Bring to the boil, and add salt to taste. Wring through a tammy. Re-heat, add the cream, and use. If preferred, half white stock may be used instead of all milk.

Béchamel Sauce (Thick)

1 gill Milk.	**1 oz. Butter.**
1 small Onion.	Mace.
1 oz. Flour.	Cayenne. Salt.

UTENSILS—Two saucepans, wooden spoon, strainer, gill measure.

Put the milk in a saucepan, and boil with a very small piece of mace, a small onion, and a dust of cayenne pepper. Melt the butter in a saucepan. Mix with it the flour. Strain the seasoned milk, add to it the flour and butter by degrees, and stir till it boils. Add a pinch of salt, and use.

Bread Sauce

½ **pint Milk.**	**6 Peppercorns.**
2 oz. White Breadcrumbs.	A small blade of **Mace.**
1 oz. Butter.	Cayenne Pepper.
3 oz. Onion.	1 tablespoonful Cream, if
2 Cloves. Salt.	procurable.

UTENSILS—Saucepan, wire sieve, knife, baking tin, strainer, wooden spoon, gill or pint measure.

First of all, season the milk as follows : Put it into a saucepan with the halved onion, the cloves, peppercorns, mace and a very little cayenne. Bring it almost to the boil, then draw the pan to one side, and let the ingredients infuse for 15 minutes. If the milk boils away, add sufficient to make up half a pint.

See that the breadcrumbs are very fine and thoroughly dry. They can be dried in the plate rack or in a cool oven. Strain the milk on to the crumbs and add the butter. Bring the sauce to the boil, and season with salt to taste. Lastly, add a tablespoonful of cream if procurable.

Brown Sauce

2 oz. Butter or good Dripping.	A bunch of Herbs (Bayleaf,
2 oz. Flour.	Thyme and Parsley).
1 quart Brown Stock.	½ teaspoonful Celery Seed.
4 oz. Onion.	1 teaspoonful Meat Extract.
½ **a Carrot.** ½ **a Turnip.**	Pepper and Salt.

UTENSILS—Saucepan, knife, wooden spoon, teaspoon, large metal spoon, piece of muslin, fine strainer or tammy cloth, pint measure.

Melt the butter or dripping in a saucepan, add the onion, finely chopped, and fry together gently until the onion is a nice rich brown. Then add the flour and brown that also. Draw the pan to one side and gradually stir in the brown stock.

Return the pan to the fire and stir until its contents are quite boiling. Remove all the scum as it rises. Add the remainder of the vegetables, thinly sliced, also pepper and salt to taste. Tie the herbs and celery seed in a piece of muslin, and put them in. Also add the meat extract. Bring to the boil and simmer gently for $\frac{3}{4}$ hour, keeping it skimmed while boiling, also stirred occasionally. Strain through a fine strainer, or wring through a tammy-cloth. Re-heat and use.

Caper Sauce (1)

½ pint Melted Butter Sauce. | 3 tablespoonfuls Capers.
1 tablespoonful Vinegar.

UTENSILS—Saucepan, knife, tablespoon, wooden spoon, pint measure.

Make melted butter sauce, as in the recipe on page 145, but instead of using water use the broth from the mutton. Chop the capers slightly. Add the capers and vinegar to the sauce, bring to the boil and serve. If the sauce is required for fish, make it with fish stock and add a teaspoonful of anchovy essence.

NOTE.—Pickled nasturtium seeds make an excellent substitute for capers.

Caper Sauce (2)

1 dessertspoonful Capers. | ½ pint hot Water or Milk.
1 oz. Butter. | 1 tablespoonful Lemon Juice or
¼ oz. Flour. | Vinegar. Salt.

UTENSILS—Saucepan, wooden spoon, measuring spoons, gill or pint measure, knife.

Melt the butter in a small saucepan. Mix in the flour and the salt, with a wooden spoon. Then add by degrees the hot water or milk, also the vinegar or lemon juice, stirring well all the time. Boil for 5 minutes. Add the capers, finely chopped, and serve in a sauce-boat.

Celery Sauce

4 small heads of Celery. | ½ pint White Stock.
2 oz. Butter. | ½ pint Milk.
1 oz. Flour. | A blade of Mace.
White Pepper. Salt.

UTENSILS—Knife, 3 saucepans, wooden spoon, pint measure.

Clean and nicely trim the heads of celery, washing them thoroughly. Use only the white parts, and shred these finely. Put all into a saucepan and cover with cold water. Add a teaspoonful of salt and boil till tender. Boil the milk with the mace, then remove the mace from it. Melt the butter in a saucepan Stir in the flour, add the stock, then the milk, and bring to the boil. Season with white pepper and salt. Add the boiled celery and serve. This sauce is used with boiled fowl, turkey, etc.

Celery Sauce (Brown)

3 heads of Celery.	1 oz. Flour.
2 oz. Butter.	1 pint Brown Stock or Gravy.

Pepper and Salt.

UTENSILS—Knife, 2 saucepans, wooden spoon, metal spoon, hair sieve, basin, pint measure.

Cut the young white parts of the celery into pieces one inch long. Wash thoroughly, and put them into a stewpan with one ounce of butter. Let them cook gently at the side of the stove for ½ hour. Melt the butter in a saucepan. Add the flour and fry together until a nice golden brown.

Add the brown stock or gravy to this. Season with pepper and salt to taste, and bring to the boil. Put in the cooked celery and simmer gently until the celery is quite tender, skimming off any scum that may rise. Rub all through a hair sieve, re-heat and use.

Chestnut Sauce (Brown)

½ lb. Chestnuts.	4 tablespoonfuls Espagnol Sauce.
½ pint good Brown Stock.	Pepper and Salt.

Proceed for this sauce in exactly the same way as for WHITE CHESTNUT SAUCE, next described, but substitute brown stock for white, and heighten the seasoning. And instead of the cream add Espagnol sauce.

Chestnut Sauce (White)

½ lb. Chestnuts.	½ pint Cream.
½ pint White Stock.	1 oz. Butter.

Salt. Cayenne.

UTENSILS—Knife, saucepan, hair sieve, wooden spoon basin, pint measure.

Cut off the tops of the chestnuts. Roast them in the oven for 20 minutes, or, if necessary, a little longer, until the skins will come off easily, then peel off the outer and inner skins. Put the chestnuts into a saucepan with the white stock and the butter. Cook gently for about 1½ hours, until quite tender.

Rub the whole through a hair sieve, and return to the saucepan. Add the cream and seasoning. Stir until it almost comes to the boil, then serve. Milk may be used instead of cream, then it may be necessary to add a little thickening.

Chutney Sauce

¼ pint Brown Stock or Gravy.	1 oz. Butter.
1 small Onion.	½ oz. Flour.
2 tablespoonfuls Chutney.	Salt to taste.

UTENSILS—Knife, saucepan, wooden spoon, tablespoon, pint measure, basin, fine strainer.

Chop the onion finely. Melt the butter in a saucepan, put in the onion, and fry gently for 10 or 15 minutes, then stir in the flour. Add, by degrees, the stock, and stir until it boils. Now add the chutney, and salt to taste, and simmer gently for another 15 minutes. Strain through a fine strainer. If a very sweet chutney is used, a few drops of lemon juice should be added.

Crayfish Sauce

2 dozen Crayfish.	12 Peppercorns.
½ a Carrot.	1 gill Cream.
1 Onion. 1 Bayleaf.	1 teaspoonful Anchovy Essence.
1 sprig of Parsley.	A few drops of Carmine.
2 oz. Flour.	1½ pints Fish Stock, as described.
2 oz. Butter.	2 quarts Water.
½ blade of Mace.	Cayenne.

UTENSILS—Two saucepans, knife, wooden spoon, tammy-cloth or fine hair sieve, teaspoon, gill or pint measure, basin.

Wash the live crayfish thoroughly in several waters to get out all the sand. It is good to stand them under a running tap for some time. Put two quarts of water into a saucepan with half a scraped carrot, one sliced onion, the mace, peppercorns, bayleaf and parsley. When boiling fast, drop in the crayfish and cover immediately. Boil for 20 minutes.

Melt two ounces of butter in a saucepan, stir in the flour,

F

and fry together without browning. Add a small dust of cayenne pepper, then pour in the fish stock, and stir until it boils. Boil for 5 minutes, then add the cream, a few drops of carmine, and the anchovy essence.

Shell the crayfish, put the meat from the claws and tails aside to add to the sauce later. Scrape out any meat from the heads, and add it to the sauce. Now pass the sauce through a tammy, or rub it through a very fine hair sieve. Re-heat it, add the meat from the crayfish tails and claws, and serve.

FOR THE FISH STOCK

Trimmings and Bones of any White Fish.	A bunch of Herbs (Bayleaf, Thyme and Parsley).
1 Onion.	6 Peppercorns.
1 small blade of Mace.	2 teaspoonfuls Lemon Juice.
1 teaspoonful Salt.	

Take the trimmings and bones of any white fish such as plaice, soles, whiting, etc., and any shells of crayfish or shrimps. Put them into a saucepan with one sliced onion, a small blade of mace, a bunch of herbs (bayleaf, thyme and parsley), the lemon juice, salt, peppercorns, and about a pint of cold water. Bring the stock to the boil, and skim it. Boil gently for 1 hour. Strain, skim off any fat, and then use.

Cucumber Sauce

3 medium-sized Cucumbers.	½ pint White Stock.
2 oz. Butter.	Cayenne. Salt.
1 oz. Flour.	A few drops Lemon Juice.

UTENSILS—Knife, saucepan, hair sieve, basin, wooden spoon, gill or pint measure.

Peel the cucumbers, take out the seeds, and cut the cucumbers into small pieces. Put the pieces into a stewpan with one ounce of butter, and cover closely with a lid. Draw to the side of the stove, and cook gently until quite tender.

Melt the remaining ounce of butter in a saucepan, and stir in the flour. Add to this the white stock (or milk, if stock is not available), and season with cayenne pepper and salt. Add this to the cucumber and then rub the whole through a hair sieve. Re-warm, and just before serving add a few drops of lemon juice.

NOTE.—The same saucepan that the cucumbers are cooked in will do for making the sauce, provided it is not too large, as it can be made after the cucumbers are cooked.

Curry Sauce

1 pint Stock.	1 small dessertspoonful best
1 oz. Butter or fresh Dripping.	Ground Rice.
2 tablespoonfuls Desiccated Cocoa-	1 small Apple.
nut.	2 teaspoonfuls Curry Powder.
½ teaspoonful Meat Extract.	1 teaspoonful Curry Paste.
1 Onion.	1 saltspoonful Salt.

UTENSILS—Knife, saucepan, wooden spoon, measuring spoons, basin, hair sieve.

Peel the onion and the apple, and mince them quite finely. Melt the butter or dripping in a stewpan, then add the onion and apple, and fry very gently over a low fire until the onion turns a pale brown. Now stir in the curry powder and paste. (If paste is not procurable, put double the quantity of powder.) Fry very gently for 5 minutes. Next add the rice flour, and cook gently for another 5 minutes.

Now stir in the stock by degrees, also add the cocoanut, meat extract, and salt. Simmer all gently for ½ hour, or until the onion and apple are quite soft. Rub the whole through a hair sieve, and return it to the saucepan to re-heat before using.

If a perfectly smooth sauce is not required, it need not be rubbed through the sieve, but in that case cocoanut milk must be added instead of the nut itself. For cocoanut milk put two tablespoonfuls of the desiccated cocoanut into a basin and pour on it half a pint of boiling water. Let it infuse for some time, then strain off the liquid and use. If this is used, then half a pint of the stock must be omitted. If liked, a few drops of lemon juice may be added, and a table-spoonful of cream improves the sauce greatly.

Egg Sauce

½ pint White Sauce.		4 Eggs.

UTENSILS—Two saucepans, wooden spoon, knife, pint or gill measure.

Make half a pint of white sauce, but season the milk as for bread sauce. Put four eggs into cold water, bring them to the boil and continue boiling for 10 minutes. Then put them into cold water to get cold. Remove the shells and chop the eggs rather coarsely. When the sauce boils, stir in the chopped eggs and serve.

Espagnol Sauce

1 Carrot. **1** large Onion.
1 Turnip. **2** Tomatoes.
3 or 4 Mushrooms.
A bunch of Herbs.
2 oz. lean Ham.
2 oz. clarified Dripping.

A pinch of Castor **Sugar.**
1 teaspoonful Lemon **Juice.**
12 Peppercorns.
2 or 3 tablespoonfuls Sherry **or** Madeira.
1 pint Brown Stock.

1 tablespoonful Flour.

UTENSILS—Knife, saucepan, wooden spoon, measuring spoons, pint measure, fine sieve or tammy, basin.

Wash and scrape a small carrot and a turnip, slice the onion and mushrooms, and cut up the ham into dice shapes. Melt the dripping in a saucepan, put the vegetables in this, and fry gently until nicely coloured. Add the flour, then tomatoes (sliced), herbs, peppercorns, castor sugar and stock.

Stir continually until boiling, then allow it to simmer gently for about an hour, until the sauce coats the spoon nicely. Rub through a fine sieve or tammy. Return to the saucepan to re-heat, and add the wine and lemon juice. Put a little piece of butter on the top, and stir this into the sauce just before using.

Fennel Sauce

Is made in the same way as TARRAGON SAUCE (see page 169), with three teaspoonfuls of chopped or pounded fennel.

Genoa Sauce

½ pint Brown Sauce.
½ wineglassful Red Wine.
½ oz. good Butter.

1 teaspoonful Mushroom Ketchup.
Castor Sugar.
1 teaspoonful Anchovy Sauce.

½ teaspoonful Pepper.

UTENSILS—Saucepan, sieve, wooden spoon, teaspoon, wineglass, pint or gill measure, basin.

Put the brown sauce into a saucepan with claret or other light, red wine, pepper, one teaspoonful of mushroom ketchup, and a pinch of castor sugar. Boil for 10 minutes. Strain through a sieve. Then work well into it the butter, and a teaspoonful of anchovy sauce. It is then ready to be served.

Genoese Sauce

1 pint Brown Sauce.
1 tablespoonful Mushroom Ketchup.
1 Shallot. Cayenne Pepper.

1 teaspoonful Anchovy Essence.
1 wineglassful Claret.
2 teaspoonfuls chopped Parsley.
2 oz. Butter.

UTENSILS—Saucepan, knife, wooden spoon, measuring spoons, pint measure, wineglass, hair sieve, chopping board, basin.

Chop the shallot finely. Put it into a saucepan with the brown sauce, and add the ketchup, anchovy essence, claret and a dust of cayenne pepper. Boil all together gently for 20 minutes. Rub it through a very fine hair sieve, then re-heat and add the finely chopped parsley. Work the butter well in, by degrees, in small pieces.

NOTE.—The butter must not on any account be added in the whole lump, or the sauce will become oily and be spoiled.

German Sauce

2 oz. Flour.	3 Yolks of Eggs.
2 oz. Butter.	Lemon Juice.

1 pint White Stock.

UTENSILS—Saucepan, wooden spoon, basin, egg-beater, pint measure, bain-marie or double boiler.

Melt one ounce and a half of butter in a saucepan. Stir in the flour and cook together for 2 or 3 minutes. Then gradually stir in one pint of well flavoured white stock. Stir until it boils, then let it cook for 10 minutes.

Beat the yolks of the eggs well in a basin, and pour the boiling sauce on to them, stirring all the time. Add a few drops of lemon juice, the remainder of the butter, and serve. If liked, two tablespoonfuls of shredded button mushrooms may be added. They must be heated in the sauce before adding it to the eggs. Do not let the sauce boil after adding the eggs, or it will curdle. If it is to be kept hot, stand it either in the bain-marie, or in a double boiler with hot water below.

Gooseberry Sauce

½ pint green Gooseberries.	2 lumps of Sugar.
½ oz. Butter.	½ pint Water.
½ oz. Flour.	Green Colouring.

UTENSILS—Enamelled saucepan, hair sieve, wooden spoon, pint measure, basin.

Top and tail the gooseberries. Put them to cook in an enamelled saucepan with two tablespoonfuls of water, and when quite soft, rub them through a fine hair sieve. Melt the butter in a saucepan, stir in the flour, then half a pint of boiling water, and add the gooseberry pulp, the sugar, and

sufficient green colouring to give the sauce a good colour.
Bring to the boil and serve.

Green Sauce

2 sprigs of Parsley.	1 hard-boiled Egg.
2 sprigs of Tarragon.	1 teaspoonful Capers.
2 sprigs of Fennel.	1 tablespoonful Salad Oil.
6 Chives.　2 Gherkins.	½ pint Mayonnaise Sauce.

Green Colouring.

UTENSILS—Saucepan, strainer, pestle and mortar, tammy-
cloth and spoons, measuring spoons, pint or gill measure.

Take the parsley, tarragon, fennel and the green part of
the chives and wash them. Put all into a saucepan, with cold
water sufficient to cover, and add a very small piece of soda.
Bring all to the boil quickly. Then strain, rinse them in
cold water, and drain as dry as possible.

Press all the moisture out, then put them into a mortar
with the chopped gherkins, capers, the yolk of egg, salad oil,
and a very little green colouring to give a good colour.
Pound all until quite smooth. Mix in the mayonnaise sauce,
rub all through a tammy, and keep in a cool place until
required.

Hollandaise Sauce

1 teaspoonful Lemon Juice.	1 oz. Butter.
1 teaspoonful Vinegar.	2 Yolks of Eggs.
½ teaspoonful Tarragon Vinegar.	Cayenne Pepper.
2 tablespoonfuls Cream.	Salt.

UTENSILS—Basin, saucepan, wooden spoon, knife, measuring spoons.

Put the vinegars, the yolks of eggs, and the cream into
a basin, and stand the basin over a saucepan of boiling water.
Stir the ingredients constantly with a wooden spoon until
the mixture thickens. Be very careful not to let it boil, or it
will curdle and be spoilt. Draw it to the side of the stove, and
stir in the butter in small pieces, one at a time, not adding a
fresh piece until the previous one has quite melted. Then add
the lemon juice, cayenne, and salt to taste, and serve in a hot
sauce-boat.

Cold Horseradish Sauce

1 teacupful grated Horseradish.	2 tablespoonfuls French Vinegar.
1 teaspoonful Mustard.	1 gill Cream.
1 teaspoonful Castor Sugar.	½ teaspoonful Salt.

UTENSILS—Knife, grater, kitchen spoon, teacup, measuring spoons.

Wash and scrape the stick of horseradish, and grate a teacupful finely. Mix it thoroughly with the mustard, sugar, cream and salt. Lastly, mix in the vinegar and serve.

Hot Horseradish Sauce (1)

½ teacupful grated Horseradish.	2 oz. Butter.
½ pint Milk. Salt. Nutmeg.	1 tablespoonful Flour.

UTENSILS—Knife, grater, 2 saucepans, wooden spoon, tablespoon, teacup, pint or gill measure.

Wash and peel a stick of horseradish, then grate it finely. Put half a teacupful of this on to boil, with just enough water to cook it. This will take about 15 minutes. Melt the butter in a saucepan, and stir the flour into the butter, add the milk, and bring to the boil. Stir in the cooked horseradish, and a grate of nutmeg, and boil for 5 minutes. Add salt to taste, and serve hot in a hot sauce-boat.

Hot Horseradish Sauce (2)

4 tablespoonfuls grated Horse-radish.	1 teaspoonful Tarragon Vinegar.
	1 teaspoonful French Vinegar.
½ pint common White Stock or Broth.	2 Egg Yolks.
	A dust of Cayenne Pepper.
½ teaspoonful Sugar.	½ teaspoonful Salt.

UTENSILS—Knife, grater, saucepan, basin, egg-beater, wooden spoon, measuring spoons, gill or pint measure.

Well wash a stick of horseradish and scrape off the outer skin. Now grate four tablespoonfuls very finely. Put this into a saucepan with the stock, and simmer until cooked, in about 30 minutes. Take it off the fire.

Beat the yolks of eggs well and add them to the sauce, stirring well all the time. Return the saucepan to the side of the stove until the sauce thickens like custard, but be most careful not to boil it. Take the saucepan off the stove, and add the vinegars and seasoning. Serve in a hot sauce-boat. The tarragon vinegar may be omitted, and all French vinegar used, if more convenient.

Imitation Dutch Sauce

½ pint Milk.	1 teaspoonful Lemon Juice.
½ oz. Flour.	1 Yolk of Egg.
1 oz. Butter.	Salt. Cayenne.

UTENSILS—Saucepan, basin, wooden spoon, egg-beater, teaspoon, gill or pint measure.

Boil the milk, with a small dust of cayenne pepper, then pour it into a basin. Melt the butter in the same saucepan, and stir in flour with a wooden spoon. Add the boiled milk to this by degrees, stirring continuously. When it comes to the boil, let it cook for 5 minutes, so that the flour may be thoroughly done. Salt, to taste, can now be added.

When it is quite boiling, add the yolk of one egg or, preferably, of two eggs, well beaten. Remove from the fire immediately, and when off the fire add the lemon juice. Serve in a hot sauce-boat.

Italian Sauce

2 oz. Butter.
½ oz. Flour.
½ pint White Stock.
1 gill Chablis.
2 tablespoonfuls Cream.
1 dessertspoonful chopped Parsley.

2 tablespoonfuls finely chopped Mushrooms.
1 saltspoonful Salt.
1 dessertspoon chopped Shallots
½ teaspoonful Sugar.
½ saltspoonful Pepper.

UTENSILS—Two saucepans, knife, wooden spoon, measuring spoons, pint or gill measure, chopping board, bain-marie or double boiler.

Put one ounce of butter in a saucepan with the chopped parsley, mushrooms, shallot, and the Chablis. Boil these until the wine is reduced to half the quantity. In another saucepan melt one ounce of butter, and stir in the flour. Moisten this with the white stock, and bring to the boil. Then stir in the reduced wine, shallot, and parsley, and add the sugar, salt and pepper. Simmer for 15 minutes. Then pour the cream on the top, and keep hot by standing it in a bain-marie, or double boiler, until wanted. When wanted, stir in the cream and use.

Liver Sauce for Hare

Liver from Hare.
1 Chicken's Liver.
1 pint good Stock, made from Game Trimmings.
2 oz. Butter.
1 dessertspoonful Mushroom Ketchup.
1 oz. Flour. 1 Shallot.

1 wineglassful Port Wine.
2 teaspoonfuls Red Currant Jelly.
1 teaspoonful Lemon Juice.
A bunch of Herbs (Bayleaf, Thyme and Parsley).
2 Cloves. Salt.
6 Peppercorns.
Black Pepper.

UTENSILS—Knife, saucepan, strainer, pestle and mortar,

hair sieve, wooden spoon, measuring spoons, pint measure, wineglass, basin, plate.

Cut the liver into dice. Melt one ounce of butter in a small saucepan, and add the shallot, finely chopped, and fry gently until it begins to colour. Then add the liver and stir it in the pan for a minute. Now add the stock by degrees, also add the peppercorns, cloves and herbs, and simmer until the liver is tender.

Strain the broth, pound the liver, and rub it through a sieve. Melt one ounce of butter in a saucepan, add the flour and fry together without browning. Stir in a little of the broth, then mix in the pounded liver and shallot. Add the remainder of the broth, then the red currant jelly, wine, ketchup, lemon juice, salt and pepper to taste. Bring almost to the boil, then serve.

Lobster Sauce

1 medium-sized Lobster.	1 teaspoonful Anchovy Sauce.
1¼ oz. Butter.	A little Lemon Juice.
¾ oz. Flour.	1 or 2 tablespoonfuls Cream.
½ pint. Milk.	Cayenne. Salt to taste.

UTENSILS—Knife, pestle and mortar, hair sieve, saucepan, wooden spoon, measuring spoons, 2 basins.

Choose a hen lobster. Pick the meat from the shell, cut it into very small square pieces, take out the coral which will be found under the tail, and wash and drain it well.

Put this into a mortar with half an ounce of butter, pound it quite smooth, and rub through a hair sieve. Cover it and put by till wanted.

Melt three-quarters of an ounce of butter in a small saucepan. Add the flour and mix well. Cook together without browning for a minute or two. Then add the milk by degrees, and bring to the boil, stirring constantly. Add the seasoning and cream. Boil for a few minutes longer, then add the lobster butter and the cut up lobster meat. Do not let it boil after this, but allow it to get thoroughly hot again. Lastly, when it is off the fire, add a few drops of lemon juice.

NOTE.—If preferred, white stock can be used instead of milk, and tinned lobster instead of fresh. The latter is not so nice nor so wholesome. If it is used, a drop or two of carmine must be added to afford the necessary colouring.

Maître d'Hôtel Sauce

½ oz. Flour.	1 dessertspoonful chopped **Parsley**.
½ oz. Butter.	½ teaspoonful Shallot.
¼ pint Milk.	1 teaspoonful Lemon Juice.
¼ pint Stock.	Thyme. Pepper. Salt.

UTENSILS—Saucepan, knife, wooden spoon, measuring spoons, gill or pint measure, chopping board.

Melt the butter in a saucepan. Add the shallot and thyme, which should be very finely chopped. Cook them together gently at the side of the stove for 10 minutes. Mix in the flour, then gradually stir in the stock and milk. Add pepper and salt to taste, then the finely chopped parsley, and last of all, when it is off the fire, add the lemon juice. If for fish, add the gravy which has run from the fish in cooking, and then pour the whole over the fish and serve.

Mayonnaise Sauce

2 Yolks of Eggs.	1 teaspoonful **Tarragon Vinegar**.
½ pint Salad Oil.	1 teaspoonful **White Vinegar**.
½ teaspoonful Mustard.	1 tablespoonful **Cream**.
A dust of Cayenne.	A pinch of Salt.
½ teaspoonful Chilli Vinegar.	A pinch of Sugar.

UTENSILS—Two basins, wooden spoon, measuring spoons.

Put the raw yolks of the eggs into a basin, being careful not to let in any of the white. Add the mustard, salt, sugar and cayenne. Work these ingredients well together with a wooden spoon. Add the oil, drop by drop, stirring the mixture well all the time, and always one way, until it becomes the consistency of batter.

Be very careful about the oil going in slowly, or it will curdle, and then it is spoilt, though sometimes it can be rectified by putting another yolk into a basin and adding the sauce slowly to it. This, however, makes much trouble, while if care is taken at first, in adding the oil slowly, the sauce is quite simple. When it is quite stiff, add the vinegars, and lastly, the cream. Keep in a cool place.

MAYONNAISE ASPIC

¼ pint Aspic Jelly.	3 tablespoonfuls Mayonnaise Sauce

UTENSILS—Basin, wooden spoon, tablespoon, pint or gill measure.

Let the jelly be cool, yet just in a liquid state. Mix the

mayonnaise sauce well into it, and stir until it just begins to thicken.

Mint Sauce

2 tablespoonfuls chopped Mint.	1 dessertspoonful Sugar.
Boiling Water.	2 tablespoonfuls Brown Vinegar.

UTENSILS—Knife, measuring spoons, chopping board.

Chop the mint very finely. Melt the sugar with one table-spoonful of boiling water, in the sauce-boat, then add the mint and vinegar, and serve cold.

Mushroom Sauce

¾ pint Button Mushrooms.	Lemon Juice.
1 oz. Butter.	½ pint Creamy Béchamel Sauce.

UTENSILS—Knife, cloth, basin, stewpan, wooden spoon pint or gill measure, tammy-cloth, if required.

Take the mushrooms, trim off their stalks, and rub them with a coarse cloth to get them perfectly clean and free from grit. Put them to soak for about 10 minutes, in cold water containing about a tablespoonful of lemon juice. Drain well, then shred them finely. Put them into a stewpan with the butter, and cover closely with a lid, then cook gently until tender.

Do not let them cook longer than is just necessary to get the required tenderness, or they will lose colour and flavour. Now add the Béchamel sauce, and simmer for 10 minutes. Rub all through a tammy if required smooth, though the sauce may be used as it is. Add a little more salt if required.

Mustard Sauce

1 teaspoonful English Mustard.	½ pint Water.
1 teaspoonful French Mustard.	1 dessertspoonful Vinegar.
2 oz. Butter.	2 tablespoonfuls Cream or Milk.
1 tablespoonful Flour.	Small Seasoning of Salt and Sugar.

UTENSILS—Saucepan, wooden spoon, measuring spoons, fine strainer or sieve, pint or gill measure, basin.

Melt the butter in a saucepan. Stir in the flour and the mustards, then the water and vinegar. Add seasoning of salt and sugar to taste. Rub through a fine strainer or sieve, then put all back into the saucepan again, re-warm, and add the cream or milk. Serve either in a sauce-boat, or it can be poured round fish, pork, etc.

Onion Sauce

6 oz. Onions. | ½ pint White Sauce.
Milk. Water. | Salt and Pepper.

UTENSILS—Knife, basin, 2 saucepans, colander, wire sieve, wooden spoon, basin, pint or gill measure.

Peel the onions and throw them, as they are peeled, into slightly salted water to preserve their colour, then put them into a saucepan with sufficient cold water to cover them. Bring to the boil, then strain. Put the onions back into the saucepan with milk and water in equal parts. Simmer until the onions are tender, then drain well and press out all the water. Rub them through a sieve.

Make half a pint of good white sauce, with milk. When it boils, add the onion pulp, and stir it until it almost boils again. Season with salt and a little white pepper, and serve.

Onion Sauce (Brown)

3 large Onions. | ¾ pint good Gravy.
2 oz. Butter. | Pepper and Salt.
¾ oz. Flour. | Lemon Juice, if liked.

UTENSILS—Knife, stewpan, wooden spoon, fine sieve, pint measure, basin.

Peel and slice finely the onions, and put them into a stewpan with the butter. Stir them gently over the fire until they are a light brown. Sift the flour over them and mix it well in. Now add the gravy, and let it simmer gently until the onions are quite tender.

Rub all through a fine sieve, return to the saucepan, and add seasoning to taste. If it should not be quite thick enough, reduce it by boiling quickly. A few drops of lemon juice may be added just before serving.

Orange Sauce

2 Seville Oranges. | 1 tablespoonful Red Currant Jelly.
1 Lemon. | Cayenne. Salt.
1 wineglassful Port Wine. | 1 small breakfastcupful Gravy.

UTENSILS—Grater, saucepan, pointed strainer, tablespoon, kitchen spoon, wineglass, breakfast cup, lemon squeezer.

Grate the rinds of the oranges. Put this into a saucepan

with the gravy, the strained juice of the oranges, the juice of the lemon, the red currant jelly, and the port wine. Season with a dust of cayenne, and salt to taste. Simmer for 5 minutes. Pass the sauce through a pointed strainer, and serve.

Oyster Sauce

1 oz. Butter.	½ oz. Flour.
½ pint Fish Stock.	A pinch of Salt.
9 Oysters.	Cayenne.

UTENSILS—Basin, knife, 2 saucepans, strainer, wooden spoon, pint or gill measure.

First carefully prepare the oysters for the sauce—open them, and save all the liquor. Put them into a small saucepan, or sauté pan, with the liquor and enough fish stock just to cover them. Put the pan on the fire, and watch carefully until you see the first signs of boiling. On no account let them actually boil, or the oysters will be leathery.

Directly there are signs of the liquor being about to boil, draw the pan to the side of the stove, and let it stand there for 2 minutes. Take it up, strain off the liquor into a basin, and stand the saucepan with the oysters on one side until wanted. Melt half an ounce of butter in a small saucepan, stir in the flour, and fry together for 1 or 2 minutes without browning. Stir the liquor strained from the oysters into this saucepan with the fried flour and butter. Add the fish stock, a dust of cayenne pepper, and a little salt, if required. Stir until it boils.

If not quite thick enough mix a little more flour quite smooth with a little cold water, and pour it through a pointed strainer into the sauce until it is the required thickness. A very little will do, and it would not need any extra thickening, only that flours vary very much in this respect. When it is the required thickness, add the remaining half ounce of butter and the oysters. Do not let the sauce remain on the fire after the oysters and butter are added. Pour into a heated sauce-boat, and serve.

Parsley Sauce

2 oz. Butter.	½ pint Boiling Water, Milk or Stock.
1 oz. Flour.	1 tablespoonful finely chopped Parsley.
White Pepper.	
Lemon Juice. Salt.	

UTENSILS—Saucepan, wooden spoon, knife, chopping board, tablespoon, pint or gill measure.

Put one ounce of butter into a saucepan and melt it. Stir in the flour, and fry together without browning. Then pour in gradually the water, milk, milk and water, or stock. Stir it over the fire until it re-boils.

Move the saucepan to the side of the fire, and add the parsley, thoroughly washed, dried, and very finely chopped. Add the second ounce of butter, and season to taste with salt and white pepper. Boil for 2 or 3 minutes longer. Squeeze in a few drops of lemon juice just before serving, or this may be omitted if preferred. If making the sauce for boiled mutton, fowls or fish, it is best partly to use the liquor they were cooked in.

Piquant Sauce

1 tablespoonful Worcester Sauce.	1 oz. Flour.
2 tablespoonfuls French Vinegar.	1 pint Brown Stock.
1 oz. Butter.	1 Onion. Castor Sugar.

A few drops Carmine.

UTENSILS—Knife, saucepan, wooden spoon, tablespoon, tammy-cloth, basin, bain-marie or double boiler.

Peel the onion and chop it. Melt the butter in a saucepan, and fry the onion in it. When nicely browned, stir in the flour, and fry together for a few minutes. Then stir in by degrees one pint of brown stock, two tablespoonfuls of French vinegar, and one tablespoonful of Worcester sauce. Add also salt to taste, a dust of castor sugar, and a few drops of carmine to give it a colour.

Boil until the mixture is the consistency of cream, then wring it through a tammy. Re-heat in the bain-marie and use. If liked, a few finely chopped gherkins may be added after it has been wrung through the tammy; also a little finely chopped parsley.

Poivrade Sauce

1 oz. Butter.	1 Tomato.
1 oz. Flour.	1 gill Vinegar.
¾ pint Brown Stock.	1 bunch of Herbs (Bayleaf, Thyme and Parsley).
1 oz. lean Ham.	
3 oz. Onion.	12 Peppercorns.
1 oz. Carrot	4 Cloves. Salt.

UTENSILS—Saucepan, knife or vegetable cutter, wooden spoon, large metal spoon, strainer, pint measure.

Melt the butter in a stewpan. Cut up the vegetables into dice, also the ham, and add them to the butter; fry gently until they are slightly brown. Add the herbs, cloves and peppercorns, and cook again for a few minutes. Then add the vinegar, and boil until reduced to half the quantity.

Mix in the flour smoothly. Add the stock by degrees and simmer for $\frac{1}{2}$ hour, skimming when required. Season to taste with salt, and add a few drops of browning if required to make it a good colour; but if a nice brown stock is used the colouring can be omitted. Strain and serve.

Prawn Sauce

1 dozen Prawns.	2 tablespoonfuls **Cream.**
$\frac{3}{4}$ pint Fish Stock.	Cayenne.
$\frac{3}{4}$ oz. Butter.	A few drops **Carmine.**
$\frac{1}{2}$ oz. Flour.	Salt to taste.

UTENSILS—Saucepan, strainer, basin, wooden spoon, tablespoon, pint or gill measure, knife.

Remove the shells from the prawns, and put the shells on to boil in three-quarters of a pint of well-flavoured fish stock. When reduced to half a pint, strain it. Melt three-quarters of an ounce of butter in a saucepan, and stir in half an ounce of fine flour. Then gradually mix in the fish stock. Bring to the boil, let it simmer gently for 10 minutes, then add the cream.

Cut up the meat of the prawns into small pieces, and add them to the sauce. Add cayenne and salt to taste, also one or two drops of carmine to give it a pale pink colour. If liked, add a few drops of lemon juice, but this must not be added until just before serving.

Reform Sauce

2 oz. Flour.	1 small Onion.
1 oz. Butter.	1 pint Brown Stock.
2 oz. Tomatoes.	1 tablespoonful Red Currant Jelly.
Pepper and Salt to taste	2 tablespoonfuls Port Wine.
A few drops Lemon Juice.	

UTENSILS—Saucepan, knife, wooden spoon, hair sieve, basin, tablespoon, pint measure.

Melt the butter in a saucepan. Add the onion, finely chopped, and fry till a nice golden colour. Then add the flour, and fry until a rich brown. Slice the tomatoes and add them to the above ingredients, together with a pint of brown stock made from meat bones. Stir all together until it boils. Let it simmer for ¾ hour, then stir in the red currant jelly, wine, lemon juice, and the seasoning. Rub the mixture through a fine hair sieve, and re-heat and use.

Rémoulade Sauce

½ pint Mayonnaise Sauce.
1 dessertspoonful chopped Gherkins.
1 dessertspoonful chopped Capers.
1 dessertspoonful chopped Tarragon.
1 chopped Anchovy.
1 teaspoonful French Mustard.

UTENSILS—Basin, wooden spoon, knife, measuring spoons, pint measure, chopping board.

Make mayonnaise sauce, as described on page 162. Chop all the above ingredients well, add them to the mayonnaise and mix well. Serve in a cold sauce-boat.

Robert Sauce

2 oz. Onion.
2 oz. Butter.
½ pint Stock.
1 oz. Flour.
1 teaspoonful made Mustard.
1 teaspoonful Vinegar.
Castor Sugar.
1 teaspoonful Lemon Juice.
Pepper and Salt.

UTENSILS—Knife, saucepan, wooden spoon, teaspoon, strainer, basin, pint or gill measure.

Chop the onion finely. Melt the butter in a saucepan. Put in the minced onion and fry together until the onion turns a pale brown. Add the flour and mix well together. Stir in the stock by degrees. Add seasoning of salt and pepper, also a pinch of castor sugar.

Mix thoroughly, and simmer for 20 minutes. Pour through a strainer. Lastly, stir in the vinegar, lemon juice, and mustard. This sauce is very good with roast pork, goose, cutlets or a grill.

Shrimp Sauce

¼ pint Picked Shrimps.
½ oz. Flour.
¾ oz. Butter.
½ pint Milk.
Cayenne.   Salt.

UTENSILS—Saucepan, wooden spoon, pint measure.

Melt the butter in a small saucepan, then stir in the flour and cook together for a few minutes. Then gradually stir in the milk. If preferred, the same quantity of fish stock can be substituted for the milk. Stir continuously until sauce boils. Add seasoning of cayenne pepper and salt to taste, then stir in the picked shrimps, bring to the boil, and use. A few drops of anchovy essence may be added if liked.

Tarragon Sauce

1 Yolk of Egg.	½ pint White Sauce.
½ oz. Butter.	1 teaspoonful blanched Tarragon.

UTENSILS—Saucepan, wooden spoon, basin, egg-beater, sieve or knife.

First blanch the tarragon. To do this, first wash a few sprigs in cold water, then pick off all the leaves. Put these into a saucepan with sufficient cold water to cover them, and add a piece of salt the size of a small pea, and a very small piece of soda. Bring the water to the boil, then strain and press all the moisture from the leaves. Rub the leaves through a sieve, or chop them finely.

Mix with them half an ounce of butter, then add them to the white sauce, and bring to the boil. Beat the yolk of an egg and pour the sauce over it. Do not put the sauce near the fire after the egg is in, or it will curdle. The egg may be omitted if preferred, but it makes the sauce much richer.

Tartare Sauce

1 teaspoonful Chives, finely chopped.	1 teaspoonful Parsley, finely chopped.
1 teaspoonful Tarragon, finely chopped.	1 teaspoonful Capers, finely chopped.
1 teaspoonful Gherkins, finely chopped.	½ pint Mayonnaise Sauce.

UTENSILS—Chopping board, knife, basin, wooden spoon, teaspoon, pint measure.

The chives, tarragon, gherkins, parsley and capers must be very finely chopped. Mix them thoroughly into the mayonnaise sauce. If chives and tarragon are not procurable they may be left out. When finished, the sauce should have a nice finely speckled green appearance.

Tomato Sauce (1)

1 lb. Tomatoes.	1 dessertspoonful Chopped Onion.
¾ oz. Butter.	¼ teaspoonful Castor Sugar.
1 oz. Rice Flour.	1 teaspoonful Lemon Juice.
½ pint well-flavoured Stock.	Pepper and Salt.

UTENSILS—Saucepan, cloth, knife, basin, wooden spoon, fine hair sieve or tammy-cloth, measuring spoons, pint measure.

Melt the butter in a saucepan. Wipe the tomatoes and remove the stalks. Slice them and put all into the saucepan with the butter. Add the finely chopped onion. Fry gently for 10 minutes. Then add the sugar, and half the stock.

Mix the remainder of the stock with the rice flour, and stir this into the pan also. Add the lemon juice, also pepper and salt to taste. Let all simmer gently for 30 minutes, or a little longer. Then rub all through a tammy, or a fine hair sieve. Put it back into a saucepan to re-heat, then use. Tinned tomatoes do quite well for this, and need not be cut up, but can be put in whole.

Tomato Sauce (2)

2 lb. Tomatoes.	1 oz. Butter.
½ oz. Flour.	¼ teaspoonful Castor Sugar.
6 Peppercorns.	½ teaspoonful Salt.
2 oz. Onions.	White Pepper.

UTENSILS—Cloth, saucepan, basin, hair sieve, wooden spoon, teaspoon, knife.

Wipe the tomatoes and pull off their stalks. Melt the butter in a saucepan. Finely chop the onion, add it to the butter, and fry together without browning for about 10 minutes. Then add the flour, and stir well together.

Now add the tomatoes, sliced, also the peppercorns, salt, and sugar, and simmer until the tomatoes are quite tender. Rub all through a hair sieve, using a wooden spoon. Re-heat, and if liked add a little pepper.

Tomato Butter Sauce

4 large Tomatoes.	1 oz. Butter. Carmine.
1 teaspoonful chopped Shallot.	Pepper and Salt.

UTENSILS—Knife, saucepan, fine sieve, wooden spoon, basin, teaspoon.

Slice the tomatoes, and put them in a pan, with the butter, three drops of carmine, shallots, and salt and pepper to taste. Cover with a lid, and cook them gently at the side of the stove, until they become a pulp. Rub the pulp through a fine sieve, re-warm and serve.

Veloute Sauce

1½ oz. Butter. | 1 pint well-flavoured Stock.
1½ oz. Flour. | Salt.

UTENSILS—Saucepan, wooden spoon, pint measure.

Melt the butter gently over a low fire, and when melted add the flour by degrees. Stir and cook gently for 5 minutes. Then add the stock by degrees. (Stock made from either veal, rabbit, or chicken bones.) Stir till boiling, and afterwards allow the sauce to simmer gently for ½ hour. Add salt to taste.

Veloute, without Meat

4 oz. Onion. | 1 oz. Flour.
1 stick Celery. | A bunch of Herbs.
½ a Carrot.   Salt. | ½ pint Milk.
1 oz. Butter. | ½ pint Water.

UTENSILS—Knife, saucepan, wooden spoon, basin, fine sieve or tammy-cloth, pint measure.

Wash the celery well, cut off the green ends, and slice the white part finely. Peel and slice the onion and carrot. Melt the butter in a saucepan, and stir in the vegetables and herbs. Cover the saucepan tightly, and let the vegetables cook gently for 5 minutes. Stir in the flour and fry all together gently.

Stir in the milk and water by degrees, bring to the boil then allow it to simmer for about ¾ hour. Add salt to taste. Strain through a fine strainer, or, better still, wring through a tammy, and use as required.

White Sauce, without Meat
(*For Cauliflower and other Vegetables*)

1 oz. Butter. | ⅛ saltspoonful Salt.
½ oz. Flour. | White Pepper.
½ pint Milk. | A few drops Lemon Juice.

UTENSILS—Saucepan, wooden spoon, saltspoon.

Melt half an ounce of butter in a small saucepan. Stir in the flour, mixing it thoroughly with a wooden spoon until it is quite free from lumps. Then draw the saucepan to one side of the stove, and let it cook for a few minutes without letting it colour. Stir in the milk by degrees, then bring the sauce to the boil, stirring all the time.

Let it cook for a few minutes so that the flour may be done thoroughly, then add salt to taste. Just before serving, add the remainder of the butter in small pieces.

SWEET SAUCES

Almond Sauce

3 oz. Ground Almonds.	1 dessertspoonful Flour.
2 oz. Castor Sugar.	3 drops Essence of Almonds, or
1 pint Milk.	2 Bitter Almonds.

2 Yolks of Eggs.

UTENSILS—Pestle and mortar, saucepan, 2 basins, wooden spoon, egg-beater, dessertspoon.

Put the ground almonds, and the bitter ones, finely pounded, into a saucepan with half a pint of milk, and bring them to the boil. Then keep the saucepan over a moderate heat for 15 minutes. Strain off all the milk, leaving the almonds as dry as possible. Remove the almonds, and pour the almond-milk back into the saucepan.

Mix the flour smoothly with the remaining cold milk, and add this to the milk in the saucepan, also add the sugar. Stir constantly until boiling, and let it boil for 5 minutes. Beat the two yolks of eggs well, mix a little of the sauce with them, then add them to the sauce in the saucepan, but do not let it boil after the egg is added.

Lastly, if it is used, add the essence of almonds, but it is much better to use the bitter almonds. In fact it is preferable to use fresh almonds altogether, but then they require to be blanched and finely chopped. To blanch almonds, put them into a saucepan with cold water to cover them. Bring to the boil, and, as soon as boiling, rinse them in cold water and rub them in a coarse cloth to remove the skins.

Apricot Sauce

1 lb. Apricot Jam.	1 wineglassful Sherry.

1 gill Water.

UTENSILS—Saucepan, hair sieve or tammy, wooden spoon, wineglass, gill measure, basin.

Melt the jam slowly in the sherry and water, and let it boil for 10 minutes. Then rub it through a hair sieve or tammy. Re-heat and use.

Chocolate Sauce

2 or 3 oz. Vanilla Chocolate.	½ pint Milk.
2 Eggs.	3 oz. Castor Sugar.

UTENSILS—Grater, 2 basins, saucepan, egg-beater, wooden spoon.

Grate the chocolate, and mix it with the milk and two ounces of sugar, then bring it to the boil. Well beat the yolks of two eggs, and pour the boiling milk on to them. Return all to the saucepan, and whisk well until it thickens, but do not let it boil. Beat the whites to a stiff froth, and add the remainder of the sugar. Pour the sauce on to them, and stir gently until partly mixed. Do not dissolve all the white of eggs as the sauce should have a frothy appearance. Cream can be added, a quarter or half pint.

Custard Sauce

2 Eggs. ½ pint Milk.	1 teaspoonful Vanilla Essence or
1½ oz. Castor Sugar.	1 tablespoonful Brandy.

UTENSILS—Saucepan, basin, wooden spoon, egg-whisk, teaspoon, tablespoon.

Put the milk on to boil in a very clean saucepan. Beat the eggs and the sugar together in a basin, then pour the boiling milk on to them and whisk well. Return the mixture to the saucepan, and continue whisking until the custard thickens. Do not let it boil, or it will curdle. Add the flavouring after the custard is taken off the fire.

Lemon Sauce

Half the Rind of a Lemon.	1 tablespoonful White Sugar.
Juice of the Lemon.	½ oz. Butter.

1 dessertspoonful Arrowroot.

UTENSILS—Saucepan, basin, strainer, knife, wooden spoon, measuring spoons, lemon squeezer.

Simmer, in about half a pint of water, half the rind of a lemon (which should not be chopped) for about 10 minutes, then take out the peel. Add to the flavoured water the sugar and the strained lemon juice. Mix the arrowroot with a little cold water, and pour the boiling syrup on it.

Return it to the saucepan, with the butter, and boil it up.

Punch Sauce

2 oz. Sugar.	½ wineglassful Marsala.
1 oz. Butter.	½ wineglassful Brandy.
1 teaspoonful Rice Flour.	Lemon. Orange.
½ wineglassful Rum.	1 gill Water.

UTENSILS—Saucepan, knife, basin, wooden spoon, strainer, teaspoon, wineglass, gill measure, lemon squeezer.

Put the sugar on to boil with the water, the rind of half a small lemon (pared very thinly) and a rather smaller quantity of orange peel. Let them simmer for 15 minutes, then take out the peel.

Mix the rice flour quite smoothly with a little cold water, and stir it into the boiling syrup. Add the butter in small pieces, then the strained juice of half the orange, also a teaspoonful of the lemon juice. Boil for 10 minutes, then add the rum, Marsala and brandy, but do not let the sauce boil after they are added.

Raspberry Sauce

¼ lb. Raspberry Jam.	½ pint Water.
Juice of 1 Lemon.	Sugar to taste.
1 tablespoonful Arrowroot.	A few drops Carmine.

UTENSILS—Saucepan, strainer, basin, fine sieve, wooden spoon, tablespoon, lemon squeezer.

Dissolve the jam in nearly all the water. Bring it to the boil and let it boil for 5 minutes, then strain, and rub it through a fine sieve. Mix the arrowroot with a little of the cold water.

Re-boil the sauce, stir in the mixed arrowroot, also the strained juice of a lemon. Add sugar to taste, and a few drops of carmine to make it a good colour. Boil for a few minutes.

Sweet Sauce (1)

½ pint Milk.	1 oz. Castor Sugar.
2 oz. Butter.	A strip of Lemon Peel.
¾ oz. Flour.	A small stick of Cinnamon.

UTENSILS—Saucepan, knife, strainer, basin, wooden spoon.

Boil a strip of lemon peel and a piece of cinnamon in the milk for 10 minutes, then strain it. Melt one ounce of butter in the saucepan, stir in the flour and cook together for a minute or two. Then gradually stir in the flavoured milk. Add the sugar, and the remainder of the butter in small pieces. If liked, a little grated nutmeg may be added as well.

Sweet Sauce (2)

1 tablespoonful Sugar.	2 Cloves. ½ pint Water.
1 teaspoonful Lemon Juice.	A piece of Cinnamon.
1 dessertspoonful Arrowroot.	A strip of Lemon Peel.
A few drops Cochineal.	

UTENSILS—Saucepan, strainer, basin, wooden spoon, measuring spoons, knife.

Simmer half a pint of water with the cloves, lemon peel, and a small piece of cinnamon stick. When the water is well flavoured, strain, and put it back into the saucepan. Add the sugar and lemon juice. Mix the arrowroot with a little cold water, and stir it into the syrup when boiling. Colour with a few drops of cochineal, and pour over the pudding.

Wine Sauce (1)

1 gill Sherry.	2 oz. Castor Sugar.
1 tablespoonful Apricot Jam.	1 gill cold Water.

1 teaspoonful Lemon Juice.

UTENSILS—Saucepan, wooden spoon, strainer, measuring spoons, gill measure.

Put the jam and sugar into a small saucepan with the cold water, and stir it over the fire until the sugar has quite dissolved, then bring it to the boil. Add the lemon juice and sherry, and bring to the boil again. Strain the sauce, and it is ready for use.

Wine Sauce (2)

1 wineglassful Sherry.	1½ oz. Sugar.
1 wineglassful Brandy.	1 teaspoonful Arrowroot.
1 oz. Butter.	1 strip of Lemon Peel.

1 gill Water.

UTENSILS—Knife, basin, wooden spoon, saucepan, wineglass, teaspoon, gill measure.

The lemon peel must be very thin. Put it on to boil for 5 minutes in the water, then take out the peel and add the sugar. Mix the arrowroot with a tablespoonful of cold water. Stir this into the boiling syrup, and add the butter in small pieces. Lastly, add the sherry and brandy.

FISH

Fish may be bought whole, by the pound or filleted. When buying fish without bone, four ounces per person is the usual allowance. When buying fish with bone, or fish that is to be filleted, six ounces per person should be allowed.

To Clean Fish

Insert scissors or a sharp knife at the gills and cut the fish open down to the vent. Scrape out all the inside, being careful that no blood is left on the backbone. Remove the gills and, if required, take out the eyes by pushing the point of a skewer under and lifting them out.

If the fish requires to be scaled, scrape it with a knife, beginning at the tail and working towards the head. Cut off the fins and tail quite close. In cutting off the fins, cut towards the head, otherwise the fins will lie close to the body.

Wash the fish well in fresh water, then put it into salted water for a few minutes. Dry it thoroughly and stand it in as cool and airy a place as possible until required for use. Turbot should be hung up by the tail, if a whole fish.

Oily fish, such as herrings and mackerel, should certainly be cooked as fresh as possible. White-fleshed fish may be kept for a day or two, in cold weather, if a little salt is rubbed on the inside along the backbone after they have been thoroughly dried. Fish that have a muddy flavour are much improved by being soaked for some time in salt and water, prior to cooking.

RULES FOR COOKING FISH

Boiling

A large fish should be tied to the strainer to keep it in position and to prevent its getting broken.

Put the fish on in cold water, adding a dessertspoonful of salt, a dessertspoonful of vinegar and a dessertspoonful of lemon juice to each quart of water. The vinegar and lemon juice help to keep the fish white and firm. Fish that is cut, or small fish, should be put on in boiling water, plunged in, as by this means the cut surfaces are hardened, the pores closed, and the juices do not escape. Do not have more water in the fish kettle than is necessary to cover the fish, or the skin may crack, and the fish lose much of its flavour. Remove all scum as it rises, or it will spoil the appearance of the fish.

When the fish is cooked, the flesh will easily leave the bone and it will have lost its watery appearance. It will be firm and white. Be sure it is well cooked, for underdone fish is quite uneatable and most unwholesome. On the other hand, if it is overdone it will be soft and flabby. The time usually allowed for boiling fish is 8 minutes to the pound, and 8 minutes over, for fish put into boiling water, but this may be varied according to whether the fish is thick or thin. Fish put into cold water will take longer to cook, but will only need actually to boil a short time.

If a fish kettle with a strainer is not available, the fish must be tied up in a thin cloth. It is a good plan to stand the fish on an enamelled plate or dish, and then tie both fish and plate in the cloth. Lower it gently into a saucepan, large enough to hold it, but not larger than necessary. Always take fish up as soon as it is cooked, for it readily spoils if left standing in the water.

To keep boiled fish hot, stand the strainer, with the fish upon it, across the kettle, lay a clean cloth over, then cover with the lid. Serve the fish on a hot dish lined with a folded napkin, and, if possible, on a strainer. Garnish according to taste.

Frying

The fish are cleaned in the same manner as for boiling, but may afterwards be cut in slices, filleted, or left whole. They may also be either dipped in batter or egged and breadcrumbed. Have a pan two-thirds full of boiling fat, and plunge the fish in. The fat is at a proper temperature when a light blue vapour—blue smoke, it is generally called—is rising from it. The fat is quite still then, not bubbling.

If the fish or the pieces are small they should be put in a basket, as it is then easier to lift them out. Whitebait would be put in a frying basket. If large, the fish is generally fried in a fish-fryer. This is a deep oval pan, which has a wire strainer in it to lay the fish on. These pans are not used in the ordinary way, as large fish are generally filleted or cut.

If not too large they can be cooked in an ordinary frying pan, but in this case a broad fish-slice must be used to lift them out. When the fish is lifted out of the fat, place it on a wire pastry rack to drain, or if a rack is not handy lay the fish on kitchen paper.

Steaming

Some fish are much improved by being steamed instead of boiled. This is the case with rather tasteless watery fish, such as small haddock and whiting. They then retain their flavour more than they do if boiled. Sprinkle the fish with a little salt, both on the inside and outside.

Have plenty of fast boiling water in the saucepan or pot, place the fish in the steamer, cover it down tightly, then place the steamer on top of the saucepan. Fish cooked in this manner takes longer than boiling—about half as long again.

Broiling

Fish is broiled by means of a gridiron which is placed either in front or on top of a clear fire.

Wipe the fish quite dry after cleaning. When thoroughly dried roll them in flour, and shake off the loose flour afterwards. Or, instead of rolling in flour, brush them over with salad oil. Oil the bars of the grid (a double one is best for fish), then spread it thickly with straws which have also been oiled. Lay the fish on, put more straws on top, and close the gridiron. Hang it in front of a bright fire, putting it close to the fire first, then drawing it away, so that it finishes cooking more slowly. Turn the gridiron over frequently while cooking.

If straws are not procurable, the fish can be wrapped in oiled paper; or the fish can be well oiled, and the grid well oiled and heated before the fish is laid on. But straws are quite the easiest method, and can, of course, be used over and over again, provided that care is taken not to scorch them too much.

Grilling Fish

Wipe the fish quite dry after cleaning, then brush it over with melted butter or salad oil, and place it carefully on an oiled or greased gridiron, under the grill. Have the gas turned on full, and cook quickly for a moment or two until the surface is sealed.

Reduce the flame, and cook, turning constantly, to keep the surface set and the juice from escaping, until the fish is cooked. The time required depends on the thickness of the fish. Serve with a pat of butter or maître d'hôtel or anchovy butter melted on top, and garnished with parsley.

FISH DISHES

Boiled Fresh Haddock

1 Haddock.	**1 Egg. Parsley.**
1 oz. Butter.	**Salt. Water. Vinegar.**

UTENSILS—Knife, fish-kettle, fish-slice, skewer, brush for butter, saucepan, sieve, plate, cloth, chopping board, measuring spoons. *Enough for 1 to 4 persons, according to size of fish.*

Scrape the fish, remove the inside and the eyes, and trim the fins and tail. Put sufficient cold water into the fish-kettle or saucepan just to cover the fish, then add a large dessert-spoonful of salt and a teaspoonful of vinegar to every quart of water. Put the fish in, and if it is a medium-sized one it will be done soon after the water comes to the boil. If it is a large fish it should be allowed to boil for 15 minutes.

When done, lift the strainer out with the fish on it and let it rest across the top of the kettle to drain off the water. Take out the skewer from the head, then slide the fish carefully on to a dish. Brush the fish over with oiled butter, then decorate it with alternate lines of hard-boiled yolk of egg (previously rubbed through a sieve), and finely chopped parsley which has been wrung dry in a cloth. Garnish with a bunch of fresh green parsley. Serve with either anchovy, shrimp, tomato or mushroom sauce.

Stuffed Fillets of Fresh Haddock

2 small Haddocks.	¼ teaspoonful chopped Lemon Peel.
3 oz. Breadcrumbs.	1 tablespoonful finely chopped Suet.
3 oz. Butter.	
1 Egg, or Milk.	½ teaspoonful Mixed Herbs.
1 teaspoonful finely chopped Parsley.	Lemon Juice.
	Pepper. Salt.

Tomato Sauce, as described.

UTENSILS—Knife, chopping board, basin, wooden spoon, measuring spoons, egg-beater, baking tin, saucepan, fireproof dish, hair sieve, grater, fish-slice. *Enough for 4 persons.*

First make the stuffing. Chop the suet finely, also the parsley, mixed herbs, and lemon peel. Put three tablespoons of the crumbs into a basin. Add the suet, herbs, parsley, lemon peel, half a teaspoonful of salt, a quarter teaspoonful of pepper. Mix these dry ingredients together, then moisten with either a well-beaten egg of a little milk.

Skin and fillet the haddock. Lay the fillets on the board, with the skinned side downwards, and sprinkle them with a few drops of lemon juice. Then spread each fillet with some of the forcemeat. Roll them up, beginning at the broad part, rolling towards the tail. Have ready some strips of buttered paper a little broader than the fillets. Roll each fillet in a strip and tie round with strong cotton, then lay them in a well-buttered baking tin, and cook in a moderate oven for about 10 minutes.

Melt two ounces of butter in a saucepan, and stir in the remainder of the crumbs. Take the fillets up, remove the papers, and roll each one in the buttered crumbs. Slightly butter the bottom of a fireproof dish, and stand the rolled fillets in it. Put into a quick oven, and when the crumbs are a nice brown take them out. Serve with tomato sauce poured round.

FOR THE TOMATO SAUCE

1 lb. Tomatoes.	1 dessertspoonful chopped Onion.
¾ oz. Butter.	½ teaspoonful Castor Sugar.
1 oz. Rice Flour.	1 teaspoonful Lemon Juice.
½ pint well-flavoured Stock.	Pepper. Salt.

Melt the butter in a saucepan. Wipe the tomatoes and remove the stalks. Slice them and put all into the pan with the butter, then add the finely chopped onion, and fry gently for 10 minutes. Then add the sugar, and half the stock.

Mix the remainder of the stock with the rice flour, and stir this into the pan also. Add the lemon juice, also pepper and salt to taste. Let all simmer gently for 30 minutes, or a little longer. Then rub all through a fine hair sieve. Put it back into a saucepan to re-heat, then use. Tinned tomatoes do quite well for this ; they need not be cut up, but put in whole.

Fried Fillets of Haddock

2 Haddocks. | White Breadcrumbs.
1 Egg.   Flour. | Frying Fat.
Pepper and Salt.

UTENSILS—Knife, cloth, 2 plates, basin, egg-beater, grater, frying pan, wire sieve, fish-slice. *Enough for 4 to 6 persons.*

Trim the fillets neatly, wash them thoroughly, then roll them in a cloth to dry. Season some flour with white pepper and salt, and roll the fillets in this, afterwards shaking off as much of the loose flour as possible. Dip them into whole beaten-up egg, then into finely made white breadcrumbs.

Plunge these prepared fillets into a pan three-parts full of boiling fat or lard, and fry a nice golden colour. Five minutes will be sufficient time for these. Take them up and drain on a wire sieve, or piece of kitchen paper. Arrange neatly on a dish, with a fish-paper under them, and garnish with a little parsley. Serve with anchovy sauce. (For SAUCES, see Index.)

Haddock, Newlyn

1 Fresh Haddock. | 1 oz. Butter.
1 Lemon.   Salt. | Coralline Pepper.
Sauce, as described.

UTENSILS—Knife, baking dish, saucepan, pan to contain baking dish, wooden spoon, lemon squeezer, strainer, fish-slice. *Enough for 3 or 4 persons.*

Wash and clean a nice large haddock, and fillet it. Butter a baking dish, and lay the fillets in it side by side, then melt the butter, and pour it over them. Sprinkle with a very little salt, some coralline pepper and the strained lemon juice.

Lay a well buttered paper over the fish, and stand the tin containing the fish in another tin containing hot water. Cook in a moderate oven for 10 or 12 minutes. Take the fillets up, and lay them on a hot dish. Save the liquor from the fish to add to the sauce.

TO MAKE THE ANCHOVY AND SHRIMP SAUCE

1 oz. Butter. | 1 teaspoonful Anchovy Sauce.
$\frac{3}{4}$ oz. Flour. | 2 drops of Carmine.
$\frac{1}{2}$ pint Milk. | 1 tablespoonful Capers.
Liquor from the Fish. | 2 tablespoonfuls Cream.
$\frac{1}{2}$ pint picked Shrimps.

Melt the butter in a saucepan. Stir in the flour, and mix well together, then stir in by degrees the milk and the liquor from the fish. Add the anchovy sauce, carmine, cream, and three-fourths of the picked shrimps, well chopped.

The remainder of the shrimps must be fried very gently in a little butter, just for a minute or two to become warmed through, and used for garnishing the fish. When the sauce is ready, pour it over the fillets, then garnish with the capers and sautéd shrimps in alternate little heaps. The cream may be omitted if desired, but, of course, its presence is a great improvement.

HAKE may be cooked in most of the ways described for haddock.

Grilled Fresh Haddock with Mustard Sauce

1 Fresh Haddock. Butter. | Pepper and Salt.

UTENSILS—Knife, brush for butter, grill, saucepan, wooden spoon, strainer or sieve. *Enough for 1 to 3 persons, according to size of haddock.*

Take a rather small haddock and slit it down the back by the side of the bone. Clean it, and remove the bone by slipping the point of a knife just underneath and gently working away the flesh. Cut off the head, tail and fins.

Pepper and salt the haddock inside, and leave it until time to cook, then brush it well over with melted butter. Butter a grill, and grill the fish over a slow fire or under the gas for 10 to 15 minutes, according to size. Serve with mustard sauce. Dish the fish up on a hot dish lined with a fish-paper, and garnish with a little parsley.

THE MUSTARD SAUCE

1 teaspoonful English Mustard.	1 dessertspoonful Vinegar.
1 teaspoonful French Mustard	2 tablespoonfuls Cream or Milk.
2 oz. Butter.	Small seasoning of Salt and
1 tablespoonful Flour.	Sugar.

½ pint Water.

Melt the butter in a saucepan, and stir in the flour and mustards, then the water and vinegar. Add a seasoning of salt and sugar, to taste. Rub through a fine strainer or sieve, then put all back into the saucepan again, re-warm, and add the cream or milk. Serve either in a sauce-boat or poured round the fish.

Boiled Dried Haddock

| 1 dried Haddock. | Pepper. Salt. |
| Milk. Butter. | Chopped Parsley. |

UTENSILS—Knife, stewpan, fish-slice, frying pan, chopping board. *Enough for 2 to 5 persons.*

Cut off the fins of the haddock, then skin it. The skin can be pulled off quite easily if the skin side of the haddock is first held to the front of the fire for a minute. Divide the fish into neat pieces about two inches square. Put these into a stewpan, with enough cold milk and water (in equal parts) to cover them well, allowing for their curling up a little in cooking. Bring to the boil, and let them simmer gently for 5 minutes or less, according to the thickness, and the extent to which the fish is cured.

Take up the pieces and arrange them neatly on a hot dish. Have ready about two tablespoonfuls of butter, just melted, and seasoned with white pepper. Pour this over the fish, and sprinkle with a little finely chopped parsley on the top. Serve very hot.

Baked Fillets with Tomato Sauce

3 large Tomatoes.	8 fillets of Plaice or Sole.
1 chopped Onion.	Seasoning.
1 tablespoonful Milk.	Tomato Sauce.

UTENSILS—Basin, knife, tablespoon, baking dish. *Enough for 4 persons.*

Mix the chopped tomatoes and onion together. Season the fillets of fish, then spread the tomatoes and onion on them. Fold them over and place in a buttered baking dish with a tablespoonful of milk, and cook for 20 minutes. Serve with tomato sauce.

Fish à la Dijon

1½ lb. Lemon Sole.	A few small **Mushrooms** or
½ gill Milk.	Prawns.
2 oz. Butter or Margarine.	A little grated **Parmesan Cheese.**
1 dessertspoonful Flour.	Salt and Pepper.

UTENSILS—Two small saucepans, fish-slice, entrée dish, wooden spoon, gill measure, dessertspoon. *Enough for 4 persons.*

Roll the fillets of fish with the skin inside, and place in a small saucepan with milk and seasoning, and simmer very gently for 10 minutes. Remove the fillets carefully with a slice and place them in an entrée dish.

Melt the butter in another small saucepan, add the flour, cook together for about a minute, then gradually add the milk in which the fish was cooked, stirring constantly. Add the mushrooms or prawns. Pour the sauce over the fish, grate a little Parmesan cheese on top, and brown under the grill.

Casserole of Smoked Fish

1 lb. Smoked Fillets.
1 oz. Margarine.
1 oz. Flour.
½ pint Milk.
¼ pint Water.

1 teaspoonful finely chopped Onions.
1 tablespoonful finely chopped Ham.
Pepper to taste.

UTENSILS—Casserole, knife, basin, wooden spoon, measuring spoons, gill measure. *Enough for 3 or 4 persons.*

Place the milk, water, onion, ham, margarine and pepper in the casserole. Cover and simmer for 10 minutes. Wash the fillets and cut them into neat pieces. Add to the mixture in the casserole and simmer for 20 to 30 minutes.

Mix the flour to a smooth paste with a little milk. Add it to the casserole and stir till boiling. Serve with mashed potatoes or thin fingers of toast.

Stewed Fresh Fillets

1 lb. fresh Fillets.
1 oz. Margarine.

½ pint Milk and Water mixed.
1 oz. Flour.

Salt and Pepper.

UTENSILS—Basin, wooden spoon, saucepan, fish-slice, wire rack. *Enough for 3 or 4 persons.*

Mix the flour to a smooth paste with a little of the milk and water. Place the remaining milk and water in a saucepan, and bring to the boiling point. Add the margarine, seasoning and fresh fillets.

Keep under boiling point till the fish is cooked (10 to 20 minutes), then remove the fish and drain thoroughly. Add the blended flour to the liquid remaining in the saucepan, and stir till boiling. Pour over the fish and garnish with lemon and parsley.

Soused Fillets of Herring

6 Fresh Herrings.
2 teaspoonfuls chopped Chives.
2 teaspoonfuls chopped Parsley.
2 Bayleaves.
12 Peppercorns.

Allspice. Pepper. Salt.
Boiling Water.
Vinegar. Salad Oil.
Garnish of Shredded Celery and Watercress.

How to fry fish (1)—(*Below*) Fillets should be cut across if too long. (*Above*) Dipping the fillets in beaten egg.

How to fry fish (2)—(*Below*) Placing the breadcrumbed fillets in the basket for frying in deep fat. (*Above*) Ready for the table.

UTENSILS—Knife, chopping board, pieces of tape, earthenware pie-dish, plate, teaspoon, gill or pint measure. *Enough for 6 persons.*

Fillet the herring, then wash and dry the fillets, and lay them on a board with the skin side down. Sprinkle with chopped chives, parsley, pepper and salt. Roll up the fillets, and bind each one round firmly with tape. Put them in an earthenware pie-dish, and sprinkle the spices, bayleaves and a teaspoonful of salt on the top. Fill the dish with vinegar and water mixed in the proportions of three parts of vinegar to one of water, and cover with an old plate.

Bake slowly in a very moderate oven for 1 hour. When cold remove the tapes and wipe off any spices that may be adhering to the fish. Arrange the fillets on a dish, and garnish them with shredded celery and bunches of watercress. Season with vinegar, salad oil, a little pepper and salt.

Boiled Cod

| A piece of Cod. | | Parsley. | Salt. |
| Vinegar. | Horseradish. | Lemon. | Sauce. |

UTENSILS—Fish-kettle, piece of tape, large kitchen spoon, cloth, knife, grater, brush, fish-slice.

Choose a nice thick middle cut, or the head and shoulders, as these are the best parts for boiling. (The tail is rather insipid if boiled, but can be satisfactorily fried in slices.) Wash and cleanse the fish thoroughly, and rub the inside well with salt ; this will harden the flesh, which is otherwise rather soft when quite fresh. Let it stand for an hour before boiling.

After this lay the fish on the strainer of the fish-kettle, and tie it in position with broad tape. Have sufficient cold water in the fish-kettle to cover the fish, with a quarter of a pound of salt and one tablespoonful of vinegar to every gallon. Lower the fish gently into the water, and bring to the boil. Simmer gently until done.

When done skim off any scum that may have risen, then lift the strainer out and stand it crosswise on top of the fish kettle. Lay a cloth over all just for a few minutes while it thoroughly drains. Place the fish on a dish with a fish-paper under, and brush it over with oiled butter. Garnish with scalloped lemon, grated horseradish, and chopped parsley, Serve with it either oyster, shrimp, anchovy or lobster sauce. (For SAUCES, see Index.)

C.I.O. G

Boiled Cod with Anchovies

Crimped Cod. | Parsley.   Salt.
12 Anchovies. | Potato Balls.

Dutch Sauce.

UTENSILS—Fish-kettle, fish-slice, fork.

Place a nice piece of crimped cod on a dish, and sprinkle it liberally all over with salt. Then place it on the strainer in a fish-kettle, with sufficient water to cover. Bring to the boil, and allow it to boil fast for 3 or 4 minutes. Draw to one side of the stove, and cook gently until done. Lift the strainer and fish out, and let it drain.

Lay the fish on a hot dish lined with a lace paper d'oyley, and garnish with potato balls (see Index), fresh parsley and filleted anchovies. Serve with Hollandaise sauce. (For SAUCES, see Index.)

Boiled Cod's Roe

Cod's Roe.   Vinegar. | Salt.   Peppercorns.

Sauce.

UTENSILS—Piece of muslin, saucepan, measuring spoons, *Enough for 2 or 3 persons.*

Wash the roe well in cold water, then tie it up in a piece of muslin. Put about a pint of water into a saucepan with one tablespoonful of vinegar, one teaspoonful of salt, and twelve peppercorns. Bring this to the boil, and then put the roe in. Boil for 15 minutes, then lift the roe out and let it drain.

Place on a hot dish, and pour parsley sauce or melted butter sauce over, with lemon juice, and a little cayenne added. The sauce can be either poured over, or the roe can be served on a hot dish lined with a lace paper d'oyley, garnished with parsley and scalloped lemon, and the sauce served separately in a sauce-boat.

Fried Cod's Roe

1 Cod's Roe.   1 Egg. | 2 oz. Butter.
White Breadcrumbs. | Parsley.

UTENSILS—Saucepan, piece of muslin, tablespoon, knife, basin, egg-beater, grater, frying pan, wire strainer. *Enough for 2 or 3 persons.*

Boil the roe as in the foregoing recipe, and let it get quite cold. Cut it into slices about half an inch thick. Dip the pieces into well-beaten egg, and then into fine white breadcrumbs.

Melt the butter in a frying pan, and when boiling put in the slices of roe. Fry them a nice golden brown on one side, then turn them and fry the other. Lay them on a wire strainer to drain, then arrange them in a circle on a dish with a fish-paper under, and place a bunch of parsley in the centre.

Cod's Steaks

3 Cod Steaks.   Breadcrumbs.
1 Egg.   Flour.   Pepper.   Salt.
                   Frying Fat.

UTENSILS—Two plates, basin, egg-beater, grater, frying pan, wire pastry rack, fish-slice. *Enough for 3 persons.*

Cut three nice steaks from the tail end of the cod. Dip them into flour highly seasoned with salt and pepper. Then dip them into whole beaten-up egg. Lastly, coat them well with fine white breadcrumbs.

Have ready plenty of boiling fat, lay in the steaks, and fry a nice golden colour. Lift them out, and let them drain on a wire pastry rack. Arrange the steaks on a hot dish, with a fish-paper under, and garnish with parsley. Serve with anchovy sauce. (For SAUCES, see Index.)

Baked Plaice

1 Plaice.   1 teaspoonful chopped Parsley.
3 oz. Butter.   Breadcrumbs.
                  Pepper and Salt.

UTENSILS—Knife, cloth, baking dish, brush for butter, basin, grater, basting spoon, fish-slice, frying pan, chopping board, measuring spoons. *Enough for 2 to 4 persons.*

Select a nice thick plaice. Wash and cleanse it thoroughly, trim off the fins and tail, then dry it. Butter a baking dish thickly, and lay the plaice in it. Brush it over with oiled butter. Mix together the finely chopped parsley, four tablespoonfuls of finely made white breadcrumbs, a small teaspoonful of salt, and a quarter of a teaspoonful of white pepper. Sprinkle the top of the fish thickly with this, and put small pieces of butter thickly over the top. Bake in a brisk oven, basting it once or twice with a little of the butter. This will take from 20 to 30 minutes, according to the size of the fish.

When cooked lift the fish out carefully with a fish-slice, and lay it on a dish. Garnish with fried parsley and lemon. (For FRIED PARSLEY, see Index.) Serve anchovy sauce with it. (For SAUCES, see Index.)

Stewed Plaice

1 or 2 Plaice.	½ Lemon.
2 Eggs.　　2 Onions.	Cayenne.　　Salt.
1 oz. Butter.	½ pint Water.
½ blade of Mace.	Garnish, as described.

UTENSILS—Stewpan, knife, basin, egg-beater, kitchen spoon, fish-slice. *Enough for 2 to 6 persons, according to size of fish.*

Cut the fish into pieces about two inches wide. Lay them on a dish, and sprinkle well over with salt. Let them remain ½ hour. Peel the onions, and slice them thinly. Fry them in a stewpan with the butter, until they are a nice golden brown.

Scrape as much of the salt off the fish as possible, but do not wash it. Lay the pieces in the stewpan, on the top of the onions. Add the mace and the half-pint of water. Cook gently for about 20 minutes, until the fish is done. Do not let it boil fast or the fish will break. Take the pieces out carefully, lay them on a hot dish, and keep them hot.

Beat the yolks of eggs well. When the fish liquor has cooled a little, stir in the beaten eggs with the juice of half a lemon and a dust of cayenne pepper. Return it to the fire until it thickens, but do not let it boil. Now pour it all over the fish. Garnish with parsley and forcemeat balls ; or with button onions which have been boiled, then stewed in brown gravy.

Fried Plaice with Caper Sauce

1 Plaice.　　2 Eggs.	Flour.　　Salt.

UTENSILS—Knife, cloth, 2 basins, egg-beater, stewpan, wire sieve, fish-slice, frying pan, frying basket, saucepan, wooden spoon, measuring spoons. *Enough for 2 to 4 persons.*

Clean and scrape a nice thick plaice, and trim the fins, head and tail. Cut the fish right down the centre, from head to tail. Then cut the fish on the slant into slices, 2 inches broad, so that they form almost diamond-shaped pieces. A moderate sized fish will make six pieces, each half making three, or a large will cut into eight. Wash, and let the pieces lie in salt water for 10 minutes, then dry well in a cloth.

Have some flour ready on a sheet of paper, put the fish into it, take the four corners of the paper and roll the pieces backwards and forwards in the flour, so that all parts are well coated. Dip each piece into the beaten egg.

Put enough clarified fat or lard into a stewpan, so that the fish will be well covered, first making sure that there is no moisture on the fat. Heat the fat slowly over the fire, and when quite boiling drop in the pieces of fish. When the fat is really boiling it will be quite silent, and a slight blue vapour will arise from it. As soon as the fish is put in, draw the pan rather to one side, so that the fish may not get too brown before being cooked through, but it must boil all the time. It will take about 10 minutes.

When nicely browned and cooked, take it out and drain it on a sieve. Keep it hot, either on the plate-rack or in front of the fire. If properly fried, the fish should be quite dry and free from fat. Pile the pieces up high on a dish lined vith a lace paper d'oyley, and garnish with fried parsley and lemon cut into butterflies.

THE FRIED PARSLEY

Wash the parsley quite clean, pick it free from long stalks, dry it thoroughly, and put it into a frying basket. Plunge it into plenty of fat that is just boiling, and let it remain for 1 or 2 seconds till crisp. Do not keep it in longer than is just necessary to make it crisp, or it will lose its colour.

THE CAPER SAUCE

1 dessertspoonful Capers.	½ pint hot Milk or Water.
1 oz. Butter.	1 tablespoonful Lemon Juice
¾ oz. Flour. Salt.	or Vinegar.

Melt the butter in a small saucepan, then mix in the flour and salt with a wooden spoon. Add by degrees the hot water or milk, also the vinegar or lemon juice, stirring well all the time. Boil for 5 minutes, then add the finely chopped capers, and serve in a hot sauce-boat.

Broiled Whitings

2 Whitings. | Butter.   Oil.
Pepper and Salt.

UTENSILS—Cloth, basin, knife, brush, gridiron, fish-slice. *Enough for 2 persons.*

Wash the whitings in salt and water and dry them well. Split each fish open all down the backbone, and cut off the heads. Brush them over with salad oil, and sprinkle with pepper and salt. Oil the bars of the gridiron, and lay the fish on. Broil for 5 minutes, turning once during the cooking.

If the fish are very thick, they will take a few minutes longer. Take them off the fire, and lay on a hot dish. Pour about a tablespoonful of oiled butter over each fish, and serve very hot. Garnish with a little fresh parsley.

Baked Whitings

3 or 4 Whitings.	1 gill Fish Stock.
A bunch of Sweet Herbs.	½ oz. Flour.
2 oz. Butter.	Carmine.
1 gill White Wine.	Salt and Pepper.

Garnish, as described.

UTENSILS—Knife, chopping board, baking tin, larger baking tin, basting spoon, dish, saucepan, wooden spoon, pointed strainer, fish-slice. *Enough for 3 or 4 persons.*

Clean and skin the fish, then lay them in a well buttered baking tin. Finely chop the herbs and sprinkle the fish with them, also with pepper and salt. Pour the wine round the fish. Lay a buttered paper over, and stand the tin in another one containing water. Bake in a moderate oven from 10 to 15 minutes, basting them frequently with the wine.

Lift the fish out, and lay them on a hot dish. Add a gill of fish stock to the liquor in the baking tin. Melt half an ounce of butter in a small saucepan, stir in half an ounce of flour, then pour in the stock, etc., from the baking tin. There should be a half-pint altogether. Stir this until it boils, and add salt and pepper if required, and two or three drops of carmine.

Pour this sauce through a pointed strainer round the fish. Garnish with button mushrooms, warmed in a little stock, and scalloped lemon, or with parsley.

Fried Whitings

3 Whitings.	1 Egg.	Breadcrumbs.	Flour.

UTENSILS—Knife, plate, basin, egg-beater, grater, frying pan, fish-slice. *Enough for 3 persons.*

Skin and clean the whitings, and truss them with their tails through their mouths. Flour them and dip them into whole beaten-up egg, and then in white breadcrumbs. Fry in plenty of boiling fat until they are nicely browned all over. Take them up, and drain on a sheet of kitchen paper. Serve them on a hot dish lined with a lace paper d'oyley. Serve with Hollandaise sauce. (For SAUCES, see Index.)

Soufflé of Whiting

9 oz. Whiting, free from skin and bone.	2 gills Milk.
	Parsley.
1 gill Fish Stock.	Browned Breadcrumbs.
3 oz. Butter.	Pepper. Salt.
Flour. 4 Eggs.	Cayenne.

UTENSILS—Pestle and mortar, saucepan, wooden spoon, 2 basins, egg-beater, soufflé tin, grater, baking tin. *Enough for 4 to 6 persons.*

Put the meat from the whiting into a mortar, and pound well. Melt butter in a saucepan. Add flour, and fry together without browning, then add fish stock and milk. The fish stock can be made from the bones and skins of the whiting. Cook at the side of the stove for 10 minutes.

Take the saucepan off the fire, and beat in the yolks of the eggs one by one. Then add the pounded whiting, and pepper, salt and cayenne, to taste. Beat all well together; then, lastly, add the whites of the eggs beaten to a stiff froth, with a tiny pinch of salt. Tie a well-buttered band of stiff paper round the outside of a well-buttered soufflé tin, so that the paper stands about two inches above the tin. Pour in the mixture immediately the whites of eggs are added, and sprinkle the top with browned breadcrumbs.

Bake in a moderate oven for ¾ hour. Remove the paper, fasten a folded napkin, or fancy paper, round the tin. Sprinkle the soufflé with finely chopped parsley and send to table at once, or it will sink. Almost any white fish may be treated in the same way.

Baked Gurnet

2 Gurnets.	2 tablespoonfuls browned Breadcrumbs.
1 oz. Butter.	
2 tablespoonfuls chopped Mushrooms.	Lemon Juice.
	3 tablespoonfuls White Wine.
1 Shallot.	Pepper and Salt.

Garnish, as described.

UTENSILS—Knife, fireproof dish, basting spoon, tablespoon. *Enough for 2 persons.*

Clean and skin the gurnets, and cut off the heads and fins. Score them across three times on each side.

Sprinkle them with two teaspoonfuls of finely chopped shallot, the finely chopped mushrooms, a little pepper and salt and lemon juice. Lay them in a well-buttered, deep fireproof dish. Pour the wine over the fish, and put the butter, in small pieces over the top. Lay a thickly buttered paper over them, and bake in a quick oven until they are cooked, basting them frequently with the wine.

About 5 minutes before they are done, sprinkle the browned breadcrumbs on top so that they get thoroughly hot through. Wipe the edges of the dish, and serve the fish in it, standing it on another. Garnish with fresh parsley and lemon. If preferred, the wine may be omitted, and milk or fish stock be substituted.

NOTE.—Gurnet may also be plainly fried, or boiled, or filleted and dressed in several different ways.

Boiled Mackerel

| 3 Mackerel. | Salted Water. | Sauce. |

UTENSILS—Scrubbing brush, stewpan, fish-slice. *Enough for 3 persons.*

These fish ought, properly speaking, to be cooked and eaten almost immediately after being caught. They do not keep at all well; and a mackerel wanting in freshness is most unwholesome.

Clean three good-sized mackerel, scrubbing them well with a brush to get off the gelatinous outer skin which they have instead of scales. Put them into boiling salted water, and boil gently until done. This will take about 10 to 15 minutes. When cooked, drain the fish, and lay them on a hot dish, on a lace paper d'oyley. Serve with Fennel sauce. (For SAUCES, see Index.)

NOTE.—Mackerel may also be pickled in the same way as herrings, or grilled, and served with black butter.

Baked Red Mullet

4 Red Mullet.	1 dessertspoonful chopped Parsley.
2 oz. Butter.	Pepper. Salt.
Tomato Sauce.	3 tablespoonfuls Breadcrumbs.

UTENSILS—Gratin dish, knife, grater, plate, saucepan, chopping board, spoons, basting spoon. *Enough for 4 or 8 persons.*

Clean the fish and lay them in a well-buttered gratin dish. Some people prefer to leave the trails and liver in these fish, and only remove the gills, but this is optional. Season with a sprinkling of pepper and salt. Pour three or four tablespoonfuls of tomato sauce over them.

Mix the finely chopped parsley with the breadcrumbs. Melt the butter, and stir it into the crumbs and parsley. Mix these well together, then sprinkle them over the fish. Put the dish in the oven, and bake till the fish are done (about 15 to 20 minutes), frequently basting them with their own liquor. When cooked stand the gratin dish in another, and serve very hot.

Baked Mullet in Paper Cases

3 Red Mullet.	1 teaspoonful Lemon Juice.
Salad Oil.	½ oz. Flour.
2 tablespoonfuls Sherry.	½ oz. Butter.
1 teaspoonful Anchovy Sauce.	Salt. Cayenne.

UTENSILS—Measuring spoons, baking tin, saucepan, wooden spoon, strainer, knife. *Enough for 3 persons.*

Sprinkle each mullet with a little salt. Cut three pieces of kitchen paper large enough to roll the fish in, and oil the paper well. Roll each fish up in a piece of the paper, tie the ends firmly, and twist the string once or twice round to keep the paper together. Lay them in a baking tin, and bake in a moderate oven.

Medium-sized fish will take 20 minutes, large ones a little longer. When cooked, keep them thoroughly hot. Melt the butter in a saucepan, add the flour, then the gravy which has run from the fish, the anchovy sauce, the lemon juice, a dust of cayenne pepper, and lastly, the sherry. Bring to the boil, strain and pour into a hot sauce-boat, ready to be served with the fish.

Remove the strings from the fish carefully, but let the fish remain in the papers. Lay them on a very hot dish, and send to table garnished with parsley.

Halibut Steaks

1½ lb. Halibut.	Pepper. Salt.
1½ oz. Butter.	Maître d'Hôtel Sauce.
Lemon Juice.	Garnish, as described.

UTENSILS—Knife, baking tin, fish-slice, saucepan, wooden spoon, measuring spoons, pint measure. *Enough for 4 persons.*

Wash the fish and cut it in slices half an inch thick. Butter a baking tin, and lay the slices of fish in it. Squeeze over them the juice of half a lemon, and sprinkle with pepper and salt. Lay a well-buttered paper on the top of the fish, and bake in a moderate oven for 10 to 15 minutes.

Lift out the slices of fish, and lay them on a hot dish. Pour the maître d'hôtel sauce over, so as to coat the fish well. Garnish with fresh parsley, and sprinkle with coralline pepper.

THE MAÎTRE D'HÔTEL SAUCE

½ oz. Flour.	1 dessertspoonful chopped
½ oz. Butter.	Parsley.
¼ pint Milk.	½ teaspoonful Shallot.
¼ pint Stock.	1 teaspoonful Lemon Juice.

Pepper and Salt.

Melt the butter in a saucepan, add the shallot, very finely chopped, and cook gently at the side of the stove for 10 minutes. Mix in the flour, then gradually stir in the stock and milk. Add pepper and salt to taste, then the finely chopped parsley, and, last of all, when it is off the fire, add the lemon juice. Pour in the gravy, which has run from the fish in cooking, and then pour the whole over the fish and serve.

Boiled Halibut

5 lb. Halibut.	A bunch of Herbs (Bayleaf,
1 Carrot.	Thyme and Parsley).
1 Onion. 1 Leek.	2 tablespoonfuls Vinegar.
½ head of Celery.	2 large tablespoonfuls Salt.
6 Peppercorns.	Garnish, as described.

UTENSILS—Saucepan or fish-kettle, fish-slice, tablespoon. *Enough for 6 or 7 persons.*

Put the piece of halibut into a saucepan, and cover it with fresh cold water. Add the carrot, onion, leek and celery, all sliced. Add also the herbs, peppercorns, salt and vinegar. Put the lid on the saucepan, and bring it to the boil. When it boils, draw to one side, and let it simmer gently until the fish is cooked. It will take about 10 minutes.

Lift out the fish, drain, then lay it on a hot dish. Spread anchovy butter over all the fish. Garnish with hard-boiled yolk of egg, and filleted anchovies.

Boiled Brill

1 Brill.	Lemon.	Parsley.	Salt.
Butter.	Vinegar.	Lobster Coral.	

Garnish, as described.

UTENSILS—Knife, fish-kettle, brush for butter, fish-slice, dessertspoon, chopping board. *Enough for 4 to 6 persons.*

Clean the fish, and trim off the fins, then rub the fish over with lemon juice. Lay it in a fish-kettle with sufficient water to cover it, adding salt and vinegar in the proper proportions. (For BOILING FISH, see p. 176.) Bring it to the boil, then draw the fish-kettle to one side, and let it simmer gently until the fish is done.

If it is a rather small fish, it will take about 10 minutes after it comes to the boil. Lift it out, drain, then brush it over with oiled butter. Lay it on a very hot dish, and garnish with chopped parsley and lobster coral laid in alternate bars across the fish. Arrange bunches of parsley, and scalloped lemon around the fish. Serve with lobster, shrimp, Hollandaise or any suitable sauce. (For SAUCES, see Index.)

Baked Brill, with Crayfish

1 Brill.	2 oz. Butter.
2 tablespoonfuls finely chopped Shallot.	1 teaspoonful finely minced Herbs.
¼ lb. Mushrooms.	Breadcrumbs.
1 gill Gravy.	6 Crayfish, and garnish, as
1 gill Madeira.	described.

Pepper and Salt.

UTENSILS—Knife, baking dish, saucepan, grater, strainer, measuring spoons, kitchen spoon, gill measure. *Enough for 6 persons.*

Choose a good-sized fish, and clean it well. Score it across the back. Chop the shallot and mushrooms very finely. Butter a baking-dish with one ounce of the butter, and spread the minced shallot and mushrooms over the inside of the dish. Pour in the gravy and Madeira. Now lay the fish in with the back downwards.

Melt the remaining ounce of butter in a saucepan, and stir in as many finely made white breadcrumbs as will absorb it. Season the crumbs with pepper, salt and the finely minced herbs, then spread them over the fish. Put the dish in the oven, and bake for ½ hour, frequently basting with gravy.

When done, lift the fish carefully on to a dish. Strain the gravy and pour it gently round. Garnish with half a dozen crayfish, some sprigs of fresh parsley and slices of scalloped cucumber.

Brill à la Tyrol

¾ lb. Boiled Brill.	Parsley.
½ pint thick Veloute Sauce.	1 oz. grated Cheddar Cheese.
2 oz. grated Parmesan Cheese.	Coralline Pepper.

UTENSILS—Saucepan, wooden spoon, knife, gratin dish, baking tin, chopping board. *Enough for 2 or 3 persons.*

Take half a pint of thick Veloute sauce (for SAUCES, see Index), and stir into this the grated Parmesan cheese, a teaspoonful of finely chopped parsley, and a dust of coralline pepper. Cut the brill into dice shapes, and mix this in also. Thickly butter a gratin dish and pour in the fish mixture. Sprinkle one ounce of grated Cheddar cheese on the top. Stand the dish in a tin containing boiling water, and bake in a quick oven for 10 to 15 minutes.

When cooked, take out the dish, stand it on another, and sprinkle the top with finely chopped parsley, and coralline pepper. Serve immediately.

John Dory

UTENSILS—Knife, fish-kettle, fish-slice.

This fish is best boiled. Clean the fish thoroughly, trim off the fins, but do not remove the head. Put it into a fish-kettle, and cook as described in the directions for boiling fish (page 176). Garnish with parsley, cut lemon, prawns or any suitable garnish. Serve with anchovy, shrimp, lobster, or Genoese sauce. (For SAUCES, see Index.)

Boiled Skate

1½ lb. crimped Skate.	½ a stick of Celery.
A bunch of Herbs.	12 Peppercorns.
½ a Carrot.	French Vinegar.
1 Onion. Salt.	Black Butter, or Sauce.

UTENSILS—Trussing needle and string, basin, stewpan, knife, piece of muslin, large kitchen spoon, measuring spoons, fish-slice. *Enough for 4 or 5 persons.*

Roll up the pieces of skate either in rounds or like the letter S. Secure them in shape with a trussing needle and string. Lay them in well-salted cold water for about an hour, then wash and rinse well. Put the pieces into a stewpan, with sufficient water to cover.

Slice the onion, carrot, and celery. Tie them all up in a

piece of muslin with the herbs and peppercorns. Put them in with the fish, and add two dessertspoonfuls of salt, and one tablespoonful of French vinegar to every quart of water. Put the pan on the stove, bring to the boil, and skim well. Let it simmer for 5 minutes, until the fish is cooked.

Lift the fish out carefully, arrange it prettily on a hot dish, cut the strings and pull them gently out. Pour black butter over the fish, and serve immediately. (For BLACK BUTTER, see Index.) Or a garnish of parsley can be used and Tartare sauce can be handed in a hot sauce-boat with it. (For TARTARE SAUCE, see Index.)

Boiled Smelts

12 Smelts. Fish Stock.	Lemon Juice.
Melted Butter.	Coralline Pepper.
Chopped Parsley.	Croûtons of fried Bread.

UTENSILS—Cloth, fish-kettle, fish-slice, saucepan, strainer, knife, frying pan, chopping board. *Enough for 4 to 6 persons.*

Clean the smelts by drawing them through the gills. Wash, and wipe them well. Arrange them on their stomachs on the fish-drainer.

Place them in the stewpan, and cover with fish stock. Bring almost to the boil, then draw them to the side of the stove for 5 minutes. Do not let them boil. Lift the fish out carefully, drain well, and arrange them on a hot dish.

Make half a pint of melted butter, add one teaspoonful of strained lemon juice, and pour this over the fish. (For MELTED BUTTER, see Index.) Sprinkle finely chopped parsley and coralline pepper on each alternate fish. Arrange fried croûtons of bread round the fish, garnishing the croûtons with chopped parsley and coralline pepper.

Fried Smelts

12 Smelts.	Breadcrumbs.
Beaten Egg.	Frying Fat.

UTENSILS—Cloth, plate, basin, egg-beater, grater, frying pan, fish-slice, wire rack. *Enough for 4 to 6 persons.*

Smelts should be very fresh, and must not be washed more than is absolutely necessary. Dry them in a cloth, then roll them in a little flour, afterwards shaking off as much as possible. Dip them in whole beaten-up egg, then into finely made white breadcrumbs. Fry them in plenty of boiling fat, until they are a pale golden colour. Drain them, arrange on a dish lined with a lace paper d'oyley, and garnish with fresh parsley

Fried Whitebait, Plain and Devilled

Whitebait.		Coralline or Cayenne Pepper.
Flour.	Frying Fat.	Brown Bread and Butter, as
Lemon.	Salt.	described.

UTENSILS—Two basins, stewpan, frying basket, cloth, wire sieve, knife, egg-beater, 2 saucers, brush, fish-slice.

The whitebait should be carefully picked over, and freed from weed, etc. Then put them into a basin of cold water, with a lump of ice, until wanted. Have ready a deep stewpan, quite half-full of boiling fat. Put two tablespoonfuls of flour on a dry cloth, then put in a handful of the whitebait drained free from water. Shake them about in the flour, then put them in a frying basket. Shake off all the superfluous flour, and plunge them into the boiling fat for about a minute and a half. Take them out, and turn on to a wire sieve.

Do another handful of the whitebait in the same way, and so continue until all are cooked. Now put them all into the frying basket. See that there is plenty of fat in the stewpan to cover all the fish well, and see that it quite boils up again (with a slight blue vapour coming from it). Put the basket containing all the fish back into the fat, and fry for a minute or two until they are quite crisp.

Keep half the fish plain, and sprinkle the other half with salt and coralline pepper or cayenne. Dish them in two piles on a hot dish lined with a fish-paper, and garnish with slices of lemon and a few little sprigs of fresh green parsley. Keep very hot and serve quickly, for being so small they soon get cold.

BREAD AND BUTTER ROLLS

Cut about one dozen very thin slices of brown bread and butter from a loaf not more than one day old. Roll the slices neatly, and trim the ends. Beat the white of an egg slightly, then chop about a dessertspoonful of parsley very finely, wring it quite dry in the corner of a cloth, and put it into a saucer. Put about a teaspoonful of coralline pepper in another saucer. Brush over the ends of the rolls of bread and butter with the white of egg, and dip one end of each into the chopped parsley, and the other ends into the coralline pepper. Arrange the rolls on a lace paper on a plate, in a circle; one resting on the other, with alternate colours showing up, and stand a little bunch of parsley in the centre.

Boiled Trout

1 or 2 Trout.	Butter. Sauce.
2 tablespoonfuls Vinegar.	Parsley. 4 Cloves.
½ a Carrot. 1 Onion.	A bunch of Herbs.
1 tablespoonful Salt.	

UTENSILS—Knife, cloth, fish-kettle or saucepan, fish-slice. *Enough for 1 or 2 persons.*

Scale, clean and draw the trout, and wipe them dry in a cloth. Put them in a fish-kettle or saucepan, and pour in sufficient water to cover the fish. Add the vinegar, salt, carrot, onion, cloves and herbs. Set the fish-kettle on the fire, and gently bring to the boil. Let it continue boiling gently for 10 to 15 minutes, according to the size of the fish. If the water boils hard the skins may break.

Take the fish out, drain well, and lay them on a folded napkin on a hot dish. Rub a little butter over them, garnish lightly with fresh parsley, and serve with Hollandaise sauce.

Mayonnaise of Trout

1 good-sized Trout.	Mayonnaise Sauce.
Court Bouillon, as described.	Mayonnaise Aspic.
Aspic Jelly. Lettuce.	Beetroot and other garnish.

UTENSILS—Knife, fish-kettle, wire sieve, fish-slice, saucepan, strainer, measuring spoons. *Enough for 2 persons.*

Clean a good-sized trout, draw it by the gills, and wipe it thoroughly inside and out. Put it into a fish-kettle with sufficient boiling court bouillon to cover it. Boil gently until the fish is done, in about 20 minutes. Lift it carefully out on to a sieve, and leave until cold.

Have ready a block of aspic jelly the length and breadth of the fish, and one and a half inches deep, or cut a croûton of bread from a stale tin loaf the same size, fry it a pale golden colour, and let it get quite cold. When the fish is quite cold, mask it with mayonnaise aspic, and let it set.

Stand the border (aspic or bread) on a dish, and sprinkle it thickly with shredded lettuce. Lay the trout carefully on it and garnish down the centre of the fish with shredded chillies, gherkins, beetroot, or any pretty garnish. Arrange prettily round the croûton the hearts of three or four small lettuce, cut in halves or quarters, quarters of hard-boiled egg, slices of beetroot and chopped aspic jelly. Serve mayonnaise sauce in a sauce-boat. (For SAUCES, see Index.)

THE COURT BOUILLON

¼ of a Carrot.	1 tablespoonful Salt.
¼ of an Onion.	1 teaspoonful Basil.
2 large sprigs of Parsley.	1 oz. Butter.
1 teaspoonful Thyme.	½ pint Vinegar.

Slice the carrot and onion, and put them with the parsley, thyme, salt, basil, and butter, into a saucepan. Stand them on the stove for 10 minutes. Now add two quarts of water and half a pint of vinegar and simmer all together gently for about an hour, then strain and use.

NOTE.—White wine, such as Chablis or Sauterne, may be used instead of vinegar, but in that case more wine must be used than vinegar, say half wine and half water.

Fried Sole

1 Sole. 1 Egg.	Frying Fat.
Breadcrumbs.	Flour. Garnish.
Pepper and Salt.	Maître d'Hôtel Butter.

UTENSILS—Knife, cloth, plate, basin, egg-beater, grater, frying pan, wire rack, fish-slice. *Enough for 1 or 2 persons.*

Skin and clean a sole, and trim off the fins with a pair of scissors. Wash the fish and dry in a clean cloth. Dip it in flour, seasoned with pepper and salt, then shake off all superfluous flour, dip the fish into whole beaten-up egg, and finally into fine white breadcrumbs.

Have ready a pan with plenty of boiling lard sufficient to cover the fish well. Plunge the fish in, and fry until it is a nice golden brown. Take up the fish and place it on a wire rack, or kitchen paper, so that it may drain perfectly free from fat. Lay it on a hot dish, either on a d'oyley or fish-paper, and garnish with cut lemon and parsley. Hand small blocks of maître d'hôtel butter with it.

Great care should be taken to have the fat boiling (with blue vapour rising), and to drain the fish thoroughly.

Fried Filleted Sole

UTENSILS—Knife, frying pan, frying basket, fish-slice.

After filleting the fish, and trimming the fillets neatly, fry them in the manner described in the foregoing recipe. Instead of the butter, serve anchovy sauce, or some other suitable sauce, with it. (FOR SAUCES, see Index.)

Sole à la Béchamel

1 large Sole.	Lemon. Parsley.
1 Egg. Butter.	Béchamel Sauce.

UTENSILS—Knife, baking tin, larger baking tin, saucepan, sieve, wooden spoon, 3 saucers, chopping board, fish-slice. *Enough for 2 or 4 persons.*

Skin and fillet a large sole, or two small ones. Cut the fillets into neat pieces of about the same size. Well butter a baking tin. Lay the fillets in it, folding one-third of each fillet back underneath, so that the fillet is double the thickness at the broad end. Squeeze over them the juice of half a lemon, and sprinkle with pepper and salt. Lay a buttered paper over, and stand the tin in another containing hot water. Cook in a moderate oven for 10 minutes.

Boil one egg hard, and rub the yolk through a sieve. Lift the fillets carefully out, and dish them in two rows down a hot dish, with the thick end of one fillet resting on the thin end of the next one. Pour about half a pint of creamy Béchamel sauce over them. (See page 149.) Next sprinkle each alternate fillet with the rubbed yolk of egg and finely chopped parsley. Garnish round the edges with slices of hard-boiled egg and sprigs of fresh parsley.

NOTE.—This is a good way of cooking fish for an invalid, but you must then be careful with the pepper and salt.

Soles with White Wine

2 Soles.	Parsley. Chives.
½ lb. Button Mushrooms.	6 Peppercorns.
3 oz. Butter.	1 teaspoonful Rice Flour.
A bunch of Herbs.	Fish Cuttings. Salt.

½ pint White Wine.

UTENSILS—Knife, pie-dish, saucepan, strainer, large kitchen spoon, basin, wooden spoon, gill or pint measure, teaspoon, pointed strainer. *Enough for 4 persons.*

Choose two moderate-sized soles. Skin and clean them,

cut off the heads, and with a sharp pair of scissors cut off the fins running down each side-edge of the fish, also cut about one inch off the tail. Put the trimmings into a saucepan with the stalks and peelings of the mushrooms, a bunch of herbs, parsley, three-pennyworth of fish cuttings, half a dozen peppercorns, one gill of white cooking wine (Chablis or Sauterne), three-quarters of a pint of water and half a teaspoonful of salt. Bring these to the boil, and simmer for $\frac{3}{4}$ hour.

Thickly butter a pie-dish large enough to hold the soles side by side. Sprinkle it thickly over the bottom with the mushrooms, finely chopped, and a teaspoonful of finely chopped chives. Lay in the fish, and strain the stock round them. Lay a buttered paper over the top, and bake in a moderate oven for 20 minutes. Take out the dish, and pour the stock carefully from it into a clean saucepan. Skim it, and reduce until it is half the quantity.

Add one gill of fish stock, and one gill of white wine. Bring to the boil, then thicken with a teaspoonful of rice flour mixed in a little cold water. Lastly, add a piece of fresh butter the size of a pigeon's egg. Lay the fish on a hot dish, and pour the sauce over them, through a pointed strainer, so that they are well masked with it. Garnish with a few of the button mushrooms kept whole, and cooked in a little of the stock. On the top of each mushroom sprinkle a pinch of coralline pepper, and serve.

Boiled Turbot

| 1 Turbot. | Sauce. | 3 large Lemons. |
| Parsley. | | Salt. |

UTENSILS—Turbot-kettle, basin, knife, lemon squeezer, fish-slice. *Enough for 6 to 8 persons.*

For boiling a whole turbot it is necessary to have a turbot-kettle, a fish-kettle of special shape, to allow this broad fish to lie conveniently in. After thoroughly cleaning the fish let it lie in salt and water for an hour, then rinse it in fresh cold water. Do not cut off the fins. Rub the fish all over with lemon-juice. This whitens the flesh and keeps it firm. Make two or three incisions or notches in the dark side of the skin to prevent it cracking.

Lay the fish in the kettle with a bunch of parsley and the juice of two large lemons. Cover the fish with water salted in the proportion of a quarter-pound of salt to each gallon of water. When the water begins to boil draw the kettle to the side of the fire, and let it simmer until the fish is tender. When cooked drain it carefully.

Lay it on a fish-paper on a hot dish, and garnish with a border of fresh parsley round the fish, and slices or quarters of lemon. Serve lobster, tartare, shrimp, prawn, or white sauce with it. (For SAUCES, see Index.) If liked, the fish may be garnished with lobster coral, when lobster sauce is served with it.

Baked Fillets of Turbot

Cold Turbot.	1 Egg.	Breadcrumbs.
½ lb. Salt Butter.		Coralline Pepper.
Lemon.	Parsley.	Lobster or Shrimp Sauce.

UTENSILS—Fish knife and fork, basin, egg-beater, plate, grater, fireproof dish, fish-slice, spoon, wire rack, saucepan.

This is a very good way of re-heating boiled turbot. Remove all the bones and skin from the cold turbot—if possible do this while the fish is still warm. When cold, cut it into neat squares. Dip them into whole beaten-up egg, then into finely made white breadcrumbs which have been seasoned with pepper and salt.

Thickly butter a fireproof dish, and lay in the fillets. Put them into a moderate oven, and keep constantly basted with the butter. Bake a nice golden brown, which will take about 15 minutes. Lift out the fillets, and drain well. Arrange them on a hot dish, and sprinkle over with finely chopped parsley and coralline pepper. Pour the sauce round and garnish with a few bunches of parsley.

THE SAUCE

Take the remains of any shrimp or lobster sauce that was served with the boiled turbot ; half a pint will be sufficient. Re-heat thoroughly, add a few drops of lemon juice, and serve in a hot sauce-boat.

Turbot with Cream Sauce

Remains of Turbot.	4 tablespoonfuls Cream.
1½ oz. Flour.	Yolk of Egg.
1½ oz. Butter.	Parsley. Salt.
1 small Onion.	1 blade of Mace.
¾ pint Milk.	Cayenne Pepper.

Potato Border, as described.

UTENSILS—Three saucepans, wooden spoon, strainer, knife, sieve, baking sheet, basin, egg-beater, brush, grater, fork or potato masher, tablespoon.

Put the milk, onion, mace, and a dust of cayenne pepper in a saucepan, and boil for 15 minutes. Melt the butter in another saucepan, and stir in the flour. Strain the seasoned milk into this, and stir until it re-boils. Season to taste with pepper and salt.

Remove the bones and skin from the fish (while warm if possible). Cut the fish into dice shapes, and put these into the saucepan with the milk, etc. Add the cream, and just bring all to boiling point.

Put a potato border (prepared as below) on to a dish. Pour the contents of the saucepan into it. Sprinkle with hard-boiled yolk of egg (rubbed through a sieve), and a little finely chopped parsley, and serve. This turbot mixture may also be scalloped, but then there must not be too much sauce. Or it may be put in a vol-au-vent.

THE POTATO BORDER

Prepare some potato purée (see Index.) Well butter a flat baking sheet, and form an oval border on it two inches high and large enough to contain the fish in the middle. Brush it over with well-beaten egg.

Prepare some buttered breadcrumbs, by putting fresh white crumbs in a saucepan, and heating them with just as much butter as they will absorb. Strew these thickly on top of the border after it is brushed over with the egg. Put the border into a moderate oven, and bake until it is a golden brown. Keep it thoroughly hot until it is required for use.

Grilled Salmon in Paper

| 3 slices of Salmon. | Parsley. Sauce. |
| Salad Oil. | Pepper and Salt. |

UTENSILS—Brush, grill, white paper, fork or fish-slice. *Enough for 3 persons.*

The slices of salmon should be an inch and a half thick. Brush them over with salad oil, and season with pepper and salt. Wrap each slice in a well-oiled piece of white paper, and twist the ends of the paper well to keep it firm.

Oil the bars of the grill, and make it thoroughly hot, then lay the fish on. (See BROILING FISH, page 178.) Grill over a clear fire for about 15 minutes, turning once in the cooking.

When done, carefully remove the papers, and quickly lay the slices on a hot dish. Garnish with a little fresh parsley. Serve with Tartare sauce in a sauce-boat. (For SAUCES, see Index.)

Boiled Salmon

1 Salmon.		A sprig of Thyme.	
½ teacupful French Vinegar.		A blade of Mace.	
1 Onion.	Butter.	12 Peppercorns.	
3 Cloves.	Salt.	Water.	Cucumber.
	Garnish.	Sauce.	

UTENSILS—Piece of muslin, fish-kettle, fish-slice, knife.

Cleanse and scald the salmon. Butter a piece of muslin, and roll the fish in it. Lay it in a fish-kettle with sufficient slightly salted water to cover. Add the vinegar, sliced onion, the cloves, thyme, mace, and peppercorns. Boil the salmon with these, and allow 10 minutes' boiling to each pound weight of fish. A little less time can be allowed if the fish is very thin.

When done, take it up and remove the muslin. Lay the fish carefully on a hot dish with a lace paper d'oyley. Garnish with cut lemon and sprigs of parsley, and serve with Hollandaise, lobster, or any suitable sauce. Hand sliced cucumber with the fish as well as the sauce. (For SAUCES, see Index.)

Boiled Salmon Cutlets

3 slices of Salmon.	Potatoes.	
Fish Stock.	Sauce.	Garnish.

UTENSILS—Cloth, saucepan, wire rack, fish-slice. *Enough for 3 persons.*

The slices of salmon should be about one inch thick. After being washed and dried put them into a saucepan with sufficient boiling fish stock to cover. Watch the stock re-boil, then draw to one side and simmer gently until cooked, which will take about 10 minutes, then take up the cutlets and drain well. Arrange them on a fish paper on a hot dish, one cutlet resting on the other, and garnish with very small new potatoes, sprinkled with parsley, and with scalloped cucumber. Serve with Piquant sauce in a sauce-boat. (For SAUCES, see Index.)

Cold Salmon, with Montpelier Butter

Salmon.   Sauce. | Fried Croûtons.
Aspic Jelly. | Montpelier Butter.

UTENSILS—Fish-kettle, fish-slice, frying pan, kitchen
spoon, knife, forcing-bag.

Boil either a whole salmon or a piece of one, according to
the recipe given for boiled salmon, and let it get cold. Coat
it thinly with aspic jelly, and let it set. Fry a croûton of
bread large enough to hold the salmon (or two of the same
size if the fish is large enough to require them). When cold
stand the croûton on a dish, and coat it with Montpelier
butter, then lay the salmon carefully on it.

Garnish with narrow strips of aspic jelly laid right across
the fish. Between the strips of jelly force out roses of Montpelier butter, using a forcing-bag and rose-pipe. Garnish round
the croûton with blocks of aspic jelly and Montpelier butter.

NOTE.—This is only suited for a large cold luncheon or
supper. It can be made very elaborate by garnishing with
small moulds of aspic in which are set prawns, pea-cut
cucumber, etc. Mayonnaise or any suitable cold sauce can
be served with it.

Mayonnaise of Salmon

Cold Salmon. | Mixed Salad.
4 hard-boiled Eggs. | Cucumber.   Beetroot.
4 small Lettuces. | Mayonnaise Sauce.

UTENSILS—Cloth, knife, kitchen spoon.

Thoroughly wash and dry the lettuces, and cut them in
quarters. Take out the hearts and lay the other leaves on
the dish upon which the salmon is to be served. Cut the salmon
into neat pieces about two inches square, and lay some of
the pieces in a circle in the centre of the lettuce leaves. Coat
them thickly with mayonnaise sauce. (For SAUCE, see Index.)

Then lay some more pieces on top in a smaller ring and
coat these with sauce. Lay still more on top in the same
way, until all the fish is used up. On the top of the pyramid
place the very small whole heart of one of the lettuces.
Arrange the other pieces round the base alternately with
groups of small salad, sliced cucumber, hard-boiled egg and
beetroot.

NOTE.—Turbot, lobster and many other fish may be
served in the same way.

Stewed Eels

2 large Eels.
1 pint Brown Gravy.
1 oz. Butter.   1 oz. Flour.
1 Onion.   3 Cloves.
A blade of Mace.
                Vinegar.   Salt.

A bunch of Herbs (Bayleaf,
    Thyme and Parsley),
6 Peppercorns.
1 dessertspoonful Ketchup.
A strip of Lemon Peel, 2 in. long.
Button Onions.

UTENSILS—Basin, knife, stewpan, wooden spoon, cloth, strainer, knife, pint measure, dessertspoon.

Skin and clean the eels, and cut them into pieces about three inches long. Put them into salted vinegar for a short time. Put the butter, the flour and the sliced onion into a stewpan and fry together until they are a light brown. Dry the pieces of eel, and put them in the stewpan with the fried onion, etc. Add gently the gravy, the herbs, mace, cloves, peppercorns, ketchup, lemon peel and (if liked) a little wine.

Stew gently until tender, but do not cook until the pieces of eel break, about 35 minutes is the time. Take out the pieces of eel, and pile them on a hot dish. Strain the gravy, add a few drops of lemon juice, and re-heat. If required, add a little more thickening. Pour it over the fish, and serve very hot. Garnish with button onions, which may be cooked with the fish. Put these in heaps round the fish, and sprinkle with a little finely chopped parsley.

Fried Eels

2 lb. Eels.   1 Egg.
Breadcrumbs.
                Tartare Sauce.

Flour.   Frying Fat.
Salt and Pepper.

UTENSILS—Saucepan, knife, basin, cloth, plate, grater, egg-beater, frying pan, wire rack. *Enough for 6 persons.*

Skin and clean the eels, then cut them into pieces three inches long. Put them into a saucepan with cold water, bring to the boil, and boil for 5 minutes. Strain, then wash them in cold water. Dry them thoroughly in a cloth.

Roll the pieces in flour highly seasoned with salt and pepper. Next dip them into whole beaten-up egg, then into finely made white breadcrumbs. Fry them in plenty of boiling fat for 6 to 10 minutes, according to the thickness of the pieces. Drain well, and dish the pieces in a pile on a dish-paper. Garnish with fried parsley. Serve with Tartare sauce in a sauce-boat. (FOR TARTARE SAUCE, see Index.)

To Boil a Crab

UTENSILS—String, saucepan, tablespoon, quart measure.

Crabs, like lobsters, should be chosen for their weight, and the medium-sized ones are best. Having selected the crab tie the large claws firmly closed. Have ready a saucepan with plenty of fast boiling water, salted in the proportion of one tablespoonful of salt to each quart of water. Plunge the crab quickly in, and boil fast from 20 to 30 minutes, according to size.

LOBSTERS are cooked in the same way.

Dressed Crab

1 boiled Crab.	1 tablespoonful French Vinegar.
2 tablespoonfuls Breadcrumbs.	2 tablespoonfuls Salad Oil.
1 hard-boiled Egg.	1 small teaspoonful Mustard.
Parsley.	Pepper.

UTENSILS—Knife, fork, chopping board, basin, kitchen spoon, grater, saucepan, sieve, measuring spoons. *Enough for 2 to 6 persons, according to size of crab.*

Open the crab, and carefully remove the small stomach bag and uneatable parts. Pick out the white meat from the body portion (which is pulled out of the shell in opening the crab) and chop it finely. Mix with it the oil, vinegar, breadcrumbs, and mustard and pepper. Remove the contents of the back shell, and mix with the above.

Wash the shell out clean, then put the mixture back into it, garnish with finely chopped parsley and hard-boiled yolk of egg (which has been rubbed through a sieve) in alternate stripes, all leading towards the tail of the crab. Stand it on a bed of shredded lettuce, or else just garnish round with sprigs of parsley.

Buttered Crab

1 boiled Crab.	1 tablespoonful Vinegar.
2 oz. Breadcrumbs.	A grate of Nutmeg.
1½ oz. Butter.	Seasoning of Salt, Cayenne and
1 teaspoonful chopped Parsley.	White Pepper, to taste.

UTENSILS—Knife, fork, chopping board, basin, wooden spoon, saucepan, grater, baking tin, measuring spoons.

Take out the meat from a large boiled crab. Chop it finely, removing any small pieces of shell. Weigh the meat, then mix with it a third of its weight of seasoned breadcrumbs, etc., as follows : To every two ounces of breadcrumbs take one ounce and a half of butter, one tablespoonful of vinegar, one tablespoonful of chopped parsley, a grate of nutmeg, and a seasoning of salt, cayenne and white pepper.

Melt the butter, and add it to the breadcrumbs (which must be fresh and finely made). Mix in the other ingredients, then mix all in with the meat of the crab. Pack it back into the shell, and cover with a thick layer of buttered breadcrumbs. Set the finished crab in a rather slow oven until done, then take it out, and serve very hot. It will take about 20 minutes in the oven.

NOTE.—This mixture may also be baked in small china cases, or in scallop shells, either for a savoury or for luncheon.

Boiled Crayfish

12 Fresh-water Crayfish.	1 teaspoonful Vinegar.
½ a Carrot.	A sprig of Parsley.
1 small Onion.	1 tablespoonful Salt.

A bunch of Herbs.

UTENSILS—Saucepan, knife, sieve. *Enough for 3 or 4* persons.

Wash fresh-water crayfish thoroughly. It is a good plan to stand them in a basket under a running tap. Put sufficient water to cover the crayfish into a saucepan, and add to this the vegetables and other ingredients given above. Bring this to the boil, then quickly plunge the crayfish in. Boil fast for ¼ hour. When done take them out, and drain thoroughly.

NOTE.—Fresh-water crayfish are often used for garnishing, for which purpose they are particularly well adapted. They are delicious when curried or in a vol-au-vent or in patties.

SEA CRAYFISH (similar to a large lobster, with a mottled shell) are boiled in the manner just described, but are allowed more time in cooking as required by their much larger size.

Sea Crayfish Curry

1 Sea Crayfish.	1 teaspoonful Curry Powder.
2 Onions. 1 Apple.	1 teaspoonful Curry Paste.
½ pint of Milk.	1 oz. Flour. 2 oz. Butter.
1 tablespoonful Cocoanut.	Boiled Rice. Salt.

UTENSILS—Knife, fork, chopping board, stewpan, two basins, wooden spoon, strainer, grater, baking tin, saucepan, measuring spoons. *Enough for 2 or 3 persons.*

Split open a boiled sea crayfish, remove the uneatable parts, then pick out all the meat from the body and claws, also the creamy parts from the head. Cut the flesh up into dice. Peel and chop two onions finely, also the apple. Melt the butter in a stewpan. Add the onion and apple, and cook together for 15 minutes without browning. Then add the curry powder and paste mixed in a little milk.

When the vegetables are thoroughly cooked, add the crayfish to them. Soak the grated cocoanut in the remainder of the milk for about ½ hour. Strain the milk from the cocoanut, and mix the flour into a smooth paste with the flavoured milk. Stir this flour paste into the curry, then bring to the boil, and add salt to taste.

Stand the curry saucepan in a tin containing boiling water so that the curry cannot boil hard, or use a double boiler. Let it simmer gently for ½ hour. Have ready a very hot dish, and put the curry in it. Garnish with slices of cut lemon and parsley. Serve plain boiled rice with it.

Scalloped Oysters

2 dozen Oysters.	2 tablespoonfuls Milk.
2 oz. Butter.	2 tablespoonfuls Cream.
½ oz. Flour.	Nutmeg. Salt.
Breadcrumbs.	Cayenne Pepper.

UTENSILS—Knife, 2 basins, strainer, 2 saucepans, wooden spoon, scallop shells, grater, tablespoon. *Enough for 4 or 6 persons.*

Open the oysters, and save all the liquor. Rinse them in the liquor, then strain the latter. Put the oysters in a saucepan with the strained liquor. Bring them almost to boiling point. They must be carefully watched to ensure their being removed before boiling actually occurs. Take them off the fire, and drain away the liquor. Remove the beards and the hard pieces of gristle from the oysters.

Melt one ounce of butter in a saucepan, then stir in the flour, add the milk and liquor from the oysters, and lastly the cream. Season with cayenne, salt, and a very little grated nutmeg. Bring this mixture to the boil, then remove from the fire, and add the oysters.

Butter some scallop shells, and sprinkle with white breadcrumbs. Put some of the oysters and sauce into each shell, and cover with a layer of buttered breadcrumbs. Put them at the top of a quick oven to brown; or brown them under the grill. Serve quickly and very hot. Arrange the scallop shells on an ornamental dish-paper, on a dish.

Oyster Fritters

2 dozen Oysters.	Peppercorns.
1 small Onion.	Cayenne.
1 Lemon. Parsley.	Frying Batter.
Mace. Salt.	Frying Fat.

UTENSILS—Knife, 2 saucepans, basin, strainer, soup-plate, cloth, skewer, egg-beater, wooden spoon, lemon squeezer, frying pan, sieve, pint measure. *Enough for 4 persons.*

Open the oysters, drain them from the liquor, and beard them. Make a broth with the liquor, the beards, half a small onion, half a blade of mace, three or four peppercorns, a sprig of parsley, half a teaspoonful of salt, and sufficient water to make three-quarters of a pint in all. Reduce this one-fourth part, then strain. When cool put it into a small saucepan, and add the oysters. Stand the saucepan over the fire until the first indications of boiling are seen, then take them off at once. Let them stand for 3 minutes.

Strain the oysters, and lay them in a soup-plate. Pour over them the strained juice of a lemon, and add a small sprinkling of cayenne. Let the oysters remain thus for 1 hour, turning them two or three times. Remove the oysters from the plate, and drain them thoroughly on a cloth. Stick a skewer into one, dip it into frying batter, then drop it into plenty of boiling fat. Do them all like this. Fry until they are a pale golden brown, then take them up and drain well on a sieve.

Dish them in a pile on an ornamental paper, and serve immediately, garnished with a few slices of lemon and fresh parsley. These oyster fritters make a good hot hors d'œuvre.

To Boil a Lobster

UTENSILS—Saucepan, large kitchen spoon.

See that the lobster is alive when purchased. In selecting lobsters choose those that are heaviest for their size ; and let them be as active as possible, which shows that they have not been out of the sea very long. Lobsters which are light in weight for their size are in poor condition and watery. The heavier the lobster the better its condition. Medium-sized lobsters are best.

Have ready a saucepan quite large enough to hold the lobster, and put in sufficient water to cover it well. Salt the water with one ounce of salt to each quart. When the water is quite boiling, drop the lobster in and boil quickly from 20 to 40 minutes, according to size. Skim well during the boiling. When cooked, take it up at once or the flesh will become stringy. Rub the shell over with a little salad oil or butter, then wipe it. This brightens the colour of the shell.

TO DRESS A LOBSTER

UTENSILS—Knife, fork, hammer or cracker.

Break off the two large claws, and crack them well. Separate the body from the tail. Split the tail in half right down the middle, and remove any uneatable parts. Stand the head upright on a dish and arrange the cracked claws and split tail round it. Garnish with fresh parsley or salad.

Devilled Lobster

1 large Lobster.	1 teaspoonful Worcester Sauce.
1 teaspoonful Chutney.	3 tablespoonfuls White Sauce.
1 oz. Butter.	A dust of Cayenne.
½ teaspoonful Mustard.	Breadcrumbs. Salt.

UTENSILS—Knife, fork, pestle and mortar, saucepan, wooden spoon, fireproof shells, baking sheet, measuring spoons. *Enough for 3 or 4 persons.*

Take all the meat from a large lobster (which has been boiled). Cut the meat up into small dice. Pound the coral in a mortar with the mustard, butter and other flavourings. Put the sauce into a saucepan, and add the pounded coral, etc., to it. Let it get thoroughly hot, then stir in the fish. Bring all to smoking point.

Have ready buttered some fireproof shells on a dish. Put the mixture into these, and sprinkle over the top with brown breadcrumbs. Stand them in the oven for a few minutes; or brown them under the grill. Arrange on a dish with a paper d'oyley beneath them. Garnish with fresh parsley.

Lobster Soufflé

1 large Lobster.	1 gill Cream.
½ lb. Cod Fish.	2 oz. Butter.
3 Eggs.	1 gill Fish Stock.
2 oz. Flour.	Salt. Cayenne.

UTENSILS—Knife, pestle and mortar, wire sieve, wooden spoon, saucepan, 2 basins, soufflé dish, egg-beater, gill measure. *Enough for 4 to 6 persons.*

Cut sufficient meat off a cod to weigh half a pound, and put it in a mortar with the coral of the lobster. Pound them well, then rub through a wire sieve. Put the butter and flour into a saucepan, and fry together without browning. Add the fish stock gradually, also the cream. Add a small quantity of salt and cayenne. Draw the pan to one side of the stove, and cook the contents gently for 10 minutes. Take the pan off the fire, and drop in the yolks of three eggs one by one, beating the mixture well between each yolk. Now add the pounded cod-fish and the meat from the lobster, finely chopped.

Well butter a soufflé dish and tie a well-buttered paper round the outside of it with the edge standing up two and a half inches above the top of the dish. Whip the whites of the eggs to a stiff froth with a small pinch of salt, and lastly add these to the fish mixture. Pour it all into the soufflé dish, and bake in a moderate oven for ¾ hour. Quickly remove the paper, place on a dish, and send to table immediately, or it will sink. CRAYFISH may be done this way.

Lobster Salad

1 nice-sized Lobster.	1 hard-boiled Egg.
2 Lettuces.	1 small Beetroot.
1 small Cucumber.	Small Salad.

Mayonnaise Sauce.

UTENSILS—Knife, fork, cloth, basin, wooden spoon, gill measure or cup, saucepan. *Enough for 2 or 3 persons.*

Pick the meat from the body of a nice-sized hen lobster, and cut it up into dice shapes, but save the head intact, and the shell, for garnishing. Wash the lettuces thoroughly, and dry by shaking them in a cloth. Keep the small hearts of the lettuces for garnishing, and shred the remainder finely. Put a layer of the shredded lettuce in a salad bowl.

Mix about a gill of mayonnaise sauce with the lobster. Put a layer of the lobster on top of the lettuce in the bowl. Put a little more sauce over it, then put another layer of the salad, lobster and sauce. Have a layer of finely shredded lettuce on top, stand the head of the lobster in the centre, and garnish round it with the claws, boiled beetroot cut into fancy shapes, and hard-boiled egg cut into quarters lengthways. Sprinkle over with lobster coral, which has been previously rubbed through a sieve. Add sliced cucumber, small salad (cress, etc.), or any suitable garnish that may be procurable. If wanted a little more elaborate, a few prawns have a pretty effect.

NOTE.—The chief things to remember are, to see that the lettuce is thoroughly clean and dry, that there is plenty of good mayonnaise sauce, and that it is not prepared long before it is wanted. It will soon lose its freshness.

Fricassee of Fish

1 lb. any White Fish.	Parsley. Salt.
1 Shallot or small Onion.	A blade of Mace.
1 pint Milk.	A dust of Cayenne.
2 hard-boiled Eggs.	A strip of Lemon Peel, 1 inch
1 oz. Butter.	long.
1 oz. Flour.	6 drops Lemon Juice.

UTENSILS—Stewpan, knife, basin, fish-slice, 2 saucepans, strainer, wooden spoon. *Enough for 3 or 4 persons.*

Put the milk into a stewpan with the shallot, mace, cayenne and lemon peel and bring to the boil. Be careful not to add too much cayenne. Skin and bone the fish, and cut it up into pieces, one and a half inches square. When the milk boils, carefully lay in the fish, and let it simmer until it is done. This will be from 10 to 15 minutes.

Lift out the fish into a basin, cover it over, and stand the basin over a saucepan of boiling water to keep thoroughly hot, while you make the sauce. Put the butter in a saucepan. When melted add the flour, and fry together without browning. Strain the milk on to this, and stir well. Boil for 2 or 3 minutes, and add salt to taste.

Arrange the fish neatly in the centre of a very hot dish. Take the sauce off the fire, add the lemon juice, then pour it over the fish. Cut the eggs each into eight pieces lengthways. Put two pieces on the top of the fish, with a sprig of parsley between, then with the others form a border round the dish, placing a sprig of parsley between each piece of egg.

Fish Cutlets

1 lb. cooked Fish.	White Breadcrumbs.
1 oz. Butter.	1 teaspoonful chopped Parsley.
1 oz. Flour.	1 teaspoonful Anchovy Essence.
½ pint Milk.	Frying Fat. Pepper.
2 Eggs.	Salt. Cayenne.

UTENSILS—Knife, fork, 2 basins, grater, saucepan, wooden spoon, pastry board, frying pan, fish-slice, egg-beater. *Enough for 4 persons.*

The remains of any cold boiled fish may be used for making fish cutlets. Free the fish from skin and bone, and flake it. Weigh it after the bone and skin are removed. Put the flaked fish into a basin with 1 oz. of breadcrumbs and the parsley. Melt the butter in a saucepan, add the flour, and stir the milk into this. Season it with pepper, salt, a very little cayenne, and the anchovy essence. Bring it to the boil, then stir in the yolk of one egg. Pour this sauce on to the fish in the basin, and mix it all thoroughly together, then allow it to get quite cold.

When cold, take a piece of the mixture the size of an egg, and place it on a slightly floured board. Form it into the shape of a cutlet, dip it into well-beaten egg, and then into fine white breadcrumbs. Fry in plenty of boiling fat till crisp and brown.

Arrange the cutlets on a dish-paper. Put a miniature cutlet frill in the end of each, a bunch of either fried or fresh parsley in the centre, then serve. The frills used are very little larger than wooden matches and can be purchased in boxes ready to stick into the cutlets. They are very dainty and easy to arrange.

NOTE.—If cutlet shapes are not desired, the mixture can be formed into balls or cakes, and cooked in the same way.

ENTRÉES[1]

IN ordering entrées, if two are required, it is always best to think them well over beforehand, for it is a decided tax on a cook's capabilities to get two ready at the same time. It is never necessary to have more than two entrées even at a very large dinner party. Two, carefully selected, are ample for any occasion, while one is quite sufficient for an ordinary good dinner. As previously remarked, it is decidedly better to have one dish really well done than to have two which are inferior owing to haste and to attempting too much.

A thing to be specially remembered is that everything must be kept quite *hot*. Whatever the garnish may be for a hot entrée, be sure that it is kept hot until the last moment. If possible, it should be put in the oven for a minute before sending to table.

Sauces for entrées must be particularly good of their kind, and should be kept warm in a bain-marie or double boiler and poured round at the last minute, and not before. In summer, it is very nice to have a cold entrée, and when convenient, an iced entrée may be prepared, and prove very acceptable.

Many little pieces of meat, vegetables, poultry, game, etc., can be used up in this way when the material is not sufficient for a more substantial class of dish. Entrées, therefore, can be a very economical item in the hands of a careful cook.

To Prepare Frying Batter

½ lb. Flour.
2 Eggs.   Salt.

1 tablespoonful Salad Oil.
1 gill tepid Water.

Sift the flour, and put it into a basin. Mix it gradually into a paste with rather more than a gill of tepid water. The water must only be just tepid, not warm. Add the yolks of the eggs and the salad oil. Beat the mixture well, use a wooden spoon for this if possible. Let it stand for an hour or two before using. When you are ready to use it, add the whipped whites of eggs with a pinch of salt.

[1] See also LUNCHEON and SUPPER DISHES, page 75; LOCAL DISHES, page 635; LUNCHEON MENUS, page 721; DINNER MENUS, page 768.

PREPARING LAMB CUTLETS—All the fat should be trimmed from the end of the bone before dipping the meat in egg and breadcrumbs. Cutlet frills add to the appearance of the dish.

A HOT ENTRÉE FOR DINNER—Left-over veal, chicken or ham and tongue can always be used up with a white sauce and peas or mushrooms as patties (p. 227) or as a vol au vent (p. 91).

This batter is excellent for fritters and kromeskies of all kinds. Always have plenty of fat for frying anything in that has been dipped in batter. The fat is boiling when the blue smoke rises from it, but for thick fritters the fat should not be quite smoking or the fritters will be cooked on the outside before being sufficiently cooked in the middle.

To Trim Mutton Cutlets

The best end of the neck of mutton is used ; and it is best if small, provided it is prime meat. Get the butcher to saw off the chine bone, then the cutlets can be easily dealt with. Take a sharp knife and divide the meat into cutlets by cutting down between each bone. If this makes them too thick then cut down close to the bone on each side. This will leave a cutlet between without a bone, which can be used ; but as a rule one cut between each bone makes them of the right thickness. When all are cut, lay them on a wet board and " bat " them out with a cutlet bat or with the side of a heavy chopping knife or a wet rolling-pin. To bat out a cutlet simply means to flatten it out to an even thickness, not to pound it into an unsightly mass.

After flattening the cutlets out, commence to trim them. To do this neatly the knife *must* be sharp. Cut off all the superfluous fat and skin, leaving an edge of fat rather more than a quarter of an inch thick. When this is done, place the knife just above where the round piece of lean ends, and make a straight cut through to the bone, then remove the meat from the thin end. Scrape the bone perfectly clean, then chop off the little piece at the other end of the bone if there is any that projects beyond the end of the meat. There may be, if the chine bone has not been sawn off quite close enough. Even if it has, there may still remain a piece to be cut off when trimming the cutlet.

To make the base of the cutlet a nice shape, some people prefer to round off the top end of the meat, instead of leaving it cut off straight and square, but that is a matter of taste. Keep them all the same size as much as possible, and do not let the scraped projecting bone be too long. The cutlets are now ready for grilling, egg and crumbing, or for using in any way that may be wished. If they are egged and crumbed, be careful not to get the egg and crumbs on the scraped bone as that must be kept perfectly clean. If not, the general effect will be quite spoiled.

Some cutlets are improved by being marinaded, particularly if the meat is of inferior quality. It is, however, a mistake to try improving prime meat, for its natural flavour wants no additions. A nice juicy cutlet, properly grilled, with a nice crisp, slightly burnt taste, and accompanied by a few crisply fried chip potatoes and a delicate purée of vegetables, is a dish fit for a king. To marinade cutlets, lay them in a seasoning of salad oil, herbs and spices, for some time before cooking. This is largely done on the Continent.

Mutton Cutlets, with Tomatoes

6 Mutton Cutlets.	Pepper and Salt.
8 medium-sized Tomatoes.	Salad Oil or Butter.

Mashed Potato.

UTENSILS—Knife, plate, saucepan, baking-dish, grill. *Enough for 6 persons.*

Cut cutlets from the best end of a neck of mutton. Trim them neatly and scrape the end bone. Put a little salad oil or butter in a plate, and season it highly with pepper and salt. Dip the cutlets in it and let them remain in it for an hour or two if convenient.

Skin the tomatoes (after submerging them in boiling water). Put them into a buttered baking-dish, season them with pepper, salt, and a pinch of castor sugar, lay a buttered paper over them, then cook in a moderate oven for 15 to 20 minutes. Lay the cutlets on a grill and cook quickly over a clear fire.

Prepare some mashed potato, and arrange a straight border neatly down the centre of a dish. Quickly place the cutlets down the centre of the border, letting one cutlet overlap another. Arrange a border or row of tomatoes down each side. Put a frill on the bone of each cutlet, and serve at once. If liked, this dish can be improved by pouring a sauce round, say, tomato butter or a nice sharp sauce. (For SAUCES, see Index.)

Epigrams of Mutton

1½ lb. Breast of Mutton.	2 large Mushrooms.
1 small Carrot.	1 Egg. Parsley.
A bunch of Herbs.	Breadcrumbs.
1 Onion. 1 Shallot.	Pepper and Salt.

Sauce, as described.

UTENSILS—Stewpan, knife, 2 dishes, strainer, large kitchen spoon, saucepan, wooden spoon, measuring spoons, round cutter, basin, egg-beater, grater, sieve, pointed strainer. *Enough for 4 persons.*

Put the thin end of a breast of mutton in a stewpan with the sliced carrot, peeled onion, herbs, bayleaf, thyme and parsley, four peppercorns and half a teaspoonful of salt. Just cover with water, bring to the boil, and then draw the stewpan to the side of the stove to simmer till quite tender. The meat must not be boiled to rags, but must be done well enough to allow of the bones being drawn out easily.

Lift the meat on to a dish, remove the bones, and season it well by sprinkling it with the chopped mushrooms, shallot and parsley, and with cayenne and salt to taste. Let the meat lie flat on the dish, then place another dish on top with a weight on it, so as to press the meat, and leave it for some hours.

Strain the broth, and when quite cold, remove the fat from the top. Take ½ pint of this, and thicken it in a saucepan with a large teaspoonful of flour mixed with a little of the stock, then add to it 1 teaspoonful of red currant jelly, 1 teaspoonful mushroom ketchup, and 1 dessertspoonful sherry. This sauce can be omitted if desired, and just the plain gravy served with the meat, or any other suitable sauce that is more convenient can be used. In any case, it should be made a nice rich brown (with a few drops of browning), or it may be coloured with a few drops of liquid carmine.

When the mutton is cold and set, take a plain round cutter, about the size of the top of a tumbler, and cut the meat out into rounds with it. Dip these into well beaten-up egg, then into finely made white breadcrumbs. Half-fill a stewpan with frying fat and, when this is smoking hot, put the pieces of mutton in and fry them a nice golden colour. Take them up, and lay them on a sieve in front of the fire to drain for a few minutes. See that the sauce is nice and hot ; then dish the mutton in a circle, resting one piece on the one in front of it, on a border of mashed potatoes. Strain the sauce, through a pointed strainer, round the meat on the dish.

NOTE.—The trimmings can be used for rissoles, cold meat curry, shepherd's pie, or many other dishes.

Mutton Fritters

1 lb. Breast of Mutton.	Frying Batter.
1 Carrot. 1 Turnip.	Frying Fat.
½ stick of Celery.	A bunch of Herbs (Bayleaf,
1 large Onion.	Thyme and Parsley).

Pepper and Salt.

UTENSILS—Knife, saucepan, large kitchen spoon, chopping board, basin, 2 dishes, frying pan. *Enough for 4 persons.*

Trim off all the superfluous fat from the thin end of a breast of mutton. Put the meat into a saucepan. Clean and slice the vegetables, and put them into the saucepan with the meat. Add the herbs and seasoning, and cover all with cold water. Bring to the boil, and remove all scum as it rises.

As soon as it boils, draw the pan to the side of the stove, and let it simmer gently until the meat is tender. When tender, lift it from the saucepan, and take out the bones. Lay the boned meat on a flat dish, and sprinkle it well with very finely chopped parsley, a little very finely chopped onion or shallot, also pepper and salt. Put another dish flat on top of the meat, with a heavy weight on it, and let it stand until cold.

When cold, cut the meat into fingers about two inches long by one and a half inches wide, dip them into frying batter, have ready a pan of boiling fat, and fry the fingers until the batter on them is a golden brown. Arrange neatly on a hot dish and sprinkle a little finely chopped parsley on the top. Pour Reform sauce round, and serve at once. (For SAUCES, see Index.)

Cutlets of Breast of Mutton

1½ lb. Breast of Mutton.	1 Egg.
¼ lb. Onions.	Breadcrumbs.
¾ oz. Flour.	Frying Fat.
½ pint Milk.	Green Peas or French Beans.
½ oz. Butter.	Pepper and Salt.

UTENSILS—Stewpan, basin, wooden spoon, saucepan, knife, cutlet cutter, egg-beater, grater, frying pan, fork, 2 dishes. *Enough for 3 or 4 persons.*

Boil the mutton as in the recipe just given for breast of mutton fritters, and put it away to press as described. Boil the onions in salted water until they are tender, then squeeze them perfectly dry.

Make a white sauce with the milk, flour and butter.

Finely chop the onions and add them to the white sauce, also add salt and pepper to taste.

When the meat is cold, stamp it out into shapes with a cutlet cutter, or, failing this, cut into neat cutlet or other shapes with a knife. Well mask each cutlet with the sauce, and set them aside to get quite firm. Then dip each one into whole beaten-up egg and then into finely made white breadcrumbs. Fry in plenty of boiling fat until they are a nice golden colour. Make a pile of freshly boiled green peas, or French beans, in the centre of a dish. Arrange the cutlets *en couronne* round the vegetables. Pour Espagnol sauce round the base, and serve.

Mutton Ragoût

1 lb. Mutton.	2 small young Carrots.
1 oz. Flour.	1 small Turnip.
Spaghetti or Macaroni.	1 Tomato.　　Herbs.
1 oz. Butter.	1 pint weak Stock, or Water.
6 or 8 button Onions.	Pepper and Salt.

UTENSILS—Knife, stewpan, wooden spoon, piece of muslin, saucepan, pint measure. *Enough for 3 persons.*

Cut up the mutton into small pieces. Melt the butter in a stewpan, then put in the meat and the vegetables. The onions may be whole if very small, about the size of marbles. If large, use fewer, and cut them into slices. Slice the carrots and turnip. Fry all until they are a nice golden colour. Then stir in the flour. Add the stock or water, pepper and salt to taste, and a bunch of savoury herbs tied up in muslin. Bring to the boil, and skim well. Draw to one side of the stove, and simmer gently for 1 hour or rather longer.

Boil some spaghetti, or macaroni, in salted water with an onion, and make a border of it round the dish. Pour the ragoût in the centre. Arrange a twist of the spaghetti on the top, and serve.

Kromeskies (1)

½ lb. cold Meat.	Lemon Rind.
1½ gills Milk.	1 teaspoonful Parsley.
1 oz. Butter.	Frying Batter.
1 oz. Flour.	Frying Fat.
Bacon.　　Nutmeg.	Pepper and Salt.

UTENSILS—Knife, grater, basin, saucepan, wooden spoon, stewpan, pastry rack, chopping board. *Enough for 2 persons.*

Take the remains of any cold white meat such as veal, rabbit, chicken, or even lamb. Free it from skin and bone, and remove any dry parts. Add a few slices of ham, but only making half a pound in all. Mince it very finely. Add pepper and salt to taste, a grate of nutmeg, a very little finely chopped or grated lemon peel, and the chopped parsley. Melt the butter in a saucepan. Stir in the flour and cook it for a few minutes without browning.

Add the milk by degrees and bring to the boil. When it comes to the boil, draw it to one side, and let it stand for 5 minutes to cook the flour thoroughly. Stir in the seasoned meat, then turn it all out on to a dish, and let it get cold. When cold, divide the meat into portions about the size of a hen's egg, and roll them into long-shaped rissoles.

Cut as many very thin slices of fat bacon as you have rissoles. Wrap a slice of bacon round each, then dip them one by one into frying batter. Drop them quickly into a stewpan of boiling fat, and fry them until the batter is a nice crisp golden brown. Drain them well on a pastry rack or folded paper. Arrange in a pile on a dish-paper. Garnish with fried parsley, or a little fresh parsley, and serve.

Kromeskies (2)

¼ lb. cold Game or Chicken.	Pounded Mace.
¼ lb. Bacon.	Parsley.
White of 1 Egg.	Frying Batter.
Flour. Garlic.	Frying Fat.

Pepper and Salt.

UTENSILS—Knife, 2 basins, kitchen spoon, egg-beater, frying pan. *Enough for 3 persons.*

Take any cold game or white meat, and pick it free of skin and bone. Mince it finely. Season it well with pepper, salt, a very small pinch of pounded mace, and a very little of the juice of a clove of garlic. Mix all well together, and bind with the beaten white of an egg. Form into small rolls and flour them slightly.

Cut a thin slice of rather fat bacon for each roll, and wrap it up in this. Now dip each roll separately into frying batter and at once drop them into plenty of boiling fat. Fry until they are a nice golden colour. Dish up prettily on a fancy paper, and garnish with fried parsley.

Mutton Mould

1 lb. cold Mutton.
1 Egg.
2 oz. Breadcrumbs.
1 dessertspoonful finely chopped
    Onion.
1 teaspoonful chopped Parsley.

½ teaspoonful finely chopped
    Thyme.
1 teaspoonful Chutney.
½ oz. Butter or Dripping.
1 tablespoonful Gravy.
Pepper and Salt.

UTENSILS—Knife, mincing machine, 2 basins, cloth, kitchen spoon, egg-beater, mould, chopping board, 2 saucepans. *Enough for 3 or 4 persons.*

Take the remains of any cold cooked mutton, and free it from skin, bone, and any hard pieces. Mince the meat very finely. Soak the bread in cold water, and when thoroughly soaked, wring it quite dry in a clean cloth. Mix the bread well with the meat, and add the chopped onion, thyme, parsley, chutney, pepper and salt.

Beat the egg well. Mix the dry ingredients with the egg thoroughly, then add the gravy. Grease a mould thickly, put the mixture in, and lay a greased paper over the top.

Steam for 1 hour in a saucepan with the water reaching three-fourths the way up the mould. Keep the lid tightly on the saucepan all the time. When cooked, turn the mould out, and pour a good rich gravy round. Garnish with a border of plainly boiled macaroni or spaghetti twisted round the base of the shape, or serve with a curry sauce.

Mutton and Chutney Sauce

1 lb. cold Mutton, cut in slices.
1 oz. Butter.   ½ oz. Flour.
3 tablespoonfuls Chutney.

½ pint Stock.
Mashed Potato.
Parsley.   Salt.

UTENSILS—Knife, frying pan, dish, wooden spoon, saucepan. *Enough for 3 or 4 persons.*

Cut the mutton into neat slices, all about the same size and shape. Melt the butter in a frying pan. Lay in the slices of mutton, and fry them slightly. When thoroughly heated, and slightly browned, lift them out, and place them somewhere to keep hot.

Stir the flour into the pan. Mix in the chutney with it, and if there are any pieces in the chutney, chop them finely. Add the stock, and stir until it boils. Add salt to taste, and if a sweet chutney is used, add a few drops of lemon juice.

Make a straight border of mashed potato down the middle

of a dish. Let the border be about five inches wide and hollowed out slightly in the middle. The hollow part should be about three inches wide, leaving one inch margin of the full height on each side.

German Cutlets

1 lb. cold Lamb.	1 small Onion.
2 oz. lean Ham.	2 Cloves. 4 Peppercorns.
1 teaspoonful Parsley.	A bunch of Herbs.
1 teaspoonful Meat Extract.	Pepper and Salt.
⅛ oz. Gelatine.	Cayenne. 1 Egg.
2 oz. Butter.	Breadcrumbs.
1 oz. Flour.	Frying Fat.
¾ pint weak Stock.	Mashed Potato.

UTENSILS—Mincing machine, 2 saucepans, strainer, wooden spoon, dish, basin, grater, egg-beater, teaspoon, frying pan, frying basket. *Enough for 4 to 6 persons.*

Mince the lamb, and the ham, very finely. Put the stock into a saucepan, with herbs (bayleaf, thyme and parsley), meat extract, one onion, two cloves, and four peppercorns. Boil until the stock is reduced to half a pint, then strain it off and dissolve the gelatine in it.

Melt the butter in a saucepan and stir in one ounce of flour. Add the stock to this by degrees. Now thoroughly mix in the minced ham and lamb, also the parsley, and seasoning of cayenne and salt to taste, and turn it out on to a flat dish to cool.

When it has set, take pieces the size of an egg, roll them in flour, and form them into cutlet shape. When formed, dip them into whole beaten-up egg, then into fine white breadcrumbs. Dip them into the egg and crumbs a second time so that they may be well coated. The cutlets should not be flattened out too much, but kept nice and thick. When all are crumbed, lay them in a frying basket, and fry in plenty of boiling fat until they are a nice brown.

Stick one of the dainty little cutlet frills in the thin end of each; or, failing these, a piece of macaroni with a frill on it. Dish them on a round potato border, and fill the middle of the border with boiled French beans. Pour tomato sauce round, and serve. Or, the cutlets may be arranged standing up round a pyramid of mashed potatoes, and a good gravy poured round. In this case a few sprigs of parsley may be placed on top of the potato.

Mutton and Tomato Pie

1 lb. cold Mutton.
6 Tomatoes.
¼ pint Gravy.

1 clove of Garlic.
1 oz. Butter.
Breadcrumbs.

Pepper and Salt.

UTENSILS—Knife, pie-dish, saucepan, breakfast cup, grater. *Enough for 4 persons.*

Cut the mutton into nice slices, not too thin. Cut the tomatoes into slices. Grease a pie-dish. Put a layer of tomatoes at the bottom of the dish, sprinkle them with pepper and salt. Cut a clove of garlic and scrape out a few drops of the juice on to the tomatoes. Then put in the meat and season this with pepper and salt.

Put a layer of tomatoes on top of the meat, and season them in the same way as with the bottom layer. Pour in the gravy. Melt the butter and mix it in a breakfastcupful of white breadcrumbs. Spread these buttered crumbs over the top layer of tomatoes, and bake in a moderate oven for ¾ hour.

Ayrshire Pasties

⅓ lb. Veal.   2 oz. Bacon.
1 teaspoonful chopped Parsley.
½ oz. Butter.
½ oz. Flour.
4 tablespoonfuls Milk.
2 Eggs.   Nutmeg.

½ teaspoonful chopped Shallot.
White Breadcrumbs.
¼ lb. Puff Paste.
Lemon Peel.
Frying Fat.
Cayenne.   Salt.

UTENSILS—Knife, saucepan, wooden spoon, grater, measuring spoons, basin, pastry board, rolling pin, brush, cutters, egg-beater, frying pan. *Enough for 4 persons.*

Chop the veal very finely, also the bacon, but do not pass either through a mincing machine. Melt the butter in a saucepan, and mix in the flour. Stir in the milk by degrees, and continue stirring until it thickens. Season well with cayenne pepper, a little nutmeg, salt, a grate of lemon peel, a teaspoonful of finely chopped parsley, and the chopped shallot. Mix all these ingredients well together, then stir in the finely chopped meat thoroughly. Turn all out on a plate and leave till cold.

Roll out the puff paste thinly, and stamp it out into rounds with a plain cutter about two inches across. Put a good teaspoonful of the meat mixture into the centres of half of them, and wet the edges of the paste with cold water. Lay a round of paste on the top of each one. Take a cutter two sizes smaller than the one the rounds were cut with, and with the blunt edge (the cutter turned upside down) press gently on the top piece of paste so that it is well pressed on to the lower one. Be careful not to press so hard as to cut through the paste. Pinch the edges all round.

Dip these rissoles into well beaten-up egg, then into fine white breadcrumbs. Fry in fat that is very hot but not quite smoking, until the rissoles are a nice golden brown colour. If the fat is quite smoking (boiling), the rissoles will be browned before the paste is properly cooked.

NOTE.—1. Any cold meat is nice done in this way.

2. Sometimes stock may be used instead of the sauce made of butter, flour and milk, described above. In this case the stock is stiffened by melting a very little gelatine in it, so that when cold the mixture is firm. When the rissoles are fried the gelatine melts, and this forms a gravy inside the coating of egg and breadcrumbs. The result is very nice.

Véal Patties

THE CASES

2 lb. Potatoes.	1 whole Egg.
3 oz. Butter.	Pepper.
2 Yolks of Eggs.	Salt.

THE FILLING

½ lb. cooked Veal.	½ pint Milk.
2 oz. cooked lean Ham.	1 Onion. Lemon Peel.
1 oz. Butter.	1 blade of Mace.
1 oz. Flour.	Cayenne. Salt.

UTENSILS—Two saucepans, sieve or potato masher, wooden spoon, forcing-bag, baking sheet, brush, 3 basins, egg-beater, strainer, knife. *Enough for 6 persons.*

To prepare the cases, rub boiled potatoes, as dry and floury as possible, through a wire sieve, or pass them through a potato masher. While they are hot, mix in two ounces of butter, the egg yolk, and pepper and salt to taste. When well mixed, put this into a forcing-bag with a medium-sized rose-pipe.

Thickly butter a baking sheet with the remainder of the butter. Force out the potato mixture, working the bag round and round so as to form several small patty cases. Brush these cases over with well-beaten whole egg. Bake them in a moderate oven until a nice golden brown colour. These cases may be made a little time before required, and kept hot on the rack.

To prepare the filling ; boil the onion, the mace, a small strip of lemon peel, and a dust of cayenne with the milk for 5 minutes, then strain the milk. Melt the butter in the saucepan, and stir in the flour. Fry together for a few minutes to cook the flour, but without browning. Pour in the boiled milk by degrees, stirring all the time. When it comes to the boil, cook for 5 minutes, then stir in the veal and ham, cut into very small dice. Bring all to the boil again, and season with salt to taste. If too thick, add a little more milk, for some flours thicken more than others.

Fill the cases with the mixture. A little coralline pepper and finely chopped parsley can be sprinkled on the top of each ; or a little hard-boiled yolk of egg and parsley. Arrange them prettily on a dish-paper, and serve. These cases may be filled with any kind of mince, or even with vegetables. They make a pretty little entrée out of comparatively nothing.

Patties à la Reine

¾ lb. Puff Paste.	½ pint Béchamel **or** Veloute
½ pint Chicken, Tongue and Mushroom.	Sauce.
	1 Egg.

UTENSILS—Basin, wooden spoon, knife, pastry board, rolling pin, pastry cutters, brush, egg-beater, baking sheet, half-pint measure. *Enough for 6 persons.*

Roll the puff paste to a quarter of an inch in thickness. Take two round cutters, one three inches and the other two inches across. Cut out rounds with the largest cutter, then place the smaller cutter in the centre of these and nearly cut through them. Dip the cutters in hot water before using, so that they may cut clean. Brush over the rounds of paste with whole beaten-up egg, lay them on a wet baking sheet, and bake in a quick oven.

When cooked, remove the centre tops carefully. Cut up into dice shapes sufficient chicken, ham, and button mushrooms to fill a half-pint measure. Make these thoroughly hot in the sauce, then fill the cases with the mixture. Put the tops on again, arrange on a dish-paper and serve.

Little Fillets of Beef

1½ lb. Fillet of Beef.	Grated Horseradish.
2 Gherkins.	Pepper and Salt.
2 teaspoonfuls chopped Chives.	Potato border.
2 tablespoonfuls Salad Oil.	Garnish, as described.
Horseradish Sauce.	

UTENSILS—Knife, cutter, basin, gridiron, saucepan, forcing-bag. *Enough for 6 persons.*

Cut the beef into slices three-quarters of an inch thick. Bat them out with a heavy knife dipped in cold water, then stamp out the slices into rounds two and a half inches in diameter. Put the oil in a dish, and season it highly with pepper and salt, and the gherkins and chives finely chopped.

Dip the fillets in this so that both sides are well covered, and let them lie in it for an hour or longer.

Make a round potato border. Lift the fillets out of the oil, and place them on an oiled gridiron. Grill over a clear fire for about 6 minutes, turning them only once during cooking. Lay them round on the top of the potato border, and sprinkle a little grated horseradish on the top of each. Pour horseradish sauce round, and fill the centre of the border with either cooked mushrooms, braised button onions, or any suitable vegetable. (For HORSERADISH SAUCE and for POTATO BORDER, see Index.)

Little Fillets, with Mushrooms

1 lb. Fillet of Beef.	Potato Purée.
½ lb. Mushrooms.	Tomato Sauce.
2 oz. Butter.	Pepper and Salt.

UTENSILS—Knife, 2 frying pans, saucepan, forcing-bag, fork. *Enough for 4 persons.*

Cut the fillets into slices about half an inch thick, and flatten them out with a cold, wetted, heavy knife. Trim neatly into rounds from two to two and a half inches in diameter and sprinkle each with pepper and salt.

Melt one ounce of butter in a sauté pan or frying pan. When melted and hot, lay in the fillets and cook for 8 minutes, turning them once or twice during the cooking.

In another pan melt the remaining ounce of butter. Peel and trim off the stalks of as many nice large mushrooms as you have fillets, and of about the same size. Season them with pepper and salt, and fry them in the second pan.

Make a potato purée, and put it into a forcing-bag with a large rose-pipe. Force out six or eight rounds of the purée on to a hot dish (as many rounds as fillets), and, if possible, keep the rounds quite separate. On top of each round lay one of the cooked mushrooms, the stalk side uppermost. On top of the mushrooms lay a fillet. In the centre of each fillet force out a rose of potato purée. Pour tomato sauce round, and serve very hot. (For TOMATO SAUCE and POTATO PUREE, see Index.)

Fillets of Beef, with Oysters

1½ lb. Fillet of Beef.	Cayenne. Pepper.
12 Oysters.	Salt. Salad Oil.
Lemon Juice.	Potato Straws.

½ pint Béchamel Sauce.

UTENSILS—Knife, small skewers, gridiron, frying pan, fork, saucepan, wooden spoon. *Enough for 8 persons.*

Trim the fillets in the same way as for fillets with mushrooms, but let them be nearly an inch thick. Make eight fillets. Cut the fillets in half, flat-ways (the same as you would cut a scone for buttering), but do not cut them right through. Cut through the centre part as much as possible, leaving as much of the edge uncut as you can. This will make a sort of pocket or purse of the fillet.

Season each oyster with a few drops of lemon juice, and a small dust of cayenne pepper. Put one seasoned oyster into the pocket of each fillet, and then close up the open edge of the fillet with a very small skewer. Brush the fillets over with salad oil and season them with pepper and salt.

Oil the bars of a gridiron, and lay the fillets on. Broil them over a clear fire from 8 to 10 minutes. Take them off the fire, and remove the small skewers. Make a pile of potato straws in the centre of a hot dish. Arrange the fillets in a circle round the pile, with the cut edges uppermost, so as to retain the gravy in the pockets.

Make half a pint of creamy Béchamel sauce. (For BECHAMEL SAUCE, see Index.) Strain the liquor from the oysters into this sauce. Cut up the four remaining oysters quite small, and put them in also. Make the sauce almost boil, then pour it round the fillets on the dish, and serve at once.

Mutton Cutlets, with Macedoine of Vegetables

8 Cutlets.	Butter or Salad Oil.
¾ pint White Sauce.	Glaze. Salt.
Larding Bacon.	Macedoine of Vegetables.

Potato border.

UTENSILS—Knife, larding needle, gridiron, baking dish, brush, basin, tablespoon, saucepans, double boiler. *Enough for 8 persons.*

Trim the cutlets neatly, and flatten them. Prepare some strips of bacon for larding, but do not have them too thick as the cutlets are not large. With a larding needle commence to lard the cutlets on one side at the top, say two lardons in the first row, if the cutlets are very small, or three if they are of a usual size. Put three or four lardons in the second row, and two or three in the third. Trim the ends of the lardons.

Brush over the cutlets with either salad oil or dissolved butter, then grease the bars of a very clean gridiron, and grill the cutlets over a clear fire for 5 minutes. Take them up quickly, lay them on a baking dish, sprinkle lightly with salt, and put them in a quick oven for 4 minutes longer to crisp up the lardons. Have ready a potato border. Just slightly brush over the larded side of the cutlets with liquid glaze. Arrange the cutlets in a circle on the border.

Make three-quarters of a pint of good white sauce. (For SAUCES, see Index.) Into half of this sauce put equal portions of any four suitable vegetables, say two tablespoonfuls of each. Suitable vegetables would be, carrots, asparagus points, peas, French beans, or young turnip cut into small dice (not chopped). Each vegetable must be cooked separately, and be quite distinct, so as not to give the sauce a mashy appearance. Keep four or five tablespoonfuls of the vegetables to garnish the dish with.

Put the macedoine (the vegetables in the sauce) into the centre of the cutlets. Pour the remaining sauce round the cutlets. Put the remaining vegetables in little heaps at each end of the dish. The macedoine of vegetables must be prepared before the cutlets are cooked, and be kept hot in a double boiler. If fresh vegetables cannot be obtained, then bottled vegetables may be used. They can be purchased already prepared for use. It is only necessary to scald them in boiling water, strain, then cook them for a little in the sauce.

Cannelon of Beef

2 lb. topside of Beef.	½ teaspoonful Nutmeg.
1 lb. Bacon.	Pepper and Salt.
Rind of 1 Lemon.	Thyme. Parsley.
2 Yolks of Eggs.	Brown Gravy.

Garnish of fried Potato Balls.

UTENSILS—Knife, mincing machine, basin, tape, wooden spoon, chopping board, baking tin. *Enough for 6 persons.*

Chop the beef very fine and pass the bacon twice through the mincing machine. Mix both thoroughly together. Thinly pare the rind off a small lemon, and chop it finely. Mix the chopped rind with the parsley and thyme. Add to these the grated nutmeg, pepper and salt to taste. The quantity of salt must be according to the saltness of the bacon. Add all these ingredients to the chopped meat, and mix them thoroughly well together with the yolks of eggs.

Form the mixture into a roll and wrap it round with a well-buttered paper. Bind round the paper with tape to keep it together and in shape. Put it into a well-greased baking tin, and bake in a moderate oven for an hour or rather longer. When cooked, remove the binding and paper. Place the roll on a dish and pour a rich brown gravy round it. Garnish with some fried potato balls arranged to form a border round.

VEAL is delicious cooked in this way, but instead of the gravy serve a purée of cucumber or vegetable marrow.

Braised Steak

1½ lb. Beefsteak.	6 Peppercorns.
1 Carrot. 1 Onion.	2 Cloves.
2 oz. Dripping.	A few pieces of Celery.
A bunch of Savoury Herbs.	1 pint Brown Gravy or Stock.

UTENSILS—Stewpan, knife, strainer, pint measure, kitchen spoon. *Enough for 4 or 5 persons.*

Thickly grease the bottom of a stewpan. Prepare the vegetables, and slice them roughly. Lay the sliced vegetables in the bottom of the stewpan with the herbs and spice, and place the piece of meat on top of them. Put the lid on the pan, and fry contents for 10 minutes, until the vegetables are a nice golden brown.

Pour in half a pint of the stock, and cover down closely with the lid. Stand the stewpan either in a moderate oven, or cook gently on the stove, for 1½ to 2 hours. Baste the steak

frequently with the stock or gravy, and add more as that in
the pan reduces.

When cooked, take up the steak, lay it on the dish on
which it is to be served, and keep it hot. Lift out the best
of the vegetables, trim a few into neat pieces to garnish the
steak with. Strain the gravy, and skim off all the fat. Put
the trimmed vegetables round the meat, pour the gravy
over, and serve. If liked, this dish may be made more elaborate
by being garnished with potato olives, plainly boiled, dipped
in a little dissolved butter, and having a sprinkling of finely
chopped parsley.

Veal Mould

1½ lb. cooked Veal.	Butter. Sauce.
½ lb. cooked Ham or Bacon.	A thick slice of Bread.
2 Onions. 1 Egg.	Milk. Nutmeg.

Pepper and Salt.

UTENSILS—Knife, basin, stewpan, wooden spoon, grater,
egg-beater, mould. *Enough for* 6 *persons*.

Take the veal, and the ham, and chop them very finely.
Soak the bread in some milk. Peel the onions and chop them
finely. Melt a little butter in a stewpan, and fry the onions
in it until slightly browned. Now mix in the meat and the
bread, well pounded up. Add about a saltspoonful of grated
nutmeg, also pepper and salt to taste. Stir all over the fire
until thoroughly well mixed and heated.

Take the pan off the fire, and then stir in a well-beaten
egg thoroughly. Butter a mould thickly. Put in the mixture,
press it firmly in, and bake in a moderate oven for 1 hour.
Turn it out, pour German sauce round, and serve. (For
SAUCES, see Index.)

Creams of Veal

¾ lb. raw Veal.	4 tablespoonfuls Béchamel Sauce.
4 oz. Panard. 1 oz. Butter.	Thyme. Cayenne.
2 Eggs. Spaghetti.	Lemon Peel.
6 Sauce Oysters.	Pepper and Salt.
Tongue. Onion.	¼ pint Italian Sauce.

UTENSILS—Knife, mincing machine, pestle and mortar,
measuring spoons, wooden spoon, sieve, 6 dariole moulds,
fancy cutter, stewpan, saucepans, entrée dish. *Enough for*
6 *persons*.

Take some fillet of veal, trim it quite free from skin and bone. Mince three-quarters of a pound of it very finely, passing it twice through the mincing machine. Put it into a mortar with the panada (for PANADA, see Index), the butter, Béchamel sauce, a saltspoonful of very finely chopped lemon peel, a teaspoonful of salt, a quarter-teaspoonful of white pepper, a very little cayenne, 1 teaspoonful of finely chopped onion and a little thyme. Pound all thoroughly in the mortar until quite smooth. Add the eggs, and mix them in thoroughly also. If time will allow, the mixture ought now to be rubbed through a sieve, but this is not always practicable.

Butter very thickly, six dariole moulds. Cut out six stars, or any fancy shapes, from a slice of boiled tongue or ham. Lay one in the bottom of each mould, in the centre ; and if you have them, put a ring of plainly cooked peas round the shapes. Take some plainly boiled spaghetti in long pieces. Begin at the bottom of each mould and wind it round and round the sides, keeping each row close together, and pressing it well to the sides, so that the sides of the mould are entirely lined with it. When all the moulds are done, fill in the centres with the veal farce.

Make a hole in the centre of the farce in each, with the end of a teaspoon dipped in cold water. Put an oyster in each hole, first removing the beards and hard pieces. Cover the oysters well over with the farce. Knock the bottoms of the moulds well on the table, so that the mixture sinks into the shape. Smooth over the open end of each mould with a wet knife, then stand them in a stewpan on a fold of paper. Lay a buttered paper over them, and put sufficient boiling water in the pan to reach about three-fourths of the way up the moulds. Watch the water re-boil, then put the lid on the pan and poach for about 25 minutes.

Make six cones of mashed potato, the size of these timbales, on a hot entrée dish. Flatten the tops so that the timbales will stand securely on them. Take the timbales up, turn them out gently, and stand one on each potato cone, the cones being high enough to raise the timbales above the level of the entrée dish. Pour Italian sauce round, and serve.

NOTE.—All small entrées are best dished on a border of some kind, either an artichoke bottom, croûton of bread, border of vegetables, or anything suitable that will go with them. If this is not done they do not show to advantage at all.

Timbales of Beef

¾ lb. Fillet of Beef.	4 oz. Panada.
1 oz. Butter.	Pepper and Salt.
3 Eggs.	Brown Sauce, as described.

UTENSILS—Knife, mincing machine, 2 wire sieves, pestle and mortar, small moulds, stewpan, saucepan, wooden spoon, forcing-bag, fancy cutter. *Enough for 4 to 6 persons.*

Free the fillet of beef from all skin and pass it twice through a mincing machine. Take ten ounces of it (the other two ounces being probably lost in the trimmings, which can, of course, go in the stock-pot), and put them into a mortar with the panada (for PANADA, see Index), the butter, and seasoning, and pound all well together, with a pestle. Then mix in the eggs and two tablespoonfuls of brown sauce thoroughly. Pound again for a little, then rub all the mixture through a coarse wire sieve.

Take some small timbale or dariole moulds, any small plain moulds will do, and well butter them. Put a star of plainly boiled carrot in the bottom of each, and three or four round the sides. Put the beef farce into a forcing-bag with a plain pipe, and fill the moulds carefully with the farce. Knock them on the table to make the mixture settle down well.

Place the moulds on a folded paper in a stewpan. Pour boiling water into the pan sufficient to reach three-fourths of the way up the moulds, then lay a buttered paper over them. Watch the water re-boil, then draw the pan carefully to one side and steam for 20 to 25 minutes. Turn the timbales out of the moulds, dish them on a potato border, and pour brown sauce round.

TO MAKE THE BROWN SAUCE

1 oz. Butter.	1 teaspoonful Meat Extract.
1½ oz. Flour.	1 pint Brown Stock.
1 Onion. 2 Tomatoes.	Pepper and Salt.

Slice the onion and put it, with the butter and flour, into a pan. Fry these together until they are a rich brown. Then add the brown stock, the meat extract, the sliced tomatoes, and the pepper and salt. Simmer these together for ½ hour, then rub all through a fine sieve. Two tablespoonfuls of this sauce is used in making the beef farce as already described ; the remainder is kept hot and poured round the timbales on the dish.

Escallops of Chicken

2 Legs and the Liver of a Chicken.	Celery. Bacon Rind.
½ lb. Veal.	A bunch of Herbs.
¼ lb. Fresh Pork.	6 Peppercorns.
1 tablespoonful chopped Ham.	¼ teaspoonful Pepper.
3 Mushrooms.	½ teaspoonful Salt.
2 Yolks of Eggs.	Potato border.
2 oz. Butter.	Purée of Peas.
1 Onion. 1 Carrot.	1 pint White Stock.

UTENSILS—Knife, mincing machine, sauté pan or frying pan, forcing-bag, needle and cotton, basin, stewpan, kitchen spoon, measuring spoons. *Enough for 6 persons.*

Cut the legs off a chicken, keeping the skin as whole as possible. Trim the veal free from skin and fat. Pass the veal, together with the pork, twice through a sausage machine, then put it into a basin.

Sauté the liver of the chicken, and the mushrooms, in a little butter for about 7 minutes. Then chop them, and the ham, finely. Add these to the minced veal and pork, and season with pepper and salt. Add the yolks of eggs and mix all well together.

Put this mixture, or farce, into a forcing-bag having a plain pipe. Fill the chicken legs with the mixture, but not too full or the skin may burst in cooking. With a needle and cotton sew up both ends of the legs, then wrap them in buttered papers. Put one ounce of butter in the bottom of a stewpan with the sliced onion, sliced carrot, half a stick of celery, a piece of bacon rind, herbs (bayleaf, thyme, and parsley) and peppercorns. Lay the farced legs, in their papers, on the top, cover the pan and put it on the stove.

Let all fry gently for ¼ hour. Then add half a pint of white stock and let the legs cook gently ¾ hour, basting them frequently with the stock, and adding more as that in the pan diminishes. When cooked, take the legs up, and remove the papers and the cottons.

Make a straight border of mashed potato on a dish. Have ready a purée of green peas in a forcing-bag with a plain pipe. Cut the legs into slices rather less than half an inch thick. Arrange them on the potato border, one slice lapping on the next. Fix the slices in place by forcing out the purée of peas around them, making a rose of the purée on each side and at the bottom of the escallops. Pour Genoa sauce round, and serve. (For SAUCES, see Index.)

Fricassee of Chicken

1 Fowl. 2 Onions.	4 Cloves. Salt.
2 oz. Butter.	6 Peppercorns.
2 Yolks of Eggs.	Cayenne Pepper.
¾ pint Milk.	A bunch of Herbs (Bayleaf,
½ teaspoonful Lemon Juice.	Thyme and Parsley).
1½ oz. Flour.	Garnish of Croûtons and Rolls
2 blades of Mace.	of Bacon.
½ pint button Mushrooms.	Rice Border, as described.

UTENSILS—Knife, 3 saucepans, strainer, wooden spoon, 3 basins, egg-beater, fork, frying pan, border mould. *Enough for 6 persons.*

Prepare a nice large fowl, cut it into neat pieces, and trim off the skin. Put the pieces of fowl into a saucepan with sufficient cold water to cover them. Bring just to the boil, then strain. Wash the pieces of fowl in cold water. Put them on again with fresh water to cover; with one large onion stuck with cloves, mace, peppercorns, a bunch of herbs (bayleaf, thyme and parsley), and a teaspoonful of salt. Simmer gently until the pieces are tender, in about ½ hour.

Take them out of the stock, then strain the latter and save it for white soup, etc. Pour some hot water over the pieces of fowl to cleanse them thoroughly from any scum, or pieces of herb, that may be adhering. Put the milk on to boil with the onion, a blade of mace, a very small thin strip of lemon peel, and a dust of cayenne pepper. As soon as it boils, draw to one side and let it infuse for 15 minutes. Now strain this.

Melt the butter in a saucepan. Stir in the flour, and fry together without browning. Stir into this, by degrees, the boiled flavoured milk ; also the same quantity of the strained stock. Stir continually until it boils, add the mushrooms, sliced, and season with a little salt if required. Lay the pieces of fowl in, and let them get thoroughly hot, then lift them out, and arrange them neatly in the centre of a rice border.

Beat the yolks of two eggs, stir them into the sauce off the fire, add the lemon juice, then pour all over the chicken. Garnish with croûtons of bread fried a pale golden colour and with small rolls of bacon. The croûtons may be brushed over on one side with white of egg and dipped in finely chopped parsley and tongue.

TO PREPARE THE RICE FOR THE BORDER

1 breakfastcupful of Rice.	½ teaspoonful White Pepper.
2½ oz. Butter. 2 Eggs.	3 breakfastcupfuls of Water or
1 teaspoonful Salt.	White Stock.

Thoroughly wash the Carolina rice in two or three waters. Put it into a saucepan with the water or white stock. Boil it gently for ¾ hour, stirring frequently to prevent it sticking. When cooked, add one and a half ounces of butter, the salt, and the white pepper.

Beat all up together with a wooden spoon until quite smooth, then add two eggs, previously well beaten, and mix well. Thickly butter a border mould and put the mixture in. Knock the mould well, to settle the rice closely into the shape. Put it in a moderate oven for 15 minutes. Turn out the rice border on to a hot dish, and fill the centre with the fricassee, as described. This rice border is also very nice for filling with mince, curry, or any kind of ragoût.

Creams of Chicken

1 Chicken. 3 Eggs.	2 tablespoonfuls thick Béchamel
1 oz. Butter.	Sauce.
1 tin Artichoke Bottoms.	6 oz. Panard.
2 tablespoonfuls Cream.	Sauce Suprême, as described.
Salt.	White Pepper.

UTENSILS—Knife, mincing machine, basin, wooden spoon, pestle and mortar, fine wire sieve, small bombe moulds, forcing-bag, tablespoon, 2 saucepans, gill measure, tammy-cloth. *Enough for 6 persons.*

Cut all the meat from a raw chicken and free it from skin and bone. Pass the meat twice through a sausage machine. Take twelve ounces of the meat, and mix with it the panard, Béchamel sauce, butter, three whole raw eggs, one teaspoonful of salt and half a teaspoonful of white pepper. Pound all quite smooth in a mortar. Then mix in the cream. Rub all the mixture through a fine wire sieve.

Thickly butter some small bombe moulds, or any small plain mould will do. Put the chicken cream into a forcing-bag having a plain pipe, then fill the moulds with it. Knock the mixture well down by striking the bottoms of the moulds on the table. If this is not properly done there will be cracks in the cream when turned out. When the moulds are filled, smooth over the open tops with a knife that has been wet by dipping it in boiling water.

Lay a fold of paper in the bottom of a stewpan, and stand the moulds on it. Pour sufficient boiling water in the pan to reach three-fourths of the way up the moulds. Cover the pan closely with a lid, watch the water re-boil, then let them poach for 30 minutes. Turn the creams out, and stand each one on an artichoke bottom. Pour Suprême sauce over, sprinkle a little chopped truffle on each, and serve.

THE SUPRÊME SAUCE

Chicken Bones and Trimmings.	2 tablespoonfuls Mushroom
2 Onions.	Essence.
1 small stick of Celery.	3 oz. Butter. 2 oz. Flour.
½ a small Carrot.	A pinch of Mignonette Pepper.
A bunch of Herbs.	½ teaspoonful Salt. Water.

Slice up the onion. Melt one ounce of butter in a stewpan. Add the onion, the chicken bone, and trimmings cut up small, a small bunch of herbs, the carrot and celery, both cut up, the mignonette pepper, and salt. Cover the ingredients with cold water, bring to the boil, skim, simmer for 1 hour, then strain.

Melt two ounces of butter in a saucepan, add the flour, and fry together without browning. Add to this by degrees three-quarters of a pint of the stock, and stir till boiling. Add the mushroom essence, then season to taste with salt. Wring the sauce through a tammy. Add a gill of cream, then re-heat and use when almost boiling.

Chicken in Shells

1 Chicken.	2 tablespoonfuls cooked Tongue.
1 gill of Button Mushrooms.	½ pint German Sauce.
2 oz. Butter.	Buttered Breadcrumbs.

UTENSILS—Knife, sauté pan, scallop shells, grater, saucepan, tablespoon, pint or gill measure. *Enough for 6 persons.*

Remove the fillets from a nice large chicken, and cut them into dice shapes. Melt one ounce of butter in a sauté pan. Put in the pieces of chicken, and fry them gently without browning. When cooked, stir them into half a pint (or rather more) of German sauce. Add the button mushrooms cut in slices, and the cooked tongue, cut into the same sized pieces as the chicken. Heat all together until almost boiling.

Butter some scallop shells, and fill them with the mixture. Sprinkle buttered breadcrumbs thickly on the top. Put them into a moderately quick oven for a few minutes, until the crumbs get a nice golden brown. Arrange the shells on a folded napkin, or on an ornamental dish-paper, on a hot dish. Garnish with either fried or fresh parsley, and serve.

Fillets of Fowl, Sautés

1 Fowl.	Peas.	Lemon Juice.	Salt.
1 pint of Velouté Sauce.		Coralline Pepper.	
1 oz. Butter.		Border of Chicken Farce, or	
Truffle.	Tongue.	Potato.	

UTENSILS—Knife, sauté pan, saucepans, wooden spoon. *Enough for* 6 *persons.*

Remove the fillets from a good-sized fowl. With a very sharp knife cut them into as many smaller fillets as possible. One fowl should make nine fillets or more. Butter a sauté pan, lay in the fillets, and sprinkle them with lemon juice, salt and coralline pepper. Lay a thickly buttered paper over, and cook them in a moderate oven for 6 or 8 minutes.

Make a plain round or oval border, either of chicken or veal farce ; or, if these are considered too expensive, a potato border will do. Turn out the border on to a hot dish. Lift the fillets with a broad flat knife, and arrange them on the border, one overlapping the other. Pour Veloute sauce over them and the border, seeing that they are masked with it. In the centre of every other fillet place a round thin slice of cooked tongue about the size of a shilling. On the other fillets place a similar sized slice of truffle. Fill the centre with plainly boiled green peas which have been tossed in a little warmed, seasoned butter.

Chicken Cutlets

1 Chicken.	Egg.	Espagnol Sauce.
1 oz. Butter.		Ground Mace.
Breadcrumbs.		Cayenne Pepper.
Mushroom Purée.		Salt. Frying Fat.

UTENSILS—Knife, 2 dishes, sauté pan, basin, egg-beater, grater, wire rack, saucepan, wooden spoon, teaspoon. *Enough for* 6 *persons.*

Bone a chicken, then divide the meat into neat pieces to make cutlets. Mix together one teaspoonful of salt, a quarter-teaspoonful of ground mace, and a little less of cayenne pepper. Season the cutlets with this, rubbing it well in. When all are seasoned put them into a well-buttered sauté pan, and sauté them over a quick fire for 7 minutes. Take the pan off the fire, put the cutlets on a dish with another dish on top (the same way up) and place a heavy weight on this.

When cold trim them neatly if required. Dip each one into whole beaten-up egg, then into finely made white bread-crumbs. Have ready plenty of boiling fat. Plunge the cutlets in, fry until they are a nice golden colour, then drain them on paper or a sieve.

Make a purée of mushrooms. Put this in the centre of the dish, and arrange the cutlets round it. Pour Espagnol sauce round the cutlets. Garnish with heart-shaped croûtons brushed over with glaze, and sprinkled with grated Parmesan cheese and chopped tongue.

Devilled Fowl

1 cold cooked Fowl.	1 teaspoonful Worcester Sauce
1 teaspoonful French Mustard.	A dust of Cayenne.
1 teaspoonful English Mustard.	½ teaspoonful Salt.
2 oz. Butter.	½ pint Gravy.
1 dessertspoonful Chutney.	1 teaspoonful Flour.

UTENSILS—Knife, basin, wooden spoon, saucepan, sauté pan, strainer, measuring spoons. *Enough for* 6 *persons.*

Cut the fowl into neat joints and score them well, making deep cuts in the meat, so that the sauce can soak right in. Mix together the mustards, chutney, sauce, cayenne and salt. The chutney must be chopped fine. Melt half of the butter, stir it into the mustard mixture, and mix well together. Spread the fowl with this, rubbing it well into the cuts.

Butter the bottom of a sauté pan. Put the pieces of fowl in, and lay a buttered paper on top. Stand the pan in a moderate oven for 10 minutes. Take it out, remove the paper, place the pan on the top of the stove, and sauté briskly for 5 minutes. Take up the pieces of fowl, and arrange them on a hot dish.

Pour half a pint of gravy into the pan. Mix one teaspoonful of rice flour, or ordinary flour, with a little cold gravy, and pour it into the pan. Bring all to the boil. Strain this sauce round the fowl, sprinkle a little finely chopped parsley over.

Sweetbreads (to Blanch)

Before cooking sweetbreads in the various ways that they can be done, they should always be blanched. To do this, trim the sweetbreads, and remove all fibrous skin. Soak them in luke-warm water, having a pinch of salt in it, for a couple of hours or longer, changing the water two or three times during the soaking. Drain them, then prepare a stewpan of cold water, place them in and just bring to the boil. Then drain them again, and put in fresh cold water to cool. When cold, dry the sweetbreads in a cloth and use in any way required.

NOTE.—Both lambs' and calves' sweetbreads are treated in this way.

Baked Sweetbreads

1 Calf's Sweetbread.   Beaten-up Egg.
Gravy. Salt.   Breadcrumbs.
    1 oz .Butter.

UTENSILS—Saucepan, cloth, knife, basin, egg-beater, plate, grater, baking tin, basting spoon. *Enough for 6 persons*.

Boil the sweetbread for 15 minutes in slightly salted water. Dry it, then cut it in half lengthwise. Dip each half into whole beaten-up egg, then into finely made white breadcrumbs.

Butter a baking-tin, lay the pieces in, and place a buttered paper over the top. Bake in a moderate oven for 20 minutes, basting them constantly with the butter. When done, lay the pieces side by side on a hot dish, pour a nice brown gravy round, garnish with fried parsley, and serve.

Fricandeau of Sweetbread

1 large Sweetbread.   6 Peppercorns.
Fat Bacon. 2 oz. Butter. A bunch of Herbs.
½ a Carrot.   Stock. Sauce.
½ a Turnip. 1 Leek. Croûton of Bread.
½ a stick of Celery.   Purée of Peas.

UTENSILS—Saucepan, basin, knife, 2 plates, larding needle, stewpan, basting spoon, baking dish, brush, forcing-bag. *Enough for 6 persons*.

Blanch a nice large sweetbread. Trim it neatly, then put it to press between two plates, with a weight on top, until it is cold. Cut about three dozen strips of fat bacon for larding. Lard the top of the sweetbread, holding it in a cloth whilst doing it. (For LARDING, see page 19.) Keep the larding even. If liked, alternate rows of tongue may be used instead of all bacon. When larded, wrap the sweetbread up in buttered paper.

Put the butter in a stewpan, and add the cleansed and sliced carrot, turnip, leek, celery, peppercorns and herbs. Lay the sweetbread on these, and cover the pan. Put it on the stove and fry for 15 minutes. Now add half a pint of white stock and put the pan in a moderate oven for an hour, basting the sweetbread continually with the stock. As the stock reduces, add more if required.

When cooked, take up the sweetbread, put it in a baking dish, and return it to the oven for 5 minutes to crisp the lardons. If convenient brush over the top of the sweetbread lightly with liquid glaze or a little of the reduced stock from the pan. Lay the sweetbread on a croûton of fried bread the same size as the sweetbread. Fill a forcing-bag, having a rose-pipe, with either pea or chestnut purée. Force roses out all round the edge and sides of the sweetbread. Pour Veloute sauce round the dish. Garnish with bunches of tongue cut into Julienne shreds, and warmed in a little white stock.

Creamed Sweetbreads

1 lb. Lambs' Sweetbreads.	½ pint creamy Béchamel Sauce.
2 French Rolls.	Butter. Parsley.
Lemon.	

UTENSILS—Two saucepans, knife, basin, basting spoon, toasting fork or toaster, wooden spoon, lemon squeezer, strainer. *Enough for 4 persons.*

Blanch and trim the lambs' sweetbreads. Put them into a pan with two ounces of butter and the strained juice of a lemon. Cover them with a buttered paper. Put the lid on the pan and cook gently for ½ hour, basting continually. When cooked, take the sweetbreads up, and cut into slices about half an inch thick.

Have ready half a pint of creamy Béchamel sauce, and make the sweetbreads thoroughly hot in this. Cut eight slices, about a quarter of an inch thick, from two French rolls. Toast and butter them, lay them on a hot dish, and put some of the sweetbreads on each. If possible, sprinkle a little finely chopped truffle on the top of each. Garnish with a little fresh parsley, and serve. Failing the truffle, use finely chopped parsley, but the other looks better.

Cutlets of Pigeon

3 Pigeons.	Egg and Breadcrumbs.
2 or 3 Mushrooms.	Pepper and Salt.
1 Shallot.	Purée of Peas.
Butter.	Purée of Potato.
1 tablespoonful chopped Chives.	Sauce.

UTENSILS—Knife, chopping board, sauté pan, 2 plates, brush, basin, egg-beater, grater, frying pan, wire sieve, forcing-bag. *Enough for 3 persons*.

Prepare three small pigeons as described on page 11, leaving enough of the leg to form the bone of the cutlet. Do not remove the claw. Bat them out with a heavy wetted knife, and trim them neatly into shape. Chop the mushrooms, chives, shallots and herbs, very finely, and season them highly with pepper and salt. Sprinkle the undersides of the cutlets with these ingredients.

Thickly butter a sauté pan and lay the cutlets in. Sauté them briskly for 7 to 8 minutes, turning them once during the cooking. Take up the cutlets and lay them on a dish or plate. Put another dish or plate on top, and weight it so as to press the cutlets. Set aside until they are cold.

When cold, trim them again into neat shapes if they require it. Brush them over with well-beaten whole egg, being careful not to egg the leg bone or claw, for these must be kept perfectly clean. After egging, dip them into finely made white breadcrumbs. Have ready plenty of boiling fat, plunge in the cutlets, and fry them until they are a nice golden colour. When done, drain them on a wire sieve, or on two or three folds of kitchen paper.

Put a purée of peas and of potato into a forcing-bag with a large rose-pipe. Force out a straight border down the centre of the dish. Arrange the cutlets down the centre and keep them in place by forcing a rose of purée on each side of them. Pour Veloute sauce round, and serve.

NOTE.—It is best for two persons to put the purée into the forcing-bag. One holds the bag, the other puts the purée in. The rose-pipe must be held firmly in the left hand while, with the right hand, the mouth of the bag is held out in a horizontal position tightly and firmly. The purée is then put in, one kind being laid along the bottom side of the bag almost extending from the pipe to the mouth, the other being laid evenly on top of this. The mouth is then gathered up and the bag used in the ordinary way. As the contents are forced out they come together beautifully blended, yet the two colours are distinct. It is essential that the bag be held horizontally, or laid on a table, when filled, otherwise the two purées cannot be laid evenly, and they will not come out together in equal quantities.

Cutlets of Pigeon à la Hagel

2 or 3 Pigeons.	1 teaspoonful Arrowroot.
1 teaspoonful Meat Extract.	½ teacupful Gravy.
A stick of Celery.	Parsley. Butter.
1 Shallot.	A few drops of Carmine.
1 wineglass Sherry.	Pepper. Salt.
1 wineglass White Wine.	Sauce, as described.

UTENSILS—Knife, chopping board, sauté pan, 2 plates, stewpan, measuring spoons, wineglass, cup, wooden spoon, basin, tammy-cloth. *Enough for 2 or 3 persons.*

Bone the pigeons. (See page 11.) Season the flesh sides with chopped shallot, parsley, salt and pepper. Put them into a buttered sauté pan and fry briskly for 7 minutes. Take them up and press between two plates, with a weight on top, until they are cold. Now put them into a stewpan with the sherry, white wine, extract of meat, and a few drops of carmine.

Simmer the cutlets in this for 15 minutes, then add the arrowroot slaked in clear gravy. Bring all to the boil. Mask the birds thickly with this sauce and dish them up on a round potato border. Put a little shredded and blanched celery on each cutlet (or shredded cucumber will do), and fill the centre with braized carrots and pour the following sauce round:

THE SAUCE

1 Tomato. 1 Onion.	The Bones and Trimmings of the
A bunch of Herbs.	Birds.
2 oz. Butter.	½ pint Gravy.
1 oz. Flour.	1 dessertspoonful Chutney.
1 wineglassful Sherry.	1 teaspoonful Lemon Juice.
1 wineglassful White Wine.	A pinch of Mignonette Pepper.

1 teaspoonful Meat Extract.

Put one ounce of butter into a stewpan and add the sliced tomato, onion, a strip of celery, the herbs, mignonette pepper, and the trimmings and bones of the birds. Fry all together for 15 minutes, then add the wines, meat extract, chutney and gravy. Simmer all together for ½ hour, then strain.

Melt one ounce of butter in the pan, and stir in the flour. Fry together without browning. Pour in the strained gravy and lemon juice, and stir until it boils. Wring through a tammy, and use.

Salmis of Pigeons

2 or 3 cold cooked Pigeons.	1 Onion. 1 oz. Flour.
Bones of any roast or raw Birds.	2 Mushrooms.
1 wineglassful Port Wine.	Parsley. Thyme.
1½ oz. Butter.	A pinch of Mignonette Pepper or
1 teaspoonful Meat Extract.	12 Peppercorns.
1 pint Second or Brown Stock.	Pepper. Salt. Garnish.

UTENSILS—Saucepan, knife, flour-dredger, wooden spoon, large kitchen spoon, hair sieve, stewpan, frying pan, teaspoon, basin, wineglass. *Enough for 2 or 3 persons.*

Melt the butter in a saucepan. Slice the onions and mushrooms. Add these, also the bones, parsley, thyme and mignonette pepper, and fry together for about 20 minutes with the lid on the pan. Now dredge in the flour and add the port wine, meat extract, stock, a quarter-teaspoonful of pepper and a little salt. Boil all up together for ½ hour, keeping it skimmed during this time. Remove the bones, then rub through a fine hair sieve.

Cut the cold pigeons into nice pieces. Lay them in a stewpan and cover well with the sauce. Bring almost to the boil, then simmer for 10 minutes so that the pigeon may get thoroughly hot. Arrange the pieces of pigeon neatly on a dish and garnish with button mushrooms and croûtons of bread. The croûtons of bread should be fried in the usual way, then brushed over with white of egg and dipped one side in finely chopped parsley, the other side in grated Parmesan cheese. If mushrooms are not procurable a few drops of mushroom ketchup may be used instead. In this case be careful not to overdo the salt. It is only necessary to heat the meat thoroughly in the sauce, not to cook it, as it is supposed to be quite cooked before being put in.

SALMIS OF GAME, are prepared in the same way as Salmis of Pigeons just described.

Aspic of Chicken

Cold Chicken.	Mayonnaise Sauce.
Tongue. Oysters.	Aspic Jelly.
½ oz. Gelatine.	Hard-boiled Egg.
1 pint creamy Béchamel Sauce.	Truffle, or Small Salad.

UTENSILS—Charlotte mould, saucepan, knife, fancy cutter, kitchen spoon, strainer, wooden spoon, tammy-cloth, basin. *Enough for* 6 *persons.*

Take a plain Charlotte mould and line it evenly with aspic jelly. Cut thin slices off the white of a hard-boiled egg and out of these cut diamond shapes. Cut the yolk in slices with a wet knife. Put a round of the yolk in the centre of the mould, and set it with a few drops of jelly. Then arrange the white diamonds round it, so as to form the petals of a flower, and set these with plain jelly.

Put a similar design in two or three places round the sides, and in between these arrange sprigs of cress, mustard, chervil, or any small salad. Or use stars of truffle. Be careful to set each garnish firmly to the mould with more of the plain jelly. It is a rather tedious process unless you have ice to stand it in. When the mould is garnished, line it with white Béchamel sauce (half a pint will be sufficient) in which has been dissolved a quarter of an ounce of good gelatine. Use the sauce when it is quite cool and just before it begins to set. If used at all warm, it will melt the aspic and spoil the effect of the garnish.

Take a quarter of the white meat of a boiled chicken, also two ounces of tongue, and cut these into dice shapes. Scald one dozen oysters in their own liquor until they are nice and plump, then drain and let them get cold. Prepare some mayonnaise aspic, made by mixing a gill of mayonnaise sauce (from which the plain vinegar has been omitted, and only the tarragon vinegar put in) with half a pint of aspic jelly. Mix both in a cool liquid state, and it is best to wring the mixture through a tammy. Mix the chicken, tongue and oysters thoroughly with this mayonnaise aspic, and, when the lining of Béchamel sauce in the mould has set, fill the mould with the mixture and put it away to become cold.

When cold and set, dip the mould for an instant into very hot water, pass a cloth quickly over the bottom to remove any moisture, then turn the aspic of chicken out on to a cold dish. Garnish with a few crisp hearts of lettuce, prawns or radishes. If preferred, several small moulds may be used, and the garnish may be of chopped aspic jelly.

Prawns in Aspic

2 dozen Prawns.	Lobster Coral.
Aspic Jelly.	Gherkins. Ice.

UTENSILS—Small square moulds, knife, kitchen spoon, basin. *Enough for 6 persons.*

Line some small square moulds thinly with aspic jelly. Decorate the bottoms with a little bunch of lobster coral in the centre of each. Round the coral arrange a ring of chopped gherkins. Set these with some of the plain jelly. Arrange a layer of prawns neatly, cover them with jelly and let them set. Then arrange another layer, and so on. It takes about six prawns to each mould, according to the size of the moulds.

When set, turn the moulds out and stand them on a block of aspic jelly. Garnish round the base with small, finely shredded lettuce tossed in mayonnaise sauce, and surmount this with prawns in their shells.

Salmis of Duck

1 Duck.	2 teaspoonfuls Crème-de-riz.
1½ pints Gravy.	1 bitter Orange.
1 wineglassful Port Wine.	Cayenne. Salt.
1 Onion. Olives.	Potato Border.

Orange Salad.

UTENSILS—Saucepan, roasting pan, basting spoon, strainer, basin, wineglass, teaspoon. *Enough for 4 to 6 persons.*

Clean and draw a duck. Put the giblets on to boil with one onion, a very little salt, a dust of cayenne and the gravy or stock. Economical stock will do if it has a teaspoonful of meat extract added. Put the duck in a roasting pan, and cover it well with melted dripping. Roast it in a brisk oven, keeping it constantly basted, until half done. When half done take it up and cut into neat joints. Strain the boiled gravy in the saucepan, return it to the saucepan and thicken with the crème-de-riz which has been slaked in the port wine. Put the pieces of duck into the sauce and cook gently for 10 to 15 minutes.

Have a round potato border ready on a dish and arrange the pieces of duck neatly on it. Squeeze the juice of a bitter orange into the sauce. Pour the sauce well over the duck, and fill the centre with compôte of oranges. Garnish round the outside of the border with alternate bunches of turned olives, which have been heated, and bunches of the orange.

POULTRY AND GAME

It is only necessary to give directions for cooking here, as full particulars of trussing, boning, etc., are given in the chapter on PROCESSES, pages 8 to 20.

Roast Chickens

2 Chickens.	Dripping. Gravy.
12 slices of Bacon.	Watercress.

Bread Sauce.

UTENSILS—Roasting tin, basting spoon, skewers, frying pan. *Enough for 8 to 10 persons.*

Truss the fowls for roasting, and stand them in a roasting tin. Melt half a pint of good dripping, and pour it over the chickens. Put a well-greased paper on top. Roast in a moderate oven, basting frequently. Fairly large fowls take 1 hour, small ones about ¾ hour.

When cooked, and nicely browned, take them out, and remove the skewers and strings. Stand the fowls on a hot dish, with the feet towards one another and the breasts pointing to the ends of the dish. Well wash and pick over a bunch of watercress, and arrange it between the two fowls. Have ready the slices of bacon, rolled and cooked, and arrange them round the fowls. Serve the gravy in a hot sauce-boat. Serve bread sauce also with the fowls (in a sauce-boat). For BREAD SAUCE, see page 150.) If liked, fowls may be stuffed with the same forcemeat as used for veal. (For VEAL FORCE-MEAT, see page 135.)

Boiled Fowl

1 Fowl. 1 Onion.	1 pint Creamy Béchamel or
6 Peppercorns.	Veloute Sauce.
1 teaspoonful Salt.	A blade of Mace.
A bunch of Herbs.	Chopped Parsley.
Lemon Juice.	1 hard-boiled Yolk of Egg.

Tongue or Bacon.

UTENSILS—Skewers, muslin, stewpan, knife, saucepan, sieve, wooden spoon. *Enough for 4 to 6 persons.*

Truss a nice plump fowl for boiling, and rub it over with lemon juice. Wrap it in buttered muslin. Put it into a stew-pan, with one sliced onion, the herbs (bayleaf, thyme and parsley), salt, peppercorns, mace, and sufficient boiling water to cover Watch the water re-boil, then draw the pan to one side. Simmer very gently for 1 to 1¼ hours, according to size and age of the fowl.

When done, take it up, remove the cloth, stand the fowl on a hot dish, and remove the skewers and trussing strings. Pour the sauce over the bird, using more if the bird is very large. Rub the hard-boiled yolk of egg through a sieve. Sprinkle finely chopped parsley down the centre of the breast, and the yolk of egg down the two sides, and garnish round the dish with rolled bacon and sprigs of fresh parsley. Or slices of tongue, warmed between two plates placed over a saucepan of boiling water, may be used instead of the bacon.

NOTE.—If a fowl is boiled without the muslin wrapper great care must be used in removing the scum as it rises, so that it may not adhere to the bird. If more convenient, a buttered paper, then a floured cloth, can be used instead of the muslin. Another important detail is the simmering, which must be very slow and gentle, to make the bird plump and white when cooked.

Chicken à la Cannes

1 Fowl. 2 Eggs.	2 teaspoonfuls chopped Parsley.
6 oz. Ham or Tongue.	¼ teaspoonful chopped Thyme.
1 lb. Veal or Rabbit.	1 teaspoonful chopped Onion or
½ lb. Fresh Pork.	Shallot.
3 hard-boiled Yolks of Eggs.	1 Onion.
1 dozen Oysters.	1 bunch of Herbs.
2 oz. Breadcrumbs.	1 blade of Mace.
1 pint Béchamel Sauce.	1 teaspoonful Pepper. Salt.

UTENSILS—Knife, mincing machine, saucepan, sieve, grater, basin, wooden spoon, forcing-bag, needle and thread, cloth, stewpan. *Enough for* 6 *or* 7 *persons.*

Bone a fowl. (See page 11.) Mince the ham or tongue, the veal or rabbit, and the pork, passing them twice through the mincing machine. Rub the hard-boiled yolks of eggs through a sieve. Put the minced meat, the egg-yolk, breadcrumbs, chopped parsley, pepper, a teaspoonful of salt (or rather less if the ham is salt), onion and thyme, into a basin, and mix all thoroughly well together. Cut the oysters into small pieces, and add them to the ingredients in the basin, also the whole raw eggs, and mix well together.

Put the mixture into a forcing-bag with a large plain pipe. Fill the fowl with the mixture, commencing first with the wings and legs, then the body. Do not fill it too full, or the skin will crack in the boiling. When filled, press the fowl into the shape for boiling, as near as possible, and sew up the ends. Rub the breast with lemon juice, and wrap up the fowl in a well-buttered cloth. Put it into a stewpan, with boiling water to cover it, and add the bones from the fowl, one onion, one teaspoonful of salt, a bunch of herbs, and a blade of mace. Watch the water re-boil, then simmer very gently for 1 hour, or longer, if the fowl is large.

When cooked, remove the cloth, stand the bird on a dish, pour the sauce over it, and garnish in the same manner as boiled fowl. If liked, coralline pepper can be used instead of yolk of egg (for the garnish), and slices of lemon may be used. If wanted for a cold luncheon, mask the fowl with Béchamel sauce, let it get quite cold, then pour liquid aspic jelly over it. Garnish with pieces of aspic jelly and fresh salad or tomatoes.

Chicken, Breadcrumbed

| 1 Chicken. | 1 Egg. | | Dripping. |
| A slice of fat Bacon. | | | Breadcrumbs. |

Espagnol Sauce.

UTENSILS—Skewers, roasting tin, basting spoon, brush, basin, egg-beater. *Enough for* 6 *persons.*

Truss a chicken for roasting, and pour half a pint of melted dripping over it. Lay a slice of fat bacon on the breast. Roast it, either in the oven or in front of a nice brisk fire, for 30 minutes, basting it well frequently. Take it out of the oven, and brush the chicken over with whole beaten-up egg. Sprinkle it thickly with lightly browned breadcrumbs.

Put it back into the oven, and roast for 20 minutes longer. Take it out, carefully remove the skewers, and replace them with silver ones, if you have them. Stand the chicken on a dish, pour Espagnol sauce round, and serve. (FOR ESPAGNOL SAUCE, see page 156.)

Grilled Chicken

| 1 young Chicken. | | 1½ oz. Butter. |
| | Pepper and Salt. | |

UTENSILS—Knife, saucepan, gridiron, brush. *Enough for* 4 *persons.*

Pluck, draw and singe a young fowl, then split it right down

he back. Take out the breast-bone, and chop off the legs.
ust above the joint. Melt the butter, dip the fowl in it, and
prinkle well with pepper and salt. Grease the bars of a hot
ridiron and lay the fowl on it, with its back next to the fire.
Broil it over a clear fire for 20 minutes, turning it frequently
.uring this time. Brush it over again with the butter, just
»efore it is finished cooking. When cooked, lay it on a very
iot dish, garnish with fried chip potatoes, pour tomato or
nushroom sauce round, and serve.

Roast Turkey

Directions for roasting a turkey are given, under the
heading of COLD ROAST TURKEY (below). The only difference
s, that when served hot it may be garnished with sausage
meat balls, and a good gravy and bread sauce served with it.
A hot boiled Bath chap, or ham, should accompany it.

Turkeys may also be boned, in the same manner as fowls
(pages 11 and 12), but then the oysters are put in whole,
with large pieces of tongue, etc. Cold turkey can be glazed,
f desired.

Trussing and Stuffing Turkeys is fully described on page
.5.

Cold Turkey

1 Turkey. 1 Egg.	1 dessertspoonful chopped Parsley.
½ lb. Sausage Meat.	½ teaspoonful chopped Lemon
¼ lb. White Breadcrumbs.	Peel.
2 oz. chopped Suet.	¼ teaspoonful Pepper.

½ teaspoonful Salt.

UTENSILS—Basin, trussing needle, skewers, grater, measur-
ng spoons, wooden spoon, baking tin, basting spoon, sauce-
»an or frying pan.

Draw, singe and truss a medium-sized turkey, for roasting ;
»r, if ordered from the poulterers', they will deliver it ready
:russed, if asked. Put the breadcrumbs into a basin with the
iuet and seasoning, and well mix with them ½ lb. of sausage
meat. If sausages are used, the meat must be squeezed out
»f the skins. Work all into a soft ball with one large raw
»gg. If only small eggs are handy, two will be necessary.
Fill the crop of the turkey with this stuffing, draw the skin
»ver, and fasten it at the back of the neck.

Put the bird on a trivet in a baking tin with water in the

tin. Melt half a pint of dripping, and pour it over the breast of the bird. Tie a buttered paper over the breast. Roast in a moderate oven for about $1\frac{1}{2}$ hours. Keep it constantly basted, for if the skin is allowed to get hard it is spoiled. About $\frac{1}{2}$ hour before it is cooked, remove the paper and brown up the bird nicely.

When cooked, put it away to cool, without removing the strings or skewers—remove these when cold. If liked, the breast and legs can be brushed over with liquid glaze, or they can be left quite plain. Put two little frills round the legs where the feet were cut off, and garnish with some nice fresh parsley. Serve with salad, and cold ham or tongue.

Devilled Turkey

2 Turkey Legs (raw).	**1 tablespoonful Chutney.**
1 tablespoonful Salad Oil, or	**$\frac{1}{2}$ teaspoonful Salt.**
Oiled Butter.	**$\frac{1}{2}$ teaspoonful Pepper.**
1 tablespoonful dry Mustard.	**Worcester Sauce.**

UTENSILS—Basin, wooden spoon, knife, gridiron. *Enough for 2 to 4 persons.*

Put the mustard, chutney, salad oil, salt and pepper, into a basin, and make them into a soft paste with Worcester sauce, mixed with a little gravy or water. Divide the legs of the turkey and score them well and deeply. Spread the legs over with the paste mixture, rubbing it well in, and let them stand for some hours, to absorb the flavour.

Oil the bars of a gridiron, lay the legs on it, and broil, either over or in front of a nice clear fire, for 10 to 12 minutes. Take them up, arrange on a hot dish, put one or two small piece of fresh butter on them, and serve at once. A little fresh parsley can be used as a garnish.

Roast Ducks

2 Ducks.		**Sage and Onion Chutney.**
Dripping.	**Gravy.**	**Apple Compôte.**

UTENSILS—Knife, skewers, string, roasting tin, saucepan, kitchen spoon. *Enough for 6 to 8 persons.*

Cleanse, draw and truss the ducks (page 16), but before fastening up the flap at the tails partly fill the insides with the stuffing. They are never stuffed at the crop end, like fowls and turkeys; the stuffing of ducks and geese is always inside the body or frame. Fasten up the flaps, then pour

alf a pint of melted dripping over the birds. Roast, either
i front of the fire or in a brisk oven, for about an hour.
f quite young they will take a little less.

When cooked, put the ducks on a hot dish, and remove
he skewers. Pour on a good brown gravy, garnish with a
ompôte of apples round the dish, and serve. Apple sauce,
n a sauce-boat, may be handed with the duck instead of
arnishing with the compôte, if liked, but the latter is pre-
erable. Green peas should always accompany ducks, if
ossible.

DUCKLINGS are prepared and cooked in the same manner,
nd served with gravy and compote. Ducks should not be
iressed and cooked too soon after being killed. They should
)e kept a day, or longer if in a cold place. If it is thought
hat the flavour of the sage and onion may be objectionable
o some, then one bird may be cooked without the stuffing.

Roast Wild Duck

1 Wild Duck.	Watercress.
1 slice of fat Bacon.	Port Wine Sauce.

UTENSILS—Knife, roasting tin, basting spoon, flour
dredger. *Enough for 2 to 3 persons.*

Prepare and truss a wild duck (see page 16). Tie a slice
of fat bacon over the breast. Roast the duck in front of a
brisk fire or in a gas oven for 20 minutes. When it has been
cooking 10 minutes, remove the bacon, baste well, then
dredge the bird over with flour. When cooked, arrange a bed
of watercress on a hot dish, remove the strings, and lay the
duck on the cress. Serve with port wine sauce, in a hot sauce-
boat, and accompanied by orange salad.

Salmi of Wild Duck

2 Wild Ducks.	A bunch of Herbs (Bayleaf,
2 large Onions.	Thyme and Parsley).
4 Cloves.	**1** pint Brown Sauce.
½ pint Claret.	**3** or **4** Oranges.

UTENSILS—Knife, saucepan, kitchen spoon, pointed
strainer, basin, pint or gill measure. *Enough for 6 persons.*

Cut the flesh neatly off two rather undercooked wild
ducks. Put the bones and trimmings into a saucepan, with
the onions, cloves, herbs, claret, and brown sauce. Boil
these together, until reduced about a fourth part, or until

the sauce coats the spoon. Only let it boil gently, and skim well. When reduced enough, strain through a pointed strainer.

Put the strained sauce into a saucepan, and lay in the pieces of duck. Let all get thoroughly hot, and, if necessary, add a little salt. When hot, squeeze the juice of a small Seville orange into the sauce. Take out the pieces of duck, arrange them neatly in the centre of a hot dish, then pour the sauce over. Arrange bunches of orange salad round, and bunches of the peel, cut into thin shreds.

THE ORANGE SALAD

Pare three oranges with a knife, so that all the outside white skin is cut off with the peel. Then cut down each side of the natural divisions of the oranges, so that the pulp comes away without any skin. Remove the pips. Season the pulp with brandy, and serve.

Roast Goose

1 Goose.	½ lb. Brussels Sprouts.
Sage and Onion Stuffing.	Gravy. Salt.
Apple or Gooseberry Sauce.	

UTENSILS—Knife, skewers, saucepan, kitchen spoon, roasting tin, basting spoon. *Enough for 6 persons.*

Pluck, singe and draw the goose. Make three-quarters of a pound of sage and onion stuffing (see page 135), and put this inside the body of the bird, through the opening at the tail end. Truss the bird (see page 15). Sprinkle the breast with salt, then lay the fat taken from the inside of the bird on top of the breast. Overlay this fat with a well-buttered paper, then stand the goose in a roasting pan. Roast in a moderate oven, and baste frequently, also turn it several times. About half an hour before it is cooked remove the paper, and brown it up nicely.

Make a gravy from the giblets, with onions, herbs, seasoning, etc. Stand the goose on a hot dish, garnish round with plainly-boiled Brussels sprouts, pour a little gravy round the bird, and serve. The remainder of the gravy can be served in a sauce-boat. Serve also apple or gooseberry sauce, in another sauce-boat. Do not pour much gravy on to the dish, as the goose is a rather difficult bird to carve.

YOUNG GEESE are not stuffed; the insides are just seasoned with pepper and salt, and watercress is used as a garnish, instead of sprouts.

Chicken Pie

1 large Chicken.
4 hard-boiled Eggs.
¼ lb. cooked Ham.
½ lb. Puff Paste.
White Stock.   1 Onion.

1 tablespoonful finely-chopped Parsley.
1 teaspoonful Salt.
1 small teaspoonful White Pepper.
6 Peppercorns.   Mace.

UTENSILS—Knife, saucepan, 2 basins, chopping board, pie-dish, pastry board, rolling pin, pastry brush, wooden spoon, egg-beater, strainer. *Enough for 6 persons.*

Pluck, singe and draw a large chicken, and cut it into neat joints. Put all into a saucepan, with the trimmings and giblets, also one onion, peppercorns, and a small blade of mace. Cover with cold water, bring to the boil, and simmer for ½ hour. Lift out the best pieces of chicken, and put them aside to cool. Boil the trimmings and giblets for gravy, until reduced to about three-quarters of a pint.

Allow the pieces of chicken to get cool. Cut the ham into very thin slices. Remove the whites from the yolks of the eggs, and roll the yolks in finely chopped parsley. Put a layer of chicken in the bottom of a pie-dish, then a layer of ham, and season with pepper and salt. Put the yolks of eggs on the ham, then add another layer of chicken, ham and seasoning. Pour in about half a pint of white stock.

Roll the paste out to about a quarter-inch in thickness. Wet the edge of the pie-dish, cut a strip of the paste, and lay it on the edge. Wet this paste edge, then cover the whole pie with paste. Trim the edges neatly, press them down, and make a hole in the centre of the cover. Cut leaves, or any suitable designs, out of the trimmings of paste, and ornament the top of the pie with them. Brush over with beaten egg.

Put the pie into a quick oven, bake until the paste has well risen, then reduce the heat, and finish cooking. This will take from ¾ to 1 hour. Strain the gravy made from the giblets, and fill the pie up with it, through the hole in the centre. Stand it on a dish, put a pie-dish collar round, and serve.

Raised Game Pie

1 lb. Paste (for RAISED PIE PASTE, see Index).
Grouse.   Pheasant.
Hare (or other suitable game).
¼ lb. Calf's Liver.
¼ lb. Ham.
½ lb. Fresh Pork.
½ lb. Bacon, cut thin.

¼ lb. Panard.
2 Eggs.   1 Onion.
1 Calf's Foot.
A bunch of Herbs.
12 Peppercorns.
Mushroom Ketchup.
1 small Shallot.
Black Pepper.   Salt.

UTENSILS—Knife, mincing machine, basins, wooden spoon, pestle and mortar, hair sieve, wire sieve, stewpan, large metal spoon, pie mould, pastry board, rolling pin, pastry brush, egg-beater, saucepan. *Enough for 6 to 8 persons.*

Make a forcemeat of the calf's liver, ham, fresh pork and shallot, passing them twice through a mincing machine, then pounding them in a mortar. When well pounded add the panard, one whole egg, and seasoning of black pepper and salt. Pound thoroughly together, then rub all through a wire sieve, moistening it, if required, with a little sherry, and then put aside until wanted.

Cut sufficient meat from the game mentioned (or other suitable game) to make a pound weight, and cut this into neat pieces. Break up small all the bones and inferior parts. Put these into a stewpan with a calf's foot, a bunch of herbs, the peppercorns, one onion, a saltspoonful of mignonette pepper, a teaspoonful of salt, a dessertspoonful of mushroom ketchup, and cover with cold water. Bring to the boil, skim well, then boil until a good strong gravy is made from it, say 2 or 3 hours. Strain the gravy through a hair sieve, set it aside to cool, then remove any fat there may be on the top. If, when it cools, it is not a stiff jelly, reduce still more by rapid boiling.

Butter a raised pie mould and line it with the paste rolled out to one-third of an inch in thickness. Spread a layer of the forcemeat on the bottom and sides. Pack the remaining space tightly with slices of ham or bacon, the pieces of grouse, hare, pheasant, or any kind of game, and season all with salt and pepper.

If a more expensive or elaborate kind of pie is required, then truffles, pistachio nuts and mushrooms, also a tin of pâté de foie gras, may be added. When the pie is filled right up, and high in the centre, cover the top with thin slices of bacon, and over this spread a layer of forcemeat. Cut a piece of paste large enough to cover the top, lay it on, and wet the edges. Fold the other edges well up over it, being careful that the paste does not bulge over the mould. Make a hole in the centre, and ornament round it with leaves cut out of paste. Brush it over with whole beaten-up egg, and fix a buttered band of paper round, standing up two or three inches above the pie. Put it into a moderate oven for 2½ to 3 hours. It will take some time to cook through.

When cooked and almost cold, just liquefy the gravy, which should be a stiff jelly. Do not make it hot. Pour half a pint of it into the pie through the hole at top, seeing that it is quite free of fat. Place the pie in a cool place until wanted, but just before it gets quite cold remove the mould. Garnish with a few sprigs of parsley or a little chopped aspic jelly, and serve.

NOTE.—The pies may also be made with mutton and pork. The important thing is to season the meat well and to have the gravy good. The bones for the gravy should be put on some time before the pie is commenced.

Stewed Duck

1 Duck. 1 Onion.	1 teaspoonful Meat Extract.
3 oz. fat Bacon.	A bunch of Herbs.
2 oz. Butter.	1 dessertspoonful Rice Flour.
1 gill Port Wine.	Cayenne. Salt.
1 pint Brown Gravy.	Olives, or Green Peas.

UTENSILS—Knife, skewers, stewpan, basin, wooden spoon, strainer, measuring spoons, pint measure. *Enough for 3 or 4 persons.*

Draw and prepare a duck, as for roasting. (See page 13.) Melt the butter in a stewpan. Chop the bacon finely, and add it to the butter. Lay the duck in the pan, breast downwards, then fry gently, until the breast is a pale brown, then turn it over, and brown the back and sides in the same way. Now add a bunch of herbs, one onion, seasoning of cayenne and salt, brown stock, or gravy, and meat extract. Bring to the boil, and let it stew gently for about ¾ hour.

Take up the duck, and keep it hot. Strain the liquor, put it on again, and bring to the boil. Mix the rice flour thoroughly with the port wine, then stir it into the gravy.

Stir till it boils, then pour it round the duck. Garnish, with either turned olives or green peas. If liked, cold duck may be used up in the same way, but then, if it is not a whole one, it should be cut up into neat joints. As it has been thoroughly well cooked it only needs to be warmed through in the gravy.

Chicken, with Savoury Rice

1 Chicken.	½ pint White Stock.
½ lb. Rice.	Larding Bacon.
1 gill Tomato Pulp.	Pepper.
4 oz. Butter.	Salt.

UTENSILS—Knife, skewers, larding needle, stewpan, saucepan, colander or strainer, basting spoon, roasting pan, pint measure. *Enough for 4 to 6 persons.*

Truss the chicken, as for roasting, and lard the breast. Melt two ounces of butter in a stewpan, put in the chicken, with its breast upwards, and sprinkle with a little salt and pepper. Lay a buttered paper over the fowl, and cover down closely. Draw the pan to a moderately hot part of the range, or on a low flame, and let the bird cook gently for about $1\frac{1}{4}$ hours, or rather less if small. Baste the fowl frequently, with the gravy which runs from it, but be careful to cover the pan closely again each time the lid is replaced.

While the fowl is cooking, prepare the rice. Blanch the rice, strain it, rinse in cold water, and drain it. Put it back into a saucepan, with two ounces of butter, the tomato pulp, and white stock, coloured with a few drops of carmine. When the stock boils, cover the rice with a buttered paper, and put the lid closely on the pan.

Let the rice cook gently, for $\frac{1}{2}$ hour to $\frac{3}{4}$ hour. If required, add a little more stock during the cooking, but, when done, the grains of rice should be quite separate, and all the stock absorbed. Put the fowl into a quick oven for a few minutes, to crisp the lardons. Make a border of the rice, remove the skewers and strings from the chicken, stand it in the centre of the dish, and serve.

Roast Guinea Fowl

1 Guinea Fowl.	Dripping.
Larding Bacon.	Bread Sauce.
Flour. Gravy.	Watercress.

UTENSILS—Knife, skewers, larding needle, roasting pan, basting spoon. *Enough for 3 or 4 persons.*

Pluck, singe and draw a guinea fowl. Truss it like a pheasant, and lard the breast. Pour about half a pint of melted dripping over the bird. Roast, in front of a brisk fire, or in a gas oven, for 1 hour, basting it frequently. About 10 minutes before it is done, baste it well, then sprinkle it with flour. Let it hang in front of the fire a few minutes longer, to froth up well. Place the bird on a hot dish, remove the skewers, etc., and garnish with bunches of watercress. Serve with a good gravy and bread sauce, in separate sauce-boats.

Boiled Rabbit

1 Rabbit.   1 Onion. | 6 Peppercorns.
Pickled Pork, or Bacon. | Milk.   Salt.
1 pint Soubise Sauce.

UTENSILS—Knife, basin, skewers, saucepan, frying pan. *Enough for 4 or 5 persons.*

Choose a young rabbit. If the claws are on, see that they are smooth and sharp. If the claws have been chopped off, see that the inside fat is white. If this fat is yellow the rabbit is old, though occasionally old rabbits have white fat. After cleaning and skinning the rabbit, soak it well in warm water for ½ hour. Thoroughly cleanse it by the tail, rinse it well, then truss it for boiling. (See page 18.)   Put it into a saucepan, with cold water to cover. When it comes to the boil strain it, and rinse again. Then put the rabbit on, with sufficient milk and water to cover (in the proportions of one part milk to two parts water), and add the onion, peppercorns, and one teaspoonful of salt. Bring to the boil, and simmer gently for ¾ hour.

Take out the rabbit, place it on a dish, and remove the skewers. Pour the Soubise sauce over, and garnish with croûtons of fried bread and slices of lemon, placed alternately. Rolled slices of bacon can also be served on the same dish ; or else a piece of boiled pork on a separate dish. If liked, parsley, mushroom, or plain onion sauce, may be served instead. (For SAUCES, see Index.)

Ragoût of Rabbit

1 Rabbit.   6 Cloves. | 12 Peppercorns.
1 wineglassful Port Wine. | A bunch of Herbs (Bayleaf,
2 oz. Butter. | Thyme and Parsley).
1 pint Brown Gravy or Stock. | 1 thin slice of Lemon Peel.
1 large Onion. | Pepper and Salt.
Garnish of Forcemeat Balls.

UTENSILS—Knife, saucepan, cloth, plate, kitchen spoon, wineglass, pint measure. *Enough for 4 or 5 persons.*

Cleanse the rabbit thoroughly, and cut it into neat joints. Blanch these, then dry them well in a cloth. To blanch the pieces of rabbit, put them into a saucepan with sufficient cold water to cover. Bring to the boil, then rinse the pieces in cold water. When quite dry, roll the pieces in flour.

Melt the butter in a saucepan, put in the pieces of rabbit, and fry a rich golden colour. Now add the gravy or stock, the onion, herbs, peppercorns, cloves and lemon peel (the herbs and spices tied in a piece of muslin), and pepper and salt to taste. Bring gently to the boil, then draw the pan to one side, and let it simmer gently from $\frac{1}{2}$ to $\frac{3}{4}$ hour. Take out the onion, bag of herbs and spices, and the lemon peel, then put in the glass of port wine. If required, thicken the gravy with a little rice flour, mixed in a little cold stock or wine. Bring all just to the boil again. Arrange the pieces of rabbit in a dish, pour the gravy over, and garnish with forcemeat balls.

Roast Pigeons

3 Pigeons.	Gravy.	Pepper and Salt.
3 slices fat Bacon.		3 slices Buttered Toast.
3 oz. Butter.		Garnish of Fried Parsley.

UTENSILS—Knife, toasting fork or toaster, roasting tin, basting spoon. *Enough for 3 persons.*

Singe and draw the three pigeons. Put about three-quarters of an ounce of butter inside each pigeon, and season them with pepper and salt. Then truss them for roasting, with a slice of fat bacon tied over the breast of each. (See page 17.) Toast the slices of bread, butter them, and stand one pigeon on each. Roast them, in front of a brisk fire or in a gas oven, for 20 minutes, basting them continually with butter.

When the pigeons are cooked, remove the strings and the bacon, or, if liked, the bacon can be left on the breasts. Place the pigeons and toasts on a hot dish, and garnish with bunches of fried parsley. Serve, with a good gravy, flavoured with a little port wine, and a compôte of fresh or dried apricots, if liked.

Braised Pigeons

3 Pigeons.	1 Onion.	A bunch of Herbs.
$\frac{1}{2}$ lb. Breadcrumbs.		A slice of Bacon.
3 oz. Butter.		$\frac{1}{2}$ pint Stock.
2 oz. Bacon.		Sauce, as described.
3 oz. Mushrooms.		A pinch of grated Nutmeg.
$\frac{1}{2}$ a Carrot.	$\frac{1}{2}$ a Turnip.	Pepper and Salt.

UTENSILS—Knife, grater, basin, plate, stewpan, basting spoon, brush, strainer, wooden spoon. *Enough for 3 persons.*

Draw and wash three young pigeons. Make the breadcrumbs, and chop the bacon and the mushrooms finely.

Melt one ounce of butter, and mix the breadcrumbs into it thoroughly. Add the chopped bacon and mushrooms, pepper, salt, and grated nutmeg. Stuff the pigeons with this mixture, and truss them. (See page 17.)

Melt two ounces of butter, or good dripping, in a stewpan. Put in with the butter, one onion, the carrot, turnip (cleaned and sliced), herbs, and bacon. Lay the pigeons on top of these ingredients, put the lid on the pan, and fry for 10 minutes. Now add the stock, lay a buttered paper over the birds, and cover closely with the lid. Stand the pan in a moderate oven, and braise for ¾ hour, basting the birds frequently with the stock, and adding more as that in the pan reduces.

When cooked, take the pigeons up and brush them over with a little liquid glaze, or the gravy in the pan can be reduced by rapid boiling and used in place of the glaze. Stand the birds on a hot dish, and garnish round with turned olives, or small potatoes or turnips. Strain the liquor from the pan, skim off all the fat, add a little more stock and salt to taste, and thicken with a little flour, mixed quite smooth with sherry to taste. Bring to the boil, pour it round the pigeons, and serve.

NOTE.—Pigeons, to be good, should be quite fresh, and, if possible, they should be drawn directly they are killed.

Stewed Pigeons

3 Pigeons.
¼ lb. lean Ham.
½ pint Button Mushrooms.
2 oz. Butter.
2 tablespoonfuls Flour.

1 dessertspoonful Lemon Juice.
A bunch of Herbs (Bayleaf, Thyme and Parsley).
Pepper and Salt.
Garnish, as described.

UTENSILS—Knife, stewpan, wooden spoon, measuring spoons, pint measure, frying pan. *Enough for 3 persons.*

Draw and truss the pigeons. (See page 17.) Cut the ham into dice shapes. Melt the butter in a stewpan, put in the ham and the pigeons, and fry together, until they are a nice golden colour. Take out the pigeons and the ham. Stir the flour into the saucepan. When well mixed, pour in, by degrees, a pint and a half of brown stock. Stir until it boils, then put in the pigeons, ham, lemon juice, herbs (tied in muslin), mushrooms, pepper and salt, to taste, and simmer all gently for ½ hour.

Take out the pigeons, and stand them on a hot dish.

Remove the herbs. Arrange the mushrooms round the birds, alternately with slices of cooked tomato and fried croûtons.

Roast Blackcock

2 Blackcock.   Gravy. | 3 oz. Butter.
2 slices of fat Bacon. | Watercress.

UTENSILS—Knife, skewers, saucepan, roasting tin, basting spoon. *Enough for 4 to 6 persons.*

Blackcock should be hung for a few days, the time varying according to the weather. Pluck and draw the birds, wipe them inside and out, and truss like fowls.   (See page 13.) Lay a slice of fat bacon on the breasts. Melt the butter, and pour it over them. Hang in front of a brisk fire, or put them into a moderate oven, and roast for about ¾ hour.

About 10 minutes before they are done, remove the bacon, so that the breasts may brown, and baste them continually. When finished cooking, remove the skewers and strings, stand them on a hot dish, and garnish with a few sprigs of watercress. Serve with a sauce-boat of rich gravy, and, if liked, one of bread sauce as well.

Roast Grouse

2 Grouse.   Butter. | Buttered Breadcrumbs.
Gravy.   Watercress. | 2 croûtons of Fried Bread.
                    Bread Sauce.

UTENSILS—Knife, skewers, cloth, roasting tin, basting spoon, frying pan, grater, baking sheet. *Enough for 4 persons.*

Pluck, singe and truss the grouse.   (See page 16.) Wipe them with a clean cloth. Put a piece of butter, about the size of a pigeon's egg, inside each bird. Roast them, either in front of a quick fire or in the oven, for ½ hour, and baste constantly. When cooked, remove the strings.

Have ready the croûtons of bread, cut large enough to stand the birds on nicely, scooped out a little in the centre, and fried a golden brown. Stand the birds on these, placed on a dish, and garnish with watercress. Hand a rich gravy, made from game bones, with these, and also bread sauce and buttered breadcrumbs, nicely browned in the oven.

Larded Grouse

1 Grouse. | Browned Breadcrumbs.
¼ lb. Larding Bacon. | Croûton of Fried Bread.
Fried Parsley. | Bread Sauce.

UTENSILS—Knife, larding needle, skewers, basting spoon, grater, roasting tin, frying pan, baking sheet. *Enough for 2 persons.*

Prepare a nice young grouse and lard the breast and legs, trimming the lardons neatly. Roast it for 30 minutes, basting continually. When cooked, remove the skewers, and stand the bird on a croûton of fried bread on a hot dish. Pour bread sauce all round. Around the edge of the dish arrange a border of bunches of fried parsley alternately with little heaps of browned breadcrumbs. Garnish round the croûton in the same manner.

NOTE.—Grouse also makes an excellent Salmi, as directed for pigeons, page 245.

Roast Partridges

2 Partridges.		Browned Breadcrumbs.
Fat Bacon.	Gravy.	Butter, or Dripping.
	Chip Potatoes.	

UTENSILS—Knife, skewers, roasting tin, basting spoon, grater. *Enough for 2 to 4 persons.*

Prepare the partridges for roasting. (See page 17.) Pour some butter, or good dripping, over them, and roast in front of a brisk fire or in a gas oven for 15 minutes. Now remove the fat bacon, sprinkle with flour, baste well, and continue roasting. Roast for another 10 minutes. Take them up, and remove the strings, etc. Place the birds on a hot dish, and garnish with chip potatoes. Hand a sauce-boat of gravy with them, also either bread sauce or browned breadcrumbs.

Boiled Partridges

| 2 Partridges. | Parsley. | 1 pint creamy Béchamel Sauce. |

UTENSILS—Knife, skewers, saucepan. *Enough for 2 to 4 persons.*

Truss the partridges for boiling, with the legs inside. Put them into a saucepan, with sufficient boiling water to cover, and a teaspoonful of salt. Watch the water re-boil, then draw to one side, and simmer gently for 20 minutes. Lift the birds out, drain well, then remove the strings. Arrange them on a hot dish, and pour creamy Béchamel sauce over them. (For BÉCHAMEL SAUCE, see page 149.) Garnish with a few sprigs of fresh parsley, and serve.

Grilled or Broiled Partridge

| 1 Partridge. | Cayenne and Salt. |
| Salad Oil, or Butter. | Fried Parsley. |

Lemon Juice.

UTENSILS—Knife, skewers, soup plate, gridiron, brush, measuring spoons, frying pan. *Enough for 2 persons.*

Truss the partridge for roasting. (See page 17.) Then split it right down the back in halves. Put about two table-spoonfuls of salad oil, or oiled butter, in a soup plate, and season it well with salt, cayenne, and a teaspoonful of very finely minced parsley. Lay the two halves of the bird in this, and let them season well, turning once or twice. They should remain in it for ¼ hour.

When ready, oil the bars of a hot gridiron and lay the halves on it, cut side to the fire. Broil them over a clear, but not very fierce, fire for 15 minutes, turning them frequently. When cooked, brush them over with oiled butter, and squeeze a few drops of lemon juice on. Arrange a bunch of fried parsley in the centre of a dish. Lay the pieces of partridge one on each side of it, and serve at once. If liked, a good game gravy may be handed with this dsh.

Roast Hare

1 Hare.	Gravy.	1 large slice of Fat Bacon.
6 thin slices of Bacon.		½ pint Milk.
1 lb. Forcemeat.		4 oz. Butter.

Red Currant Jelly.

UTENSILS—Basin, cloth, chopping board, wooden spoon, knife, frying pan, skewers, needle and thread, larding needle, roasting tin, basting spoon. *Enough for 5 or 6 persons.*

Choose a young hare, and soak it in warm water for 1 hour. Rinse it well, dry it, and lay it on a board. Line the inside of the hare with thin slices of bacon. Make about one pound of forcemeat, the same as for veal. (See page 135.) Cook the liver and kidneys of the hare in a little butter. Chop them finely, and mix in with the forcemeat. Fill the inside of the hare with this, reserving sufficient to make about a dozen balls for garnishing. Sew the hare up, and truss it for roasting. (See page 17.)

Tie a slice of fat bacon over the back, or lard it. Lay a well-buttered paper over, and stand it on a trivet in a roasting pan. Pour the butter and milk over. Cream is better than milk if obtainable. Put to roast, in a moderate oven, for about 1½ hours. Baste frequently, adding more milk as that in the pan reduces.

About a quarter of an hour before it is cooked, take off the paper and bacon fat. Baste and flour it well, then put it back into the oven to froth up. When ready, remove the skewers, stand the hare on a hot dish, and garnish with the forcemeat balls which have been fried in a little butter. Hand red currant jelly and a good gravy with it.

NOTE.—1. Hares should be well hung before being cooked.

2. Liver sauce is very good handed with roast hare. (See page 160.)

Jugged Hare

1 Hare. 2 oz. Butter.	½ dozen Peppercorns.
½ pint Claret. ½ pint Gravy.	1 Onion. 3 Cloves.
1 wineglassful Port Wine.	Flour. Lemon Peel.
1 tablespoonful Red Currant Jelly.	Salt and Cayenne.
A few slices of Bacon.	Forcemeat Balls.
A bunch of Herbs (Bayleaf, Thyme and Parsley).	Fried croûtons of Bread, as described.

UTENSILS—Knife, stewpan, frying pan, pint or gill measure, 2 basins, saucepan, pointed strainer, wooden spoon, teaspoon, tablespoon, wineglass. *Enough for about 6 persons.*

Skin and paunch a hare, cut it up into convenient-sized joints, and dredge them over with flour. Melt the butter in a frying pan, put in the pieces of hare, and fry until they are a nice brown. Cut some very thin slices of bacon, and lay them in the bottom of a stewpan, then pack in the pieces of hare on top of these, and sprinkle with a seasoning of salt and a very little cayenne pepper.

Now put in the herbs (one bayleaf, and a sprig of thyme and parsley), also a strip of lemon peel, one onion stuck with cloves, and 6 peppercorns, moisten with half a pint of claret and half a pint of beef gravy, cover tightly with a lid, and simmer very gently until quite tender. This will take from 1½ to 2 hours. Then take out the pieces of hare, and stand them in a basin over a saucepan of boiling water to keep hot.

Strain the gravy, thicken it with about a large teaspoonful of flour mixed quite smooth in a little claret, and add the red currant jelly. Boil the gravy, stir in the thickening, and add a wineglass of port wine. Put the hare back into the gravy, to get thoroughly hot, then dish it up. Garnish with forcemeat balls and fried croûtons of bread.

THE FORCEMEAT BALLS.

1 oz. lean Bacon.	1 teaspoon minced **Parsley.**
2 oz. Suet. 1 Egg.	¼ teaspoonful minced **Herbs.**
¼ teaspoonful Lemon Peel.	3 oz. White Breadcrumbs.

Pepper and Salt.

UTENSILS—Knife, grater, basin, wooden spoon, teaspoon, frying pan, chopping board.

Chop the bacon and suet very finely. Make the breadcrumbs, and mix them with the grated lemon rind, minced herbs, suet, bacon and seasoning. Bind all with one raw egg, and roll into balls the size of a marble. Fry them in butter and use for garnishing.

THE CROÛTONS

UTENSILS—2 cutlet-shaped cutters, frying pan, wire rack, basin, egg-beater, knife, saucepan, sieve, 2 plates, wooden spoon, brush.

Take some slices of stale bread a quarter of an inch thick, cut them out with a cutlet-shaped cutter about two and a half inches long. Then take a cutter two sizes smaller, and cut out the centres so as to leave cutlet-shaped rings. Fry these rings in plenty of boiling fat until they are a pale golden colour, then drain them well.

When cold, brush over one side with beaten-up white of egg. Dip one-half of this side on to finely chopped parsley, and the other half on to hard-boiled yolk of egg, which has been rubbed through a sieve. Arrange these prettily round the hare, with little piles of forcemeat balls in between.

Roast Pheasant

1 Pheasant. Gravy.	Croûton of fried Bread.
1 slice Fat Bacon.	Bread Sauce.
½ pint Dripping.	Browned Breadcrumbs.

Watercress.

UTENSILS—Knife, skewers, roasting tin, basting spoon, frying pan, grater, baking sheet. *Enough for* 4 *or* 5 *persons.*

When the pheasant has been properly hung, pluck, singe, draw and truss it. Pheasant is trussed like grouse. (See page 16.) Cut a slice of fat bacon, large enough to cover the breast. Slit the bacon in five or six places, then fasten it on the breast of the bird. Or the breast can be larded. Pour clarified dripping over it.

Roast the bird either in the oven or in front of a clear fire for ½ hour to ¾ hour, or longer if the bird is a very large one. About 10 minutes before it is cooked remove the bacon, so that the breast may brown up nicely. Baste constantly during the cooking. If the bird is once allowed to get dry, it will be spoiled, as the skin gets hard, and no amount of basting afterwards will remedy this. All birds must have very frequent basting. When cooked, place the pheasant on a croûton of fried bread, which has been slightly hollowed out in the centre. Garnish with a few sprigs of watercress at each end. Serve with a sauce-boat of rich gravy, made from game bones, a sauce-boat of bread sauce, and some browned breadcrumbs, and an apple and celery salad if liked.

NOTE.—It is necessary for pheasant to be hung several days, otherwise it will be wanting in the excellent flavour associated with this bird. Pheasant newly killed tastes little different from chicken. From six to seven days is the period they are usually hung, at which time blood appears at the bird's beak. The cock bird is generally considered best, while there are some who think the hens more delicate and better eating, particularly if they are laying. The age of the bird can be judged by its spurs ; they are short and blunt with young birds.

Stewed Pheasants, with Rice

2 Pheasants.	2 oz. Butter.
4 oz. lean Ham.	A bunch of Herbs.
2 Onions. Flour.	Pepper and Salt.

Rice Border,

UTENSILS—Knife, stewpan, large kitchen spoon, wooden spoon, saucepans, soup plate, basin, strainer, pint measure. *Enough for 8 to 10 persons.*

Singe and draw two young pheasants, then cut them into neat joints. Put the giblets on to boil with an onion, a bunch of herbs, pepper and salt, and sufficient water to cover. Bring all to the boil then skim and boil gently. Melt the butter in a stewpan, and put in the pieces of pheasant, the other onion (sliced), the ham cut into dice shapes, a little pepper and salt. Cover tightly, and draw the pan to where its contents will cook gently in their own juices. Turn the pieces two or three times during the cooking, which will take about $\frac{3}{4}$ hour. Take the pieces up, put them in a soup plate, cover with a basin, and stand the plate over a saucepan of boiling water to keep hot while the gravy is being made.

Sift one large tablespoonful of flour into the pan in which

the pheasants were cooked, and stir it well. Then strain a
pint of the gravy, made from the giblets, into it. Bring all
to the boil for 5 minutes, then strain. Rinse out the stewpan,
and put the pieces of pheasant in it with the sauce, and boil
up again. Prepare the rice border, arrange the pieces of
pheasant in the centre, pour the sauce over, and serve.

Quails in Cases

3 Quails.	4 Eggs.	Sprinkling of Sherry.	
4 oz. fat Bacon.		1 Shallot.	
½ lb. Calf's Liver.		Nutmeg.	Herbs.
Butter.	Salad Oil.	Pepper and Salt.	

UTENSILS—Knife, frying pan, kitchen spoon, muslin bag,
grater, pestle and mortar, forcing-bag, 2 baking tins, fireproof
china cases, basin, egg-beater. *Enough for 3 persons.*

Bone the quails, with the exception of the leg bones.
The boning is done the same as with chicken (see page 11).
Cut the bacon into small dice, and fry it for a few minutes.
Then add the calf's liver (cut small), one shallot (finely chopped)
a bunch of herbs, tied up so that they can be removed, a
small quarter-teaspoonful of grated nutmeg, and seasoning
of pepper and salt. Fry these together gently, stirring often.
When thoroughly well cooked, remove the herbs, and pound
all the rest in a mortar until quite smooth.

Allow the mixture to get cold, then put it in a forcing-bag
with plain pipe. Fill the quails with this, and truss them.
Cut three bands of stout paper, about two inches and a half
wide, and eight or nine inches long, and butter them well.
Bind these round the sides of the birds to keep them in good
shape.

Well butter a baking dish, and stand the quails in it.
Sprinkle a little sherry on the top of each, and lay a well-
buttered paper over them. Cook in a moderate oven for 15
minutes, then take them out and remove the papers. Brush
three oval fireproof china cases with salad oil. Put a layer
of the pounded forcemeat in the bottom of each. Put a
quail in each one, and sprinkle a little more sherry over
them.

Beat the whites of four eggs to a stiff froth, with a pinch
of salt. Put this into a forcing-bag with a plain rose-pipe,
and garnish the tops of the quails with it. Be sure to leave
the feet of the birds showing through this garnish. Stand the
cases on a clean baking pan, placed in another containing

boiling water. Put them in a moderate oven, until the white of the egg is a pale gold colour. Take them out, sprinkle a few browned breadcrumbs on top, and serve. If liked, the egg can be omitted, and a few browned breadcrumbs sprinkled over instead. Arrange the cases, with the birds in them, on a dish ; garnish with a few sprigs of watercress, and serve.

Ptarmigan

This is a kind of grouse, and can be cooked in the same manner. (FOR GROUSE, see page 262.)

Roast Snipe

4 Snipes.   Butter. | Toast.   Gravy.
Watercress.

UTENSILS—Skewers, knife, toaster, roasting tin, basting spoon. *Enough for 2 to 4 persons.*

Truss the snipes (see page 16), and thread the four of them on a skewer. Prepare two slices of buttered toast, to place beneath the birds while they are roasting, to catch the dripping from the trail. Roast in front of a brisk fire or in the oven for about 12 minutes. Baste continually with butter while roasting. When cooked, remove the skewers, cut the pieces of toast in half, and put a bird on each. Stand them on a dish, and garnish with a few sprigs of watercress. Hand good brown game gravy, and serve very hot. They are spoiled if allowed to get cool.

Woodcock

These are cooked in the same manner as snipe, but must be allowed 15 to 20 minutes roasting, unless required very underdone. They should never be cooked very much.

Roast Teal

This is prepared and roasted in the same manner as wild duck. Garnish with cut lemon and watercress. It is also very good made into a Salmi.

Hazel Hen

Prepare and roast like partridge. Serve on a hot dish garnished with cut lemon and watercress.

JOINTS

THIS is the substantial course of the dinner, and many people would not consider the meal complete without it. There are, however, many dishes which can be served in place of an actual joint, for this course. The chief thing to be remembered in regard to a joint is that it must be well basted during the cooking, and this applies whether roasting it in front of the fire or in the oven. If the cooking is done in an oven, the meat must be turned, unless the oven happens to have an exceptionally even heat on all sides. But the basting is the chief thing, and most inexperienced, and frequently experienced, cooks fail in this. It should be done certainly every 10 to 15 minutes, unless a self-basting roaster is used.

It is not sufficient just to put the meat in the oven or in front of the fire, and leave it to cook. Of course, it will cook, but the results will be nothing like what they should be. The skin will be hard, the meat will be wasted, and the flavour will be spoiled also.

When the meat is placed on its stand ready for the oven, pour some melted dripping thickly over it. It can then be placed in the oven to roast. To obtain the proper roasted flavour the ventilators of the oven must be opened so that the vapours escape freely into the flues. The oven must also be very clean.

When it is proposed to roast a joint in front of the range the fire must be made up a proper time beforehand, so that it is burning clear and bright when wanted.

Cover the meat well with melted dripping and hang it close to the fire at first, in order to seal up the pores and so prevent the juices escaping. It is the same as when grilling a steak, if the meat is subjected to a good heat for a short time at first the outer surface is made to resemble a thin skin or envelope which retains the juices and the succulent qualities of the meat. After a little time the joint must be drawn farther away. Keep it constantly basted whilst cooking.

UTENSILS REQUIRED

A set of roasting pans.   A set of skewers.
One basting spoon.   A flour dredger.
A pointed strainer.   Saucepans for pot roast.
A forcing-bag.   Knife.   Measuring spoons.

Roast Leg of Mutton

A leg of Mutton. | Gravy.   Flour.
Dripping. | Salt.

Enough for 8 to 10 persons (6 lb. leg).

Choose a plump leg of mutton, weighing about six to seven
pounds. Wipe it quite dry, remove all thick skin and trim
it neatly. Cut off any thin flap and chop off the knuckle bone.
Place it on the stand of a roasting pan. Have some dripping
melted, and pour this well over, then place all in a brisk
oven.

When the joint has been cooking about $\frac{1}{2}$ hour, sprinkle
it with a dessertspoonful of salt. Baste regularly about every
10 to 15 minutes. About $\frac{1}{2}$ an hour before the leg is cooked,
dredge it liberally with flour and then baste it again. When
cooked, take up the joint and put it on a hot dish. Strain the
gravy and remove every particle of fat. Re-heat the gravy
with sufficient other gravy added to make it three-quarters
of a pint, and serve in a hot sauce-boat. The dish and the
gravy must be thoroughly hot, and the joint should also be
kept hot while the gravy is being made. Red currant jelly
can be served with this joint in a separate small fancy dish.
If liked, the leg may be garnished with a few roast potatoes
and braised carrots placed alternately round the dish.

Allow about 20 minutes to every pound of mutton, unless
required rather underdone, for which 15 minutes to the pound
will be sufficient. A leg weighing about six pounds will
therefore take about $1\frac{3}{4}$ hours.

Boned Leg of Mutton

A leg of Mutton. | Forcemeat, as described.
1 Cucumber.   Salt. | 6 stuffed Tomatoes.

Enough for about 10 persons.

Take a leg of mutton weighing about seven pounds, and
bone it. To do this, begin on the under side of the joint at
the thick end. Have a very sharp knife and pass it under the

skin until it Is over the bone, then cut right down to the bone and loose the meat from it. Keep the knife close to the bone all the time. Continue this until you get to the joint, then cut the skin, fold the flesh back, and remove the bone. When the principal bone is removed, take out the knuckle, but this must be done from the other end as it comes out that way more easily.

Fill the cavity in the leg with forcemeat. Replace the knuckle bone and tie the skin round to keep it in place. Fasten up the opening at the other end, either by darning in a skewer, which can be drawn out afterwards, or with a needle and thread. Cover the leg well with melted dripping, sprinkle lightly with salt, and put it to roast either in the oven or in front of the fire.

When cooked, place it on a hot dish and garnish round with stuffed tomatoes and cucumber. Pour a good gravy round, and serve.

Allow 20 minutes to the pound for roasting.

THE FORCEMEAT

½ lb. cold Boiled Bacon or Ham.	¼ teaspoon powdered Thyme.
1 Egg.	Rind of half a Lemon chopped
¼ lb. White Breadcrumbs.	finely.
¼ teaspoonful grated Nutmeg.	1 teaspoonful Salt.

½ teaspoonful Pepper.

Mince the bacon finely and mix it with the breadcrumbs, nutmeg, thyme, lemon peel, salt and pepper. Work these thoroughly well together, then bind them with one whole raw egg. Fill the leg with this as directed.

TO COOK THE CUCUMBER

Peel the cucumber and cut it in four, lengthways. Remove the seeds, then cut it into pieces two inches long. Melt two ounces of butter in a stewpan. Lay in the cucumber, season it well with pepper and salt, and cook gently until tender ; this will take about 15 minutes. Arrange in a dish alternately with stuffed tomatoes. (For STUFFED TOMATOES, see page 393.)

Boiled Leg of Mutton

A leg of Mutton.		A bunch of Herbs.
1 Carrot.	1 Turnip.	1 pint of Caper Sauce.
2 Onions.		2 dessertspoonfuls Salt.

Enough for 8 *to* 10 *persons.*

To prepare a leg of mutton for boiling, cut off the shank bone, trim the leg and make an incision at the first joint. This cuts the sinews and keeps the leg a better shape. Put it into a saucepan with sufficient cold water, slightly salted, to cover. Add the herbs and vegetables, washed and cleaned. Bring to the boil and cook for about 1½ hours, or according to size. This time is suited for a leg weighing six pounds (15 minutes to the pound). When it comes to the boil, draw to one side so that it only simmers gently for the remainder of the time.

When cooked, take out the leg, remove the cloth, put the leg on a dish, and place the dish over the saucepan to keep hot. Lift out the vegetables and trim and cut them into neat shapes. Pour caper sauce thickly over the leg of mutton and garnish round the dish with the trimmed vegetables.

NOTE.—1. The broth is kept for making mutton broth or any white soup.

2. If preferred, parsley sauce may be used instead of the caper sauce poured on the leg.

Braised Boned Leg of Mutton

A leg of Mutton.	1 Carrot. 2 Onions.
¼ lb. Bacon. 1 Egg.	Celery. 1 Turnip.
¼ lb. Breadcrumbs.	1 bunch of Herbs.
¼ lb. Mushrooms.	Peppercorns. 1 Shallot.
2 oz. Dripping.	Pepper and Salt.

Enough for 8 *to* 10 *persons.*

Bone a leg of mutton as described with Boned Leg of Mutton, page 271, but remove the knuckle entirely. Fill the cavity in the leg with stuffing. Turn in the meat at the knuckle end, then sew up both openings so that the stuffing will not come out. Make the leg into as compact a shape as possible, resembling a roly-poly pudding, and bind it well into shape with broad tape.

Put the dripping in the bottom of a stewpan, with the sliced carrot, sliced onions, a few pieces of celery cut up, a sliced turnip, a bunch of herbs (bayleaf, thyme and parsley), and about ten black and white peppercorns. Put the leg on these and fry it for about 20 minutes. Lay a well-buttered paper over the meat, then add about half a pint of stock. Put the pan into the oven and braise for about 1½ hours, keeping it constantly basted over the paper, adding more stock as that in the pan reduces.

When cooked, take up the leg, remove the tapes and brush it over with liquid glaze ; or with a little of the gravy in the pan, boiled down quickly to a glaze state. Dish up the leg, strain the gravy from the braise and remove all the fat. Put this gravy into a saucepan with half a pint of ordinary gravy or stock, and one teaspoonful of red currant jelly. Bring it to the boil, pour some of it round the meat, and serve the remainder in a sauce-boat. Garnish round the meat with alternate piles of potato balls and plainly boiled Brussels sprouts.

Roast Shoulder of Mutton

A shoulder of Mutton.	Salt and Pepper.
Dripping. Gravy.	Onion Sauce.

Enough for 8 to 10 persons.

Trim the shoulder neatly, place it on the stand in a roasting pan with the cut side upwards, and melt about half a pint of dripping and pour it over. Place the joint in the oven and baste it constantly, at least every 15 minutes. When it has been in about ½ hour, sprinkle it well with salt and pepper.

When cooked, take it up, stand it on a hot dish, and serve, accompanied by hot gravy in a sauce-boat. Onion sauce or Soubise sauce should always accompany roast shoulder of mutton.

Allow 15 minutes to the pound for roasting.

Boned Shoulder of Mutton

A shoulder of Mutton.	12 Mushrooms.
4 Sheep's Kidneys.	3 Tomatoes.
½ lb. Bacon.	Dripping. Butter.
2 Eggs. Onion.	Pepper and Salt.
½ lb. Breadcrumbs.	Gravy, as described.

Enough for 8 to 10 persons.

Bone a shoulder of mutton as described on page 271, and trim off some of the fat. Put the breadcrumbs into a basin. Skin and core the kidneys and chop them finely. Chop the bacon and a teaspoonful of onion, mix these ingredients and the crumbs well together, and season them with pepper and salt, then bind the whole with the well-beaten eggs. Fill the cavity in the shoulder with this stuffing, and roll and tie the shoulder (the meat) into a nice shape. Place it on the stand in an oven pan, and pour about half a pint of melted dripping over it. Place it in the oven to roast and baste it frequently, at least every 15 minutes.

Peel the mushrooms, remove the stalks and wash them in salted water. Melt about two ounces of butter in a stew-pan, lay in the mushrooms, the dark sides upwards, and dust them over with pepper and salt. Put on the lid, stand the pan on a moderately hot part of the stove, and cook until tender. Slice the tomatoes and cook them in the same way as the mushrooms.

For the gravy melt half an ounce of butter in a small saucepan. Add half an ounce of flour, and fry together without browning. Add half a pint of stock by degrees, and the liquor from the mushrooms and tomatoes. When the shoulder is cooked, take it up, strain the gravy and pour some round the joint. Garnish with the mushrooms and sliced tomatoes, putting them alternately, and resting one slightly on the other.

Allow 15 minutes to the pound for roasting.

Stuffed Loin of Mutton

Loin of Mutton.	Onions, cooked as described.
Dripping. Flour.	Veal Forcemeat.
Red Currant Jelly.	Pepper and Salt.

Enough for 8 *to* 10 *persons.*

Take a loin of mutton with the flap left on, and not jointed, and remove the outside skin. Cut out the fillet (which is the piece that is called the under-cut of a sirloin of beef). This is useful for noisettes of mutton and many small dishes, either as an entrée or a luncheon dish. Cut out all the bones from the loin and lay the joint out flat on a board with the cut side upwards.

Spread it all over with forcemeat as made for veal (for VEAL STUFFING, see page 135), then roll the loin up tightly. beginning from the thick side, bind it round firmly with tape, place it on the stand in a roasting pan, pour melted dripping over it, and sprinkle well with pepper and salt. Put it into a moderate oven to roast, and baste it frequently.

About ½ hour before the meat is cooked, dredge it over with flour, then baste again. When done, place it on a hot dish, and pour gravy round. Garnish with onions, and hand red currant jelly with the loin.

Allow 15 minutes to the pound for roasting.

TO COOK THE ONIONS

Choose Spanish onions, rather small, and skin them. Put them into a stewpan with two ounces of butter, or good dripping, and fry them until browning. Then dredge in three-quarters of an ounce of flour. Add one pint of brown stock and cook until the onions are tender. Arrange them round the meat.

Roast Neck of Mutton

| 4 lb. best end of Neck of Mutton. | Dripping. | Flour. |
| Potato Purée. | Salt. | |

Enough for 8 *persons.*

Take about four pounds of the best end of a neck of mutton. Chop off the bones evenly, and scrape off all the meat for about two inches up, just the same as if it was divided into cutlets. Now joint the meat. Dust it over with salt, then with flour, pour melted dripping over and place it in a brisk oven to roast.

When cooked, fill a forcing-bag, having a large rose-pipe, with a purée of potato. Force out two rows close together down the centre of the dish. Stand the neck of mutton on this with the thick end of the joint downwards. Then between each bone force out a rose of purée. Pour plenty of nice gravy round, in which may be dissolved a teaspoonful of red currant jelly.

Allow 15 minutes to the pound for the roasting.

Roast Hind-quarter of Lamb

A hind-quarter of Lamb.	Buttered Breadcrumbs.
Dripping. Gravy.	Watercress.
Mint Sauce.	Salt.

Enough for 10 *persons.*

Take a hind-quarter of lamb, saw off the knuckle bone, then fix the joint on a spit, or put it on the stand in a roasting pan. Cover it well with melted dripping and, if cooked in an oven, lay a greased paper over. Baste it regularly about every ¼ of an hour or rather less. About ½ an hour before the cooking is finished remove the paper and cover the top of the joint thickly with buttered breadcrumbs. Put it back in the oven to get nicely browned.

Garnish the joint with watercress nicely picked over and seasoned with pepper, salt, salad oil, and vinegar. Send to table with a clear gravy and mint sauce served in separate sauce-boats.

Allow 15 minutes to the pound for the roasting.

Roast Fore-quarter of Lamb

A fore-quarter of Lamb.	Maître d'Hôtel Butter.
Dripping.	Garnish of Peas.
Hot Mint Sauce.	

Enough for 7 or 8 persons.

Cut all the discoloured veiny parts from underneath the neck portion of a fore-quarter of lamb. Cover the joint well with melted dripping, and if there are any pieces of fat sent with the joint lay these on top. Roast in a moderate oven and baste it regularly every 10 to 15 minutes.

When cooked, take it up, cut round the shoulder, partly raise it from the neck part, and put in about two ounces of maître d'hôtel butter. Place it quickly on a hot dish, garnish with four little heaps of green peas round the dish. Serve with hot mint sauce, and a gravy may also be served with it if liked. (For SAUCES, see Index.)

Allow 15 minutes to the pound for the roasting.

Roast Neck of Lamb

| A neck of Lamb. | Stewed Cucumber. |
| Butter.   Parsley. | Maître d'Hôtel Sauce. |

Enough for 4 to 6 persons.

Trim the neck neatly, then wrap it up in a well-buttered paper and roast it in a brisk oven. When cooked, remove the paper, lay it on a hot dish and sprinkle a little finely chopped parsley on the top. Pour maître d'hôtel sauce round. (For SAUCES, see Index.) Garnish with stewed cucumber arranged round the dish.

Allow 15 minutes to the pound for the roasting.

Stewed Breast of Lamb

A breast of Lamb.	1½ pints Green Peas.
White Stock.	Potato Balls. Salt.
2 oz. Butter.	1 blade of Mace.
¾ oz. Flour.	½ teaspoonful White Pepper.

Enough for 3 persons.

Cut a breast of lamb into pieces and remove the skin. Lay the pieces in a stewpan, with a blade of mace, and sprinkle with a teaspoonful of salt, and half a teaspoonful of white pepper. Add sufficient white stock to cover, and place the lid on the pan and simmer very gently for $\frac{3}{4}$ hour. Skim well and remove the mace. Add one pint of the peas, and simmer again for $\frac{1}{2}$ hour.

Work the butter and the flour together, then stir them into the gravy in small lumps so that all dissolves. Simmer again for 10 minutes. Take the meat out carefully and arrange pieces prettily on a dish. Pour the sauce over them. Garnish the dish with potato balls, and the remaining half-pint of peas, plainly boiled.

Roast Saddle of Lamb

A saddle of Lamb. | Dripping. Salt.

Enough for 5 or 6 persons.

Wrap the saddle in a well-buttered paper. After sprinkling salt on the joint put it to roast in a moderately hot oven, and baste it frequently, at least every 10 to 15 minutes. About $\frac{1}{2}$ hour before it is cooked, remove the paper so that it may brown up nicely.

When done place it on a hot dish and pour a rich gravy round. Serve mint sauce with this joint. If liked, it can be garnished with watercress and fresh salad handed with it.

Allow 15 minutes to the pound for roasting.

Irish Stew

3 lb. Neck of Mutton. | $\frac{1}{2}$ lb. Suet Paste.
5 lb. Potatoes. | 1 teaspoonful Pepper.
3 large Onions. | 1 dessertspoonful Salt.
1$\frac{1}{2}$ pints Water.

Enough for 6 to 8 persons.

Cut the neck of mutton into neat pieces and trim off some of the fat. Pare the potatoes, and if large halve them lengthways. Peel the onions and slice them. Put a layer of the potatoes at the bottom of a stewpan, then a layer of the meat, then a layer of the onions. Sprinkle with part of the salt and pepper. Put another layer of the potatoes, meat and onions, but finish with a layer of potatoes on the top, then pour in the water gently. Put the lid closely on the pan and stew the contents very slowly for about 2 hours or rather longer. Do not let it cook fast.

About ½ hour before it is done make half a pound of suet paste into balls the size of a pigeon's egg and put them into the stew. When cooked, lift out the meat carefully and arrange it in the centre of a hot dish. Garnish round the meat with the potatoes and suet dumplings, and serve.

Roast Sirloin of Beef

A piece of Sirloin of Beef. | Flour. Salt.
Horseradish.

Allow a 10 *lb. joint for* 12 *persons.*

Choose a sirloin with a good undercut, but it should not exceed 16 lb. in weight. If larger it will be difficult to roast, the outside being apt to become overcooked by the time the middle is sufficiently done. Sprinkle it with flour.

TO ROAST THIS JOINT IN FRONT OF THE FIRE, hang it on the spit and have a dripping-pan beneath. Let the fire be clear. As this joint takes some time to cook, the fire must be properly attended to before putting the meat to it, and must be well kept up afterwards. Baste the meat carefully at about 10 to 15 minutes' intervals.

When done, sprinkle a small quantity of salt over it, and stand the joint on a hot dish. Empty the dripping-pan of all the dripping, and add about a quarter-pint of boiling water to the gravy in the pan. Remove every particle of fat, then strain the gravy round the meat, not over it. Garnish the joint with tufts of grated horseradish. Serve horseradish sauce with it, and Yorkshire pudding.

TO ROAST THIS JOINT IN THE OVEN, it is necessary to watch it carefully while cooking. It must be well basted at 10 to 15 minutes' intervals. The oven must not be allowed to overheat, neither must the joint be overdone, or it will prove to be most extragavant. Beef dripping should always be kept separate, as, when clarified, it is excellent for making cakes and pastry.

Allow 15 minutes to the pound for the roasting.

NOTE.—Joints should never be roasted in an oven without using a double pan. The water in the lower pan prevents the gravy or dripping boiling, as fat does not boil at the temperature of boiling water. Consequently the dripping does not waste, nor does it bubble and spit on to the hot oven plates, and the smell of burnt fat is absent.

Boiled Round of Beef

13 lb. silverside of Round of Beef.	6 Carrots. 6 Turnips.
	Suet Dumplings.

The whole round of beef is usually too large for a moderate sized family, and it is therefore best to have a piece of the silverside. After taking the meat out of the pickle (in which it should have been lying for about 10 days), wash off the salt, skewer it up into a nice round shape and bind it round firmly with tape, or buy it ready for cooking. As this is not a very fat part of the beef, it is best to skewer a piece of fat in as well.

When the meat is well bound up, put it into a saucepan with cold water to cover, and bring to the boil. Remove the scum as it rises. The skimming should be carefully attended to, as the appearance of the joint will be much spoiled if it is neglected. When the meat comes to the boil, draw the pan to one side and let it simmer gently for 3 hours. Two hours before it is done, put in the carrots and turnips, previously scraped and peeled and cut into convenient pieces. If the vegetables are young, they will not require so long a time to cook. About ½ hour before all is done, add about six suet dumplings the size of hens' eggs.

When the meat is done, take it up, remove the tape and skewers, and, if possible, replace the skewers with silver ones. Stand the meat on a hot dish and arrange the vegetables and dumplings neatly round. Pour a little of the liquor from the saucepan over the beef, and serve. The remainder of the liquor should be kept, as it is excellent for making pea soup.

NOTE.—If wanted to serve cold, return joint to pan containing liquor and leave till cold.

Roast Fillet of Beef

4 lb. Fillet of Beef.	1 dozen Olives.
½ pint Button Mushrooms.	½ pint Tomato Sauce.
Pepper and Salt.	

Enough for 6 to 8 persons.

Trim off all unnecessary fat and skin from the meat, season it with pepper and salt, and tie it up, across the fillet, with two or three pieces of tape to keep the meat in a nice compact form. Roll it in a well-buttered paper, and place it in a roasting pan. Pour some melted dripping over, and put it into a quick oven to roast. Baste it constantly.

Turn a dozen olives, or choose stoned olives, and heat these with half a pint of button mushrooms, in a little stock. When the meat is half cooked, remove the paper and dredge the fillet over with flour. Return it to the oven to brown up nicely. When cooked, place it on a hot dish, and pour half a pint of tomato sauce round. (FOR TOMATO SAUCE, see page 169.) Garnish with the button mushrooms and turned olives.

Allow 15 minutes to the pound for the roasting.

Braised Fillet of Beef

3 lb. Fillet of Beef.
1 Carrot. 2 Onions.
1 small Turnip. 12 Allspice.
½ stick Celery.
A bunch of Herbs (Bayleaf, Thyme, and Parsley).
8 Peppercorns.

1 tablespoonful Mushroom Ketchup.
1 wineglassful Sherry.
3 oz. Butter or good Dripping.
Slices of fat Bacon.
½ pint Stock or Gravy.
Garnish.

Enough for 5 or 6 persons.

Melt three ounces of butter or dripping in a stewpan. Slice the carrot, onions, celery and turnip, and add these to the butter. Add also the herbs, sherry, ketchup and spices. Trim the fillet neatly, and free it from skin and unnecessary fat. Tie it up neatly with tape and lay it on top of the vegetables. On top of the meat place two or three slices of fat bacon. Put the lid close down on the pan, and let all fry together for about 15 minutes.

Now pour into the pan, by the side of the beef, about half a pint of stock or gravy. Let the meat braise gently for about 2½ hours, and keep it well basted with the liquor, adding more as it reduces.

When cooked, take out the fillet, remove the tapes, then lay it on a hot dish. Lift the vegetables out of the pan. Boil the gravy rapidly until reduced to a glazy state. Brush the meat over with this, and pour a rich gravy round. Garnish with fried potatoes and mushrooms in alternate heaps.

Stewed Steak and Oysters

1½ lb. Steak.
1½ dozen Oysters.
2 oz. Butter.
1 Onion.

½ wineglassful Port Wine.
1 teaspoonful Flour.
½ pint of Water.
Pepper and Salt.

Enough for 4 or 5 persons.

Melt the butter in a stewpan. Slice the onion, put it in

with the butter, and fry until it is a golden brown, then lay
in the steak, cut into thick pieces. Fry for about 15 minutes
then add the water and season with pepper and salt to taste
Add the liquor from the oysters, cover the pan closely
and let it simmer gently for 1 hour.

Then mix the flour smoothly with the port wine, and
thicken the gravy with this. Draw the pan from the fire, add
the oysters, and stir until they are plump. Do not let it
boil after the oysters are in or they will be leathery. Dish
up the steak, put the oysters round and pour the gravy over
Garnish with croûtons of fried bread, brushed over with
white of egg, and dipped in grated Parmesan cheese.

Beefsteak and Kidney Pudding

2 lb. Steak.	1 Shallot. Vinegar.
1½ lb. Suet Crust.	1 teaspoonful Parsley.
1 Ox Kidney.	Salt and Pepper.

Enough for 5 or 6 persons.

Beat the beefsteak well with a wet rolling pin, and cut
into pieces about two ounces each. Put the kidney in sufficient
cold water to cover it, with about a tablespoonful of vinegar
added, and soak it for 10 minutes, then take out the kidney,
rinse it in fresh, cold water, dry it thoroughly, core it and slice
it.

Well butter a pudding-basin and line it with suet paste,
leaving a good margin of paste hanging over the edge. Put
in a layer of the steak and kidney, sprinkle it with a little
of the chopped parsley, shallot (or onion), pepper, and salt.
If liked, a mushroom or two can be used. Put in another
layer of the steak, kidney and seasoning, and so on until the
basin is full. Pour in about a gill and a half of cold water.

Cut out a piece of paste the size of the basin and lay it
on top. Wet the edges, then fold over the margin of paste
lining and press down firmly so that gravy may not escape.
Lay a buttered paper over the top, then a pudding cloth, and
tie cloth firmly on. Have ready a saucepan three-parts full
of boiling water, and put the pudding in. Boil for at least
4 hours. If the water boils away, add more that is boiling.
The pudding must be kept well covered with boiling water.

Turn the pudding out on to a hot dish, sprinkle a little
chopped parsley on top, then serve. Or serve in the basin
with a folded table napkin pinned round.

NOTE.—When cooked, take off the cloth and the paper,

and cut out a small piece of the paste, about the size of a shilling, from the centre of the pudding. This will prevent the pudding breaking when it is afterwards turned out.

Beefsteak and Oyster Pie

2 lb. Fillet Steak.		½ lb. Puff Paste.	
2 dozen Oysters.		White Stock.	Cayenne.
	Salt.	White Pepper.	

Enough for 5 or 6 persons.

Cut the fillet steak into thin slices, flatten them out, then wrap up an oyster in each slice. Put a layer of this in a pie-dish and season with white pepper, salt, and a dust of cayenne.

Put another layer and season, and so on, until the dish is full, then pour in white stock until the dish is nearly filled with it. Wet the edge of the dish, and line the edge with a strip of puff paste rolled out to about a quarter of an inch thickness and cut to the width of the dish edge. Wet this rim of paste, then put a cover of paste of the same thickness over the pie, make a hole in the centre of the cover to let the steam escape, ornament the edge of the paste, cut four leaves from the trimmings of paste, and arrange them round the centre hole. Brush the pie over with whole beaten-up egg, then stand the pie-dish in a tin containing boiling water, place this in a moderately quick oven, and bake until the paste has well risen.

After that put the pie down at the bottom of the oven, still keeping it in water, until the meat is cooked. The pie will take about an hour and a half altogether. When cooked, take the pie out of the oven, and whilst still hot fill it quite up with more of the gravy by pouring it through the hole in the centre of the top crust. Be sure to add the liquor from the oysters.

Broiled Steak

| 1½ lb. Rump Steak. | | Salad Oil. | Pepper. |
| | Maître d'Hôtel Butter. | | |

Enough for 4 to 6 persons.

Have a prime rump steak, not cut too thin. Wipe it, also trim off any superfluous fat. Rub it over with salad oil, and sprinkle it with pepper only. Rub the bars of the gridiron or grill over with a piece of suet. Make the bars quite hot, then lay the steak on it. Have a very clear fire—one made partly with coke is best. Stand the gridiron over it, and grill the steak from 8 to 10 minutes, according to whether it is required underdone, or moderately well done, or cook under an electric or gas grill.

When the steak is to be turned use steak tongs (made for the purpose) if you have them. If not, then arrange to turn the steak some other way, but on no account should a fork be stuck into it. Only turn steak once whilst grilling. It is a mistake to think it requires frequent turning.

Have ready a very hot dish, cover, and plates. Take the steak up, lay one or two pieces of maître d'hôtel butter on top and serve quickly. Steak should never be kept waiting after it leaves the fire. It may also be served with tomato or horseradish sauce. (For SAUCES, see Index.)

NOTE.—Some people like a piece of butter melted in the dish, and a teaspoonful or two of Worcester sauce or ketchup heated with it. The gravy which runs from the meat is, however, generally sufficient.

Roast Fillet of Veal

8 lb. Fillet of Veal.	Dripping.
1 lb. Veal Forcemeat.	Pepper.　Salt.
¼ lb. fat Bacon.	Flour.

Garnish of Bacon and Lemon.

Enough for 10 to 12 persons.

Cut out the centre bone of the fillet and fill the cavity that this leaves with forcemeat. Cut the bacon into thin slices, tie it round the meat and skewer it firmly. Put the joint on the stand of a roasting pan, and pour half a pint of melted dripping over it. Half fill the lower pan with water, and put it all into a moderate oven and baste frequently, at least every 10 or 15 minutes.

When the meat has been in the oven for 2 hours, remove the bacon, sprinkle the veal with pepper and salt, and dredge it over with flour. Baste frequently and roast for 1 hour longer. When cooked, place the veal on a hot dish, and garnish round with small rolls of thin bacon and slices of lemon. Strain the gravy from the pan and put it into a saucepan. Skim all the fat off, then add sufficient gravy stock or boiling water to it to make up half a pint. Stir well, and when boiling pour it round the joint.

Veal should be cooked slowly, and constantly basted, for,

like lamb, it requires to be thoroughly well cooked. Some prefer to have bread sauce served with the veal, but it is by no means necessary.

Roast Loin of Veal, with Cream Gravy

5 or 6 lb. of Loin of Veal.
Pepper and Salt.

Macaroni Sauce.
½ pint Single Cream.

Enough for 6 to 8 persons.

Bone the loin of veal, remove any unnecessary fat, but leave the kidney. Season with pepper and salt. Fold the flap under so as to cover the kidney entirely, then tie the joint round with string to keep it in place. Wrap it in a sheet of well-buttered paper and roast in a moderate oven for about 1½ hours, keeping it well basted.

After 2 hours' roasting, remove the paper, and put the veal into a baking tin with the cream. Cook it for ½ hour longer and baste it with the cream. When cooked put the joint on to a hot dish. Serve with cream gravy in a hot sauce-boat.

Braised Breast of Veal

3 lb. Breast of Veal.
Veal Forcemeat.
Stock.   1 oz. Butter.
1 Onion.   1 Carrot.
½ stick of Celery.

A bunch of Herbs (Bayleaf,
    Thyme and Parsley).
6 Peppercorns.
1 teaspoonful Salt.
Cucumber Sauce.

Enough for 6 persons.

Bone the breast of veal, and lay the meat out flat on a board, with the skin side downwards. Spread a layer of forcemeat over, then roll, and tie it up into a neat shape. Make a few slights cuts in the skin.

Put the butter into a stewpan with the carrot, onion and celery (all sliced), and the bunch of herbs, peppercorns and salt. Lay the meat on top, put the lid on closely, and fry about 15 minutes. Now lay a buttered paper on top of the meat, pour about half a pint of stock into the pan and baste the meat with it. Put the lid on closely again, stand the pan in a moderate oven, and cook gently for about 2 hours, basting frequently, and adding more stock as that in the pan reduces.

When cooked, take it up, remove the strings and brush it over with liquid glaze. Stand the joint on a hot dish, pour cucumber sauce round, and serve.

Calf's Head

Half a Calf's Head.	1 tablespoonful Salt.
1 large Onion.	½ stick of Celery.
1 Carrot. 1 Leek.	1 pint Parsley Sauce.

Enough for 5 or 6 persons.

Put half a calf's head to soak in well-salted cold water for two or three hours, during which time the water should be changed once or twice. Then take it out and rinse well in cold water. Remove the brains and tongue, soak and wash brains, blanch them, then boil for 15 minutes. Take a small pointed knife and bone the head, leaving on the ear. When the bone is removed, roll up the flesh lengthways, put it into a well-buttered cloth, and bind firmly with tape to keep it in a good shape. Put it into a stewpan with cold water to cover.

Wash and pare the vegetables, cut them into pieces about an inch and a half long, put them in with the head and add the bones. Bring to the boil and skim well, being careful to remove the scum as it rises. Add salt, also put the tongue in, tied in a piece of muslin. Boil for 2½ to 3 hours, or even longer, according to size.

Take it up, and remove the cloths. Lay the head on a hot dish, and cut the ear into strips with a pair of scissors. Make a pint of good parsley sauce. Chop the brains, and put these into the parsley sauce. Pour the sauce over the head. Skin the tongue, lay it by the side of the head, and serve very hot. The whole head may be cooked and served in the same way. If liked, tomato sauce may be poured over the head instead of parsley sauce. Garnish with fresh parsley and lemon.

Chump of Veal

4 or 5 lb. of the chump end of a Loin of Veal.	½ oz. Glaze.
	1 Onion. 1 Carrot.
3 oz. Bacon Trimmings.	½ stick of Celery.
1 oz. Butter.	½ a Turnip.
1 quart Stock.	Salt and Pepper.

Stuffing, as described.

Enough for 6 or 7 persons.

Take four or five pounds of the chump end of a loin of veal, and bone it. Then stuff it with the stuffing described below. Chop up the bones and trimmings, and prepare and slice the vegetables. Put the vegetables, chopped bones, bacon trimmings, and one ounce of butter into a stewpan.

After stuffing the veal, tie it up firmly into a good shape with tape and lay it in the pan with the vegetables. Put the pan over a moderate fire, and fry gently until the veal is a pale brown all over. Turn the veal frequently, and baste it with the butter. When it is a good colour, add a quart of stock, season with pepper and salt, put the lid on the pan, and let it simmer gently for about $1\frac{1}{2}$ to $1\frac{3}{4}$ hours.

When cooked take out the meat and keep it hot. Strain the gravy, take off the fat, add the glaze, and boil until it reduces about a third. Pour this over the veal, and garnish round the dish with potato balls.

THE STUFFING

6 oz. fine Breadcrumbs.	1 teaspoonful Lemon **Peel, chopped.**
1 dessertspoonful chopped **Thyme.**	3 oz. Beef Suet.
1 teaspoonful chopped **Marjoram.**	2 Eggs.
1 tablespoonful chopped **Parsley.**	1 teaspoonful **Salt.**

$\frac{1}{2}$ teaspoonful Pepper.

Wash the parsley, thyme and marjoram and dry them well in a cloth, then mince them and the lemon peel very finely. Chop the suet finely, too. Put all the ingredients into a basin, add salt and pepper, and mix thoroughly whilst in a dry state. When thoroughly mixed, bind the whole with two well-beaten eggs, then use it for stuffing the veal.

Dried herbs may be used if fresh ones are not procurable, but they must be thoroughly well powdered and sifted, so that they are quite fine and free from stalks. Remove the strings from the meat before putting it on the dish. If glaze is not procurable, use a teaspoonful of meat extract instead, but then the gravy should be thickened with a little potato flour.

Boiled Knuckle of Veal

4 to 6 lb. Knuckle of Veal.	$\frac{1}{4}$ lb. Rice.
1 oz. Butter.	1 tablespoonful chopped **Parsley.**
$\frac{3}{4}$ oz. Flour.	A blade of Mace.
2 Onions.	Salt. Pepper.

Enough for 6 persons.

Break the shank-bone of the knuckle, and wash it clean. Put this into a stewpan, with sufficient water to cover, let it gradually come to the boil, and remove the scum. After skimming well, add the rice, onions, blade of mace, pepper and salt. Simmer the whole gently for about $2\frac{1}{2}$ hours. When cooked, take up the meat, put it on a dish, and keep hot while the sauce is being made.

Melt the butter in a saucepan, add the flour, and fry together for 5 minutes, without browning. Mix in gradually one pint, or rather more, of the stock and rice in which the knuckle has boiled, and add the chopped parsley. Pour this over the knuckle, then garnish round with plainly boiled olive potatoes. If liked, a piece of pickled pork may be boiled separately and served with the veal.

Roast Ox Heart

| 1 Ox Heart. | Veal Forcemeat. |
| Dripping. | Tomato Sauce. |

Enough for 6 persons.

Take an ox heart that has hung for 2 or 3 days. Wash and soak it very thoroughly, to remove the blood. Cut away the pipes, and fill the cavities with veal forcemeat, securing it well with needle and twine. Pour half a pint of melted dripping over the heart. Wrap it in a well-buttered paper, and put it in a roasting tin. Roast it in a moderate oven, for $2\frac{1}{2}$ hours.

About $\frac{1}{2}$ hour before it is done, remove the paper, baste the heart well with dripping, sprinkle it over with salt and pepper, then dredge it thoroughly with flour. Put it back into the oven for the remaining $\frac{1}{2}$ hour, to brown nicely. When cooked, lay the heart on a very hot dish, pour tomato sauce round, and serve immediately.

Ox heart is spoiled if not sent to table directly it is cooked; and very hot plates should accompany it. If liked, a good brown gravy may be poured round the heart on the dish instead of tomato sauce. In this case, red currant jelly should be served with it.

ROAST SHEEP'S HEARTS are served in the same way as ox heart, but they only require 1 hour to cook.

VEGETABLES

THERE are two details in the preparation of vegetables that should have the best attention always. Firstly, the vegetables should be quite fresh. Secondly, they must be thoroughly well cleaned. Stale flabby vegetables never repay one for the trouble of cooking, and are quite the dearest in the end, however cheaply they may have been purchased in the first place.

Practically all vegetables, with the exception of old potatoes and dried (haricot) beans, require to be put into boiling water (unless otherwise directed) and be kept boiling all the time. If allowed to go off the boil they get watery. They must also be taken out of the water directly they are cooked, never allowed to stand in the water.

Cabbage, cauliflower, lettuce, or any vegetable that may contain insects, should be soaked in strongly salted water for a little time, and then be well rinsed in fresh water. All tuber or root vegetables should be well scrubbed before peeling. As the vegetables are prepared for cooking, they should be put into cold water and allowed to remain in it until required.

Boiled Potatoes

UTENSILS—Basin, scrubbing brush, knife or potato peeler, saucepan, skewer, cloth. *Allow 2 medium-sized potatoes per person, and 1 or 2 over.*

Choose potatoes of as nearly the same size as possible, wash and brush them in cold water to remove the earth, then throw them into a basin of clean cold water. Peel the potatoes as thinly as possible, cutting out the black spots (eyes). As they are peeled throw them into cold water, and if very large cut them in half lengthways. Put them into a saucepan with just enough water to cover, and bring quickly to the boil.

Draw the pan to one side, or lower the gas flame, and allow it to boil gently for 20 minutes to 30 minutes, or until a skewer can be rather easily run through them. The time varies with the age and the kind of potato.

When cooked as much as this, pour off every drop of water holding the lid against the pan to prevent the contents falling out. When strained, cover the potatoes with a clean cloth and put the lid close on the pan for 10 minutes to finish cooking, shaking the pan occasionally during this time Then put the lid half on, and leave for another 5 or 10 minutes, and the potatoes should then be quite dry and floury. Do not boil potatoes too long, as they will finish cooking in their own steam when the water is drained off.

Baked Potatoes

UTENSILS—Basin, scrubbing brush, baking tin. *Allow 2 medium-sized potatoes per person, and 1 or 2 over.*

Choose potatoes that are perfectly sound, wash and brush them in cold water, and rinse them in fresh cold water. Put them into a baking tin without drying them, and bake in a moderate oven for about 1 hour.

Fold a serviette, put it in a hot vegetable dish, arrange the potatoes and draw the serviette well up over them.

Roast Potatoes

UTENSILS—Basin, scrubbing brush, knife or potato peeler, saucepan, cloth, baking tin. *Allow 2 potatoes per person, and 1 or 2 over.*

Prepare the potatoes as for boiling, page 289. Put them into a saucepan with cold salted water, and bring to the boil. Then strain and dry them well in a cloth. Either put them into the dripping-tin beneath the joint with which they are to be served, or put them into a baking tin with three or four tablespoonfuls of dripping. Sprinkle them with salt and bake in a quick oven for ¾ hour to 1 hour, or until they are soft and nicely brown.

New Potatoes

UTENSILS—Two basins, scrubbing brush, knife, saucepan, teaspoon. *Allow 3 per person, and 3 or 4 over.*

Wash and brush the potatoes, then put them into clean cold water. Either scrape off the skins with a knife or, if they are very fresh, it is easier to rub the skins off with a coarse cloth. As they are skinned throw them into cold water. They turn brown quickly if left out of water. Put them into a saucepan with boiling water, salted in the proportion of a teaspoonful of salt to every quart of water. Put in a sprig of mint.

Boil from 15 to 20 minutes, according to size. When soft, pour off the water, lay a cloth over the potatoes, and let them steam for 10 minutes, then remove the mint. Put one ounce of butter on the top of the potatoes, and when it is quite melted turn them out into a hot vegetable dish. Sprinkle with a little finely chopped parsley, and serve.

Sauté Potatoes

1 lb. Boiled Potatoes.		**1 teaspoonful finely-chopped**
2 oz. Butter.	**Salt.**	**Parsley.**

UTENSILS—Knife, plate, sauté pan, fork, teaspoon. *Enough for 3 persons.*

Cut the boiled potatoes into slices about a quarter of an inch thick. Melt the butter in a sauté pan. Lay in the slices of potato, only putting in sufficient at one time to cover the bottom of the pan. Fry until they are a nice golden colour, moving them constantly.

When nicely coloured, turn them on to a hot dish. Keep these hot while frying the others in the same manner. When all are done and on the dish, pour the butter that is left in the pan over them. Sprinkle with chopped parsley and salt, then serve.

Potatoes à la Française

2 lb. Potatoes.	**Chopped Parsley.**
Frying Fat.	**Coralline Pepper.**

UTENSILS—Knife, basin, cloth, stewpan, frying basket, wire sieve, fork. *Enough for 6 persons.*

Let the potatoes be of uniform size, and pare them evenly, trimming the sides until they are quite smooth. Now cut the potatoes into even slices an eighth of an inch thick. Wash the slices well in cold water, then dry them thoroughly in a cloth. Have ready a stewpan half full of frying fat, hot enough to frizzle a piece of bread dropped into it, but not smoking. Lay the slices of potato in a wire basket, only putting enough to cover the bottom, and not overlapping one another. Plunge the basket into the fat and cook till tender, but do not brown them. They should only be a pale gold colour.

When cooked, drain on a wire sieve, and repeat this process until all the slices are done. This part of the cooking can be done some time before they are wanted. The following completes the cooking when the potatoes are required. Have ready a pan of clarified boiling fat. This must be quite boiling (with blue smoke coming from it). Put the partially cooked potatoes into the basket, plunge them into the fat, and move them about. The slices will then swell out, if the potatoes are good. Pick out those that are swelled, drain them quite dry, and arrange prettily on a dish-paper. Sprinkle with chopped parsley and coralline pepper.

In the second frying it is not necessary to do only one layer at the time, a larger quantity can be done at once. The important things to be remembered are—firstly, that the slices must all be of the same thickness ; secondly, the second lot of frying fat must be quite boiling. The slices which have not swelled out with the second frying may be tried again in the boiling fat, but success is doubtful.

Potatoes à la Maître d'Hôtel

1½ lb. Potatoes.	1 tablespoonful chopped **Parsley.**
1 oz. Butter. ½ oz. Flour.	1 Yolk of Egg.
½ pint White Stock.	Salt and Pepper.
1 teaspoonful strained Lemon Juice.	

UTENSILS—Knife, saucepan, colander, measuring spoons, wooden spoon, basin, egg-beater, lemon squeezer, strainer. *Enough for 4 or 5 persons.*

Peel the potatoes, and put them into a saucepan, with sufficient cold water to cover. Bring to the boil, strain, then wash them in cold water. Put them on again, with sufficient cold water to cover, and add one teaspoonful of salt. Boil until the potatoes are barely tender, strain, and let them dry thoroughly. When cold, cut into thick slices.

Melt the butter in a saucepan, dredge in the flour, and stir until smooth. Add the stock by degrees, and stir until it boils. Put in the potatoes, the finely-chopped parsley, and salt and pepper to taste, unless the stock is already highly seasoned. Simmer the potatoes in this for 5 minutes.

Beat the yolk of an egg, add about a teaspoonful of cold stock or water, also the lemon juice. Draw the saucepan to the side of the stove or lower the gas flame, stir in the beaten-up egg and lemon juice. When the stock thickens, turn all out into a hot dish, and serve.

Chip Potatoes

Potatoes. | **Frying Fat.   Salt.**

UTENSILS—Knife, basin, cloth, stewpan, fork, sieve or kitchen paper. *Allow about 2 potatoes per person.*

Wash the potatoes well, and peel them. Slice very thinly, keeping the slices as nearly as possible of the same thickness. As they are sliced, put them into a basin of cold water, and leave them in this for about 15 minutes. Rinse, and dry them thoroughly in a cloth. Have ready a stewpan, half full of good clarified fat quite boiling, and put the slices in this. Stir constantly, so that they colour evenly. When they feel quite crisp, and are of a pale golden colour, lift them out quickly, and drain thoroughly. Do not let them get too brown, as they darken slightly after being taken out of the fat. When quite dry, turn them into a very hot dish, sprinkle with salt, and serve.

Mashed Potatoes

1 lb. cooked Potatoes. | **3 tablespoonfuls Milk or Cream.**
2 oz. Butter. | **White Pepper.   Salt.**

UTENSILS—Two saucepans, wire sieve, wooden spoon. *Enough for 3 persons.*

The potatoes should be plainly boiled, and floury. Rub them through a wire sieve, or put them through a potato masher. Melt the butter in a saucepan, put the potatoes in, and season with pepper and salt to taste. Add the milk or cream, and mix with a wooden spoon until quite white and smooth. Put them into a hot dish, and mould into any form preferred.

Green Peas

1 quart shelled Green Peas. | **1½ oz. Butter.   Pepper.**
2 teaspoonfuls Salt. | **A sprig of Mint.**
1 teaspoonful Sugar. | **2 quarts Water.**

UTENSILS—Enamelled saucepan, knife, colander, teaspoon, quart measure. *Enough for 3 or 4 persons.*

When the water is boiling fast, season it with the salt and sugar, put in the peas and the sprig of mint. Boil rapidly, with the lid off the pan, for 15 to 25 minutes, according to the age of the peas. When cooked, drain the peas in a colander, remove the mint, then return them to the saucepan. Add the butter and sprinkle with a little salt, pepper, and castor sugar, and shake the peas gently until the season-ings are thoroughly mixed. Serve them in a hot dish.

NOTE.—Peas should never be boiled in a tin saucepan if they are to be of a good colour.

Peas with Bacon

1 quart shelled Peas.	3 oz. Streaky Bacon.
1 sprig of Mint.	1 oz. Butter.
1 small Lettuce.	1 oz. Flour. 1 quart Water.
1 small Onion.	1 teaspoonful Salt.

UTENSILS—Two saucepans, basin, wooden spoon, knife, quart measure, frying pan. *Enough for 3 or 4 persons.*

Wash the shells or pods of the peas and put them on to boil in one quart of water with the sprig of mint, the lettuce, salt and onion, and let these boil together for 20 minutes. Strain the liquor from the above into a stewpan, and when it boils put in the shelled peas. Boil until the peas are tender. When the peas are cooked, work up one ounce of butter with one ounce of flour, and stir this into the peas by degrees. Cut the bacon into small dice, and fry them crisp. Mix the bacon in with the peas, place all in a hot dish, and garnish with fried croûtons of bread.

French Beans

UTENSILS—Knife, basin, saucepan, colander. *Allow 1 quart for 4 or 5 persons.*

Choose fresh young beans, rinse them in cold water, and cut off the heads and tails, also the thin strip of fibre down each edge of the bean. If the beans are very young, there will be nothing to trim off the edges, in which case only the ends need be cut off. Then cut the bean either into thin slices, or across in a slanting direction.

When prepared, plunge them into fast-boiling salted water. They will take about 20 minutes to cook, during which time the pan should be left uncovered to keep the beans a good colour. When on the point of being cooked, the beans will sink to the bottom of the pan. They must then be taken off at once and drained in a colander. Return them to the saucepan ; put some pieces of butter on top, add pepper and salt, and shake the saucepan until the butter is melted. Turn all out into a hot dish, and serve.

Broad Beans

UTENSILS—Basin, saucepan, colander, large spoon. *Allow*
1 *peck for* 6 *or* 7 *persons.*

Shell the beans, and, if old, skin them. To skin the beans,
throw them into a basin of boiling water, and let them remain
in it for a few minutes. Strain them off, and they can be
skinned quite easily.

To cook the beans, put them into a saucepan of fast-
boiling salted water, and boil for about 15 to 20 minutes,
until tender. Remove any scum that may rise. When cooked,
drain in a colander, then return them to the saucepan, with
a piece of butter and seasoning of pepper and salt. Toss
them about while the butter melts and the beans get
thoroughly hot, then serve.

Cabbage

UTENSILS—Knife, teaspoon, basin, saucepan, colander,
saucer, mould. *Allow* 1 *large cabbage for* 3 *or* 4 *persons.*

Cut off the outer leaves of the cabbage and the hard part
of the stalk. Put it to soak, for about ½ hour, in sufficient
water to cover, to which must be added two teaspoonfuls
of vinegar. This is to draw out any insects there may be
in it. Have ready a saucepan of boiling salted water. Take
the cabbage out of the vinegar and water, rinse it in fresh
water, then plunge it into the saucepan of boiling salted
water. Boil rapidly, with the lid off the pan, until the cabbage
is quite tender. This will take from 20 minutes to ½ hour,
or even longer.

Drain thoroughly in a colander, and, with the under side
of a saucer or plate, press out all the moisture. If the cabbages
are young, cut them across once or twice with a knife, put a
small piece of butter in each, then turn them into a hot dish,
and serve. If older, chop the cabbage up well, and put into
a saucepan with an ounce of butter and seasoning of pepper
and salt. Make it thoroughly hot, then put it into a well-
buttered plain mould or pudding basin. Press the cabbage
in firmly, turn it out into a hot dish, sprinkle the top with
coralline pepper, and serve.

Peas à la Française

1 quart shelled Peas.	1 teaspoonful Cream.
1 Onion. 1 Lettuce.	½ teaspoonful Castor Sugar.
2 Eggs. Pepper and Salt.	2 oz. Butter. Mint.

UTENSILS—Knife, stewpan, basin, egg-beater, wooden spoon, teaspoon. *Enough for 3 or 4 persons.*

Peel the onion. Cut the heart of a well-washed lettuce into fine shreds. Put the butter into a clean stewpan, add the peas, pepper, salt, lettuce, onion and a sprig of mint, but no water except that which hangs upon the lettuce. Cover up the pan, and let its contents cook gently from 20 to 30 minutes. When the peas are tender, remove the mint and onion from the pan.

Well beat the yolks of eggs with the cream. Stir this into the peas, with about half a teaspoonful of castor sugar. Shake the pan until the peas are nicely thickened, but on no account allow the mixture to boil after the eggs are added.

Boiled Turnips

UTENSILS—Basin, scrubbing brush, knife, saucepan, colander. *Allow 2 medium-sized turnips per person.*

First wash and brush the turnips well. Pare them rather thickly, as the outer skin is very often bitter, and, unless the turnips are very young, the outside is generally stringy. If large, cut them in halves, or in quarters. Put them into a saucepan, with plenty of boiling water, salted in the proportion of one large teaspoonful of salt to every quart of water. Boil about $\frac{3}{4}$ hour, until they can be easily pierced with a fork. Drain well in a colander, place them in a vegetable dish, pour half a pint of white sauce over, and serve.

Purée of Turnips

3 lb. Turnips.	2 tablespoonfuls sifted Flour.
4 tablespoonfuls Cream.	4 Whites of Eggs. Parsley.
1 oz. Butter.	Salt and Pepper.

UTENSILS—Two basins, scrubbing brush, knife, 2 saucepans, colander, cloth, wire sieve, wooden spoon, sieve or flour sifter, fireproof dish, tablespoon, egg-beater, forcing-bag, baking tin. *Enough for 5 or 6 persons.*

Pare and slice the turnips. Put them into a saucepan of cold water, with half a teaspoonful of salt. Bring to the boil, then strain, and rinse them in cold water. Now put the slices into fast-boiling salted water, and boil until tender. When cooked, drain well, then wring them perfectly dry in a strong cloth. Rub the whole through a wire sieve. Put this purée into a saucepan, with the butter, half the cream, and the white pepper and salt, then sift in the flour. Stir with a wooden spoon, until boiling.

Well butter a deep fireproof dish, and put the purée into it. Pour over the purée two tablespoonfuls of cream. Whip the whites of four eggs stiffly, with a pinch of salt. Put these into a forcing-bag with a large rose-pipe, and ornament the top of the turnips with it. Stand the dish in a tin of boiling water, and place it in a moderate oven until the egg is a nice gold colour. Sprinkle the top with finely chopped parsley, stand the dish on another, and serve.

Turnips à la Béchamel

1 bunch of Turnips.	**½ pint Creamy Béchamel**
Water. Salt.	**Sauce.**

UTENSILS—Basin, knife, scrubbing brush, 2 saucepans, colander, wooden spoon. *Enough for 2 or 3 persons.*

Wash, pare and quarter the turnips, put them into a saucepan of cold water, with a pinch of salt, and bring them to the boil. As soon as they boil strain them, and rinse in cold water. Now put them into a saucepan of boiling salted water, and boil until tender. Drain thoroughly, and arrange the turnips in a hot vegetable dish. Pour half a pint of creamy Béchamel sauce over, and serve.

Chicory

1 lb. Chicory.	**Salt.**	**Water.**
	Melted Butter.	

UTENSILS—Basin, 2 saucepans, colander. *Enough for 2 or 3 persons.*

It is, of course, the bleached tops of chicory that are used. Wash the chicory well in salted water, then put it into a saucepan of cold water. Just bring to the boil, then strain, and rinse it in cold water. Now put it in boiling salted water, and boil until tender. When cooked, drain thoroughly, and place in a hot vegetable dish. Pour plain melted butter sauce over, and serve.

NOTE.—Chicory also makes excellent salad in its raw state, with a dressing of oil and vinegar. It is also very nice stewed in a good brown gravy.

Cauliflower au Gratin

1 Cauliflower.	2 oz. buttered Breadcrumbs.
¾ pint Béchamel Sauce.	4 oz. grated Cheese.
2 oz. Butter.	Cayenne. Salt.

UTENSILS—Basin, knife, 2 saucepans, wooden spoon, fireproof gratin dish, pint measure, grater. *Enough for 2 or 3 persons.*

Trim the cauliflower neatly, blanch it, then plainly boil it, and when cooked, drain it well. Thickly butter a fireproof gratin dish, and lay the cauliflower in it.

Make three-quarters of a pint of Béchamel sauce (for SAUCES, see Index). Grate four ounces of a dry cooking cheese. Stir the cheese into the sauce, and season well with salt and cayenne. Pour this over the cauliflower, then sprinkle the top with buttered breadcrumbs. Bake it in a moderately hot oven for 15 to 20 minutes, until it is a nice golden brown. Serve in a silver dish or on a plate with a paper collar round its neck. Serve at once.

Vegetable Marrow

2 young Vegetable Marrows.	2 oz. Butter.
	Pepper and Salt.

UTENSILS—Knife, basin, saucepan or fireproof dish. *Enough for 4 to 6 persons.*

The following recipe is for very young marrows. Scrape the outsides, then cut them into quarters, and remove the seeds. Rinse the quarters in cold water. Melt the butter in a saucepan. Put in the pieces of marrow, and sprinkle with pepper and salt. Cover closely with the lid of the saucepan, and cook gently over a low flame, or cook the marrow in a covered fireproof dish in the oven. Time required by either method—about ½ hour.

Lift out the marrows, and put them into a hot vegetable dish. Make half a pint of white sauce, add the liquor from the saucepan to it, and pour over the marrow in the dish. To cook marrows when not so young, they have simply to be pared and quartered, then boiled in plenty of boiling salted water. (For WHITE SAUCE, see Index.)

Tomatoes au Gratin

1 lb. Tomatoes.	1 small teaspoonful Pepper.
4 oz. Breadcrumbs.	1 teaspoonful Salt.
2 oz. Butter.	½ teaspoonful Castor Sugar.
1 teaspoonful chopped Shallot.	

UTENSILS—Basin, knife, pie-dish, grater, teaspoon. *Enough for 3 or 4 persons.*

Scald and skin the tomatoes, then cut them in slices. Well butter a pie-dish, and line it thickly with buttered breadcrumbs. Put in a layer of tomatoes, sprinkle with pepper, salt, sugar and a little finely-chopped shallot. Then put a layer of breadcrumbs, and on this another layer of tomatoes and seasoning, and so on, until the dish is full. Finish with a layer of well-buttered breadcrumbs on top. Wipe round the edge of the dish, then bake in a quick oven for about ½ hour.

Baked Tomatoes

UTENSILS—Knife, baking dish. *Allow 2 tomatoes per person.*

Choose tomatoes of as nearly the same size as possible. Cut out the stalks. Well butter a baking dish, and stand the tomatoes in, stalk side upwards. In the holes left by the stalks being cut out, put a small piece of butter, also seasoning of pepper and salt. Lay a well-buttered paper on the top, and bake in a moderate oven from 10 to 15 minutes.

Asparagus

UTENSILS—Knife, basin, tape, saucepan, dessertspoon, wire sieve or rack.

Asparagus should always be fresh, but it may be kept for a day or two if stood with the cut ends in a soup plate of cold water. To prepare asparagus for cooking, trim all the pieces to the same length, then scrape the white part lightly with a knife. Wash thoroughly in cold water. Tie it into bundles, of about a dozen heads each, with tape, keeping the heads all the same way, and as near the same thickness as possible. When ready, let them lie in cold water for ½ hour, then drain, and put them into a saucepan with plenty of fast-boiling water, salted in the proportion of one dessertspoonful of salt to every quart of water.

Boil gently from 25 to 30 minutes, according to the size of the heads. When the green part is tender, take the asparagus out, drain it thoroughly, and remove the tapes. Lay it gently in a hot vegetable or asparagus dish. Serve with either plain melted butter, or Hollandaise sauce, or green sauce, in a sauce-boat.

Iced Asparagus

Allow 50 *heads for* 4 *or* 5 *persons*.

Prepare and cook the asparagus in the manner just described. When cold, stand it on ice, or in a refrigerator, for some time. Lay the asparagus in a dish and serve. Prepare a quarter-pint of cream, slightly whipped, and stood on ice until thoroughly cold. Serve this with the asparagus.

Asparagus Points

1 bundle of Asparagus.	1 Yolk of Egg.
2 oz. Butter.	1 small teaspoonful Castor Sugar.
1 tablespoonful Flour.	1 dessertspoonful Lemon Juice.
1 Onion. Salt.	2 tablespoonfuls Cream.

UTENSILS—Two basins, knife, saucepan, wooden spoon, egg-beater, lemon squeezer, measuring spoons. *Enough for* 2 *or* 3 *persons*.

Take some nice fresh asparagus, wash it well, and cut off the green parts into pieces one inch long. Put these into a saucepan, with plenty of boiling salted water, cook for 10 minutes, then strain. Put them back into the saucepan, with one ounce of butter, half a pint of water, one peeled onion, and the sugar. Place the saucepan at the side of the fire, and simmer gently for about 20 minutes.

Rub the remaining ounce of butter well into the flour, and when the asparagus is cooked stir this in, in small pieces. Beat the yolk of egg and the cream together, and when the butter has quite dissolved stir this mixture in also. Stir until it thickens, then take it off the fire. Add the lemon juice, and serve in a hot dish.

Globe Artichokes

2 or 3 Artichokes.	Salt. Water.
	Sauce.

UTENSILS—Knife, basin, saucepan, cloth, teaspoon. *Enough for* 2 *persons*.

Cut off the tips of the leaves, remove a few of the smallest outside bottom leaves, and trim off the stalks evenly. Soak for about ½ hour in salted water, then wash them well. Put them into a saucepan of fast-boiling salted water, and boil until quite tender. This can be ascertained by pulling one of the leaves off, and if it comes off easily they are cooked. When cooked take them out, and stand upside down (stalk side up) on a cloth to drain.

Serve whole or cut them right through in halves, or even quarters, if large. Take a teaspoon and scoop out the choke, or fluffy part, which grows in the bottom. Keep the parts hot whilst you are doing this, then arrange them neatly on a dish. Serve with either melted butter sauce, Béchamel sauce, or Hollandaise sauce. They can be eaten cold, with pepper, oil and vinegar. (FOR SAUCES, see Index.)

Artichokes, with Parmesan Cheese

6 or 8 Artichoke Bottoms.	½ pint Béchamel or Veloute
2 oz. grated Parmesan Cheese.	Sauce.
6 or 8 croûtons of fried Bread.	Cayenne. Salt.

UTENSILS—Knife, saucepan, frying pan, fireproof dish, baking tin. *Enough for 6 persons.*

If using fresh artichokes, remove the leaves and chokes, and trim the bottoms into good shapes. Put them into boiling salted water, boil until tender, then drain them. Tinned artichoke bottoms answer the purpose just as well. Cut the required number of croûtons of bread, and fry them a pale golden colour. Butter a fireproof dish, and lay the croûtons in, side by side.

When the artichokes are ready, stand each one on a croûton. Take half a pint of Veloute or Béchamel sauce, stir the cheese into it, and season with cayenne, and pour over the artichokes. Sprinkle the top thickly with grated cheese, then stand the dish in another one, containing water. Put both into a quick oven, near the top, and when the cheese has melted and browned a little take it out. This will take 10 to 15 minutes. Sprinkle with a little finely-chopped parsley, and serve at once in the dish in which it was cooked.

NOTE.—If liked, artichoke bottoms may be plainly cooked, and served with any of the sauces that are used for the whole artichokes.

Jerusalem Artichokes

2 lb. Artichokes.	Salt. Milk.
Water.	Sauce.

UTENSILS—Two basins, scrubbing brush, knife, saucepan. *Enough for 6 to 8 persons.*

Thoroughly wash and brush the artichokes, and put them into clean cold water before beginning to peel them. Peel carefully, and as they are done throw them into fresh cold water, acidulated with pure malt vinegar. They should not be left out of water longer than necessary after they are peeled, as they turn black very quickly. The water should also be changed if it becomes dirty while the artichokes are being peeled.

Have ready, boiling on the fire, sufficient milk and water, mixed in equal proportions, to cover the artichokes, and slightly salted. Drain the artichokes, and throw them into the boiling milk and water. Boil gently, with the lid on, for 15 to 20 minutes, until they are tender. Strain, and put them into a hot vegetable dish. Serve with either melted butter sauce, white sauce, or any suitable sauce, poured over them. The liquor the artichokes are boiled in can be used as a foundation for white soups.

Artichoke Fritters

6 Jerusalem Artichokes.   Frying Fat.
Frying Batter.   Cayenne.
Anchovy Sauce.

UTENSILS—Two basins, scrubbing brush, knife, saucepan, stewpan, kitchen paper. *Enough for 2 or 3 persons.*

Boil the artichokes plainly. When cold, cut them into rather thick slices. Season with a little cayenne and a few drops of anchovy sauce. Dip the slices of artichoke into frying batter, then plunge them into a stewpan half full of boiling fat. Fry, until they are a pale gold colour. Take them up, and drain thoroughly.

Arrange the fritters prettily on a dish, with a fancy paper beneath them, and serve. These fritters are suited for luncheon or can be served as a dressed vegetable. If liked, the slices may be rolled in flour, dipped in egg, then in breadcrumbs, and fried. This would be instead of using frying batter.

Baked Artichokes

2 lb. Jerusalem Artichokes.   2 oz. Butter.
Pepper and Salt.

UTENSILS—Basin, knife, scrubbing brush, cloth, baking dish, basting spoon. *Enough for 6 to 8 persons.*

Peel and trim the artichokes neatly, then dry them thoroughly. Melt the butter in a baking dish. Put the artichokes in, and season with pepper and salt. Stand the dish in a moderately hot oven and bake for about ½ hour, basting them frequently. They should be a nice brown, and quite tender when cooked.

Scalloped Artichokes

6 Jerusalem Artichokes.	2 oz. Butter. Cayenne.
White Sauce. Breadcrumbs.	Anchovy Essence.

UTENSILS—Knife, two saucepans, scallop shells, grater, kitchen spoon, basin. *Enough for 2 or 3 persons.*

Peel the artichokes, boil them plainly, and cut them into slices as nearly the same size as possible, and not too large. Butter three or four scallop shells with one ounce of butter. Melt the remaining ounce of butter in a saucepan, and stir in sufficient fine white breadcrumbs to absorb it. Line the shells with a layer of these buttered crumbs. Put the slices of artichoke into a basin, and season them with a few drops of anchovy essence, cayenne, and three tablespoonfuls of white sauce.

Put a layer of the artichokes and sauce in the shells, then cover with buttered crumbs. Stand them in a moderate oven until they become a nice golden brown. Arrange the shells on a dish and garnish with a few sprigs of parsley, and serve.

Haricot Beans

1 pint Beans.	1 teaspoonful chopped Parsley.
1 Onion. ½ oz. Butter.	Pepper and Salt.

UTENSILS—Basin, saucepan, measuring spoons, colander, pint measure. *Enough for 4 persons.*

Wash the beans, then put them in cold water to soak all night, or for at least 12 hours. When soaked, put them into a saucepan with sufficient cold water to cover, and salted in the proportion of one tablespoonful of salt to every two quarts of water. Add the onion, then bring to the boil, and simmer very slowly until the beans are tender, which will take about 2½ hours.

When cooked, remove the onion, strain the beans thoroughly, then let them stand in the saucepan by the side of the fire, with the lid partially off, that they may dry.

Add the butter, parsley, and seasoning of pepper and salt. Shake the beans about for a minute or two, then turn them into a hot dish, and serve. Do not stir the beans, as they break so easily. If liked, parsley-butter may be poured over, instead of putting the chopped parsley in with them.

Beetroot

UTENSILS—Knife, saucepan, vegetable brush. *Allow* 1 *large beetroot for* 3 *persons*.

Beetroots must be washed very carefully, and the skin must not be broken. It is also important that the top should not be cut off too closely. If either is done, the root will " bleed " when being cooked, and lose its colour. Put the beetroots into a saucepan of fast-boiling salted water, keep the saucepan well covered, and boil until cooked. They take 2 to 3 hours' boiling, according to size.

To see if they are cooked, lift them out of the saucepan gently and press with the fingers. If done they will be quite soft. On no account try them with a fork, or injure them in any way. When cooked, peel quickly, and then slice them. Lay the slices evenly in a vegetable dish, pour white sauce over, and serve.

Brussels Sprouts

| 1 lb. Sprouts. | Vinegar. |
| 1 oz. Butter. | Pepper and Salt. |

UTENSILS—Two basins, knife, teaspoon, saucepan, pint measure, fork, colander. *Enough for* 2 *or* 3 *persons*.

Wash the sprouts, carefully trimming off all the outside and discoloured leaves. As they are done, throw them into a basin of cold water, in which has been put one teaspoonful of vinegar. This is to draw out any insects that may be in them. Let them soak in this for ½ hour, then strain and rinse them in fresh cold water. Have ready a saucepan containing plenty of fast-boiling water, salted with one dessertspoonful of salt to every quart of water, and put the sprouts in this. Keep them boiling rapidly, with the lid off, until cooked. This will be about 20 to 25 minutes. Try them with a fork, and if the stalk ends are quite tender they are done. Do not cook them longer than is necessary, or they will lose their colour.

Drain thoroughly in a colander, then return them to the

saucepan, with the butter and a sprinkling of pepper, and toss them about in the melted butter for a few minutes.

Turn them out into a hot dish, in as much a pyramid shape as possible. If liked, they may be served with either a few tablespoonfuls of maître d'hôtel sauce poured over them, or some cream stirred in with them. It is a great improvement.

Carrots

4 or 6 Carrots. | **1 oz. Butter.** **Salt.**
1 teaspoon chopped Parsley.

UTENSILS—Knife, scrubbing brush, basin, saucepan, fork or skewer, colander. *Enough for 2 to 4 persons.*

Cut off the green tops, well wash the carrots, then scrape them and remove all the black specks. If large, they may be cut in halves or quarters, lengthways, then into convenient sized pieces. Keep in cold water until wanted. To cook them, have ready a saucepan of fast-boiling water, salted with one dessertspoonful of salt to every quart of water, and throw the carrots in this. Let them boil until tender, which will take an hour, or rather less if the carrots are young. Try if they are done by running a fork or skewer into them. If quite tender, take them up.

Drain well, then return them to the saucepan, with the butter. Shake them about gently for a minute or two. Arrange them prettily on a dish, sprinkle a little finely-chopped parsley over, and serve. If liked, carrots may be mashed, as directed for turnips (see Index).

New Carrots and Cream

1 bundle of new Carrots. | **1 Yolk of Egg.**
1 oz. Butter. | **½ gill Cream.**
Pepper and Salt.

UTENSILS—Knife, basin, scrubbing brush, saucepan, cloth, egg-beater, wooden spoon. *Enough for 2 persons.*

Trim off the green tops, and wash the carrots thoroughly. Throw them into plenty of boiling salted water, and boil for 20 to 30 minutes, until tender. Drain well, then take them in a coarse cloth and rub very gently, to remove the skins.

When skinned, return them to the saucepan, with the butter and the seasoning of pepper and salt. Beat up the yolk of one egg slightly with the cream, and stir this mixture into the carrots until it thickens. Then arrange them neatly in a hot dish, pour the sauce from the pan over, and serve.

Celery

1 or 2 heads of Celery.　　|　　Salt.　　Milk.
White Sauce.

UTENSILS—Knife, basin, tape, saucepan, toaster or toasting fork. *Enough for 4 or 5 persons.*

Strip off the very coarse outside leaves from the heads of celery (these leaves can be used for flavouring soups, etc.), then thoroughly wash them. Trim neatly, and cut the heads into lengths, four inches long. Tie each piece round with a piece of string or tape, and throw them into cold water, until wanted. When required, put them into a saucepan, with sufficient cold water to cover, bring to the boil, then strain, and rinse them in cold water. After this, put them into a saucepan of boiling milk and water, slightly salted, and boil gently till tender. This will take $\frac{3}{4}$ to 1 hour.

When cooked, take up, drain thoroughly, and remove the tapes. Lay the celery on a slice of buttered toast in a vegetable dish. Pour white sauce over, and serve. The liquor in which the celery is boiled is nice for white soups. Celery may also be stewed in brown gravy instead of milk and water, but it should first be blanched in the same way ; then, instead of pouring white, pour a brown sauce over.

Stewed Cucumber

1 large Cucumber.　　|　　1 oz. Butter.　　$\frac{1}{2}$ oz. Flour.
$\frac{3}{4}$ pint Brown Stock.　　|　　Pepper and Salt.

UTENSILS—Knife, cloth, stewpan, wooden spoon, pint measure. *Enough for 2 persons.*

Pare the cucumber, cut it into pieces about 3 inches long, then cut these in halves, lengthways, and take out the seeds. Dry the pieces well, in a cloth. Melt the butter in a stewpan, and lay the cucumber in. Fry, until it is a pale golden colour, then lift the pieces out. Stir the flour into the butter, fry together for a minute or two, then gradually stir in the stock. When boiling, put in the pieces of cucumber, and simmer until they are tender. If the stock is not flavoured enough, add a little pepper and salt. When done, lift the cucumber out carefully, and lay it on a hot vegetable dish. Pour gravy over, and serve.

Cucumber au Gratin

1 Cucumber.	¼ oz. Butter.
1½ gills Béchamel Sauce.	Breadcrumbs.
2 oz. grated Cheese.	Cayenne. Salt.

UTENSILS—Knife, 2 saucepans, colander or sieve, pie-dish or gratin dish, wooden spoon, grater, pint or gill measure, baking tin. *Enough for 2 persons.*

Pare the cucumber, cut it into two-inch lengths, then cut these in halves, lengthways, and scoop out the seeds. Put these pieces into a saucepan of slightly salted boiling water. Boil slowly, until tender, then drain thoroughly. Well butter a fireproof gratin dish, or an ordinary shallow pie-dish will do. Lay the pieces of cucumber in it neatly.

Stir the grated cheese into the Béchamel sauce, and add a very small dust of cayenne pepper. Pour the sauce over the cucumber, then spread the top thickly with breadcrumbs. Stand the dish in another, containing water, and bake in a moderate oven until the crumbs are a golden brown. Take the dish out of the one containing water, stand it on another dish, with a fancy paper under, and serve.

Stuffed Cucumbers

1 Cucumber. Butter.	Buttered Breadcrumbs.
4 or 5 croûtons of Bread.	Tomato Sauce.
Forcemeat, as described.	

UTENSILS—Knife, round cutter, grater, 2 baking dishes, frying pan, palette knife or egg slice, measuring spoons, 2 basins, egg-beater. *Enough for 2 persons.*

Cut the cucumber into two-inch lengths, and pare them. Scoop out the seeds, without spoiling the shape of the cucumber. This is best done with a plain round cutter. Fill the holes with forcemeat. Stand these stuffed pieces of cucumber on their ends in a well-buttered baking dish, and sprinkle a few buttered breadcrumbs on the top of each, lay a well-buttered paper over, then stand the tin in another, containing water. Bake in a moderate oven, until the cucumber is tender. This will take about 15 to 20 minutes.

Cut as many round croûtons of bread as you have pieces of cucumber. Let the croûtons be a little larger than the cucumber. Fry them a pale golden brown, then drain thoroughly. Lift the pieces of cucumber with a palette knife, or slice, and stand one on the centre of each croûton. Arrange neatly on a dish, pour tomato sauce round, and serve.

THE FORCEMEAT

2 tablespoonfuls any nice Cold Meat or Game, minced.	½ teaspoonful finely chopped Parsley.
¼ teaspoonful finely chopped Onion.	1 teaspoonful Breadcrumbs.
	1 Egg. Pepper and Salt.

Mix the dry ingredients well together, and bind the whole with a well-beaten egg. Do not press the forcemeat too tightly into the pieces of cucumber, or they will crack in the cooking. A little mound can be made in the centre. Smooth the mound of forcemeat at the upper end, with a wetted knife, before putting the breadcrumbs on.

Aubergine Fritters

1 Aubergine.	Salt.	Frying Batter. Frying Fat.

UTENSILS—Knife, 2 basins, frying pan, wire rack, egg slice. *Enough for 2 persons.*

Peel a medium-sized aubergine and cut it in slices, about half an inch thick. Soak these in salt and water for ½ hour, then drain thoroughly. Dip them into frying batter, then fry in boiling fat for 5 or 6 minutes. Drain on a wire pastry rack, or fold of kitchen paper, then dish them neatly in a pile on a hot dish. Sprinkle a little coralline pepper over, if liked, and serve.

NOTE.—The slices may also be egged and crumbed, and fried in fat. When young and quite small, these fruits may be boiled until tender, and served with white sauce.

Stuffed Aubergines

2 Aubergines.	½ teaspoonful chopped Parsley.
4 tablespoonfuls Breadcrumbs.	1 large Mushroom.
2 filleted Anchovies. Pepper.	1 oz. Butter. 1 Egg.

UTENSILS—Knife, saucepan, chopping board, 2 basins, kitchen spoon, egg-beater, grater, baking tin, frying pan, measuring spoons. *Enough for 4 persons.*

Stem the aubergines, and split them in halves, lengthways. Scoop out the insides, leaving the rind about half an inch thick. Melt the butter in a saucepan. Chop the insides of the fruits (which have been removed) finely, and put this in with the butter, with two tablespoonfuls of breadcrumbs, the chopped anchovies, parsley, mushrooms, and seasoning of pepper. Cook all together for a few minutes, then remove the mixture from the saucepan, and add sufficient well-beaten egg to bind all together.

Fill the centres of the egg-fruits with this, and sprinkle buttered breadcrumbs on the tops. Place them in a well-greased baking tin, and lay a buttered paper over. Bake in a moderate oven, for about 30 minutes. Serve very hot on a hot dish, and garnish with a few sprigs of fresh parsley.

Greens, to Boil

| 2 lb. Greens. | Butter. | Vinegar. |
| Pepper and Salt. | | |

UTENSILS—Two basins, knife, saucepan, dessertspoon, colander, saucer, chopping board. *Allow 2 lb. greens for 4 or 5 persons.*

Wash the greens thoroughly and cut off the thick stalks and any decayed or blemished leaves. As they are washed throw them into a pan of cold water, with a little vinegar in it, and let them remain in this about ½ hour. Rinse well, and put them into a saucepan of fast-boiling water, salted with one dessertspoonful of salt to every quart of water. Have the lid on the pan until the water boils again, then remove it and let the greens boil rapidly, with the lid off, until they are tender, which will take about ½ hour. Be careful to remove any scum that may rise.

When cooked, drain in a colander, then take a small plate or saucer, lay it on the greens, and press out every drop of moisture that you can. Now turn the greens on to a clean board, and chop them up finely. Return them to the saucepan, with a piece of butter, about the size of a walnut, and a seasoning of pepper and salt. Let them thoroughly re-heat, then turn them neatly into a hot vegetable dish. If liked, a basin may be well greased with either butter or dripping, and the greens (after being chopped and seasoned) pressed into this, after which they are turned out on to a dish, so that they keep the shape of the basin.

Leeks

| 4 Leeks. | White Sauce. | A slice of Buttered Toast. |

UTENSILS—Knife, saucepan, colander. *Enough for 2 to 4 persons.*

Trim off the outsides of the leeks, and cut away most of the green part. Also, cut them straight off at the roots. Slit leaves down a little way at the top, so that they can be easily washed. Wash them thoroughly. It is a good plan to hold them under a running tap. When ready, throw them into a saucepan of boiling salted water, and boil until tender, which will be ½ hour, or longer. Then drain well, halve, and arrange in a hot dish. Pour a good white sauce over, and serve.

Leeks may also be stewed in a brown gravy. If leeks are well cooked, they do not taint the breath. SPRING ONIONS can be cooked in this manner, and will be found very palatable.

Boiled Lettuce

1 large white Cos Lettuce. | Melted Butter. Salt.
Buttered Toast.

UTENSILS—Knife, basin, tape, saucepan, dessertspoon, pint measure, colander. *Enough for 2 persons.*

Trim off the green outside leaves from a large lettuce. Wash the heart well, then tie round with a piece of tape. Put it into a saucepan of boiling salted water (one dessertspoonful of salt to each quart of water), boil quickly, until tender—from 20 to 30 minutes. Lift the lettuce out carefully, drain well, and remove the tapes. Cut it in halves, lengthways, then across, and lay it in a hot vegetable dish. Pour melted butter sauce over, and serve.

Lettuces are really excellent served in this way, but only the bleached hearts must be used. Lettuce may also be stewed and served with a brown gravy.

Baked Mushrooms

12 or 14 Mushrooms. | 2 oz. Butter.
Pepper and Salt.

UTENSILS—Cloth, knife, fireproof dish. *Enough for 2 or 3 persons.*

Choose large flat mushrooms for this, if possible. Wipe them with a clean cloth, peel them, and cut off the stalks close up to the crowns. Do not wash them, unless absolutely necessary, but if they must be washed let it be done lightly in a basin of salted water, and drain them well.

When ready, well butter a fireproof dish, and lay the mushrooms in, edge to edge, dark sides upwards. Put a small piece of butter on each, and sprinkle with pepper and salt. Cover, or lay a well-buttered paper over, then stand them in a moderate oven to cook, for about 20 minutes, or a little longer if very large or thick. Serve the mushrooms piled up in the centre of a hot dish, after pouring round the gravy which has run from them.

Stewed Mushrooms

1 lb. Mushrooms.	2 tablespoonfuls Cream.
2 oz. Butter.	Pepper and Salt.
½ pint Milk.	1 teaspoonful Flour.

UTENSILS—Knife, stewpan, basin, wooden spoon, measuring spoons, frying pan or toaster. *Enough for 4 or 5 persons*

Peel and trim the mushrooms. Melt the butter in a stewpan, then put in the mushrooms, season with pepper and salt, and add nearly all the milk. Cover tightly, and simmer gently until done (about 25 minutes). When cooked, pour in the cream. Mix the flour smoothly with the remainder of the milk, and thicken the mushrooms with this. Let it all boil for a minute or two, then turn into a hot dish. Garnish with croûtons of bread, and serve very hot.

If liked, the stewed mushrooms may be served on rounds of buttered toast for breakfast. They are then garnished with small rolls of bacon and a little parsley. The peelings and stalks of mushrooms should be washed in salt and water, and used for flavouring gravies, etc.

Grilled Mushrooms

8 or 10 large Mushrooms.	Lemon Juice.
Butter.	Pepper and Salt.

UTENSILS—Knife, basin, cloth, saucepan, dish, gridiron. *Enough for 2 persons.*

Choose large mushrooms for this. Peel and trim them. Rinse in salted water, then dry well in a cloth. Lay them on a dish; melt some butter and pour over them. Season with pepper and salt, and let them remain thus for ½ hour, or longer. Grease the bars of a gridiron, a double one, if possible. Lay the mushrooms on, white sides downwards.

Broil over a clear fire, from 8 to 10 minutes, turning them once during cooking.

When cooked, squeeze a few drops of lemon juice on each, arrange neatly on a very hot dish, and serve at once. If liked, a little chopped onion can be used as seasoning, as well as pepper and salt, but some consider that this somewhat spoils the flavour of the mushroom.

Spanish Onions, Braised

4 or 5 Spanish Onions. | **1 pint** Brown Gravy.

UTENSILS—Knife, saucepan, wooden spoon. *Enough for 3 or 4 persons.*

Peel the onions, and put them in a saucepan, with cold water to cover. Bring to the boil, then strain. Pour a pint of brown gravy into the saucepan, and stew gently for 1½ to 2 hours. Lift out the onions on to a hot dish, thicken the gravy slightly, pour it round the onions, and serve.

Boiled Spanish Onions

4 Spanish Onions. Salt. | Parsley. White Sauce.

UTENSILS—Knife, saucepan, colander, dessertspoon, pint measure. *Enough for 3 or 4 persons.*

Peel the onions, put them into a saucepan, large enough to hold them side by side, and cover with cold water. Bring to the boil, then strain, and rinse them in cold water. Now put them into a saucepan of boiling salted water (one dessert-spoonful of salt to each quart), and boil gently until tender. This will be in 1½ to 2 hours. Drain well, and put them into a hot vegetable dish. Pour half a pint of white sauce over, then sprinkle a little chopped parsley on top, and serve.

Stuffed Onions

4 Onions. **3 oz.** Butter. | **½ lb.** Sausage Meat. Salt.

UTENSILS—Knife, saucepan, cloth, metal spoon, baking dish, brush. *Enough for 4 persons.*

Choose the onions as much the same size as possible. Peel them, then blanch in the manner described in the two previous recipes. Put them into boiling salted water, and boil for 15 minutes. Take them up, and drain well, standing them.

RICE AND SHRIMP SALAD (p. 326)—Salads are economical and
attractive, and can be served all the year round.

upside down, on a cloth. Scoop out the centres of the onions with a spoon. Fill the cavities with sausage meat.

Melt the butter in a baking dish, and stand the onions in, side by side. Bake in a quick oven, until nicely browned, basting occasionally with some of the butter. When cooked, brush over the tops with a little liquid glaze, if you have it. Stand the onions on a hot dish, garnish with a few sprigs of parsley, and serve. Onions are also excellent stuffed with mushroom purée, and baked in the same way.

Fried Onions

1 or 2 large Onions. | Flour.   Frying Fat.   Salt.

UTENSILS—Knife, saucepan, cloth, plate, frying pan, wire rack. *Enough for 1 person.*

Peel and blanch the onions, in the manner described with previous recipes (see previous page). Put them into boiling salted water, and boil for 15 minutes. Dry thoroughly, then cut them into rings. Dry these well in a cloth, and roll them in flour. Shake off as much of the flour as possible, then fry in boiling fat, until they are a pale golden brown. Drain well, and use them as a garnish. They should be quite crisp.

Seakale

Allow 1 lb. seakale for 3 persons.

This is cooked in exactly the same way as celery (page 306). It is generally plainly boiled, but it may also be parboiled, and then stewed in brown gravy.

Salsify

1 bundle of Salsify. | Melted Butter Sauce, or White
1 oz. Butter. | Sauce.   Vinegar.   Salt.

UTENSILS—Knife, basin, saucepan, teaspoon, pint measure, cloth. *Enough for 3 or 4 persons.*

Trim the salsify, and wash well in cold water. Prepare a saucepan of boiling water, in which is put one teaspoonful of vinegar and one teaspoonful of salt to every quart; put the salsify in this, and boil gently until tender. This will take about ½ hour. Strain, then rub it with a clean coarse cloth, and the skin will easily come off. Cut the salsify into pieces, two inches and a half long, and return them to the saucepan, with the butter. Shake over the fire, until they get thoroughly hot again.

Arrange neatly in a vegetable dish, and pour either white sauce, or melted butter sauce over, and serve. If liked, after boiling, the salsify can be egged and crumbed, or dipped into batter and fried. Or it is excellent if scalloped in the same way as oysters, but with a few drops of anchovy sauce added.

SCORZONERA may be cooked in exactly the same way.

Spinach

| 2 lb. Spinach. | Croûtons of fried Bread. |
| 1 oz. Butter. | Pepper and Salt. |

UTENSILS—Knife, basin, saucepan, wire sieve, wooden spoon and basin or chopping board, plate, frying pan. *Enough for 2 or 3 persons.*

Spinach is, of all vegetables, one which requires the most careful washing. First strip the leaves off the stalks, then wash them thoroughly in several waters, handling as lightly as possible. Have ready a large saucepan, empty ; lift the spinach out of the water, and put it straight into the saucepan. It requires no more water than that which adheres to the leaves. Cover the lid closely, and cook very gently for about ½ hour, stirring frequently, to prevent its adhering to the saucepan.

When ready, turn it out into a sieve, put a plate on it, and squeeze as much moisture out as possible.

If there is time, the spinach can be rubbed through the sieve into a clean basin, using a wooden spoon for the purpose. If not, turn it on to a board and chop it finely. Return it to the saucepan with the butter, and pepper and salt to taste. When thoroughly hot, dish it up in a pyramid, in a hot dish, and garnish it round with fried croûtons of bread. Do not use a tin saucepan for cooking spinach in.

Spinach, with Cream

| 2 lb. Spinach. | Castor Sugar. | 2 oz. Butter. | 1 oz. Flour. |
| 4 tablespoonfuls Cream. | | Pepper and Salt. | |

UTENSILS—Knife, saucepan, wire sieve, wooden spoon, tablespoon, basin, stewpan. *Enough for 2 or 3 persons.*

Boil the spinach, as in the last recipe, then rub it through a wire sieve. Melt the butter in a stewpan, stir in the flour, and fry together, without browning. Put in the spinach purée, and mix it well with the butter and flour. Add the cream, and seasoning of white pepper, salt, and a dust of castor sugar. Dish up on a hot dish, and garnish either with leaves of puff paste, baked a golden brown; or with heart-shaped croûtons of bread, brushed over with white of egg, and sprinkled with grated Parmesan cheese and finely chopped parsley.

Indian Corn (Maize)

2 heads of Corn. | 1 oz. Butter.
Pepper and Salt.

UTENSILS—Basin, saucepan, knife. *Enough for 1 or 2 persons.*

The heads must be quite young. Strip the husks off, and wash the heads in cold water. Put them into a saucepan of boiling salted water, and boil about ¾ hour, until they are tender. Drain, then with a sharp knife slice off the corn from the hard green cob or core. Return the corn to the saucepan, with the butter, and season it with pepper and salt. Toss, in the saucepan over the fire, until quite hot, then turn all into a hot dish, and serve.

Corn can also be served on the cob, boiled in the same way, with melted butter sauce.

To Boil Rice

UTENSILS—Saucepan, colander, cloth. *Allow 1 cupful for 2 persons.*

Wash the rice, put it into a saucepan, with a little salt, and sufficient cold water to cover, bring just to the boil, then strain it. Now wash the rice well in cold water, then put it into a saucepan three-fourths full of fast-boiling water. Boil rapidly for 15 minutes, or rather less, until the rice is tender.

Strain through a colander, then pour about a quart of hot water over it. Let it remain in the colander, lay a cloth over, and dry it in front of the fire, or on the rack. Cooked in this way each grain will be quite separate, and beautifully white.

Parsnip Balls

1 pint mashed, boiled Parsnips. | 2 Eggs. Frying Fat.
2 tablespoonfuls Butter. | Breadcrumbs.
1 tablespoonful Milk. | ½ teaspoonful Pepper.
1 teaspoonful Salt.

UTENSILS—Saucepan, fork, basin, egg-beater, kitchen spoon, measuring spoons, grater, plate, frying pan. *Enough for 3 or 4 persons.*

Melt the butter in a saucepan, add the cold mashed parsnip, pepper, salt and milk. Stir this over the fire, until it begins to bubble, then take it off, and add one beaten egg, to bind it. When cool, form into balls, about half the size of an egg; roll these in egg and breadcrumbs, and fry in boiling fat. Drain them; place neatly in a vegetable dish, with a paper under them, and serve.

NOTE.—Parsnips may also be plainly boiled, or mashed, like turnips. This vegetable is much improved when the frost has been on it.

Seakale, with Melted Butter Sauce

15 heads of Seakale. Salt.	Melted Butter Sauce, as
1 tablespoonful Vinegar.	described.

UTENSILS—Basin, knife, tape, 2 saucepans, tablespoon, strainer, wooden spoon, pint measure. *Enough for 3 persons.*

Wash and rinse the seakale thoroughly to remove the grit. Cut away any brown or discoloured parts. Tie the heads up into small bundles with tape, and put them into a basin of cold water until wanted. Have a saucepan of boiling salted water, sufficient to cover the seakale well, and put two tablespoonfuls of vinegar into the water.

Put in the seakale, and boil until it is quite tender—this will take about 20 minutes. Lift out the bundles into a strainer, drain well, and remove the tapes. Lay the seakale in a hot vegetable dish, and pour the following sauce over.

THE SAUCE

¼ lb. Butter.	½ teaspoonful Lemon Juice.
1 oz. Flour.	Salt and White Pepper.
¾ pint Water.	

Melt half the butter in a saucepan, add the flour, and mix with a wooden spoon until quite smooth. Add, by degrees, three-quarters of a pint of boiling water, stirring all the time. Cook the sauce for a few minutes, then add the lemon juice. Season to taste, with salt and white pepper. Lastly, add the remainder of the butter in small pieces. Pour the sauce over the seakale, and serve.

Vegetable Curry

1 large Apple. 2 Onions.	1 teaspoonful Curry Powder.
½ Cucumber. ½ lb. Rice.	1 small teaspoonful Curry Paste.
French Beans, Cauliflower, or Peas, etc.	1 teaspoonful Salt.
1 tablespoonful Cocoanut.	2 oz. Butter.
½ teaspoonful Ground Ginger.	½ pint Milk.
	Flour.

UTENSILS—Knife, stewpan, wooden spoon, breakfast cup, measuring spoons, saucepan. *Enough for 4 to 6 persons.*

Peel the onions, apple, cucumber, or a piece of vegetable marrow the same size, and slice the onion and apple thinly. Cut the cucumber into pieces one inch and a half long by one inch broad. Melt the butter in a stewpan, dust the prepared vegetables over with flour, and put the apple and onions into the butter. Put on the lid, and cook without browning for 20 minutes, then add the cucumber and fry for another 15 minutes. Now add the grated cocoanut, the curry powder, curry paste, ground ginger, salt and milk.

Take, and mix together, any plainly boiled vegetables such as cauliflower, French beans, broad beans, peas, salsify, etc., sufficient to make a large breakfastcupful. If cauliflower is used, it must be cut into small pieces the size used for pickles, and broad beans must be skinned. Cut French beans and salsify into dice, add them to the curry, and simmer for ½ hour. Prepare some plainly boiled rice, and put a border of it down each side of the dish, but not at the ends, and the curry in the centre. Sprinkle a little grated cocoanut over the top, and serve.

NOTE.—It is not necessary to use all of the vegetables named, but the greater the variety of suitable vegetables the better. The rice may be served on a separate dish.

SALADS

Salads are not only good for you, but they are an addition to the menu, and are economical, especially Russian salads and others of that kind, which depend to a great extent on left-over vegetables for their attraction. Fruit Salads, too, equally good and coming into favour for breakfast, can be worked up into delectable sweets with the aid of left-over tinned fruit and delicious flavourings.

When making salads there are one or two points you must closely observe :

1. The different constituents should be kept entirely apart till it is time to prepare the salad.
2. All fresh vegetables like cabbage, celery, chicory, endive, lettuce, sorrel, and watercress, should be well washed in clean cold water to crisp them up, then carefully and thoroughly dried on a cloth, or hung up to dry in the open air in salad baskets.
3. Shred vegetables with your fingers, as much as possible, using a silver knife when a knife is necessary.
4. If celery is unobtainable, but the flavour of celery is desired, shred the firm, white heart of a cabbage very finely, sprinkle with celery salt and use instead.
5. Always stand your tomatoes for a minute or two in boiling water, then peel them and leave until cold before using in salads.

SALAD DRESSINGS

French Dressing

4 tablespoonfuls Olive Oil.	¼ teaspoonful Pepper.
½ teaspoonful Salt.	Sugar. Lemon Juice.
2 tablespoonfuls Vinegar.	½ teaspoonful Mustard.

UTENSILS—Basin, wooden spoon, measuring spoons.

Mix the oil into the pepper, mustard, and sugar, and stir well ; then add the vinegar and a few drops of lemon juice, if liked. A little tarragon vinegar can be used instead of some of the malt or wine vinegar. Use very cold.

Cream Salad Dressing

2 hard-boiled Eggs.	2 teaspoonfuls Tarragon
½ teaspoonful made Mustard.	Vinegar.
2 tablespoonfuls Cream.	Cayenne.
1 tablespoonful Vinegar.	White Pepper. Salt.

UTENSILS—Saucepan, fine sieve, wooden spoon, measuring spoons, basin.

Boil the eggs thoroughly hard, and afterwards chill them in cold water, then rub the yolks through a fine sieve. Put the yolks and all the other ingredients together, except the vinegars, and mix them thoroughly well. Then add the vinegars by slow degrees, mixing well all the time. The sauce should be of the consistency of thick cream when finished. If cream is not procurable, salad oil may be used in its place.

Mayonnaise Sauce

2 Yolks of Eggs.	Salt and Pepper.
¼ teaspoonful French Mustard.	½ pint Salad Oil.
Vinegar.	

UTENSILS—Basin, wooden spoon, teaspoon.

Put the egg yolks into a basin, and add salt and pepper to taste, and French mustard, if liked. Stir the yolks with a wooden spoon, then add the oil, a drop at a time at first, and then more quickly, stirring steadily all the time. When the sauce is of the consistency of thick cream, slowly add vinegar to taste. Keep all utensils and ingredients very cold when making the sauce, so as to prevent curdling.

Eggless Mayonnaise

¾ cupful Olive Oil.	1 teaspoonful Salt.
1 teaspoonful Icing Sugar.	1 small Baked Potato.
1 teaspoonful Mustard.	2 tablespoonfuls Mustard.

UTENSILS—Knife, fork, 2 basins, wooden spoon, measuring spoons, fine sieve.

Peel and mash the potato, then stir in the mustard, icing sugar, and salt. Add the vinegar, and rub the mixture through a fine sieve, then slowly stir in the oil and the remainder of the vinegar.

Russian Cream Dressing

1 cupful Cream.	2 tablespoonfuls Vinegar.
1 tablespoonful Sugar.	2 tablespoonfuls Lemon Juice.
1 teaspoonful French Mustard.	1 teaspoonful Salt.
Dash of Paprika.	

UTENSILS—Two basins, wire whisk, wooden spoon, measuring spoons, lemon squeezer.

Beat the cream till smooth and thick, then mix together in a basin the vinegar, sugar, lemon juice, French mustard, salt, pepper, and paprika, and beat the mixture into the cream. If liked, tomato ketchup or Worcester sauce can be used to flavour this dressing.

Sour Cream Dressing

1 cupful Sour Cream.	2 tablespoonfuls Olive Oil.
½ cupful Tomato Ketchup.	1 teaspoonful Salt.
Sugar to taste.	2 tablespoonfuls White Vinegar.

UTENSILS—Basin, wooden spoon, measuring spoons, cup.

Mix the salt, oil, sugar and vinegar together in a basin. If preferred, use 1½ tablespoonfuls white vinegar and 1 dessertspoonful tarragon. Beat in the ketchup, then gradually beat in the cream, and serve with fish and vegetable salads.

Roquefort Salad Dressing

¼ lb. Roquefort Cheese.	¼ teaspoonful Paprika.
2 tablespoonfuls Lemon Juice.	4 tablespoonfuls Cream.
1 tablespoonful Vinegar.	

UTENSILS—Knife, fine sieve, wooden spoon, measuring spoons, basin, lemon squeezer.

Chop and rub the cheese through a fine sieve. Gradually stir in the lemon juice, paprika, and vinegar, and when well blended, lightly mix in the cream, or olive oil, if preferred.

Thousand Island Dressing

1 tablespoonful Mayonnaise.	1 tablespoonful Chilli Sauce.
1 teaspoonful chopped Parsley.	1 teaspoonful hard-boiled Egg.
1 teaspoonful Ketchup.	1 teaspoonful chopped Beetroot.
1 teaspoonful Tarragon Vinegar.	1 teaspoonful Onion Juice.
½ teaspoonful Paprika.	1 saltspoonful made Mustard.
3 chopped Olives.	

UTENSILS—Basin, wooden spoons, measuring spoon, knife, large-necked bottle.

Mix gradually and in small quantities the mayonnaise with the chilli sauce, parsley, hard-boiled egg, beetroot, mushroom ketchup, tarragon vinegar, onion juice, paprika, mustard and olives. Pour the mixture into a large-necked bottle, cork, and shake until smooth. Then serve on crisp lettuce heads carefully washed and drained.

SAVOURY SALADS

A Simple Salad

2 Lettuces.
French Dressing.

½ lb. Tomatoes.
½ teaspoonful Castor Sugar.

UTENSILS—Knife, basin, cloth, teaspoon, kitchen spoon, salad bowl. *Enough for 6 persons.*

Remove the outside or any withered leaves and worts from the lettuce. Quarter the lettuces, if hearted, otherwise pull them apart into leaves, r tear into small portions if the leaves are large. Wash in clear, cold water, and if not crisp, stand 1 hour in salted water. Dip the tomatoes in boiling water, peel, stand till cold, then slice.

Dry the lettuce very carefully on a cloth, taking care not to bruise it. Moisten the tomato and lettuce with any French salad dressing, then transfer them to the salad bowl. Half a teaspoonful of castor sugar an be added to the salad dressing before using with simple salad.

Potato Salad

1 tablespoonful chopped Gherkin.
6 good-sized Potatoes.
3 large tablespoonfuls Mayonnaise.
1½ tablespoonfuls Vinegar.

1 medium-sized Onion.
1 teaspoon French Mustard.
1 cupful chopped Celery.
2 tablespoonfuls chopped Pimento.

UTENSILS—Saucepan, knife, basin, wooden spoon, measuring spoons. *Enough for 3 or 4 persons.*

Boil the potatoes in their skins in salted water. Cool, peel, slice and chop them roughly, then mix with the minced onion, celery and pimento. Sprinkle lightly with paprika, and pepper and salt to taste. Stir in the vinegar, mayonnaise mixed with French mustard, and the gherkin. If liked, 2 tablespoonfuls chopped walnut can be added.

Potato and Tomato Salad

6 cold Potatoes.
6 large Tomatoes.
6 teaspoonfuls Salad Oil.
2 teaspoonfuls French Vinegar.
1 teaspoonful Tarragon Vinegar.

1 teaspoonful chopped Shallot.
A dust of Castor Sugar.
½ small teaspoonful Salt.
Watercress. Filleted Anchovies, Olives, or Pickles.

UTENSILS—Knife, basin, wooden spoon, teaspoon, salad bowl. *Enough for 4 persons.*

Trim cold cooked potatoes all to the same size, and cut them into slices, a quarter of an inch thick. Skin the tomatoes by dipping first into hot water, and cut them into slices, the same thickness as the potatoes. Chop the shallot very finely, and put it into a basin with the salad oil, vinegars, sugar, pepper and salt, and mix thoroughly well together.

Arrange slices of potato in a salad bowl, alternately with slices of tomato, pour some of the dressing over them, then arrange another layer of potatoes and tomato, put more dressing, and so on. On top of all put a bunch of well-picked watercress, which has been seasoned with the dressing. If liked, filleted anchovies, olives or pickles may be chopped up and added.

Beetroot Salad

| 1 Beetroot. | Vinegar. | Salad Oil. |
| Celery. | Salt and Pepper. | |

UTENSILS—Knife, basin, glass dish, wooden spoon, tablespoon. *Enough for 2 or 3 persons.*

Take one large or two small beets, cooked and cold, and cut them into slices. Lay the slices in a glass dish. Make a dressing of two tablespoonfuls of salad oil, four of brown vinegar, and a little salt and white pepper, pour this over the salad, then garnish with small bunches of shredded celery.

Cucumber Salad (1)

| 1 Cucumber. | 1 tablespoonful Salad Oil. |
| 2 tablespoonfuls Vinegar. | Pepper and Salt. |

UTENSILS—Knife, salad bowl, basin or cup, tablespoon, teaspoon. *Enough for 2 to 4 persons.*

Pare the cucumber, then slice it thinly and arrange the slices neatly in a salad bowl. Sprinkle ½ teaspoonful of salt over, and a little pepper. Just before serving, mix the oil and vinegar together and pour it over.

NOTE.—1. Cucumbers should be quite fresh and stiff. If a trifle limp, stand them in a jug containing a little water, with the stalk ends downwards.

2. They should always be pared from the point, towards the stalk.

Cucumber Salad (2)

1 Cucumber.	2 tablespoonfuls French Vinegar.
3 Spring Onions.	1 tablespoonful Salad Oil.

Pepper and Salt.

UTENSILS—Knife, dish, basin, wooden spoon, tablespoon.
Enough for 2 to 4 persons.

Peel a cucumber, beginning at the point and peeling towards the stalk, otherwise it is liable to be bitter. Slice the cucumber very thinly, also the onion. Place them on a dish and sprinkle them with salt, cover them with a piece of paper, wetted with cold water, and let them stand for ½ hour, then pour off all the liquid that has been drawn from the cucumber.

Make a dressing of the oil and vinegar, mixing salt and pepper and oil together then stirring in the vinegar gradually, and mix well. Lay the cucumber neatly on a dish, and pour the dressing over it. Decorate with sprigs of watercress or minced parsley.

Salad of Cooked Vegetables

1 teacupful cooked French Beans.	1 teacupful young cooked Carrots.
1 teacupful cooked Peas.	1 teaspoonful finely-chopped
1 teacupful cooked Asparagus Points.	Chives, or the green of Spring Onions.

Salad Dressing, as described.

UTENSILS—Saucepans, knife, salad bowl, hair sieve, wooden spoon, basin, teacup, measuring spoons, fine strainer.
Enough for 4 to 6 persons.

Cook these vegetables separately. Do not shred the French beans finely, only trim off the ends and a thin strip from each edge. Cut the carrots into thin round slices. When the vegetables are quite cold, arrange them prettily in layers, in a salad bowl. Pour the salad dressing over, sprinkle with the finely chopped chives or spring onion, and serve. Any suitable vegetable may be used in the same way.

THE DRESSING

2 hard-boiled Yolks of Eggs.	A few drops Chilli Vinegar.
4 tablespoonfuls Cream.	1 small teaspoonful Tarragon
¼ teaspoonful French Mustard.	Vinegar.

1 saltspoonful Salt.

Rub the hard-boiled yolks through a hair sieve, put them into a basin with the seasonings, and mix well together.

Next, add the cream, by degrees, stirring all the time. Lastly, add the vinegars, a little at a time. If liked, more vinegar can be used, but do not overdo it. It is a common fault to be too lavish with vinegar, and then to attempt to correct it by adding sugar.

Salad oil may be used instead of cream, but some people do not like this so well. After the dressing is mixed, strain it through a fine strainer to remove any lumps in the egg. If a more elaborate dish is required, the salad may be garnished with shredded celery or chopped aspic jelly.

Salad Varsovienne

6 **Tomatoes.** Mayonnaise.
¼ cupful cooked **Peas.**
2 tablespoonfuls **Capers.**
1 tablespoonful chopped **Gherkin.**

½ cupful cooked **Veal.**
¼ cupful diced **Cucumber.**
½ cupful **Tomato Pulp.**
Salt, Pepper, Paprika, Vinegar.

UTENSILS—Knife, sieve, wooden spoon, basin, cheese-cloth, cup, tablespoon. *Enough for 3 or 4 persons.*

Peel the tomatoes, remove thin slices from the top of each, scoop out the seeds and pulp, then rub the pulp through a sieve. Sprinkle the insides with salt, turn them upside down, and stand ½ hour.

Mix together in a basin the diced cucumbers, peas, gherkin, tomato pulp, and capers. Season to taste and place in a cheese-cloth to drain off any liquid. Add ½ cupful of cold cooked veal, cut in fine dice, and moisten with mayonnaise. Stuff the tomatoes, sprinkle them with minced parsley and serve each on an individual plate lined with lettuce leaves.

Water Lily Salad

6 hard-boiled **Eggs.**
6 stuffed **Olives.**
Vinegar. Seasoning.

1 large **Lettuce.**
1 teaspoonful chopped **Parsley.**
Olive Oil. Radishes.

UTENSILS—Saucepan, knife, basin, wooden spoon, tea-spoon. *Enough for 4 persons.*

Boil the eggs for 30 minutes, chill in cold water, shell, and cut lengthways, from small end nearly to the other, into six petals. Take out the yolks and beat them till smooth with vinegar, oil, and seasoning to taste, or with a little mayonnaise, and form into cone-shaped balls.

Lay the white petals in the centre of a bed of heart of lettuce leaves arranged on individual salad plates, place a cone in centre of each lily, and sprinkle it lightly with fine parsley. Garnish with one or two tiny radishes and small olives to resemble buds, and mask with a little French dressing.

Asparagus Salad

Asparagus Tips.
½ cupful Cream.

¼ teaspoonful Salt.
¼ cupful Tomato Pulp.

2 teaspoonfuls Lemon Juice.

UTENSILS—Basin, wooden spoon, teaspoon, cup, lemon squeezer, knife.

Stir the tomato, salt, and lemon juice lightly into the cream. Arrange the asparagus tips, allowing from seven to ten to each, on individual plates lined with heart of lettuce leaves. Pour dressing over the cold, cooked tips, and sprinkle with minced parsley.

Spanish Salad

6 hard-boiled Eggs.
1 cupful diced cooked Beetroot.
Lettuce Leaves.   Mayonnaise.

2 cupfuls cold boiled Rice.
1 chopped Pimento.
½ teaspoonful grated Shallot.

UTENSILS—Knife, saucepan, kitchen spoon, teaspoon, basin, cup, grater. *Enough for 4 or 5 persons.*

Mix the rice, eggs cut into dice, beetroot, pimento and shallot together, and season lightly with pepper, salt, celery salt and paprika. Mix, and toss up lightly with plenty of thick mayonnaise. Serve heaped on lettuce leaves, garnished with thin strips of pimento and chopped chervil.

Crayfish or Lobster Mayonnaise

½ pint Mayonnaise.
1 gill whipped Cream.

1 large Crayfish or Lobster.
Lettuce.

UTENSILS—Knife, fork, 2 basins, wire whisk, salad bowl, wooden spoon, pint measure. *Enough for 2 to 4 persons.*

Remove the meat from a lobster or crayfish, stir half the whipped cream into the mayonnaise. Line a salad bowl with heart of lettuce leaves, lightly mix the fish with prepared mayonnaise and arrange it in the bowl. Cover with the remainder of the whipped cream, and decorate with lobster coral, chopped gherkin, and mustard and cress, and picked shrimps.

Mock Lobster Salad

1 oz. cooked Rice.	½ teaspoonful **Worcester Sauce.**
4 oz. cooked **Fish** (Hake or Skate).	Salt and Pepper.
	Lettuce and Cress.
1 large Tomato.	Salad Dressing.

UTENSILS—Knife, basin, wooden spoon, teaspoon. *Enough for* 1 *or* 2 *persons.*

Skin and slice the tomato. Mix the cooked rice, fish, Worcester sauce, tomato and seasoning together. Add sufficient salad dressing to bind the ingredients. Serve heaped up in a bowl or on a dish, garnished with lettuce and cress and sliced tomato.

Rice and Shrimp Salad

¼ lb. Carolina Rice.	2 hard-boiled **Eggs.**
1 gill picked Shrimps.	1 Lettuce.
1 tablespoonful Vinegar.	3 tablespoonfuls Salad Oil.
Salt and Pepper.	Chopped Parsley.

UTENSILS—Saucepans, sieve or colander, 2 basins, wooden spoon, tablespoon, knife. *Enough for* 2 *or* 3 *persons.*

Cook the rice in fast-boiling salted water, as you would for curry. When done, drain, dry, and let it get cold. Mix the rice, shrimps and chopped hard-boiled eggs together in a basin. Pour over them the oil mixed with the vinegar and stir well. Pile up in a salad bowl lined with lettuce leaves and sprinkle with chopped parsley.

Ham and Egg Walnuts

¼ lb. Ham.	A few Walnuts.	½ teaspoonful chopped **Chives.**
2½ hard-boiled **Eggs.**		Mayonnaise. Seasoning.

UTENSILS—Saucepan, fork, knife, basin, wooden spoon, teaspoon, mincing machine. *Enough for* 2 *persons.*

Separate the yolks from the whites of eggs, and mash the yolks. Add the chives, salt, pepper and paprika to taste. Mix to a smooth paste with mayonnaise.

Put the ham through a mincer, add the chopped walnuts, then mix them with the other ingredients into a paste before forming into balls the size of a walnut. Serve on lettuce leaves with a jug of mayonnaise.

SWEET SALADS

Fruit Salad

1 Egg Yolk.
¾ cupful whipped Cream.
1 cupful chopped Banana.
Juice of 1 Orange.
A handful of Muscatel Grapes.

¼ cupful Maple Syrup.
Juice of ½ Lemon.
1 cupful diced Pineapple.
2 diced Pears.
1 cupful Strawberries or Cherries.

UTENSILS—Double boiler, wooden spoon, lemon squeezer, strainer, cup, knife, salad bowl.

Beat the yolk well in a double boiler, add the syrup, and stir till the mixture thickens and is cooked. Cool, fold in the cream, and when required, stir in strained lemon juice. Mix the banana, pineapple, pears, grapes and orange juice in a salad bowl with the dressing. Stand for 30 minutes, then add the strawberries or cherries, and serve at once.

NOTE.—A quarter of a cupful of chopped walnuts can be added to this mixture.

Californian Fruit Salad Dressing

½ cupful Castor Sugar.
3 Yolks of Eggs.
½ pint Whipped Cream.

Juice of 1 Orange.
Juice of 1 Lemon.
Butter the size of an Egg.

¼ teaspoonful Orange-flower Water.

UTENSILS—Double boiler, basin, teaspoon, cup, lemon squeezer, wooden spoon, wire whisk.

Cook the butter, egg yolks, lemon and orange juice, and sugar in a double boiler till smooth, and when cool fold in the whipped cream. Flavour with orange-flower water and serve with any fruit salad.

Harlequin Salad

½ pint Water or Red Currant Juice.
Juice of ½ tin Peaches.
½ lb. Grapes.   ½ tin Peaches.
1 handful ripe Strawberries.

Rind of 1 Lemon.
Juice of 1 Orange.
¼ lb. stoned Cherries.
1 handful Raspberries.
¼ lb. Loaf Sugar.   Cream.

UTENSILS—Tin-opener, saucepan, knife, lemon squeezer, strainer, glass dish, wire whisk, kitchen spoon, basin. *Enough for 4 to 6 persons.*

Boil the water or red currant juice with the loaf sugar and the thinly pared rind of lemon till it will spin a thread. Add the peach juice and orange juice, then strain the syrup and flavour with Maraschino to taste. Skin and seed the grapes, stone the cherries and pile all in a glass dish. Add the strawberries and raspberries, and the tinned peaches cut into fingers. Pour over the syrup, and serve with whipped cream, sweetened, and flavoured with vanilla, and delicately tinted pink with cochineal.

My Favourite Fruit Salad

1 lb. Colmar Grapes.	3 Canary Bananas, sliced.
1 tablespoonful Maraschino Syrup.	2 tablespoonfuls Maraschino
1 tablespoonful Pineapple Juice.	Cherries.
2 Peaches.　　1 Pear.	Juice of 2 Tangerines.

UTENSILS—Knife, salad bowl, basin, wire whisk, table-spoon, lemon squeezer, strainer. *Enough for 4 to 6 persons.*

Halve and seed the grapes, and mix them in a bowl with strained juice of tangerines. Add the halved cherries, syrup, diced pineapple and juice, peeled and sliced bananas, peeled and diced peaches and pears. Stand for 30 minutes on ice, and serve with whipped cream, sweetened and flavoured with vanilla.

NOTE.—A little Maraschino liqueur can be added to the salad, and strawberries can be substituted for cherries.

PASTRIES
AND PUDDINGS

PASTRY

UTENSILS FOR PASTRY-MAKING—Sieve, measuring spoons, basin, lemon squeezer, strainer, wooden spoon, pastry board or marble slab, rolling pin, cloth, pastry brush, cutters, knife, baking sheet, pie-dish or pie-plate, pastry rack.

Puff Paste (1)

½ lb. Flour.　　½ lb. Butter.　│　Lemon Juice.　　Salt.

Take the flour, butter, juice of half a lemon, and half a teaspoonful of salt, sift the flour and salt into a basin ; strain the lemon juice, add a little cold water to it, and stir it lightly into the flour. Mix with sufficient cold water, about a teacupful in all, to make it into a dough, as near the consistency of butter as possible. Turn the dough out on to a slightly floured marble slab or pastry board, and knead it until air-bubbles can be seen in it, then roll it out lightly.

Flour a cloth, put the butter on it, and squeeze out as much moisture as possible. Press the butter out to about half the size of the dough, and then put it in the centre of the paste. Dust it lightly with flour, and fold over the edges so that the butter is well wrapped in the paste. Now put it away in a cool place for an hour (on ice if you have it), and when it has stood long enough, roll it out straight and evenly, lengthways of the paste, not crossways. Next, turn it right over and roll the other side, keeping it even. Fold it into three and turn it half round, so that three raw edges face you, and roll again ; then turn over as before and roll again, making four times in all. Fold once more into three, and put away again for ½ hour.

If you have no ice, dip a *linen* cloth in the coldest water available, wring it very dry, and lay it over the paste. When the paste has stood for ½ hour, roll it out four times again in exactly the same manner as at first. Put it away for another

½ hour, then roll again four times. The rolling out is done three times, and there are four rollings each time. Paste made like this is never a failure if the oven is right, but much of the success of the pastry is in the baking. The oven must be hot, but not hot enough to burn it. If too cool, the butter melts and runs out of the paste, which makes it heavy and tough.

TO MAKE PATTIES.—Roll out the pastry to a quarter of an inch in thickness. Take a plain round cutter, two inches and a half across, also a cutter one inch across. Cut out rounds with the large cutter; then, with the small one, cut the centres out of half of the large rounds. Brush over the rings with cold water on one side, and then lay them evenly, wet side down, on the large rounds. Brush them over on the other side with whole beaten-up egg, also the small rounds which are to form the tops of the patties.

Wet a baking sheet with cold water, lay the patty cases on it, also the little tops, and bake in a moderate oven, opening the door as little as possible. The tops will be done before the cases. When the pastry is baked sufficiently, take it out, fill the cases, and put the tops on.

Puff Paste (2)

1 lb. Flour.   Lemon Juice.
¾ lb. Butter.   Water.   Salt.

Sift the flour and salt through a fine sieve. Divide the butter into three parts. Squeeze the juice of a lemon into ½ pint of very cold water. Put the sifted flour and salt into a basin and mix it lightly into a dough with the lemon-water. Sprinkle a pastry board, or preferably a marble slab, with a little flour, just enough to prevent the paste from sticking. Puff paste can be made heavy by using too much flour in the rolling-out process.

Roll the paste out, then divide one of the three portions of butter into small pieces, and dot them lightly and evenly about the paste. Sprinkle over a little more flour. Fold all the edges of the paste into the centre, then set aside in a cool place for 15 minutes. Roll it out again, and put the second portion of butter, divided into small pieces, on it in the manner just described. Fold all the edges of the paste into the centre again, and leave for another 15 minutes. Repeat the process with the third portion of butter, and leave it for 15 minutes again. Now roll out three times, and use.

Flaky Pastry

½ lb. Flour.   3 oz. Butter. | 4 oz. Lard.   **Water.**
1 teaspoonful Baking Powder. | A pinch of Salt.

Sift the flour with the baking powder and salt. Rub in the butter and mix to a stiff paste with cold water. Put the lard on a well-floured board and press it out into thin pieces with a rolling pin. Roll out the pastry to a squarish shape, cover it with lard, and fold the sides to the centre both ways, then over in half. The pastry should then be folded into eight. Roll out and use as required.

Short Paste

½ lb. Flour. | 4 oz. Butter.
1 oz. Rice Flour. | 1 Yolk of Egg.
1 teaspoonful Baking Powder. | A little cold Water.

Sift the flour and the rice flour through a sieve, into a basin or on to a marble slab. Rub in the butter until quite smooth, then mix in the baking powder. Make into a stiff dough with the yolk of an egg and a little cold water. Roll out to the required thickness, and use.

This pastry is especially suitable for fruit tarts.

Dripping Paste

6 oz. good Beef Dripping. | 1 teaspoonful Baking Powder.
6 oz. Flour.   A pinch of Salt. | A little cold Water.

Work up the dripping into a creamy state with a wooden spoon. Sift a pinch of salt and the baking powder with the flour, then rub it into the dripping. Add sufficient cold water to make it into a stiff dough. Roll out, and use.

Suet Paste

1 lb. Flour. | 6 oz. Beef Suet.
Pinch of Salt. | ½ pint cold water.

Free the suet from all skin and shreds, and chop it very finely. Put the flour, and a pinch of salt, into a basin, and rub the chopped suet well into it. Mix into a smooth dough, with about half a pint of cold water, then roll out, and use.

Less suet may be used for a very plain paste, or for a very rich one use a little more. The quantities first given are for a good ordinary paste for boiled fruit or meat puddings, or suet dumplings. The most important point in obtaining a successful paste is chopping the suet very finely.

Raised Pie Paste

1 lb. Flour.   1 Egg. | ¼ lb. Butter.   Salt.

Rub the butter with the flour and salt, mix these with one whole egg, and sufficient cold water to make a stiff dough, then roll out, and use.

Choux Paste for Eclairs, etc.

4 Eggs.   3 oz. Butter. | 1 breakfastcupful Boiling Water.
5 oz. Flour.

Put the butter and water into a saucepan, and boil them up ; when quite boiling, put in all the flour at once. Stir well and beat, until it leaves the sides of the pan, then let it cook slowly, at the side of the stove, for 10 minutes. Beat the eggs well, and add them, by degrees, to the mixture, beating all the time—beat well, for quite 10 minutes.

Put the mixture into a forcing-bag, with a plain pipe, and force out in the required shapes on to a greased baking sheet. Bake in a rather steady oven for about ½ hour. The oven should have a steady heat, and the door should not be opened for the first 15 minutes, neither must the éclairs be taken out before they are properly cooked through, or they will be spoiled.

TO ICE PASTRY

Eggs. | Icing or Castor Sugar.

Beat the whites of one or two eggs to a stiff froth, and spread this over the pastry when it is cool. Sift icing or castor sugar thickly over, put the pastry back into the oven, and let the icing become a pale golden brown.

Apple Tart

2 lb. Cooking Apples. | 4 Cloves.   Castor Sugar.
¾ lb. Short Paste. | 1 teaspoonful chopped Lemon
4 oz. moist Sugar. | Peel.
1 teacupful Cold Water.

Enough for 6 persons.

Make three-quarters of a pound of short paste (see page 331). Pare and core the apples, and slice them into thin slices. Put a layer of the apple in the bottom of a pie-dish, sprinkle some of the moist sugar over, some of the chopped lemon peel, and one or two of the cloves ; now put another layer of apple, etc., and fill the dish in this way, piling up the apple high in the centre, then pour in about a teacupful of cold water.

Roll out the paste to about a quarter of an inch in thickness. Cut a strip, and lay it round the edge of the dish, first wetting the edge it lies on. Now wet the paste edging, and put the paste cover over the whole pie. Press the edges gently, then trim them neatly. Brush the top paste over with cold water, stand the dish on a paper, then sprinkle the top thickly with finely-crushed loaf sugar. Put the pie into a moderate oven to bake, and when the loaf sugar begins to colour, lay a wet sheet of paper over the top. If the apples are a good cooking kind, the pie will be baked in $\frac{1}{2}$ to $\frac{3}{4}$ hour.

NOTE.—All FRUIT TARTS may be made in this way, except that cloves are used only with apples.

Apple Meringue Pie

3 cupfuls, hot, sweetened stewed Apples.	2 Eggs. Pastry.
$\frac{1}{2}$ teaspoonful grated Lemon Rind.	2 tablespoonfuls melted Butter.
	2 tablespoonfuls Castor Sugar.

Enough for 6 persons.

Line a pie-plate with short paste, prick it all over to prevent the crust from rising, and bake it in an oven of 375° F. till crisp and pale golden. Mix the apples with the melted butter, lemon or orange rind, or cinnamon, and the well-beaten yolks of eggs. Fill this mixture into the pastry shells when it is cold.

Beat the whites of eggs till stiff, beat in two-thirds of the sugar until very stiff, fold in the remainder of the sugar, and pile on top of the pie. Put in a slow oven to set for 10 minutes.

Apple Puffs

1 lb. good Cooking Apples.	Sugar. Cold Water.
$\frac{1}{2}$ lb. Flaky or Puff Paste.	A small piece of stick Cinnamon.

Enough for 4 persons.

Pare and core the apples, then slice them. Put the slices into a saucepan, with two tablespoonfuls of cold water, and the piece of cinnamon, and stew until the apples are quite pulpy. Remove the cinnamon, sweeten to taste, and put the pulp away to cool.

When the apple is cold, roll out the puff paste to an eighth of an inch in thickness. Cut strips four inches wide, then cut these across to make four-inch squares; brush the edges of the squares over with cold water ; put a tablespoonful of the apple pulp on one half of a square, then fold the other half over, corner to corner, so as to form a triangle. Press the edges firmly together, brush the puffs over with beaten-up white of egg, and sift icing sugar thickly over the top.

Wet a clean baking sheet with cold water, lay the puffs on it, and bake in a fairly quick oven for 15 minutes, opening the door as little as possible. If the oven door is opened too often while puff pastry is being baked, the pastry is spoiled completely, and the cold draught makes it rise unevenly, more on one side than the other.

Open Apricot Tart

1½ lb. Apricots. | 3 oz. Sugar.
¾ lb. Short Paste. | 1 pint Water.

Enough for 6 persons.

Cut the apricots in halves, and remove the stones. Make a syrup of the sugar and water, and cook the apricots gently in it. Well butter a tin pastry-ring, or a tin cake-ring will do. Stand it on a buttered baking sheet, then line the sides and bottom with short paste, all in one piece—the sides should be about two inches deep, not more. Butter a sheet of paper, and line the paste with it, butter side downwards, then fill it with raw rice. This is to prevent the paste from rising out of shape.

Bake in a moderate oven for about 20 minutes, then take out the rice and the paper, remove the ring, and put the pastry back in the oven to finish cooking the inside. When done, lift it gently on to a pastry rack, and fill the centre with the cooked apricots. Ornament the edges with royal icing (see Index for this), or omit the icing, and put a wreath of green leaves, cut out of angelica, round. If liked, whipped cream may be put on the top of the apricots.

Fruit Tartlets

½ lb. Short Paste.   Water. | 1 cupful Castor Sugar.
Fruit and Fruit Syrup. | ¼ pint whipped Cream.

Enough for 6 persons.

Make half a pound of short paste, as described on page 331. Butter some small tartlet tins, and line these with paste, a quarter of an inch thick. Now put buttered papers over the paste, fill in these with raw rice, and bake in a moderate oven for 15 minutes. Remove the rice and papers, then return the tins to the oven for the paste to dry in the centres. When this is done, turn them out of the tins and put them aside to cool.

Make a syrup with a cupful of castor sugar and a cupful of water. Stew any suitable fruit in this, such as cherries, apricots, gooseberries, etc., and when cooked, fill the tartlets with the fruit. Reduce the syrup by rapid boiling, then pour a little over the fruits to glaze them.

Lemon Cheesecakes

¼ lb. Butter.	1 lb. Castor Sugar.
Puff Paste.	3 Lemons. 6 Eggs.

Enough for 6 to 8 persons.

Dissolve the butter in a stewpan, add the sugar, the grated rinds of two lemons, and the strained juice of three. Beat the eggs and add these, then stir without ceasing until the sugar is dissolved and it begins to thicken. When of the consistency of honey, the mixture is ready for use—it will keep good for three months if put in a jar and covered tightly.

Line some patty-pans with good puff paste, mix a few biscuits or ratafias with some of the mixture, and fill the patty-pans half full. Bake for 30 minutes.

Ground Rice Puffs

1 oz. Margarine.	1 oz. Sugar. 1 Egg.
1½ tablespoonfuls Ground Rice.	½ teaspoonful Baking Powder.
Raspberry Jam. Puff Paste.	A little Vanilla Essence.

Enough for 2 persons.

Line a small pie-dish with pastry, spread over it a layer of raspberry jam, and then fill with the mixture.

THE MIXTURE.—Beat the margarine and sugar to a cream, stir in the other ingredients, and mix well together with a beaten egg. Bake for 15 minutes in a moderate oven, till a golden brown.

Mince Pies

¾ lb. Flaky Pastry.	Castor Sugar.
Mincemeat.	White of 1 Egg.

Enough for 5 or 6 persons.

Roll out the pastry and cut it into rounds. Line buttered tartlet tins with the rounds, fill them up with mincemeat, moisten the edges with cold water, and cover with rounds of pastry. Cut the pies across in the centre, and bake in a quick oven. If the mince pies are to be glazed, brush them with beaten white of egg or water and dredge them with castor sugar when the pastry is half cooked.

NOTE.—Mince pies can also be made without using tartlet tins.

THE MINCEMEAT

1 lb. Valencia Almonds.	1 lb. Sultanas.
6 oz. Mixed Peel.　　Spices.	1 lb. Currants.
¾ lb. Demerara Sugar.	¼ lb. Crystallised Fruits.
1 lb. Beef Suet.	1 lb. Cooking Apples.
2 Lemons.　　1 Tangerine.	1 gill Brandy.　　1 gill Rum.

UTENSILS—Knife, chopping board, basin, gill measure, grater, teaspoon, lemon squeezer, wooden spoon, strainer.

Stone and chop the raisins and peel, clean the other dried fruit, and peel and chop the apples. Mix the fruit in a large basin with the finely shredded suet, 2 oz. blanched and chopped almonds, the sugar, salt, ½ teaspoonful grated nutmeg, ½ teaspoonful ground cloves, ¼ teaspoonful ground mace, 1 teaspoonful each of ground cinnamon and ginger, the grated rinds of two lemons and of one tangerine. Add the strained juice of the lemons and the tangerine, the brandy and the rum. Pot and cover.

HOT PUDDINGS

Roly-Poly Pudding

1 lb. Suet Paste.　　　　|　　　　**Jam, or Treacle.**

UTENSILS—Basin, knife, pastry board, rolling pin, wooden spoon, pudding-cloth, saucepan. *Enough for 6 persons.*

Make 1 lb. of good suet paste, as described on page 331, and roll it out to a quarter of an inch in thickness. Spread it evenly over with any kind of jam, or with treacle, to within an inch of the edges, and roll it up carefully. Wet the paste and press it firmly together at the ends. Fold a well-buttered cloth round, tie it at the ends, and tightly pin it in the centre.

Boil the pudding for 1½ hours, and when cooked, remove the cloth carefully.

A nice, sweet sauce can be poured over and around the roly-poly ; and, if liked, the top can be sprinkled with castor sugar and shredded pistachio nuts.

Christmas Pudding

3 oz. Flour.	6 oz. Suet.	5 oz. Sugar.	3 Eggs.
3 oz. Breadcrumbs.		2 oz. Candied Peel.	
6 oz. stoned Raisins.		½ teaspoonful Spice.	
6 oz. Currants.		1 small wineglassful Brandy.	
4 oz. minced Apple.		A pinch of Salt.	

UTENSILS—Basin, wooden spoon, grater, knife, chopping board, mould, teaspoon, tablespoon, wineglass, pudding-cloth, saucepan, sugar sifter. *Enough for 6 or 7 persons.*

Mix together the flour, white breadcrumbs, beef kidney suet, stoned raisins (weighed after they have been stoned), well-cleaned currants, minced apples, sugar, peel (minced small), half a teaspoonful of nutmeg mixed with the pounded mace, a pinch of salt, the brandy and the whole eggs. Mix and beat these ingredients well together, pour them into a well-buttered mould or basin, spread a buttered paper over, then tie a cloth firmly over the top.

Boil for 4 hours, keeping the pudding well covered with boiling water, then turn it out, sift icing sugar thickly over the top, pour two or three tablespoonfuls of brandy round, and, just before sending to table, set this alight. At Christmas time a piece of holly can be stuck in the centre. This pudding may be served with wine or punch sauce, or with rum or brandy butter.

Ascot Pudding

1¼ pints Milk.	3 Eggs.	3 oz. Sugar.	
3 oz. Rice.	3 oz. Suet.	1 oz. Mixed Peel.	
6 oz. Sultana Raisins.		Sauce, as described.	

UTENSILS—Two saucepans, knife, chopping board, 2 basins, wooden spoon, egg-beater, strainer, double boiler, mould. *Enough for 4 or 5 persons.*

Stew the rice in the milk until it is very tender and has absorbed all the milk. When it has cooled a little, mix with it the finely chopped beef suet, the sugar, the finely chopped mixed candied or orange and lemon peel, the sultana raisins,

and the eggs well beaten and strained. Put the mixtur
into a well-buttered mould or basin. Lay a buttered pape
over the top, stand it in a saucepan with sufficient boilin
water to reach three-quarters of the way up the mould, an
boil for 3 hours. More boiling water must be added to tha
in the saucepan as it boils away. When done, turn th
pudding out on to a dish, and pour the following sauc
over :

THE SAUCE

1½ oz. Loaf Sugar.	1½ gills Sherry, or other
3 Yolks of Eggs.	White Wine.
1 teaspoonful Lemon Juice.	

Dissolve the sugar in the wine made hot. While quit
hot, stir in the beaten yolks of three eggs. Put this sauc
in a double saucepan, and stir until it thickens, like custard
but do not let it boil, or it will instantly curdle. Pour thi
over the pudding ; or, if preferred, serve in a hot sauce-boat
A teaspoonful of lemon juice added is an improvement.

NOTE.—If wine is not liked, a plain custard sauce
flavoured with lemon peel or vanilla, may be substituted.

Small Baked Rice Puddings

2 tablespoonfuls Rice.	¼ Pint Thick Cream.
¾ Pint Milk.	Sugar, to taste. Citron.
2 oz. Butter. 4 Eggs.	Nutmeg. Lemon.

UTENSILS—Saucepan, basin, egg-beater, grater, smal
cups or tins. *Enough for 2 or 3 persons.*

Wash the rice, and put it to simmer, with the milk, unti
thick and tender. Add a piece of butter, the size of an egg, the
cream, and milk. Just bring to the boil. and then allow it to
get cold. When cold, mix in the well-beaten eggs, sugar to
taste, and a little nutmeg and grated lemon peel, if liked
Butter little cups or tins, put some slices of citron at the
bottom and fill them three-parts full of the mixture. Bake
in a rather slow oven for ¾ hour. Serve with a sweet sauce

Alma Pudding

½ lb. Breadcrumbs.	4 oz. Sultana Raisins.
6 oz. finely-chopped Suet.	6 Eggs. 1 gill Rum.
2 oz. Sago. 5 oz. Sugar.	1 tablespoonful Apricot Jam.

UTENSILS—Two basins, grater, egg-beater, wooden spoon,
tablespoon, gill measure, mould, saucepan. *Enough for 6
persons.*

Put the breadcrumbs in a bowl, with the sago, suet,

sugar, picked sultana raisins, and apricot jam. Well beat six eggs, and add a gill of rum to them. Put these in with the other ingredients, and mix all well together. Well butter a basin or mould, and put in the mixture. Tie a buttered paper over the top, and stand in a saucepan, with boiling water reaching a little more than half-way up the mould. Steam gently for 2 hours, adding more boiling water as that in the saucepan boils away.

Winter Pudding

½ lb. Flour. 2 Eggs. | ¼ lb. Sugar.
1 teaspoonful Carbonate of Soda. | 2 tablespoonfuls Jam.
2 tablespoonfuls Butter.

UTENSILS—Basin, wooden spoon, measuring spoons, mould, saucepan. *Enough for 6 persons.*

Mix together the sugar, butter, eggs, and carbonate of soda, for about 5 minutes. Then add the flour, and mix again. Lastly, add the jam.

Fill a buttered mould three-parts full with this mixture, and lay a buttered paper over the top. Stand the mould on a fold of paper, in a saucepan, with sufficient boiling water to come three-fourths the way up the mould. Watch the water re-boil, and then let the pudding steam for 2 hours. Turn it out on to a hot dish, and pour any sweet sauce—a custard or wine sauce—over, and serve. (For SWEET SAUCES, see pages 172 to 175.)

Imperial Pudding

6 Eggs. | The weight of the Eggs in Butter.
The weight of the Eggs in Flour. | The weight of the Eggs in Currants.
The weight of the Eggs in Castor Sugar. | Candied Peel, to taste.

UTENSILS—Two basins, wooden spoon, egg-beater, knife, mould, saucepan. *Enough for 6 persons.*

Beat the butter to a cream, add the castor sugar, and beat again. Thoroughly beat the eggs, then add them, by degrees, to the butter and sugar. Add the flour, and beat again. Lastly, add the currants and peel. The important point in making this pudding is to beat it thoroughly after adding the different ingredients.

Put the mixture into a well-buttered basin, or mould, and lay a buttered paper over the top. Stand the basin on a fold of paper in a saucepan, with boiling water reaching three-fourths the way up the basin. Steam for 6 or 7 hours, gently adding more boiling water as that in the saucepan boils away. Turn the pudding out on to a hot dish, pour wine sauce over, and serve. (For WINE SAUCE, see page 175.)

Baked Lemon Pudding

| 1 Lemon. | 2 Eggs. | 2 small tablespoonfuls Arrow- |
| 1 breakfastcupful White Sugar. | | root. |

1 dessertspoonful Butter.

UTENSILS—Two basins, wooden spoon, measuring spoons, breakfast cup, egg-beater, lemon squeezer, strainer, saucepan, grater, pie-dish. *Enough for 2 or 3 persons.*

Mix the arrowroot smoothly with a little cold water. Add the yolks of eggs, not beaten, half the sugar, the strained juice of the lemon, and the grated rind. Add one pint of boiling water, and boil for 5 minutes. Mix the butter well with the other ingredients, then put the mixture into a buttered dish.

Beat the whites of the eggs to a stiff froth, and add the remainder of the sugar to them. Spread this on top of the pudding, and bake in a moderate oven until it is a light brown.

Plain Rice Pudding, Baked

| 3 oz. Rice. | 2 oz. Butter. | 2 oz. Sugar. | 2 Eggs. |
| 1¼ pints Milk. | | Grated Rind of half a Lemon. |

UTENSILS—Saucepan, wooden spoon, grater, basin, egg-beater, pie-dish. *Enough for 5 or 6 persons.*

Wash the rice, and about half cook it in boiling water. Drain off the water, and put the rice into a stewpan, with the milk. Stew slowly until the rice is quite tender, and before it is taken from the fire, stir in the butter and sugar. Remove it from the fire, and when it has cooled a little add the well-whisked eggs and the grated lemon rind. Grated nutmeg can be used instead of the lemon, if preferred. Pour into a well-buttered pie-dish, and bake in a slow oven from 30 to 40 minutes.

Snowdon Pudding

½ lb. Breadcrumbs.	6 oz. Sugar.	4 Eggs.
½ lb. Beef Kidney Suet.	A few split Raisins.
1½ oz. Rice Flour.	5 oz. Orange Marmalade.

A pinch of Salt.

UTENSILS—Two basins, grater, wooden spoon, egg-beater,

mould, pudding-cloth, saucepan. *Enough for* 6 *persons.*

Ornament a well-buttered mould with some split raisins (or they may be omitted, if preferred). Mix together the suet, finely minced, the breadcrumbs, rice flour, salt, orange marmalade, sugar, and well-whisked eggs. Beat the whole until all the ingredients are thoroughly well mixed. Pour the mixture gently into the mould, cover it with a buttered paper and a floured cloth, and boil gently for 1½ hours.

When turning out, if the ornamentation of split raisins sticks to the mould it will show that the mould was not buttered well. Serve with wine sauce or arrowroot sauce. (For ARROWROOT SAUCE, and WINE SAUCE, see Index.)

Bread and Butter Pudding

Slices of Bread and Butter.
2 oz. Sugar.   3 Eggs.
1½ pints Milk.

¼ lb. Currants, or Sultana Raisins.
A grate of Nutmeg or Lemon.

UTENSILS—Pie-dish, knife, basin, egg-beater, saucepan, grater. *Enough for* 6 *persons.*

Have some thickly-buttered slices of bread, and put a layer in the bottom of a pie-dish. Sprinkle a few currants or raisins over, lay more slices of bread and butter, and sprinkle again, and repeat until the dish is filled. Boil the milk, and pour it hot on to the well-beaten eggs. Add to this the sugar and spice, then pour it over the bread and butter in the dish. Bake slowly for 1 hour.

Cocoanut Pudding

1 pint Milk.   2 Eggs.
3 oz. Desiccated Cocoanut.

2½ cupfuls Sponge Cake Crumbs or Breadcrumbs.
3 oz. Castor Sugar.

UTENSILS—Two basins, grater, wooden spoon, pie-dish, egg-beater. *Enough for* 3 *or* 4 *persons.*

Mix the cocoanut, crumbs and sugar well together in a large basin with the milk, then turn into a buttered pie-dish. Beat up the eggs and pour them on top, then cook until brown.

Old-Fashioned Apple Charlotte

3 lb. Apples.   1 Lemon.
3 oz. Butter, clarified.
Slices of Bread.

3 oz. Butter for Marmalade.
¾ lb. Sugar.
½ teaspoonful powdered Cinnamon.

UTENSILS—Round cake tin, knife, stewpan, lemon squeezer, strainer, tin plate. *Enough for* 6 *persons.*

Butter a round cake tin, or a deep pie-dish will do. Cut some thin oblong slices of stale bread suitable for lining the tin or dish, dip these in clarified butter, and line the tin with the slices, either with the ends coming together exactly, or with the ends lapping over one another. This is to prevent the escape of the fruit.

Pare, quarter and core the apples. Put them into a stewpan with the fresh butter, sugar, powdered cinnamon, and the strained juice of a lemon. Let these stew gently until they form a smooth and dry marmalade, stirring often to prevent burning. Let this mixture cool, then put it into the lined tin or pie-dish, filling it to the brim. Cover the top with slices of bread, dipped in clarified butter, and let these slices fit exactly together also. Put a tin plate on top, with a weight on it. Bake in a brisk oven for ¾ to 1 hour. When cooked, and before removing the charlotte from the mould, drain the butter from it. Turn out gently on to a dish, and sift sugar over.

Baked Apple Dumplings

| 6 Apples. | ½ lb. Flour. | Castor Sugar. | Cloves. |
| ¼ lb. Butter. | Yolk of 1 Egg. | ½ teaspoonful Baking Powder. | |

UTENSILS—Knife, apple corer, 2 basins, wooden spoon, pastry board, rolling pin, pastry brush, baking sheet. *Enough for 4 to 6 persons*.

Pare the apples, and remove the cores without cutting the apples in halves or breaking them. Put the flour in a basin, rub in the butter until it is quite worked in, add the baking powder, then the yolk of egg, and mix into a stiff paste with a very little cold water. Roll the paste out to about a quarter of an inch in thickness, and then cut it into rounds large enough to cover the apples.

Put an apple in the centre of a round of paste, and fill the hole left by the core with castor sugar and one clove, then gather the paste up all round the apple, and work it round so that the apple is completely covered. Put the joined side down, brush over the top of the dumpling with cold water, and sprinkle thickly with castor sugar. Bake in a moderate oven for ½ hour. To prevent the sugar becoming too brown, lay a sheet of wet paper over. Serve in a glass dish with a custard sauce poured round.

Tapioca Pudding

2 tablespoonfuls Tapioca.
1½ pints Milk.
2 oz. Sugar.   3 Eggs.

½ teaspoonful Vanilla Flavouring, or a few drops of Lemon and Ratafia.

UTENSILS—Saucepan, basin, wooden spoon, measuring spoons, pie-dish, baking tin. *Enough for 6 persons*.

Simmer the tapioca in the milk until it is swelled, then pour it into a bowl and let it cool a little. Add the sugar and flavouring, and beat in three eggs. Take a pie-dish holding a quart, and butter it. Pour in the tapioca, and bake slowly in a moderate oven for an hour.

NOTE.—All milk puddings should be cooked slowly, and it is best to stand the baking dish in a baking-pan containing water.

SAGO PUDDING is made in the same manner as the Tapioca Pudding just described.

Vermicelli Pudding

4 oz. Vermicelli.   4 Eggs.
1 quart Milk.   2 oz. Butter.
¼ lb. Castor Sugar.

½ teaspoonful Vanilla Flavouring or 1 dessertspoonful Orange-flower Water.

UTENSILS—Stewpan, wooden spoon, measuring spoons, basin, pie-dish, baking tin. *Enough for 8 persons*.

Put the milk on to boil in a stewpan. When boiling, drop the vermicelli in, little by little, slightly crushing it in the hand. Keep stirring, to prevent the vermicelli forming into lumps. Boil gently until tender and thick, stirring frequently. This will take about 25 minutes.

Now add the butter, sugar and the flavouring, turn the mixture into a bowl and let it cool, then beat in the eggs, and whisk all well together. Butter a pie-dish (three-pint size), and pour in the mixture. Bake slowly in a moderate oven for 1 hour, standing the dish in a tin containing a little water. The pudding should be a nice pale brown.

SEMOLINA PUDDING is made in the same manner as in the foregoing recipe for Vermicelli Pudding.

Rustic Pudding

1 quart ripe Greengages (or Currants and Raspberries, mixed, can be used ; or Cherries, or any juicy fruit).

Breadcrumbs, or thin slices of Bread.
½ lb. Castor Sugar.
Lemon Juice.

UTENSILS—Knife, pie-dish, grater, dessertspoon. *Enough for 6 to 8 persons.*

Stone the fruit. If slices of bread are used, cut off the crust. Take a deep pie-dish and fill it with alternate layers of fruit, well sprinkled with sugar, and the slices or crumbs of bread. The last layer to be breadcrumbs and sugar. A dessertspoonful of lemon juice sprinkled over the last layer of fruit is an improvement. Put the pudding into a rather brisk oven to bake for ½ to ¾ hour.

Ground Rice Pudding

2 pints Milk.	4 Eggs.	2 oz. Castor Sugar.
3 tablespoonfuls Ground Rice.	Lemon Peel, or Bayleaf.	

UTENSILS—Stewpan, knife, 2 basins, wooden spoon, tablespoon, egg-beater, pie-dish. *Enough for 6 persons.*

Put one pint and a half of milk into a stewpan, with a strip of lemon peel or a bayleaf, and bring it to the boil. Mix the ground rice into a smooth batter with the remaining half-pint of milk. Strain the boiling milk on to this, and stir over the fire until the mixture thickens. Sweeten with the castor sugar. When it is nearly cold, add four well-beaten eggs and a pinch of salt. Butter a pie-dish, pour in the mixture, and bake in a slow oven for 1 hour.

Boiled Batter Pudding

½ lb. Flour.	4 Eggs.	1 pint Milk.
1 oz. Butter.		½ teaspoonful Salt.

UTENSILS—Three basins, wooden spoon, teaspoon, saucepan, egg-beater, pudding-cloth. *Enough for 4 or 5 persons.*

Mix the yolks of eggs smoothly with the flour, then thin this with a pint of milk. Melt the butter and stir it in, and add the salt. Whisk the whites of the eggs to a froth, and stir these in gently also. Butter a basin, pour the mixture in, and tie a buttered and floured cloth over. Boil the pudding for 1 hour and 10 minutes. The pudding should cut smoothly. If it sticks to the knife it is not done sufficiently. Serve with plain butter and sugar, or with sweet sauce.

APPLE MERINGUE PIE—The meringue may be decorated with stoned raisins before it is put in the oven to set (p. 333).

Batter and Fruit Pudding

½ lb. Apples. | 4 large tablespoonfuls Flour.
3 Eggs. | ½ pint Milk.

UTENSILS—Three basins, wooden spoon, tablespoon, egg-beater, knife, saucepan. *Enough for 2 or 3 persons.*

Mix the flour smoothly with a small portion of the milk. Add the rest of the milk by degrees, also the well-beaten eggs. Butter a basin thickly, and fill nearly to the brim with apples, pared, quartered, and cored, then pour the batter into the fruit, and fill up the basin quite full. Tie a buttered and floured cloth tightly over the top, and boil for 1¼ hours.

Turn out on to a hot dish, and strew thickly with sugar. If sugar is added in the making, it will make the pudding heavy. This pudding is equally good made and baked in a pie-dish.

NOTE.—Cherries, gooseberries, and plums may be used instead of apples.

Sir Watkin Pudding

3 oz. Suet.   2 Eggs. | 2 tablespoonfuls Orange or Lemon Marmalade.
2 oz. Sugar. |
4 oz. Breadcrumbs. | Lemon Juice.
1 tablespoonful Flour. | Brandy or Rum.
Arrowroot Sauce, as described.

UTENSILS—Knife, grater, wooden spoon, tablespoon, liqueur glass, 3 basins, egg-beater, lemon squeezer, saucepan. *Enough for 3 persons.*

Chop the suet finely. Mix together the suet, breadcrumbs, flour, sugar, marmalade, a small liqueur glass of rum or brandy, the juice of half a lemon, and the well-beaten eggs. When thoroughly mixed, put all into a buttered mould or basin and steam for 3 hours. Serve with arrowroot sauce, as follows :

THE ARROWROOT SAUCE

2 teaspoonfuls Arrowroot. | A large wineglassful Sherry or
2 oz. Loaf Sugar.   1 Lemon. | other wine.

UTENSILS—Knife, saucepan, teaspoon, wineglass, basin, lemon squeezer, strainer, wooden spoon.

Put the thin rind of half a lemon, and the loaf-sugar, into half a pint of water, and boil gently for 10 minutes. Mix the arrowroot very smoothly with the strained juice of the lemon. Take out the rind of the lemon from the sugar-

C.I.O.   M

water in the pan, and then stir in the arrowroot. Take the sauce from the fire, and add a large wineglass of sherry, Marsala, or similar light wine. If preferred, a small glass of brandy can be substituted for the wine.

Boiled Bread Pudding

4 oz. stale Breadcrumbs.	4 oz. dry finely-minced Suet.
½ pint boiling Milk.	A pinch of Salt.
3 Eggs.	A few drops Ratafia Essence, or
2 oz. Sugar.	a strip of Lemon Peel boiled
Ratafias.	in the milk.

UTENSILS—Grater, 3 basins, 2 saucepans, knife, rolling pin and board, egg-beater, wooden spoon, cloth. *Enough for 3 persons*.

Put the breadcrumbs into a basin. Prepare the boiling milk, flavoured with a few drops of ratafia essence, or with a strip of lemon peel boiled in it. Pour this over the crumbs in the basin, cover with a plate, and let the crumbs absorb the milk, and get cold. Now stir in the minced suet, a pinch of salt, and about six or eight crushed ratafias.

Whisk the eggs with the sugar, and continue to whisk them until the sugar is dissolved. Pour this into the basin, with the other ingredients, and mix together thoroughly. Turn all into a buttered basin, put a buttered paper over the top, then a cloth, tie securely, and boil for 2 hours. Serve with raspberry sauce, or custard sauce flavoured with ratafia, or bayleaf.

Cornflour Pudding

4 tablespoonfuls Cornflour.		1 oz. Castor Sugar.
1 quart Milk.	2 Eggs.	1 oz. Butter.
	Vanilla Flavouring.	

UTENSILS—Two basins, saucepan, wooden spoon, tablespoon, egg-beater, pie-dish. *Enough for 6 persons*.

Mix the cornflour smoothly with a little of the milk, and put the remainder of the milk on to boil. When the milk boils, pour it on to the slaked cornflour, add half an ounce of butter, and return all to the saucepan, then bring to the boil again, stirring all the time.

Beat the eggs well, with the sugar. Take the boiling cornflour from the fire and pour it on to the eggs and sugar, add flavouring to taste and mix well. Butter a pie-dish, pour the mixture in, and bake in a moderate oven for 20 minutes. When cooked, sift castor sugar over the top, and serve.

Cornflour Meringue

1 tablespoonful Cornflour.	4 tablespoonfuls Castor Sugar.
1 quart Milk. 4 Eggs.	6 drops Essence of Lemon.

UTENSILS—Two basins, saucepan, Wooden spoon, tablespoon, egg-beater, pie-dish. *Enough for 6 persons.*

Mix the cornflour to a smooth paste with a little cold milk. Boil the milk and pour it on to the slaked cornflour. Return this to the saucepan and boil for 20 minutes, stirring all the time, then remove the pan from the fire, and let its contents cool slightly. Separate the yolks from the whites of the eggs, and beat the yolks well with two tablespoonfuls of the sugar and the lemon flavouring. Stir this by degrees into the boiled cornflour.

Butter a pie-dish, pour the mixture into it, and bake for 15 minutes. Beat the whites of the eggs to a stiff froth, with a pinch of salt. Stir the remaining two tablespoonfuls of sugar lightly into the white, and when the pudding is cooked, heap the whites of the eggs lightly on, and set it in the oven to brown slightly. Ornament with a few little patches of red currant jelly, and serve either hot or cold.

Plain Cabinet Pudding

¼ lb. Bread-crusts. 2 Eggs.	A few Raisins.
½ pint Milk. Sugar.	A few drops of Vanilla.
Sauce, as described.	

UTENSILS—Pudding basin, 2 small basins, egg-beater, knife, 2 saucepans, wooden spoon, pint measure, measuring spoons, strainer. *Enough for 3 or 4 persons.*

Butter a basin well. Stone the raisins, and ornament the basin with them. Cut the bread-crusts into dice, and put them in the basin. Beat the eggs, and add to them the milk, sugar and flavouring. Pour this over the bread in the basin, and let it soak some time before cooking, then lay a fold of buttered paper over the top.

Stand the basin on a fold of paper in a saucepan with boiling water, enough to come half-way up the basin or mould. Put on the lid, and steam for 1¼ hours. The fold of paper in the bottom of the saucepan prevents the basin from moving about in the boiling. Serve, with sauce poured over.

THE SWEET SAUCE

Simmer half a pint of water with two cloves, a strip of lemon peel and a small piece of a stick of cinnamon. When the water is well flavoured, strain, and put it back into the saucepan. Add a tablespoonful of sugar and a teaspoonful of lemon juice. Mix one dessertspoonful of arrowroot with a little cold water, and stir it into the syrup when boiling. Colour with a few drops of cochineal, and pour over the pudding.

Pancakes

4 Eggs. 1 pint Milk.	A pinch of Salt.
2 oz. Butter.	4 tablespoonfuls Flour.

UTENSILS—Two basins, sieve, wooden spoon, tablespoon, egg-beater, frying pan, broad knife. *Enough for 3 or 4 persons.*

Sift the flour. Separate the whites and yolks of the eggs. Mix the flour into a smooth batter with the milk and the yolks of the eggs, adding a pinch of salt. It is best to make this batter some time before it is wanted for use. When ready to cook the pancakes, whip the whites of the eggs to a still froth, with a pinch of salt, and stir these well into the batter.

Melt the butter, and pour sufficient into a small frying pan to grease it well. When the butter boils in the pan, pour in sufficient batter to cover the bottom thinly. When quite set and lightly browned, turn it with a broad knife ; or, better still, toss it over ; but this requires a little practice. Lightly brown the pancake on the other side, then roll it up, lay it on a hot dish, and proceed with the next one. When all are done, pile them neatly on a hot dish with a fancy paper. Sprinkle icing sugar over, and serve with cut lemon and sugar.

NOTE.—Pancakes should be served quickly after they are made, and eaten at once.

COLD SWEETS

Cornflour Blancmange

| 3 tablespoonfuls Cornflour. | 2 breakfastcupfuls new Milk. |
| ¼ oz. Butter. | Sugar. |

UTENSILS—Basins, saucepan, wooden spoon, tablespoon, breakfast cup, moulds. *Enough for 3 persons.*

Take three level tablespoonfuls of cornflour, and mix it quite smoothly with a little of the milk, then bring the remainder of the milk to the boil. When it boils, remove the saucepan from the fire, and pour it on to the blended cornflour slowly, stirring all the time. Then add the butter and return it to the fire.

Boil the mixture for 10 minutes, stirring continually. If liked, sugar and flavouring may be added, but it is quite nice without. When sufficiently boiled, pour into one large or several small moulds. The moulds must be previously dipped in cold water. When the blancmange is cold, turn it out and serve, either plain or with fruit or jam.

NOTE.—The important point is to pour the boiling milk on to the cornflour, then to return it to the saucepan and boil it well.

Princess Mary Pudding

¼ lb. Rice. 1 oz. Gelatine.	¼ lb. minced Dried Fruits, such
1½ pints Milk. ¼ pint Cream.	as Cherries, Angelica, Citron
6 oz. Sugar.	(if liked), Ginger, Apricots,
6 Yolks of Eggs.	etc.
Vanilla or Ratafia Flavouring.	1 tablespoonful Rum or Liqueur.

UTENSILS—Saucepan, wooden spoon, tablespoon, knife, chopping board, plate, 4 basins, mould, breakfast cup. *Enough for 5 or 6 persons.*

Put the rice into boiling water, and boil until about half done. Then drain, and put it into a stewpan, with the boiling milk, the sugar, and flavouring of vanilla, ratafia, or lemon. Stir well, and simmer at the side of the range, or on a low gas flame, until the rice is quite tender, then let it get cold.

Mince the assortment of dried fruits, and moisten them with the liqueur or rum. Put this away on a plate. Strain the milk from the rice, and if this milk is not sufficient three-parts to fill the size of mould that is chosen, add a little more to it. Stir the yolks of six eggs into this milk, and heat it until a custard is formed, stirring in also the dissolved gelatine.

Put the custard into a bowl, and beat it to a froth. Blend with it a breakfastcupful of whipped cream. When the mixture begins to set, work into it, by degrees, the rice and the fruit. Fill the mould with the mixture, and put it into a cool place until next day.

Old-fashioned Trifle

1 pint Cream.	Strawberry Jam.
1 pint Custard.	$\frac{1}{2}$ pint Sherry.
6 penny Sponge Cakes.	$\frac{1}{4}$ pint Brandy.
12 Macaroons. $\frac{1}{4}$ lb. Ratafias.	$\frac{1}{4}$ pint Water.

UTENSILS—Saucepan, wooden spoon, egg-beater, 2 basins, pint measure, glass dish, knife, forcing-bag. *Enough for* 6 *persons*.

The sponge cakes should be stale. Mix the sherry, brandy, and water together. Spread a layer of jam on the bottom of a glass dish. Cut the cakes in half, dip them into the wine and water, and put a layer of them on the jam, then dip some macaroons and ratafias in the wine, and put them with the layer of sponge cake. Pour some good thick custard over.

Now put more jam, soaked cakes and custard, letting the cakes pile high in the centre. Whip and flavour the cream, put it into a forcing-bag having a large rose-pipe, and force this out on top of all. The top of the cream can be ornamented with crystallised fruits, sweets or anything that may be suitable and convenient. The trifle should be prepared some hours before it is to be served, except the cream which goes on at the last minute.

Plain Junket

2 quarts tepid Milk.	2 tablespoonfuls Rennet.
1 tablespoonful Castor Sugar.	Nutmeg.
Clotted or Thick Cream.	

UTENSILS—Bowl, tablespoon, quart measure, grater. *Enough for* 6 or 8 *persons*.

Take two quarts of milk warm from the cow. Put the castor sugar into a bowl, pour the milk on to this, and stir. Now put in the rennet and give another stir. At once place the bowl where it will not be disturbed until required for the table.

Just before serving, lay some clotted cream gently on top, or pour one-third of a pint of very thick cream over it. Finally, grate a little nutmeg over. If milk cannot be had warm from the cow, then warm some very new milk to the same temperature, taking care not to make it too hot.

NOTE.—Junket should always be made in a deep bowl, not in a shallow glass dish.

Orange Caramel

6 large Oranges.	Castor Sugar. Angelica.
½ lb. Cane Sugar.	Brandy or Liqueur.
½ pint whipped Cream.	2 tablespoonfuls cold Water.

UTENSILS—Two basins, knife, serving dish, saucepan, wire whisk, forcing-bag. *Enough for 4 to 6 persons.*

Peel the oranges, thoroughly free them from all white skin, remove the pips, then put the pieces into a basin. Sprinkle a little castor sugar and some brandy or liqueur over them, and let the orange steep in this for 20 minutes, then arrange the pieces neatly on top of one another in a circle on a dish.

Put ½ lb. cane sugar on to boil with 2 tablespoonfuls of cold water. Boil until it turns to caramel—that is, just after it has boiled to the crack and is a pale golden colour, and when dropped into cold water it will harden immediately. When the sugar is boiled to this point pour it over the oranges. Cut a dozen pieces of angelica to represent leaves. Dip the ends of these into the caramel, and arrange them between the pieces of orange. The angelica must be got ready and placed handily for use, as the caramel sets very quickly.

When the caramel is cold, whip the cream, sweeten it very slightly, and put it into a forcing-bag with a large rose-pipe. Fill the centre of the oranges with it, then serve. If liked, the brandy may be omitted, and the oranges just steeped in sugar water.

Orange Custard

2 Oranges.	2 Eggs.	¾ oz. Gelatine.
1¼ pints Milk.		2 oz. Castor Sugar.
	¾ gill cold Water.	

UTENSILS—Three basins, saucepan, egg-beater, wooden spoon, mould with pipe in centre, knife, pint measure, glass dish. *Enough for 3 or 4 persons.*

Soak the gelatine in the water for about 10 minutes. Simmer the milk, with the thin rind of one orange, for 10 minutes, then remove the rind. Well beat the yolks of the eggs, and stir them into the milk, over the fire, until it thickens. Do not let it boil. Now add the sugar and the gelatine, and stir until these are dissolved.

Whip the whites of the eggs to a stiff froth. Allow the custard to become cool, and just before it begins to set, stir in the whipped whites. Pour the mixture into a wet mould with a pipe in the centre. Peel the oranges, divide them in their natural divisions, and sweeten them with castor sugar. When the custard has set, turn it out into a glass dish, fill the centre with the pieces of orange, and serve.

A Simple Charlotte Russe

9 penny Sponge Cakes, or 18 Savoy Fingers.	2 oz. Castor Sugar.
1 pint Cream.　1 Egg.	1 Lemon.　Garnish.
	1 oz. Gelatine.　Salad Oil.

UTENSILS—Round mould, brush, knife, grater, lemon squeezer, strainer, basin, wire whisk, saucepan. *Enough for 6 persons.*

Take a round mould and brush it over inside with salad oil. Cut off the outsides of the cakes and line the mould with them. Let the pieces of cake be arranged to join neatly together. Brush over the inner surfaces of the cakes with white of egg, to join them together, but do not let any of the egg touch the mould. Flavour the cream with the strained juice and grated rind of a lemon and the castor sugar, then whip the cream for 20 minutes.

Dissolve the gelatine in a little boiling milk. When cool, add this to the cream, whisking all the time until it thickens, pour it into the mould, and lay slices of cake on the top. When quite cold and firm, turn the charlotte out on to a glass dish, and garnish the top prettily with leaves of angelica and dried cherries.

Surprise Pudding

1 pint Milk.　1 oz. Sugar.	½ oz. Gelatine.　Angelica.
2 Eggs.　1 penny Sponge Cake.	A few Glacé Cherries.
1 tablespoonful Jam.	Pineapple Flavouring.

UTENSILS—Two basins, saucepan, egg-beater, wooden spoon, tablespoon, knife, mould. *Enough for 4 persons.*

Dissolve the gelatine in a small quantity of milk and put the rest of the milk on to boil. Beat the eggs well and stir in the boiling milk. Return the milk and egg mixture to the saucepan, and stir till the custard thickens but does not boil, then add the dissolved gelatine, sugar, and the pineapple flavouring.

Slice the sponge cake rather thinly, spread the slices with jam and then place them together again. Pour half the custard into a mould, put in the sponge cake, and leave until it is setting, then fill up the mould with the remainder of the custard. When cold and set, turn it out by dipping the mould for a second into hot water. (The water should be of a temperature that you can only just bear your hand in.) Garnish the pudding with rings of glacé cherries, or whole cherries, and a few strips of angelica.

NOTE.—Tin moulds are best, as mixtures turn out of them so much more satisfactorily, and they only require to be dipped into the hot water. Earthenware moulds require to stay in the water much longer, with the result that greater risk is run of the pudding turning out unsatisfactorily.

Spanish Pudding

1 quart New Milk.	A few drops Almond Flavouring.
3 oz. Castor Sugar.	½ oz. Gelatine.
3 tablespoonfuls Arrowroot.	Garnish of Fruits.

UTENSILS—Two basins, saucepan, wooden spoon, table-spoon, knife, mould. *Enough for* 6 *persons*.

Soak the gelatine in half a pint of the milk ; mix the arrow-root with a little of the milk, and put the remainder of the milk on to boil. When it boils, add the sugar, stir in the slaked arrowroot, and almond flavouring to taste. Add also the soaked gelatine. Set the milk on the fire again, and stir until it boils. Pour it into a wetted mould and allow it to get cold, then turn out, and garnish with any stewed or crystallised fruits.

Princess Pudding

2 tablespoonfuls Arrowroot.	2 Yolks of Eggs.
1 large Lemon.	Compôte of Fruits.
½ cupful White Sugar.	1 pint Boiling Water.

UTENSILS—Grater, lemon squeezer, 2 basins, wooden

spoon, tablespoon, cup, saucepan, egg-beater or fork, mould. *Enough for 3 persons*.

Blend the arrowroot with a little water, then add the sugar and the grated rind and juice of the lemon. Mix all well together, then pour a pint of *boiling* water on to it. Beat the yolks of the eggs slightly, then stir them in, and pour the mixture into a mould having a pipe in the centre. When cold and quite set, turn it on to a dish rinsed with cold water. Fill the centre of the pudding with a compôte of fruits, arrange some of the fruits round outside, and serve.

NOTE.—If wanted plainer, the fruits may be omitted, and the whites of the eggs whipped to a stiff froth, sweetened and flavoured, and used instead of the fruits.

Stone Cream

3 oz. Arrowroot.	1 oz. Almonds. A little Jam.
1 quart Milk. ½ gill Cream.	3 oz. Granulated Sugar.

UTENSILS—Basin, wooden spoon, saucepan, glass dish, wire whisk, knife. *Enough for 5 or 6 persons*.

Mix the arrowroot with a little of the milk, then boil the remainder of the milk with the sugar in it, pour it on to the arrowroot, return it to the saucepan, and boil for 10 minutes, stirring hard all the time. When nearly cold, pour into a glass dish, previously spread over with jam. Whip the cream, spread it over, and stick almonds, cut into shreds, all over the top.

Coffee Sponge

1 tablespoonful Gelatine.	⅔ cupful Castor Sugar.
1 White of Egg. Salt.	3 cupfuls strong hot Coffee.
2 tablespoonfuls cold Water.	½ teaspoonful Vanilla Essence.

UTENSILS—Two basins, saucepan or coffee percolator, wooden spoon, cup, measuring spoons, wire whisk, mould. *Enough for 5 persons*.

Cover the gelatine with the cold water, and set aside for 10 minutes, then add the sugar and pour the hot coffee over, stirring until the gelatine is dissolved. Cool, add vanilla, and when about to set add the white of egg, beaten to a stiff froth. Beat until spongy and light. Turn into a mould to set, and serve with vanilla or lemon custard.

Russian Jelly

6 Lemons. 6 Cloves.	4 Whites and Shells of Eggs.
½ stick Cinnamon.	2 wineglassfuls Brandy.
4 oz. Gelatine.	2 wineglassfuls Sherry.
1 lb. Loaf Sugar.	Carmine. 2 quarts Water.

UTENSILS—Knife, lemon squeezer, strainer, enamelled saucepan, wineglass, wire whisk, quart measure, jelly-bag, basin, 2 moulds. *Enough for* 8 *persons*.

Pare the lemons very thinly, and squeeze out the juice and strain it. Put the peel and juice into a bright or an enamelled saucepan, more than large enough to hold all the ingredients, as they boil up very much. Add the sugar, cloves, cinnamon, and the whites and shells of eggs, and whisk all well up together ; then add the gelatine and two quarts of warm water. Stand the pan over the fire or gas ring, and continue whisking until it comes to the boil. Simmer for 5 minutes, then remove it from the fire.

Hang up the jelly-bag, and pour about two quarts of boiling water through it. When the jelly has stood off the fire for 10 minutes, strain it through the bag. When it is through, put it back into the bag and strain again, and do this a third time, to get the jelly quite bright and clear, then put aside to cool a little, but not to set. Line two moulds with this clear jelly, and divide the remaining jelly into two parts ; add the brandy to one half, and the sherry and a few drops of carmine to the other.

Whip these separate jellies over ice until they are quite frothy and spongy. Just before they commence to set, pour them into the moulds, first a layer of the white ; then, as soon as that sets, a layer of the pink, followed with another layer of white, and ending with a layer of pink. Let the moulds stand on ice until the jelly sets. When ready to serve, dip the moulds, just for an instant, into a large basin of very hot water. Only just dip them, then dry off any water on the bottom of the jelly and turn out on to the dish.

Italian Jelly

4 Lemons. 6 Cloves.	1 inch Cinnamon Stick.
2 oz. Gelatine.	1 quart Water.
½ lb. Loaf Sugar.	1 wineglassful Noyeau Syrup.
3 Whites and Shells of Eggs.	Candied Fruits. Oranges.

UTENSILS—Knife, lemon squeezer, strainer, tin or enamelled saucepan, 3 basins, wire whisk, jelly-bag, wineglass, tin mould. *Enough for* 6 *persons*.

Pare the lemons very thinly, squeeze out the juice and strain it. Soak the gelatine in half a pint of the water for 15 minutes. Put the sugar, lemon peel, lemon juice, whites and shells of eggs, the cinnamon and cloves into a clean bright tin or enamelled stewpan. Let the stewpan be large enough to hold three or four quarts, and the jelly will not then boil over. Whisk these ingredients together with a wire whisk, then put in the soaked gelatine, and the remaining water. Place the stewpan on the fire to boil, whisking all the time and until it is about to boil. Just before it boils, cease whisking, and let it boil for 10 minutes. Then take the pan off the fire, and let it stand for 5 minutes.

While it is standing, get the jelly-bag ready. If you have a stand, then hang the bag on it ; if not, it can be tied up between two chairs. Stand a perfectly clean basin beneath it, and first pour two quarts of boiling water through the bag, then empty this away. When the bag is clear, pour a little of the jelly in, and when this has run through, remove the basin and put another one in its place to receive the remainder. Pour the first jelly into the bag again. If necessary, put all the jelly through the bag a second and a third time, to get it quite bright and clear. When cool, but not set, add the syrup.

Take a bright tin mould and line it with jelly, letting the jelly be half an inch thick at the bottom. On this bottom layer arrange some crystallised fruits and pieces of orange. Set these with jelly, then pour in another layer of jelly half an inch thick. Put more fruits and jelly until the mould is filled, then, if possible, stand it on ice to set. When quite set, dip the mould for an instant into water which is of a heat that you can only just bear your hand in. Pass a cloth quickly over the top to absorb any moisture there may be, then turn the jelly out into a pretty glass or silver dish. Garnish round the base with a few more of the crystallised fruits, and serve. If preferred, all fresh fruits may be used.

Jelly à la Monaco

1 quart Lemon Jelly.	A few drops Carmine.
1 wineglassful Sherry.	A few drops of Green Colouring.
1 wineglassful Kirsch Syrup.	½ pint whipped Cream.

UTENSILS—Saucepan, basin, fancy jelly moulds, wineglass, wire whisk, forcing-bag. *Enough for 6 persons.*

Make a quart of plain lemon jelly. Flavour half of this

with sherry (or brandy), and colour it pink. Flavour the other half with Kirsch syrup, and colour it a pale green. Fill some small fancy jelly moulds with the different jellies, and set them aside to cool, then turn them out on to a pretty dish. Whip the cream stiffly, and put it into a forcing-bag with large rose-pipe. Force a rose out in the centre of each jelly, then serve. If preferred, other flavourings can be used.

Meringues

| 4 Whites of Eggs. | | ½ pint Cream. |
| ½ lb. Castor Sugar. | | Icing Sugar. |

UTENSILS—Baking sheet, egg-beater, 2 basins, tablespoon, sharp-pointed knife, wooden spoon, sieve, teaspoon. *Enough for 4 or 5 persons.*

Before commencing to make the meringues, see that the oven is right. It is best to make them after the oven has been used for something else, as it is then of a nice, steady, moderate heat. Get ready a perfectly clean baking sheet, and cover it entirely with strips of white paper four inches wide. Separate the whites from the yolks of the eggs, and put the whites into a basin, with a pinch of salt, and whip until quite light and stiff. Do not leave off whipping, when you have once commenced, until they are finished. With a wooden spoon, mix the sugar in lightly and quickly, but do not beat the eggs after the sugar is added.

Take the mixture up with a tablespoon, and drop it in spoonfuls on the paper or tin, dropping each one as much in the shape of an egg as possible. A little practice is all that is required to shape them nicely. Sift icing sugar over them, and put into a very moderate oven, and bake for 2 or 3 hours. The oven may be allowed to cool down a little the latter part of the time. The meringues should be a pale fawn colour when they are done, and can be lifted off the tin without sticking.

When removed from the oven, take each one and hollow out the centre a little with a sharp-pointed knife, scraping gently from the underside. Put a teaspoonful of stiffly whipped cream, flavoured to taste, into each, then put two together, cream to cream. Pile prettily on a glass dish, with a dessert paper beneath them, and serve.

NOTE.—(1) The Meringue cases—that is, the meringues before the cream is put in—can be made some days before they are wanted, if kept in a tin in a dry place, but the cream must not be put in until the last minute. (2) In hot weather, the meringue cases can be filled with ice cream.

Prune Shape

1 lb. Prunes (weighed without the stones).	Rind of ½ Lemon.
	½ oz. Gelatine. 2 oz. Almonds.
3 oz. Sugar. 1 pint Water.	Custard, as described.

UTENSILS—Stewpan, knife, basin, kitchen spoon, pint measure, mould. *Enough for 6 persons.*

Put the prunes into a stewpan with the water, the lemon rind, pared very thinly, and the sugar. Simmer till tender, stirring occasionally, to prevent the fruit from sticking. Dissolve the gelatine in some of the liquid, and mix it thoroughly with the prunes. Bring the mixture just to the boil, and add a few of the almonds, blanched and shredded, then pour into a wet mould, and when set turn out into a glass dish. Shred the remainder of the almonds finely, and stick them all over the shape, to represent a hedgehog. Pour custard round the base of the shape, and serve.

THE CUSTARD

½ pint new Milk.	A small piece of Lemon Rind.
3 Yolks of Eggs.	Sugar to taste.

UTENSILS—Saucepan, double boiler, tablespoon, wooden spoon, basin, egg-beater.

Boil the lemon rind in the milk. As soon as the milk boils, reduce the heat and let the lemon infuse for 15 minutes. Beat the yolks of eggs well in a basin. Add one tablespoonful of sugar to the eggs, and mix thoroughly.

Strain the boiling milk on to the eggs and sugar, stirring briskly all the time. Then pour all into a double boiler, and stir the mixture until it thickens, *but on no account let it boil.* Pour it out at once, and stir again for a few minutes, to prevent the eggs from cooking too much and curdling.

Toasted Marshmallows

1 tablespoonful Granulated Gelatine.	1 cupful Castor Sugar.
	3 Whites of Eggs.
1½ teaspoonfuls Vanilla Essence.	Crushed Macaroons.
1 cupful boiling Water.	Cream.

UTENSILS—Basin, wooden spoon, wire whisk, cup, measuring spoons, square shallow pan, knife. *Enough for 4 persons.*

Pour boiling water over the gelatine, stir in the sugar, and stand until it is dissolved, stirring occasionally. Place the basin containing the mixture on ice, add the egg whites and beat till thick, then turn into a square shallow pan, dipped in cold water, and leave till set and ice cold. Remove from pan, cut into pieces the size of a marshmallow, and roll in dried macaroon crumbs. Serve piled up, on a pretty dish, accompanied by sugar and cream. (For OTHER JELLIES, see Index.)

Gooseberry Fool

2 quarts unripe Gooseberries. | $\frac{1}{2}$ **pint Cream.**
4 oz. Sugar. **Water.** | $\frac{1}{2}$ **pint new Milk.**

UTENSILS—Basin, saucepan, coarse sieve, wooden spoon. *Enough for 6 persons.*

Wash the green gooseberries, and put them on to boil in half a pint of water. When the gooseberries turn yellow and are quite soft, turn them out into a coarse sieve placed over a bowl. Press the pulp through the sieve, occasionally scraping it off the underside of the sieve, as this quickens the process. When all is through, stir in a quarter of a pound of moist sugar (or more if liked very sweet), and allow it to get cold. When cold, add the milk and cream, and mix thoroughly. Serve in a glass dish, or in melba glasses.

Banana Mould

1 packet Pineapple Jelly. | **4 large Bananas.**
$\frac{1}{4}$ **pint Cream (fresh or tinned).**

UTENSILS—Knife, 2 basins, kitchen spoon, fork, glass dish. *Enough for 4 persons.*

Cut up the jelly and dissolve it completely in $\frac{1}{4}$ pint of hot water. When nearly cold, but before it has begun to set, stir in the cream gradually. Peel the bananas, mash them with a fork and then beat until quite light and smooth. Stir this lightly and thoroughly into the jelly and cream. Pour into a glass dish, and stand in a cool place to set.

NOTE.—1. If the mixing is done before the jelly is sufficiently cool, the jelly, banana and cream will separate into layers.

2. Strawberries and raspberries may be substituted for the bananas. Of these fruits, ¾ lb. will be enough.

Raspberry Slices

1 large oblong Sponge Cake.	Whipped Cream.
1 cupful Castor Sugar.	1 White of Egg. Vanilla.
1¾ cupfuls Raspberries.	1 tablespoonful Lemon Juice.

UTENSILS—Oblong tin, knife, 2 basins, wire whisk, cup, lemon squeezer. *Enough for 6 persons.*

Make a sponge cake in the usual way and bake it in an oblong tin. When quite cold, cut it with a sharp knife cross-wise in half-inch slices. Beat the raspberries, sugar, lemon juice and egg white with a wire whisk for over ½ hour over ice, till the mixture will keep its shape, then spread it between the slices of the cake, and sandwich them together.

Whip ¾ pint of cream to a stiff froth, and sweeten and flavour it with vanilla. Mask the cake all over the top and sides with it and decorate with one or two perfect raspberries and with shavings of angelica.

Strawberries in Ranelagh Way

1 pint Strawberries.	Icing Sugar.
3 gills thick Cream.	Pistachio Nuts.
Orange and Lemon Juice.	Orange-flower Water.

UTENSILS—Two basins, silver fork, knife, wire whisk, teaspoon, kitchen spoon. *Enough for 2 persons.*

Break up the strawberries in a bowl with a silver fork, but do not mash them. Sprinkle them with a few drops of lemon and orange juice. Two-thirds fill custard glasses with the mixture, then shake a teaspoonful of icing sugar into each. Fill up with thick, half-whipped cream, delicately flavoured with orange-flower. Decorate with chopped, blanched pistachio nuts.

Quince Snow

2 large Quinces.	Sponge Cake. Sugar.
2 Whites of Eggs.	Custard, as described.

UTENSILS—Knife, saucepan, hair sieve, wooden spoon, 2 basins, wire whisk, measuring spoons. *Enough for 2 persons.*

Pare and core two large quinces, slice them thinly, and boil till quite soft in a very little water, then rub them through a hair sieve. Whip the whites of eggs to a froth, and add the quince purée to the eggs, by degrees, and sugar to taste. Whip all together till quite smooth.

Take two penny sponge cakes and cut them in half, lengthways. Lay them in the bottom of a glass dish, and pour one pint of custard over them. Drop the quince snow on, in large rocky tablespoonfuls.

TO MAKE THE VANILLA CUSTARD SAUCE

¾ pint Milk.	2 Eggs.	1 tablespoonful Castor Sugar.
1 large teaspoonful Flour.		A few drops Vanilla Essence.

Boil the milk. Mix the flour and sugar quite smoothly with a little cold milk, and stir this into the boiling milk, and just bring to the boil again. Beat the two eggs well, and when the milk is boiling again, pour it on to the beaten eggs. When slightly cooled, flavour with a few drops of vanilla essence, and while still warm, pour the mixture over the sponge cake. This should all be done before you begin to make the snow.

A few slices of stale sponge cake, of any kind, will do for the foundation if you have it by you. If a plain custard will do, the yolks of the two eggs not used when making the snow will be sufficient, or the two yolks and one whole egg can be used.

Provence Apples

8 red Apples.	1 cupful Castor Sugar.
Juice of 1 Orange.	Rind of ½ Lemon.

UTENSILS—Saucepan, fork, grater, lemon squeezer, knife, serving dish. *Enough for 4 persons.*

Cook the apples in boiling water until soft, turning them often, then remove them and take off the skins. Add to the water the sugar, grated lemon rind and orange juice. Simmer till reduced to a cupful, then cool and pour over the apples arranged in a serving dish. Serve with cream.

Stuffed Cantaloup

Melons.	1 pint whipped Cream.
Sliced Peaches.	Pistachio Nuts.

UTENSILS—Knife, basin, spoon, wire whisk. *Allow* 1 *small cantaloup for 2 persons.*

Choose ripe cantaloups and cut them in halves, carefully remove all seeds, and fill each hollow with sliced peaches and whipped cream, sweetened and flavoured with vanilla essence.

If the weather is very hot, substitute ice cream for whipped cream, but mask the top of the ice cream with lightly whipped fresh cream, and garnish with tiny fingers of peaches. When whipped cream and peach filling is used, garnish with chopped, blanched pistachio nuts.

Chestnut Flake

1 lb. Chestnuts.	2 cupfuls Castor Sugar.
1 cupful Water.	1 pint Cream.
1 tablespoonful Maraschino.	1 teaspoonful Butter.

UTENSILS—Knife, 2 saucepans, kitchen spoon, potato masher, measuring spoons, cup. *Enough for 6 persons.*

Slit the chestnuts and place them in a saucepan, then add the butter and shake till it is melted. Cover the pan and stand it at the side of the fire for 5 minutes, then shell the chestnuts and cook them till half done in boiling water.

Meanwhile boil the sugar and water for 10 minutes, add the chestnuts and cook till soft, then put them through a potato masher. Serve with whipped cream, very slightly sweetened and flavoured with maraschino.

Stewed Pears

12 cooking Pears.	¾ lb. Loaf Sugar.
1 Lemon. 6 Cloves.	Cochineal, if desired.

UTENSILS—Knife, stewpan, lemon squeezer, kitchen spoon, strainer. *Enough for 6 persons.*

Pare, cut in halves and core the pears. Put them in a stewpan with a close-fitting lid with the thinly pared rind and the juice of a lemon, the cloves, loaf sugar, and as much water as will just cover them. If a bright colour is required, add a teaspoonful of cochineal essence.

Stew the fruit as gently as possible until perfectly tender. When the pears are tender, lift them out, then reduce the liquid by rapid boiling. Strain the syrup over the pears, and when cold serve in a glass dish.

Nougat Baskets

½ lb. Castor Sugar.	Pistachio Nuts.
2 tablespoonfuls Lemon Juice.	Glazed Fruits.
¼ lb. Almonds. Royal Icing.	Whipped Cream. Salad Oil

UTENSILS—Two saucepans, cloth, knife, baking tin, lemon squeezer, strainer, tablespoon, kitchen spoon, marble slab or large dish, palette knife, 6 basket moulds, forcing-bag, pastry rack, basin, wire whisk. *Enough for 6 persons.*

Put the almonds into a saucepan with sufficient cold water to cover them, and bring them just to the boil. Strain, then rub them in a cloth to remove the skins. Split the almonds in halves, shred them very finely, and put them to dry. When dry, bake the shreds to a very pale golden colour. Put the castor sugar into a saucepan with the strained lemon juice and boil until it is a pale yellow, stirring all the time. Then add the almonds, mixing them in gently, and just let the mixture boil up. Have ready a marble slab or large dish, well rubbed over with salad oil. Well oil six little basket moulds, also oil your fingers. Take a small piece of the nougat and turn it on to the slab or dish, flatten it quickly with a well-oiled palette knife, lay it in the mould, press it to the shape and trim the edges. Line the mould as thinly as possible, and let it be done quickly. The small moulds to form the pedestals are filled entirely with the nougat, and when filled they are rubbed on the slab to ensure the bottom being quite smooth. A little practice is needed to mould nougat well.

When the baskets are set, loosen them from the moulds and stand them on a pastry rack until quite cold. When cold, the baskets and pedestals can be joined. To do this, boil some sugar to the crack (the same as for glazing fruits), dip the bottoms of the baskets in this, and then stick them on to the pedestals. Only sufficient nougat for one basket must be taken from the saucepan at the time, the remainder being kept warm. To ornament the baskets, fill a small forcing-bag, having a small rose or leaf-pipe, with royal icing, force this out round the edges of the baskets, then shred some blanched pistachio nuts very finely and stick these all round in the icing.

Fill a large forcing-bag having a rose-pipe with stiffly whipped and flavoured cream. Fill the baskets with this, and stick glazed fresh fruits in it, such as grapes, cherries, strawberries, etc. Stand the baskets on a dish with fancy paper beneath, garnish with a few sprigs of maidenhair fern, then serve. The baskets may also be filled with ices, or broken jelly and cream, differently flavoured and coloured.

Gateau à la Victoria

1 breakfastcupful Castor Sugar.	½ pint whipped **Cream.**
1 breakfastcupful Flour.	6 Eggs.
Macedoine of Fruits.	¾ lb. Plain Icing.
A small quarter-cup Water.	Brandy or Liqueur Syrups.

UTENSILS—Two basins, wooden spoon, flour sifter, saucepan, egg-beater, cake tin, knife, forcing-bag, cup. *Enough for 6 to 8 persons.*

Take a good-sized basin, and break the eggs into it. Sift the flour, and set it to warm. Put the sugar on to boil with the water. Beat the eggs for about 5 minutes, then pour the sugar on (when it boils), beating well all the time. Keep the mixture warm, and whisk it for 20 minutes.

Now stop whisking, and with a wooden spoon, gradually stir in the sifted flour. Pour the mixture into a deep cake mould or tin, which has been well buttered and dusted over with equal parts of flour and castor sugar. Bake in a moderate oven. This is best made a day or two before it is required.

When wanted, hollow out the centre of the cake, leaving a wall about one inch thick all round. Stand it on the dish on which it is to be served. Soak the cake with brandy or liqueur syrups. (These can be purchased quite inexpensively.) Fill a forcing-bag having a medium-sized rose-pipe, with two-coloured plain icings (a white and a pink), and ornament the edge and sides of the cake with it. Fill the centre with a macedoine of fruits, prepared as for a fruit salad (see Index). Put the whipped cream into a bag with a large rose-pipe. Ornament the tops of the fruits with this, and serve.

Baba Rings

½ lb. Flour.	½ oz. Yeast.	½ gill tepid Milk and Water.
5 oz. Butter.	3 large Eggs.	Pinch of Salt.
1 oz. Castor Sugar.		Syrup, as described.

UTENSILS—Sieve, 3 basins, saucepan, knife, cloth, wooden spoon, pastry board, ring moulds, baking sheet, pastry rack, dish. *Enough for 6 to 8 persons.*

Rub the flour through a fine sieve, then put a quarter part of the flour into a basin. Dissolve the yeast and a pinch of salt in the tepid milk and water. Mix this well into the portion of the flour in the basin, work it into a round ball, and cut a cross on the top. Then put the remaining flour into a basin, make a well in the centre, put the ball of dough into it, and draw the flour up round. Cover the basin with a cloth, and stand it in a warm place for the dough to work.

When it has risen well up through the flour (this will be in about 20 minutes if the yeast is good), turn it all out on to a pastry slab or board. Break the eggs into it, and add the butter and sugar. Now mix the paste thoroughly well with the hands, drawing it well through the fingers, and lifting it up well in order to work in as much air as possible. Continue working and beating this well, but lightly, for 20 minutes— by this time it will leave the hands perfectly clean.

Well butter some ring moulds, and dust them over with fine flour. Half fill the moulds with the mixture, stand them on a baking sheet, lay a cloth over, and place them in a warm place to rise. When the mixture has risen well in the moulds and looks very light, put into a rather quick oven and bake until a pale golden brown. When cooked, turn the rings out and stand them on a pastry rack over a dish. Pour boiling syrup over them once or twice. Ornament the tops with a few pieces of candied fruits, and serve either hot or cold.

THE SYRUP

6 oz. White Sugar. | $\frac{1}{2}$ gill Rum, or Flavouring.
$\frac{3}{4}$ pint Water.

Put the sugar and water into a saucepan, and boil until reduced to half the quantity. Now add the rum or any flavouring that may be preferred, and pour over the rings as described.

NOTE.—The baba mixture may be baked in one large mould, and a few crystallised fruits, almonds or raisins chopped up and worked into it.

Stewed Dried Fruit for Dessert

UTENSILS—Basin, stewpan, kitchen spoon.

Place fruit in cold water for 12 hours, drain and turn into a pan with fresh water. Stew or simmer over a slow fire for 20 minutes, adding sugar to taste in the last 5 minutes only. Serve when cold.

ICES

Allow 1 *quart of ice cream for* 8 *persons*.

Ices may be roughly divided into three classes, *i.e.*, dessert ices, in which cream is the chief ingredient ; the common ice cream, in which milk and eggs are the chief ingredients ; and, lastly, water ices, consisting chiefly of syrup and fruit juice. The Neapolitan is not a distinct kind of ice. It is made up by placing layers of different ices in a mould, and then freezing the whole firmly enough to be cut into blocks.

Whether good or cheap, ices can be served in a variety of forms, by means of different fancy moulds and accompaniments. A variety of attractive ice dishes can now be made very easily by buying ready-made ice cream blocks and serving them with sauces, fruits, or chopped nuts.

The contents of a large mould, when turned out, are generally designated an ice pudding, and portions are served from this. Dessert ices are made in smaller moulds. All mould ices have to be frozen firm enough to keep their shape when turned out. The method of moulding ices is described a little further on.

UTENSILS FOR FREEZING

Ice cream freezer.   Large and individual ice moulds.
Ice pack. Ice scoop.   Sundae glasses.
Spatula or palette knife. Ice cream plates.

TO FREEZE ICE CREAM

When making ice cream, remember that the ice to go in the tub around the freezer should be broken into pieces about one inch in size, not much larger, and to this is added about one-fifth to one-fourth part of freezing-salt (or a little more in hot weather). The ice can be easily broken if placed in a coarse cloth or sack, and beaten with a mallet. The ice and salt are well shaken down, and the tub filled up to well above the level of the mixture inside ; the ice should not, however, reach quite up to the lid.

The object of mixing salt with the ice is to make the temperature still lower. Salt has a melting effect on ice, and this is accompanied by a rapid and considerable lowering of the temperature. If it were not for this, it would be a difficult matter to freeze the contents of the pot, some ingredients not freezing at ordinary ice temperature. The use of suitable salt puts this right.

Having put the cold mixture in the freezer, and this being packed round with ice and salt in the tub, the handle of the pot must then be turned to keep the contents agitated until it begins to congeal. After the first 10 minutes' turning, take the lid off the pot, and, with a spatula, scrape to the centre any cream that is frozen on the sides ; then turn the freezer again for a few minutes, and mix again. The turning and agitation are to prevent some of the mixture, the sugar for instance, sinking to the bottom ; also to ensure all parts being frozen equally, and so prevent lumps. It is important that the stirring be properly done until the whole begins to congeal. When all is frozen, ice can be heaped on top of the pot, and allowed to remain so until its contents are wanted.

FREEZING POWDERS

Ice, in combination with salt, is the best material for making ices ; but when travelling, or in remote districts where ice is difficult to procure, freezing powders are of the greatest service, and those of the best makers are perfectly satisfactory in their action. Indeed, there is no doubt that freezing powders would be more largely used than they are at present, were it not that they are more expensive than ice. For cooling water and other liquids, and for refrigerating food in the sick chamber, where it is sometimes impossible either to keep or manage ice for this purpose, freezing powders are invaluable. They are useful, also, when a very rapid and strong freezing mixture is required, being used instead of salt with the ice. In choosing a freezing machine, it is desirable to ascertain if it is as well adapted for the use of powders as of ice, as some of the metal-lined machines are corroded by the action of the powders.

Some little care is required in determining the amount of sugar or syrup that should be used to sweeten the mixtures. There should be sufficient, of course, but an excess of sugar greatly retards the freezing process, or may even prevent it. The correct amount can be judged with practice, but it is better to use a Saccharometer. This instrument is quite inexpensive, and admits of precise results being obtained. If the instrument sinks too low in the mixture, the sweetening —sugar or syrup—may be increased, but if it does not sink to the mark, then the sweetening is already too great. To decrease the sweetening and make the instrument sink, milk must be added to a cream ice, or water to a water ice.

TO MOULD ICES

Dessert ices are not only served in glasses now. They may be served in small fluted porcelain cups or servers, or in stamped paper holders ; but it is more the rule to mould them, if time and circumstances will allow. The patterns and shapes of moulds are almost numberless, but they may be simply divided into two kinds, *viz.*, those that are hinged, and those that are not. The design of the moulds is a matter of choice.

Ices that are moulded, whether in one large mould, or in the small dessert moulds just referred to, have to be put in before they are frozen firm. Press the semi-frozen mixture into the design of the mould, so that it is filled. The mixture will not run into the design. When this is done, see that the remaining space is quite full, then close the mould firmly.

If the mould is of the kind that takes into several pieces, it can be easily arranged to have the moulded ices in two or more colours ; different colours in the cover, body and base, for instance. If the mould is of pudding-size, and does not open or take apart, then one or two thin pieces of cardboard can be stood down inside the mould to make divisions, and the spaces filled with different ices. The cards are then withdrawn before the ice is frozen firm. When the mould is ready, place it in a refrigerator to freeze firm. If you have no refrigerator, then bury it in ice and salt ; but in this case, the joints of the mould must be made water-tight with melted mutton fat. Some consider it sufficient to wrap the mould in oiled paper. In any case, it will not do for the salt to get inside the mould. To turn the ice out, dip the mould in luke-warm water for a moment, wipe off the drops, and turn out at once. If preferred, a cloth wrung out in warm water and wrapped round the mould for a moment will serve the purpose.

TO KEEP ICE

A refrigerator is the best thing to keep ice in, but, failing this, much can be done with paper and woollen cloths. Wrap the ice in paper first (newspaper will do), then cover as thickly as possible with woollen or other cloths (a woollen blanket is best), and keep it out of draughts. Each time the packet is opened renew the paper. If ice is kept in a vessel of any kind it is best not to let it lie in its water. It melts more quickly when it does. It can be stood on a stand of some kind, or on crossed sticks—anything to keep it from resting in water.

Ice Cream made with Custard

4 Eggs.	1 oz. Butter.	$\frac{1}{2}$ lb. Loaf Sugar.	
1 quart Milk.		Flavouring.	Colouring.

UTENSILS—Two basins, egg-beater, saucepan, wooden spoon, fine hair sieve or muslin, freezing utensils.

The basis of this is a custard. Beat up the eggs, and add these to the milk, with the sugar and butter. Put the mixture into a saucepan and place it over the fire. Keep it well stirred until it thickens, but on no account let it boil or it will be spoiled. When cooked, strain through a fine hair sieve or through muslin, and put aside to get quite cold.

When about to freeze this mixture, it may be coloured and flavoured according to the nature of the ice required. Only vegetable colourings should be used. These are obtainable at all good provision merchants and stores. For VANILLA, the essence can be used with a small quantity of saffron colouring to give it a rich appearance. For RASPBERRY, the essence can be used, and a little carmine for colouring. STRAWBERRY essence can also be used, with carmine for colouring, but the latter should be used more sparingly to give it a lighter tint than for raspberry.

Once the mixture is quite cold, and flavoured and coloured, put it into the pot and freeze, as described on page 366.

Ice Cream made with Gelatine

2 Eggs.	1 quart Milk.	$\frac{1}{4}$ oz. Gelatine.	
$\frac{1}{2}$ lb. Loaf Sugar.		Colouring.	Flavouring.

UTENSILS—Basin, egg-beater, wooden spoon, saucepan, hair sieve, freezing utensils.

This is a little smoother in the eating and has a rather better substance than the preceding. Whisk the eggs, stir them into the milk, and add the loaf sugar. Put the mixture into a saucepan, and place it on the stove or gas ring. Stir well until it thickens, but on no account let it boil or it will be spoiled.

Remove from the fire, and add the gelatine. then stir until
the gelatine is dissolved. Strain through a fine hair sieve,
and allow it to get quite cold. When quite cold, add flavouring
and colouring ; then freeze, as described on page 366.

CREAM CUSTARD DESSERT ICES

The basis of these is a CREAM CUSTARD. Whisk four large
or five small eggs, mix these into one quart of fresh cream,
and add half a pound of castor sugar. Put these into a saucepan, and place it over a moderate heat. Stir well until it
thickens, but on no account let it boil or it will curdle and
spoil. Strain through a fine hair sieve, and allow it to get
quite cold, then add the fruit pulp or flavouring and colouring (as follows), and freeze.

UTENSILS FOR CREAM CUSTARD ICES

Basins.	Saucepan.
Egg-beater.	Fine hair sieve.
Wooden spoon.	Wire sieve.
Lemon squeezer.	Freezing utensils.

Measuring Utensils.

Raspberry Ice Cream

1 quart Cream Custard (as described above).	**1 pint fresh Raspberry Pulp.** Carmine. Lemon Juice.

Make cream custard, as described on this page. Rub
sufficient fresh raspberries through a sieve to make a pint of
pulp, add the pulp to the custard, and colour with carmine.
A little lemon juice may be added, if liked. Freeze as
described.

Strawberry Ice Cream

This is made in exactly the same way as raspberry, just
described. A bright coloured strawberry is best ; but even
then some colouring must be used. Lemon juice may be
added, if liked.

Pineapple Ice Cream

1 quart Cream Custard (as described on this page).	**1 small Pineapple. 2 Lemons.** Saffron Colouring.

Make cream custard, as described on page 370. Peel and bruise a small pineapple, and rub it through a wire sieve, or the pineapple may be cut up and boiled for 10 minutes in a gill of water, and then rubbed through the sieve. Squeeze the juice from the lemons, add the fruit pulp and lemon juice to the custard, and mix well. Colour with a little saffron colouring and freeze as described.

Vanilla Ice Cream

1 quart Cream Custard (as described on page 370).	Vanilla Extract, or 2 Vanilla Pods. Saffron Colouring.

If vanilla pods are used, they must be put into the saucepan when the custard is made. If extract is used, this is added to the unflavoured custard just before freezing. A desirably pure extract can be made at home, by cutting up a few vanilla pods, and putting them into a small bottle, with a tablespoonful of brandy to each pod. This is ready for use in a week or longer, if the bottle is shaken occasionally. Do not use too much extract. Let the flavouring be delicate. Vanilla ices require a good custard, and it is better to increase the eggs given in the recipe on page 370 from four to six.

NOTE.—Water ices cannot be satisfactorily flavoured with vanilla.

Ginger Ice Cream

1 quart Cream Custard (as described on page 370).	4 oz. Preserved Ginger. Flavouring of Ground Ginger.

Make cream custard, as described on page 370. Mix in with the custard, during the making, the ginger cut up finely, and add a little ground ginger to flavour the whole well. Allow it to get quite cold, then freeze as directed. The ground ginger should be very good and fresh, or it may impart a mouldy flavour.

Noyeau Ice Cream

1 quart Cream Custard (as described on page 370).	1 wine glass Noyeau. 1 wine glass Sherry.

Make cream custard, as described on page 370. When quite cold, mix in the noyeau and sherry, then freeze as directed.

Chocolate Ice Cream

| 1 quart Cream Custard | 4 oz. Cocoa, or best Chocolate |
| (as described on page 370). | Paste. |

Vanilla Flavouring, if liked.

Make cream custard, as described on page 370. Stir into
it the cocoa, or an equal weight of good chocolate paste. These
ingredients should be made of proper consistency with milk
before being added. Flavour with vanilla, if liked, and freeze
as described on page 366.

Almond Ice Cream

| 1 quart Cream Custard | ¾ lbs. Almonds. |
| (as described on page 370). | |

Make cream custard, as described on page 370. Blanch
the almonds, then grate them finely, and add to the custard
just as it is finished making. When the custard is cooked,
allow it to stand a time, then strain through a fine sieve,
and allow to get quite cold. When quite cold, freeze as described on page 366.

WALNUT, COCOANUT, BRAZIL-NUT and PISTACHIO-NUT ICE
CREAMS may be made in the same manner as the almond.

Coffee Ice Cream (1)

| 1 quart Cream Custard | ½ pint Strong Coffee. |
| (as described on page 370). | 3 oz. Castor Sugar. |

Make one quart of cream custard, as described on page
370. Add to this a strong infusion of Mocha coffee, sweetened
with castor sugar. When quite cold, freeze as described.

Coffee Ice Cream (2)

1 quart Cream Custard (as described	½ lb. freshly roasted Mocha Coffee
on page 370, but made with 6	Berries.
Eggs.)	

Make cream custard, as described on page 370. When
made, and just removed from the fire, put the coffee berries
in it. The berries must be freshly roasted, and, if possible,
hot, to ensure obtaining the delicate flavour and aroma.

Cover the pan closely, and put a cloth over to keep in the
steam ; let it infuse for 1 hour, then strain. When quite
cold, freeze as described. The colour of the custard is not
altered by this method. If carefully made, it is very delicate.

Tutti Frutti Ice Cream

1 quart Vanilla Ice Cream.
2 candied Pears.
2 candied Prunes.
6 candied Cherries.
2 candied Figs.
4 Marrons Glacés.
1 tablespoonful Rum.
1 tablespoonful Maraschino.
1 tablespoonful Kirsch.
1 oz. Angelica.

Enough for 8 persons.

Chop up the fruit very finely, place it in a basin, and season it with the kirsch, maraschino, and rum. Mix, and let it stand for 10 minutes. Add the mixture to the vanilla ice cream, and stir.

Fill a quart brick ice cream mould with the cream. Cover both sides lightly with buttered paper. Cover mould, and bury it in broken rock salt and ice for 3 to 4 hours. Remove the mould and dip it in luke-warm water for a second or two. Remove the cover and paper, and unmould on to a silver dish.

Jack Frost Sundae

3 sliced Bananas.
½ cupful Maraschino Cherries.
½ tin shredded Pineapple.
1 tablespoonful chopped Dates.
1 tablespoonful Lemon Juice.
2 tablespoonfuls Maraschino Syrup.
Vanilla Ice Cream.
Whipped Cream.

Enough for 12 persons.

Mix the fruit with the lemon juice and syrup, and put a teaspoonful in the bottom of each sundae glass. Cover with a scoop of vanilla ice cream, then with a tablespoonful of whipped cream flavoured with maraschino. Garnish each with a maraschino cherry and blanched chopped pistachio nuts.

Coupe Margot

1 Pear.   ½ Orange.
1 slice of Pineapple.
1 Peach.   ½ Banana.
Vanilla Ice Cream.
6 Maraschino Cherries.
2 tablespoonfuls Lemon Juice.
1 teaspoonful Sugar.
2 teaspoonfuls Maraschino.
Whipped Cream.

Enough for 6 persons.

Dice the pear, pineapple, banana, cherries, peach and orange, place them in a mixing bowl with the lemon juice, maraschino, and sugar, and stand for 5 minutes. Use this mixture to cover the bottoms of six punch glasses. Fill with vanilla ice cream, and garnish with whipped cream and maraschino cherries.

Caramel Ice Cream

½ pint Milk.   1 pint Cream. | ¼ cupful Brown Sugar.
¼ cupful Flour.   1 Egg. | ½ cupful Castor Sugar.

UTENSILS—Double boiler, saucepan, basin, wooden spoon, teaspoon, cup, egg-beater. *Enough for 6 persons*.

Bring the milk to the boil in a double boiler. Stir the castor sugar and flour into the beaten eggs. Remove the double boiler from the fire, then stir the egg mixture into the milk and return the pan to the fire and cook for 20 minutes, stirring frequently. Make a caramel with the brown sugar and a teaspoonful of water. Add this to the other mixture and allow to cool, then add the cream and freeze.

Mousse au Chocolate

¼ lb. Grated Chocolate. | ¼ lb. Castor Sugar.
½ pint Thick Cream. | 1 teaspoonful Vanilla Essence.
½ pint Water.

UTENSILS—Double boiler, wooden spoon, teaspoon, grater, basin, wire whisk, freezing utensils. *Enough for 4 persons*.

Put the chocolate, vanilla, sugar and water into the top of a double boiler. Stir over boiling water in the lower part until the mixture is well blended. Remove and allow to cool. Add the cream, stiffly frothed, a little at a time, stirring slowly while doing so. Drop the mixture into a mould lined with a sheet of white paper, cover tightly, and bury in broken ice and rock salt. Freeze for 1½ hours, then serve unmoulded with vanilla wafers.

Ice Pudding

1 pint Milk. | ½ lb. Crystallised Fruit.
8 Yolks of Eggs. | Rind of ½ Lemon.
½ pint whipped Cream. | 1 wineglassful Kirsch or Noyeau
4 oz. Castor Sugar. | Syrup.

UTENSILS—Saucepan, knife, 2 basins, egg-beater, strainer, fine hair sieve, wooden spoon, wineglass, wire whisk, freezing utensils. *Enough for 8 persons*.

Put the milk into a saucepan with the castor sugar and the thinly peeled rind of half a lemon, bring it to the boil, and simmer for 5 minutes. Strain it on to the beaten yolks of eight raw eggs, then return the mixture to the stove, and stir until it thickens, but on no account let it boil. Rub it through a fine hair sieve and put aside until quite cold. Freeze as directed, but when of the consistency of batter,

dd the whipped cream, also half a pound of any nice
rystallised fruits cut up small, and the kirsch or noyeau
yrup. Mix well, and continue freezing. Fill a fancy mould
vith the frozen mixture, and put it in a refrigerator or pile
t round with ice until wanted.

Biscuits Tortoni

6 fresh Eggs.	3 oz. crushed Macaroons.
2 oz. Sugar.	½ pint whipped Cream.
2 tablespoonfuls Maraschino.	1 teaspoonful Vanilla Essence.

UTENSILS—Two basins, wire whisk, saucepan or double
boiler, board, rolling pin, measuring spoons, large spoon, 6
round paper cases. *Enough for 6 persons.*

Separate the whites from the yolks of eggs and put the
yolks into a basin. Whisk them for 10 minutes over a pan
of hot water, or in a double boiler over hot water. Remove
them from the hot water and whisk for another 5 minutes,
then set on ice, and stir till cold. Add the maraschino, 1 oz.
crushed macaroons, and cream flavoured with vanilla. Mix
lightly, and divide the mixture between six round paper
cases and sprinkle with the remainder of the crushed
macaroons. Freeze as described on page 366.

UNCOOKED DESSERT ICES
(MADE WITH CREAM AND WITHOUT EGGS)

These are made without eggs, and require no cooking.
Two simple recipes are first given, from which it will be seen
that the ices described in the previous pages can all be made
in this manner, it being merely necessary to substitute
sweetened cream for the custard.

Chocolate Ice Cream

1 quart Cream.	¾ lb. Castor Sugar.
1 pint Milk.	8 oz. Chocolate.

UTENSILS—Grater, basin, wooden spoon, strainer, freezing
utensils.

Scrape and reduce the chocolate to powder, and mix it
into the milk thoroughly. Add the cream and sugar, then
strain, and freeze as directed on page 366.

Raspberry Ice Cream

1 quart Cream.	1½ lb. Raspberry Pulp or Rasp-
1 pint Milk.	berry Jam.
¾ lb. Castor Sugar.	Carmine.

UTENSILS—Basin, wooden spoon, strainer, freezin,
utensils.

Sweeten the pulp with the sugar, and add this to the mil
and cream. If jam is used, the sugar can be omitted. Th
jam requires to be beaten up in the milk and cream. Add th
colouring, then strain. Lemon juice may be added if liked
Freeze as directed.

Trilby Bombe

1 large tin Apricots.	1 cupful Cream.
1½ pints Water.	1 White of Egg.
1 oz. Pistachio Nuts.	2¼ cupfuls Castor Sugar.
1 teaspoonful Vanilla Essence.	1 oz. Almonds.
½ teaspoonful Almond Essence.	Juice of 1 Lemon.

UTENSILS—Fine sieve, 2 basins, wooden spoon, lemon
squeezer, wire whisk, knife, teaspoon, cup, freezing utensils.
Enough for about 8 *persons.*

Press the apricots through a fine sieve, add the apricot
syrup and water, 2 cupfuls of the sugar, the lemon juice,
and stir until dissolved. Freeze, then beat the cream until
stiff and beat the egg white until dry. Beat the remainder
of the sugar into the white of egg, and add the essences,
blanched and chopped almonds and pistachio nuts, then
fold and beat in the cream.

Line a 1½ pint melon mould with the apricot mixture.
Cover with some of the apricots, filling the mould to over-
flowing. Spread paper over the ice, and press the cover in
place beyond the mould, then pack it in equal quantities of
salt and ice. Stand for 2 or 3 hours, and serve with vanilla
wafers.

Jam or Fruit Syrup Ices

If fresh fruit is not obtainable, cream ices can be made
with jams or fruit syrups. The flavour is inferior to fresh
fruit, yet most people consider it preferable to using essences
or some of the doubtful flavouring preparations. A single
example is given here to show the method employed.

As a rule ices are most needed when fresh fruit is easily
obtainable, but as the ice is such a welcome refreshment at

winter dances and festivities, recourse must then be had to preserves or extracts.

Among the recipes for Syrups on pages 460 to 468 will be found many suitable for flavouring ices; and as they are easily prepared, keep well and give no trouble when the time comes for using them, they can be strongly recommended for the purpose. The syrup must not be too heavy with sugar.

Raspberry Ice Cream

1 pint Cream.	1 lb. Raspberry Jam.
½ pint Milk.	1 Lemon. Carmine.

UTENSILS—Lemon squeezer, 2 basins, strainer or sieve, kitchen spoon, freezing utensils. *Enough for 8 persons.*

Squeeze the juice from the lemon and add it to the jam, then add the cream and milk, and beat up in a basin. Press through a sieve, or strain, add carmine colouring to give the required pink shade, and freeze as directed.

If preferred, the jam can be dissolved in a little boiling water, then strained before adding the other ingredients. No sugar is needed.

Neapolitan Ices

The Neapolitan ice consists of three or four different ordinary ices placed in layers, then frozen hard enough to permit of the mass being cut into blocks and served on a plate or paper. For this purpose a pewter mould is needed, and those constructed for the purpose have every convenience for arranging the layers of ice.

Supposing it is decided to have a Neapolitan of four colours, the four different ices are first prepared in separate freezers. These may be raspberry, lemon, chocolate and plain cream; and this might be the order in which they are put in the mould. A suitable ice-spoon is supplied with the mould, this being requisite for the levelling of the layers. The mould is filled up and the cover pressed down to make the ice solid and firm.

If you have an ice refrigerator this will suffice to complete the freezing so that the block when turned out is firm. If no refrigerator is available, the mould is surrounded and covered with ice and salt; but before doing this, the joints in the mould must be made water-tight. Melted mutton fat is generally used for this, but some consider that an oiled paper wrapped round the mould is sufficient. Whatever is done, the object to be attained is the exclusion of salt water from the ice in the mould. If it enters, it will spoil the ice.

To remove the ice, dip the mould for a moment in luke-warm water, wipe off the drops, then turn out the contents. Turn the block on to a board, cut it into oblong pieces, and serve. The cut pieces must be put into a refrigerator or freezer if they cannot be served at once.

WATER ICES

The basis of these is a syrup, which is made as follows. It can be kept a considerable time if bottled.

SYRUP FOR WATER ICES

3 lb. Loaf Sugar. | 1 quart Water.
½ the White of an Egg.

UTENSILS—Saucepan, basin, egg-beater, metal spoon, strainer. *Enough for 8 to 10 persons.*

Melt the sugar in the water, place it over a gentle heat and bring to the boil. Add the white of egg, well beaten, boil for 10 minutes, then skim and strain. When cool, it is ready for use, or can be bottled. If a saccharometer is handy, the syrup can be tested. It should register 30 to 36 on the scale.

Lemon Water Ice

1 pint of Syrup (as described above). | 5 Lemons.

Squeeze the juice from the lemons, and strain it. Stir this into the syrup, and freeze as directed. This ice can be greatly improved if the sugar with which the syrup is made can be rubbed on to the rinds of two or three of the lemons.

ORANGE WATER ICE can be made in the same manner as Lemon Ice, just described.

Raspberry Water Ice

1 pint Syrup (as described on this page). | ½ pint Water.
5 oz. Raspberry Pulp.

Rub sufficient raspberries through a fine sieve to make five ounces of pulp. Mix this in with the syrup and water, then freeze as directed on page 366.

STRAWBERRY WATER ICE is made in the same manner as Raspberry Ice, just described.

Melon Water Ice

1 pint Syrup (as described on page 378).
½ pint Water.

½ lb. ripe Melon.
Juice of 2 Lemons.
1 glass Noyeau.

Take the melon, with the pips, and bruise it in a mortar. Add the lemon juice, syrup and water, and noyeau. Mix well together, then strain, and freeze as described. If liked, this ice can have a little colouring added before freezing.

Pineapple Water Ice

1 pint Syrup (as described on page 378).
Juice of half a Lemon.

½ pint Water.
½ a small Pineapple.

Put the pineapple in a mortar and well bruise it. Add the lemon juice, syrup, and water, and mix well together, then strain. Freeze as directed.

Cherry Water Ice

1 pint Syrup (as described on page 378).
½ pint Water.

1 lb. Black Cherries.
Juice of a Lemon.
1 wine glass Noyeau.

Bruise the cherries in a mortar, with their stones. The flavour of the stones (kernels) should come out well in this ice, or if preferred, a few drops of extract of bitter almonds may be used. Add the lemon juice, noyeau, syrup and water, mix well together, then rub through a sieve or strain. Freeze as described. This ice can be coloured just before freezing, if necessary.

Green Gooseberry Sorbet

1 quart Green Gooseberries.
¾ lb. Loaf Sugar.
4 Lemons.

2 wineglassfuls Brandy.
Green Colouring.
1½ pints Water.

Top and tail the gooseberries, put them on to boil with the sugar and water and cook them until quite soft. Now add the strained juice of the lemons, and sufficient green colouring to make it a pretty colour. Rub all through a fine hair sieve.

Prepare the freezing machine, then pour in the mixture and partly freeze. When partly frozen, add two glasses of brandy (or maraschino if preferred). Now freeze well until it is in a dry state. Have ready some glass sorbet cups or small tumblers, which should have been standing in a very cool place to get thoroughly cold. Divide the sorbet into the glasses, stand them on lace papers on two glass or silver dishes, and serve at once.

SAUCES FOR ICE CREAMS

Chocolate Sauce

3 oz. Unsweetened Chocolate.	1 cupful Evaporated Milk.
1 cupful Icing Sugar.	½ cupful Water.
1 teaspoonful Vanilla Essence.	

UTENSILS—Knife, double boiler, wooden spoon, teaspoon, cup.

Cut the chocolate into small pieces. Melt it in a double boiler over boiling water. Stir in the sugar, milk, and water. Keep on stirring till smoothly blended—the sugar must be quite dissolved. Cook slowly without stirring till a little tested in cold water forms a soft ball. Flavour with vanilla, and keep the sauce warm over boiling water until required. This sauce can be served poured over any vanilla-flavoured ice cream.

Chocolate Velvet Sauce

1 oz. Chocolate.	1 tablespoonful Butter.
¾ cupful Castor Sugar.	½ cupful Marshmallows.
⅓ cupful boiling Water.	

UTENSILS—Saucepan, knife, wooden spoon, tablespoon, cup.

Melt the chocolate in a saucepan with the water. Add the butter, stirring constantly till you get a smooth paste. Stir in the sugar, and cook till slightly thick. Add the chopped marshmallows, stirring till melted and smoothly blended, then use hot.

Mocha Sauce

1½ cupfuls Milk.	½ cupful ground Coffee.
⅓ cupful Castor Sugar.	¾ tablespoonful Arrowroot.

UTENSILS—Saucepan, basin, wooden spoon, tablespoon, cup, strainer.

Scald the milk with the coffee, then stand for 20 minutes. Mix the sugar, arrowroot, and a few grains of salt together, then stir in the strained coffee. Pour the mixture into a saucepan. Cook, stirring constantly, for 5 minutes, and serve in a hot sauce-boat with vanilla ice cream.

Orange Sauce

1 cupful Orange Juice.
1 teaspoonful grated Orange Rind.

1 cupful Castor Sugar.
Juice of 1 Lemon and grated Rind of ½ Lemon.

UTENSILS—Saucepan, lemon squeezer, teaspoon, metal spoon, cup, grater.

Cook all ingredients together for 15 minutes. Skim, cool, and serve with vanilla ice cream.

Peach Sauce

1 cupful Peach Syrup.
⅓ cupful Tinned Peaches.

2 teaspoonfuls cold Water.
1 teaspoonful Arrowroot.

UTENSILS—Double boiler, basin, wooden spoon, teaspoon, cup, knife.

Heat the peach syrup in the top of a double boiler. Thicken with the arrowroot, blended with the cold water, add the chopped peaches, and boil for 5 minutes, stirring all the time. Then cool, and pour 2 tablespoonfuls of sauce over each portion of vanilla ice cream, placed in a sundae glass.

Walnut Sauce

1½ cupfuls Castor Sugar.
1 cupful chopped Walnuts.

1 teaspoonful Vanilla Essence.
½ cupful Water.

UTENSILS—Double boiler, wooden spoon, teaspoon, cup, knife.

Boil the sugar and water to a thick syrup in the top of a double boiler. Add the walnuts, a pinch of salt, and vanilla. Serve poured over vanilla ice cream.

SAVOURIES, CHEESE and EGG DISHES

When preparing savouries, remember to make them as dainty as possible. All that is usually wanted at the end of a dinner is a small and piquant tit-bit to remove the sweetness from the mouth. Most cheese dishes, such as cheese straws, cheese tartlets, macaroni au gratin, cheese soufflé, and fondue, can be served as a savoury, as well as cauliflower au gratin.

Finnan haddock and kidney and mushroom toasts, herring roes, and bacon toasts, mushrooms on toast, sardines on toast, and chicken livers cut in four rolled in bacon and fried, besides angels on horseback, are also suitable. All hot savouries must be served *very* hot.

Golden Cheese Marbles

1¼ cupfuls grated Cheddar or Edam Cheese.
2 tablespoonfuls Flour.

½ teaspoonful Celery Salt.
2 Whites of Eggs.
Paprika.

UTENSILS—Basin, egg-beater, wooden spoon, pastry board, frying pan, measuring spoons, cup, grater. *Enough for 3 or 4 persons.*

Beat the whites of eggs till light but not stiff, add the flour, cheese, paprika and celery salt, then roll the mixture into balls the size of marbles and fry till golden brown in deep fat at 375° F. Serve on a hot dish lined with a lace paper d'oyley.

Cheese Straws

¼ lb. Puff Paste.
2 oz. Grated Cheese.
A dust of Cayenne.

UTENSILS—Basin, pastry board, rolling pin, grater, knife, baking sheet, wire pastry rack. *Enough for 3 or 4 persons.*

Roll out the puff paste on a slightly floured board or slab. Sprinkle the cheese over it, and a dust of cayenne, and roll these in as if they were flour. When quite rolled in, cut the paste into thin strips, a quarter of an inch wide and five inches long. Lay these side by side on a wet baking sheet.

Cut three or four strips, about seven inches long, and tie

hese into loose knots, so as to form rings for the straws to
tand in. Put these on the baking sheet also. Bake in a
moderate oven until cooked, keeping them a very pale golden
colour. When cooked, lay them on a wire pastry rack, and as
soon as they are cold put the straws into the paste rings, to
orm bundles. Arrange the bundles on a dish, with fancy
ace paper underneath, and serve. They may be kept in a
in, if desired, and either warmed when wanted or served
cold.

NOTE.—Cheese straws can also be made by mixing
ogether equal weights of butter, flour, breadcrumbs and
grated cheese, with a little salt and cayenne. These ingredients
are made into a paste, then cut into strips and baked, as
described above. Straws made in this manner will not keep
so well.

Cheese Fondue

| 3 Eggs. 1½ oz. Butter. | 1 oz. Grated Cheese. |
| 1 tablespoonful Cream. | Fried Croûtons of Bread. |

Cayenne and Salt.

UTENSILS—Basin, egg-beater, saucepan, wooden spoon,
tablespoon, grater, frying pan, knife. *Enough for 3 or 4
persons.*

Break the eggs into a basin, season them with cayenne
and salt, then beat them until they run easily through the
fork of whisk. Put three-quarters of an ounce of butter
into a small saucepan, and, when melted, stir in the eggs.
Stand the saucepan over a moderate heat, and continue
whisking until the mixture begins to thicken. Then take a
wooden spoon and stir in the remaining three-quarters of an
ounce of butter, a small piece at a time, stirring continuously.
Now stir in the grated cheese and cream.

Keep the mixture constantly moving, until it is lightly
set, then turn it out quickly into a hot china or silver dish.
Have ready some dainty croûtons of bread, fried a pale
golden brown, in clarified butter, and garnish with these.
Serve quickly. If liked, crescents of puff pastry may be served
instead of the bread croûtons.

Bread and Cheese Fondue

| 1 Egg. ½ pint Milk. | Thin slices of Bread. |
| Thin slices of Cheese. | Seasoning. |

UTENSILS—Knife, pie-dish, basin, egg-beater. *Enough fo*
1 *or* 2 *persons.*

Butter each slice of bread and cover it with sliced cheese
sprinkling with salt, pepper and dry mustard. Lay th
slices, buttered side up, on top of one another in a pie-dish
Beat the egg and milk, pour over, and bake in a moderate
oven.

Cheese Custard

1 cupful **Breadcrumbs.**	1 **Egg.** ½ pint **Milk.**
1 cupful **Grated Cheese.**	**Pepper and Salt.**

UTENSILS—Basin, egg-beater, grater, cup, fireproof
dish. *Enough for* 2 *persons.*

Beat the egg and add the milk. Pour these over the cheese
and breadcrumbs and season to taste with pepper and salt.
Pour into a greased fireproof dish, and bake in a moderate
oven about ½ hour. Serve hot and eat at once.

Cheese Soufflé

3 oz. grated **Parmesan Cheese.**	4 **Eggs.** 1 gill **Milk.**
1 oz. **Butter.** 1 oz. **Flour.**	**Cayenne Pepper.**

UTENSILS—Saucepan, wooden spoon, basin, grater, egg-
beater, soufflé cases. *Enough for* 3 *persons.*

Melt the butter in a saucepan, stir in the flour, without
browning it, then gradually mix in the milk, and season with
a pinch of cayenne pepper. Stir constantly, until it boils,
then let it cook for 10 minutes. Take the mixture off the
fire, drop in the yolks of three eggs, one by one, beating the
mixture well between each yolk, then beat in the grated
cheese.

Whisk the whites of eggs to a stiff froth, with a pinch of
salt, and stir these lightly into the mixture at the last
moment. Have ready some small soufflé cases, with buttered
papers fastened round them standing an inch and a half
above the tops of the cases. Pour the mixture into these, and
bake for 10 to 15 minutes in a hot oven.

Take them out, quickly remove the papers, arrange the
soufflés on a hot dish, and serve immediately. If preferred
the whole can be baked in one large soufflé case, and will then
have to be 20 to 30 minutes in the oven.

Cheese Eggs

3 oz. stale Cheese. | **3** Eggs. **1 oz.** Butter.
Pepper and Salt.

UTENSILS—Fireproof dish, knife, cup, grater. *Enough for 2 persons.*

Put the butter into a fireproof dish, and let it melt, then cut some very thin slices from the cheese and place them at the bottom of the dish. Put this into the oven, and when the cheese has melted, break the eggs one by one into a cup and slip them into the dish.

Return the dish to the oven and let the whites just set, then cover with the remainder of the cheese, grated. Sprinkle with pepper and a little salt, put a few pieces of butter here and there over the top. Return to the oven to brown, and serve immediately. This makes a good luncheon dish.

Gnockie

1 pint Milk. **6 oz.** Semolina. | **1** Yolk of Egg. **1 oz.** Butter.
2 oz. grated Cheese. | Salt and Pepper.

UTENSILS—Saucepan, wooden spoon, grater, plate, knife. *Enough for 3 persons.*

Put the milk on to boil, stir in the semolina and cook slowly for 10 minutes. Add the cheese and butter, and salt and pepper to taste. Take off the fire and add the yolk of egg. Turn all on to a plate, and when cold cut into shapes. Sprinkle with a little grated cheese, then bake in the oven till brown and serve very hot.

Eggs à l'Adlon

6 hard-boiled Eggs. | **1 teaspoonful** Butter.
1 teaspoonful Tomato Ketchup. | Pepper and Salt, to taste.
6 Tomatoes. Lettuce. | Mayonnaise Sauce.

UTENSILS—Saucepan, knife, basin, fork, teaspoon. *Enough for 6 persons.*

Shell the eggs and cut them in halves crosswise, then remove the yolks and mash them till smooth with butter, tomato ketchup, and pepper and salt to taste. Stuff the empty half whites with this mixture, hollow out the centre of the tomatoes, season lightly with pepper and salt, and sink in each the stuffed half egg, masked with mayonnaise.

Serve for lunch or Sunday night supper prettily arranged in a crystal dish, on a bed of crisp chicory or lettuce leaves.

Eggs in Ramekins

3 Eggs.   Cream. | Chopped Gherkins, Truffle, and
Pepper and Salt. | Pickled Cherries.

UTENSILS—Three ramekins, knife, kitchen spoon, baking
tin, enamelled saucepan, wooden spoon, dessertspoon. *Enough
for 3 persons.*

Butter 3 small ramekins or as many as you want to use,
and break a fresh egg into each. Sprinkle the eggs with
chopped gherkins, truffle, pickled cherries, and pepper and
salt. Lay a spoonful of cream on top, and stand the casseroles
on a Yorkshire tin half filled with hot water. Poach in the
oven till set, then pour a little of the following sauce over
each and serve as a second course at dinner.

The SAUCE is just ½ pint of white sauce put in an enamelled
saucepan, 1 egg yolk stirred in and 1 dessertspoonful of lemon
juice. Stir well while adding, then break in ½ oz. of butter,
a bit at a time, and stir till very hot, but do not boil.

Eggs au Gratin

4 Eggs.   Breadcrumbs. | Chopped Onions.
4 tablespoonfuls Tomato Ketchup | Butter.

UTENSILS—Gratin dish, knife, frying pan, grater, tablespoon. *Enough for 2 persons.*

Sprinkle a shallow gratin dish with chopped onions,
which you have already sautéd in a frying pan till tender.
Break in the eggs very carefully, then pour over tomato
ketchup. Dot with pieces of butter, sprinkle breadcrumbs
lightly fried in butter, over the top, and bake in a moderate
oven until the eggs are set. Serve as a luncheon dish.

Varsovienne Eggs

½ pint tinned Sugar Corn. | 2 saltspoonfuls Salt.
1½ gills Cream. | ½ saltspoonful grated Nutmeg.
½ saltspoonful Cayenne. | 1 tablespoonful grated Parmesan
6 Eggs.   ½ oz. Butter. | Cheese.

UTENSILS—Enamelled saucepan, grater, wooden spoon,
6 cocotte dishes, measuring spoons. *Enough for 6 persons.*

Place the corn in an enamelled saucepan with the butter,
cream, salt, cayenne and grated nutmeg. Lightly mix with
a wooden spoon, then simmer for 10 minutes, stirring all
the time. Divide the mixture evenly between six fireproof

cocotte dishes, well buttered, then carefully crack the eggs into each. Season equally with ½ teaspoonful salt and 2 saltspoonfuls white pepper, evenly sprinkle the cheese over them, then bake in an oven for 5 minutes. Serve as a luncheon dish.

Surprise Eggs

3 Eggs.   Parsley. | 6 small rounds of Bread.
Sausage Cakes, half cooked.

UTENSILS—Saucepan, basin, knife, round cutter, frying pan, plate. *Enough for 3 persons.*

Boil the eggs for 15 minutes, then place them in a bowl of cold water, and when cold remove the shells. Fry six rounds of bread to a golden brown in hot fat. Dip the eggs in a little flour and wrap each one in a partly cooked sausage cake. Work this round the egg until it is entirely enveloped in the sausage meat. Roll lightly in flour, drop into boiling fat, fry until golden, and drain on paper.

Lastly, cut the eggs in halves, and stand them on the rounds of fried bread and arrange on a silver entrée dish, garnished with plenty of parsley.

Serve either hot or cold with or without salad.

Spanish Eggs

3 Eggs.   1½ tablespoonfuls Milk.
1 chopped Pimento.   Pepper and Salt.
1 dessertspoonful Butter.   1 tablespoonful Cream.

UTENSILS—Basin, egg-beater, double boiler, knife, wooden spoon, measuring spoons, toaster. *Enough for 2 persons.*

Beat the eggs lightly with an egg-beater, then turn them into a double boiler along with the milk, chopped pimento, pepper and salt to taste, and butter. Cook slowly, stirring all the time till the mixture begins to thicken. Then quickly stir in the cream, allow it to thicken, and serve at once on squares of hot buttered toast.

This can be used as a supper or breakfast dish

Devonshire Eggs

4 hard-boiled Eggs.   Cooked Sausages, **or Sausage-**
1½ cupfuls hot White Sauce.   meat Cakes.
2 tablespoonfuls Buttered Crumbs.

UTENSILS—2 saucepans, knife, baking dish, grater, frying pan, tablespoon, cup. *Enough for 4 persons.*

Slice the eggs thickly. Add them to the white sauce. Turn into an oiled baking dish, and sprinkle buttered crumbs over the top. Bake in a moderately hot oven for 15 minutes, then garnish with sausages or sausage meat cakes.

Egg and Ham Pie

4 hard-boiled Eggs.	1½ cupfuls finely-diced Ham.
¼ cupful fine dried Breadcrumbs.	1 pint White Sauce.
1 tablespoonful Butter.	

UTENSILS—Saucepan, baking dish, basin, wooden spoon, tablespoon, cup, pint measure, grater, knife. *Enough for 4 or 5 persons.*

Butter a baking dish. Add the white sauce to the meat, put a layer in the bottom of a baking dish, and then a layer of sliced eggs. Continue in this way until the savoury mixture and the eggs have been used. Finish with the crumbs dabbed with butter, and brown in a moderate oven for about 10 minutes. Serve as a luncheon dish.

Lyonnaise Eggs

6 Eggs. 1½ cupfuls Milk.	¼ cupful Breadcrumbs.
1 chopped Onion.	2 tablespoonfuls Butter.
1 tablespoonful Flour.	Salt and Pepper, to taste.

UTENSILS—Stewpan, wooden spoon, tablespoon, cup, deep baking dish, grater. *Enough for 6 persons.*

Cook the onion in butter for 10 minutes. Add the flour, and cook until the mixture is smooth, stirring constantly. Gradually pour in the milk, and cook for 3 minutes, stirring constantly. Season with pepper and salt, and pour into a deep, hot baking dish.

Carefully break into it the six eggs. Cover the eggs with breadcrumbs, or if liked, cream cracker crumbs can be used. Bake in a moderate oven until the eggs are set—in about 10 minutes. Serve as a luncheon dish.

Buttercup Eggs

4 hard-boiled Eggs.	1 tablespoonful Flour.
½ teaspoonful Salt.	Parsley. Pepper.
1 tablespoonful Butter.	1 cupful Milk.
4 slices of Toast.	

UTENSILS—Saucepan, wooden spoon, measuring spoons, basin, knife, toaster, strainer. *Enough for 2 or 3 persons.*

Make a thin white sauce with butter, flour, milk and seasonings. Separate the yolks from the whites of eggs. Chop the whites finely and add them to the sauce. Cut the slices of toast in halves lengthways and pour sauce over them. Force the egg yolks through a strainer or a potato slicer, letting them fall on to the sauce, making a mound of yellow. Garnish with parsley and toast, cut into points.

Breton Eggs

8 fresh Eggs.	½ gill Cream.
2 slices of Bread.	2 saltspoonfuls White Pepper.
1 tablespoonful melted Butter.	3 skinned Pork Sausages.
½ teaspoonful Salt.	2 tablespoonfuls cooked Peas.

UTENSILS—Basin, fork, frying pan, knife, measuring spoons. *Enough for 8 persons.*

Beat the eggs, cream, salt and pepper in a bowl with a fork for several minutes. Heat melted butter in a frying pan. Add the sliced parboiled sausages—the slices should be ½ inch thick. Fry for 2 minutes, then add the bread, cut in ¼ inch squares, and the peas.

Cook gently for 5 minutes, occasionally tossing while cooking. Drop in the eggs, slightly beaten, stir till thickened, and serve in a hot dish, garnished with sippets of fried bread or toast.

Curry and Olive Eggs

3 hard-boiled Eggs.	Anchovy Paste.
Curry Powder. Olives.	Capers. Butter.
8 croûtons of Bread.	Salt. Cress.

UTENSILS—Basin, wooden spoon, knife. *Enough for 4 persons.*

Mix the yolks of eggs with enough butter to moisten them into a soft paste, and flavour with curry powder and salt, then make the mixture into eight flat pats. Stone eight olives, fill each with anchovy paste, and top with a caper. Set them upright in the butter mixture, and garnish with capers and cress.

Chinese Rice

¾ cupful Rice.	2 teaspoonfuls Salt.
3 tablespoonfuls Butter or Lard.	½ cupful diced, lean Ham.
1 Green Pepper.	2 tablespoonfuls Soy Sauce.

UTENSILS—Stewpan, pint or quart measure, silver fork, wire strainer, frying pan, kitchen spoon, measuring spoons. *Enough for 2 persons.*

Wash the rice until the water is clear, then put it into a pan with 2 quarts of cold water and the salt, and cook until the grains are soft enough to be mashed with a silver fork. Then pour the rice into a wire strainer and pour cold water over it, and drain.

Put the butter or lard in a frying pan and when smoking hot, add the ham and fry for 5 minutes. Add the rice, green pepper, seeded and minced very small, and fry for another 5 minutes, stirring occasionally. Lastly, add the soy sauce and mix all thoroughly. Serve piled up in a hot dish.

Creole Rice

1 cupful Rice.	2 cupfuls diced, cold Cooked Beef.
Rashers of Bacon.	1 tin Tomatoes.
6 large peeled and chopped Mush-rooms.	2 Onions, peeled and diced.
	6 Pimentoes.

1 Green Pepper.

UTENSILS—Stewpan, cup, knife, double boiler, frying pan. *Enough for 3 or 4 persons.*

Well wash the rice and parboil it in 6 cupfuls of cold water. Heat the contents of a small tin of tomatoes in a double boiler. While the rice is cooking, cut up thin rashers of bacon into dice, fry them slowly, and then add the onions, and allow them to cook until a delicate brown.

Turn the bacon and onions into a double boiler, then sauté the mushrooms in the bacon fat, and add them and the fat in which they were cooked to the tomato mixture. Next add the pimentoes, seeded green pepper, parboiled rice, and beef, and serve when piping hot in a hot dish.

Curried Rice and Tomatoes

1 lb. Rice. ½ Lemon.	1 tablespoonful Curry Powder.
½ pint Brown Gravy.	1 Onion. 1 tin Tomatoes.

UTENSILS—Saucepan, quart measure, basin, wooden spoon, tablespoon, knife, lemon squeezer. *Enough for about 8 persons.*

Wash the rice well in three waters, then parboil it in ½ gallon of cold water. Mix the curry powder with gravy, then boil it and the sliced onion for 30 minutes. Add the tomatoes and rice, and simmer all together at the side of the fire till well done. Just before serving, pour over the juice of ½ a lemon.

Macaroni à la Crème

¼ lb. Macaroni.	¼ lb. Mushrooms.
½ pint Cream. 1 pint Stock.	3 tablespoonfuls Butter.
1 slice of Onion.	2 teaspoonfuls Salt.
1 slice of Carrot.	2 large tablespoonfuls Flour.

UTENSILS—Two saucepans, pint measure, measuring spoons, knife, wooden spoon, basin, strainer, colander. *Enough for 2 or 3 persons.*

Break the macaroni into three-inch pieces and put it into a saucepan with 2 quarts of boiling water and salt, and boil for 30 minutes. Mix the flour with a small quantity of stock, then add the remainder of the stock. Pour this into a small saucepan, add quickly the carrot, onion, pepper and salt to taste, mushrooms and butter. Bring slowly to the boil, then move the pan to the side of the fire, and allow to simmer for 20 minutes.

Rub the mixture through a strainer, and add the cream. Drain the macaroni well, put it back in the sauce, cook for 5 minutes longer and serve very hot.

Macaroni à la Teddie

2 oz. boiled Macaroni.	1 oz. Butter. ½ pint Milk.
1 oz. Flour. Chopped Ham.	½ a chopped, fried Onion.
1 tablespoonful Tomato Sauce.	Pepper and Salt.

UTENSILS—Saucepan, wooden spoon, tablespoon, knife, frying pan. *Enough for 1 person.*

Cut the boiled macaroni into one-inch lengths, and make a sauce with butter, flour and milk. Add to the sauce a little chopped ham, onion, and tomato sauce, mix all well together, season with pepper and salt, make very hot, and pile on a dish. Garnish with parsley. When fresh tomatoes are in season, they should be used instead of sauce.

Spaghetti Veronese

¾ lb. Spaghetti.	1 small tin Tomatoes.
1 cupful diced Cheese.	2 chopped Pimentoes.
1 Green Pepper.	2 cupfuls cold, chopped Pork.

UTENSILS—Saucepan, spoon, colander, knife, cup. *Enough for 4 persons.*

Parboil the spaghetti in plenty of boiling, salted water, stirring occasionally. Drain, add the tomatoes, cheese, pimentoes, green pepper, finely minced, and let this simmer for a few minutes before stirring in the pork. Sprinkle with cayenne before serving very hot.

Chinatown Macaroni

½ lb. cut Macaroni.	2 oz. Salt Pork.
2 oz. Beef Steak.	1 large tin Tomatoes.
Salt. Pepper. Cayenne.	2 medium-sized Onions.
2 oz. Fresh Pork.	½ clove of Garlic.

UTENSILS—Saucepan, colander, mincing machine, knife, frying pan. *Enough for 4 persons.*

Throw macaroni into boiling, salted water till tender. Drain, pour a cupful of cold water through the macaroni, then return it to the saucepan. Put the beef and fresh pork through a mincer and cut up the salt pork. Heat the minced meat in a frying pan till the fat is melted, add the onion and fry till brown, then stir in the chopped meat. Brown slightly, add a finely minced clove of garlic, the tomatoes, and pepper and salt to taste.

Cook all together till the meat is tender, then pour the sauce over the hot macaroni and serve.

Macaroni a l'Italienne

¼ lb. Macaroni. 2 oz. Butter.	½ pint Tomato Purée.
2 oz. grated Cheese.	Pepper and Salt.

UTENSILS—Stewpan, colander, grater, wooden spoon. *Enough for 3 or 4 persons.*

Put the macaroni into a stewpan of fast-boiling salted water or white stock. Boil rapidly, until tender, in about 20 minutes. Drain thoroughly, and return it to the saucepan, which must be quite dry, then put in half the cheese, and mix it well, then stir in the other half. Now stir in the butter and seasoning of pepper and salt, then the tomato purée (fresh or tinned tomatoes will do), and let all get thoroughly hot together. Turn it on to a hot dish and serve. Rice is excellent done in the same way.

Macaroni au Gratin

¼ lb. Macaroni.	2 tablespoonfuls Buttered
½ pint Béchamel Sauce.	Crumbs.
2¼ oz. Cheese. ½ oz. Butter.	Pepper and Salt.

UTENSILS—Two saucepans, fireproof gratin dish, wooden spoon, tablespoon, grater, baking tin, pint measure. *Enough for 3 or 4 persons.*

Boil the macaroni well. Thickly butter a fireproof gratin dish, or a shallow pie-dish, with half an ounce of butter. Make the Béchamel sauce, then stir into it the grated cheese (one ounce of Parmesan and one ounce of Gruyere preferred), and season with pepper and salt.

Lay the macaroni in the buttered dish, pour the sauce over, and sprinkle with the remaining cheese and the buttered crumbs on top. Stand the dish in a pan containing water, and put both into a quick oven, near the top. When the macaroni is quite hot and nicely browned on top, take it out, stand the dish of macaroni on another dish, with fancy paper beneath, and serve quickly.

Stuffed Tomatoes

2 large Tomatoes. | 1 Egg. | 1 large tablespoonful fresh
1 grated Onion, to taste. | | Breadcrumbs.
1 heaped teaspoonful Butter. | | ½ teaspoonful minced Parsley.
A pinch of Sweet Herbs.

UTENSILS—Knife, enamelled saucepan, basin, fork or egg-beater, grater, fireproof dish, measuring spoons. *Enough for 2 to 4 persons.*

Cut the tomatoes in halves and scoop out the middles. Put the middles into a saucepan, together with the butter, onion, herbs, a roughly beaten egg, the parsley, and breadcrumbs, season to taste with pepper and salt, and stir till thick, but do not let it boil. Then pile the mixture into the tomato halves. Bake on a buttered fireproof dish in a moderate oven for 10 minutes.

Scotch Nips

6 oz. cooked, Dried Haddock. | 1 gill thick Cream.
2 Yolks of Eggs. | White Pepper and Salt.

UTENSILS—Knife, stewpan, frying pan, wooden spoon. *Enough for 3 or 4 persons, as a savoury.*

Chop the cooked dried haddock up finely and place it in a stewpan. Add the cream, yolks of eggs, pepper and salt to taste, and stir over a moderate heat till the mixture thickens. Pile it on fried croûtes, sprinkle with a little paprika, and dish up in a circle on a paper d'oyley and serve hot.

Sardines en Fritot

6 Sardines. | Frying Batter.
Parmesan Cheese. | Parsley.

UTENSILS—Knife, frying basket, frying pan, basin, egg-beater, wooden spoon. *Enough for 2 or 3 persons.*

Wash, wipe and skin the sardines, dip them in frying batter, then place them in a wire basket and fry in deep, smoking fat until golden brown.

Fry the parsley, dipping it in the hot fat three times before the final immersion, to prevent it from scorching. Pile the sardines on a hot dish, lined with a lace paper d'oyley. Sprinkle with grated Parmesan cheese and serve garnished with fried parsley.

Devilled Sardines

6 Sardines. | Salt.   Lemon Juice.
½ teaspoonful Curry Powder. | Buttered Toast.
½ teaspoonful Mustard. | Chopped Parsley.

UTENSILS—Knife, basin, wooden spoon, teaspoon, baking dish, brush, toaster or toasting fork. *Enough for 2 or 3 persons.*

Scrape off the skins from the sardines. Mix the curry powder, mustard, and a very small pinch of salt into a thin paste with some of the oil from the sardines, then brush the fish well over with the paste. Lay them on a buttered baking dish in a hot oven for 5 minutes.

Cut six fingers of buttered toast, lay the sardines on them, sprinkle with a few drops of lemon juice and a little finely chopped parsley. Serve very hot, laying them side by side on a paper d'oyley.

Stuffed Bacon on Toast

½ cupful stale Breadcrumbs. | ½ small Onion.
Lamb's Kidneys.   Beaten Egg. | ½ tablespoonful Parsley.
Salt and Pepper. | 10 slices Bacon.

UTENSILS—Grater, 2 basins, knife, egg-beater, small skewers, cup, tablespoon. *Enough for 4 persons, as a savoury.*

Mix the crumbs with the chopped onion, and add parsley and seasonings, moisten with beaten egg, then spread the mixture on thin slices of bacon. Fasten each slice round a piece of lamb's kidney with the help of small skewers, and bake in a hot oven for 20 minutes.

Serve on rounds of hot buttered toast with the crusts

removed. Garnish with halved tomatoes, baked or grilled,
sprinkled with breadcrumbs, pepper and salt, and dabs of
butter.

Mexican Toast

1 cupful Milk.	½ lb. Cheese.	¾ cupful chopped **Walnuts.**
1 well-beaten Egg.	Paprika.	¼ cupful chopped **Olives.**
1 tablespoonful Butter.		½ teaspoonful Worcester Sauce.

UTENSILS — Double boiler, grater, basin, egg-beater,
measuring spoons, cup, toasting fork or toaster, wooden
spoon. *Enough for 4 persons, as a savoury.*

Heat the milk in a double boiler or chafing dish, and add
the grated cheese. Stir till melted. Add the butter, paprika,
Worcester sauce and beaten egg. Cook gently for a few
minutes, still stirring, then add the nuts and olives. Cook for
5 minutes longer, and serve on buttered toasts with the crusts
removed.

Lobster Toast

1 small Lobster.	Pounded Mace.
1 tablespoonful Cream.	Cayenne. Salt.
Buttered Toast.	

UTENSILS—Knife, fork, saucepan, kitchen spoon, tablespoon, small round cutter, toasting fork or toaster. *Enough
for 4 persons, as a savoury.*

Remove all the meat from a small boiled lobster, and
chop it finely. Put it into a saucepan with the cream, salt
and cayenne to taste, and the smallest possible pinch of
pounded mace.

Have ready some rounds of hot buttered toast the size
of crown pieces, and spread the lobster on these. Now arrange
them on a hot dish, with a fancy paper, and serve. If the
lobster has any coral, rub it through a sieve and sprinkle it
over the toasts before serving.

Strasbourg Toast

5 Eggs.	Foie Gras.	Parsley.
	5 squares of Buttered Toast.	

UTENSILS—Toasting fork or toaster, knife, stewpan, cup,
egg-slice. *Enough for 3 to 5 persons.*

Make some nice buttered toast, and spread it rather
thickly with pâté de foie gras. Cut it into five neat squares,

large enough to hold one egg each, and keep them hot. Have ready a stewpan of slightly salted boiling water.

Break the eggs, one at a time, into a cup, and slide them gently into the water. Draw the pan to one side of the stove, and poach until the eggs are firm. Lift them out carefully, trim neatly, and place one on each piece of toast, sprinkle a little finely chopped parsley on top of each, and arrange neatly on a hot dish and garnish with parsley.

Kidney Toast

2 Sheeps' Kidneys.	1 oz. Butter or Salad Oil.
1 tablespoonful chopped Bacon.	3 tablespoonfuls Milk or Cream.
¼ teaspoonful chopped Parsley.	A dust of Cayenne.
1 small teaspoonful Flour.	Nutmeg. Toast. Salt.

UTENSILS—Knife, stewpan, sieve, wooden spoon, measuring spoons, toasting fork or toaster, round cutter. *Enough for 2 to 5 persons.*

Skin the kidneys and chop them finely. Melt half an ounce of butter in a pan, put in the chopped kidney, bacon and parsley, and cook together gently for 10 minutes, then sift in the flour, a dust of cayenne, a small pinch of grated nutmeg, and salt to taste. Lastly, stir in the milk or cream, gradually. After it thickens, let it cook very gently for 5 minutes.

Butter the toast well, and stamp it out into four or five rounds, the size of a small teacup. Spread the kidney on the rounds of toast, arrange neatly in a hot dish, garnish with fresh parsley, and serve very hot.

Ham Toast

8 tablespoonfuls lean Ham.	6 tablespoonfuls Cream or Milk.
2 Yolks of Eggs.	Butter. Cayenne.
Squares of Toast.	

UTENSILS—Knife, tablespoon, basin, egg-beater, saucepan, toasting fork or toaster. *Enough for 3 persons.*

Take the lean part of the remains of a ham, and chop it finely. To eight tablespoonfuls of this add the yolks of two eggs well beaten, the cream or milk, a piece of butter about the size of an egg, and a seasoning of cayenne pepper. Stir over a moderate heat until the mixture begins to thicken, then spread it on squares of toast and serve very hot.

OMELETS

TO make a perfect omelet, melt the necessary amount of butter in an omelet pan until it begins to bubble. Whisk the eggs for a second or two, add seasoning required, then pour gently into the bubbling butter. As soon as the eggs set underneath, keep lifting the omelet with a palette knife to allow the liquid on top to run underneath and cook. When almost set on top, put any filling to be used, such as that required for a kidney omelet, in the centre, and fold over. Serve at once.

When the ingredients that give the omelet its name have to be mixed with the eggs, serve the omelet when almost set on top. If you wait until the omelet is dry on top, it will taste too dry. When making an omelet in which the yolks and whites of eggs are beaten separately, you may find it necessary to finish the cooking of the omelet for a second or two under the grill before folding.

Serve the omelet on a hot dish lined with a lace paper d'oyley. Some consider that the addition of a tablespoonful of cold water to every two or three eggs used makes the omelet lighter.

UTENSILS REQUIRED FOR OMELET MAKING—Omelet pan, palette knife, two basins, egg-beater, knife, spoon.

Apricot Omelet

| 6 Yolks of Eggs. | 1 oz. Butter. |
| 4 Whites of Eggs. | Apricot Jam. |

Enough for 3 persons.

Beat up the whites of four and the yolks of six eggs, with a very small pinch of salt. Put the butter in the omelet pan, and when it bubbles, pour in the eggs. Stir until they set, then fold the omelet, inserting within the fold as much apricot jam as will lie in it. Let it remain in the pan until it is nicely browned on the under side, then lift out the omelet neatly on to its dish, sprinkle with powdered sugar, and glaze it under the grill.

Brussels Sprouts Omelet

| 25 Brussels Sprouts. | 1 oz. Butter. |
| 6 Eggs. Sauce. | Pepper and Salt. |

Enough for 4 or 5 persons.

Boil some young Brussels sprouts until they are tender, then divide each sprout into four or more portions, according to size, and dry on a cloth. Beat up six eggs, yolks and whites, and mix the sprouts with them, adding pepper and salt to taste. Melt the butter in the pan, and when hot, put in the mixture, sprinkle with pepper and salt, and fry until of a nice brown colour. Serve quickly, sending butter sauce, sharpened with a dash of lime juice, to table with it.

Cheese Omelet (1)

| 4 Eggs. | 1 oz. Butter. |
| Parmesan Cheese. | |

Enough for 2 persons.

Beat up the eggs with one or two tablespoonfuls of grated Parmesan cheese, and pepper and salt to taste. Put a piece of butter the size of an egg into a frying pan. As soon as it is melted, pour in the omelet mixture, and, holding the pan with one hand, stir the omelet with the other by means of a spoon.

The moment it begins to set, cease stirring, but keep on shaking the pan for a minute or so. Then with the spoon double up the omelet, and keep shaking the pan until the under side of the omelet has become of a golden colour. Turn it out on a hot dish and serve with plenty of grated Parmesan cheese strewn over it.

Cheese Omelet (2)

6 Yolks of Eggs.	4 oz. cooking Cheese.
4 Whites of Eggs.	½ pint Cream.
½ oz. Butter.	Pepper and Salt.

Enough for 3 or 4 persons.

Grate the cheese and beat up the yolks of six eggs and the whites of four. Add the grated cheese to them, and, by degrees, the cream. Season well with pepper and salt, using cayenne pepper if liked. Fry with butter in the ordinary way, and serve as quickly as possible when ready.

Ham Omelet

| 2 tablespoonfuls Ham, minced. | 6 Yolks of Eggs. |
| 4 Whites of Eggs. | Butter. Pepper. |

Enough for 3 persons.

Mince two tablespoonfuls of lean ham finely. Fry this in a little butter for a few minutes. Whisk up the yolks of six eggs and the whites of four together, with pepper, and a very small pinch of salt. Stir in the cooked ham, then put a piece of butter, about the size of an egg, into the pan, and when it bubbles pour in the mixture. Proceed as for CHEESE OMELET (1) (see above).

NOTE.—Tongue can be used instead of ham, if preferred.

Haricot Beans Omelet

½ pint Haricot Beans.	2 tablespoonfuls Breadcrumbs.
½ teacupful Milk.	½ oz. finely-chopped Parsley.
4 Eggs. 2 oz. Butter.	Pepper and Salt.

Enough for 2 or 3 persons.

This makes a very nourishing omelet, but requires to be prepared beforehand. The beans should steep at least 6 hours in cold, slightly salted, water. It is a good plan to set them to steep overnight, especially if they are required for luncheon or early dinner. When steeped, boil in fresh water until perfectly soft, and then mash them in milk. When mashed, rub through a sieve or fine colander.

Then add the finely grated breadcrumbs, parsley, eggs, yolks and whites, well beaten, a tablespoonful of melted butter or olive oil, and salt and pepper to taste. Mix the whole thoroughly, and pour into a buttered pan or enamelled dish. Bake from ¾ hour to 1 hour in the oven, which should not be too hot. Send a sharp brown sauce to table with it.

Jam Omelet

This omelet is made with any suitable jam, as described with APRICOT OMELET, on page 397.

Macaroni Omelet

2 oz. Macaroni.	4 Eggs.
2 tablespoonfuls Flour.	½ oz. Parsley.
½ pint new Milk.	Pepper and Salt.

Enough for 2 persons.

Boil the macaroni until it is perfectly tender, then drain it. Rub the flour into a smooth paste with a little cold water.

Boil the milk in a lined saucepan, and when boiling, pour it on the flour paste, and stir well until it thickens, then add the macaroni, cut up into small pieces.

Have ready four eggs, well beaten, and the parsley, chopped fine. Add these to the milk, at the same time as the macaroni, and season with white pepper and salt. Pour the mixture, while hot, into an enamelled pie-dish, well buttered. Bake in a moderately hot oven, until browned over, then turn out. Serve with onion sauce, if liked, or with brown sauce.

Plain Omelet

4 Eggs.   Parsley. | Butter.   Pepper and Salt.
Enough for 2 *persons.*

Beat up the eggs, with one dessertspoonful of parsley, very finely minced, and pepper and salt to taste. Put a piece of butter, the size of an egg, into a frying pan. As soon as it is melted, pour in the omelet mixture. Hold the handle of the pan with one hand, stir the omelet with the other, by means of a spoon. The moment it begins to set, cease stirring but keep on shaking the pan for a minute or so. Then, with the spoon, double up the omelet, and keep shaking the pan until the under side of the omelet has become of a golden colour. Turn it out on a hot dish, and serve.

ANOTHER METHOD

Break three eggs, yolks and whites, into a basin, add salt and pepper to taste, and beat them with a whisk, till thoroughly blended. Have the frying pan previously on the fire, with a lump of butter the size of a walnut in it. Pour in the beaten eggs just before the butter boils. Let them set, and then fold up the omelet, and serve on a hot dish. A few chopped herbs and parsley may be added to the eggs before frying.

Plain Sweet Omelet

3 Eggs.   2 oz. Butter. | 1 oz. Castor Sugar.
Enough for 1 *or* 2 *persons.*

Beat up well three eggs (whites and yolks). Add to them one ounce of butter, broken up into small pieces, and the sifted sugar. Stir well together. Put one ounce of fresh butter into the omelet pan. When it fritters, pour in the mixture, and continue stirring until it begins to set. Then turn the edges over until the omelet is of an oval shape.

Lift it on to a dish, brown it under the gas grill, sift sugar over, and serve at once. This will only make a small omelet. If a larger one is required, double the proportions of the ingredients.

Potato Omelet

6 Potatoes.	4 Whites of Eggs.
1½ oz. Butter.	Breadcrumbs.
6 Yolks of Eggs.	Pepper and Salt.

Enough for 3 or 4 persons.

Boil six mealy potatoes, dry them well, and mash with half an ounce of butter, add one ounce of breadcrumbs, very finely grated, the yolks of six eggs and the whites of four, and season to taste with white pepper and salt. Melt one ounce of butter in the omelet pan, and when it is quite hot pour in the mixture. Fry a nice golden brown colour, over a not too fierce fire. For omelet making a gas boiling-burner is far preferable to a stove, for the heat can be so well regulated.

Rice Omelet (Savoury)

3 oz. Rice.	3 Eggs. Parsley.

Enough for 2 persons.

Wash the rice well in two or three waters, then boil it in one pint of water, until the water is entirely absorbed. When it is nearly cold, add to it three well-beaten eggs and a quarter of an ounce of chopped parsley. Butter an enamelled pie-dish, pour in the omelet, and bake in a moderate oven.

Serve with fine herbs sauce.

Rice Omelet (Sweet)

Follow the above recipe, but use, instead of chopped parsley, one ounce of sifted white sugar, and omit the sauce.

Rum Omelet

6 Yolks of Eggs.	3 oz. Butter.
4 Whites of Eggs.	2 oz. Castor Sugar.
1 wineglassful Rum.	

Enough for 3 persons.

Make a plain sweet omelet, with four whites and six

yolks of eggs. When cooked, strew sugar over, and, instead of glazing it, pour the hot rum over it. Set it alight as it is being put upon the table.

Savoury Omelet

| 4 Eggs. | Parsley. Shallot. |
| 1 oz. Butter. | Pepper and Salt. |

Enough for 2 persons.

Beat up three or four eggs with one dessertspoonful of parsley, very finely minced, half a clove of shallot, also finely minced, and pepper and salt to taste. Put a piece of butter, the size of an egg, into a frying pan ; as soon as it is melted, pour in the omelet mixture, and, holding the handle of the pan with one hand, stir the omelet with the other by means of a spoon. The moment it begins to set, cease stirring, but keep shaking the pan for a minute or so. Then, with the spoon, double up the omelet, and keep shaking the pan until one side of the omelet has become a golden colour. It is now ready to serve.

ANOTHER METHOD

Besides parsley, add a very few fresh sweet herbs and a few chives, all very finely minced. Powdered sweet herbs may be used, but in either case great care should be taken not to put in too many.

Shallot Omelet

| 3 Eggs. 3 oz. Butter. | Parsley. Shallot. |
| 1 tablespoonful Cream. | Pepper and Salt. |

Enough for 1 or 2 persons.

Break the eggs into a basin, add the cream, a small pat of butter, broken into pieces, a little chopped parsley, some shallot, well chopped, and some pepper and salt. Put two ounces of butter into the omelet pan, and while the butter is melting, whip the eggs and other ingredients well together, until they become frothy.

As soon as the butter begins to fritter, pour the eggs into the pan, and stir the omelet. As the eggs appear to set, roll the omelet into the form of an oval cushion. Allow it to acquire a golden brown colour on one side over the fire, and then turn it out on its dish. Pour a thin sauce, or gravy, under it, and serve.

Soufflé Omelet

6 Eggs.	2 tablespoonfuls Castor Sugar.
Lemon Juice.	2 oz. Butter.

Enough for 2 or 3 persons.

Separate the yolks and whites of six eggs. Strain the yolks and add to them the sugar and a little lemon juice or orange-flower water, and stir well together. Whip the whites into a stiff froth, and then mix lightly with the rest. Melt the butter in the pan, and pour in the mixture. When cooked, sprinkle over with sugar, and either put into the oven for a few minutes to rise, or else hold a salamander over it, or hold it under the gas grill.

Spinach Omelet

¼ lb. Spinach.	1 large tablespoonful Flour.
¼ lb. Beetroot.	4 Eggs.　2 oz. Butter.
½ oz. Parsley.　½ oz. Leeks.	4 tablespoonfuls Milk.
¼ oz. Lemon Thyme.	Pepper and Salt.

Enough for 3 or 4 persons.

Chop up, together, the spinach (it should be young and tender), beetroot, parsley, leeks, and lemon thyme, then season the mixture with salt and pepper. Add, by degrees, the flour, milk, eggs, well beaten, and butter, melted. Mix the whole well together, put into an enamelled pie-dish, and bake for 20 minutes in the oven.

NOTE.—If beet is not liked, Brussels sprouts can be used instead.

Sweet Omelet, with Jam

6 Yolks of Eggs.	1 oz. Butter.
4 Whites of Eggs.	Strawberry Jam.　Castor Sugar.

Enough for 3 persons.

Beat up the whites of four and the yolks of six eggs, with a very small pinch of salt. Put a piece of fresh butter in the omelet pan, and directly it is melted pour in the eggs. As soon as they are set, fold up the omelet, inserting within the fold as much strawberry jam as will lie in it. Turn out the omelet neatly on its dish, sprinkle thickly with powdered sugar, and glaze under the grill. (See also APRICOT OMELET, page 397.)

Swiss Omelet

2 oz. Parmesan Cheese.	1 oz. Breadcrumbs.
3 oz. Butter.	¼ pint Milk.
½ oz. Parsley.	4 Eggs.

Enough for 2 persons.

Made with grated cheese, in the following manner : Grate Parmesan cheese ; melt two ounces of butter ; add this to the cheese, also the finely-chopped parsley, the breadcrumbs, finely grated, the milk, and the eggs, well beaten. Fry in the usual way, with a little butter in the pan, which must be properly heated before the mixture is put in.

Tomato Omelet

| 6 Tomatoes. | 4 Eggs. Sauce. Milk. |
| 2 oz. Breadcrumbs. | Salt and Pepper. |

Enough for 2 persons.

Scald six ripe tomatoes, skin them, and remove the seeds. Stew until tender, then mash, and rub through a sieve. Add the breadcrumbs, well-beaten eggs, four tablespoonfuls of milk, and salt and pepper to taste. Mix all thoroughly, pour into a buttered dish, and bake in a moderately hot oven. Serve with vinegar or brown sauce, not made with stock, as is ordinary brown sauce, but merely browned butter thickening, thinned with vinegar.

Celery Fritters

1 bunch of Celery. | 1 cupful sifted Flour.
1 cupful Milk.　2 Eggs. | 1 teaspoonful Baking Powder.

UTENSILS—Knife, saucepan, cloth, sieve, 2 basins, egg-beater, wooden spoon, teaspoon, cup, frying pan. *Enough for about* 6 *persons*.

Clean, scrape, and cut the celery into 4 inch lengths. Stand it in boiling water for 10 minutes, then wipe it dry. Sift the flour and baking powder into a basin, then gradually stir in the milk and beaten eggs. Beat well. Dip the celery fingers into this batter, and fry them in deep, smoking hot fat.

Cheese and Lentil Rolls

½ lb. Rough Puff Pastry. | 1 cupful Breadcrumbs.
1 cupful Lentils. | 1 oz. Butter.
2 Tomatoes. | Salt.　Beaten Egg.
2 oz. Cheese. | Pepper and Mustard.

UTENSILS—Cloth, saucepan, wire sieve, knife, wooden spoon, cup, grater, egg-beater, pastry board, rolling pin, basins, pastry brush, baking sheet. *Enough for* 6 *to* 8 *persons*.

Wash the lentils, then tie them loosely in a cloth. Cook them for 1 hour in boiling salted water, then rub them through a wire sieve. Add the butter, the skinned and sliced tomatoes, grated cheese and enough breadcrumbs to thicken.

Roll the pastry into a thin strip, cut it into squares, brush it with beaten egg, and place on the centre of each square a roll of the lentil mixture. Fold the pastry over, trim the edges, brush with beaten egg, and bake for 20 minutes in a hot oven.

Cheese and Tomato Toast

1 medium-sized Tomato. | 2 tablespoonfuls grated Cheese.
½ oz. Butter.　2 Eggs. | Salt and Pepper to taste.

UTENSILS—Saucepan, knife, egg-beater, grater, table-spoon, wooden spoon, plate, basin. *Enough for* 2 *or* 3 *persons*.

Melt the butter in a saucepan. Add the skinned and sliced tomato, and fry until cooked. Add the cheese, and beaten eggs, and stir over the fire until the mixture thickens. Season. Pour over slices of hot buttered toast, and serve.

Cheese Soufflé Omelet

1 gill Milk.	1 oz. Cheese.	1 oz. Butter or Margarine.
2 Eggs.	½ oz. Cornflour.	Pepper and Salt to taste.

UTENSILS—Wooden spoon, 3 basins, egg-beater, 2 saucepans, omelet pan, gill measure, knife or palette knife. *Enough for 3 persons.*

Mix the cornflour smoothly with a little of the milk, using a wooden spoon. Boil the remainder of the gill of milk. Stir it into the cornflour paste, then turn the mixture into a saucepan and boil for 2 minutes, stirring constantly. Remove the pan from the fire, cool the contents slightly, then stir in the egg yolks, one at a time. Beat well, season to taste, and fold in the stiffly frothed egg whites.

Melt half the butter in an omelet pan, and when smoking hot, gently but quickly pour in the omelet mixture. Cook till lightly brown underneath, then place in a moderate oven till browned on top.

Meanwhile melt the cheese and the remainder of the butter, in a saucepan over a low heat. Stir in 1 tablespoonful of milk or cream, and season to taste. Stir till creamy, then pour on top of the omelet. Fold in two, and serve, sprinkled with grated cheese, on a hot dish.

Creamed Vegetable Toasts

¼ lb. Haricot Beans.		1 slice Toasted Bread.	
1 Onion.	½ Carrot.	2 Potatoes.	¼ Turnip.

UTENSILS—Knife, basin, 2 saucepans, wooden spoon, strainer or colander. *Enough for 2 or 3 persons.*

Soak the beans in cold water to cover overnight. Put them in a saucepan in cold water, and simmer till almost tender. Add the prepared carrot, turnip and onion, cut into dice. Cook gently for 10 minutes. Cut the potatoes into dice and cook for another 10 minutes.

THE SAUCE

1½ oz. Butter.		1½ oz. Flour.
¼ pint Milk.		Seasoning.

Melt the butter, add the flour, then the milk gradually. Stir till boiling. Add the strained vegetables, season to taste, re-heat and serve on a hot dish garnished with fingers of hot buttered toast.

Italian Risotto

1 cupful Rice.
1 tablespoonful Salt.
1 small chopped Onion.

1½ tablespoonfuls Butter.
1 cupful stewed Tomatoes.
Grated Parmesan Cheese.

UTENSILS—Colander, 2 saucepans, knife, tablespoon, cup, grater. *Enough for 3 to 4 persons.*

Carefully pick and wash the rice, turn it into a saucepan of boiling water, add the salt, and boil until tender. Drain, cover, and set at the side of the fire to steam for 5 minutes.

In the meantime the sauce should have been made. Put the butter and chopped onion into a saucepan, and cook slowly until well browned. Then add the stewed tomatoes, season to taste, and simmer for ½ hour. Put the rice in a serving dish, pour the sauce over, and sprinkle thickly with Parmesan cheese. Serve at once.

Macaroni à la Milanaise

⅓ lb. Macaroni.
2 teaspoonfuls Salt.
2 cloves of Garlic.
Grated Parmesan.

2 quarts boiling Water.
1 tin Tomato Sauce.
¼ cupful Olive Oil.
8 Peppercorns.   Bayleaves.

UTENSILS—Two saucepans, colander, measuring spoons, measuring cup, quart measure, knife, strainer. *Enough for 4 persons.*

Boil the macaroni till tender, putting it in boiling salted water. Drain it in a colander, and pour over it one cupful of cold water. Open the tin of tomato sauce, pour the juice into a saucepan with two bayleaves, the peppercorns, olive oil, minced garlic, salt, and 2 tablespoonfuls of grated Parmesan cheese. Cook slowly until well seasoned, then strain and pour over the macaroni. Re-heat, turn into a hot vegetable dish, sprinkle thickly with more grated Parmesan, and serve at once. SPAGHETTI can be cooked in the same way.

Mock Fillets of Sole

2 oz. Semolina.
2 teaspoonfuls grated Onion.
2 teaspoonfuls Butter.
4 cooked Potatoes.

½ pint Milk.
Salt and White Pepper.
White Sauce.
Chopped Parsley.

UTENSILS—2 saucepans, wooden spoon, potato masher or

fork, grater, pint measure, teaspoon, pastry board, basin, egg-beater, knife, frying pan. *Enough for 2 persons.*

Stir the semolina and milk in a saucepan over the fire till boiling. Add the butter and onion. Cook slowly for 10 minutes, then add sufficient cooked and mashed potatoes to thicken the mixture. Season with salt, pepper and paprika, if liked. Turn the mixture out on to a floured board, and form it into fillet-shaped pieces about $\frac{1}{4}$ inch thick. Dip these in beaten egg, and toss them in breadcrumbs. Fry them in deep fat until brown. Serve with white sauce mixed with 2 teaspoonfuls of finely chopped parsley.

Mushrooms à la Newburg

1 lb. Musnrooms.	1½ cupfuls Milk. Salt.
3 Yolks of Eggs.	3 tablespoonfuls Butter.
½ teaspoonful Salt.	Sherry and Paprika to taste.

UTENSILS—Knife, saucepan, wooden spoon, measuring spoons, cup, basin. *Enough for 4 to 6 persons.*

Stem the mushrooms, and cut up the peeled stems. Wipe and break the peeled caps. Fry the caps and stems in smoking-hot butter for 2 minutes, then add 1¼ cupfuls of milk, or better still, cream, if you have it. Season with salt and paprika, cover, and simmer till tender.

Remove the pan from the fire, stir in the egg yolks, diluted with $\frac{1}{4}$ cupful of milk, then return the pan to the fire, and stir constantly over a slow heat till the mixture is thick and creamy. Flavour with sherry to taste. Serve in hot pastry cases, or on rounds of hot buttered toast or fried bread.

My Favourite Macaroni Dish

1 lb. Macaroni.	1 gill Tomato Sauce.
1 gill Madeira.	¼ lb. Parmesan Cheese.
Salt, Nutmeg and Pepper to taste.	

UTENSILS—Two saucepans, gill measure, wooden spoon, grater. *Enough for 6 persons.*

Cook the macaroni in salted water for 30 minutes, without breaking it. Drain, and put it into a saucepan with the tomato sauce and Madeira. Add the cheese and seasoning. Cook slowly for 10 minutes, tossing it frequently. Serve with grated Parmesan cheese.

Nut Roast

1 cupful Brown Breadcrumbs.	1 cupful White Breadcrumbs.
1 cupful shelled Barcelona Nuts.	1 cupful Pine Kernels.
2 Eggs. 1 oz. Butter.	1 Onion, finely chopped.
2 Tomatoes, skinned and sliced.	Salt and Pepper to taste.

UTENSILS—Saucepan, knife, grater, basin, egg-beater, pie-dish, cup. *Enough for 4 or 5 persons.*

Melt the butter, and add the chopped onion and skinned and sliced tomatoes, and fry. Add the breadcrumbs and nuts finely chopped. Moisten with the beaten eggs. Season with salt and pepper. Press the mixture into a greased pie-dish, and bake for $\frac{1}{2}$ hour. Turn out and serve with apple sauce.

Potato Omelet

3 Eggs.	1 tablespoonful cooked **Potatoes**.
1 tablespoonful Breadcrumbs.	1 tablespoonful Butter.
1 tablespoonful Milk.	1 tablespoonful grated Cheese.
1 teaspoonful chopped Parsley.	Pepper and Salt.

UTENSILS—Basin, egg-beater, saucepan, omelet pan, knife, grater, fork or potato masher, palette knife. *Enough for 2 persons.*

Beat the eggs until frothy. Add the parsley, mashed potatoes, breadcrumbs, cheese, milk and seasonings. Melt the butter in an omelet pan, pour in the mixture, and fry for 2 minutes. Brown the top under a hot grill. Fold over and serve at once.

Rice with Cheese Sauce

1 quart Boiled Rice.	$\frac{1}{2}$ pint White Sauce.
$\frac{1}{4}$ cupful grated **Cheese**.	Paprika to taste.

UTENSILS—2 saucepans, colander, wooden spoon, grater, pint measure. *Enough for 4 to 6 persons.*

Boil the rice in boiling, salted water, and drain it well. Then hold it in a colander under the cold tap for a moment. Drain well, and add it to the white sauce. (See Index). Season to taste with paprika, add the cheese, and heat until the cheese is melted, stirring lightly. Serve at once.

NOTE—A $\frac{1}{4}$ cupful of cooked peas, or 2 tablespoonfuls of minced pimento, or $\frac{1}{4}$ lb. of chopped fried mushrooms can also be added, if liked.

Scalloped Corn

1 tin of Corn.	3 tablespoonfuls Cream.
½ cupful Corn Liquid.	2 tablespoonfuls Flour.
1 teaspoonful Salt.	1 tablespoonful Butter.
1 cupful Breadcrumbs.	Pepper, Paprika and Salt.

UTENSILS—Basin, flour sifter or sieve, wooden spoon, measuring spoons, cup, grater, frying pan, pie-dish. *Enough for 4 to 6 persons.*

Sift the flour, salt and pepper, and 1 teaspoonful of sugar, if liked, into a basin. Stir in the corn and the liquids. Melt the butter in a frying pan, and stir in the breadcrumbs. Cover the bottom of a fireproof pie-dish with half the fried crumbs. Add the corn mixture, seasoned to taste with paprika, if liked. Cover with the remainder of the crumbs, and bake in a moderate oven for 20 minutes.

Spanish Eggs

6 Eggs. 3 Tomatoes.	2 Onions.
1 teaspoonful Parsley.	2 Pimentoes.
1 tablespoonful melted Butter.	Salt and Pepper to taste.

UTENSILS—Saucepan, knife, tablespoon, wooden spoon, frying pan or egg-poacher. *Enough for 3 persons.*

Chop the scalded and peeled tomatoes, peeled onions, and pimentoes together, and place them in a saucepan. Add the parsley and butter, and cook for 5 minutes, stirring frequently. Pour the mixture over fried, poached or steamed eggs, arranged on a large hot dish or on individual dishes.

Spanish Toast

½ lb. grated Cheese.	1 cupful strained Tomatoes.
½ cupful soft Breadcrumbs.	½ cupful cooked Peas.
1 Pimento. 2 Eggs.	1 tablespoonful Butter.
1 dessertspoonful minced Onion.	Seasoning to taste.

UTENSILS—Saucepan, wooden spoon, measuring spoons, cup, grater, knife, basin, egg-beater. *Enough for 4 persons.*

Melt the butter in a saucepan, add the onion, and cook till soft. Stir in the tomatoes, crumbs, and chopped pimento, and when the crumbs are quite soft, stir in the eggs, beaten with a tablespoonful of milk, and the cooked or tinned peas. Season to taste. Stir till thick. Serve on rounds or squares of hot buttered toast.

Stuffed Aubergine

1 large Aubergine. 1 Egg.	1 tablespoonful Butter or
1 small Onion or Shallot.	Margarine.
2 tablespoonfuls Breadcrumbs.	$\frac{1}{2}$ teaspoonful Parsley.

Salt, Pepper and Paprika.

UTENSILS—Knife, basin, grater, wooden spoon, measuring spoons, saucepan, frying pan, fireproof baking dish, basting spoon. *Enough for 2 persons.*

Parboil the aubergine in boiling salted water till tender, but not soft. Cut it in half, lengthways, and scrape out the inside into a basin without breaking the skin. Melt the fat in an enamel pan. Stir in the minced shallot or onion, and brown them slightly. Stir in the aubergine pulp, crumbs, seasoning and egg yolk. Mix them well, and refill the shells. Place them side by side in a well-buttered fireproof dish, and bake for $\frac{1}{2}$ hour in a moderate oven, basting them frequently with a little butter, until nicely browned.

NOTE—Two or three ounces of mushrooms, peeled, chopped and fried, can be added to the stuffing, if liked.

Stuffed Onions

4 Spanish Onions, parboiled.	$\frac{1}{2}$ teaspoonful Dried Thyme.
2 oz. Breadcrumbs.	A little Milk.
1 oz. Suet, finely chopped.	Squeeze of Lemon Juice.
1 teaspoonful chopped Parsley.	Salt and Pepper to taste.

UTENSILS—Saucepan, knife, basin, wooden spoon, teaspoon, chopping board, baking tin. *Enough for 2 or 3 persons.*

Parboil the onions for about $\frac{3}{4}$ hour, then remove the centres carefully. Mix the crumbs, suet, seasoning and herbs together, and bind them with a little milk. Place a little of this forcemeat in each onion. Bake the onions gently in a greased baking tin until tender, in about 1 hour.

Tomato Rice

1 cupful Rice.	2 tablespoonfuls Butter.
6 Tomatoes.	Salt, Pepper and Sugar.

UTENSILS—Saucepan, pie-dish, knife, tablespoon, plate, cup. *Enough for 4 persons.*

Boil the rice until tender. Peel and slice the tomatoes. Butter a pie-dish and put in a layer of tomatoes. Sprinkle with salt, pepper and a little sugar, then add a layer of rice. Repeat the layers until the dish is full, having a layer of tomatoes last. Dab the butter in pieces on top, cover with paper, and bake for 20 minutes. Remove the paper, and bake for 10 minutes longer. Serve piping hot.

Tomato Toad-in-the-Hole

6 firm Tomatoes.	1 tablespoonful melted Butter.
1 tablespoonful chopped Parsley.	2 tablespoonfuls Breadcrumbs.
1 pint Milk. 3 Eggs.	½ lb. Flour. Seasoning.

UTENSILS—3 basins, wooden spoon, sieve, tablespoon, egg-beater, grater, knife, Yorkshire pudding tin. *Enough for 6 persons.*

Sift the flour and salt into a basin. Make a hollow in the centre, and stir in the well-beaten eggs, diluted with half the milk. Rinse out the egg basin with the remainder of the milk and stir this into the batter. Then beat till the batter is smooth, and let it stand while you prepare the tomatoes. Cover the tomatoes with boiling water, stand them for 1 minute, then remove them from the water and peel, with a sharp-pointed, saw-edged, stainless knife. Remove a little pulp from the centre of each.

Mix the crumbs, melted butter, parsley or chopped chives, pepper, salt, paprika, and garlic salt, if liked, to taste. Moisten with beaten egg and tomato pulp. Stuff the tomatoes with the mixture, then place them on a well-greased Yorkshire pudding tin. Cover with batter, and bake in a moderate oven for from 45 minutes to 1 hour. Serve cut into squares and sprinkled with grated cheese.

Vegetable Batter

2 Tomatoes.   Stock. | ½ gill Batter.
Cold cooked Vegetables (carrot, turnip, beans, lentils, potatoes, etc.).

UTENSILS—Pie-dish, knife, 2 basins, egg-beater, wooden spoon, teaspoon, pint or gill measure. *Enough for 4 persons.*

Butter a pie-dish. Mix and season the vegetables, and moisten them with stock. Peel and slice the tomatoes and place them on top of the other vegetables. Pour the batter over, and bake in a hot oven for ½ hour. Serve at once.

THE BATTER

2 oz. Flour.		¼ teaspoonful Salt.
¼ pint Milk.	1 Egg.	Pinch of Pepper.

Mix the flour and seasoning together. Beat the egg and add half the milk to it. Add this slowly to the flour, and beat well until of the consistency of thick cream, then add the remainder of the milk, and allow it to stand for 1 hour.

Vegetable Charlotte

3 large Carrots.	3 Eggs. ¼ cupful Flour.
6 large Potatoes.	1 teaspoonful Castor Sugar.
2 teaspoonfuls Salt.	

UTENSILS—Knife, grater, 2 basins, egg-beater, saucepan, wooden spoon, teaspoon, fireproof baking dish. *Enough for 4 to 6 persons*.

Peel and grate the potatoes. Stir in the salt, pepper and slightly beaten eggs. Grate and parboil the carrots in water to cover, with the sugar. When they are nearly tender, drain off the water, and stir in the potato mixture, flour, and seasoning to taste. Turn into a well-buttered fireproof dish, and bake very slowly till golden brown—in about 1½ hours.

NOTE—This mixture can also be baked in a border mould, and the centre can be filled, when turned out, with buttered peas or fried mushrooms.

Vegetable Custard

¾ cupful cooked Peas.	2 beaten Eggs.
¼ cupful cooked Rice.	1 cupful Milk.
1 teaspoonful grated Onion.	Salt, Paprika and Celery Salt.

UTENSILS—Saucepan, double boiler, basin, egg-beater, grater, wooden spoon, teaspoon, cup, custard cups, baking tin. *Enough for 3 persons*.

Boil the rice in salted water, and drain it well. Stir in the peas and onion, and add seasoning to taste, and the milk and eggs. Stir the mixture in the top of a double boiler, with water boiling below, till tepid. Turn into buttered custard cups, set these in a pan of hot water, and bake in a moderate oven till set.

BISCUITS AND CAKES

TIME-TABLE FOR BAKING		Oven.
Small cakes	15 to 25 minutes	Quick.
Sponge cakes	45 to 60 minutes	Fairly quick.
Large fruit cakes	2 to 4 hours	Moderate.
Layer cake	20 to 30 minutes	Fairly quick.
Biscuits	5 to 12 minutes	Quick.
Muffins and scones	15 to 30 minutes	Fairly quick.
Pastry	35 to 40 minutes	Quick.

Ginger Biscuits

1 lb. Flour. 2 Eggs. | ½ lb. Butter.
½ lb. Castor Sugar. | 1 tablespoonful Ground Ginger.

UTENSILS—Sieve or flour sifter, 2 basins, egg-beater, wooden spoon, tablespoon, pastry board, rolling pin, fancy cutters, baking tin, pastry rack.

Sift the flour and ginger into a basin, and rub in the butter. Stir in the sugar and well-beaten eggs. Knead to a soft dough, then turn on to a lightly-floured pastry board, and roll out thinly. Cut into fancy shapes, place in a buttered baking tin, and bake in a moderate oven till crisp and golden.

Ginger Snaps

¼ lb. Butter. 1 lb. Flour. | ½ pint Treacle.
½ tablespoonful Ground Ginger. | ¼ lb. Brown Sugar.

UTENSILS—Basin, wooden spoon, tablespoon, pastry board, rolling pin, round cutter, small tins, pastry rack.

Rub the butter into the flour, then stir in the ginger and sugar. Mix in the treacle by degrees, you may not need it all, for the dough must be quite stiff. Knead thoroughly on a lightly floured board, then roll into a thin sheet. Cut into small rounds, and bake in small buttered tins in a moderate oven till brown and crisp.

Yarmouth Biscuits

¼ lb. Currants. ¾ lb. Flour. | ½ lb. Castor Sugar. 3 Eggs.
½ lb. Fresh Butter.

UTENSILS—Two basins, egg-beater, wooden spoon, baking tin, pastry rack.

Put the flour into a basin, and rub the butter well into it. Beat the three eggs well, then add the eggs and other ingredients to the flour and mix well. Drop in rough pieces on to a baking tin, and bake in a fairly quick oven.

French Biscuits

3 Eggs. **Castor Sugar.** | **The weight of the Eggs in Flour.**
1 oz. Candied Peel.

UTENSILS—Two basins, egg-beater, knife, wooden spoon, metal spoon, baking sheet, sieve, pastry rack.

Beat the whites of the eggs to a stiff froth, then stir in the candied peel cut very small. Beat well, then add by degrees the weight of three eggs in flour, also the same weight of castor sugar. Well beat the yolks of the eggs, add these and mix all well together.

Drop spoonfuls of the mixture on to a buttered paper, and shape them as neatly as possible with the spoon. Sift powdered sugar over them, then bake in a moderate oven until they are a pale gold colour. Remove them from the paper before they cool.

Rice Biscuits

7 oz. Castor Sugar. | **8 oz. Ground Rice.**
7 oz. Butter. | **7 oz. Flour.** **2 Eggs.**

UTENSILS—Two basins, egg-beater, baking sheet, pastry rack.

Rub all the dry ingredients thoroughly well together. Beat the eggs well, and mix the dry ingredients into a dough with the eggs. Drop the mixture in little lumps on to clean buttered baking sheets, and bake in a moderate oven from 10 to 15 minutes.

Oatmeal Crackers

7 oz. sifted Flour. | **3 oz. Castor Sugar.**
3 oz. Medium Oatmeal. | **3 oz. Butter or Margarine.**
¼ teaspoonful Baking Powder. | **1 Egg.** **Cold Water.**

UTENSILS—Saucepan, sieve, 2 basins, wooden spoon, teaspoon, egg-beater, pastry board, rolling pin, round cutter, baking tin, cake rack.

Mix the flour, oatmeal, sugar and soda together in a basin.

Stir in the butter or margarine, melted and warmed in a saucepan. Beat the egg and 1 tablespoonful of cold water together, and moisten the mixture of oatmeal and sugar, etc. Turn the paste on to a floured board and roll it out very thinly with a rolling pin. Cut it into crackers with a cutter or the top of a wine glass, and bake for 20 minutes on a greased baking tin in a hot oven. Cool on a cake rack.

Genoese Baskets

3 Eggs.	½ teaspoonful Baking Powder.
The weight of the Eggs in Butter.	Lemon Peel. Angelica.
The weight of the Eggs in Sugar.	¼ lb. Plain Icing.
The weight of 4 Eggs in Flour.	Compote of Fruits.

UTENSILS—Two basins, egg-beater, wooden spoon, teaspoon, knife, castle pudding tins, wire sieve, forcing-bag.

Beat the butter and sugar to a cream. Whip the eggs well, then add the eggs and the flour, alternately, to the butter and sugar. Mix in half a teaspoonful of finely chopped lemon peel and, lastly, add the baking powder.

Well butter some castle pudding tins, and sift them over with flour and sugar mixed in equal parts, half fill the tins with the mixture, and bake them in a moderate oven for 15 to 20 minutes. When cooked, turn them out on to a wire sieve to cool. It is best to make these the day before they are required. When cold, cut the tops off flat and straight, then hollow out the centres.

Make a quarter of a pound of plain icing, and colour it half pink and half green. Put it into two small forcing-bags with a rose and a leaf-pipe, and ornament the sides and edges of the baskets with this. Fill the centres with any nice fruit stewed in syrup. Cut six or eight strips of angelica on the slant, so as to form handles, and stick these on. Arrange the baskets on a pretty dish with fancy lace paper, and serve.

American Doughnuts

1 breakfastcupful new Milk.	1½ teaspoonfuls Cream of Tartar.
1 breakfastcupful Castor Sugar.	2 Eggs. 2 Nutmegs.
1½ teaspoonfuls Carbonate of Soda.	½ teaspoonful Salt.
Flour.	Frying Fat.

UTENSILS—Basin, grater, wooden spoon, teaspoon, breakfastcup, pastry board, stewpan, wire spoon, egg beater.

Beat the eggs well, add the sugar, the grated nutmegs, salt, carbonate of soda (freed from lumps), and cream of tartar, and mix. Add the milk, and beat all well together, then, by degrees, mix in enough flour to make a soft dough, and roll into balls the size of a small egg.

Have ready a stewpan of boiling lard, and when it is quite boiling (with the blue smoke coming from it) drop in the balls. Fry from 8 to 10 minutes, until they are a nice golden brown, then lift them out with a wire spoon or skimmer. Roll them, while they are hot, in sifted sugar, and serve either hot or cold. The lard can be used over and over again if properly strained.

Iced Petits Fours

6 oz. Flour.	4 oz. Butter.	½ lb. fresh Eggs.
½ lb. Castor Sugar.		1 Lemon. Flavourings.
1 small teaspoonful Baking Powder.		Icing, as described. Crystallised Fruits.

UTENSILS—4 basins, wooden spoon, teaspoon, tablespoon, sieve, egg-beater, knife, 2 sandwich tins, brush, pastry rack, plate, saucepan.

Separate the whites from the yolks of the eggs. Put the yolks into a basin with the castor sugar, and well beat together for 10 minutes. Rub the flour through a sieve, and just melt the butter, but do not oil it. Add this to the other ingredients, then stir in the flour. Whip the whites of the eggs to a stiff froth with a pinch of salt. then stir them into the mixture. Divide the mixture in half, flavour one half with a teaspoonful of finely chopped lemon peel, and the other with either almond or vanilla.

Brush two sandwich tins over with warm butter, and dust them over with flour. Put the mixtures into the tins, and bake in a moderate oven from 10 to 15 minutes. Turn them out on to a sieve to cool, and when cool, cut up into small, fancy shapes.

Take one pound of best icing sugar, and divide it into four parts. Add to each part two tablespoonfuls of liquid, a different liquid to each, so as to get four distinct icings. The liquids may be water with a few drops of essence, equal parts of rum and water, liqueur syrup and water, etc. ; and they may be coloured with a few drops of different colourings. Warm the icings thoroughly, and mix each one well. Stand one-fourth of the little cakes on a pastry rack over a dish, pour one of the icings over these, then ornament with crystallised fruit ; do another fourth with another icing, and so on. When the icings are set, put the cakes into small paper cases, arrange them on a fancy plate, and serve.

Raisin Girdle Cakes

1½ cupfuls Flour.
1 Egg.   1 cupful Milk.
½ cupful halved Raisins.

2 teaspoonfuls Baking Powder.
1 tablespoonful melted Butter.
½ teaspoonful Salt.

UTENSILS—Sieve, 2 basins, egg-beater, saucepan, wooden spoon, knife, measuring spoons, cup, girdle.

Sift all the dry ingredients into a basin. Stir in the slightly beaten egg mixed with the milk, and the melted butter. When well mixed, add the raisins, and cook in spoonfuls on a hot, greased girdle, turning the cakes when they are browned underneath.

Gingerbread

1¼ lb. Flour.   ¼ lb. Butter.
⅜ lb. Moist Sugar.
½ oz. Powdered Allspice.
1 lb. Treacle.   Milk.

¼ oz. Powdered Cinnamon.
1 oz. Candied Peel or Orange
   Peel, cut small.
½ oz. Ground Ginger.

UTENSILS—Basin, wooden spoon, cake tin, saucepan, pastry rack.

Rub the butter into the flour, add the other ingredients, and mix well. Make into a dough with the treacle and a little warm milk, put this into a buttered tin and bake in a moderate oven for ¾ to 1 hour.

NOTE.—Two eggs can be added to the ingredients if desired.

Scotch Christening Cake

1¼ lb. Flour.
¾ lb. Rice Flour.
8 oz. Castor Sugar.
6 oz. Butter.
¼ teaspoonful Baking Soda.

¾ lb. cleaned Currants.
¼ lb. minced Orange Peel.
¼ lb. cleaned Sultanas.
1 teaspoonful Essence of Lemon.
A little Milk.

UTENSILS—Two basins, wooden spoon, teaspoon, knife, egg-beater, cake tin.

Rub the butter into the flour. Stir in the sugar and baking soda until properly mixed, then add the fruit. Pour in the well-beaten eggs and enough milk to make the cake quite moist. Turn the mixture into a greased cake tin lined with two layers of buttered paper, and bake in a moderate oven for about 3 hours.

Shortbread

¾ lb. Flour. | ½ lb. Sugar. | ¼ lb. Butter.

UTENSILS—Basin, wooden spoon, pastry board, rolling pin, fancy cutters, baking sheet, pastry rack.

Beat the butter and sugar to a cream, then, by degrees, work in the flour. Turn this dough on to a lightly floured board, and roll it out to half an inch in thickness. Stamp out any fancy shapes, and, if liked, put a small piece of candied peel on top of each. Place the shortbreads on a greased baking sheet, and bake in a moderate oven. Do not let them get too brown—they should be quite pale when cooked.

Raisin Slab Cake

6 oz. Butter. 2 Eggs.	¼ teaspoonful Almond Essence.
6 oz. Castor Sugar.	½ teaspoonful Vanilla Essence.
½ lb. Flour. 5 oz. Raisins.	1 teaspoonful Baking Powder.
1 oz. Lemon Peel.	A little Milk.

UTENSILS—Basin, wooden spoon, teaspoon, knife, oblong baking tin, pastry rack.

Cream the butter and sugar together, then add the eggs and cream the mixture again. Stir in the essences, and then all the dry ingredients, and beat to a stiff batter. Spread in an oblong buttered baking tin, and bake for about 1 hour in a moderate oven. If desired, a few blanched almonds may be put on top before the cake is put in the oven.

Plum Cake

½ lb. Butter.	3 oz. Candied Peel.
¼ lb. Raisins.	3 oz. Almonds.
½ lb. Castor Sugar.	½ lb. Sultanas.
¾ lb. Flour. 4 Eggs.	1 teaspoonful Baking Powder.

UTENSILS—2 basins, wooden spoon, teaspoon, knife, egg-beater, cake tin, rack.

Cream the butter and sugar, then add the yolks of the eggs one by one, and beat for 10 minutes. Next, mix in three-fourths of the flour, also the stiffly frothed whites of eggs. Chop the peel and raisins. Mix the remainder of the flour, and a small teaspoonful of baking powder, with the fruit, and then stir this into the cake. Put the mixture into a well-buttered tin lined with buttered paper, and bake for 2 hours.

NOTE—The oven should be rather quick at first, but allowed to cool off towards the end.

Pikelets

1 Egg. 1½ cupfuls Flour.	½ teaspoonful Carbonate of Soda.
1 cupful Milk. 1 oz. Sugar.	1 teaspoonful Cream of Tartar.

UTENSILS—2 basins, egg-beater, wooden spoon, teaspoon, girdle or oven sheet, knife.

Put the flour into a basin, mix in nearly all the milk, then add a well-beaten egg and the sugar. Dissolve the soda in the remainder of the milk, and add this to the batter. Lastly, add the cream of tartar. Grease a girdle with mutton suet, or, failing a girdle, lay an oven sheet on top of the stove and grease it. Put the mixture on in spoonfuls. When well risen, turn them and cook on the other side. When cooked, butter them and serve either hot or cold.

Seed Cake

3 Eggs. ½ lb. Flour.	1 teaspoonful Baking Powder.
6 oz. Castor Sugar.	2 tablespoonfuls Milk.
6 oz. Butter.	2 teaspoonfuls Carraway Seeds.

UTENSILS—2 basins, wooden spoon, measuring spoons, egg-beater, cake tin, pastry rack or sieve.

Beat the butter and sugar in a basin till light and white, then add the eggs, well-beaten, and the milk. Mix the seeds and the baking powder with the flour, stir in the egg mixture, and pour into a greased tin lined with buttered paper. Bake till ready in a slow oven—for about 1½ hours.

Coffee Cake

5 cupfuls Flour. 1 Egg.	1 cupful Treacle.
2 cupfuls Currants (or 1½ cupfuls stoned and chopped Raisins).	1 cupful Brown Sugar.
	1 small cupful Lemon Peel.
2 cupfuls Sultanas.	2 cupfuls boiling Coffee.
1 cupful Butter.	2 teaspoonfuls Carbonate of Soda.
1 dessertspoonful Ginger.	

UTENSILS—Basin, wooden spoon, measuring spoons, cup, saucepan or coffee percolator, knife, cake tins, pastry rack.

Mix the butter with the flour, then add the fruit, egg, sugar, lemon peel, ginger and treacle. Mix the soda into the boiling coffee, then stir the coffee, still boiling, into the mixture. Stir quickly and thoroughly, pour into buttered tins, and bake in a quick oven for about 2 hours.

NOTE.—As this mixture rises very much, it is better only to half-fill the tins.

Cherry Cake

3 Eggs.	The weight of 4 Eggs in Flour.
The weight of 3 Eggs in Butter.	1 small teaspoonful Baking
The weight of 3 Eggs in Sugar.	Powder.

3 oz. Glacé Cherries.

UTENSILS—2 basins, wooden spoon, teaspoon, egg-beater, knife, cake tin, pastry rack.

Beat the butter and sugar to a cream, then add the eggs, well beaten. Next add the flour, then the cherries cut into slices, and lastly the baking powder. Beat all up together. Butter and flour a tin, put the mixture in, and bake in a moderate oven.

Christmas Cake

1¾ lb. Flour.	12 Eggs.	½ lb. Sultanas
1 lb. Butter.	1 lb. Sugar.	½ lb. Mixed Peel.
1 lb. Raisins.		½ lb. Glacé Cherries.
½ lb. Currants.		1 teaspoonful Baking Powder.

½ lb. ground Almonds.

UTENSILS—Knife, sieve, basin, plates, wooden spoon, teaspoon, pastry rack, utensils for icing.

Prepare all the ingredients before making the cake. Stone the raisins and chop them roughly, and rub the flour through a fine sieve, clean the currants and sultanas, and chop the cherries and peel. Beat the butter and sugar to a cream, and break in two eggs, and beat well. Put in a handful of flour, and beat again.

Continue so, until all the eggs and nearly all the flour are used up. Mix in the rest of the flour with the fruits and ground almonds and work all into a cake mixture, by degrees, beating it well. Lastly, add the baking powder. Well butter a tin, and line it with well-buttered papers. Dust it with equal parts of flour and sugar, then put the mixture in. Bake in a moderate oven for 3 to 4 hours.

Turn it out on to a pastry rack or sieve to cool. When cool, brush the cake over with white of egg slightly beaten. Spread a layer of almond paste on the top and sides, then put it to set. When set, spread over a thin coating of royal icing, and let this set. Lastly, ornament the cake with different coloured icings (from different forcing-bags), in any fancy designs, as described on page 20.

THE ROYAL ICING

White of 1 Egg.		½ lb. of Icing Sugar.

½ teaspoonful of Lemon Juice.

UTENSILS—Basin, sieve, wooden spoon.

Sift the icing sugar into a basin, and stir in the white of egg and lemon juice. Work all together with a wooden spoon, till quite smooth and white. To do it properly this will take about 15 minutes. If not wanted for use at once, cover it with a piece of paper just dipped in water.

Rock Cakes

1 lb. Flour.	6 oz. Butter.		½ lb. Moist Sugar.
2 Eggs.	¼ lb. Currants.		Essence of Lemon.

UTENSILS—3 basins, wooden spoon, egg-beater, baking sheet, pastry rack or wire sieve.

Put the flour into a basin, and rub the butter well into it, then mix in the sugar thoroughly. Well wash and dry the currants, then add these, and also add a few drops of essence of lemon. Beat two eggs well, stir them in, and mix all well together with a wooden spoon.

Drop the mixture in lumps on a buttered baking sheet, and bake in a moderate oven. If liked, seeds may be used instead of currants.

Scotch Jam Sandwich

6 oz. Flour.	1 gill Milk.		4 oz. Castor Sugar.
1 teaspoonful Baking Powder.			Jam. Pinch of Salt.
2 oz. Butter.	1 Egg.		Essence of Lemon.

UTENSILS—Two sandwich tins, teaspoon, sieve, 2 basins, wooden spoon, egg-beater, knife.

Measure out all the ingredients ready before beginning to mix any of them. Butter and flour two round shallow sandwich tins; sift the flour, baking powder and salt well together, dry, in a bowl; beat the sugar and butter to a cream; beat the egg separately, then add it to the sugar and butter; work into this the flour, and add the milk and lemon flavouring.

Pour this mixture at once into the two tins, half in each, put it into a hot oven, and bake for about 10 minutes. When done, turn the two out; spread jam on one, place the other on top, sift icing sugar over, and serve.

Rice Buns

4 oz. Butter.	2 Eggs.		4 oz. Castor Sugar.
4 oz. Ground Rice.	Milk.		2 lb. sifted Flour.

UTENSILS—2 basins, wooden spoon, sieve or flour sifter, egg-beater, baking sheet, pastry rack.

Beat the butter to a cream, add the sugar, and beat again. Now mix in slowly the ground rice, then the flour. Well beat the eggs, and mix them in, adding sufficient milk to make the whole into a stiff batter. Butter a clean baking sheet, and drop the mixture on in pieces the size of a walnut. Bake in a brisk oven until they are a nice golden colour.

Simnel Cake

½ lb. Butter.	¾ lb. Flour.		¼ cupful Milk.
½ lb. Sultanas.			¼ lb. Castor Sugar.
2 oz. Citron Peel.			1 teaspoonful Baking Powder.
2 oz. Cherries.			Almond Paste, as described.
6 Eggs.	¼ oz. Spice.		White Icing and Decorations.

UTENSILS—Knife, wooden spoon, teaspoon, 4 basins, cake tin, cup, sieve, rack.

Beat the butter and sugar to a cream. Add alternately the flour sifted with the spice, and one egg at a time. Then stir in the milk, picked sultanas, washed and dried currants, chopped cherries, and baking powder. Beat well for a moment, then pack into a greased tin lined with three folds of greased paper.

FOR THE ALMOND PASTE, mix 10 oz. of ground almonds with ¾ lb. castor sugar, vanilla and orange flower water to taste, and moisten to a soft paste with whites of eggs. Spread one-third of this paste over the uncooked cake mixture in the cake tin, fill in the remainder of the cake mixture, and bake from 2 to 2½ hours in a moderate oven.

When the cake is cooked, turn it out to cool, then decorate the top with a ring of almond paste. Ornament the paste with a fork or scissors, then brown it under a moderately hot grill, taking care not to scorch. When cold, run a layer of icing into the centre of the ring. Decorate with marzipan fruits, sugar eggs, or a chicken and nest, etc.

Birthday Cake

¾ lb. Flour. 4 Eggs.	½ lb. Castor Sugar.
½ lb. Butter.	1 oz. Preserved Ginger, or
2 oz. Candied Cherries.	Orange Peel.
¼ lb. Currants.	¼ lb. Sultanas.
1 oz. chopped Walnuts.	½ teaspoonful Baking Powder.

UTENSILS—Wooden spoon, knife, sieve, 3 basins, egg-beater, cake tin, rack.

Cream the butter and sugar in a basin. Sift the flour into another basin with the baking powder and a pinch of salt. Add the flour and the beaten eggs alternately, to the butter and sugar. Stir in lightly the halved cherries, cleaned currants and sultanas, chopped walnuts, and minced ginger or peel, dusted with a little of the flour, and add a little milk if necessary. If you want a more economical recipe, you can use only 2 eggs in the mixture, and make up the liquid with milk, but in that case, use 1½ teaspoonfuls of baking powder.

Pour the mixture into a greased cake tin lined with two layers of buttered paper. Bake about 2 to 2½ hours till ready. When cold, cover with royal or plain icing, and decorate with candles and glacé cherries or halved walnuts, and pieces of crystallised fruits.

Blitz Torte

¼ cupful Butter.	1 teaspoonful Vanilla.
1 cupful Flour.	¼ cupful Milk. 4 Eggs.
½ cupful Castor Sugar.	Pinch of Salt.
2 teaspoonfuls Baking Powder.	Custard Filling, as described.

UTENSILS—Four basins, wooden spoon, teaspoon, cup, egg-beater, 2 shallow baking tins, saucepan, double boiler, knife.

Cream the butter and sugar. Add the egg yolks and vanilla. Mix the flour and baking powder together, and add to them the first mixture, alternately with the milk. Spread in two shallow buttered baking tins.

Cover the mixture with the whites of 4 eggs, stiffly frothed, mixed with ¾ cupful of sugar, and sprinkle ¼ cupful of blanched sliced almonds all over. Bake in a moderate oven for about ½ hour, and spread custard filling between the layers.

THE CUSTARD FILLING

½ cupful Sugar.	1 Egg. Salt.
1 tablespoonful Flour.	1 cupful Milk or Cream.
½ teaspoonful Vanilla.	

Mix the dry ingredients, add the egg, slightly beaten, and pour on the scalded milk or cream gradually. Cook in a double boiler, stirring constantly till thick. Cool, then add vanilla or lemon essence to taste.

Ribbon Cake

½ cupful Butter. 4 Yolks of Eggs.	½ teaspoonful Mace.
4 Whites of Eggs.	⅙ teaspoonful Cinnamon.
3½ cupfuls Flour.	¼ teaspoonful Nutmeg.
2 cupfuls Sugar.	1 cupful Milk.
⅓ cupful Raisins.	⅓ cupful Figs.
1 tablespoonful Treacle.	5 teaspoonfuls Baking Powder.

UTENSILS—Three basins, egg-beater, wooden spoon, measuring spoons, cup, knife, sieve, 3 layer cake tins, rack.

Cream the butter and sugar. Add the yolks of eggs, beaten and mixed with the milk. Sift in the flour and baking powder, and lastly add the stiffly beaten whites of eggs. Put two-thirds of this mixture in two layer cake tins. Add to the remainder of the mixture the mace, cinnamon, nutmeg, raisins and treacle. Bake the three mixtures in the oven for 30 minutes. When ready, put the layers together with apple jelly, placing the dark layer in the centre.

Marble Cake

LIGHT PART

6 oz. Sugar.	¼ lb. Butter.
½ lb. Flour.	4 Whites of Egg.
Pinch of Salt.	1 gill Buttermilk.
1 teaspoonful Baking Powder.	6 drops Essence of Lemon.

UTENSILS—Three basins, wooden spoon, teaspoon, grater, egg-beater, gill measure, cake tin, rack.

Cream the butter and sugar in a basin. Add half the flour and salt, stir in the whites of egg, well beaten, then the remainder of the flour and baking powder and the essence of lemon. Mix with the buttermilk.

DARK PART

4 oz. Dark Sugar.	2 oz. Butter.
6 oz. Flour.	2 oz. grated Chocolate.
4 Yolks of Eggs.	1 teaspoonful Vanilla.
1 teaspoonful Baking Powder.	1 gill Buttermilk.

Beat the butter, sugar and eggs in a basin till light. Add the flour and milk gradually. Beat till smooth, then add the chocolate, vanilla essence and baking powder. Butter a cake tin and line it with greased paper. Put in alternate layers of light and dark mixture till both are used up. Bake in a moderate oven.

This cake can be cut in three crosswise, and then the layers can be put together with fillings in the following order : first, apricot jam ; second, almond paste ; third, raspberry jam. Confectioner's custard can be substituted for the almond paste.

Chocolate Cream Cake

4 Yolks of Eggs.	3 Whites of Eggs.
2½ cupfuls Flour.	1 cupful thick, Sour Cream.
1 teaspoonful Baking Soda.	1¼ cupfuls Castor Sugar.
Pinch of Salt.	2 oz. Chocolate.

1 teaspoonful Vanilla Essence.

UTENSILS—Saucepan, 3 basins, egg-beater, wooden spoon, teaspoon, cup, sieve, 2 shallow layer cake tins, rack.

Beat the sugar and yolks of eggs till very light. Melt the chocolate in part of the cream over the fire. Cool, then add it to the remainder of the cream. Sift the soda with the flour and salt, and add it alternately with the cream to the yolks and sugar. Flavour with the vanilla essence, then fold in the stiffly frothed whites of eggs. Bake in two square, shallow, buttered layer tins. When cold, put the halves together with American frosting.

Lemon Layer Cake

2¼ cupfuls sifted Flour.	¾ cupful Castor Sugar.
1 Egg. 1 cupful Milk.	½ teaspoonful Salt.
¼ cupful melted Butter.	1 teaspoonful Vanilla Essence.
4 teaspoonfuls Baking Powder.	Lemon Cheese.

UTENSILS—Two basins, egg-beater, wooden spoon, teaspoon, cup, sieve, 2 layer cake tins, rack.

Add the sugar to the well-beaten egg, then stir in alternately the milk, and flour sifted with the baking powder and salt. Add the melted butter and vanilla. Beat well. Bake in two buttered layer cake tins in a moderately quick oven for about ½ hour until quite firm and light. When cold, put the layers together with lemon cheese.

Fudge Layer Cake

1¾ cupfuls Flour.	½ cupful Butter.
2 Yolks of Eggs.	1 cupful Castor Sugar.
½ cupful Milk.	2 Whites of Eggs.
3 teaspoonfuls Baking Powder.	1 teaspoonful Ground Cinnamon.

UTENSILS—Four basins, egg-beater, wooden spoon, tea-spoon, cup, sieve, 2 layer cake tins, cake rack.

Beat the butter and sugar to a cream. Sift the flour, baking powder and cinnamon together. Beat the egg yolks, and stir the milk into them. Add the egg and milk and the flour alternately to the butter and sugar. When all are stirred in, lightly fold in the stiffly frothed whites of eggs. Bake in two well-buttered layer cake tins. Cool on a cake rack, then put together and ice on top with fudge frosting (see page 435).

Caramel Layer Cake

2 tablespoonfuls Butter.	2 teaspoonfuls Baking Powder.
1 cupful Castor Sugar.	½ teaspoonful Vanilla.
1 Egg. ¾ cupful Water.	Grated Rind of ½ Lemon.
2 cupfuls Flour.	Jam, Cocoanut and Filling.

UTENSILS—Three basins, egg-beater, wooden spoon, tea-spoon, cup, grater, sieve, tablespoon, 2 layer cake tins, rack.

Cream the butter and sugar. Stir in about 1 tablespoonful of the water, then add the beaten egg and beat well. Let the mixture stand while you sift the flour and baking powder three times. Stir in the flour and the remainder of the water, then beat the mixture thoroughly. Bake in two buttered layer cake tins for about 15 to 20 minutes. When cold, put together with chocolate nut filling, sprinkle the top of the cake with apricot jam, and sprinkle over with desiccated cocoanut.

THE CHOCOLATE NUT FILLING

¾ cupful Brown Sugar.	½ cupful Milk.
3 tablespoonfuls Cream.	1 oz. grated Chocolate.
¼ cupful Butter.	½ cupful chopped Walnuts.

UTENSILS—Saucepan, wooden spoon, tablespoon, cup, knife, grater, basin.

Put the butter, cream, milk and sugar into a saucepan and bring to the boil. Stir till thick, then remove the pan from the fire and stir till cool. Add the chocolate, melted in 1 dessertspoonful of hot water, and the nuts.

George Washington Pie

3 cupfuls Flour.	6 Eggs.
4 teaspoonfuls Milk.	2 cupfuls Castor Sugar.
1 level teaspoonful Baking Soda.	2 teaspoonfuls Cream of Tartar.

UTENSILS—Three basins, wooden spoon, teaspoon, cup, sieve, egg-beater, 2 layer cake tins, cake rack.

Beat the yolks till they are honey coloured. Sift the flour three times with the cream of tartar, then sift it with the castor sugar. Beat this lightly into the egg yolks. Add the stiffly frothed whites, then the soda dissolved in the milk. Bake in buttered layer cake tins till firm and golden, in a quick oven. Cool on a cake rack, and fill with strawberry jam or mocha cream.

TO MAKE THE MOCHA CREAM

6 oz. Fresh Butter.	¼ lb. Icing Sugar.
4 Yolks of Eggs.	1 tablespoonful Coffee Essence.

1 heaped teaspoonful Almonds.

Cream the butter and sugar together. Beat in the egg yolks, one by one, and when thoroughly mixed, add, drop by drop, the coffee essence and the almonds, blanched, roasted and finely chopped. Allow the filling to harden in a cool place.

Uncle Tom's Layer Cake

2 Eggs. 2½ cupfuls Flour.	1 cupful Treacle.
2 tablespoonfuls Butter.	1 teaspoonful Ground Cinnamon.
1 cupful Castor Sugar.	1 teaspoonful Baking Soda.
1 cupful Sour Milk.	1 small teaspoonful Ground Cloves.

UTENSILS—Sieve, 4 basins, egg-beater, wooden spoon, measuring spoons, cup, 2 layer cake tins, cake rack, knife.

Sift the flour and spices into a basin. Cream the butter and sugar, stir in the slightly beaten eggs, and the treacle, then the flour and milk alternately, after dissolving the soda in the milk. Bake in two buttered layer cake tins in a moderate oven until firm—usually from 30 to 45 minutes. Cool on a cake rack, then put the halves together with butter icing. Spread the top with a very thin layer of sifted icing sugar, moistened with tepid water and flavoured with rum.

Mahogany Layer Cake

⅓ cupful Butter.	¼ teaspoonful Salt.
2 Eggs. 1 cupful Milk.	1 teaspoonful Nutmeg.
1¼ cupfuls Sugar.	4 teaspoonfuls Baking Powder.
2½ cupfuls Flour.	1 tablespoonful Cocoa.
1 teaspoonful Cinnamon.	1 tablespoonful cold Water.

UTENSILS—Three basins, egg-beater, wooden spoon, measuring spoons, cup, sieve, 3 layer cake tins, cake rack.

Cream the butter, add the sugar gradually, and the well-beaten eggs. Mix thoroughly. Sift the flour, salt, baking powder and spices together, then add a little to the liquid mixture. Add the milk, a little at a time, then the remainder of the dry ingredients.

Bake two-thirds of the mixture in two greased and floured layer cake tins. To the remaining third, add 1 tablespoonful of cocoa mixed with 1 tablespoonful of water. Use this for the middle layer. Bake the three layers in a moderate oven from 15 to 20 minutes. Cool and cover the sides and top, and between the layers, with chocolate butter icing.

Marshmallow Layer Cake

1 cupful Butter.	2 teaspoonfuls Lemon Juice.
3 Eggs. 1 cupful Milk.	Grated Rind of ½ Lemon.
3½ cupfuls Flour.	½ teaspoonful Salt.
2 cupfuls Castor Sugar.	3 teaspoonfuls Baking Powder.

UTENSILS—Three basins, wooden spoon, teaspoon, cup, sieve, grater, egg-beater, lemon squeezer, 3 layer cake tins, cake rack, knife.

Beat the butter and sugar till light. Add the eggs, thoroughly beaten, then the milk, lemon rind and juice. Sift the flour, salt and baking powder together, and add to the mixture. Divide into three portions, and put into three buttered layer cake tins. Bake in a moderate oven for about 25 minutes.

When cold, spread two layers with white icing, and embed in the icing quartered or halved marshmallows. Put the cakes together and sift icing sugar over the top, or put the layers together with marshmallow cream and dust with grated shelled walnuts.

Spiced Layer Cake

1½ cupfuls Castor Sugar.	¾ cupful Coffee.
¾ cupful Butter. 3 Eggs.	1 teaspoonful Vanilla.
3 cupfuls sifted Flour.	1½ teaspoonfuls Cinnamon.
3 teaspoonfuls Baking Powder.	¼ teaspoonful Nutmeg.
¼ teaspoonful Cloves.	1 teaspoonful Salt.

UTENSILS—Two basins, wooden spoon, teaspoon, cup, sieve, 2 layer cake tins, cake rack.

Cream the butter and sugar together and add the eggs, one at a time, then beat well. Mix the dry ingredients together and sift them, then stir them into the liquid mixture. Add the vanilla. Pour into two buttered layer cake tins. Bake in a moderate oven, and when cooked turn out on to a cake rack to cool. When cold, put the layers together and ice with vanilla icing.

Chocolate Nougat Cake

¼ cupful Butter.
1 Egg. 1 cupful Milk.
3 teaspoonfuls Baking Powder.
½ teaspoonful Vanilla.
½ lb. Flour.

1½ cupfuls Castor Sugar.
⅓ cupful Castor Sugar.
2 oz. melted Chocolate.
⅔ cupful Almonds, blanched and shredded.

UTENSILS—Saucepan, 2 basins, wooden spoon, teaspoon, cup, sieve, knife, round layer cake tins, cake rack.

Cream the butter, add 1½ cupfuls of sugar gradually, then the egg, unbeaten. When well mixed, add two-thirds of the milk, and the flour, sifted with the baking powder, then the vanilla essence. Stir in the melted chocolate and the remainder of the sugar, then place on the fire. Add the remainder of the milk by degrees and cook, stirring constantly, till smooth. Cool slightly, then add to the cake mixture. Bake for from 15 to 20 minutes in round, buttered layer cake tins. When ready, turn out, lay on a cake rack to cool, then put together with butter icing.

Valentine Layer Cakes

¾ cupful Butter.
4 Eggs. 1 cupful Milk.
3 cupfuls of Flour.
2 cupfuls Castor Sugar.

¼ lb. grated Chocolate.
½ teaspoonful Ground Cloves.
1 teaspoonful Cinnamon.
½ teaspoonful Vanilla Essence.

4 teaspoonfuls Baking Powder.

UTENSILS—Two basins, wooden spoon, teaspoon, cup, grater, sieve, baking tins, heart-shaped cutter, knife, rack.

Beat the butter to a cream, add the sugar, beat well, then add the eggs, one at a time. Sift the baking powder and spices with the flour, and add these alternately with the milk to the butter and sugar. Stir lightly till smooth, then add the grated chocolate and vanilla essence. Turn into buttered baking tins and bake till firm but not dried up. Cool on a cake rack. Cut into hearts with a heart-shaped cutter. Split in two and fill with walnut filling.

Frost the tops with icing sugar, sifted and mixed with 1 tablespoonful of boiling water, the grated rind of ½ lemon, and flavoured to taste with strained lemon juice. Garnish with a glacé cherry or a strip of angelica cut to form an arrow.

THE WALNUT FILLING

¼ lb. minced Walnuts.	¼ cupful Castor Sugar.
⅜ cupful Milk.	1 Yolk of Egg.
½ teaspoonful Vanilla.	

UTENSILS—Double boiler, wooden spoon, cup, knife, teaspoon.

Mix the egg and sugar in a double boiler, add the milk, and stir over boiling water till the mixture thickens. Add the vanilla and finely chopped nuts, and spread between the hearts.

Scotch Lawn Tennis Cake

6 oz. Flour.	2 oz. Cornflour.
5 oz. Sugar.	4 oz. Sultanas.
4 Eggs. 4 oz. Butter.	2 oz. Candied Peel.
3 oz. Glacé Cherries.	1 teaspoonful Baking Powder.

UTENSILS—Two basins, wooden spoon, teaspoon, egg-beater, knife, 2 layer cake tins, skewer, cake rack.

Cream the butter, add the sugar, then the flour, gradually moistening with yolks and stiffly beaten egg whites. Stir in the cornflour, and lastly add the fruit. The cherries should be halved and the sultanas well dried, and the peel should be finely minced.

Pour the mixture into two well-buttered layer cake tins and bake in a hot oven for about 10 minutes, then cook slowly till done. Try with a skewer, and as soon as it leaves the sides of the tin clean, remove from the oven. When the cake is cool, put the layers together with almond paste, and sprinkle the top with castor sugar.

Canadian Layer Cake

1½ cupfuls sifted Flour.	1 cupful Castor Sugar.
½ cupful Butter.	1 teaspoonful Vanilla Essence.
2 Eggs. ½ cupful Milk.	¼ teaspoonful Salt.
2 teaspoonfuls Baking Powder.	

UTENSILS—Three basins, wooden spoon, egg-beater, sieve, teaspoon, cup, 2 layer cake tins, cake rack, knife.

Beat the butter to a cream. Add the sugar gradually. Beat the eggs well, and stir them into the mixture, then add the vanilla, and the milk alternately with a little of the flour sifted with the baking powder and salt, till all the dry mixture is combined with the moist. Give one quick, short beat.

Turn the mixture into two buttered layer cake tins, and bake in a quick oven from 25 to 30 minutes. When cold, put the layers together with jam, and sprinkle the top with icing sugar, or spread lightly with jam and sprinkle with desiccated cocoanut or shredded walnuts.

Chocolate Iced Cake

2½ cupfuls sifted Flour.
2 Eggs. ½ cupful Butter.
½ cupful grated Sweet Chocolate.
½ cupful cold Water.
3 tablespoonfuls Castor Sugar.

1½ cupfuls Brown Sugar.
¼ teaspoonful Salt.
1 teaspoonful Vanilla Essence.
⅔ cupful Milk.
2 teaspoonfuls Baking Powder.

UTENSILS—Saucepan, wooden spoon, measuring spoons, cup, grater, sieve, egg-beater, 2 basins, 2 sandwich tins, cake rack, knife.

Put the chocolate, castor sugar and water in a saucepan. Bring to the boil. Beat the brown sugar and butter together. Stir in the eggs, well beaten, and when the cooked mixture is cool add it, with the vanilla and milk, and beat thoroughly. Sift the flour, salt and baking powder together and add to the other mixture. Beat hard, then turn into two large buttered sandwich tins. Bake for about 30 minutes in a moderate oven.

When cold, put the layers together with vanilla ice cream, and cover with whipped sweetened cream and chopped nuts. Serve with forks.

ICINGS FOR CAKES

Almond Paste (Marzipan)

1½ lb. Ground Almonds.
½ lb. Castor Sugar.
1½ lb. Icing Sugar.
About 5 Whites of Eggs.
½ teaspoonful Orange-flower Water.

¼ teaspoonful Orange Essence.
¼ teaspoonful Rose Essence.
3 drops Almond Essence.
1½ tablespoonfuls Lemon Juice.
¾ teaspoonful Vanilla Essence.
¼ teaspoonful Violet Essence.

UTENSILS—Sieve, 2 basins, egg-beater, teaspoon, lemon squeezer.

Sift the sugars into a basin. Add the ground almonds, lemon juice and almond essence. Flavour to taste with the essences. Knead well with the hands, adding only sufficient beaten egg to moisten. Both yolks and whites, or whites or yolks only, can be used, according to whether the icing is liked white, pale yellow, or dark yellow. Knead until the icing is free from cracks, then use as required.

American Frosting

¾ cupful Castor Sugar. | 1 teaspoonful Pineapple Essence.
1 White of Egg. | ½ cupful Water.

UTENSILS—Saucepan, wooden spoon, teaspoon, cup, basin, egg-beater.

Stir the sugar and water in a saucepan over the fire till dissolved. Cook for 10 minutes, counting from the time that the icing begins to bubble. Add a pinch of salt to the egg white, and beat till stiff and quite dry, then pour the bubbling syrup into the beaten egg. Continue beating for a few minutes, then spread between and on top of the cake.

Caramel Icing

cupful Castor Sugar. | 1½ cupfuls Brown Sugar.
tablespoonful Butter. | 1 cupful Milk.

UTENSILS—Saucepan, wooden spoon, tablespoon, cup.

Boil the brown sugar, castor sugar, and milk together until the syrup is sufficiently thick to form a soft ball when tested in cold water. Add the butter and remove the pan from the fire. Cool till the mixture is lukewarm. Now beat thoroughly until thick and creamy, and the right consistency to spread. Put a layer of the icing between the cake and cover the top and sides also. Decorate with halved walnuts and crystallised violets.

Fudge Frosting

1½ cupfuls Castor Sugar. | ½ cupful Milk.
1 teaspoonful Butter. | ½ teaspoonful Vanilla.
1½ oz. Chocolate. | Pinch of Ground Cinnamon.

UTENSILS—Saucepan, wooden spoon, teaspoon, cup.

Melt the butter in a saucepan. Add the sugar and milk, and stir to make certain that the sugar does not adhere to the saucepan. Add the chocolate and cinnamon, after heating to boiling point, and boil without stirring for 13 minutes. Remove the pan from the fire. Beat the icing till it is of the right consistency, add the vanilla, and use at once. The cake can be decorated with mocha icing or with halved walnuts.

Orange Frosting

1 Yolk of Egg. Icing Sugar. Grated Rind of 1 Orange.	1 teaspoonful Lemon Juice. 1 tablespoonful Orange Juice.

UTENSILS—Basin, lemon squeezer, strainer, grater, measuring spoons, kitchen spoon.

Mix all ingredients except the sugar together. Stand the mixture for 1 hour, then strain, and add sugar till the frosting is thick enough to spread. Use.

Plain Icing

1 cupful Icing Sugar. 2 tablespoonfuls boiling Milk or Water.	¼ teaspoonful Vanilla, Lemon, or other Essence, or 1 tea- spoonful Lemon Juice.

UTENSILS—Saucepan, basin, sifter, wooden spoon, measuring spoons, cup.

If the cake is cold, heat the liquid. Stir the liquid into the sifted sugar, adding more liquid, a few drops at a time, if needed. A little lemon juice added to any other fruit juice gives icings a better flavour. Icing is the proper consistency for using when it coats the spoon.

Uncooked Butter Icing

1 cupful Confectioner's Sugar. 2 tablespoonfuls Milk.	2 tablespoonfuls Butter. ½ teaspoonful Vanilla.

UTENSILS—Basin, cup, measuring spoons, wooden spoon.

Beat the butter and sugar to a cream. Flavour with vanilla essence. CHOCOLATE BUTTER ICING needs only the addition of 1 oz. of chocolate, melted over boiling water, and COFFEE BUTTER ICING the addition of 2 tablespoonfuls of strong coffee and 1 teaspoonful of dry cocoa.

Vanilla Icing

1 cupful Castor Sugar. 1 White of Egg.	⅛ teaspoonful Salt. ½ teaspoonful Vanilla.
4 tablespoonfuls cold Water.	

UTENSILS—Double boiler, wooden spoon, measuring spoons, cup.

Put the sugar, water and unbeaten egg white into the upper part of a double boiler. Have boiling water in the lower part. Begin to beat the mixture at once, and continue while it cooks for 7 or 8 minutes. It should be thick enough to spread.   Remove the mixture from the fire and continue beating for about 5 minutes, or until it has thickened.   If the icing is not cooked enough, return it to the double boiler and re-cook for a short time.   If it is too stiff, add a small quantity of water and cook again.   This is sufficient to ice a three-layer cake on the tops.

BREAD AND ROLLS

Loaf Bread

8½ lb. Flour.   1 oz. Yeast. | 1 teaspoonful Salt.
1½ pints tepid Water. | 1 teaspoonful Sugar.

UTENSILS—Two basins, wooden spoon, teaspoon, knife, cloth, sieve, pint measure, 3 loaf tins.

Sift the flour and salt into a warm bowl.   Work before the fire until the chill is off.   Make a well in the centre.   Cream the yeast and sugar together, and add the tepid water, then pour this mixture into the well in the flour.   Work enough flour into the well from the outside to form a batter, then sprinkle flour on top, cover with a cloth and set in a warm place for 20 minutes, when it should be covered with bubbles and be quite spongy.

Now mix in the remainder of the flour, knead well with the hands, and, if required, add more tepid water.   The mixture should be stiff enough to leave the bowl and the hands clean.   Turn up the smooth side, make two cuts across it, and set it to rise again, this time for at least 1½ hours. Divide it into three pieces and knead each well.   Put these into buttered tins and set again for ½ hour, or till double the size.   Put into the hot part of an oven for 15 minutes, then in a cooler part till ready.

Dinner Rolls

2 lb. Flour.   1 oz. Yeast. | ¼ pint tepid Milk and Water,
1 small dessertspoonful Salt. | mixed.
                   1 teaspoonful Sugar.

UTENSILS—Two basins, wooden spoon, measuring spoons, pint measure, cloth, knife, baking sheet, brush, pastry board.

Put the flour and salt in a basin.   Beat the yeast and sugar to a cream, then add half the milk and water to the yeast.   Make a hole in the centre of the flour and mix in the

yeast. Stir in enough flour to make a stiff batter and sprinkle
a little over the top. Cover with a clean cloth, put in a warm
place for 10 minutes to sponge, then stir in all the flour from
the sides, and add the remainder of the milk and water.
Knead well, cut across the top, and set to rise for 1 hour.

Divide the dough into equal portions and knead up into
small rolls. This quantity will make about 2½ dozen rolls.
Place them on a slightly floured tin, and set to rise for
15 minutes. Bake in a quick oven for 15 minutes, and just
before they are done brush with a little milk or beaten egg.

Brown Bread

12 oz. Wheaten Flour.	1 Yeast Cake.
14 oz. White Flour.	1 tablespoonful Butter.
2 tablespoonfuls Brown Sugar.	5 gills Milk or Water.

UTENSILS—Saucepan, 2 basins, tablespoon, wooden spoon,
cup, sieve, knife, pastry board, gill measure, loaf tins.

Dissolve the yeast in ¼ cupful of the milk or water, heated
till tepid. Bring the remainder of the liquid to the boiling
point and add the salt, sugar, and melted butter. Cool, then
add the yeast. Sift the flours into a basin, make a hole in the
centre and pour in the liquid to make a dough that can be
handled. Mix thoroughly, and knead on a floured board
until it is smooth. Stand in a warm place to rise until it is
fully twice its original size, then divide into suitable pieces
and knead. Place in greased tins and stand again to rise.
Bake in a moderately hot oven for 50 to 60 minutes.

Brown Muffins

¼ lb. Wholemeal Flour.	1 tablespoonful Castor Sugar.
¼ lb. White Flour.	2 tablespoonfuls Butter.
1 Egg. ½ pint Milk.	½ teaspoonful Salt.
3 teaspoonfuls Baking Powder.	

UTENSILS—Two basins, egg-beater, measuring spoons,
wooden spoon, sieve, saucepan, 12 muffin tins.

Beat the egg until light, and add the milk. Sift the flours
together, add the salt and sugar, and stir into the egg
mixture. Blend thoroughly, then stir in the melted butter.
Place in buttered muffin tins, and bake in a hot oven—400
degrees Fahr.—for 20 to 25 minutes. This quantity is
enough to make 12 muffins.

Rye Bread

¾ cupful Cornmeal.	1 tablespoonful Sugar.
6 cupfuls Rye Flour.	½ cupful tepid Water.
2 cupfuls Wheaten Flour.	3 cupfuls boiling Water.
2 cupfuls mashed Potatoes.	2 tablespoonfuls Butter.
1 cake of Yeast.	½ tablespoonful Salt.

UTENSILS—Saucepan, 2 basins, wooden spoon, tablespoon, cup, knife, potato masher, cloth, pastry board, bread tins.

Pour boiling water over the cornmeal, stir till smooth, and cook, stirring constantly, for about 2 minutes, till mushy. Add the sugar, salt and butter, then stand the mush till lukewarm. Add the potatoes, the yeast dissolved in the lukewarm water, then the rye and wheaten flour. Mix and knead to a stiff, smooth dough, using ordinary flour to mould with.

Cover, stand in a warm place till the dough is double its size, then shape into three or four loaves, and place in buttered bread tins. When the dough has risen to the top of the tins, bake for 1 hour or more in a moderate oven. Cross cuts should be made with a knife on each loaf before baking.

Buttermilk Loaf

4 cupfuls Flour.	½ teaspoonful Salt.
1 beaten Egg.	1 teaspoonful Sugar.
1½ cupfuls Buttermilk.	2 teaspoonfuls Cream of Tartar.
1 teaspoonful Baking Soda.	

UTENSILS—Sieve, 2 basins, egg-beater, cup, teaspoon, wooden spoon, loaf tin.

Sift the flour, salt, soda and cream of tartar together into a basin. Stir in the beaten egg mixed with half the milk. Add the remainder of the milk, and mix well. Place in a well-buttered loaf tin and bake in a moderate oven for 35 minutes.

You can make brown bread loaf with buttermilk too, using half this quantity of flour and the other half wheaten meal. To enrich it, rub a tablespoonful of butter into the flour before mixing.

Coffee Bread

Flour to make Batter.	¼ cupful Castor Sugar.
3 tablespoonfuls Flour.	⅓ cupful Castor Sugar.
1 cupful hot Milk.	1 Egg. ⅓ Yeast Cake.
½ cupful tepid Milk.	½ teaspoonful Salt.
3 tablespoonfuls Butter.	1 teaspoonful Ground Cinnamon.
¼ cupful Butter.	½ cupful Raisins.

UTENSILS—Saucepan, 3 basins, egg-beater, wooden spoon, measuring spoons, cup, knife, brush, baking tins.

Bring the cupful of milk almost to the boil, add ⅓ cupful of butter, ¼ cupful of castor sugar, and the salt. When luke-warm, add the yeast dissolved in the tepid milk, the well-beaten egg, and enough flour to make a stiff batter, then the raisins, stoned and roughly chopped. Cover, and let rise overnight.

In the morning spread buttered baking tins with the mixture, ½ inch thick. Cover, and allow to rise again. When quite light, brush over with beaten egg, and cover with the following mixture : Melt 3 tablespoonfuls butter, add the ⅓ cupful castor sugar, the cinnamon, and, when the sugar is partly melted, the flour. If you heat the flour slightly first, the bread will be all the better.

In baking bread, allow the heat of the oven to increase slightly during the first 20 minutes, and gradually to decrease for the last 20 minutes. Store when cold in a dry box with a tightly fitting lid, and in a dry cupboard.

Prairie Bun Loaf

1½ pints Flour.	1 heaped tablespoonful Butter.
5 Yolks of Eggs.	2 tablespoonfuls Castor Sugar.
1 cupful Sour Milk.	1 teaspoonful Baking Powder.
½ teaspoonful Salt.	

UTENSILS—Two basins, sieve, egg-beater, wooden spoon, measuring spoons, cup, loaf tin.

Sift the baking powder, flour and salt together. Rub in the butter with the tips of the fingers, add the sugar, sour milk, and the beaten egg yolks. If you have some cream to spare, use fewer egg yolks, or less milk if you want a rich loaf. Mix all, and bake in a lightly greased tin in a moderate oven.

Southern Corn Bread

2 cupfuls Cornmeal.	2 tablespoonfuls Butter.
2 Eggs. 2 cupfuls Milk.	½ teaspoonful Salt.
3 teaspoonfuls Baking Powder.	

UTENSILS—Sieve, saucepan, 3 basins, egg-beater, deep loaf tin, cup, measuring spoons, wooden spoon.

Sift the cornmeal, salt and baking powder into a basin. Scald the milk and add the butter, and when the butter is melted, add the milk and butter, mixed with the beaten egg

FOR SUMMER TIME—Ice cream forms the basis of a variety of dainty sweets, and can be served with petits fours, which are easily made at home (p. 419).

How to prepare dinner rolls—The dough can be kneaded up into a variety of shapes after it has risen, or simply cut into rounds (p. 437).

yolks, to the cornmeal. Fold in the stiffly frothed whites of eggs, and bake in a deep, buttered loaf tin for about ½ hour.

To vary the recipe, half cornmeal and half flour can be used ; or ½ tablespoonful more butter and only one egg.

Breakfast Loaf

1 lb. Flour.	½ pint hot Milk.
1 tablespoonful Butter.	2½ teaspoonfuls Baking Powder.
1 teaspoonful Salt.	

UTENSILS—Sieve, saucepan, basin, wooden spoon, measuring spoons, pint measure, pastry board, baking tin.

Sift the flour, salt and baking powder into a basin. Dissolve the butter in the hot milk, stir this into the dry ingredients, and quickly make into a soft dough. Knead for a moment on a lightly floured board. Take a small piece from the dough to form the top. With floured hands lightly shape the bulk of the dough into a flattish cake. Place on a greased tin, flatten the small piece of dough in a round on the top, and bake in a hot oven for about ¾ hour, until the loaf is golden, and ready in the centre. The more quickly and lightly the loaf is mixed, the better it will be.

Milk Bread

4½ lb. best Flour.	1 oz. Yeast. 1 oz. Salt.
1 oz. Margarine or Lard.	1 quart Milk or Milk and Water.

UTENSILS—2 basins, wooden spoon, pint measure, loaf tins.

Put the flour in a bowl, then rub the margarine into it. Take a little of the milk and water, just warm, and dissolve the yeast in it. Take the remainder of the milk and water, which should be at about 110 degrees Fah., add the salt to it, and the dissolved yeast, then add it to the flour and margarine, and make into a firm dough.

Knead well, leave for 1 hour, and knead well again. Leave for another 20 minutes, break into six parts, shape according to your tins, leave in the tins for another 35 minutes, then bake in a hot oven for 45 minutes.

Spoon Bread

3 tablespoonfuls Cornmeal.	½ teaspoonful Salt.
1 cupful Milk. 1 Egg.	1 teaspoonful Baking Powder.

UTENSILS—Basin, egg-beater, wooden spoon, measuring spoons, cup, baking tin.

C.I.O.   P

Beat the egg, add the milk, stir in the cornmeal and salt, and, lastly, add the baking powder. Bake in a moderate oven for about 25 minutes—like a custard. This is delicious and nourishing, and a great change from toast and rolls for breakfast or dinner.

Carievale Nut Bread

4 cupfuls Flour. 1 Egg.
1 cupful Castor Sugar.
1 large tablespoonful Butter.
½ lb. chopped Walnuts.

1 teaspoonful Salt.
1 level tablespoonful Baking Powder.

UTENSILS—3 basins, sieve or flour sifter, wooden spoon, measuring spoons, cup, egg-beater, knife, loaf tin.

Sieve the flour, baking powder and salt into a basin. Cream the butter and sugar together. Add the egg, well beaten, to the milk, then stir the egg and milk alternately with the sifted flour, into the butter and sugar. Add the walnuts, and beat well to a stiff batter.

Turn the mixture into a well-buttered loaf tin, stand it in a warm place for 20 minutes until the loaf has risen half as high again, then bake from 30 to 45 minutes until cooked.

SANDWICHES AND POTTED MEATS

Do not be content with using only white bread and bridge rolls for sandwiches. Use as well brown bread, unsweetened cheese biscuits and crisp rye and wheat bread. Bread should not be more than thirty-six hours old. Cream the butter before using, but on no account let it oil.

Afternoon tea sandwiches should be cut into dainty shapes ; for luncheons and picnics, sandwiches can be simply cut into oblongs. Sponge drops and sponge fingers can also be used for afternoon tea sandwiches, and rounds of cooked flaky pastry, with sweet fillings such as strawberry jam and lemon cheese. Decorate savoury sandwiches with mustard and cress, or with watercress, or with nasturtium flowers and leaves, and decorate sweet sandwiches with maidenhair fern.

Write the names of the varieties on sandwich flags, and plant a flag in each plate of sandwiches. The plate should be lined with a lace paper d'oyley.

UTENSILS FOR SANDWICH MAKING

Stainless saw-edged bread knife.	Saucepan
Bread board	Basin
Chopping knife and board	Plate
Spreading knife	Sandwich flags
Fork	Serving dishes
Pestle and mortar	Lace paper d'oyleys
Hair sieve	Sandwich set
Wooden spoon	Set of sandwich cutters

Whitstable Sandwiches

1 cupful picked Shrimps.	½ cupful chopped Spring Onions.
½ cupful finely-chopped Lettuce and Watercress.	3 hard-boiled Eggs.
	2 tablespoonfuls French Dressing.

Marinate a tightly packed cupful of shrimps for 2 hours in French dressing, then add the lettuce and watercress. Mix in the sifted yolks and finely chopped whites of eggs, and moisten with mayonnaise. Use this mixture as a filling between thin slices of brown or white bread, spread thinly with mayonnaise.

Crab and Tomato Sandwiches

1 cupful Crab.	Mayonnaise.
¾ cupful finely-minced Celery.	Tomatoes.

Finely chop the crab, add the celery, and moisten with some mayonnaise. Spread half the slices of bread with mayonnaise and with the mixture ; then spread the remainder of the slices with mayonnaise and with thin slices of peeled tomatoes, and put the slices together.

Bloater Cream Sandwiches

1 Bloater.	1 tablespoonful Worcester Sauce.
4 to 6 drops Tobasco.	¼ cupful Butter.

Free the meat of the bloater from skin and bones, and mash it to a paste with a fork. Season with sauce, allowing the quantity of ingredients mentioned to each cupful of bloater paste. Stir in the softened butter and tobasco, then use this paste as a filling for buttered bridge rolls or for toast, together with mustard and cress.

Potted Salmon Sandwiches

1 lb. Salmon.	½ lb. Butter.	½ a Cucumber.	1 tin Loaf.
½ teaspoonful pounded Cloves.		1 teaspoonful Lemon Juice.	
2 teaspoonfuls Anchovy Sauce.		Cayenne Pepper.	Black Pepper.

Pound the salmon in a mortar, with two ounces of best butter, pounded cloves, anchovy sauce, a seasoning of cayenne, half a teaspoonful of black pepper, and the lemon juice. When well incorporated, spread this mixture on thin slices of bread and butter. On half the slices lay some thinly cut slices of cucumber, then cover with the other slices and press firmly down. Trim, and cut into small fingers, and serve on a paper d'oyley, garnished with watercress.

NOTE.—Tinned salmon may be used for this, which will make the recipe cheaper.

Egg and Anchovy Sandwiches

3 hard-boiled Eggs.	Bread and Butter.
¼ lb. Butter. Cayenne Pepper.	2 teaspoonfuls Anchovy Sauce.

Pound the yolks of the hard-boiled eggs in a mortar, adding, by degrees, the butter (slightly warmed), the anchovy sauce, and a rather high seasoning of cayenne. Chop the whites of egg very finely, and add them to the mixture.

Spread between slices of thin brown bread and butter, or in bridge rolls with mustard and cress.

Mustard and Cress Sandwiches

| Brown Bread. ¼ lb. Butter. | Potted Meat (any kind). |
| Mustard and Cress. | Cayenne and Salt. |

Cut some thin slices of brown bread, butter them well, and season with cayenne and a little salt. Spread with potted meat, then with minced mustard and cress. Cover these with slices of bread, spread first with butter, then with potted meat; press firmly down, trim the edges, and cut into diamonds and triangles.

Dish the sandwiches " en couronne " (lying in a circle, lapping over one another), on a lace paper d'oyley. Garnish with a bunch of mustard and cress in the centre.

Savoury Colebrook Sandwiches

| 3 oz. Boiled Beef. | ½ teaspoonful Pepper. |
| ½ lb. Butter. | 1 tin Loaf of Bread. |

1 oz. Pickled Cabbage.

Let the beef be about half-fat and half-lean, and mince it finely. Pound the minced meat in a mortar, adding by degrees the pepper and butter, and incorporate these thoroughly well together. Cut the loaf into thin slices, and butter them, then spread the slices of bread and butter with the mixture.

Cut some wafer slices of boiled beef, cut them into strips, and lay some on the pounded meat, then cut some thin short strips of pickled cabbage, and lay these on top. Cover with a second slice of the spread bread and butter, press down, and trim off the crusts. Cut the sandwiches into squares, and arrange on a fancy lace paper, or d'oyley, garnish with parsley, and serve.

Potted Beef

Remains of Cold Beef.	½ teaspoonful Nutmeg.
1 teaspoonful Salt.	1 blade of Mace.
½ teaspoonful Pepper.	Butter.

The cold beef can have been either roasted or boiled. Mince it finely, then put it in a mortar with the pepper, salt, mace (pounded), nutmeg, and a piece of butter about the size of an egg. This is a good way of using up the remains of a large joint.

Potted Game

The remains of any Cold Game.	Allspice. Castor Sugar.
The same weight of finely-chopped fat Ham.	Cayenne. White Pepper.
	Salt.
Powdered Mace.	Clarified Butter.

UTENSILS—Knife, mincing machine, pestle and mortar, small pots, kitchen spoon, saucepan.

Free the remains of the cold game from skin, bone and any hard parts, then pass it twice through a mincing machine. Pass the ham through twice also, then put all into a mortar, and season highly with the spices, cayenne, white pepper, salt, and a small quantity of castor sugar, and pound thoroughly.

When well pounded, press the mixture into small earthenware or china pots, pour clarified butter over the tops, and put away in a dry place. If ham is not procurable, butter may be used instead.

Potted Cheese

1 tablespoonful Butter.	¼ lb. Cheddar Cheese.
1 Yolk of Egg.	¼ cupful Cream.

UTENSILS—Saucepan, wooden spoon, tablespoon, cup, basin, egg-beater, grater.

Melt the butter in a saucepan, and stir in the grated cheese and pepper. When melted, beat in gradually the egg yolk, beaten and diluted with cream. Season with cayenne, and cook till thick and smooth, then use for sandwiches.

Spanish Rarebit

½ lb. grated Cheese.	1 cupful strained Tomatoes.
2 Eggs.	1 dessertspoonful minced Spring
½ cupful soft White Breadcrumbs.	Onions.
¼ cupful cooked Peas.	1 chopped Pimento. Butter.

UTENSILS—Saucepan, measuring spoons, cup, knife, chopping board, basin, egg-beater, wooden spoon.

Melt a tablespoonful of butter in a saucepan, and cook the onions until soft. Stir in the tomatoes, breadcrumbs and chopped pimento, and when the crumbs are quite soft, add the eggs, beaten with a tablespoonful of milk, very gradually, and the peas. Season with pepper, paprika and salt to taste, and stir till thick. Serve between slices of buttered toast or dry bread.

Lemon Cheese

3 Whites of Eggs.	½ lb. Fresh Butter.
4 yolks of Eggs.	Rind of 3 Lemons.
¼ lb. Castor Sugar.	Juice of 2 Lemons.

UTENSILS—Grater, 2 basins, egg-beater, double boiler, wooden spoon, lemon squeezer, pots and covers.

Grate the lemon rinds, and mix them with the beaten yolks and whites of eggs, place the mixture in the top part of a double boiler, and add the lemon juice, stirring it in gradually. Heat slowly, stirring continually, till the mixture is as thick as honey. Pot like jam, and use for layer cakes, biscuits, pastry cases, or with bread and butter or toast.

Tutti Frutti Sandwiches

1 cupful chopped Glacé Fruits.	½ cupful finely-shredded Almonds.
Lemon Cheese.	Sponge Fingers.

UTENSILS—Knife, chopping board, basin, cup, saucepan, cloth.

Finely chop equal quantities of glacé cherries, pineapple, apricots, and pears, and, if liked, add a few chopped muscatel raisins. Mix the fruit with prepared blanched almonds, then moisten with lemon cheese so that the mixture can be spread.

Spread newly baked sponge fingers with the mixture, and sandwich two together. Insert a few baked, blanched almonds round the edge of each sandwich, and serve for afternoon tea.

CONFECTIONERY

ANY kinds of sweets can be made quite quickly and inexpensively at home—the uncooked confectionery being especially simple and permitting of many variations. The most important point in making these sweets is to use only the finest icing sugar, but this is not an expensive item.

Uncooked sweets have for their basis a dough made of icing sugar moistened with equal parts of white of egg and water, and this dough is rolled out and coloured and flavoured, and then cut into shapes. The finished sweets only take a few hours to dry and are then ready for use. Cooked sugar creams are smoother and more delicate than the uncooked, but they require a little practice before you can rely upon good results. Several recipes for toffees, candied fruits and fudges, etc., are also given, and these form most wholesome sweetmeats which are very interesting to make.

UNCOOKED CONFECTIONERY

SUGAR CREAM BASIS FOR UNCOOKED CONFECTIONERY

UTENSILS—Basin, mixing spoon, pastry board, rolling pin, knife, smooth metal sheet or tray.

Put the white of an egg and an equal quantity of cold water into a basin, and add sufficient icing sugar, gradually, to make into a stiff dough. The white of one egg and the water will take up about $1\frac{1}{2}$ pounds of sugar, so that, if the whole of this is not wanted of one colour and flavour, it can be separated into parts when the dough is quite soft, and each given its distinctive colour or flavour before stiffening it with more sugar.

Vanilla or any of the usual flavourings answer perfectly, and dry powdered chocolate can be worked in in the same way as the dry sugar. Chocolate gives an attractive brown shade ; carmine can be used for pink ; and other vegetable colourings serve equally well.

When the flavouring and colouring are done and more sugar has been worked in to stiffen the mass, roll it out at once and cut it into shapes. The finished sweets seem to improve with one or two days' keeping, but are eatable, if required, in about 6 hours.

Plain Cream Squares

Make some plain sugar cream, as described, and flavour with a few drops of vanilla essence, raspberry, almond, or other flavouring. Dust a pastry board over with icing sugar, and rub the rolling pin with the latter. Put the cream on the board, roll out to three-quarters of an inch in thickness, and cut it into square or oblong pieces with a knife. Dust over a smooth metal sheet or tray with icing sugar, and place the squares on to dry.

Chocolate-flavoured Cream Squares

Make some sugar cream, as described on page 448, but when quite a soft dough has been made, cease to add sugar, and finish it with chocolate powder instead. Add vanilla or almond extract, then roll out the mass and cut into squares, as described in the last recipe.

Neapolitan Squares

Make some plain sugar cream, as described on page 448, and separate it into three or more parts. Flavour one part with vanilla, and leave this white ; flavour a second part with raspberry or rose, and colour this pink with two or three drops of carmine ; add powdered chocolate to a third part, and mix it thoroughly in, adding a few spots of water if necessary.

Roll each out on a board, previously dusted over with icing sugar, and rub this sugar on the rolling pin. When a quarter of an inch thick, place the layers on top of one another, the white one in the middle, and lightly press together. Cut into squares, and place them on a smooth tin or tray, dusted over with sugar.

Peppermint Creams

Make some plain sugar cream, as described on page 448. Leave this white, and flavour it with peppermint, roll it out to a quarter of an inch in thickness, then cut it into small rounds. Place to dry, as described with the last recipe.

Nut Cream Squares

Make some plain sugar cream, as described on page 448. Flavour this with vanilla or almond. Or it is very nice if a small quantity of chocolate is mixed in, as the flavour of this latter goes very well with nuts. Chop up, not finely, some mixed nuts such as almonds, walnuts and filberts, in quantity nearly equal to the cream, and while the cream is moderately soft, add the nuts and gently knead them in.

Roll or flatten out the mass to about three-quarters of an inch in thickness, then cut it into square or oblong pieces with a sharp knife. Place these to dry on a tray or smooth surface, dusted over with icing sugar.

Cream Almonds

These are simply made by wrapping the almond in a casing of flavoured sugar cream, made as described on page 448.

OTHER NUTS can be treated in the same manner.

Fruit Cream Bars

Make some plain sugar cream, as described on page 448, and flavour it if desired, though it is not very necessary with this sweet. Chop up some assorted preserved fruits such as glacé cherries, figs, raisins (previously stoned), and a little peel. Work this into the sugar cream, then roll or flatten it out to three-quarters of an inch in thickness. Cut it into bars, and place to dry on a smooth surface dusted over with icing sugar.

Almond Creams

Make some plain sugar cream, as described on page 448, and flavour it with almond or vanilla essence. Colour it with a few drops of carmine for a pale pink, or with sufficient chocolate to give it a pale fawn colour, then make it into balls. Insert the point of a knife to make an opening, and insert a bleached almond in each, or make small egg-shaped balls, and press an almond on top of each. Place to dry, as described in the last recipe.

Walnut Creams

Take some plain sugar cream, as described on page 448. Add powdered chocolate to this, and knead up together to make a firm dough, using a drop or two of water if necessary. The chocolate should be about one-fifth or one-sixth of the whole amount, say 1 oz. chocolate to 5 oz. of sugar cream Flavour slightly with almond or vanilla, make into balls, and press half a walnut on top of each, then place to dry.

Coffee Creams

These are made in the same way as Walnut Creams just described ; but instead of using chocolate, the sugar cream is flavoured with coffee extract. Half-walnuts are pressed on just the same.

Cream Cherries

Take some plain sugar cream, as described on page 448, flavour it with a few drops of vanilla, and form it into balls the size of small cherries. Take some glacé cherries, and cut them in halves, then press a half-cherry on each side of the ball. This will slightly flatten the ball, which is rather desirable. Cut some strips of angelica to form the stalks, and insert one in the end of each ball, then put the cherries to dry on a sugared tray.

Cocoanut Cream Drops

Make some plain sugar cream, as described on page 448, but before it becomes a firm dough, cease adding sugar, and finish it with desiccated cocoanut, kneading it well in. The quantity of cocoanut should be about one-third of the whole. Flavour with a few drops of vanilla, or the flavouring can be omitted with this sweet.

Form into balls, and either leave them plain, or lightly brush over with syrup or white of egg, and roll them in some dry cocoanut. Place away to dry.

Chocolate Creams

UTENSILS—Double boiler, fork, buttered paper, sugar cream utensils (page 448).

Make some plain sugar cream, as described on page 448, and flavour it with vanilla, rose, lemon, or any essence preferred. Make balls or pyramids, and put these aside to dry for about 4 hours or longer.

Melt some chocolate in a double saucepan, or in any vessel over steam. When the creams are dry, dip one in the melted chocolate, letting it rest on the end of a narrow fork. With a knife scrape off the chocolate beneath the fork, then slip the cream on to buttered paper to cool and set. Do all like this. The chocolate should not be too hot. It must be thick enough to coat the creams well, and not to run thin at the tops.

Dominoes

UTENSILS—Double boiler, small pointed brush, sugar cream utensils (page 448).

Make some plain sugar cream, as described on page 448, and flavour it with vanilla. Roll this out to a little less than a quarter of an inch in thickness. Cut it into oblong domino-shaped pieces, and set aside to dry for about 4 hours.

Melt some chocolate, as described in the last recipe ; and with a camel-hair or any small pointed brush, draw lines across the centres of the squares, then make chocolate dots. Put them aside again for the chocolate to set hard.

ANOTHER METHOD

UTENSILS—3 basins, wooden spoon, egg-beater, sandwich tin, palette knife.

This is perhaps the method to be preferred for children's eating. Make a thin layer of sponge or light cake, and cut this into domino shapes, ice the top and sides with royal icing, and when this is dry, put the chocolate lines and spots on, as just described.

ROYAL ICING is made by mixing the white of an egg, half a teaspoonful of lemon juice, and half a pound of finest icing sugar thoroughly well together, until they are of the consistency of thick batter. The mixing should be done with a wooden spoon, and take not less than 15 minutes. Spread it on the cake with a palette knife, and set aside to dry.

Uncooked Marzipan

UTENSILS—Basin, lemon squeezer, saucepan, cloth, pestle and mortar, knife.

Take $\frac{1}{2}$ lb. of blanched almonds, $\frac{3}{4}$ lb. of finest icing sugar, the white of one egg and the juice of half a lemon. Pound the almonds to a paste in a mortar, then add the other ingredients, and pound all well together. This confection can be eaten alone, cut into small squares, or it serves excellently as a filling for chocolate sweets. One layer of this could be used with advantage in making the Neapolitan squares described on page 449.

Assorted Creams
(MADE WITH FRESH CREAM)

Take some finest icing sugar and free it perfectly from lumps. Put it into a basin, and work in sufficient thick sweet cream to make into a ball or dough which can be cut or worked into shapes. Divide into three or four parts and flavour them differently. Any of the shapes described in the preceding pages can be made with this sugar cream. These creams are delicious flavoured with any fresh fruit juice, but, if this is done, either more sugar or less cream must be used.

NOTE.—These sweets do not keep more than a day or two.

COOKED SWEETS
SUGAR BOILING DEGREES

					°Fah.
To boil to a short thread	..	..	..		216
To boil to a long thread	..	..	..		218
To boil to a small pearl	..	..	..		220
To boil to a large pearl	..	..	..		222
To boil to the blow stage	..	..	..		230
To boil to the feather stage	..	..	..		233
To boil to the soft-ball stage	..	..	..		238
To the hard-boiled stage	..	..	..		248
To boil to the brittle or crack stage, soft crack					280–290
To boil to the brittle or crack stage, hard crack					290–300
Caramel stage	..	..	..	..	312–330

UTENSILS FOR MAKING COOKED SWEETS—Enamelled saucepan, wooden skewer, wooden spoon, basin, knife, pint measure, sugar-boiling thermometer, sugar scraper, dipping fork, dish, marble slab or greased tin, strainer.

Cooked Sugar Creams

These are the basis of cooked cream confectionery and fondants, similar to the uncooked described in preceding pages. In appearance there is little distinction between the uncooked and the cooked sugar cream sweetmeats, but the latter are superior in smoothness and delicate eating, though more trouble to make. Given a sugar-boiling thermometer, there should be no failures, but if working without a thermometer, carefully attend to the following directions and you cannot go wrong.

Put 1 lb. of the best loaf sugar into an enamelled saucepan with a small teacupful of cold water. See that the sugar melts, and when it begins to boil do not stir or touch it in any way for 10 minutes—it will not burn. Dip a wooden skewer gently in and lift it out again, and take a small drop of the sugar from the end of the skewer between the finger and thumb. The fingers should first be wetted to save burning them. Open the finger and thumb, and if the sugar threads, it is done. The boiling time may vary from 8 to 11 minutes, according to how fast it is. It is better to boil gently.

Up to now the boiling sugar has not been stirred or shaken, and the pan should now be lifted gently from the stove without shaking it, and placed somewhere to cool until the sugar can be just touched with the fingers without their being burned. This will be in about 15 minutes in a cool kitchen, depending on whether the sugar is spread out in a large pan or more in bulk in a small one, and also depending on the quantity cooked at one time. When cooled to this extent pour it into a bowl and beat well with a wooden spoon until it becomes a thick, white and glossy cream. When stiff enough, take it out into the hands and knead well. It then becomes a soft, manageable dough, very smooth and not in the least grainy in the mouth like uncooked sugar cream.

The important points are correct boiling, no disturbance or shaking before it is cool enough, yet it must not be allowed to get too cool. If it goes hard or grainy it shows too much boiling, disturbance of some kind, or allowing it to get too cold. If this should happen the sugar can be used up again for the same purpose quite satisfactorily by adding a proper proportion of water.

When the dough is ready it can be divided and used for any of the cream sweetmeats described under UNCOOKED CONFECTIONERY, fashioned into any other shapes; in fact, there is scarcely a limit to the exercise of one's ingenuity. Any suitable flavouring and any vegetable colouring may be used.

Candied Fruits

Put $\frac{1}{2}$ lb. of cane sugar on to boil with a $\frac{1}{4}$ pint of water, in a bright saucepan. Boil the sugar to the " crack." This is when a little taken in a spoon and dropped into cold water immediately sets hard and brittle, so that it will break short. When the syrup has boiled to this degree, remove it from the fire. Dip the fruits in carefully, immediately remove any sugar hanging beneath, then lay them on a dish or marble slab.

Tangerine, orange, nuts and other fresh fruits are excellent treated in this way. Preserved confections such as glacé cherries, angelica, crystallised violets, and such like, can be candied in this way, and make a very pretty ornamentation for sweet dishes. For this purpose, the fruit is first stuck on a skewer; then, when dipped, a long string of the syrup is allowed to hang from it, and this is laid on the dish. When set, the fruit is found to have a long candy spike attached, and this is stuck into the pudding mixture.

Candied Chestnuts

Take some large chestnuts, and remove the outer skins. Put the nuts into boiling water and boil for 5 minutes, then remove the inner or second skins, which should come off quite easily. Be careful to reject decayed or unsound nuts. Now throw them into some fresh boiling water, and boil until tender. Take the nuts carefully from the pan, and put them into a basin of tepid water which has the juice of a lemon in it.

When cool, dry carefully, but leaving them moist and soft, then put all into a basin and pour boiling hot syrup over them. After remaining in a little while, lift the nuts out, drain them, and lay on a dish to dry. The syrup for this purpose is boiled to the degree when it threads.

Orange Straws

Boil some orange peel for about 2 hours, changing the water once or twice during this time, as it becomes very bitter. After boiling, drain the peel, and when cool cut it into narrow strips about two inches long. Make a syrup of 1 lb. of sugar with 1 pint of water, put the cut peel into this and boil for 25 minutes, then remove the strips and lay them out on plates. Dry in a slow oven or other warm place. If required for keeping, they may take 24 hours drying.

Salted Almonds

Blanch and dry some sweet almonds. Put a piece of butter in a pan, and when melted stir in a little salt, but be careful not to overdo the salt. Put the almonds into this, and keep stirring until they are all coated with the salted butter and have become a pale brown colour. They are then done. The cooking can be done either over a very gentle heat, or in an oven. The frequent stirring is necessary in either case, particularly when over the fire or gas ring.

Sugared Almonds

Blanch and dry some sweet almonds. Put a cupful of white sugar and a quarter-cupful of water into a saucepan, and boil until it threads. To ascertain when sugar is at this degree, dip the thumb and forefinger in cold water. Dip a spoon into the sugar, and then take a drop of it between the finger and thumb. Immediately open them, and a thread will appear if the sugar is cooked sufficiently. This will take 8 to 10 minutes, according to how fast it boils. Put the almonds into this to cook, and stir them occasionally.

When the almonds turn a pale brown, remove the pan from the fire and stir until its contents cool. The syrup will then turn to powdered sugar, some of which clings to the almonds.

Chocolate Almonds

Blanch some sweet almonds. Melt some chocolate, and coat the nuts as described with chocolate creams, below.

CHOCOLATE FILBERTS can be made in the same way.

Chocolate Creams

Make some cooked sugar cream as described on page 453. Flavour it with vanilla, almond, raspberry, or any essence preferred, form balls or pyramids, and put these aside to dry for about 6 hours. Melt some chocolate, and when the balls are dry enough dip one in, letting it rest on the end of a narrow fork. With a knife scrape off the chocolate beneath the fork, then slip the cream on to buttered paper to cool. Do all like this, but do not let the chocolate be too hot, or it will run thin on top of the creams.

ANOTHER METHOD

Put 1 lb. of white sugar into a pan. Pour over it as much milk or thin cream as it will absorb. Dissolve this over the fire, then boil slowly until it will just candy if a little is dropped into cold water. Do not stir it up to this time.

Now remove the pan from the fire, and stir until it is beginning to cool, then add the flavouring. Stir or beat again until it creams and is cool enough to handle. Form into balls and shapes, and, when dry, cover with chocolate, as last described. If the boiling goes on but a minute or two too long, the sugar will not properly cream on being beaten, but will go to dry powder.

Nougat

Prepare some almonds and other nuts (or almonds alone will do) by blanching and drying them, and chopping them into moderate-sized pieces. Put $\frac{1}{2}$ lb. of castor sugar into an enamelled pan with 1 large tablespoonful of lemon juice, and melt it. As soon as dissolved, put in $\frac{3}{4}$ lb. of the chopped nuts and stir rapidly. Pour the mixture into a buttered pan and press into cakes with a buttered knife, as it cools quickly.

ANOTHER METHOD

The following is perhaps the most usual recipe for nougat, but it requires great care in making. Unless the heat is only just sufficient to melt the sugar, it will turn it brown. The heat of boiling water is barely sufficient, and to melt the sugar properly and without discolouring it requires steam under pressure.

Put $\frac{1}{2}$ lb. of castor sugar into an enamelled pan without water, place it on a very slow heat and melt it. As soon as melted throw in $\frac{1}{2}$ lb. of blanched and chopped nuts (previously well dried). Stir quickly, and turn out on to a buttered dish. The mixture can be worked a little with oiled hands.

Cooked Marzipan

This is a recipe for cooked marzipan; the uncooked is described on page 452. Blanch 1 lb. of sweet almonds. Put these into a mortar with a few bitter ones, add a few spoonfuls of rose-water, then pound the whole smooth. Put this into a stewpan with a pound of icing sugar, and stir over the fire until a smooth paste is obtained, which will not stick to the fingers when touched.

Sprinkle a pastry board with icing sugar, then roll out the paste. Divide it into cakes, then place them on sheets of paper on a baking sheet and bake in a slow oven until they are a pale yellow colour.

Rahat Lakum (Turkish Delight)

Make a syrup with 3 lb. of icing sugar and 3 pints of water, and clear it with the whites of 3 eggs and the juice of a lemon. Dissolve 6 oz. of pure wheat starch in ¾ pint of cold water, strain it, and add it to the clear syrup when it is boiling. Reduce the whole by boiling to two-thirds. It should then be very thick and stringy. Flavour the paste with attar of roses or any sweet essence.

Have ready a large dish well covered with almond oil. Empty the paste on the dish when it is cool, spread it about one inch thick. Have ready another dish covered with finely powdered sugar, and when the paste is quite cold turn it over very carefully upon the sugared dish. Absorb the oil with blotting paper, and cut the paste into pieces two inches square, powder them with sugar, and keep them very dry. A fine rahat is made with rose or cherry syrup, and with blanched almonds stirred in before the paste thickens.

Barley Sugar

Put 1½ lb. of loaf or castor sugar into a well-tinned saucepan, and add ½ pint of water and half the white of an egg. Mixed well together. Bring to the boil and skim carefully. As soon as the scum ceases to rise, the sugar is clarified, but it is best then to strain it through muslin. Put it back into the pan and boil it to the crack, so that a little dropped into cold water becomes hard and brittle.

Remove from the fire, add a teaspoonful of lemon juice, and after letting it stand for a minute, pour out on to an oiled dish. Before it is set hard, cut into strips and twist them, or small squares; or it can be dropped while hot into lozenge-shaped drops.

Butter Scotch

Put 1 lb. of Demerara sugar into a saucepan with a teacupful of water. Boil until a little dropped into cold water immediately becomes hard and brittle. Add 2 oz. of fresh butter, and boil for 4 or 5 minutes longer, then pour on to a buttered dish and cut into oblong pieces.

Treacle Toffee

Put a ¼ lb. of fresh butter into a tinned saucepan, and when partially melted add ½ lb. of treacle and ½ lb. of Demerara sugar, and mix well together. Boil for 8 or 10 minutes, then test it by dropping a little in cold water. If it immediately hardens and is brittle, pour all on to a buttered dish.

Before it is hard it can be marked into squares with the back of a knife, and it will then break evenly. If liked, almonds can be pressed in before the toffee hardens. Toffee can be pulled until it is any desired light colour, or even white. It is then, while soft, made into rolls or sticks about half an inch thick, and cut into short pieces with scissors.

Almond Hardbake

Mix together 1½ lb. of moist sugar and ¾ pint of cold water. Put these into an earthenware pan and boil until a little dropped into cold water immediately becomes hard and brittle. Have ready 3 oz. of almonds, blanched and split lengthways, and add these, with 3 oz. of butter, to the boiled sugar. Boil again, until a little dropped into cold water hardens immediately, then pour the hardbake on to an oiled or buttered dish to set.

Cocoanut Candy

Mix together 1 lb. of loaf sugar with ½ pint of cold water, in an earthenware pan, and when the sugar is dissolved, boil for about 5 minutes, carefully removing all scum as it rises. Now mix in a ¼ pound of desiccated cocoanut, or fresh-grated or sliced cocoanut. Boil up again, and when the candy rises quite up in the saucepan, remove the latter from the fire and then spread the candy about half an inch thick on well-dried and warm sheets of writing-paper.

When nearly cold, remove the papers and cut the candy up into neat squares. If desired, the candy, or part of it, can be given a pink tint by adding a few drops of carmine.

Cocoanut Fudge

| 2 lb. Barbadoes Sugar. | ½ pint Water. |
| ½ lb. tin Condensed Milk. | 2 oz. Desiccated Cocoanut. |

1 teaspoonful Vanilla Essence.

Boil the sugar in a saucepan, with a pinch of cream of tartar mixed with water, for 5 minutes. Add the condensed milk, and stir till the candy reaches the soft ball stage when a little is tested in cold water, then remove the pan, and stir in the cocoanut and vanilla. Beat the mixture until creamy, pour it into greased tins, and cut it into squares before it is quite cold.

Royal Fudge

| 1 lb. Brown Sugar. | 1 walnut of Butter. |
| 1 cupful Walnuts. | Grated rind of 1 Orange. |

Put all the ingredients into a saucepan, stir till the sugar has dissolved, and then until the mixture comes to the boil. Boil for 3 minutes, remove the pan from the fire, and beat until the mixture is thick. Pour into buttered tins, and cut into squares when cold.

SYRUPS

In the preparation of syrups, which are solutions of sugar, care should be taken to employ only the best refined sugar, and the purest water obtainable, as they will then become perfectly transparent without the trouble of clarifying. When, however, doubtful sugar is employed, clarification becomes necessary.

This is best done by dissolving the sugar in the water or fruit juices cold, and then beating up a little of this cold syrup with some white of egg and one or two ounces of cold water, until the mixture froths well ; this must be added to the syrup in the boiler. When the whole is frisked up to a good froth, heat is applied and the scum which forms is removed from time to time with a clean skimmer. As soon as the syrup begins to simmer, it must be removed from the fire and allowed to stand until it has cooled a little, when it should again be skimmed, if necessary, and finally passed through a clean flannel. By using refined sugar, however, all this trouble of clarification can be avoided.

TO PREPARE SYRUPS

The proper quantity of sugar for syrups will, in general, be found to be two pounds to every pint of water. These proportions allow for the water that is lost by evaporation during the process, and are those best calculated to produce syrup of proper consistence and possessing good keeping qualities.

In the preparation of syrup, employ as little heat as

possible. The best plan is to pour the water, cold, over the sugar, and to allow the two to lie together for a few hours in a covered vessel, occasionally stirring. Then apply a gentle heat, preferably that of steam or of a water-bath (double saucepan) to finish the solution. Syrups are sufficiently boiled when some taken up in a spoon pours out like oil, or a drop cooled on the thumb-nail just gives a thread if touched. When a thin skin appears on blowing the syrup, it is judged to be finished. These tests, however, often lead to errors, which may be easily prevented by employing the proper proportions, or by using a saccharometer or syrup gauge.

A solution of sugar prepared by dissolving two parts of double refined sugar in one of water, and boiling this a little, affords a syrup which will keep excellently.

TO STORE SYRUPS

Syrups are best kept in a cool place, and the bottles must be full, and well corked. The temperature should never rise above 55 degrees Fahrenheit. Small bottles are best unless the demand is large. When in large bottles, which are frequently opened before the contents are used up, the syrup may decompose.

To prevent fruit syrups from fermenting they should be bottled while hot, and the bottles quite filled. Take, for instance, some quart bottles and warm them. Fill these nearly full with the hot syrup, and cover or cork them temporarily until the syrup cools a little and contracts in volume. Then fill up with more hot syrup, cork the bottles securely and wax them.

A large number of different syrups are made by preparing a simple syrup, and then flavouring it with essences and colouring with carmine and other prepared vegetable colourings. When fresh fruit is used, however, the making of the syrup and the preparation and addition of the fruit go hand in hand, as a syrup to keep cannot be made by simply adding the raw fruit juice. Absolute cleanliness is essential in syrup-making.

SIMPLE SYRUP

UTENSILS—Stewpan, wooden spoon, skimmer, flannel bag, basin, quart measure.

This is the basis of most mineral water syrups and those made with essences. This is a simple method of preparing syrups, but they are not so good as those prepared with the fresh fruit. Put 8 lb. of sugar, the whites of 2 eggs and 2 quarts of water into a pan, place it on the stove and stir until the sugar is dissolved. Allow it to come to the boil, and simmer for 2 or 3 minutes, then remove from the fire, skim well and strain through a flannel bag. Add the essence as described in some of the following recipes.

FRESH FRUIT SYRUPS : A GENERAL RECIPE

UTENSILS—Preserving pan, wooden spoon or pestle and mortar, fruit press or jelly-bag, flannel bag, basin, skimmer, pint measure, corked bottles.

The fruit can be raspberries, currants (red or black), cherries, etc. Whichever is used, let it be quite fresh and sound. Put the fruit into a large pan or wooden vessel, and mash it well with a wooden instrument, mixing in ½ lb. of castor sugar with every 25 lb. of fruit. When well mashed, let it stand for 4 days in a warm room of even temperature, say 68 degrees Fahrenheit, then press out the juice, and place this to settle in a cool place, where it should remain for about 2 days.

To each 5 lb. of the clear juice add 9 lb. of loaf sugar. Put this on the stove to boil, and let it simmer for a few minutes, then remove from the fire, strain through flannel, and it is ready for bottling. Previous to bottling, let the syrup stand for a little time, then skim off any scum that may appear, and afterwards see that no residue from the bottom of the pan (if there is any) goes into the bottles. Bottle and cork as described on page 461.

The following recipes of various syrups are placed in alphabetical order.

Ambrosia Syrup

This is prepared by mixing together equal parts of Vanilla and Strawberry syrups.

Apple Syrup

Pare the apples, then mash them in a large mortar or in a strong tub, using a stone or wooden pestle. When well mashed, press out the juice. To do this effectually with this fruit, a cyder press or something of the kind is necessary, otherwise much of the juice will be lost.

For each pint of juice, take ½ pint of water and 3 lb. of loaf sugar. Bring the water and sugar to the boil and add the juice, simmer for a few minutes, then remove from the fire or gas ring. After standing a little time skim well, strain through flannel, and bottle as described on page 461.

Blackberry Syrup

Put fresh berries in a coarse jelly-bag, and press out the juice. To each quart of juice add 6 lb. of loaf sugar and 1 pint of water. Put on the stove, see the sugar dissolved, then bring just to boiling point. Remove the pan from the stove, and allow it to stand a little while.

Now skim, and strain through flannel. Bottle and cork while the syrup is hot, then place it in a cool cellar to keep. It is considered an improvement to add one ounce of French brandy to each quart of this syrup.

ANOTHER METHOD

Take 5 quarts of blackberries, 12 lb. of loaf sugar, and 1 pint of water. Place a layer of fruit in a pan, then sprinkle with sugar (castor sugar might be used for this); place another layer and sprinkle this, and so on until the fruit is all used, let this stand for several hours, then press out the juice, passing some of the water through the remaining pulp so that none be lost. Add the remaining sugar and water to the juice, and bring all to the boil. Skim, strain through flannel, and bottle as described on page 461. This will keep well.

ANOTHER METHOD

Mix together 6 pints of simple syrup (page 461), 2 pints of water, 2 ounces of tartaric acid, and 2 ounces of essence of blackberry. Colour with carmine. If necessary, strain through flannel, then bottle.

Capillaire Syrup

Put together in a pan 9 lb. of loaf sugar and 5 lb. of orange-flower water. See the sugar dissolve, then bring to the boil and simmer for a few minutes until the syrup is clear. Remove from the fire, and while hot strain through flannel. Dissolve 2 drams of tartaric acid in 8 ounces of strong orange-flower water, and add this to the syrup when it cools. Lastly, add 4 ounces of Rhine wine, then bottle.

Cream Syrup

Put together in a pan $1\frac{1}{4}$ pounds of loaf sugar, 1 pint of water, and 1 pint of condensed milk. Bring to the boil, then strain through flannel. If kept in a cool place, this will keep for a week, but not much longer.

Currant Syrup

Press out the juice from some fresh red currants. Make some simple syrup (page 461), and to each gallon add 1 pint of currant juice. Bring just to the boil, then after standing a little time, skim off any scum there may be, and strain the syrup through flannel. Bottle whilst hot, as described on page 461.

Ginger Syrup

Prepare 6 pints of simple syrup (page 461), and add to it 2 pints of water, 1 ounce of tartaric acid and 2 ounces of essence of ginger. Give it a light brown or an orange tint with burnt sugar, then bottle.

ANOTHER METHOD

Add 4 ounces of essence of ginger to 1 gallon of simple syrup, and shake well together. Colour with a few drops of tincture of curcuma, or with burnt sugar, then bottle.

ANOTHER METHOD

Put 9 lb. of loaf sugar in a pan with 5 lb. of water, when the sugar is dissolved bring to the boil, and simmer a few minutes until it is clear. When cool, mix in 8 ounces of essence of ginger and 4 ounces of Rhine wine. Mix well, let it settle, then bottle.

Imperial Syrup

This is prepared by mixing together equal parts of Raspberry and Orange syrups.

Lemon Syrup

Take some lemons, grate off the yellow rinds, and rub a little castor sugar in with this. Squeeze the juice from the lemons, and to each pint of juice add a pint of water and $3\frac{1}{2}$ lb. of castor sugar. Add the grated rind and place the whole on the stove.

Allow the mixture to get moderately hot, so that the sugar is thoroughly dissolved, but on no account let the syrup boil. The less heat there is, to effect the complete solution of the sugar, the better. Strain and bottle.

ANOTHER METHOD

Make 1 gallon of simple syrup (page 461), and allow it to get cold. Dissolve $\frac{1}{2}$ oz. of citric acid in 3 oz. of water, and dissolve 2 oz. of fine white gum arabic in 2 oz. of warm water. Mix well together the gallon of syrup, with 20 drops of fresh oil of lemon, the dissolved citric acid and the gum solution, then bottle.

Maple Syrup

Dissolve $3\frac{1}{2}$ lb. of maple sugar in 1 quart of water, and bring just to the boil. If liked, add a small quantity of gum solution, as described in the last recipe, to produce a rich froth. Strain, and then bottle.

Milk Punch Syrup

Make 1 pint of heavy syrup. This is prepared in the same manner as simple syrup (page 461), but allow 3 lb. of sugar to the pint of water. When cool, add $\frac{1}{2}$ pint of brandy and $\frac{1}{2}$ pint of Jamaica rum. Prepare a flavouring by macerating (steeping for some hours), 2 oz. of ground nutmegs in 8 oz. of alcohol, and add 2 teaspoonfuls of this to the syrup. Bottle for use.

In using this, a certain amount is put into the tumbler, and then some Cream syrup is added. The soda water follows. The proportions of the spirit syrup and cream syrup are according to taste.

Mulberry Syrup

Let the fruit be sound and ripe, and free it from stalks. Place it in a large pan, or in a wooden tub, and crush it with a stone or wooden pestle. When well mashed, let the fruit stand for 3 or 4 hours, then put all into a flannel bag, and press out the juice thoroughly. Dissolve a $\frac{1}{4}$ oz. of citric acid in 3 oz. of water, and add this quantity to each gallon of juice to acidulate it slightly. Put 14 lb. of loaf sugar to every gallon of juice, and place on a slow fire to dissolve the sugar, stirring well. See that the sugar is dissolved thoroughly, but do not let the syrup boil. Remove from the fire, strain, and bottle.

ANOTHER METHOD

Prepare 6 pints of simple syrup (page 461), and add to it 2 pints of water, 1 oz. of tartaric acid, and 2 oz. of mulberry essence. Colour with carmine, then bottle.

Nectar Syrup

One method of preparing this is to mix together three parts of Vanilla syrup, one part of Pineapple syrup and one part of Lemon syrup.

ANOTHER METHOD

Prepare a gallon of simple syrup (page 461), and add 1 oz. of extract of vanilla, 1 oz. of extract of rose, 1 oz. of extract of lemon, and 1 oz. of extract of bitter almonds. Colour with carmine, then bottle.

Orange Syrup

This can be prepared with fresh fruit, or with essence, by either of the methods described with Lemon syrup. The finished syrup can be coloured slightly with saffron colouring or tincture of turmeric.

Orgeat Syrup

Put 8 oz. of blanched sweet almonds and 4 oz. of bitter almonds into a mortar, with a little water, and beat them to a smooth cream. Now add 3 pints of water, mix thoroughly, and strain. Put the strained liquor into the boiling pan, with 6 lb. of castor sugar and 4 oz. of orange-flower water. Heat and stir sufficiently to melt the sugar thoroughly, then remove from the fire and bottle.

ANOTHER METHOD

Mix together ½ pint of simple syrup, ½ pint of Cream syrup, 1 pint of Vanilla syrup, and 5 drops of oil of bitter almonds. An imitation of Orgeat syrup is prepared by simply flavouring some Cream syrup with a few drops of oil of bitter almonds.

Pear Syrup

This is prepared in the same manner as Apple syrup. A juicy and soft pear should be chosen.

Raspberry Syrup

Let the fruit be fully ripe and free it from stalks. Put the fruit in a wooden tub and crush it with a wooden or stone pestle, or a spatula. When mashed, let it remain for 3 or 4 hours, then put it in a flannel bag and press out the juice into a suitable vessel. Dissolve ½ oz. of citric acid in 3 oz. of water, and add this quantity to each gallon of juice. Put 14 lb. of loaf sugar with every gallon of juice into the pan, and place it on a slow fire. Stir until the sugar is dissolved, but do not boil.

When the sugar is quite dissolved, remove from the fire, skim and strain if necessary, then bottle hot, as described on page 461. Keep in a cool place. Raspberry syrup is improved by adding about 1 quart of red currants to each gallon of raspberries.

ANOTHER METHOD

Take 5 quarts of raspberries, 12 lb. of white sugar and 1 pint of water. Put a layer of fruit in an earthenware pan or wooden tub, and sprinkle with some of the sugar (use castor sugar for the sprinkling). Place another layer of fruit, sprinkle with sugar, and continue until all the fruit is in, then let it stand for several hours.

Press out the juice and strain it, also wash through the pulp with some of the water. Add the remaining sugar and water to the strained juice, and put this over the fire. Bring just to the boiling point, then strain and bottle hot, as described. It is an improvement to use part red currants, as mentioned in the last recipe.

ANOTHER METHOD

Prepare 6 pints of simple syrup (page 461), and add to it 2 pints of water, 2 oz. of tartaric acid, and 2 oz. of essence of raspberry. Colour with carmine, then bottle.

Rose Syrup

Prepare one gallon of simple syrup (page 461). **Add to** this 1 oz. of essence of rose, and mix well. Dissolve ½ oz. of citric acid in 3 oz. of water, and add this. Colour pink with carmine, then bottle.

Sherbet Syrup

This is prepared by mixing together equal parts of Orange, Pineapple and Vanilla syrups.

Strawberry Syrup

This can be prepared with fresh fruit or with essence in the same manner as the Raspberry syrups. Strawberries require a little more mashing than raspberries, but the process is similiar in all other respects.

Vanilla Syrup

Prepare 1 gallon of simple syrup. Dissolve ½ oz. of citric acid in some of the syrup. Add this, and also 1 oz. of extract of vanilla to the bulk of the syrup. Mix well together, then bottle for use. If the syrup is required to be more strongly flavoured, the quantity of vanilla may be doubled.

PRESERVES

THE PRESERVATION OF FOOD

No food which contains a high percentage of moisture will keep long in good condition unless special means are taken to preserve it. Dry foods, such as tea, cocoa, rice, barley and sago, keep almost indefinitely without deterioration, since they do not provide a suitable medium for the innumerable germs by which they may be infected. These germs, in the forms of moulds, yeasts or bacteria, thrive and proliferate in moisture—and in a moderate temperature. In order, therefore, to preserve such foods as meat, fish, fruit, vegetables, eggs and milk, it is necessary either to extract their moisture, or to subject them to such extremes of temperature as will destroy the germ life which leads to their decay.

Yet another method of preservation is the addition of some substance such as salt or sugar, which is inimical to bacterial growth.

Drying

In this country it is not easy to sun-dry fruit and vegetables in any quantity, though in warmer climates this method of preserving is commonly adopted, and even such juicy fruits as peaches, apricots and plums can be sufficiently evaporated by exposure to the hot sun.

An alternative method to sun-drying, however, is presented by drying in a slow oven. All kinds of herbs, as well as beans and peas and apple rings and pears, can be dried gradually at a temperature of between 140 and 180 degrees Fahr. The fruit or vegetables should be cleaned and prepared, and placed, not too thickly, on trays—preferably wooden trays stretched with muslin so that the warm air can circulate all round. The trays can be removed from the oven when necessary, and the drying continued on the following day, as the process must not be hurried or the fruit will be shrivelled and spoilt.

When the fruit is thoroughly dry, it should be left for a few hours until quite cold, and then packed away in airtight tins or boxes. If it is subsequently allowed to become damp, all the benefit of the drying is, of course, lost.

Bottling

By this method, the foods are sterilised—that is, they are subjected to sufficient heat to destroy bacterial life, and are then sealed up in order to prevent the entry of fresh organisms. The simplest way of bottling is to use the special bottles with screw lids which are sold for the purpose, and a special steriliser, but fruit and vegetables can be bottled successfully in glass jam jars, with the help of a fish kettle. Bottles can be fitted with a cork and the tops sealed over with melted wax.

The contents of the jars must be brought up to and maintained at simmering point for a definite time until perfectly sterile, and then be made thoroughly airtight. This can be done, in the case of ordinary jam jars, by pouring hot mutton fat on top of the contents, and covering closely with bladder or strong parchment papers.

To STERILISE FRUIT, pack the bottles closely with sound, well graded specimens which have been well washed. Be careful not to bruise the fruit in the process—a silver or a wooden spoon is the best utensil to use. Fill the bottles nearly to the top either with cold water or with syrup, made by dissolving 1 lb. of loaf sugar in 1 quart of water, then stand them in a fish kettle or other large vessel such as a clothes' boiler. Protect the bottles from the heat beneath by thick layers of paper or slats of wood.

Pour cold water into the boiler till it reaches the necks of the bottles, then bring it *very* slowly to simmering point, and simmer until the fruit is cooked—in about 10 minutes in the case of small berries, 15 or 20 minutes in the case of goose-berries, and as much as 25 minutes for large plums, etc.

When screw-cap bottles are used, place the caps over the bottles before placing them in the kettle, but on no account screw them down until the cooking is completed, and they have been removed from the fire. VEGETABLES such as beans and peas are more difficult to bottle successfully than fruit, since greater and more sustained heat is necessary to render them sterile. If you have a pressure cooker, it is easy to raise them to the correct temperature, but if not, they can be soaked in a weak solution of permanganate of potash, which helps to destroy organic substances, well washed in running water, and then packed into the bottles. To the water which is to fill the bottles, salt should be added at the rate of about 3 oz. to 1 gallon of water, and in the case of peas, a little sugar can be added if desired.

Bring the water in the fish kettle slowly to the boil, boil for 1 hour, then screw up the lids. On the following day, unscrew, and bring again to the boil, boil for a few minutes, then seal the bottles and put them away. The contents will then keep for a long time, provided that the covers are perfectly airtight.

Canning

The canning of food is carried out on the same principle as bottling. The contents of the tins must be maintained at the same high temperature in order to kill all moulds and bacteria, and they must then be rendered airtight. Canning is never attempted in many households, as it is thought to be a difficult and elaborate process, but if you purchase a special hand-sealer—quite a small and inexpensive implement—you will find that it is really a quicker and less troublesome method than bottling, since there is no fear of breakages during the process.

Jam Making

In the making of jams and jellies, sterilisation is brought about by thorough boiling, and the addition of a large quantity of sugar helps to prevent the fruit from decaying.

Pickling

Vegetables that are boiled in vinegar are completely sterilised, and will keep indefinitely. Vinegar hinders bacterial growth, and helps to preserve food even without the additional safeguard of boiling, but the method adopted in pickling is similar to that in bottling—with vinegar substituted for water or syrup.

Other Methods of Preserving

Just as in extreme heat, so in extreme cold, germs are arrested or destroyed. Freezing and chilling are methods of preservation possible on a large scale, but hardly practicable for any length of time in the ordinary household. A refrigerator, however, is invaluable for keeping food fresh and pure, especially in districts where daily supplies are not available.

Other methods of preserving are bottling in alcohol, smoking and salting. String beans, for instance, will keep satisfactorily for the winter if stored in jars or tubs between thick layers of common salt. When required for eating, they need only be washed, sliced and boiled in the ordinary way.

To Pickle Eggs

The most usual method of preserving eggs for winter use is to place them in a large crock or vessel of galvanised iron or enamelware, and pour over them a solution of waterglass, which has been mixed with *hot* water and allowed to become *perfectly cold*. The proportions of water and preservative are indicated in the directions on the different brands.

The crocks should then be covered over, and looked at from time to time in case the water has evaporated to the level of the eggs, in which case more must be added. If even a small portion of the egg is left uncovered, air will penetrate the shell, and the egg will go bad.

Eggs for pickling should be perfectly fresh, the best age being between five and twelve hours.

JAMS

If sound fruit and pure granulated or preserving sugar are used, jams and jellies will always be a success. Pick the fruit on a dry day, and discard any that is bruised or over-ripe. When making jam or jelly with fruit that lacks acid, such as strawberries, either allow the juice of 2 large lemons to every 4 lb. of fruit, or use a preparation of concentrated fruit juice, which supplies the acid deficient in the fruit you are using.

Some difference of opinion exists as to the necessity of skimming the jam while it is boiling. The general rule is to remove the scum as fast as it rises while boiling ; yet there is the fact that if the jam is well stirred, and the scum stirred in, the latter will usually have disappeared by the time the jam is ready to pour off, and the jam itself will afterwards keep equally well. The point to be remembered is, that if the jam is not skimmed, it must be stirred continually while boiling. The skimming of course causes considerable waste.

HOME-MADE CONFECTIONERY—Even the amateur, with very little practice, can make successful caramels, fudges and toffees.

AN EASILY MADE SWEET—Peppermint is one of the many flavour-ings which can be given to a simple sugar cream basis (p. 449).

It is very important that the jars into which the jam is poured for keeping be perfectly dry. It should be made a rule not to pour the jam in on the day that they are washed. Let them be washed the previous day, well wiped, and then dried in front of the fire or on the rack, then covered with cloths to keep the dust out until they are wanted. *If the least trace of moisture, or even dampness, is in the pots, the jam will turn mouldy.*

The average time that different jams take will be found given in the recipes, but the time will depend on the quality or the particular growth of the fruit ; and it also depends on the heat of the fire. No precise time can, therefore, be given, and all jams must be tested to ascertain if they are finished cooking. The test consists in putting a little of the jam on a cold plate, and if it sets like a jelly, it is done.

When the jam is cooked, remove it from the fire or gas ring and let it stand a few minutes before potting. Pour it into the dry, warm pots, and label them with the name and date. Use screw-on tops, or parchment covers dipped in water and securely tied down. A special tissue paper top, usually sold with the parchment covers, should be laid on top of the jam before covering. It is important not to fill the pots too full. Store in a dry, airy cupboard.

UTENSILS FOR PRESERVING—Preserving pan, saucepan, jelly-bag on stand, flannel, scales for weighing, pint or quart measure, sharp-pointed knife, fruit bottling outfit, sugar-boiling thermometer, silver knife, skimmer, wooden spoon, jars, labels, covers, colander, grater, hair sieve, lemon squeezer.

Apple Jam

Select good cooking apples, and peel, core and slice them thinly. Weigh the slices, then put them to stew until tender. This is best done in a double pan, or by putting the fruit into a jar and standing this in a saucepan of boiling water.

Put the stewed fruit into the preserving pan, add 1 lb. of crushed preserving sugar and the juice of half a lemon to each pound of fruit. If liked, the grated rind of the lemon can be added, or 1 oz. of whole ginger and a few cloves, to each pound of fruit. Bring the jam just to the boil, then simmer for ½ hour. Test by putting a little on a cold plate. If it sets, the jam is done. Pot as described above.

C.I.O.   Q

Apple Curd

3 lb. tart Apples.	4 oz. Butter.
1½ lb. Sugar.	2 Yolks of Eggs.
½ pint Water.	⅛ teaspoonful Ground Cinnamon.

Peel, core and slice the apples, and simmer them gently in the water until thoroughly cooked, then beat them until smooth, or rub them through a sieve. Add the sugar, cinnamon, beaten eggs and butter. Stir over a gentle heat until the eggs cook and thicken, but do not boil. Pot immediately.

NOTE.—Apple curd makes a delicious filling for sandwich cakes and tarts, but has not the same keeping qualities as apple jelly, and therefore should be made when required.

Dried Apricot Jam

2 lb. Dried Apricots.	2 oz. Sweet Almonds.
4 lb. Sugar.	4 pints Water.

Wash the fruit well, and quarter it before soaking. Steep it in water for 24 hours. Turn apricots and water into a preserving pan. Add sugar and boil for 45 minutes, then add blanched and halved almonds. Boil it quickly until the fruit is soft and transparent, as well as ready to set. Pot and seal while hot.

Fresh Apricot Jam

Let the fruit be ripe. Pare it as thinly as possible, then open and remove the stones. Weigh the prepared fruit, place a layer in an earthenware pan, sprinkle with pounded preserving sugar, then place successive layers of fruit and sugar until all is used. The quantity of sugar to be allowed is 1 lb. to each lb. of prepared fruit, and when all is placed in the pan, as just described, let it remain for several hours or until the next day. After standing, put the fruit and sugar into the preserving pan, bring just to the boil, then simmer gently for about 30 to 40 minutes, when the jam will become clear.

This jam should not be stirred too much, it looks best if the halves of apricots are not much broken. In this case the scum must be skimmed off as it rises. An improvement can be made by breaking the stones, blanching the kernels, and adding these to the fruit and sugar when they go into the preserving pan. When the jam is ready, take out the pieces of apricot as whole as possible, and put them into the jars. Afterwards pour over the syrup and kernels. Cover and secure, as described on page 473.

Blackberry Jam

Let the fruit be ripe and dry when gathered, and remove all the stalks. Weigh the prepared fruit, and allow ¾ lb. of crushed preserving sugar to each lb. of fruit. Put the fruit and sugar into a preserving pan and stir well with a wooden spoon, until the juice runs from the berries, then bring just to the boil, and simmer for 30 minutes. Test by putting a little on a cold plate, and if it jellies it is done. If this jam is constantly stirred during the simmering, there is no occasion to skim it. Allow it to cool, then put in jars as described on page 473.

ANOTHER METHOD

Pare, core and thinly slice some good cooking apples (as sharp a kind as possible, but ripe), and put ¼ lb. of the slices to each lb. of berries. A little more sugar is required than in the previous method, say 1¾ lb. to every 2 lb. of mixed fruit.

ANOTHER METHOD

Use the strained juice and grated rind of lemons, instead of apples, one small lemon to each 2 lb. of berries. The larger proportion of sugar is needed with this, as with the apples.

ANOTHER METHOD

When the small seeds of the berries are objected to, cook the fruit until it is very soft, then take it from the pan and rub it through a sieve. This would be done before the sugar is added, and as the removal of the seeds reduces the weight about one-half, only about half the sugar will be required if the weight of the uncooked fruit is taken as the basis of measurement.

Cherry Jam

Use ripe fruit for this, and be careful to reject that which is over-ripe or damaged. The Kentish cherry is best, having a pleasant acid taste. The sweet kinds make it almost impossible to use the quantity of sugar necessary for preserving. Allow ¾ lb. of crushed preserving sugar to each lb. of stoned fruit. Put the fruit and sugar into the preserving pan, and stir occasionally until it just comes to the boil, then let it simmer for ¾ hour, stirring continuously.

Test by putting a little on a cold plate, and if it jellies it is done. If the stirring is well done, no skimming is needed. The scum will all disappear by the time the jam is cooked. Put into jars, let it cool, then cover as described on page 473. The flavour is greatly improved by cracking some of the stones and putting the kernels in with the jam a few minutes before it is done.

ANOTHER METHOD

When the cherries are sweet, allow ½ lb. of sugar to each lb. of fruit, and to each 7 lb. of cherries allow 1 pint of red currant juice with 1 lb. of sugar to the pint of juice.

Cranberry Conserve

1 quart picked Cranberries.	1½ cupfuls Water.
¼ lb. stoned Raisins.	½ lb. shelled Walnuts.
1½ lb. Castor Sugar.	1 Orange.

Boil the cranberries with half the water till they explode, then put them through a sieve, and add the other ingredients —the sugar, the nuts and raisins chopped, and the juice of the orange. Boil for 25 minutes, then pot and cover. Serve with hot or cold turkey or venison.

Black Currant Jam

Let the fruit be quite ripe and gathered on a dry day. Pick the fruit off the stalks. Allow rather more than ¾ lb. of crushed preserving sugar to each lb. of picked currants. Put the fruit and sugar into a preserving pan, bring just to the boil, then simmer for 40 minutes, stirring well all the time. Test by putting a little on a cold plate, and if it jellies it is done. Pour into pots, let it cool, then cover as described on page 473. This jam, having a thick juice, is very liable to burn.

RED CURRANT JAM is made in just the same manner.

Currant and Raspberry Jam

The fruit must be ripe and gathered on a dry day. This very particularly applies to the raspberries. The proportions for fruit and sugar are 1 lb. of picked currants, ¼ lb. of picked

spberries and 1 lb. of crushed preserving sugar. **Put the**
uit and sugar into the preserving pan, and bring **to the**
oil. Simmer, or boil gently, for about 40 minutes, test by
utting a little on a plate, and if it jellies it is done, then
our it into jars, let it cool, and cover as described on
age 473.

Damson Jam

See that the fruit is sound, rejecting any that is damaged.
tone the fruit, then allow ¾ lb. of crushed preserving sugar
o each lb. of stoned fruit. Put the fruit and sugar into the
reserving pan, bring to the boil, then simmer, or gently
oil, for 1 hour. It is important that this jam be well stirred,
s it is very liable to stick and burn. Test by putting a little
n a cold plate, and if it jellies it is done. Pour it into jars,
nd when cool, cover as described on page 473.

Gooseberry Jam, Red

Red gooseberries are usually sweeter than the green or
vhite, and require less sugar. Choose the rough, hairy kind
f possible. Top and tail the fruit, and to each lb. of fruit
llow ¾ lb. of crushed preserving sugar, and to each 12 lb.
f gooseberries, 1 pint of currant juice. Put the gooseberries
nd juice into the preserving pan, and boil until the fruit
egins to break. This will take about 1 hour, as the goose-
erry is a tough fruit. Now add the sugar, and continue
immering for 20 to 30 minutes. Test by putting a little on
a cold plate, and if it jellies it is done. Pour into jars, allow
it to get cold, then cover as described on page 473.

ANOTHER METHOD

Use water instead of currant juice to boil the gooseberries
in. The currant juice is not absolutely necessary.

Gooseberry Jam, Green or White

The gooseberries need not be quite ripe. Top and tail
them, and allow 1 lb. of crushed preserving sugar to each
lb. of picked fruit. Put the sugar into the preserving pan,
with 1 pint of water to each 2 lb. of sugar. Boil together
from 10 to 15 minutes, and remove the scum. Put in the

gooseberries and simmer for ¾ hour. Test by putting a litt
on a cold plate, and if it jellies it is done. Pour into po
let it get cold, then cover as described on page 473.

Greengage Jam

Remove the stones and stalks from the fruit. Allo
¾ lb. of crushed preserving sugar to each lb. of stoned frui
or a little less sugar if the fruit is fully ripe and very swee
Put the fruit and sugar into the pan and bring just to the boi
then simmer for about ¾ hour. Test by putting a little on
cold plate, and if it jellies it is done.

NOTE.—It is an improvement to crack about half th
stones, remove and blanch the kernels, and add these whe
the boiling of the jam is nearly completed. Pour the jar
into pots, let it get cold, then cover and label.

Mulberry Jam

Let the mulberries be ripe and picked dry, and remov
all stalks. It is best to make this jam partly with whol
fruit and partly with juice only, therefore allow 1 lb. o
crushed preserving sugar and 1 pint of mulberry juice t
each lb. of whole fruit. Put the juice and sugar into th
preserving pan, bring just to the boil, then simmer for £
minutes to dissolve the sugar; skim it well during this time
Add the whole fruit, and boil rather quickly for ½ hour
stirring well. Test by putting a little on a plate, and if i
jellies stiffly it is done, then put into pots, and cover when
cold.

Plum Jam

Open the plums and remove the stones, but do not use
a steel knife. Allow from ¾ lb. to 1 lb. of crushed preserving
sugar to each lb. of fruit, weighed before it is stoned. The
quantity of sugar must be judged by the sweetness of the
fruit, which varies much in this respect. Put a layer of stoned
fruit in an earthenware pan, and sprinkle with part of the
sugar. Place another layer of fruit on this, then sprinkle
and add more until all the fruit and sugar are used. Leave
them until the next day.

Put all into the preserving pan, bring to the boil, then
simmer gently for about 15 minutes. Add some blanched

kernels, which greatly improve the flavour, then boil quickly
for about 15 to 20 minutes longer. Stir well, as this jam is
liable to stick and burn. Test by putting a little on a cold
plate, and if it jellies it is done. Pour into pots, allow to get
cold, then cover as described on page 473.

Raspberry Jam

It is desirable that this fruit be picked on a dry day,
also that it be ripe and used as soon as possible. Remove
the stalks. Allow barely 1 lb. of sugar to each lb. of fruit ;
allow a full lb. of sugar and 1 gill of red currant juice to
each lb. of raspberries. The currant juice is a great improvement. Put all into a preserving pan, bring to the boil, and
then simmer gently for about 35 to 40 minutes. Test by
putting a little on a cold plate, and if it jellies it is done.
Pour into pots, allow it to get cold, then cover as described
on page 473.

Rhubarb Jam

If possible obtain young or forced rhubarb, as it does not
require stringing or peeling, neither does it require so much
boiling. Cut the rhubarb into pieces about one inch long.
Allow a pound of crushed preserving sugar to each pound of
rhubarb, and a great improvement can be made by adding
the minced rind of half a lemon (or a little lemon essence) and
a piece of whole ginger to each pound of the rhubarb. Put
all in the preserving pan, and place this on a rather cool
part of the stove until the rhubarb softens. Keep stirring.

When the rhubarb is soft and the sugar melted, bring all
to the boil, and simmer gently for about ½ hour if the rhubarb
is young, or from ¾ to 1 hour if it is old. Test by putting a
little on a cold plate, and if it jellies it is done, then remove
the pieces of ginger. If essence of lemon is used, this should
not be stirred in until the cooking is completed. The ginger
may be omitted if preferred. Pour into pots, and when cold,
cover as described on page 473.

Strawberry Jam

This is a fruit that seldom appears in a perfectly sound
condition, suited for good jam making, at the shops and at
a reasonable price. It is best obtained direct from the fields,

or from one's own gardens. It must be ripe, sound and dry
Remove all stalks.

Allow 1 lb. of crushed preserving sugar to each lb. of
fruit ; or a little more sugar if the fruit is not sweet. Put al
in the preserving pan, bring just to the boil, then simmer
gently for about 30 to 40 minutes. Test by putting a little
on a cold plate, and if it jellies it is done. If the fruit is to
be kept as whole as possible, the stirring must be no more
than is necessary to prevent it burning at the bottom, and
it must then be skimmed well. Pour into pots, let it get cold
then cover as described on page 473.

JELLIES

Apple Jelly

Choose apples with red skins if possible, wipe and cut them
into quarters, but do not peel them. To each lb. of fruit
allow 3 pints of cold water. Put fruit and water into a
preserving pan and boil rapidly for 30 minutes. This will
extract the juice from the apple, and at the same time
the water will be reduced. Strain and press through flannel.
Allow 1 lb. of loaf sugar to each pint of liquid. Put the
liquid and sugar to boil, and again boil rapidly for 30 minutes.

Test by putting a little on a cold plate, and if it jellies it
is done. If liked, a teaspoonful of lemon juice may be added
just before the last boiling is completed. Pour into jars
and, when cold, cover down, as described for jams on page 473.

Blackberry Jelly

Let the fruit be dry and freed from stalks. Put it into a
jar, place this in a saucepan of boiling water and let it simmer
for about ½ hour, until the juice comes away freely. Strain
and press out the juice through coarse flannel, then put
the juice to boil with ¾ lb. of loaf sugar to each pint, and
boil for about 40 minutes, stirring well.

Test by putting a little on a cold plate, and if it jellies
it is done, then pour into jars and, when cold, cover down
as described for jams on page 473. This jelly is improved by
using equal quantities of bullaces and blackberries. The tart
flavour of the bullace overcomes the flatness of the blackberry.

Black Currant Jelly

Free the currants from stalks, put them into a jar, place this in a saucepan of boiling water and simmer for a little more than ½ hour, when the juice should flow from the fruit freely. Strain and press out the juice through flannel.

If preferred, the cooking may be done by putting the fruit into a preserving pan with 1 gill of water to each lb., then bruising and stirring the fruit until the juice flows freely. Allow 1 lb. of loaf sugar to each pint of juice, put into a preserving pan, see that the sugar melts, then boil gently for about 30 minutes, stirring well. Test by putting a little on a cold plate, and if it jellies it is done. Pour into jars and, when cold, cover as described for jam on page 473.

Red Currant Jelly

Let the currants be moderately ripe. Free from stalks, and put them into a jar, place this in a saucepan of boiling water, and simmer for a little more than ½ hour, when the juice should flow freely. Strain through flannel, but if the jelly is wanted very clear, do not press the fruit, as the pulp which will then come through will make the jelly cloudy. If preferred, the cooking can be done in a preserving pan, as described in the last recipe.

To each pint of juice allow ¾ lb. of loaf sugar. Put sugar and juice into the preserving pan, and as soon as the sugar is melted, bring to the boil and simmer for about ½ hour, stirring well. Test by putting a little on a cold plate, and if it jellies it is done. Pour into jars and, when cold, cover as described for jams on page 473.

White Currant Jelly

Proceed exactly as with Red Currant jelly, but do not attempt to do the first cooking in the preserving pan, and see that all vessels are quite clean. Skim carefully and well to keep the jelly clear.

Gooseberry Jelly

Top and tail the gooseberries, which should not be over-ripe, slightly unripe is best. Put them into a preserving pan with 1 quart of water to each gallon of gooseberries and boil until the fruit is quite a pulp, stirring well. Strain and press through a coarse flannel, then to each pint of juice allow

1 lb. of loaf sugar. Put the sugar and juice into a pan, bring to the boil and simmer for about 40 minutes, stirring and skimming well. Test by putting a little on a cold plate, and if it sets it is done. Pour into jars, let it get cold, then cover as described for jams on page 473.

Mulberry Jelly

This is made in the same way as Blackberry jelly, allowing the same amount of sugar and the same time in cooking. A few almonds boiled with the fruit improve the flavour.

Pear Jelly

Let the pears be the most juicy kind obtainable. Cut them into quarters without paring or coring, and put them into the preserving pan with a pint of water to each 4 lb., and boil on a slow fire until they are a pulp, then strain through flannel, or a jelly-bag, and let them remain all night to drain.

The next day squeeze out any remaining juice, and to each pint of juice allow rather more than ½ lb. of loaf sugar and a very little lemon juice to flavour. Boil on a quick fire for about 30 minutes, stirring well. Test by putting a little on a cold plate, and if it jellies it is done. Pour into jars and, when cold, cover as described with jam on page 473.

Quince Jelly

The fruit must be ripe and perfectly sound. Pare and slice, and put the pieces into a preserving pan with just sufficient water to float them. Boil until the fruit is a pulp, which will take quite 2 hours, then strain through flannel, passing the juice through more than once if wanted clear.

To each pint of juice allow 1 lb. of loaf sugar. Boil the juice and sugar together for about ¾ hour, then test by putting a little on a cold plate, and if it jellies it is done. Pour into jars and, when cold, cover as described for jams on page 473. If preferred, the fruit need not be peeled, in fact, some people consider the peel improves the colour of the jelly.

Raspberry Jelly

This is prepared in the same way as Red Currant jelly, with the same amount of sugar and the same time for cooking. It is considered an improvement if some red currant juice is added, ¼ pint to each pint of raspberry juice. The sugar need not be increased if this is done.

Rhubarb Jelly

This is best made in September. Choose red rhubarb, cut it into short lengths and put them in a large jar. To each 6 lb. of rhubarb add the peel of 3 lemons. Put the jar into the oven, let the rhubarb get quite soft, and the juice will flow freely, then strain, and squeeze through flannel.

Put the juice into the preserving pan, or into an enamelled saucepan, with the juice of the 3 lemons. Add 1½ lb. of sugar to each pint of rhubarb juice, and, when dissolved, bring all to the boil and simmer for about ¾ hour, stirring well and skimming. Test by putting a little on a cold plate, and if it jellies it is done. Pour into jars and, when cold, cover as described for jam on page 473.

Strawberry Jelly

Take, say, 4 lb. of strawberries and 2 lb. of red currants or pink rhubarb. If rhubarb is used, cut it into small pieces. Put all into a jar placed in a saucepan of boiling water, and simmer for quite ½ hour, until the juice comes away freely, then strain and press through flannel, but pass it through the flannel again once or twice if wanted quite clear.

Put the juice to boil with ¾ lb. of loaf sugar to every pint, and boil for about 30 minutes, stirring well and skimming. Test by putting a little on a cold plate, and if it jellies it is done. Pour into jars and, when cold, cover as described for jam on page 473.

MARMALADES

Apple Marmalade

Choose good cooking apples, those that cook to a smooth pulp easily. Peel, core, and thinly slice them. Allow ¾ lb. of loaf sugar to each lb. of prepared apple. Put the sugar into the preserving pan with a little water, say ½ cupful to every 6 lb. of sugar, let the sugar gradually melt, then boil it for 10 minutes.

Put in the prepared apple, with a few cloves and a little lemon peel, if liked, boil for an hour, stir, and skim well. It should now be a smooth pulp, moderately clear and of a bright amber colour. Put into jars, and when cool cover and label.

Russet Apple Marmalade

Choose apples that do not cook to a soft pulp. Cut them in quarters, remove the cores (but do not peel them), then cut them into thin slices. Put 3 lb. of loaf sugar into the preserving pan with 1 pint of water, and boil rapidly for 20 minutes to make a syrup. Sufficient syrup should be made three-fourths to cover the apples that are prepared. Put the apple slices into the syrup, and boil for 1 hour, stirring frequently. Flavour with cloves or lemon, as preferred. This marmalade bears a close resemblance to orange marmalade in appearance, if a suitable apple is chosen.

Grapefruit Marmalade

| 4 Grapefruit, 10-12 oz. in weight. | 6 quarts Water. |
| 5 Lemons. | 9 lb. Sugar. |

Wipe the lemons and grapefruit and cut them in half. Remove and collect the juice, but reject the pips and centre core of the grapefruit. Shred the pith and rind of both the grapefruit and lemons thinly, either by hand or machine, then put the shredded pith or peel into a large pan with the water and juice, and soak overnight.

Next day, put into a saucepan, and simmer slowly until the contents of the pan are reduced by half—this will take about 3 hours. Add the sugar, bring to the boil, stirring meanwhile, and boil until it jellies—in about 20 to 30 minutes. Pour into pots and cover.

Lemon Marmalade

Take some lemons, slice them very thinly and remove the seeds, but no white pith or pulp need be removed. To each lb. of sliced fruit add 3 pints of cold water, and let it stand for 24 hours. After standing, put the lemon and water into a pan, and boil until the lemon is tender. Then pour all out into an earthen bowl, and let it stand until the next day.

Weigh the lemon and water, and to each lb. add $1\frac{1}{2}$ lb. of preserving or loaf sugar. Boil together until the syrup jellies—to test this, put a little on a cold plate, and if it thickens and becomes firm like jelly it is done. The lemon should be rather transparent when done.

Orange Marmalade

Choose Seville oranges. Peel them—this is best done by just cutting superficially round the orange twice, and the peel will then come off in quarters. Boil the skins for about 2 hours, changing the water two or three times. This removes the bitterness of the peel. The peel can be tied in muslin. If the peel has much white pulp on it, a little should be scraped off when it is soft, then cut the rind into thin strips about an inch long. Pull the oranges to pieces, remove the pips and cut off as much white pith as possible.

Allow the same weight of sugar as of oranges before they were peeled. Put the sugar, with ½ pint of water to every lb., into the preserving pan. Boil for about 10 minutes, remove the scum, then add the orange pulp and rind. Simmer for about 20 minutes or a little longer, test by putting a little on a plate, and if it jellies it is done.

NOTE.—Orange marmalade is improved by adding the juice and the grated rind of a lemon to the orange pulp just before boiling ; say 1 lemon to 6 oranges.

ANOTHER METHOD

Cut up 12 Seville oranges very thin and small, and pick out the seeds. Put them in an earthenware pan, and add 3 pints of cold water to each lb. of fruit. Let them stand for 24 hours, then put them on the stove and boil until tender. The seeds may be put in a muslin bag and boiled with the oranges. Remove from the fire, and let all stand until next day.

Now to each lb. of boiled fruit add 1 lb. of loaf sugar. Boil, stirring constantly, until the orange is quite clear and the syrup jellies. To test this, put a little on a cold plate and if it thickens and becomes firm like jelly, it is done. An improvement can be made by adding the juice and grated rinds of 2 lemons to this quantity of oranges.

Quince Marmalade

Pare and quarter the fruit, remove the cores, and throw each piece, as done, into cold water to preserve its colour. Put the pieces into a preserving pan with just sufficient water to float them. Stew until the fruit is reduced to a pulp, stirring occasionally—this will take quite 2 hours. Add ¾ lb. of loaf sugar to each lb. of pulp, and boil gently for ¾ hour.

Test by putting a little on a cold plate, and if it jellies it is done. Put into jars, and when cold, cover and label.

Rhubarb Marmalade

4 lb. Rhubarb.	1 gill Water.
6 lb. Sugar.	6 oz. blanched and split Almonds.
6 Lemons (rind of 6, juice of 2).	Red Colouring.

Wipe the rhubarb and lemons, then cut up the rhubarb and add the finely grated lemon rind and the water. Simmer until a pulp, add the sugar, which has been previously heated, the lemon juice and the almonds. Boil rapidly until the marmalade sets when tested on a cold plate, then pot and cover.

DRIED FRUITS AND SYRUP PRESERVES

Dried Cherries

Take large sweet cherries and stone them. The stoning can be done with a little instrument made as follows : Bend a piece of stiff wire to the shape of a rather large and long hairpin. Bind this on to a piece of wood, leaving the loop projecting about an inch. Bend the loop so that it curves over a little. The stones can be readily removed with this. Put the cherries into a preserving pan with well-crushed preserving sugar, or castor sugar, in the proportion of 1 lb. of sugar to 3 lb. of fruit. Boil very gently until the fruit shrinks a little, then strain them free from the syrup.

Put the strained cherries on a sieve, and place them in a cool oven to dry. Do not let them cook. When they are dry enough to handle, they can be stored away. Use the syrup to boil more cherries in, adding a small amount of sugar to make good that taken by the previous lot of cherries. If preferred, the cherries can be rolled in castor or icing sugar before being stored away.

Cherries Preserved in Syrup

The fruit must be sound and ripe. It can be stoned (as described in the last recipe) if preferred. Make a syrup by boiling together sugar and water in the proportion of 1 lb. of the former to $\frac{1}{2}$ pint of the latter. Boil for 15 minutes, and remove what scum there may be. Put in the cherries and boil again for 15 minutes, then strain off the cherries and put them into jars. Reduce the syrup by another 5 minutes' boiling, then pour it over. Allow to get cold, and cover tightly, as described for jam on page 473.

Preserved Damsons

Let the damsons be well picked, and quite free from bruise or blemish. Allow ¼ lb. of castor sugar to each lb. of fruit. Put the fruit in large jars or bottles, sprinkle the sugar in, then stand the jars in a boiler with water reaching well up them. Bring the water gradually to the boil, and simmer until the fruit is soft, but not broken, then take the jars out and strain the juice away. Put the juice in a pan to boil for 15 minutes, then strain it through flannel and pour it over the fruit, either in the bottles it was cooked in or in small jars—the latter is best. When cold, cover as described for jam on page 473.

Damson Cheese

The pulp must be obtained from the fruit without the skins. One method is to bake the damsons until the skin just cracks, then take each one separately and peel it. The peel comes off quite easily. Another way is to put them into a preserving pan, and stir them until they are soft enough to rub or beat through a coarse sieve.

Put the pulp into the preserving pan with ¾ lb. of loaf sugar to each lb. of pulp ; or 1 lb. of sugar if preferred quite sweet. Stir the sugar well in, simmer for 1 hour, then boil quickly for about 20 minutes. Pour into jars and, when cold, cover as described for jam on page 473. The flavour can be improved by cracking half the stones, blanching the kernels and adding these when the cooking is about half completed.

Preserved Ginger

The strength of the ginger requires to be reduced and the flesh well swollen. This is usually effected by putting the green ginger into fresh boiling water each night and morning for a fortnight. Another method is to scald the ginger until it is soft, then peel off the outer skin and soak the inner part in cold water, changing the water several times.

When the ginger is ready, make a heavy syrup with 2 lb.

of sugar to each pint of water, and clarify it. To clarify the syrup, allow the white of one egg to the amount of sugar and water stated above. Stir this in while the sugar is dissolving and before it is put on the fire. When the syrup boils, throw in a small cupful of cold water and bring to the boil again. Do not stir after this water is added. Let it boil for 5 minutes, then stand it aside for a little time and remove the scum. It is then ready for use. Put the ginger into the clarified syrup and boil until it is done, then put into jars and cover when cool.

Greengages Preserved in Syrup

Stone the fruit if preferred. Make a syrup of sugar and water; 1 lb. of the former to $\frac{1}{2}$ pint of the latter. Boil together for 10 minutes and remove the scum. Put in the fruit and simmer for nearly $\frac{1}{2}$ hour. If the stones are removed, blanch some of the kernels and add these when the boiling is half-done, then strain off the fruit and put it into jars. Reduce the syrup by 10 minutes' more boiling, and pour it over the fruit. Allow it to cool, then cover as described for jams on page 473.

Pears Preserved in Syrup

The jargonelle pear is considered best for preserving; failing this, any moderate or small-sized firm pear, not quite ripe (when the pips are just black). Put the pears in the pan over the fire with sufficient cold water to cover, bring to the boil, and simmer until they are slightly soft, then take them out and put into cold water. Pare the fruit carefully, leaving a little of the stem and the blossom or eye at the thick end. Pierce them with a skewer at the blossom end, reaching as far as the core.

Make a syrup of sugar and water, in the proportion of 1 lb. of the former to each $\frac{1}{2}$ pint of the later. Boil for 10 minutes, then remove any scum there may be. Put the pears in and let them simmer gently. If time is of importance, the simmering can be completed at once, but for best results it should be done for about 5 minutes on three successive days, allowing the fruit to remain in the syrup meanwhile. When the pears are done, drain them and put them into jars. Reduce the syrup by boiling for 10 minutes (or enrich it with more sugar if the quantity is none too great), then pour over the fruit. When cool cover tightly.

Plums Preserved in Syrup

Gather the fruit when full grown and just as it begins to ripen. Pick out the largest fruit until the remaining small ones are one-third the whole quantity. Put this third into a preserving pan with as much water as would just cover the whole, then boil and skim well. When the fruit is boiled soft, strain it through a coarse hair sieve.

To each quart of the liquid add $1\frac{1}{2}$ lb. of loaf sugar, boil up, skim well, then put in all the fruit. Scald well and remove from the fire. Put the plums into bottles with wide mouths, pour the syrup over, then lay a piece of white paper on top. Pour some melted mutton fat on top and tie down.

Prune Preserve

First wash the prunes, then put them into a preserving pan with water just to cover, and add the grated rind of a lemon. Stew until quite tender, then rub the prunes through a sieve. Weigh the pulp, and to each lb. allow $\frac{1}{2}$ lb. of sugar. Put the sugar in the pan with a little water, and when it is quite melted add the pulp and boil together for 15 minutes, stirring and skimming well. Pour into jars and, when cool, cover down as described for jams on page 473.

Strawberries

PRESERVED WHOLE IN THEIR OWN JUICE

Obtain large strawberries if possible, picked when dry ; remove all stalks. Allow 1 lb. of sugar to each lb. of fruit. Put a layer of fruit in a deep dish and sprinkle with castor sugar ; put another layer and sprinkle again, and so on. Gently shake the dish, so that the sugar may get beneath and around the fruit, then let it remain for a day, when it will be found that much of the juice will be drawn out.

On the next day drain the juice into an enamelled or copper pan, and put the remaining sugar into it. This can be loaf or castor sugar. When the sugar is melted, put in the strawberries, bring to the boil, and simmer gently for nearly 30 minutes. Test by putting a little on a cold plate, and if it jellies it is done. When the strawberries are being boiled, do not stir more than is absolutely necessary so as not to damage the fruit. Put into jars, and, when cold, cover as described for jam on page 473.

CANNED FOODS

By John Campbell, Ph.D.

The world owes a debt of gratitude to those food experts working with the manufacturers who have, by patient research and experiment, brought the preserving processes to their present state of efficiency.

The old idea that tinned foods are greatly inferior in nutritive and caloric value to the fresh foods from which they were prepared is now known to be wrong. The contrary is the truth. Generally they have a higher protein and caloric value, on account of the lower water content, the removal before preservation of waste parts (like bone, gristle, and offal), and the addition of accessory ingredients like oil, gelatine and sugar.

In fresh fish, as purchased, for example, the waste may reach 70 per cent., but when canned the whole of the contents is edible. In tinned salmon the waste falls from 40 to 14 per cent., and in lobster it is nil. In those foods which need no cooking there is a further saving of coal, gas, or electric current.

Canned fruit also yields the fruit acids and salts in their natural condition, and roughage in the form of cellulose and fibre. The latter is much softened by the preserving processes and gives the necessary intestinal bulk without undue irritation. Nor is the flavour adversely affected except in a very few instances. In many fruits the flavour is developed and preferred by most people to stewed fresh fruit. This is especially the case with stoned fruit.

VITAMINS IN CANNED FOODS

It was long thought that the high temperature to which preserved food was subjected destroyed the vitamin content. But this theory has been proved to be wrong. It was based on insufficient data and incomplete knowledge of the exact conditions under which vitamins are destroyed.

In modern canning processes, the sterilising is completed as rapidly as possible in the sealed tins, thus protecting the contents from the action of air, and the vitamins are thus preserved from destruction. In animal foods, like soups and fish, it has been proved that there is no loss of vitamin content during the preserving processes. In the brands submitted to bio-chemical tests it was found that they were richer in vitamins A and B than green vegetables or milk.

In vegetables and fruit the chief vitamin present is water—soluble, anti-scorbutic C. This vitamin is more sensitive to the action of heat than A, B, D or E, but provided the food is protected from oxidation and the action of alkalies, and the period of heating is short, little or no destruction takes place. Modern preserving operations fulfil these conditions, and recent researches show conclusively that canned fruit has a full vitamin content. Canned tomatoes, peas, apples, peaches, were found to undergo no loss of vitamin C and to be richer in that element than fresh orange juice. Canned spinach is richer in anti-rachitic vitamin D than butter and almost equal to cod-liver oil in that respect. Storage for 3 years had no deteriorating effect on the vitamin content.

FOOD POISONING

To many people all canned food is suspect on account of the fear of poisoning. But under modern processes the danger of infection may be dismissed. Occasionally cases of microbic infection have been traced to the consumption of canned foods, but these are so rare in relation to the millions of tins used for culinary purposes, that the degree of absolute safety has almost been reached. It is certain that there are far more cases of disease from the consumption of tainted or infected fresh food than from preserved foods.

Sir William Willcox, the eminent authority on toxicology and scientific advisor to the Home Office, pointed out in his address to the London Chamber of Commerce that " Ptomaine poisoning from the consumption of canned foods was so rare that we may dismiss it." In the same lecture he mentioned that in his military experience during the war not a single case of food poisoning occurred from food being infected in the unopened tin. Millions of troops were fed for years on canned foods, and the evidence of poisoning was nil. The sources of contamination were to be found in the house and not as a rule in food supplied by the provision trade. It was usually the food in the kitchen.

In the early periods of the canned industry when solder was used in conjunction with naked metal, there was evidence of a certain degree of metallic contamination from the action of the acids on the metal. Under modern processes this danger has been entirely eliminated by the use of internally lacquered tins and other precautions which prevent the formation of the deleterious metallic salts. Sir William Willcox, referring to this point in a lecture, said, "The danger of metallic poisoning from tinned foods was nil. He had never met a case in a fairly large experience of food poisoning."

Efficiently prepared tins show slightly concave ends. Tins with bulging ends should not be bought because bulging ends indicate internal fermentation and decomposition with the formation of gas. When buying canned foods remember to confine your purchases to branded goods packed by reputable firms giving the source of origin, and who assume full responsibility for them. By doing this you are assured of the purity and quality of the goods you purchase.

The entire contents of all canned foods should be emptied into glass or earthenware dishes immediately after opening, and consumed as soon as practicable.

PRESERVED FRUIT RECIPES

Fleur of Cherries

PASTRY CASE

5 oz. Flour.	Pinch of Salt.
2½ oz. Butter.	Cold Water.

FILLING

1 tin Cherries.	Vanilla Flavouring.

½ pint Cream, or ¼ pint of Cream and ¼ pint Custard.

UTENSILS—Tin-opener, 2 basins, knife, wooden spoon, pastry board, rolling pin, pie-plate, fork, egg-beater, gill measure. *Enough for 3 or 4 persons.*

Cut and rub the butter into the flour till it is like fine breadcrumbs, and add the salt. Mix to a very stiff consistency with cold water, then roll out, and line a deep plate with the pastry. Prick well, and bake in a moderate oven for about 20 minutes.

When cold, pile the cherries in the centre, cover the fruit with whipped cream, sweetened and flavoured. If custard and cream are used, whip the cream, add the custard when it is quite cold, and pour over the cherries.

Scalloped Greengages

1 tin Greengages.	**1 oz.** Butter.
4 oz. Breadcrumbs.	**½ pint** Juice from tin.

UTENSILS.—Tin-opener, grater, frying pan, kitchen spoon, ie-dish, pint measure. *Enough for about 3 persons.*

Place the breadcrumbs in a frying pan and add the utter. Fry slowly till golden brown in colour, pressing and tirring frequently with a spoon, then drain the greengages, nd place a layer of fruit in the bottom of a greased pie-dish. .dd a layer of browned crumbs, and repeat the process till he dish is filled, taking care to finish with a layer of crumbs. 'our the fruit syrup over the whole, and re-heat in a moderate ven for about 20 minutes.

Loganberries in Jelly

1 bottle or tin Loganberries.	**½ pint** Cream or Custard.
Sugar to flavour. Gelatine.	**½ oz.** chopped Walnuts.

UTENSILS—2 basins, wire whisk or saucepan, glass dish, :itchen spoon, pint measure, knife. *Enough for about 4 persons.*

Drain the loganberries, and to every ½ pint of juice from he tin, add ½ oz. of gelatine. Add sufficient sugar to sweeten, hen add half the loganberries, and pour into a glass dish. When set, cover with custard or whipped cream. Decorate with the remainder of the loganberries, and sprinkle with :hopped walnuts.

Peach " Eggs "

6 Peaches. **¼ pint** Cream.	Wine, flavoured Milk, or Fruit
6 rounds of Sponge Cake.	Syrup.
¾ oz. Sugar.	Flavouring.

UTENSILS—Knife, glass bowl or individual dishes, basin, wire whisk. *Enough for 6 persons.*

Cut a sponge into rounds. Soak the sponge with wine, milk, or fruit syrup, and place one peach on top of each portion, round side uppermost. Add sugar and flavouring to the cream, and whip it to a coating consistency and coat each peach. Sprinkle with chopped pistachio nuts.

Pear Hedgehog

1 tin Pears.	**4 oz.** Sugar.
2 Whites of Eggs.	Blanched sliced Almonds.

UTENSILS—Tin-opener, basin, wire whisk, baking tin, saucepan, knife.

Drain the pears. Whip the whites of eggs stiffly, slowl
add half the sugar and beat it well in, then stir in the remainin
sugar. Place the pears on a baking tin, cover each pear wit
the sugar and egg mixture, and insert the sliced almonds t
represent hedgehog prickles.

Bake in a very slow oven till the meringue is crisp—abou
¾ hour to 1 hour. Allow to cool, and serve accompanied b
fruit syrup from the tin served in a sauce-boat.

Strawberry Shortcake

½ lb. Flour. 4½ oz. Butter.	½ oz. Ground Almonds.
2 oz. Castor Sugar.	Pinch of Baking Powder.
1 Yolk of Egg.	1 bottle or tin of Strawberries.

Whipped and sweetened Cream.

UTENSILS—3 basins, wooden spoon, pastry board, rollin
pin, fork, wire whisk. *Enough for about 4 persons.*

Cream the butter and sugar, add the yolk of egg, an
mix, then work in the flour, ground almonds and bakin
powder. Divide into three, and roll into rounds about
quarter of an inch thick. Prick, and bake in a moderat
oven till a golden brown.

Crush the strawberries, add the sugar and a little cream
and spread on to a round of shortcake. Cover with the next
round, then repeat the process, and complete with a layer
of strawberries. Pile whipped cream on top and round the
edges of the layers of fruit. Decorate with pistachio nuts.

Basket of Fruits

1 round Sponge Cake.	Mixed bottled or tinned Fruits.
2 oz. Desiccated Cocoanut.	Cream, if liked.
4 tablespoonfuls Jam.	Angelica.

UTENSILS—Knife, saucepan, brush, baking sheet, basin,
wire whisk, metal spoon.

Hollow out the centre of the sponge cake. Melt the jam
and brush it over the outside of the cake, then roll the cake
in desiccated cocoanut which has been slightly browned in
the oven, and afterwards soak it in juices obtained from the
bottles or tins. Pile the fruits in the centre and cover with
whipped and sweetened cream, and place a thin handle of
angelica over the top of the basket.

NOTE.—Individual " baskets " can be made from penny
sponge cakes.

Raspberry Sponge

| 1 bottle or tin of Raspberries. | 1½ Jelly Squares. | Water. |

UTENSILS—Basin, saucepan, metal spoon, wire whisk, glass dish, knife. *Enough for 4 or 5 persons.*

Drain the fruit, dissolve the jelly squares in the juice, in a saucepan, and add sufficient water to make 1½ pints in all, when dissolved. Place the raspberries in the bottom of a glass dish, adding sufficient liquid jelly to set the fruit. Cool the remaining jelly, then whisk it to a stiff froth. Pour this on top of the fruit, and decorate with raspberries and chopped jelly.

Baked Plums

1 bottle or 1 lb. tin Plums.
½ oz. Butter.   4 oz. Sugar.
¼ pint Water.

Small piece of Cinnamon Stick, or ½ teaspoonful grated Nutmeg.

UTENSILS—Knife, fireproof dish, basin, jug, basting spoon, teaspoon. *Enough for 4 persons.*

Remove the fruit from its container and pour off the juice. Cut the plums in half and stone them. Arrange them in a greased casserole or fireproof dish, and sprinkle with sugar. Add the cinnamon stick or grated nutmeg, pour the water over the fruit, and place small pieces of butter on top.

Bake in a moderate oven till the fruit is soft, basting frequently with the juice, and adding more water if necessary. Serve with pastry fingers or shortbread biscuits.

Apricot Tart

1 tin Apricots.
5 oz. Flour.   2½ oz. Butter.

Cold Water.   Pinch of Salt.
Jam Glaze, as described.

UTENSILS—Tin-opener, 2 basins, knife, wooden spoon, tablespoon, pastry board, rolling pin, pie-plate, fork, saucepan, strainer. *Enough for 3 or 4 persons.*

Cut and rub the fat into the flour until the mixture resembles fine breadcrumbs. Add the salt, and mix to a very stiff consistency with cold water, then roll out thinly, and line a tin plate with the mixture. Decorate the edges with small rounds of the dough, prick and bake in a moderate oven.

Drain the apricots. When the pastry is quite cold, fill with the fruit, keeping the round sides uppermost. Coat with jam glaze, as below, and decorate with finely chopped almonds.

THE JAM GLAZE

1 gill Syrup from tin.
1¼ tablespoonfuls Jam.

¼ oz. Gelatine.
1½ tablespoonfuls Sugar.

1 tablespoonful Lemon Juice.

Boil the jam, syrup, lemon juice and sugar for 5 minutes. Cool slightly and add the gelatine, then boil again and strain into a basin. When cool, add pink colouring. Use when setting.

Chaudfroid of Pineapple

1 tin Pineapple Slices.	¼ pint Custard.
1 Jelly Square.	

UTENSILS—Tin-opener, knife, basin, 2 saucepans, tablespoon, wooden spoon, pint measure. *Enough for about 4 persons.*

Remove the pineapple from the tin and drain the slices. Cut up the jelly square, add about 4 tablespoonfuls of the fruit juice, and heat till dissolved. Prepare the custard, and when cold stir in the dissolved jelly, which should be cold but not set. Coat the slices with the mixture, and when set fill the centres with chopped jelly.

Cold Pineapple Soufflé

1 small tin Pineapple Chunks.	4 oz. Sugar.
¼ pint Syrup from tin.	½ pint Cream.
3 Whites of Eggs.	½ oz. Gelatine.
3 Yolks of Eggs.	Rind of 1 Lemon.

UTENSILS—Tin-opener, 3 basins, wire whisk, saucepan, pint measure, tablespoon, knife, soufflé case. *Enough for 4 persons.*

Place the yolks, sugar, rind and juice in a basin, and whisk over a pan of hot water till the sugar is dissolved, then remove from the pan and whisk till cold. Add the cream, slightly whipped, and fold in the stiffly beaten whites of eggs. Stir in the gelatine (previously dissolved in 3 tablespoonfuls of water or juice). When the mixture shows signs of seething, add the chunks, cut into small pieces, and pour into a soufflé case. When set, decorate with pineapple and pistachio nuts.

Empire Punch

1 quart Water. 4 oz. Sugar.	¼ pint Strawberry Juice.
¼ pint Lemon Juice.	½ pint Pineapple Juice.
Mint Leaves.	

UTENSILS—Saucepan, pint measure, lemon squeezer, jug.

Boil the water and sugar together for 20 minutes, then add the fruit juice and allow to cool. Serve in a tall jug, garnished with mint leaves.

PICKLES

Use porcelain or enamelled saucepans for pickling. On no account use brass, copper or tin pans. Use wooden spoons for mixing, and allow no metallic substance to come into contact with pickle or vinegar. If you put a piece of horse-radish into a jar of pickles, the vinegar will not lose its strength so quickly, and the pickles will keep sound much longer, especially tomato pickles. Use glass or glazed stone jars for potting pickles, and always make certain that the vinegar completely covers the pickles. If any pickles show signs of not being good, pour off the vinegar and cover with fresh vinegar and add fresh spices, first removing the damaged pickles.

TO MAKE BRINE FOR PICKLES

Put 1 gallon of water and 1 lb. of salt into a saucepan. Bring to the boil, then strain, and let the brine become quite cold before using.

UTENSILS REQUIRED FOR MAKING PICKLES—Porcelain or enamelled saucepan or preserving pan, wooden spoon, knife, strainer, flannel bag, large sieve or hamper lid, skimmer, pint measure, measuring spoons, basins, large jar, lemon squeezer, glass or glazed stone jars or bottles, bladder covers or corks and wax.

Pickled Beetroot

The beets must first be cooked. Wash the roots very carefully, so that the outside skin may not be broken. Do not trim them, for if they are damaged or cut they will lose nearly all their colour in cooking. Put them into boiling water with a little vinegar in it, and simmer gently for 1 hour to $1\frac{1}{2}$ hours, according to age. They do not require to be fully cooked. Remove the beets, and let them cool.

Take sufficient vinegar to cover the beet when it is cut up and bottled. Boil this up with $\frac{1}{2}$ oz. of whole pepper and $\frac{1}{2}$ oz. of allspice to each quart. Let it boil gently for 15 minutes. Peel the beets, cut them into slices a little more than a quarter of an inch thick, and put them into bottles or jars. When the vinegar is cold, pour it over. Cover the bottle or jar with bladder. If bottles are used they may be corked and waxed as described for bottled fruits on page 470.

Pickled Red Cabbage

Take off the outside leaves of the cabbage; quarter it; cut out the stem; then slice it rather thinly across. Lay the cut cabbage out on a large dish, or in the bottom of a tub; strew salt over and leave for about 20 hours. After this time, take out the cabbage and drain it as free from brine as possible on a sieve or clean hamper lid.

Take sufficient vinegar to cover the cabbage when it is in the jars, and boil this up with $\frac{1}{2}$ oz. of whole pepper and $\frac{1}{2}$ oz. of bruised ginger to each quart. A little allspice may be added if preferred. Put the cabbage in jars or bottles, pour the boiled vinegar (when cold) over it, then cover as described with BEETROOT above.

Pickled Cucumber

Cut the cucumbers into slices about a quarter of an inch thick. Spread these out on a dish and sprinkle with salt (as for pickled cabbage). Let them remain for about 20 hours. After this time, put the pieces on to a sieve to drain well, for 5 or 6 hours. Take sufficient vinegar to cover the cucumber when it is in jars, and boil this up with $\frac{1}{2}$ oz. of whole pepper and $\frac{1}{2}$ oz. of bruised ginger to each quart. Boil for about 10 minutes, then, while hot, pour it over the cucumbers in their jars or bottles. Cover, as described with BEETROOT on page 497.

Pickled Gherkins

Soak about 100 gherkins in a pickle of $2\frac{1}{2}$ lb. of common salt to 1 gallon of water. Let them remain in this for a day, then take them out, drain well, wipe separately, and put them in a large jar. Boil together 2 quarts of vinegar (white vinegar if obtainable), 3 oz. of common salt, 1 oz. of allspice, 1 oz. of mustard seed, $\frac{1}{2}$ oz. of cloves, $\frac{1}{2}$ oz. of mace, half a slice of nutmeg and half a stick of horseradish. Let all boil for 12 minutes, then skim well.

When cold, pour this mixture over the gherkins in the large jar, and let them stand for about 20 hours closely covered. The next day put all into a pan, bring to the boil, then simmer for 10 minutes. Put the gherkins into jars, pour the vinegar and spices over, then cover, as described for BEETROOT on page 497. This pickle is better for being kept a month.

Mixed Pickles

The following vegetables may be used : cauliflower, cucumber, gherkins, small onions, French beans and capsicums.

Pick the cauliflower into nice pieces, and cut the cucumber into small blocks. The other vegetables need only be trimmed, not cut up. It is best not to wash the vegetables, only wipe them. Put the vegetables in an earthenware pan and sprinkle well with salt. Let them remain 3 days, then drain, shake them, and put in the sun to dry.

Make a pickle as follows.—Take 1 quart of vinegar, $\frac{1}{2}$ oz. of turmeric, $\frac{1}{2}$ oz. of ground black pepper, $\frac{1}{4}$ oz. of pounded cloves, 1 oz. of ground mustard, $\frac{1}{2}$ oz. of mustard seed, 1 oz. of bruised ginger and a little cayenne to taste (a small pinch). Put the mixed vegetables into jars or bottles. Put the vinegar and spices on to boil, simmer for about 10 minutes, then pour boiling hot on to the vegetables. When cool, cover as described for BEETROOT on page 497.

Pickled Onions

The small silver onions have the best appearance, but ordinary kinds will do. Take off first the dry outside skin, then the next skin. Put the onions in a large jar. Make a strong solution of salt and water, bring it to the boil, then pour over the onions and let all get cold. Repeat this with new salt and water, then drain. Put the onions into bottles or jars, cover with cold vinegar in which is a teaspoonful of black pepper, a slice of whole ginger and a blade of mace to each pint. A bayleaf can be put in each jar or bottle if liked. Cover, as described for BEETROOT on page 497.

Piccalilli

Prepare vegetables as follows : slice a closely grown white-hearted cabbage, slice a good sound beetroot, divide a cauliflower into neat pieces, trim and wipe a few French beans, gherkins and radish pods. Lay these on a sieve or clean hamper-lid, well sprinkle with salt, and expose to the sun or fire for 3 days, that all water may be extracted. Shake off the salt, then put the vegetables into a stoneware pan, mix them well and scatter some mustard seed in also.

Put some vinegar on to boil with 1 oz. of sliced garlic and $\frac{1}{2}$ oz. of turmeric to each quart. Put the vegetables in a large jar, and when the vinegar boils, pour it over boiling hot. Tie a paper over and let all stand for 2 weeks in a warm place, preferably near a fire. Now put the pickle into the jars or bottles, but the quantity of vinegar must be such that it does not fill them. Boil some fresh vinegar with $\frac{1}{2}$ oz. of white pepper, $\frac{1}{2}$ oz. of mace, and a small pinch of nutmeg and cloves to each quart. When boiling, skim well and fill the bottles or jars with this. When cool, cover as described for BEETROOT on page 497.

Pickled Walnuts

The walnuts are picked young, before the hard shell is formed inside. Prepare a strong brine, well prick the walnuts with a fork, and put them in it. Change the brine each third day, until the walnuts have been in 9 days, then take them out and drain well. Spread them on a sieve or clean hamper-lid in the sun, until they become black. This will take about 3 days, then put the walnuts into bottles or jars, and prepare the pickle as follows :

Put some vinegar on to boil with 2 oz. of whole pepper, 1 oz. of allspice, and 1 oz. of bruised ginger to each quart. Boil for 15 minutes, then pour the mixture over the walnuts boiling hot. When cool, cover as described with BEETROOT.

Spiced Pickled Pears

4 lb. Pears.	2 lb. Sugar.	2-inch stick of Cinnamon.
2 pints Vinegar.		Juice and Rind of $\frac{1}{2}$ Lemon.
16 Cloves.	10 Allspice.	Large piece of Whole Ginger.

Peel, core, and cut the pears into pieces of equal size. Tie the spices loosely in muslin, then put the sugar, vinegar, lemon juice and spices into a saucepan and simmer for 15 minutes. Add the fruit, and cook till tender. Remove and pack into glass jars, fill these with the vinegar syrup, and tie down when cold. SPICED PLUMS can be made in the same way.

Chilli Sauce

18 ripe Tomatoes.	1 tablespoonful Celery Seed.
2 tablespoonfuls Salt.	2 or 3 Red Peppers.
2 tablespoonfuls Ginger.	1 quart Vinegar.
1 tablespoonful Cloves.	1 tablespoonful Allspice.
$\frac{1}{2}$ cupful Sugar.	1 tablespoonful Cinnamon.
2 Onions.	1 tablespoonful Mustard.

Peel the tomatoes, after dipping them in boiling water, chop them, and place them in a preserving pan. Add the peppers, finely minced, the onions peeled and minced, the round spices, and vinegar. Boil for about 2 hours until thick, stirring frequently to avoid scorching, then bottle and seal.

STORE SAUCES

A Fish Sauce

Gather about as many nasturtium blossoms as will go into a pint measure, and put these into a jar with a quart of good vinegar. Add 6 shallots, 3 teaspoonfuls of salt, and 2 teaspoonfuls of cayenne, and let these stand for 8 or 10 days. Strain off the vinegar, and to each pint of this add 2 oz. soy and 2 oz. essence of anchovies. Bottle, cork well, and wax over the corks.

Green Tomato Sauce

Slice $\frac{1}{2}$ peck of green tomatoes, sprinkle them with a cupful of salt, and let them stand all night. The next day pour off the liquor and put the slices into a saucepan with vinegar to cover. Add 3 green or red chillies, 2 large onions chopped finely, $\frac{1}{2}$ teaspoonful of brown sugar, $\frac{1}{2}$ teacupful of scraped horseradish, 1 dessertspoonful each of cloves and allspice, and $\frac{1}{2}$ teaspoonful each of red and white pepper. Bring to the boil, simmer until the tomato is quite soft, then put into wide-necked bottles, cork well and wax over the corks.

Harvey Sauce

Take 6 anchovies (some consider that sprats serve as well) and cut them up small. Take a head of garlic and a shallot and chop rather finely. Put these ingredients into a jar, and add 6 teaspoonfuls of soy, 6 teaspoonfuls of walnut or mushroom ketchup, $\frac{1}{2}$ oz. of cayenne and $\frac{1}{2}$ gallon of vinegar. Add a little carmine colouring, if liked. Let these ingredients soak together for 10 or 12 days, stirring them frequently, then strain through flannel, bottle, cork well and wax over the corks.

An Epicure's Sauce

Take ½ pint of mushroom ketchup, ½ pint of walnut ketchup, 3 oz. of chopped shallots, 2 oz. of soy, 2 oz. of port wine, ½ oz. of cloves, ½ oz. of white pepper, and ¼ oz. of cayenne. Let these soak together for 10 or 12 days, stirring frequently. Strain through flannel, then add ¼ pint of vinegar. Bottle, cork well, and wax over the corks.

A General Store Sauce

Take 10 cloves of garlic and chop them. Put these into a saucepan with 1 quart of vinegar, 1 oz. of cayenne, tablespoonfuls of soy, and 2 tablespoonfuls of walnut ketchup; bring to the boil, then simmer for ½ hour. Strain through flannel, then bottle. Cork well and wax over the corks.

Piquant Sauce

Take 3 cloves of garlic, 3 shallots, 3 anchovies, 2 table spoonfuls of mushrooms and 1 oz. of cayenne. Bruise all well together in a mortar, then pour on 1½ pints of boiling vinegar. Put all into a large bottle, and let it stand for 2 or 3 weeks, shaking occasionally. At the expiration of this time strain it through flannel, then bottle. Cork well, and wax over the corks.

Reading Sauce

Take 1 pint of liquor from pickled walnuts, 1 pint of water, a bare ½ pint of soy, 1 oz. of shallot, ¼ oz. of bruised ginger, ½ oz. of mustard seed, 1 anchovy, ¼ oz. of cayenne, and a few dried bayleaves. First bruise the shallots, put them to boil with the walnut liquor, and boil for 15 minutes, then bruise all the other ingredients that need it (except the bay-leaves), and put them together in another pan.

Boil these for about an hour, then mix in the boiled walnut juice, stirring well. Simmer all together for 15 minutes, then put all into a jar, cover closely, and let them stand for 24 hours. Now open the jar, add the bayleaves, then close down and let it stand for a week, after which strain the sauce through flannel, then bottle. Cork well, and wax over the corks.

Tomato Sauce

Choose ripe tomatoes, and bake them in the oven until they are tender, then rub them through a sieve, fine enough

keep back the seeds and skins. To every lb. of pulp allow
pint of chilli vinegar (or vinegar with a little cayenne),
oz. of garlic, 1 oz. of shallot, 1 oz. of scraped horseradish,
oz. of ground white pepper and ½ oz. of salt. Boil the whole
ogether, until every ingredient is tender, then rub all through
sieve, and to every lb. of the mixture add the juice of two
mons. Boil again until of the consistency of cream. When
old, bottle, cork well, and wax over the corks.

Apple and Tomato Chutney

6 cooking Apples.	6 large Tomatoes.
4 small Onions.	1 cupful stoned Raisins.
3 teaspoonfuls Salt.	1 quart Vinegar.
3 cupfuls Brown Sugar.	¼ cupful mixed Peppercorns,
1 Green Pepper.	Allspice Berries and Cloves.

Mix the finely chopped peeled apples, and the tomatoes,
aisins, and seeded pepper together in a saucepan. Add the
emainder of the ingredients, with the spices tied in a muslin
ag, and boil for 1½ hours very steadily. Remove the spice
ag, and pack the chutney in sterilised jars and seal down.

Green Tomato Chutney

4 lb. green Tomatoes.	1 lb. Marrow.
1 lb. Sugar.	1 lb. Sultanas.
1 lb. Shallots.	¼ oz. bruised Ginger.
3 pints Vinegar.	3 oz. Salt.
Juice of 3 Lemons.	½ oz. Chillies.
3 lb. Apples.	1 doz. White Peppercorns.

Pour the vinegar and sugar into a pan with the ginger,
peppercorns and chillies, tied in muslin, and boil for 50
minutes. Cut the vegetables into small pieces, or pass them
through a mincing machine, and add them, with the lemon
juice, to the vinegar, then simmer until the vegetables are
thoroughly cooked and the chutney is sufficiently thick—
in about 3½ to 4 hours. It may be necessary to add more
vinegar as cooking proceeds.

RED TOMATO CHUTNEY can be made in the same way,
using firm red tomatoes.

Mushroom Ketchup

Mushrooms for this purpose must be picked when dry.
Break them up into small pieces, place them in a stoneware
pan, and sprinkle with salt, allowing ¼ lb. of salt to each 3½
lb. of mushrooms. Let them stand for 3 days, frequently

stirring and mashing them, to cause the juice to flow. No
strain, and also get all the juice possible by pressure.

To each quart of juice add 2 oz. of salt, a few clove
¼ oz. of peppercorns and ¼ oz. of whole ginger. If preferrec
a pinch of cayenne and a little mace may be added. Bo
slowly for 1 hour, then strain. Bottle, cork well, and wa
the corks over. Some consider that more juice is obtaine
by heating the mushrooms in a jar in the oven.

NOTE.—Double ketchup is made by boiling ordinar
ketchup down, a quart to a pint. There is no advantage i
making this, except that smaller quantities can be used tha
of the ordinary ketchup.

Walnut Ketchup

The green outer shells of walnuts serve quite well fo
this. Take three half-sieves of these and put them in a tul
with salt sprinkled between each layer. About 1½ lb. of sal
will be the quantity required. Let them stand for 6 days
occasionally stirring and mashing them, until the shell
are soft and pulpy. Drain the liquor away as it appears
This can be done by banking up the shells on one side of th
tub, then raising that side. Continue this as long as liquo
can be obtained from them ; the quantity obtained shoul
be about 3 quarts.

Simmer the liquor in an iron boiler, until scum ceases t
rise. Now add 2 oz. of bruised ginger, 2 oz. of allspice,
oz. of long pepper and 1 oz. of cloves, and boil all togethe
for ½ hour. When cool, strain and bottle. Some prefer no
to strain, but to put the spices in the bottles with the ketchup
an equal quantity in each bottle. This ketchup is not properl
mature and fit for use until kept for 6 months. Well cor
the bottles, and wax over the corks.

VINEGARS

Tarragon Vinegar

The full-grown shoots of tarragon are used for this, anc
they should be gathered the day before they are needed
Fill a half-gallon jar with as many as will go in withou
pressing down. Add 3 cloves, and the rind of 1 lemon, cu
thinly. Fill up the jar with white wine vinegar, and tightl
cork it. Expose to the sun for 2 or 3 weeks, then open and

train off the vinegar. Wring the tarragon in a cloth, filter all the vinegar through flannel, then bottle it.

Cucumber Vinegar

Peel 3 moderate-sized cucumbers, and slice them. Put them into a jar, and pour on 1 quart of cold vinegar. Slice 2 onions and 2 shallots, and add these, together with 1 tablespoonful of pepper, ¼ tablespoonful of cayenne and about 1 tablespoonful of salt. Let this stand for a week. At the expiration of this time boil all up, then allow to get cold, strain through flannel, then bottle.

NOTE.—This vinegar can be used for salads, or as a cold meat sauce.

Garlic, Shallot, or Horseradish Vinegar

This vinegar is simply made by putting 2 oz. of finely chopped garlic, or shallot, or scraped horseradish, into 1 quart of cold boiled vinegar, and, after it has infused for about 2 weeks, the vinegar is strained off and bottled. With horseradish vinegar, a little finely chopped shallot is an improvement. Either can be used as soon as made.

Raspberry Vinegar

2 quarts fresh Raspberries.	2 quarts Vinegar.	Sugar.

Pick and wash the raspberries, then drain them well. Pour the vinegar over them, and let them stand in a covered vessel for 4 days, stirring them every morning. Strain, and add 1 lb. of sugar to every pint of juice. Bring slowly to the boil and simmer for 20 minutes. Bottle when cold, and cork tightly for winter use.

BLACK CURRANT VINEGAR can be made in the same way.

Spiced Vinegar

1 quart Vinegar.	2 oz. Black Peppercorns.
1 oz. Whole Ginger.	1 oz. minced Shallots.
2 Bayleaves. ½ oz. Allspice.	½ oz. Salt. 2 cloves of Garlic.

Crush the allspice, ginger and peppercorns and place them in a jar, add the remainder of the ingredients, and cover closely. Stand the jar in a warm place for 7 days, then place it in a saucepan containing boiling water, and simmer for 1 hour. Cool, strain the vinegar, and bottle.

BEVERAGES

CORDIALS AND LIQUEURS

Angelica Cordial

Take 1 quart of proof spirit, and dissolve in this 1 dram of calamus and ¼ oz. of oil of angelica. Add 1 quart of white sugar syrup, mix well, and bottle.

Anise Liqueur

Put 1 oz. of anise-seed in 1 quart of proof spirit or brandy, and let it macerate for 2 weeks, shaking it occasionally. If preferred, the oil of anise-seed can be used, and for this quantity half a dram will be sufficient. Strain off the seed, add 1 quart of white sugar syrup, mix well, and bottle.

Anisette

Take 1 quart of proof spirit, and dissolve in it 1 dram of oil of anise and ½ dram of oil of star anise. Add 1 pint of white sugar syrup, mix well, and bottle.

Blackberry Cordial

Take 1 quart of crushed blackberries, and macerate them in 1 quart of brandy for a week. Press out the liquor, and add ½ lb. of loaf sugar to it. Let it stand for 2 weeks, then strain through flannel, and bottle.

Caraway Liqueur

In 1 quart of brandy dissolve ½ dram of oil of caraway and add ½ pint of white sugar syrup. Mix well and bottle.

Cherry Brandy

Mash 3 lb. of black cherries with their stones. Put these in a jar with 1 gallon of proof spirit, or best brandy, and let them macerate for 2 weeks. Dissolve 2 lb. of loaf sugar in rather less than ¾ gallon of water. Press the liquor from the cherries, add the syrup to it, then strain through flannel, and bottle.

Cherry Cordial

Dissolve 2 lb. of loaf sugar in 1 quart of cherry juice. When quite dissolved, add 1 quart of best brandy. Mix well and bottle.

Cherry Liqueur

Take 1 lb. of black cherries and 1 lb. of morella cherries, and mash them with the stones. The stones should be broken. Bruise about a dozen cloves, and add these. Add $\frac{1}{4}$ oz. of cinnamon and $\frac{1}{2}$ lb. of loaf sugar. Put all into a large jar or bottle, and pour in 1 quart of brandy. Cork tightly, let it stand for 2 weeks, then strain through flannel, and bottle.

Clove Brandy

Take 2 oz. of cloves and 2 oz. of coriander seed, and bruise them. Put these with $\frac{1}{2}$ lb. of loaf sugar into 1 quart of brandy. This liqueur is greatly improved by the flavour of cherries, and either a little cherry essence or a $\frac{1}{4}$ lb. of bruised black cherries can be added. Put all into a large bottle, and let them stand for 3 or 4 weeks, then strain through flannel and bottle.

Curaçao

This liqueur as sold is made with the peel of the curaçao orange as follows :

Put $\frac{1}{2}$ lb. of the peel in 2 quarts of good brandy, and let it stand for a week. Half an ounce of sanders wood is usually put in with the peel to give the liqueur its usual reddish-brown colour. When it has stood a week, strain off the liquor ; then dissolve in it $\frac{1}{2}$ dram of oil of bitter almonds and $\frac{1}{2}$ dram of oil of cinnamon. Lastly, add 1 pint of white sugar syrup. Strain through flannel (or filter through blotting paper), then bottle. It should stand a few weeks before using, as it improves with time.

ANOTHER METHOD

Take 2 Seville oranges and $\frac{1}{2}$ a small lemon, and pare them thinly. Put the peel into a large bottle with $1\frac{1}{2}$ drams of cinnamon, $1\frac{1}{2}$ drams of coriander seed and 1 pint of good brandy or proof spirit. Cover them up and let stand for a month. Strain through flannel, then add 1 pint of white sugar syrup, a little saffron colouring, and bottle.

Currant Ratafia

Put 1 quart of brandy into a large bottle, and add to it ½ pint of black currant juice, ¼ dram of cinnamon, ¼ dram of cloves and a ¼ dram of peach kernels. Dissolve 1 lb. of white sugar in this, then cover and let stand for a fortnight. Strain through flannel and bottle.

Ginger Cordial

To 1 quart of brandy add 1 quart of white sugar syrup and 2 oz. of essence of ginger.

Noyeau

Take 2 quarts of best brandy or proof spirit, and dissolve in it ¼ oz. of oil of bitter almonds, 2 drams of oil of orange, and 1 dram of oil of cinnamon. Add 1 quart of white sugar syrup, mix well and bottle.

Orange Gin

Pare 3 Seville oranges and 1 lemon very thinly. Put the peel into a quart of gin, let it stand 4 days, then strain. Put 2 lb. of loaf sugar into 1 pint of water, and bring to the boil. When boiling, pour it on to the strained gin and stir well. When cool, bottle it, and a little saffron colouring may be added. For ORANGE LIQUEUR, brandy is substituted for the gin, and no colouring is then needed.

Peppermint Cordial

Dissolve 1 oz. of oil of peppermint in 1 gallon of pure spirit, and add to this 1 gallon of white sugar syrup.

Raspberry Cordial

Mix together 1 pint of strained raspberry juice and 1 quart of spirit. Mix into this 1 quart of white sugar syrup.

Strawberry Cordial

Take any quantity of ripe strawberries, bruise them, just cover with proof spirit, and let stand for 24 hours. Drain off the spirit and replace with fresh, letting this stand for 24 hours also. Drain this off, and then cover the strawberries with water. Strain off the water and add it to the spirit, hen mix 1 quart of white sugar syrup to each quart of spirit, .nd ¼ gill of orange-flower water. Strain and bottle.

Shrub

Mix 1 pint of Seville orange juice into 3 pints of rum. f Seville oranges are not obtainable, use three-fourths •rdinary oranges and one-fourth lemons. Strain the mixture, hen stir in 1 quart of white sugar syrup, and bottle.

Sloe Gin

Pick the sloes free from stalks and let them be quite dry. ʹill wine or other bottles with them, and put in as much ;ounded sugar as can be got in, then fill up with gin and :ork the bottles. Shake well every day for 14 days, then eave them for about 6 months. The gin can then be strained .nd put into clean bottles. It will keep for years and improve vith time. Some consider it an improvement to put about)ne drop of oil of bitter almonds in each bottle when the ;in is poured in.

Whisky Cordial

Put 1 quart of whisky into a wide-necked bottle or jar, and into this put 1 lb. of white currants, the thin rind of a large lemon or two small ones and ¼ oz. of bruised ginger. Let them remain for about 24 hours, then strain through flannel. Add 1 pint of white sugar syrup, then bottle.

AERATED DRINKS

Ginger Beer

This recipe is the customary one, in which brewer's yeast is used. Pare two lemons thinly, then cut them open and remove the seeds. Squeeze out the juice into a stoneware pan, and put the peel with it. Add to this 2 oz. of bruised ginger, 1 oz. of cream of tartar and 2 lb. of white sugar. Bring 3 gallons of water to the boil, pour this, boiling hot, over the ingredients in the pan, and allow it to cool until only lukewarm.

Now add 2 good tablespoonfuls of thick brewer's yeast, which must be quite fresh. Stir the yeast well in, then cover the pan with a cloth and let it stand undisturbed in a warm place for at least 12 hours. Skim off the yeast, bottle at once and tie the corks down. To avoid making the beer thick by disturbing the sediment, the clear liquor can be poured off into another pan after it is skimmed, and before the bottling commences. It is ready for use in 3 or 4 days. Half a pound more sugar can be used, and the ginger beer will then keep better. The extra sugar, however, may make it sweeter than most people like.

ANOTHER METHOD

In this no yeast is required, and the ginger beer takes longer to mature, but the result is superior. Take 5 oz. of bruised ginger, and boil it in 3 quarts of water for $\frac{1}{2}$ hour. Then add 5 lb. of white sugar, 1 gill of lemon juice, $\frac{1}{4}$ lb. of honey and 15 quarts of water (making 18 quarts or $4\frac{1}{2}$ gallons of water altogether). When cold strain through a cloth and add a quarter of the white of an egg, and a teaspoonful of essence of lemon. Let all stand with a cloth over for 4 days, then bottle and tie the corks down. It is ready for use in about a fortnight, but will keep for several months.

An equivalent for ginger beer can be made by putting about 10 drops of essence of ginger with a tablespoonful of simple syrup, in a tumbler, and filling up with aerated water.

Ginger Beer Powders

Enough for 1 *Powder.*

Put 1 drop of essence of lemon on $1\frac{1}{4}$ drams of icing or castor sugar. Add to this 30 grains of carbonate of soda and 5 grains of finely ground ginger. Mix these ingredients thoroughly well together, and put up in coloured paper for keeping, then take 30 grains of tartaric acid, and let this be kept in white paper.

When the tumbler of ginger beer is required, the contents of the coloured paper are first put in and dissolved, then the contents of the white paper are added, in just the same way as with seidlitz powders. The presence of the powdered ginger makes the ginger beer slightly cloudy, but scarcely more so than ginger beer usually is.

Lemonade

There is no good method of making this by fermentation,

as with ginger beer, and recourse must be had to the soda syphon, with lemon syrup, or to powders made as follows :

Put 1 dram of essence of lemon on to 6 oz. of icing or castor sugar, and mix well. Add to this 1 oz. of tartaric acid, and mix well again. Divide the whole into about 20 to 24 powders. Each one will make a tumbler of lemonade.

Sherbet

Put 40 drops of essence of lemon on to ½ lb. of icing sugar, and mix well. Take ¼ lb. of carbonate of soda and ¼ lb of tartaric acid, see that they are thoroughly dry, then mix them with the sugar. Mix well, and to ensure this the whole can be passed through a fine sieve once or twice. Put into bottles and cork well. It is important that dampness be excluded. Even a damp spoon inserted in the bottle will cause sherbet to deteriorate.

A Simple Effervescing Drink

Take the juice of several lemons, strain it, and allow ½ pint of cold water to each lemon. Add castor sugar to taste —about a dessertspoonful to the pint. When a draught is required, pour out a tumblerful and add half a small tea-spoonful of carbonate of soda. Stir and drink at once.

Mulled Cider

1 quart sweet Cider.	6 Cloves.
1 small stick Cinnamon.	½ teaspoonful whole Allspice.

Put the cider in a preserving pan. Add the cinnamon, broken in pieces, the allspice, cloves, and a small piece of ginger root, if liked. Bring to boiling point and boil for 3 minutes, then skim, and pour into a hot jug. Serve at once.

COCKTAILS

EQUIPMENT REQUIRED

Cocktail Shaker (with separate compartment for ice, when possible)	Variety of Bitters
	Lemon Squeezer
	Bottle Maraschino Cherries
Cherry Sticks	Bottle Stuffed Olives
Cocktail Glasses	Liqueurs
Tray. Ice. Dry Gin	Whisky
French and Italian Vermouth	Limes. Oranges. Lemons.

HOW TO MIX A COCKTAIL

Measure out the ingredients required into a shaker. Add ice, shake well, and pour into glasses when the mixture is properly iced. When wanted sweet, stab a maraschino with a cherry stick and plant one in each glass. If wanted dry substitute a small olive or stuffed olive, or pickled onion for the cherry. Serve at once, just before lunch or dinner, if the cocktails are a prelude to lunch or dinner.

Maiden's Prayer

2-8ths cocktailglass Cointreau. | 1½-8ths cocktailglass Orange Juice
3-8ths cocktailglass Gordon's Gin. | 1½-8ths cocktailglass Lemon Juice

N.B.—The cocktail must be well shaken.

Martini

½ cocktailglass Gin. | ¼ cocktailglass French Vermouth
¼ cocktailglass Italian Vermouth. | 1 Olive in each glass.

If wanted dry, use more French vermouth and less Italian and add a few drops of lemon juice.

Manhattan

½ cocktailglass Irish Whisky. | ¼ cocktailglass French Vermouth
¼ cocktailglass Italian Vermouth.

Bronx

½ cocktailglass Gin. | ¼ cocktailglass Orange Juice.
¼ cocktailglass Vermouth.

Use French vermouth for a dry cocktail, and Italian for a sweet one.

Orange Blossom

½ cocktailglass Gin. | ½ cocktailglass Orange Juice.

Clover Club

½ cocktailglass Gin. | ¼ cocktailglass Grenadine, or
¼ cocktailglass Orange Juice. | Raspberry Syrup.
½ cocktailglass Lemon Juice. | Few drops Angostura Bitters.
White of 1 Egg.

The quantities given are for one cocktail. Serve the cocktails in champagne glasses.

Pendennis

½ cocktailglass Gin. | ¼ cocktailglass French Vermouth.
¼ cocktailglass Apricot Brandy.

The brandy and vermouth can be varied.

Riviera

½ cocktailglass Crème-de-menthe. | ½ cocktailglass Lemon Juice.
Sugar to taste.

Shake and pour into a champagne glass, and fill with Appollinaris.

Cherry Brandy

1 cocktailglass Brandy. | ½ cocktailglass Cherry Brandy.
1 Egg.   Milk. | Angostura and Sugar to taste.

Put the ingredients in a tumbler, and fill up with milk. Put in a shaker.

Apricot Brandy

½ cocktailglass Gin. | ½ cocktailglass Orange Juice.
Dash of Apricot Brandy. | ¼ cocktailglass Lemon Juice.
Sweeten to taste.

Hong Kong Special

½ cocktailglass Gin. | ¼ cocktailglass Crème-de-caçao.
¼ cocktailglass Cream.

Shake with ice.

Charlie Lindbergh Cocktail

½ cocktailglass Kinna Lillet. | ½ cocktailglass Plymouth Gin.
2 dashes Orange Juice. | 2 dashes Pricota.
Lemon Peel.

Jersey Lightning

(SPECIAL ROUGH COCKTAIL)

½ cocktailglass Swedish Punch. | ½ cocktailglass Brandy.
Dash of Absinthe.

Serve very cold.

Leap Year Cocktail

1-6th cocktailglass Grand Marnier. | 1-6th cocktailglass Italian
⅔ cocktailglass Gin. | Vermouth.
Dash of Lemon Juice. | Lemon Peel on Top.

Pen Club Cocktail

½ portion Dry Gin. | 2 dashes Absinthe.
½ portion French Vermouth. | 2 dashes Angostura Bitters.
4 dashes Benedictine.

Will Rogers Cocktail

½ cocktailglass Plymouth Gin. | ¼ cocktailglass French Vermouth.
¼ cocktailglass Orange Juice. | 4 dashes Curaçao.

WINE CUPS

Claret Cup

1 quart Claret.	2 liqueur glasses Curaçao.
1 liqueur glass Maraschino.	Powdered Sugar to taste.
Peel of 1 Lemon.	2 or 3 bottles of Soda Water.

Cucumber and Mint.

Mix the Claret, Curaçao and Maraschino with lemon and sugar to taste. Stand for ½ hour on ice. Add soda water, with one or two slices of cucumber and one or two sprigs of mint. To vary this cup, substitute Benedictine for the Curaçao, and 2 glasses of Brandy for the Maraschino. Use 1 quart of soda water instead of the 3 bottles.

If a stronger Claret cup is wanted, let the original recipe stand, but omit the soda water, and sweeten with 2 tablespoonfuls of fine sugar. Ice well before serving, and add one or two slices of orange and one or two dices of pineapple and a small piece of cucumber rind 5 minutes before required. Garnish with mint.

Peach Cup

| 1 Peach per person. | Sparkling Hock or Moselle. |

Prick each peach, which must be very ripe, all over with a silver fork. Then place one in each large, long-stemmed goblet, and fill to within an inch of the brim with iced sparkling Hock or Moselle.

White Wine Cup

| 1 bottle White Wine. | 1 glass Curaçao. |
| 1 glass Brandy. | Powdered Sugar to taste. |

Ice.　　　Fruit.

Mix the ingredients together, and stand them on ice for 15 minutes. Add one small strip of cucumber peel, a few lumps of ice, one or two slices of orange and ½ tablespoonful of diced pineapple. Garnish with sprigs of mint. If wanted larger, add 1 pint of soda water and two or three slices of diced pineapple to the ingredients before icing.

GARNISHES FOR WINE CUPS

Borage.	Strawberries.
Sprigs of Mint.	Cherries.
Slices of Lemon, Orange, or	Raspberries.
Tangerine.	Grapes.

Strips of Cucumber Peel.

TABLE OF MEASURES

1 wineglass	=	½ gill.
2 gills	=	1 breakfast cup or ½ pint.
1 gill	=	½ breakfast cup or 8 fluid tablespoonfuls.

TEA AND COFFEE MAKING

To Make Tea

1. Draw water from the cold tap and only just bring it to the boil. It should not be boiled for more than about a minute.

2. If possible, use a stoneware teapot, and then pour the made tea off into the metal pot, but the tea can be made in the metal pot at first if necessary.

3. First pour some boiling water into the pot, and leave it there long enough to make the pot quite hot.

4. Empty out the water, then put in the tea, a teaspoonful for each person and a teaspoonful over, and put one piece of loaf sugar with it. If a large quantity of tea is to be made, it is better to make it in two or three pots rather than in one unusually large one. The pot should be of suitable size for the quantity of tea, not much too large.

5. Put the cosy on, and after two minutes take it off and stir the tea in the bottom of the pot with a spoon.

6. Replace the cosy, and let the tea remain another two minutes. It is then ready for use, and should be used at once, although some teas take longer to infuse than others.

7. Do not let tea stand more than 5 minutes before it is poured out, unless there are some means provided for removing the leaves, so that they do not remain in the liquid. With the tea-leaves removed, the made tea may stand as long as liked, and could even be re-heated. To those who require a full yet delicately flavoured tea, which will have the least prejudicial effect on the digestive organs, *it is important that the leaves do not remain in the made tea more than about 5 minutes.* Either all the tea must be poured out in this time or the leaves must be removed from the pot.

To Make Coffee

The terms " café noir " and " café au lait " mean, first, black coffee—a strong decoction of coffee without milk, and served in small cups ; second, good coffee mixed with hot milk, about half of each, and served in larger cups. Success in making coffee depends very largely upon using sufficient of the substance, and of good enough quality. When serving black coffee, after lunch or dinner, always offer cream with it.

It must never be supposed that the strength of well-made coffee is due to its being boiled. Coffee must never be actually boiled. For breakfast coffee it is usual to allow 1 tablespoonful for each person. This is about $\frac{1}{2}$ oz., and should have $\frac{1}{4}$ pint of water to it. For a breakfast coffee-cup about $\frac{3}{4}$ oz. is requisite. One ounce of coffee should not have more than $\frac{1}{2}$ pint of water to it—rather less. It is always best to have the coffee beans freshly roasted, and to grind them yourself as they are needed.

In making café au lait, do not let the milk boil, but have it scalding hot, and pour the milk and coffee into the cup together. If the milk boils, the coffee may have an unpleasant skin on it. To make good coffee, use either a percolator, or an earthenware coffee pot, choose a blend of coffee you like, and do not spare it. All good percolators are accompanied by instructions which should be carefully followed in order to make coffee of the best quality.

Turkish Coffee

Some prefer Turkish coffee as an after-dinner beverage, but the palate usually has to be accustomed to this. Take 3 tablespoonfuls of freshly-roasted berries, and pound them well ; or they may be ground, but it is not considered so good. Put these with 3 tablespoonfuls of water into a small brass pot, and just bring to the boil. Remove from the fire, stir, then bring just to the boil again. If the coffee is to be sweetened, add sufficient castor sugar to the coffee before it is put to boil. Pour into small cups.

DIET FOR HEALTH

THE CHOICE OF A HEALTHY DIET

By PROFESSOR R. H. A. PLIMMER, D.SC., *Professor of Chemistry in the University of London at St. Thomas's Hospital Medical Schools, and* VIOLET G. PLIMMER.

Oxygen from the air, water to drink, and food to eat supply all the material needs of the body. The food has to provide in suitable amounts the various substances required for the upkeep and proper working of the animal body.

Good health and resistance to infection depend upon the correct choice of foods. Badly chosen diets lead, inevitably, to ill health and lowered resistance to infection. The prevalent ailments, constipation, indigestion, heart diseases of "unknown origin," gastro-intestinal troubles, rickets, tuberculosis, can, in most cases, be traced to the consumption, for a long period, of a mixture of foods which failed to supply the body with all that it needed.

No single foodstuff is a complete food for the adult. A mixed diet is taken in the hope that the incompleteness of one food will be made good by some other kind. Even milk for the infant is not a satisfactory food unless the mother is supplied with a proper and complete diet.

The common classification of foods into four groups is convenient. The diet as a whole can be pictured as a square, and a square is not a square if the corners are cut off, as they are in the case of incomplete diets. The square represents all that the food should give to the body to maintain it in that state of good health and efficiency which every one desires.

The diagram of the square with a larger central portion and four corners shows a healthy diet. The question is how to fill the central part *and* the four corners?

The figure represents the four classes of foods as of equal size because they are equally necessary and indispensable, but the actual consumption of the different groups is not equal in weight. Attention must be given to the relative quantities of the four classes of food.

THE MEAT CLASS.—Experience has proved that 8 oz. of the meat foods per day, spread over the several meals, is the most suitable quantity. The meat foods are : Lean of meat, including poultry, game, and all flesh foods, whether fresh, dried, frozen, tinned, or salted. Fish of all kinds. Eggs, cheese, milk. The usual daily amounts are from 4 to 6 oz. of meat *or* fish, ½ pint of milk, 2 oz. egg (1 egg), and about 1 oz. of cheese. They can be interchanged as desired. Larger quantities every day are unnecessary and wasteful, though occasionally the above amount may be exceeded.

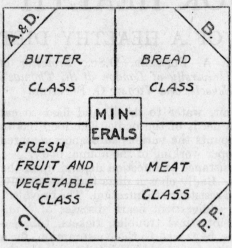

A SQUARE MEAL

The four squares represent the four types of food which are essential for a complete diet—and the centre and the corners (the vitamins) must be included.

THE BUTTER CLASS.—On the average, from 2 to 3½ oz. of butter and fats are eaten daily.

THE BREAD CLASS.—The bread class of foods, consisting of starches and sugars, forms the greater part of the daily food. The total amount corresponds to about 2 lb. of bread per day. The bread class of foods is ordinarily somewhat as follows : ½ lb. bread, ½ lb. of cakes, puddings, biscuits, ¼ lb. of sugar and sweet foods with some starch and sugar from vegetables and fruits.

THE FRUIT AND VEGETABLE CLASS.—In this class, potatoes are eaten in the greatest amount ; green and root vegetables and fruits are the other foods of this class. From ½ to 1 lb. of potatoes a day is a common daily quantity.

All the above are healthy quantities. An increase of all four groups, especially of the bread class, is wanted for any hard manual labour. An increase in the meat class only is not correct. Excess of the meat class of food is the most common mistake in the daily diet. Children need, *proportionately*, a larger quantity of the meat class than adults, best given as milk, or eggs, or fish. There should not be a great preponderance of the bread class, as is the case in the excessively starchy and sugary diet usually given to children.

Observing these correct proportions, the central part of the diagram becomes filled naturally by the dictates of the appetite. These proportions of the four classes of foods will generally give just enough of those necessary minerals which are represented by the small central square. The mineral supply is still more satisfactory if attention is given to those foods which go to fill the four corners.

Vitamins

The four corners indicate the *health* properties of the foods as contributed by the vitamins. Different vitamins are associated with each class of foods. Without vitamins a diet soon leads to disease and death. With just a little but not enough of the vitamins, death is not so soon. With more but still insufficient, there is chronic ill health of various kinds. It is only with a full amount of the several vitamins that there is proper and perfect health. It is most essential that the firm foundations of health be laid in infancy and childhood. The system thus strongly built up is then more able to withstand any errors made in later life.

Vitamins A and D come from the butter or fat class of foods. The fats vary greatly in the amount of these vitamins which they contain. Hence there is the possibility of getting too little of these vitamins. The butter class can be divided into two groups :

FATS WITH VITAMINS A AND D.—Butter, cream, milk, meat fat, fish fat, more expensive margarines, egg yolk, green vegetables.

FATS WITHOUT VITAMINS.—Bacon fat, lard, cheaper margarines. There are two possible reasons for a lack of these vitamins. We may not get enough if our fat is largely or mostly bacon fat or cheaper margarine, or there is too little of the proper fats in the diet by having an excess of the starchy foods. This is most often the case with children, and hence the prevalence of rickets.

SUNSHINE is another necessity in connection with the fat of the diet. The fat may contain the forerunner or pro-vitamin of vitamin D. The ultra-violet light from the sun makes it into vitamin D. This action takes place through the skin.

There is one other fat, though not an ordinary food, which is very rich in both vitamins A and D. This is cod liver oil. A teaspoonful daily for children will fill the corner.

Vitamin C comes from fresh fruits and vegetables, which have long been recognised as an essential part of the diet. The quantity required is, however, not so well known.

The smallest amounts consistent with health are 1 oz. of orange or lemon juice a day, or about 7 oz. of apple or banana, or 10 oz. of cooked potato. A mixture of fruits and vegetables must make up a corresponding amount.

Vitamin C is spoiled by cooking. Cooking must be for as short a time as possible, and soda or its bicarbonate should never be used. Dried and preserved fruits do not take the place of fresh ones, though tinned fruits and vegetables prepared by the modern processes are as good as the fresh material.

Vitamin PP is usually not lacking in the common daily diet. The meat class of foods which, as stated above, is often taken in excess, generally gives plenty of this vitamin. Modern researches show that it is associated with vitamin B.

Vitamin B is the one most commonly taken in too small an amount. There are two very distinct groups of the bread class of foods :

WITH VITAMIN B.	WITHOUT VITAMIN B.
Wholemeal flour.	White flour.
Wholemeal bread.	White bread.
	Oatmeal.
Brown rice.	White rice.
Brown barley.	Pearl barley.
Dried peas, beans, lentils.	Sago, tapioca.
Nuts.	Cornflour.
Potatoes.	Sugar of all kinds.

Examination of the ordinary diet will at once reveal the fact that the bulk of the bread class of foods is taken from those without vitamin B. Every effort ought to be made to consume wholemeal flour in bread and cakes, etc., at all times, but there is one other way of consuming enough vitamin B, and that is by adding to the customary deficient diet some food which is very rich in this vitamin B.

If one remembers how to choose the foods to make a square meal every day, the rest of the diet will almost look after itself, and one should be able to eat anything one likes.

APPETITE AND DIGESTION

By Sir Frederick Mott, K.B.E., M.D., B.S., LL.D., F.R.C.P., F.R.S., *Late Lecturer on Morbid Psychology at the University of Birmingham.*

We speak of food being appetising on account of its savoury smell, or because of its flavour, but flavour is largely due to the sense of smell rather than of taste, though we taste sweet and bitter things and acid and salt substances. Now a savoury odour of cooked food effects through the sense of smell a psychic process, which, starting the desire to eat, causes a flow of the digestive juices before even the food enters the mouth ; and it has been shown that not only does the mouth water at the smell or even the sight of appetising food, but that the gastric juice also begins to flow. On the other hand, if the odour of the food is unsavoury, or the food has neither flavour nor savour, and there is little or no desire to eat, this appetite juice does not flow. Fear, worry and anxiety stop the flow of the appetite juice, and therefore, unless there is a strong stimulus by a savoury smell of cooked food, a mentally tired man has little or no desire for his meal when he comes home after a long day at his work, profession or business. In some cases of insanity where there is marked mental depression, food is refused, and the late Dr. Maudsley told me that he was once called to a case of this character, when the idea occurred to him of using the stimulus of a savoury odour of cooked food to overcome this aversion, so he had some cheese toasted. The smell of the savoury toasting cheese made the man ask what was cooking, and he was induced to eat.

The sense of sight also plays an important part in the psychological anticipation stage of eating a meal. The food should not only please the sense of smell, but also the sense of sight, by the way it is put on the table ; the clean table-cloth, the napkin, the hot plates, and the garnishing of the dish with parsley, watercress, etc., all help to promote a pleasant psychic state and the flow of the appetite juices, whereas a slovenly and dirty or unpleasing table promotes a feeling of disgust and a failure of the flow of the appetite juices. An unvitiated palate is Nature's best guide for the nutrition of the individual.

VARIED MENUS

When I had charge of the Neurological Clearing Hospital in London I realised the importance of attending to these appetising influences in the promotion of convalescence of neurasthenic officers. Another very important matter in relation to the feeding of invalids, especially neurasthenics, is monotony. When a particular bill of fare is always associated with a particular day of the week, as so often occurs in hospitals and institutions, it has an unappetising effect, and to an irritable, nervous man or woman may be such a source of annoyance and irritation that it may cause discontent, and even aversion of wholesome nutritious food. A pleasant gastronomic surprise by a wife to a tired and irritable husband on coming home will often be an appetising tonic, and sometimes even be the means of preventing domestic quarrels. Indeed, doctors, if they would attend more to promoting the flow of the appetite juice by giving their attention to appetising food, might dispense with tonics, which in my opinion owe their value largely to the faith the bitter taste inspires. Cocktails and *aperitifs* are only required by persons who have lost the natural appetising influences of savoury, well-cooked food. I have often thought that doctors and nurses do not pay half enough attention to the preparation of wholesome and appetising invalid food. All nurses should have a course of training whereby they can acquire a practical knowledge of the subject and of its importance in the care of the sick and in convalescence.

INVALID COOKERY

I remember that great and experienced physician, the late Sir William Broadbent, telling me how frequently in hotels and the houses of the wealthy it was very difficult to obtain suitable food for patients. The chefs did not understand, and the nurses either had not sufficient authority or interest or knowledge to see that the food of the invalid was suitable. He, therefore, knowing the great importance attached to proper food being given to his patient, would himself go into the kitchen and instruct the cook in the preparation of suitable food. Afterwards he would, when visiting, ask for the food to be brought that he might taste it.

A delicate flavour to food often increases the desire, and, instead of making wholesome food indigestible, it makes it more digestible by the pleasant psychic influence inducing a flow of the appetite juice, and the consequent desire for more.

Cooks, however, show their intelligence and special aptitude for the art, not only by making their dishes pleasing to look upon, but by their capacity for giving a flavour to food by sweet herbs, peppers and essences. Those who leave flavouring agents and condiments out altogether are not so bad as those who use them with such a heavy hand that wholesome food is made distasteful or even disgusting. For example, garlic is a most valuable flavouring agent, but it may be disgusting to English people if more than a suspicion is in the food. It is related that a celebrated cook was once asked how he obtained this suspicion, or, as the French say, *soupçon*, in his salads. He said, " I breathe on it," but then he chewed garlic.

In conclusion, we hear a great deal about people drinking too much alcohol, but very little is said about eating too much. Physicians warn middle-aged people against the dangers of over-eating, especially red meat, resulting in high blood-pressure with thickening and loss of elasticity of the arteries and a tendency to apoplexy. The warning often comes too late, and sometimes it is disregarded.

Fortunately the public are coming more and more to see the wisdom of preventing disease, and one way is the advancement in knowledge and practice of dietetics. Lastly, we cannot do better than follow the wise and common sense principles laid down by Voltaire : " Regime in diet is better than medicine. Eat in moderation what you know by experience you can digest, for only that which you can digest is good for the body. What is the medicine which makes you digest ? Exercise. What will repair your energy ? Sleep. What will lessen incurable ills ? Patience. What will change a bad constitution ? Nothing."

RULES FOR DIET

By J. S. BAINBRIDGE, M.Sc. *Author of " Economic House-keeping,"* etc.

When planning menus, one must take into consideration certain diet rules, *which should be followed whether an economical or a more expensive diet is being planned.*

1. One pint of milk should be provided per person per day. This should be the irreducible minimum and, in the case of children, an effort should always be made to exceed this figure. Milk is the cheapest and best " all round " food available, the food *par excellence* for making good deficiencies in the rest of the diet.

2. Wholemeal cereals should always be used in preference to refined cereals. They are a much cheaper insurance premium against ill-health, and, in addition to being far more economical sources of vital mineral elements than are refined flours, etc., they contain valuable stimulating roughage and are quite definitely less acid-producing.

3. The more economical the diet must be, the larger must be the amounts spent on cereal foods. This increased expenditure on cereals must be deducted from the amount spent on animal foods, *and not from that reserved for fruits, vegetables and milk.* Where strict economy is necessary, an expenditure on cereal foods of about 30 per cent. of the food allowance secures a diet which is approximately equal to the theoretical scientific requirements.

4. Apart from the expenditure on cereal foods, the food allowance should be divided into three approximately equal parts, of which

    (*a*) One part, *or more*, should be spent on milk and its products.

    (*b*) One part should be spent on fruit and vegetables.

    (*c*) One part, *or less*, should be spent on meat and fish.

In all circumstances the maximum possible amounts of protective foods should be used, and the minimum necessary amounts of the destructive or acid-forming foods.

CONSTRUCTION OF MENUS

The fact that a selection of food is being bought which, taken as a whole, fulfils scientific requirements, does not entirely solve the problem. Each week has to be divided into seven days, and each day into three meals, all of which have to be satisfying and—equally as important—attractive. Because spinach, for example, is a very valuable food, it might be thought that it should be introduced into the dietary on every possible occasion, in spite of the fact that it is a very difficult vegetable to disguise and, to many people, really repulsive. The skilful cook works on rather different lines and, by serving meals which are at the same time scientifically correct, attractive and varied, achieves her aims without her family even suspecting that they are to some extent subjects of a dietetic experiment.

The type of meal to be provided depends on the season, and on the size and age of the family; but certain broad principles should always be borne in mind when meals are being planned. Every meal, almost without exception, comes into one of two types, (a) meals which consist essentially of carbohydrates and fats (such as breakfast) and (b) meals in which proteins and carbohydrates predominate (such as dinner). There are sound physiological reasons why meals should not consist of one type of foodstuff only, or why mixtures formed principally of fats and proteins should not be used. The following rules on the construction of menus, adapted from Professor M. S. Rose's *Laboratory Handbook for Dietetics* (Macmillan), should be followed.

First think of each day as a whole, rather than as three separate meals. Then arrange the menus so that the principal types of food material (carbohydrates, fats and proteins) are fairly evenly distributed over the day. For example, do not concentrate all the protein into one meal by serving meat, fish and cheese together.

Next, do not serve the same dish twice on the same day— in fact, except for staple foods such as bread and milk, try to avoid even serving the same food twice. It would be a mistake, for example, to begin dinner with tomato soup if a salad containing tomatoes is to appear later. Each dish should differ in colour and flavour from that served before and after it. Thus a highly-flavoured dish should be followed by a bland and comparatively tasteless one.

Meals are usually digested more easily when they contain at least one warm dish, but when it is desirable that a meal should be light—as lunch for sedentary workers, for example—

this warm dish may consist of soup or even of a drink. Except with children and hard manual workers, the heaviest meal of the day should take place in the evening. It may conveniently begin with soup, which in addition to being pleasantly warming, stimulates the production of gastric juice and so enables the stomach to be in the best " frame of mind " for dealing with later courses of the meal. The evening meal may conveniently include two hot dishes, but it should not be needlessly elaborate. There is no point, for example, in serving two green vegetables together, unless one is raw ; or in serving rice with potatoes, since both these are high calorific foods and are used essentially to supply energy. The custom of serving rice separately as a vegetable can, however, be commended.

Summer and winter menus need not differ materially. As much raw food as possible should always be taken ; but it is usual to increase the proportion of fruits, salads and light dishes generally in summer, and to provide rather more substantial puddings, etc., in winter.

BALANCING YOUR WEIGHT

If we considered that we are what we eat, or that what we eat to-day is walking about to-morrow, as the saying goes, we should all be more particular about what we do eat, or, for that matter, about what we drink. There is no doubt that we can lose weight or gain weight as we wish by taking care over our diet.

TO CUT DOWN WEIGHT

As far as losing weight is concerned, you must remember that the average slimming diet is suitable for only average cases of obesity. A diet that will slim a woman in her thirties, a woman who takes little exercise, will not suit a stout woman in her fifties. A diet that will bring down a girl in her teens, is not of much use to a middle-aged man who has lived not wisely but too well.

It is most difficult to adhere to a slimming diet, planned on recognised lines. For example, it is not easy to pass by food you like. That is why you may break the rule of "no potatoes" or other vegetables that grow under the ground, and introduce these vegetables sparingly in the week's diet. If you have the courage to refuse them altogether, substituting salad, if you like, you will hasten the slimming process.

Those who, through circumstances, find it quite impossible to follow the diet prescribed below, can still cut down their weight by paying attention to the following points :

1. Eat slowly and at regular intervals.

2. Take not more than a small cup of clear soup or $\frac{1}{2}$ glass of water at a meal. No alcoholic or malt drinks, sweet drinks, cocoa, chocolate, milk, or thick soup.

3. Drink a glass of water 1 hour before each meal.

4. Give up all condiments, ketchups, chutneys, mustard, horseradish, etc.

5. Avoid all highly seasoned foods, and eat very few sweets.

6. Drink ½ glass of hot water containing the juice of a lemon first thing in the morning and last thing at night.

7. Choose plain foods, omitting all gravies and sauces.

8. Do not eat just before going to bed, or lie down immediately after a meal.

Foods You May Take

BREAD.—Gluten bread, stale white bread, rye or wheat crispbread, toasted brown bread—all in small quantity.

DRINKS.—Water, hot or cold, mineral waters, coffee and tea without sugar, and without milk, if possible.

EGGS.—Poached, soft-boiled or steamed.

SOUP.—Clear beef or chicken soup.

FISH.—Sea bream, brill, cod, John Dorey, flounders, gurnet, haddock, plaice, skate, smelts, sole, turbot and whiting.

MEATS.—Lean boiled or grilled beef, grilled lean steak, roast beef, roast mutton, grilled mutton chops, grilled lamb chops, roast lamb, boiled or grilled chicken. Eat meat only once daily, unless on the same diet for lunch and dinner.

VEGETABLES.—Asparagus, cabbage, cauliflower, celery, lettuce, onions, peas, radishes, spinach, French beans, tomatoes, watercress cooked in a little water.

SALADS.—All green salads.

FRUITS.—Apples, berries, cherries, grapes, lemons, oranges, peaches, fresh always when possible.

PLANNING YOUR MENUS

CHOOSE FOR BREAKFAST.—Any fresh fruit except bananas. Grilled fish, or boiled, poached or steamed eggs—as much as you like. One slice of gluten bread, toasted, or one gluten biscuit, or a gluten roll, with half a pat of butter. Large cup of coffee, black or with only a little milk.

CHOOSE FOR LUNCHEON OR SUPPER.—One cup of any clear soup containing vegetables, or tomato soup. A small portion of grilled fish or meat, roast meat, boiled, poached, steamed scrambled or hard-boiled eggs, as much as wanted. Any green vegetable. A large portion of lettuce, tomato, cucumber or asparagus salad, served with vinaigrette sauce. One slice of gluten bread, with half a pat of butter. Fresh fruit. Black coffee or tea with lemon and no sugar.

CHOOSE FOR TEA.—China tea with lemon and no sugar.

One slice of thin toast scraped with butter, or two reducing biscuits.

CHOOSE FOR DINNER.—Half a grapefruit, a slice of melon, or a fruit cocktail, or one cupful of tomato bouillon, or any consommé not containing rice, macaroni, or spaghetti. Boiled, grilled or stewed fish, or boiled, grilled or roasted meat, served without sauce or gravy containing fat. Use lemon juice with fish, and pickled beetroot or any vinegary relish with meats. Green salads, or boiled or steamed vegetables, or a portion of each, spinach, celery, onions, tomatoes, cucumbers, asparagus, marrow, cabbage, are all good. Fruit salad with no cream, or fresh fruit, or dried figs. A small cup of black coffee.

BEFORE RETIRING.—Juice of 2 oranges.

A TYPICAL DAY'S DIET

BREAKFAST.—One cup of black coffee, or coffee with a little milk but no sugar. One apple, orange, or half a grapefruit. One boiled, poached, steamed or scrambled egg. Two slices of dry toast or gluten bread ; one small pat of butter.

11 A.M.—One glass of cold water.

LUNCHEON OR SUPPER.—Grilled steak, the size of the palm of your hand, or two lean lamb cutlets, or two slices of any roast meat except ham or pork, or an ordinary portion of roast poultry or game, or a large portion of boiled, steamed, baked or grilled fish. A large portion of green vegetables. Fresh fruit or a cup of coffee without milk.

4.30–5 P.M.—One cup of tea, with lemon and no sugar.

DINNER.—Choice of fish, game, meat or poultry, but not fish *and* game, meat or poultry. One slice of rye crispbread. A large portion of green vegetables. A large portion of salad dressed with seasoned lemon juice, but no oil. Any fresh fruit, or a cup of tea.

AVOID.—Oily fish, duck, goose, ham, bacon, sausages, preserved fish and meats, potatoes, beetroot, turnips, dried beans, onions, stewed sweetened fruits, bananas, jams, jellies, grapes, dates, raisins, pastries, confectionery, nuts, all hot scones and buns, as well as white bread, and puddings except junket.

There are many other ways of reducing as you eat. One writer states that, eager to reduce, she gave up bread, and all kinds of cakes and pastries, and potatoes, and lost on an average three pounds a week as long as her efforts lasted. *But as soon as she started to enjoy bread, cakes, pastries and potatoes again, up went the scales.*

If you have the strength of mind to limit yourself in quantity when you return to your old diet, allowing yourself, say, only one potato, one slice of brown bread or toast, and, perhaps, one cake or biscuit for tea, you ought to keep the slimness you have achieved.

One of the most popular forms of reducing is to eat the same food for lunch and dinner ; for example, grilled cutlets and pineapple slices. One of each for lunch, and two of each for dinner. But if you take up this kind of diet, do not eat much at breakfast. Content yourself with grapefruit or a glass of orange juice or an apple ; a little lean bacon, steamed egg or fish—preferably boiled, stewed or grilled. You can conclude with one cup of China tea, or coffee and milk, and dry toast scraped with butter.

The best way to reduce is to live on non-fattening foods, then you will soon oxygenise your blood, your elimination will become thorough, and your glands will function as they should. But to reduce in this way you must avoid sweets and starchy foods, and eat as little fat and as few fatty foods as you can. If you eat the foods here suggested, take only three moderate meals daily, and nothing between them, you will soon reduce as much as you want.

Keeping Slim while Entertaining

When entertaining, try to serve as light meals as possible. Serve rye or wheat crispbread as well as hot rolls and toast, and salads moistened with French dressing instead of your favourite mayonnaise. Have cream for your guests' coffee, but drink black coffee yourself.

For a dainty summer luncheon, you might start with a grapefruit cocktail, then follow this with lamb cutlets, grilled tomatoes, and a lettuce salad. Offer your guests potatoes, cooked in any way you please, but take none yourself. Finish with stuffed, baked apples, and custard or cream, but take nothing with your own apples.

If you wish to conclude with a fruit salad, substitute consommé or tomato soup for grapefruit. Offer cauliflower, moistened, after boiling and draining, with a good pat of butter in preference to covering it with white sauce, when tomato soup is your choice, instead of grilled tomatoes.

When tired of grapefruit, substitute chilled, strained orange juice for the usual grapefruit and juice, and allow to each person six or seven green grapes, slit and carefully seeded. Decorate each glass with a tiny sprig of mint. Better still to stand a few mint leaves in the orange juice for an hour before the cocktail is wanted, then remove them, ladle the mixture into each glass, and place a leaf of frosted mint in the centre of each.

For a vegetable, mince boiled carrot finely, add minced onion, salt and pepper to taste, and moisten the mixture with French dressing. This could be served with the cutlets instead of cauliflower or tomatoes.

To facilitate slimming, whether you entertain or not, eat nothing but fruit one day a week. Eat as much as you like, only try to keep the quantity under 4 lb. If you prefer, you can substitute a milk day for a fruit day. Here is an alternative diet for one day a week : An apple and an orange and a large cup of black coffee for breakfast. Two apples and one orange and a small cup of black coffee for lunch. Two oranges at 4. p.m. One apple and one orange and a large cup of coffee and milk, but no sugar, at 7 p.m.

To Preserve your Youthful Figure after 40

Begin by studying your diet.

MEAT.—You must limit meat to once a day, and that meat course should consist of a grilled steak, the size of the palm of your hand, or two lean lamb cutlets or one lean lamb chop, or two thin slices of roast beef or mutton, or a good portion of boiled or roast chicken or turkey or of roast game, or tripe and onions.

Neither roast pork, duck, goose nor cooked kidneys, meat stews, cold tongue, nor any tinned meats must be taken.

VEGETABLES.—You can enjoy as much green vegetable as you please, so long as it is plainly cooked. You can also eat freely of vegetables that grow *above* the ground, as well as celery, but no beetroot, carrots, turnips, potatoes or dried beans must ever be part of your diet unless you have plenty of exercise.

FRUIT.—Eat fruit freely, preferably raw. You can eat as much cooked fruit as you want as well, so long as it is not sweetened, but you must give up all preserves and dried fruits. It is wise also to eat no bananas or nuts.

LIQUIDS.—When planning your meals allow yourself only a limited quantity of liquid, no matter what it is, but remember that all sweet drinks, all alcoholic drinks, chocolate, cocoa and thick soups, unless in the shape of vegetable broths, must be avoided. Drink only black coffee, China tea with lemon and no sugar, water and still mineral water, and take a glass of water an hour before each meal, and first thing in the morning and last thing at night. You can add the juice of a lemon if you like. All foods must be plainly cooked and served without gravy, sauce or condiments. If you like buttermilk and can obtain it, drink it in place of water an hour before meals. Allow yourself only one small cup of liquid at a meal, whether it be tea, coffee or clear soup. It is better not to take any bread or toast, but substitute biscuits or loaves made of gluten flour. If you cannot do without bread, eat it stale or toasted, and preferably brown, but avoid both cold and hot rolls, muffins, cake, pastry, biscuits, pies, sweets, and puddings of all kinds. You can have boiled, steamed or grilled white fish, but no shell fish or oily kinds of fish.

TYPICAL DAILY MENU

BREAKFAST.—Apple, grapefruit, one slice of pineapple or orange. One cup of black coffee, or China tea with lemon.

LUNCHEON AND SUPPER.—A portion of boiled or steamed fish, or a boiled or steamed egg. Green salad dressed with lemon juice. A slice of gluten bread. Fresh fruit.

DINNER.—Meat, game or poultry; green vegetable; green salad dressed with lemon juice. Fresh fruit. A small cup of black coffee.

If you live a very active life, you could allow yourself a piece of cake, or a slice of bread and butter, or one or two biscuits, with your afternoon tea, and be a little less stringent with your diet. For example, you might have some stewed sweetened fruit or a little baked custard with your luncheon or dinner, or an egg or a rasher of bacon, or even a slice of buttered toast, with your breakfast. How you occupy yourself during the day should naturally be taken into consideration when planning a diet of this kind. But whatever you do, you must not take a rest after eating, and you must limit yourself to eight hours' sleep.

SLIMMING RECIPES

Reducing Bread

1 Yeast Cake.	**1** tablespoonful melted **Butter.**
5 to 6 cupfuls **Gluten Flour.**	**3** cupfuls tepid **Milk or Water.**

½ teaspoonful Salt.

UTENSILS—Basin, wooden spoon, tablespoon, cup, knife, pastry board, saucepan, cloth, 2 loaf tins.

Dissolve the yeast cake in one cupful of tepid milk or water. Stir in the remainder of the milk or water, the butter, salt and flour. Turn on to a lightly floured pastry board and knead slightly. Divide the dough into two portions, and place each in a well-greased loaf tin. Cover the tins with a clean cloth, and stand in a warm place until the loaves are twice the size—in about 1½ hours. Then bake in a moderate oven, 360 degrees Fahr., from ¾ to 1 hour. This is a plain bread which can be used regularly in place of ordinary bread.

Sweet Gluten Bread

1 Yeast Cake.	½ teaspoonful Salt.
1 pint Gluten Flour.	**2** tablespoonfuls Castor Sugar.
2 tablespoonfuls melted Butter.	**1** Egg. Gluten Flour (extra).

3 cupfuls tepid Milk or Water.

UTENSILS—Two basins, wooden spoon, measuring spoons, cup, egg-beater, pint measure, cloth, pastry board, saucepan, 2 loaf tins.

Dissolve the yeast in the tepid milk or water, and stir in the pint of gluten flour. Cover with a clean cloth, then stand in a warm place till spongy and light. Stir in the salt, the melted butter, castor sugar, beaten egg, and as much more gluten flour—probably about 2 pints—as will make the dough fit to knead. Turn on to a lightly floured board, then knead till smooth and elastic. Divide in two, and place each portion in a well-buttered or oiled loaf tin. Bake in a moderate oven, 360 degrees Fahr., for from ¾ to 1 hour. If preferred, the dough can be shaped into rolls and baked on a baking sheet.

Starch-free Bread

1½ oz. White Starch-free Flour.	**2** Eggs. A pinch of Salt.

1 walnut of Butter.

UTENSILS—Two basins, wooden spoon, egg-beater, knife, loaf tin.

Rub the butter into the flour. Stir in the salt and well-beaten eggs. Turn the mixture quickly into a well-buttered loaf tin. Bake at once in a hot oven for about 20 minutes.

Reducing Pastry

½ lb. Starch-reduced Flour. | Pinch of Baking Powder.
2 oz. Butter or Lard. | Cold Water.

UTENSILS—Basin, wooden spoon, knife, pastry board, rolling pin.

Rub the butter or lard into the flour. Stir in the baking powder and enough cold water to make a soft dough. Roll out, and use in place of ordinary pastry.

Gluten Bran Puffs

1 cupful Bran. | 1 cupful Gluten Flour.
1 Egg.   ¾ cupful Milk. | ¾ cupful Buttermilk.
½ teaspoonful Baking Soda.

UTENSILS—Two basins, egg-beater, cup, teaspoon, wooden spoon, sieve, bun tins.

Beat the egg. Stir in the buttermilk and milk. Sift the salt, gluten flour and soda together, then mix in the bran. Stir the liquid into the flour, and beat well. Bake in hot buttered bun tins in a quick oven.

Reducing Wafers

1½ oz. Starch-free Flour. | 4 drops of Vanilla Essence.
¾ oz. Butter.   1 Egg. | Pinch of Salt.

UTENSILS—Two basins, egg-beater, wooden spoon, pastry board, rolling pin, knife or cutters, fork, baking sheet.

Rub the butter into the flour, stir in the well-beaten eggs and the vanilla, then turn the mixture on to a lightly floured board. The salt can be omitted if preferred. Roll out quickly, cut into fancy shapes and prick them with a fork. Bake on a well-buttered tin in a hot oven till a rich brown.

Reducing Biscuits

1 cupful Gluten Flour. | ⅓ cupful Cream.
¼ teaspoonful Salt.

UTENSILS—Basin, wooden spoon, teaspoon, cup, pastry board, rolling pin, knife or cutters, fork, baking sheet.

Mix the flour with the salt and cream. If the dough is not very stiff, add a little more flour. Roll out, and finish like reducing wafers.

Gluten Bread

1 Yeast Cake. | 3 cupfuls tepid Milk.
5 cupfuls Gluten Flour. | 1 tablespoonful Butter.
½ teaspoonful Salt.

UTENSILS—Two basins, wooden spoon, measuring spoons, cup, sieve, saucepan, loaf tins.

Dissolve the yeast in a cupful of the milk. Stir in the remainder of the milk, then the melted butter. Beat in the flour, sifted with the salt, and knead slightly. Turn at once into well-oiled loaf tins. Let the loaves rise in a warm place till twice their size. This takes about 1½ hours. Bake in a moderate oven, 350 to 375 degrees Fahr., from 45 minutes to 1 hour.

Gluten Muffins

1 cupful Bran.　　1 Egg.	3 teaspoonfuls Baking Powder.
2 cupfuls Gluten Flour.	½ cupful Milk.
2 oz. melted Butter.	½ cupful Water.

¾ teaspoonful Salt.

UTENSILS—Two basins, wooden spoon, teaspoon, cup, egg-beater, saucepan, muffin tins.

Mix the dry ingredients in a basin. Stir in the milk and water and the well-beaten egg, then the melted butter. Bake in buttered muffin tins for 25 minutes in a hot oven.

Gluten Oven Scones

¾ lb. Gluten Flour.	½ cupful Water.
2 tablespoonfuls Butter.	½ teaspoonful Salt.
½ cupful Milk.	5 teaspoonfuls Baking Powder.

UTENSILS—Basin, sieve, wooden spoon, measuring spoons, cup, pastry board, rolling pin, round cutter, baking sheet.

Sift the dry ingredients into a basin, then rub in the butter with the finger tips. Make the mixture into a dough with the milk and water. Turn on to a lightly floured board, roll to ¼ inch in thickness, and shape into rounds with a small cutter. Bake for about 15 minutes on a buttered tin in a moderately hot oven, 375 degrees Fahr.

Baked Tomato and Egg

1 Egg.　Salt and Pepper.	1 teaspoonful Butter.

1 firm Tomato.

UTENSILS—Knife, metal spoon, teaspoon, baking tin or individual fireproof dish. *Enough for 1 person.*

Cut a slice from the top of the tomato, and scoop out some of the pulp. Break in an egg. Sprinkle with salt and pepper to taste, and add as much of the pulp as the tomato will hold, then put a piece of butter on top. Sprinkle again with salt and pepper, and bake in a moderate oven for 15 minutes.

Forfar Steaks

6 oz. minced Steak. | **1 small** Onion.
Salt and Pepper.

UTENSILS—Mincing machine, knife, basin, metal spoon, plate, frying pan. *Enough for 1 person.*

Choose steak from the round. Put it through a mincer, and mix with seasoning to taste. Shape into rather flat cakes. Brown in a little hot butter or dripping, and serve with halved tomatoes, sprinkled with pepper and salt, and baked in a tin, or with a dish of watercress. Drain the steak from fat before serving.

Fruit Salad (1)

1 Apple. **4** Walnuts. | **1 slice of** Pineapple.

UTENSILS—Knife, basin, tablespoon, fruit salad glass. *Enough for 1 person.*

Cut the pineapple into dice. Add the peeled, chopped and cored apple. Mix the fruit with 1 tablespoonful of pineapple juice, and sprinkle with chopped walnuts.

Fruit Salad (2)

½ **Orange.** ½ **Grapefruit.** | **2 Maraschino** Cherries.

UTENSILS—Knife, pointed spoon, basin, fruit salad glass. *Enough for 1 person.*

Peel the orange, divide it into fingers, and remove the seeds. Extract the grapefruit pulp. Dice the fruit, mix it together, and serve either in a glass or in a half grapefruit shell, with minced cherries on top.

Fruitade

1 Lemon. Water. **1 Orange.**

UTENSILS—Cloth, basin, lemon squeezer, strainer, jug.

Wash and dry the lemon and orange, place them in a basin, cover them with cold water, and soak for 2 hours. When thoroughly soaked, drain the fruit, and squeeze it in a lemon squeezer. Strain the juice into a jug, and add the water in which the fruit was soaked. Chill and serve. If preferred, the fruitade can be sweetened with a small saccharine tablet.

THE SLIMMING BREAKFAST—A cup of black coffee, half a grapefruit or an apple, and toast or a dry roll.

The fattening breakfast—Bananas, then fried eggs and bacon can be followed by buttered toast and marmalade, with a cup of hot chocolate.

TO PUT ON WEIGHT

Generally speaking, it is easy to prescribe a diet for leanness, which is usually caused through run-down tendencies. Very often the introduction into the diet of foods containing plenty of vitamins will build up the body, but care should also be taken to provide only food that is easy to digest. *For unless the food that is taken can be easily assimilated, the indigestion that will result will cancel the value of the food itself.*

One should start a campaign for putting on weight by planning well balanced menus, and then by adhering strictly to them.

WELL BALANCED DAILY MENU FOR WINTER

BREAKFAST.—Half a grapefruit. Cereal and milk. One steamed egg and 2 grilled rashers of bacon. Toast, butter and honey. Coffee or tea.

LUNCHEON OR SUPPER.—Tripe and onions, mashed potatoes. Baked rice pudding, stewed figs. Celery, biscuits or toast, cream cheese. Small cup of black coffee.

TEA.—Brown bread and butter, as much as liked, jam, bloater cream. Ham, tongue and celery sandwiches, or sandwiches made of brisling paste. One piece of plum, cherry, seed, madeira or sponge cake, or a choice of ginger snaps and gingerbread.

DINNER.—Barley mutton broth. Large portion of roast beef, chicken or game, large portion of buttered greens, spinach or Brussels sprouts, baked potatoes. Pancakes ; followed by fresh fruit, if liked.

If this kind of diet does not increase the weight as quickly as desired, a glass of warm milk or orange juice should be taken about 11 o'clock in the morning, again midway between the midday meal and tea, and just before retiring. It really does not matter much whether milk is taken in between meals or at meal time, so long as it is included in the daily diet.

When planning menus for those who are under weight, any of the following foods can be chosen :

C.I.O.   S

Wholemeal biscuits, bread and cereals, oatmeal, breakfast foods, eggs, milk, cream cheese, beef, lamb, chicken, liver, pheasant, tripe, all green vegetables, baked potatoes, butter, onions, dates, raisins, all milk puddings, and puddings in which milk or eggs or both are chiefly used, such as blanc-manges, custards, junket, tapioca cream, and creams, light steamed puddings and pancakes, raw and baked apples, fresh berries, grapes, grapefruit, oranges, stewed figs and prunes, cocoa, cream, etc.

You can also use a large proportion of any of these foods in preparing one course, such as boiled chicken with white sauce and boiled rice, which is also a suitable food.

When the digestion is impaired, you must avoid tongue, sausage, kidney, liver, stews, pork, duck, goose, herrings, and all shell fish except oysters, and all preserved meats and fish. Onions, cucumbers, radishes, cabbage and turnips, jams and preserves, as well as berries, all alcoholic and malt drinks, condiments, pastries, nuts, rich gravies, rich sauces and soups, and hot breads of all kinds must also be avoided. The lighter and more digestible the food, the better, so long as it is nourish-ing and well balanced, and taken at regular intervals, and not before resting or retiring.

If thinness is caused by anaemia, malnutrition or neuras-thenia, it is necessary to choose plain, nutritious food, simply prepared, to give up all condiments, gravies and sauces, and to eat plenty of red meat and vegetables. It is also advisable to drink a glass of water on arising, and an hour before each meal, as well as before going to bed, and to take note of the following hints :

1. Eat slowly, and chew thoroughly.

2. Eat at regular intervals daily, and keep to the same hours for meals every day, if you can.

3. You should only change your meal hour if you are hot or excited, after work or play or from any other cause. It is unwise to eat when hot and excited.

4. Try to sit quietly for a few minutes after every meal. Do not, whatever you do, hurry in any way after a meal.

The following menus should be studied and followed as closely as possible. It costs money, of course, to provide highly nourishing diet, but to get rid of anaemia and mal-nutrition it is essential to eat properly.

TYPICAL DAY'S DIET FOR PUTTING ON WEIGHT

BREAKFAST.—One large glass of milk, or 1 large cup of cocoa made with milk. One bowl of porridge or other cooked cereal. Two thick slices of buttered bread. Any jam, jelly, marmalade or honey, or any fresh fruit, or both jam or honey and fruit.

LUNCHEON.—Hot meat and potatoes, a second vegetable. A simple pudding. Roll and butter. Or, two large meat sandwiches, a glass of milk in which an egg is beaten, and a simple pudding.

NOTE.—If you have to lunch in a restaurant, choose the first luncheon; if you take your lunch with you to business, choose the second. Either luncheon can be taken at home.

DINNER.—Hot meat, vegetable, salad. Roll and butter. Fresh or stewed fruit.

NOTE.—It is better to have the main meal in the middle of the day. Besides the meals suggested, drink extra milk to bring the total quantity up to 1 quart a day. Drink egg and milk at 3 p.m. when possible, and again drink a glass last thing at night. Do not take any water with your meals, but drink water freely between meals. Boil, grill, steam, bake or roast the different foods, as suitable. Frying is the most indigestible method of cooking.

What Foods to Choose

MEATS.—Beef, mutton, steak, lamb and mutton chops, chicken, game, bacon, liver, tripe, sweetbreads, brains, fish.

VEGETABLES.—Artichokes, asparagus, cooked celery, cauliflower, lettuce, spinach, carrots, boiled beetroot moistened with butter, peas, young string beans and potatoes.

FRUITS.—Raw and cooked fruit. Baked and stewed apples, stewed prunes and pears, oranges, mandarins, berries, bananas, figs, melons and preserved fruits.

DRINKS.—Cocoa, milk, tea, water and mineral water.

SUNDRIES.—Beef tea, bouillon, clear soup, chicken and mutton broth, beef juice, and soups thickened with vegetables, barley, rice, vermicelli, sago, tapioca or spaghetti, except fatty soups; eggs, sour milk cheese, any puddings, except tarts and pastries; macaroni and spaghetti dishes; bread, biscuits, toast, sponge cake and other plain cakes; chocolate and a limited amount of sweets.

What Foods to Avoid

MEATS AND FISH.—Pork, kidneys, sausages, stews, duck, goose, shell fish, except raw oysters, herring, and all preserved meat and fish.

VEGETABLES.—Cucumbers, cabbages, Brussels sprouts, raw onions, radishes, turnips, coarse, old carrots, and all pickled vegetables.

DRINKS.—Ice cream sodas, alcoholic drinks and all fancy beverages.

SUNDRIES.—Rich cakes and soups, gravies, hot rolls, condiments and nuts.

FATTENING RECIPES

Cream of Lettuce Soup

3 cupfuls Chicken Stock.
1 small Onion.   1 Potato.
1 slice of stale Bread.
2 cupfuls Milk.

1½ teaspoonfuls **Salt.**
Pepper, to taste.
2 tightly-packed cups **shredded**
   Lettuce.

UTENSILS—Stewpan, basin, strainer, cup, teaspoon, wooden spoon, knife. *Enough for 3 or 4 persons.*

Place the lettuce, stock, bread, potato, and sliced, peeled onion in a stewpan. Boil for ½ hour. Strain, add the milk, bring to boiling point, and season to taste. If wanted thicker, stir into the soup, before adding the milk, a tablespoonful of cornflour mixed with 2 tablespoonfuls of cold water. Water can be substituted for part of the stock, or for all of it, but then the soup will not be so nourishing.

SPINACH SOUP, made in the same way, is equally good, and spinach is a vegetable which is to be recommended to those who are run down or anæmic.

Nut and Raisin Bread

4 cupfuls Flour.
2 Eggs.   2 cupfuls Milk.
4 tablespoonfuls melted Butter.
¾ cupful chopped Walnuts.

½ cupful chopped Raisins.
½ cupful Castor Sugar.
1 teaspoonful Salt.
4 teaspoonfuls Baking **Powder.**

UTENSILS—Two basins, sieve, egg-beater, wooden spoon, measuring spoons, cup, saucepan, knife, 2 loaf tins.

Sift the dry ingredients into a dry basin. Stir in the nuts and raisins, and add the well-beaten eggs alternately with the milk and melted butter. Bake in one large or two small uttered loaf tins, from 45 minutes to 1 hour, depending on whether you make one or two loaves.

Soda Bread

3 cupfuls Wheatenmeal.	1½ teaspoonfuls Salt.
1 cupful Flour. 2 Eggs.	1 teaspoonful Baking Soda.
½ cupful Castor Sugar.	1 pint Sour Milk.
2 tablespoonfuls melted Butter.	2 teaspoonfuls Cream of Tartar.

UTENSILS—Two basins, egg-beater, wooden spoon, measuring spoons, cup, sieve, saucepan, loaf tin.

Beat the eggs well, then beat in the sugar and salt, and stir in the butter. Add the flour, sifted with the soda and cream of tartar, to the egg mixture, alternately with the milk. Beat in the wheatenmeal. Bake in a well-buttered loaf tin from ¾ to 1 hour in a rather hot oven.

Potato Pancakes

1¼ cupfuls grated Raw Potato.	½ teaspoonful Salt.
1 Egg. Pepper to taste.	1 teaspoonful Baking Powder.
3 heaped tablespoonfuls Flour.	

UTENSILS—Basin, wooden spoon, measuring spoons, cup, egg-beater, grater, frying pan, knife or palette knife.

Mix all the ingredients well together with a wooden spoon, after beating the egg. Melt a little nut of bacon fat in a frying pan, and drop tablespoonfuls of the batter in the smoking hot fat, keeping them well apart. Turn when brown underneath, and brown on the other side. Serve with fried or grilled chops, cutlets or steaks.

Potato Soufflé

2 cupfuls hot, mashed Potatoes.	1 tablespoonful chopped Parsley.
1 tablespoonful Butter.	½ cupful tepid Milk. Mint.
4 whites of Eggs.	

UTENSILS—Saucepan, soufflé dish, knife, chopping board, tablespoon, wooden spoon, cup, basin, wire whisk, grater. *Enough for 2 persons.*

Season the potatoes very delicately with powdered mint, then stir in the parsley, butter and salt, and pepper to taste. Add the milk, and beat well till smooth, then stir in the egg whites and bake at once in a buttered soufflé dish till puffy and brown on top. Serve sprinkled with grated cheese.

Baked Honey Custard

3 Eggs. ½ teaspoonful Salt.	¼ cupful run Honey.
3 cupfuls cold Milk.	¼ teaspoonful Vanilla Essence.

UTENSILS—Basin, egg-beater, wooden spoon, teaspoon, cup, pie-dish or 6 fireproof cups, baking dish. *Enough for 3 or 6 persons.*

Beat the eggs slightly, stir in the milk, salt, vanilla and honey. Bake either in a pie-dish, or in half a dozen fireproof cups, standing them in a pan a quarter filled with boiling water. They take about ½ hour if baked in cups, and ¾ hour if baked in a pie-dish.

Rhubarb Cream

| 1 large bunch Young Rhubarb. | 1¼ cupfuls Castor Sugar. |
| 1 Lemon.   3 Cloves. | 1½ cupfuls Whipped Cream. |

A half-inch stick of Cinnamon.

UTENSILS—Cloth, knife, saucepan or double boiler, cup, grater, lemon squeezer, wooden spoon, wire whisk, basin.

Wipe the rhubarb—there should be 12 stalks. Cut them into inch lengths, and place them in a saucepan or in the top of a double boiler. Add the grated lemon rind and strain in the juice of a lemon, throw in the cloves and cinnamon, and cover the saucepan. Cook gently till the juice flows freely, then add the sugar and continue cooking until it reaches the marmalade stage. Cool, fold in the cream, and serve in tall sundæ glasses, or in the centre of a glass dish lined with sponge fingers put together with lemon curd. Decorate with whipped cream. Sponge fingers can be handed with the rhubarb cream if it is served in sundae glasses.

Walnut Gingerbread

½ cupful Butter.	½ cupful Brown Sugar.
1 cupful Treacle.	½ cupful Milk.
3 cupfuls sifted Flour.	1 cupful Chopped Walnuts.
1 level teaspoonful Baking Soda.	1 teaspoonful Ginger (ground).

UTENSILS—Two basins, wooden spoons, teaspoon, cup, knife, sieve, shallow baking tin, cake rack.

Beat the butter and sugar to a cream, stir in the treacle, ginger, and the soda dissolved in the milk, then the flour and the walnuts. Bake in a well-buttered, shallow baking tin in a moderate oven for about 45 minutes. Turn out, and cool on a cake rack.

Swiss Cocoa

| 6 teaspoonfuls Cocoa. | 5 teacupfuls Water. |
| 1 cupful Condensed Milk. | 3 or 4 grains of Salt. |

2 tablespoonfuls Castor Sugar.

UTENSILS—Basin, wooden spoon, measuring spoons, cup, saucepan. *Enough for 6 persons.*

Mix the cocoa, sugar and salt together with a wooden spoon. Stir in the water, then turn into a saucepan and bring to the boil. Boil up, draw off the fire until the cocoa falls again, then boil up again. Remove from the fire, stir in the condensed milk. Return to the fire, and bring to boiling point before serving.

Chocolate Malted Milk

1 tablespoonful Cream.
1 cupful freshly-made
   Chocolate.
	2 tablespoonfuls Malted Milk
	   Powder.
	Castor Sugar to taste.

UTENSILS—Double boiler, wooden spoon, tablespoon, cup, basin. *Enough for 1 person.*

Pour the chocolate into the top of a double boiler. Stir in the malted milk, mixed to a paste with the cream, and stir over boiling water till hot. If wanted less rich, substitute milk for the cream. If wanted richer, stir in a well-beaten egg, mixed with the malted milk and cream, and flavour with vanilla to taste.

COCOA and COFFEE MALTED MILK can be made in the same way, substituting made cocoa or coffee for the chocolate.

ICED MALTED MILK can be made with any of these flavours. It is heated in the same way, allowed to become thoroughly cold (chilled, if possible, in a refrigerator) then served with a heaped tablespoonful of vanilla ice cream floating in the glass.

FRUIT FOR HEALTH

You can eat fruit any way you like, so long as you eat it every day. The best way to take it is ripe, between meals. Cooked or tinned fruit is not so good for the health as raw fruit.

Always begin breakfast with fruit—fresh for preference. Grapefruit, oranges and apples are best, but when they are unavailable, use any fruit you like, so long as you are not suffering from any illness in which fruit is forbidden. For example, tinned and dried fruits, dates, figs, prunes and raisins are forbidden to sufferers from digestive troubles, from diabetes, and to the stout, but they are good in constipation. Raw and cooked fresh fruits, while good for anaemia and constipation, can be taken in moderation in cases of diabetes, *with the exception of grapes, figs, prunes, dates and raisins.*

Any one wanting to reduce should avoid all stewed, tinned preserved or sweetend fruit, as well as bananas, grapes, raisins, jams and jellies ; but raw apples, cherries, apricots, figs, peaches, pears, plums, grapefruit, melon and oranges, and unsweetened berries can be taken. When you are hungry, and are having a fight with your appetite, do not run to anything except fruit. An apple, an orange, or a slice of melon will stave off hunger without adding to your weight. When reducing, you can eat juicy fruit of all sorts, especially apples, oranges, berries, cherries, grapes, peaches, plums and melon, as freely as you like without fear.

If more fruit were eaten, the curse of constipation, which brings all kinds of diseases in its train, would be overcome. If more apples were eaten, not only would constipation cease to exist, but we should have sounder teeth and gums. For apples are a first-class dentifrice. Briefly, a fruit diet purifies the blood and pure blood prevents disease.

To return to the daily meals, when fresh fruit is not available for breakfast, stewed fruit, followed by brown bread and butter, is the next best substitute. Then be sure to have at least one fruit course for lunch or supper and dinner, or make fruit part of one course. If you introduce fruit to your diet in this way, and either start your day with a glass of orange or lemon juice, or a glass of half and half, all you need to do to court good health and beauty is to drink a nightcap to match. You must also remember to give your young children fruit juice daily, either orange or grape juice, and when the children grow older, teach them the same fruit habits that you have learned yourself, and then your doctor's and dentist's bills will not be worth talking about. The following are some recipes for raw and cooked fruit dishes : (Other fruit dishes will be found under PUDDINGS ; FRUITS, PRESERVED ; etc.)

Orange Daisies

6 large Seedless Oranges. | **6 Lettuce Leaves.**
2 teaspoonfuls Brown Sugar.

UTENSILS—Knife, 6 plates. *Enough for 6 persons.*
Peel the oranges with a sharp knife, taking care not to

crush. Remove each section carefully, then line six plates with a lettuce leaf and arrange all the sections from one orange on each leaf in the form of a daisy. Put a little brown sugar in the centre. The lettuce can be omitted if desired. Use for the first course at lunch or dinner.

Angel's Delight

1 South African Pineapple.
1 Grapefruit.
1 cupful Castor Sugar.

2 large Oranges.
1 Cocoanut.
Juice of 1 Lemon.

UTENSILS—Knife, fork, basin, lemon squeezer, cup, grater, glass bowl. *Enough for* 6 *persons.*

Slice and pare the pineapple, and fork out the pineapple pulp from the core into a basin, together with any juice. Peel grapefruit and oranges, remove all white pith and separate into sections, throwing away any membrane between. Place the sections over the pineapple. Sprinkle with sugar and lemon juice and stand on ice or in a refrigerator for 3 or 4 hours, then peel and grate the cocoanut and mix three-quarters of the grated nut with the prepared fruit. Place in a glass fruit bowl and cover with the remainder of the grated cocoanut. Serve as a sweet for lunch or dinner. Cream can be served with the dish if desired.

Apple Purée

10 Apples (tart).
¾ cupful Water.

½ cupful Castor Sugar.
1 teaspoonful Butter.
1 tablespoonful Lemon Juice.

UTENSILS—Knife, cloth, cup, measuring spoons, wooden spoon, lemon squeezer, sieve, basin, saucepan. *Enough for* 6 *persons.*

Wipe, quarter, core and peel the apples and place them in a saucepan. Add the water, cover, and cook slowly until the apples begin to soften, then add the sugar and lemon juice, and finish cooking. Press through a sieve and beat a moment or two. Serve alone as a breakfast dish, or in company with any sweet plain cake. If preferred, a pinch of grated nutmeg or ground cinnamon can be substituted for the lemon juice.

Golden Apples

6 good Cooking Apples.	2 oz. Ground Almonds.
1 Egg. Butter.	Juice of 1 Orange.
2 oz. Castor Sugar.	1 tablespoonful Cream.

1 tablespoonful Water.

UTENSILS—Fireproof dish, knife, apple corer, basin, tablespoon, lemon squeezer, wooden spoon. *Enough for 6 persons.*

Peel and core the apples without cutting through to the stalk. Butter a fireproof dish, and stand the apples in it. Mix together all the other ingredients except the water, and pour the mixture over the apples. Pour the water round, and bake for ½ hour. Serve the apples in the fireproof dish, and hand cream or custard with them.

Rhubarb Sauce

1 bunch of Rhubarb.	1 Orange.

Castor Sugar to taste.

UTENSILS—Knife, grater, saucepan, large spoon. *Enough for 4 persons.*

Skin and cut the rhubarb in half-inch blocks. Cover with boiling water, stand 10 minutes, then drain. Add enough water just to keep the rhubarb from sticking to the saucepan, then cover the pan and simmer till the rhubarb is soft. Sweeten to taste and sprinkle with grated orange rind. Serve cold, with any blancmange, custard, junket or milk shape. This is a good way of using up left-over stewed rhubarb.

Apricot and Prune Compôte

¼ lb. Dried Apricots.	¼ lb. Dried Prunes.

½ cupful Castor Sugar.

UTENSILS—Basin, saucepan, cup, large spoon. *Enough for 4 persons.*

Pick over and wash the fruit carefully and soak it in cold water overnight. Next day, place in a saucepan, bring to boiling point, add sugar and a dash of ground cinnamon to taste, and simmer till tender. Serve alone or with any milk shape, custard or junket.

Empire Compôte

2 large Pears.	½ pint Raspberries.
4 Plums. 4 Oranges.	½ Grapefruit.
2 Peaches. 1 Apple.	1 tablespoonful Curaçao.
3 slices of Pineapple.	2 tablespoonfuls Kirsch.

2 tablespoonfuls Castor Sugar.

UTENSILS—Silver fruit knife, tablespoon, salad bowl, basin, wire whisk. *Enough for* 6 *to* 8 *persons*.

Peel and slice the pears, peaches and plums into a salad bowl. Add the peeled, cored and sliced apple, the oranges, skinned and cut into fingers, and the raspberries. Dice the pineapple, and add the pulp of the grapefruit cut into dice, as well as any juice. Sprinkle the mixture with sugar, and stand the bowl in the refrigerator for 1 hour, or until the sugar is dissolved, then add the liqueurs. Serve with whipped cream, sweetened and flavoured with vanilla to taste.

Fruit Menus

THREE ORANGE BREAKFAST MENUS

1. Oranges ; puffed rice ; grilled ham and fried mushrooms ; toasted brown bread, lemon marmalade ; China tea or coffee (for adults), milk.

2. A glass of orange juice ; shredded wheat ; steamed eggs on toast ; rolls and butter, honey.

3. Orange slices ; muffets ; fried kindeys, bacon and tomato ; toast, red currant jelly.

NOTE.—Serve China or Indian tea, or coffee, for adults, and milk for children.

THREE GRAPEFRUIT BREAKFASTS

1. Half a grapefruit ; cornflakes ; grilled Finnan haddock with poached egg ; toast, brown bread, and lemon cheese.

2. Grapefruit hearts ; fried bacon, bread and tomatoes ; rolls ; orange marmalade.

3. Grapefruit juice ; force ; fried kippers, boiled egg ; toast, honey.

THREE ORANGE LUNCHEONS

1. Fish cakes, tomato sauce, lettuce and cucumber salad ; junket and orange compôte.

2. Sardines, watercress and brown bread ; orange marmalade pudding with custard sauce.

3. Mushrooms on toast ; orange and banana jelly with whipped cream.

NOTE.—Serve a glass of lemonade, lemon squash or orange-ade with luncheon.

THREE GRAPEFRUIT LUNCHEONS

1. Half a grapefruit; tongue salad with tomatoes; baked custard.

2. Pickled herring and potato salad; grapefruit and pineapple salad; sponge cake and hot coffee.

3. Grapefruit cocktail; devilled eggs, lettuce and tomato salad; pancakes.

NOTE.—Serve a glass of lemonade, lemon squash or orangeade with luncheon.

THREE ORANGE DINNERS

1. Melon; grilled lamb cutlets, tomato sauce, creamed potatoes, French beans; orange meringue pie.

2. Egg mayonnaise; roast ribs of beef, buttered spinach, baked potatoes; compôte of oranges with banana cream.

3. Cream of tomato soup; roast duckling with orange and watercress salad, potato crisps, and apple and onion sauce; chocolate blancmange.

THREE GRAPEFRUIT DINNERS

1. Grapefruit cocktail; grilled steak and onions, potato chips, mashed turnips; stewed plums and vanilla custard sauce.

2. Vegetable broth; casserole of rabbit, mashed potatoes, buttered French beans; stuffed grapefruit salad.

3. Half a grapefruit; braised Devonshire hake, with steamed potatoes, lettuce and cucumber salad; trifle.

INVALID COOKERY

PLANNING meals for the invalid is the most difficult of all catering, for not only are you restricted in the choice of foods, ingredients, and even methods of cooking, but you have to reckon without the appetite which helps to make a success of every-day meals.

There are two chief points to bear in mind when preparing the invalid's diet—the fact that food is part of the cure and so must be made nourishing and digestible, containing those elements demanded by the patient's condition ; and the fact that in sickness one has little appetite, and must be tempted by dainty dishes, delicately made and attractively served.

The invalid's tray will come to be regarded with pleasant anticipation if it is made colourful and varied. Cups and dishes from different services can be used in turn, and painted trays or patterned cloths are more cheerful than dark brown oak and white linen. Flowers brighten the meal considerably —a few sprays laid beside the tumbler, or a freshly gathered posy in a vase, and the food itself can be chosen with an eye to its colour and appearance. A small polished dish-cover, or a fire-proof ramekin with a lid, will help to keep the food really hot on its journey upstairs, and if ice is allowed by the doctor, a lump or two will improve the cold drinks and make them far more appetising.

Much greater variety is permitted nowadays in invalid dietary than used to be the case when beef tea and chicken broth were the nurse's main standby. Fresh foods containing vitamins are of much more value in building up strength and fighting the germs of disease, than foods which have lost all their " goodness " through long cooking. Raw milk is rich in vitamins, and most invalids are allowed fresh fruit juice, which is a source of other essential vitamins. Freshly squeezed lemon juice should be given instead of bottled lemonade ; oranges are one of the most valuable fruits, and, if necessary, the juice can be extracted and strained through fine muslin. Raw salads and raw grated vegetables, which can be served in many attractive combinations, are also more valuable than cooked, for the iron and other mineral elements in them, as well as the vitamins, then remain unimpaired.

Neither is it necessary to deny the invalid who is on a

more substantial diet, all savoury food. Steamed fish and chicken are all very well once in a way, but there are more appetising dishes. The food can be baked or fried without being rendered indigestible, provided it is not cooked in a greasy manner. In a fairly light diet, a soufflé, or a mousse made from chicken, lamb or fish, will be a welcome change from eggs and steamed fish.

If you live within reach of the large stores, it is possible to obtain many little delicacies which are, perhaps, too expensive for the ordinary table. Special game, rare fruits and unusual varieties of cheese, for instance, or vegetables out of season, will tempt the appetite in convalescence, and such little dainties as Cape gooseberry jam, guava jelly, or Cyprus honey make a delicious addition to the tea-tray.

Invalid Diets

The following are some suggestions for different diets, chosen with a view to combining suitable food elements and varying the taste and appearance of the meals as much as possible.

LIGHT MEALS

1. Unsweetened calves' foot jelly, served on an ice cream plate, with a slice of lemon and thin wheaten wafers or buttered rusks. Orange custard, made by pouring sweetened, new-laid egg custard over peeled orange quarters, arranged in a fruit salad glass, and leaving to set till cold.

2. Clear mutton broth with custard dice, served in a bouillon cup or marmite, accompanied by fingers of brown toast. Raspberry fool, in a fruit cocktail glass, or baked apple and cream.

3. Cream of chicken soup, in a cup, with brown bread and butter or dry toast. Fruit jelly with sponge fingers.

SLIGHTLY SUBSTANTIAL MEALS

1. A lightly poached egg on spinach, served on a square of lightly buttered toast. Junket and stewed apples or prunes.

2. A small fillet of sole, baked or fried, with cream sauce and brown bread and butter. Vermicelli pudding, made with fresh milk and egg, baked in an individual fireproof dish.

3. Ripe English tomato, raw, stuffed with chopped mustard and cress, moistened with mayonnaise. Fish soufflé, in individual soufflé dish, with wheaten wafers or cheese straws.

4. Scrambled egg and tomato on toast. Sponge roll and cream.

5. Lamb mousse, cold, with lettuce hearts and buttered crispbread. Chocolate blancmange, hot or cold.

NOURISHING MEALS

1. Breast of chicken, roast, with bread sauce, lettuce or watercress salad, and stewed celery or Brussels sprouts. Apple charlotte, baked in individual fireproof dish.

2. Savoury omelet, flavoured with chopped parsley and ham, brown bread and butter. Custard and stewed fruit. Biscuits and cream cheese.

3. Lamb cutlet, grilled, with potato croquette and braised onion or young buttered carrots. Ripe fruit with cream or junket.

4. Pineapple and cheese salad, made by placing a round of pineapple (fresh or tinned) on a bed of lettuce leaves, and stuffing centre with cream cheese, garnished with chopped walnuts, and accompanied by cheese straws. A little oil and vinegar or lemon juice can be sprinkled over the salad, if desired. Baked whiting and buttered crispbread or brown bread and butter.

5. Cheese soufflé, baked in individual soufflé dish. Tomato salad. Tapioca or rice pudding with jam or jelly.

An invalid's breakfast should always commence with fruit, when it is allowed in the diet. This can be varied with grapes, skinned and stoned ; orange juice, freshly squeezed ; stewed prunes with cream and cornflakes ; and fresh fruit with rusks or grape nuts. Banana and cream, served with cornflakes, makes an attractive dish when summer fruits are out of season.

SUITABLE FOODS FOR INVALIDS

Before proceeding to the recipes of dishes, etc., designed for invalids, some information upon suitable foods for invalids may be given. Of course the medical man has something to say regarding this, and his instructions must always be followed ; nevertheless the following paragraphs will afford suggestions for varying the diet, which is such a necessary and important feature of invalid catering.

The ailment that is deserving of first consideration is indigestion, for besides being a cause of suffering in itself, it may accompany other troubles, and so far as food is concerned, it must have every consideration.

Dyspepsia (Indigestion)

People suffering from indigestion or flatuence require simple and plain food, as nutritious as possible, so that the quantity need not be large ; it must be well masticated, eaten slowly, and about 3 to 4 hours should elapse between meals. It is very desirable that the previous meal be practically digested before eating again. Drink as little as possible with the meal. Do not drink for an hour before or after a meal. Avoid alcohol in every form, wine, beers, spirits, liqueurs, etc. If there is debility, a little Scotch whisky may be taken with meals.

Foods to be avoided :—Fat. Greasy substances and oils in every form. Hot or very new bread. Muffins. Buttered toast. Thick soups. Rich or highly spiced foods. Nearly all Sauces. Pork. Veal. Liver. Heart. Kidney. Goose. Duck. Rabbit. Fried fish, if cooked greasily. All oily fish, of which there are many, ranging from the humble sprat and herring to the salmon. All shell-fish, except oysters. Beef and steak with some, though not all. Potatoes. Cabbage. Peas. Dried beans (green scarlet-runners and French beans are digestible, if young and fresh). Pastry, all kinds. Substantial puddings. Preserves. Any unripe fruits. All nuts. Bananas. Cheese, unless very finely grated, when it digests with many, though not all. Cheese often brings about the pain of indigestion by being eaten with butter (on bread or biscuits) ; by omitting the butter cheese is often agreeable, and it is distinctly nourishing. Tea and coffee must not be drunk, particularly the latter. Well-made tea (see Index) does not disagree with every dyspeptic. Ices, and iced foods and drinks, must be avoided.

Foods that may be taken are :—Beef tea. Clear soups (consommé). Fish that are not fat or oily in the flesh, such as whiting, sole, haddock, plaice, brill, flounder, cod and turbot. These fish are put in the order of digestibility. They should be steamed, boiled or baked, in bad cases, but otherwise may be fried, if properly done. (For FRYING IN FAT, and for CHOOSING FISH, see Index.) Oysters may be eaten raw (but no other shell-fish), though as they so readily absorb disease germs, they are best avoided. Chicken. Turkey. Pheasant. Partridge. Pigeon. The latter should be young, or stewed, as it is close in texture. Game with brown flesh is best avoided, though not very indigestible. Mutton. Beef, occasionally, but not in bad cases. Sweetbreads, all kinds. Eggs, raw or lightly cooked. Toast, if crisp through and not buttered. Light milk puddings. Stewed fruits. Baked or stewed apples. Macaroni. Milk, boiled if necessary. Cocoa, not the thick kind, but the essence ; and other beverages, as will be described later. Everything should be taken warm. Iced, or even cold drinks, should be avoided. Bananas are not digestible.

Gout and Rheumatism

Nourishing foods are required. Clear (consommé) soups are allowed, also julienne, mock-turtle and tomato. Bean and pea soups are prohibited. All kinds of fish are allowed, if they are fresh and not canned. Young lamb, chicken, turkey and all game are allowed, but red meats such as mutton, and especially beef, are inadvisable. No ham or bacon.

Spinach, green beans, onions, new peas, lettuce, carrots, parsnips, turnips, cauliflower, rice and oatmeal, are allowed ; but not asparagus, radishes, sugar roots (as beets and swede turnips), potatoes (unless well baked), lemons (unless taken without sugar). No sweets, pastry, puddings or confectionery. Whenever sweetening is needed for anything, saccharine must be used instead of sugar. No fried meats. No strawberries, bananas, preserves, jellies, nor any sugar compounds. No alcoholic drinks, wines, beers, etc., but in cases of debility a little Scotch whisky may be taken with meals.

For drink, take tea ; milk, hot or cold ; coffee, for breakfast only. Do not drink for one hour before or one hour after meals. No hot or very new bread.

If good exercise is not taken, then the above diet requires modifying to some extent, and the following should only be taken sparingly :—Meat. Poultry. Game. Salmon. Eggs. Strong soup. It must always be remembered that sugar and starch are injurious to the gouty. And foods with albumen in them must be avoided to some extent, particularly if a fair amount of exercise is not taken.

Diabetes

Those suffering from this ailment require carefully to avoid all foods containing sugar and starch. The following must be avoided :—Milk. Sugar. Flour. Cornflour. Oatmeal. Rice. Sago. Macaroni. The various pulse foods. Fruits containing a high percentage of sugar. Potatoes. Beets. Carrots. Peas. Parsnips. Broad beans. Spanish onions.

The following are allowed :—Meat soups. Fish. Poultry. Game and meat of all kinds. Also eggs, butter, cream, cheese. Certain vegetables. Light dry wines. Weak unsweetened spirits. Tea, coffee, and cocoa having no sugar in its composition, and these may be sweetened with saccharine. There may be a plentiful use of butter, cream, fat and oils, if the digestion will allow. Oftentimes the digestion is weak, though the appetite is keen.

Obesity

Lean meat is the chief food to be taken to reduce obesity, as albumen is not conducive to fatness. The following should be avoided :—Soups (except the clear, in small quantity). Salmon, and all fish having oil in their flesh. Fatty meats, and fat in all forms. Potatoes. Bread. Butter. Cake. Sugar. Cream. All farinaceous puddings and preparations. Preserved fruits or jams. Beers. Wines. Spirits.

The following may be taken, but in moderate quantities, and with plenty of exercise. Three light meals a day :—Fish that is not oily. Poultry. Game. Lean meat. Eggs. Green vegetables in plenty (omitting peas and broad beans). Milk, preferably skimmed. Salads or tomatoes with vinegar ; no oils. Fruits. Toast, crisp right through. Tea and coffee, without milk or sugar (saccharine may be used for sweetening). Mineral waters. (See also page 527 *et seq.*)

For Extreme Thinness

This may be due to various causes, but the following flesh-forming foods are needed, and those producing fat should be taken freely.

Take :—Milk. Cream. Butter. Soups. Fish. Poultry. Game and meats of all kinds. Fat bacon. Puddings of all kinds. Most fruits. Biscuits, with butter. Bread. Cakes and sweet dishes. Eggs. A little beer or stout.

Avoid :—Lemons and all acid fruits. Vinegar. Spices. Condiments. (See also page 537 *et seq.*)

In Cases of Fever

As a rule there is a great waste of albuminous tissue from the body, and this must be made good. Meat is largely composed of albumen, but most probably it cannot be eaten. Beef tea, properly made, is therefore good, if it can be retained or causes no ill symptoms, but the best of all foods is milk, and, later on, white of egg, or whole eggs. At first the diet will probably be wholly fluid, but later these two foods can be made into puddings, and other light and digestible dishes.

Milk, at first, must be made digestible, and not likely to curdle in the stomach. The addition of barley water is very helpful in this respect. Soda-water can also be used. Or the milk may be boiled or peptonised (the materials for peptonisation are readily obtained at a chemist's). Whey is also a digestible and light nutritious milk drink if strained and the curds removed. The curds are indigestible. (For WHEY see Index.)

Stimulants are of importance, but should only be given under the medical man's directions. During convalescence a little light wine or weak spirits and water can be taken. When solid foods can be taken the following may be prepared. Preparations of milk and eggs. Beef tea. Boiled fish. Then, later, chicken. Light puddings, and then meat which is easily digestible, in small quantity. Such meats as beef and steak, also potatoes and pastry, must be strictly avoided. In no case must a full meal be given. The digestion is certain to be impaired, and overfeeding, or the taking of heavy foods, must have a prejudicial effect.

Consumption

So far as is yet known, the only hopes of cure lie in improving the health, strengthening the tissues, and making the sufferer capable of withstanding the attacks of the bacillus. It is a case of who is the strongest, and whom the conditions most favour.

In regard to conditions, one of the most essential is open air. As to climate, there is some difference of opinion, but open air living, all agree, is most important. Next to this, and equalling it in a general way, is abundance of nourishing and stimulating diet. Fats and oils should be introduced into the diet by every possible means. Cream and butter, fat bacon and oily salad dressings, are all beneficial.

Provided the patient has a good digestion, the following may be given :—Milk (preferably boiled). Beef tea. Broth. Cocoa. Chocolate. Egg, with milk. Egg, with sherry or brandy. Soda and milk. Any milk or cream and egg drinks. Wines and stimulants are beneficial, but best given under the medical man's instructions. Cream and milk in any form. Fat bacon. Butter. Sardines. Eggs (particularly yolks). Various egg dishes. Toast and dripping. Milk puddings, enriched with butter. Omelets. All farinaceous foods. Fish. Poultry. Game and digestible meats.

A FLUID DIET

Beef Tea

UTENSILS—Knife, mincing machine (optional), stewpan, skimmer, pint measure, basin, fine sieve or strainer.

The meat for beef tea must be juicy, such as steak, rump, beef or buttock, or topside. On no account use shin of beef. All skin, fat and gristle should be removed before preparing beef tea. Shred the meat, or mince it in a machine. Put the shredded meat into an enamelled saucepan with cold water, and let it stand (cold) for 15 minutes. Allow a pint of water to each pound of trimmed meat, or less if wanted strong.

Put the pan over a slow heat, and stir slowly. As the stirring progresses, it will be seen that the meat loses colour, and the water becomes first red and then a rich red-brown ; now remove from the fire and strain through a fine sieve or strainer, skim carefully, and remove all fat. On no account must the beef tea be allowed to boil, nor must it reach anything near boiling point. About 130° Fahr. is the highest temperature, a heat that the finger can only just be dipped in without actual scalding. If beef tea gets hotter than this, the albumen solidifies like white of egg, and, in the case of beef tea, it gets strained out—which should not occur.

This beef tea is not so palatable as that usually made, but it is the most nutritious. Seasoning of salt, half a teaspoonful to the pound of meat and pint of water, should be added, but no pepper unless allowed.

ANOTHER METHOD

The same meat is used, and prepared in the same way as described in the last recipe. When shredded, put it into jar with the same amount of water as given, and place his in a pan containing water. Or a double saucepan may be used. Let the water in the outer pan just simmer gently for 3 hours and it will be done. The beef tea in the jar does not boil. Strain carefully and remove all fat.

This method is not so quick as the last one, but it is reliable. Season with a little salt, as in last recipe.

Whole Beef Tea

Prepare this in a saucepan, as in the last recipe, and when the liquid is a rich red-brown, strain it off. Now put the meat in a mortar, and pound it until it can be rubbed through a wire sieve. Add this to the beef tea, and serve. This is more nourishing than ordinary beef tea, but it is a solid food, and must not be given if liquid food only is allowed.

Beef Juice

UTENSILS—Knife, grill, lemon squeezer.

Take some small pieces of juicy lean beef, about the size that will go into a lemon squeezer. Grill these, subjecting them to a sharp heat first, to scorch slightly and seal the pores. Grill them underdone, then place each piece in a strong lemon squeezer, and press out all the juice into a dainty coloured glass. Season with salt and pepper, and serve hot. The lemon squeezer should be made hot before being used, by dipping in hot water, and the same with the glass.

Mutton Tea

Make tea with lean, juicy mutton in any of the manners described for beef tea; a pound of meat, a pint of water, and half a teaspoonful of salt, being the proportions of the ingredients. It is a change from beef tea, and easily digested.

Barley Water

UTENSILS—Saucepan, strainer, knife, jug.

Blanch two ounces of barley, then strain it. This ensures the barley water being a good colour. Put the blanched barley, a thin strip of lemon rind and three pieces of loaf sugar into a jug. Pour a pint of boiling water over, cover closely, and when cold, strain it. There is some nutriment in barley water, and it serves well to dilute milk, as it prevents the milk forming indigestible curds in the stomach.

Arrowroot

UTENSILS—Basin, dessertspoon, wooden spoon, saucepan, teaspoon.

Mix a dessertspoonful of arrowroot to a smooth paste with a little cold milk. Boil half a pint of milk, and pour it gradually on to the arrowroot, stirring well all the time. Put all into the saucepan and boil for 6 minutes, stirring all the time. This amount of boiling is necessary to cook the arrowroot sufficiently. Add a teaspoonful of castor sugar, then serve. Water arrowroot can be made, but there is very little nourishment in arrowroot without milk.

Eggs and Brandy
(*For Cases of Exhaustion*)

UTENSILS—Basin, egg-beater.

Beat together the yolk of an egg and a quarter-ounce of castor sugar. Add two ounces of cinnamon water and two ounces of good brandy. If the case is not serious, half the quantity of brandy may be used. It can be given every hour in cases of extreme weakness; a teaspoonful to children, and more in proportion to those that are older.

Egg Nog
(*A Nutritious Stimulant*)

UTENSILS—Double boiler, basin, egg-beater, tumbler, dessertspoon.

Take a bare tumbler of milk, and make it very hot but not boiling. This is best done in a double saucepan, or by putting a jug in a saucepan of boiling water. Let the milk get cold. Beat up a fresh egg with a quarter-ounce of castor sugar in a tumbler until it is a stiff froth. Add a dessert-spoonful of brandy, then fill the tumbler with the cold, scalded milk.

Soda-Water with Milk, etc.

SODA-WATER AND MILK is made by taking half of each and mixing together. This is usually preferable to milk only, as it prevents the formation of indigestible curds in the stomach.

SODA-WATER AND CREAM consists of half a tumbler of soda-water, and half a gill of cream mixed together. It is generally used when milk is forbidden.

SODA-WATER AND WHITE OF EGG is made by beating up the white of an egg to a stiff froth, then adding a tablespoonful of brandy or lemon juice, and filling up the tumbler with soda-water.

Gruel

UTENSILS—Dessertspoon, basin, wooden spoon, saucepan.

Mix a dessertspoonful of patent groats or fine oatmeal with a little cold milk. Pour on half a pint of boiling milk, then put it into the saucepan and boil for 10 minutes, stirring well. Add sugar or salt as may be preferred, and, if needed, a tablespoonful of brandy can be mixed in.

Lemonade

UTENSILS—Knife, jug, strainer.

Pare a lemon very thinly, and put the rind in a jug. Cut the pared lemon and another one into slices, and put these into the jug also. Add about four pieces of loaf sugar, or more or less, according to taste. Pour a pint of boiling water over, cover closely and allow to get cold. When cold, strain, and it is ready for use. This is the best lemonade for invalids, though not so palatable as some.

Fruit Drinks

These can be made from fresh fruit juices with soda-water and sugar. Lemon squash is made by squeezing the juice of a lemon into a tumbler, adding castor sugar, then filling up with soda water. Orange juice makes an agreeable drink.

Toast Water

UTENSILS—Toasting fork or toaster, jug, strainer.

Take a slice of crust of bread and toast it hard, but do not burn it. Toast water made from crust keeps best. Put the toast into a jug with a pint of fresh cold water, let it soak 1 hour, and the water should then have a nice brown tint. Strain, and it is ready for use.

Whey

(*A Digestible Nutritious Drink*)

UTENSILS—Saucepan, strainer, jug.

Whey can be made in several manners, but, whichever is adopted, the curds must be removed by straining, as they are indigestible. Boil a pint of milk, then add either half a pint of buttermilk, or the juice of a lemon. This curdles the milk, and the curds must be strained off, as they are indigestible.

ANOTHER METHOD

Add a teaspoonful of rennet to a pint of warm milk, and when it curdles, strain off the curds as already described. The strained liquid is whey, and ready for use.

WINE WHEY

This is made by pouring two wineglassfuls of sherry into a pint of milk when it is boiling. This curdles the milk, and the curds must be removed as explained above. This is, of course, a stimulating beverage, and, being heating, it induces perspiration.

Peptonising Fluids

To peptonise a food is partly to anticipate digestion, so that a patient can take and absorb nourishing things which he could not otherwise digest. Peptonisation is resorted to in cases of severe indigestion, dyspepsia, fever, gastric trouble, etc. The peptonising agent is obtained from the chemist, and as there are several kinds, the manner of using is best obtained from the directions issued with them.

The process is exceedingly simple, and in practically all cases the directions are to heat (or cool) the liquid (beef tea, milk, gruel, etc.) to 140° Fahr. This is the temperature at which a liquid can just be tasted without burning the mouth. The peptonising agent is then put in, and the basin or jug is either stood in another vessel containing hot water, or it is covered with a cosy, and allowed to stand from 15 to 30 minutes, according to the degree of the predigestion required. It is then ready for use.

If the patient cannot take the fluid at once, it is best to bring it to the boil, which stops the peptonising process. Sometimes, if left too long, the beverage becomes slightly bitter. In peptonising soups, it is considered best to make some peptonised water gruel, which is thin, and then make the soup with this in the ordinary way.

Sterilising Milk

To effect this perfectly is not an easy matter, for ordinary boiling is not quite sufficient. It is, however, considered that all dangerous germs are destroyed if the milk is heated in a double saucepan (or in a jug placed in a saucepan of water) for $\frac{3}{4}$ hour, the water in the outer vessel simmering all this time.

SOUPS

Clear soups as a rule can be readily digested, and may be considered as excellent restoratives. Meat broths also serve well if unthickened, but probably the most generally serviceable are soups or broths made from chicken, mutton and veal. The following may be considered as soups suited for convalescents, for prior to convalescence soups may not be allowed. It depends upon the ailment and the doctor's opinion.

Chicken Soup

$\frac{1}{2}$ Chicken. 1 Yolk of Egg.	$\frac{1}{2}$ saltspoonful Salt.
1 very small Onion.	$\frac{1}{2}$ gill Cream. 1 pint Water.
1 small blade of Mace.	1 teaspoonful Ground Rice.

UTENSILS—Knife, meat chopper, stewpan, large metal spoon, measuring spoons, basin, strainer, pint measure.

Cut up the chicken into moderately small pieces, and break the bones. Put it into a saucepan with water and the salt, and bring to the boil. When boiling, add the onion and mace, and let all simmer for 3 to 4 hours, skimming occasionally, and adding more water as that in the pan evaporates.

Mix the ground rice into a smooth paste with a little cold milk. Remove all fat from the soup, then strain and pour it on to the rice, stirring well. Return it to the saucepan and simmer for 10 minutes. Mix the yolk of egg and the cream together, draw the saucepan from the fire and stir them in. Let all stand on a hot part of the stove or on a low gas flame for a minute or two (but not to boil), then serve.

Chicken Broth

$\frac{1}{2}$ Chicken (or about 2 lb.	1 quart Water.
of Chicken Giblets).	1 teaspoonful Parsley.
1 oz. Ground Rice.	$\frac{1}{2}$ teaspoonful Salt.

UTENSILS—Knife, meat chopper, basin, kitchen spoon, teaspoon, strainer, stewpan, quart measure, chopping board.

Cut up the chicken or giblets into moderately small pieces, and break the bones, put them into a saucepan with the water and the salt, and bring to the boil. Simmer for about 3 hours.

Mix the rice to a smooth paste, with a little water. Strain off the broth, remove all grease, then pour it on the rice, stirring all the time. Simmer again for $\frac{1}{4}$ hour, mix in the parsley, finely chopped, then serve.

NOTE.—It is perhaps more usual to use whole rice instead of ground rice, and serve this in the broth. An onion can be boiled in it if liked and allowed.

Mutton Broth

1¼ lb. Neck of Mutton, the leanest part.	1 tablespoonful Rice or Pearl Barley.
1 quart Water.	1 teaspoonful Parsley.
½ teaspoonful Salt.	

UTENSILS—Knife, saucepan, large spoon, measuring spoons, strainer, quart measure, chopping board.

Carefully trim off all fat from the mutton, then cut up the lean part, put it into a saucepan with the cold water and salt, bring to the boil and remove the scum. Add the rice or barley, then simmer gently for about 3 hours. Skim, then strain the broth on to the parsley (finely chopped), and serve. If meat can be taken, it may be cut up small, returned to the broth and served in it.

ANOTHER METHOD

Add vegetables, when allowed, for this makes the broth more attractive. For the quantity given above, cut up a small carrot, a small turnip, an onion and a piece of celery, and let these simmer with the meat about 3 hours. The broth is poured on to the parsley the last thing, as described above, and pepper is added.

A Restorative Soup

½ Chicken. ½ lb. Shin Beef.	3 pints cold Water.
½ lb. Knuckle of Veal.	½ teaspoonful Salt.

UTENSILS—Knife, saucepan, large spoon, teaspoon, pint measure, strainer, basin.

Remove all fat from the meat, then cut the lean up into small pieces. Put the meat, with the bones, into a saucepan with the water and the salt. Bring to the boil, and skim well, and simmer very gently for 4 hours. When cooked, strain off the soup, and as soon as cool, remove the fat from the top. Re-heat it as required, and serve.

Vegetables can be cooked in the soup if liked and allowed. The chicken may be omitted, and more of the other meats substituted, if liked. When cold, this soup is a jelly, and can be served as such.

Veal Broth

Is made in the same way as Mutton Broth (see page 570). Use knuckle or neck of veal, and remove all fat. It is considered a palatable broth of a delicate flavour.

Lamb's Head Broth

1 Lamb's Head.	1 Turnip. Salt.
1 oz. Rice or Pearl Barley.	1 teaspoonful Parsley.
1 Carrot. 1 Onion.	3 pints cold Water.

UTENSILS—Meat chopper, tape, saucepan, large spoon, teaspoon, knife or vegetable cutter, chopping board.

The vegetables may be omitted if not allowed.

Have the head chopped in half, then tie it together with tape. Put it into a saucepan with the water and half a teaspoonful of salt. Bring to the boil, remove the scum, then add the vegetables cut into small dice, and the rice or barley. Simmer for about 3 hours, then lift out the head, skim well, pour the broth on to a teaspoonful of chopped parsley, and serve.

FISH

Fish is the lightest form of solid food, and those fish which have the oil confined to their livers, and not diffused about in their flesh, are digestible and good. Fish having the oil in their flesh—as herring, mackerel and salmon—are distinctly nourishing but indigestible. People suffering from indigestion or leading sedentary lives should eat fish more often than meat.

The following sauces are usually permissible : white sauce, parsley sauce, egg sauce. If the digestion is in a weak state, it is generally ordered that sauces be omitted and the fish served plain.

Fish is more or less digestible according to how it is cooked ; and the processes in their order of digestibility are as follows : steamed, boiled, grilled, baked, fried. Fried fish is the least suitable, unless the patient is well on the road to recovery. The fish in their order of digestibility are as follows : whiting (called the chicken of the sea), soles, haddock, plaice, flounder, halibut, turbot, dory, cod, then the oily-fleshed varieties.

For particulars of Choosing, Preparing and Cooking fish, see Index.

Boiled Whiting

1 Whiting.   Salt. | Vinegar.   Garnish.

UTENSILS—Wooden skewer, fish-kettle or saucepan, tea-spoon, fish-slice, knife.

Wash the fish well, then truss it with its tail in its mouth (see page 12). Put sufficient cold water into the fish-kettle or saucepan just to cover the fish. Add a teaspoonful of salt and a teaspoonful of vinegar to each quart of water. Put the fish in, and if it is a small one it will be done by the time the water just comes to the boil. If it is a large fish, keep it in the nearly boiling water for a few minutes. It is best not to boil it. When the skin cracks the fish is done.

Drain well, then serve on a dish-paper, and garnish with fresh parsley and cut lemon. The fish may appear more dainty to an invalid if a folded napkin is substituted for the dish-paper. Parsley or white sauce may be poured over if allowed.

Boiled Sole

This is cooked in the same manner as Whiting, in the preceding recipe, but may take 3 to 4 minutes longer.

Boiled Fresh Haddock

1 Haddock.   Salt. | Vinegar.   Garnish.

UTENSILS—Knife, fish-kettle or saucepan, dessertspoon, teaspoon, fish-slice.

Scrape the fish, remove the inside and the eyes, trim the fins and tail. Put sufficient cold water into the fish-kettle or saucepan just to cover the fish. Add a large dessertspoonful of salt and a teaspoonful of vinegar to every quart of water, then put the fish in, and if it is a medium-sized one it will be done in 10 minutes after the water comes to the boil. If it is a large fish it should be allowed to boil 15 minutes.

When done, lift the strainer out with the fish on it, and let it rest across the top of the kettle to drain off the water.

Slide the fish carefully on to a dish, which has a folded napkin
or dish-paper laid on it. Garnish with a bunch of fresh
green parsley.

Boiled Plaice, or Brill

1 Plaice, or Brill.	Vinegar. Lemon.
Butter.	Salt. Garnish.

UTENSILS—Knife, fish-kettle, fish-slice, brush for oiled
butter.

Clean the fish, trim off the fins, and rub it over with
lemon juice. Lay it in a fish-kettle with sufficient water to
cover it, adding salt and vinegar in the proper proportions.
(For BOILING FISH, see above.) Bring it to the boil, then
reduce the heat, and let it simmer gently until the fish is
done.

If it is a rather small fish, it will take about 10 minutes
after it comes to the boil. Lift it out, drain, then brush it
over with oiled butter. Lay it on a very hot dish, and garnish
with parsley and cut lemon.

Fish Soufflé

4 oz. White Fish, free from skin and bone.	½ gill Fish Stock.
1 oz. Butter. 2 Eggs.	1 oz. Flour. 1 gill Milk. Pepper and Salt.

UTENSILS—Pestle and mortar, saucepan, wooden spoon,
basin, egg-beater, soufflé tin.

Put the fish into a mortar, and pound it well. Melt the
butter in a saucepan, Add to it the flour, and fry together
without browning. Add to this the fish-stock and milk.
(The fish-stock can be made from the bones and skin of the
fish.) Cook at the side of the stove or on a low gas flame
for 10 minutes. Take the saucepan off the fire, and beat in
the yolks of the eggs one by one. Then add the pounded
whiting and the seasoning of pepper and salt. Beat all well
together, then, lastly, add the whites of the eggs beaten to
a stiff froth, with a tiny pinch of salt.

Tie a well-buttered band of stiff paper round the outside
of a well-buttered soufflé tin, so that the paper stands about
two inches above the tin. Pour in the mixture immediately
the whites of eggs are added and bake in a moderate oven
for ¾ hour. When cooked, remove the paper, fasten a folded
napkin, or fancy paper, round the tin, sprinkle the soufflé
with finely chopped parsley if liked, and send to table at once,
or it will sink.

Fish Quenelles

| 8 oz. fresh White Fish. | 4 oz. Breadcrumbs. |
| 1 Egg.　2 oz. Butter. | Toast.　Pepper.　Salt. |

UTENSILS—Knife, pestle and mortar, grater, basin, egg-beater, wire sieve, wooden spoon, plate, 2 dessertspoons, frying pan, toasting fork or toaster, fish-slice.

Take ½ pound of uncooked white fish (whiting or haddock, etc.), freed from skin and bones, and break it into flakes. Put this into a mortar with the butter, seasoning and bread-crumbs, and pound them well. Beat up the egg, and add sufficient of it to bind the ingredients in the mortar. When well pounded, rub all through a wire sieve, occasionally scraping the sieve underneath, as this hastens the process.

When all is through, shape the mixture into quenelles. This is best done by taking a dessertspoonful of the mixture, then with a wet knife smoothing over the top to make it egg-shaped. Another wet spoon is then taken, and with it the contents of the first spoon are scooped out so as to resemble an egg. When all are ready, place them in a greased frying-pan, and pour boiling water gently into the pan until they are nearly covered. Cover with a buttered paper, and poach for about 10 minutes.

Have ready one or two pieces of toast on a hot dish. Lift out the quenelles with a perforated fish-slice, so as to drain them well, then arrange them neatly on the toast. Garnish with parsley, and serve. White sauce may also be served, if allowed.

The foregoing recipes will serve to show how fish is best prepared for Invalid Diet. It must be carefully cooked, so as to be appetising, delicate and digestible. Other fish recipes will be found on pages 176 to 215, a number of which can be adapted by omitting any rich ingredients and seasonings that may be given.

Fish omelet is appetising, the fish finely chopped and made savoury with a little chopped parsley ; and the whites of the eggs beaten as in omelet soufflé (see Index).

EGG DISHES

Eggs, being very rich in albumen, are decidedly nutritious, but their digestibility depends entirely on the cooking. If raw eggs can be taken in any form, they are best; but, failing this, let the cooking be done carefully. Over-cooking must be avoided.

To Boil an Egg

Put the egg on in cold water, to cover it completely, bring to the boil and simmer for 1 minute. This mode prevents, as far as possible, cracked shells and partial boiling out.

Another excellent way (probably the best way) is to have a saucepan of boiling water just removed from the fire, put the egg into this, then stand it on a cool part of the range or on a very low gas flame, where the water will keep hot, but not boil nor simmer. This cooking takes 10 minutes. Eggs should not be cooked until required for eating, as the white becomes less digestible while waiting.

Poached Egg

UTENSILS—Cup, frying pan, egg-slice, toasting fork or toaster, round cutter or tumbler.

This is perhaps the lightest way of cooking an egg. Break the egg into a small cup. Have ready a frying pan or shallow stewpan, with sufficient water to cover the egg. When the water shows signs of boiling at the edge of the pan, pour the egg in as gently as possible. Cook it for 3 minutes, or until the white is just set but not hard, then lift it out on a perforated slice, drain for a moment, and place the egg on to a square or round of buttered toast.

It is best to trim the edges of the egg before placing it on the toast. This can be done by pressing a thin-edged glass over it. Garnish with parsley. If butter is not allowed on the toast (for buttered toast is indigestible) the top surface may be moistened with a little hot milk.

Baked Egg

UTENSILS—Ramekin case or cup, teaspoon.

Butter a china or paper ramekin case, or a small earthenware cup, break an egg carefully into it, add a sprinkling of pepper and salt, and, if liked or convenient, a teaspoonful of cream. Bake in a moderate oven for 3 or 4 minutes, until the white is just set, then serve at once.

Steamed Egg

UTENSILS—Ramekin case or cup, knife, saucepan.

Butter a case or cup, as in the last recipe. If liked, a sprinkling of chopped parsley may be put in the case before the egg is broken in. Break in the egg, then put the case into a saucepan with a little boiling water, steam gently until the white is just set, then serve at once.

Scrambled Egg

UTENSILS—Dessertspoon, saucepan, cup, fork, spoon, toasting fork or toaster.

Heat a dessertspoonful of milk and a quarter of an ounce of butter in a small saucepan. Beat up an egg in a cup, with a little pepper and salt. Pour it into the saucepan, and stir sharply until it begins to thicken. Remove from the fire, and stir a little longer until you have a creamy mixture. Cook as little as possible, to prevent its becoming indigestible. Serve on a square of buttered toast, if allowed.

Omelets

A variety of these is given on pages 397 to 404. The plain and savoury omelets are usually allowed if lightly cooked. They are both appetising and nourishing. If allowed, a simple variety can be made by inserting a little hot cooked vegetable —such as cauliflower, French beans, peas, etc.—in the fold of the omelet.

POULTRY, GAME AND MEATS

Practically all meats are nourishing, but their digestible qualities vary greatly. It is understood, of course, that if food cannot be digested properly, its nourishing qualities do not count so much ; and it cannot be too often remembered that foods which digest well not only stimulate and strengthen an invalid in an agreeable manner, but also have the greatest dietetic value.

The comparative digestibility of various meats is referred to on page 552, but it may be mentioned that the following should always be avoided : pork, veal, salted meat, ducks, geese, pigeon (unless well stewed), beef (unless the invalid's

BARLEY WATER FOR THE INVALID—Barley water flavoured with lemon is nutritious as well as palatable (p. 557).

TEA FOR THE INVALID—The first essential is to make the tray dainty and gay. When milk is not allowed, tea can be served with lemon.

digestive powers are fairly good), rabbit, liver, heart and kidney. All poultry and game are readily digested, but when the digestion is very weak, game with white meat will always be found best.

BOILING

The roasting of meats, both in front of the fire and in the oven, is described in other parts of this book, and will be found from the Index, but the process of boiling, as applied to meats, has not been referred to so fully.

Fresh meats are put into boiling water, as this sudden heat seals the pores, minimises the loss of juices and ensures more tenderness when the meat is cooked. This applies to poultry and game as well as meat. When the meat is put in boiling water, the boiling ceases. The water is then brought to the boil again, and all scum removed at once. When this is done, move the pan to a cooler part of the stove, or lower the gas jet, so that the cooking is completed with the water only just simmering.

A fowl or pheasant will take about 1 hour to cook; 10 minutes more or less according to its size. Partridge takes about 40 minutes. Meat takes a good 15 minutes to the pound. Twenty minutes is necessary if it is a solid, boneless piece. In timing the cooking of meat, consideration must always be given to the thickness and the shape of the piece. To go by the weight only is wrong, for a thin piece of meat must be cooked through much more quickly than a thick piece.

Boiled Chicken

1 Chicken.   **Lemon.** | **Salt.**   **Butter.**   **Bacon.**

UTENSILS—Skewers, string, saucepan, teaspoon, knife.

Choose a small plump bird, and truss it for boiling. Rub it over with lemon juice, then wrap it in buttered paper, and tie with string. Put it into a saucepan of boiling water, with a teaspoonful of salt. If vegetable flavouring is allowed add a sliced carrot, turnip and onion.

When the water re-boils, reduce the heat and simmer gently for about 1 hour. Remove the chicken from the pan, drain well, and remove the paper and skewers. Place on a hot dish, and, if allowed, pour white sauce over. Garnish with small rolls of bacon and sprigs of fresh parsley.

C.I.O.   T

Stewed Chicken

1 Chicken.	1 Yolk of Egg.	1 piece of Celery.
1 2 pint Milk.		Pepper and Salt.
1 4 pint Water.		1 tablespoonful Flour.

UTENSILS—Knife, stewpan, pint measure, tablespoon, basin, wooden spoon.

Cut the bird into neat pieces, put it into a stewpan with the milk and water, which should cover it. If preferred, weak stock may be used instead of milk and water. Shred the celery and put it in, then bring it to the boil. Simmer gently for about 1½ hours. When cooked, lift out the pieces of fowl on to a hot dish, and keep them warm.

Rub the flour into a smooth paste with a little cold milk or water. Pour this into the liquor in the saucepan, and boil up for 5 minutes to cook the flour. If preferred, a teaspoonful of arrowroot may be used instead of the flour. Remove the pan from the fire, and stir in the yolk of egg and the seasoning, pour on to the pieces of fowl on the dish, and serve, garnished with rolls of bacon. The sauce should not be thick. It must only thinly coat the fowl.

NOTE.—Other ways of cooking chicken are described in the Poultry section, pages 248 to 269.

Turkey

ROAST TURKEY is described on page 251. It is best to omit the spices and high seasonings. Half a turkey can be cooked if desired. The same time should be allowed.

Stewed Pigeon

| 1 Pigeon. | 1 oz. Rice. | A piece of Celery. |
| 1 2 pint weak Stock or Water. | | Chopped Parsley. |

UTENSILS—Skewers, knife, stewpan, pint measure, toasting fork or toaster.

The pigeon may be trussed and stewed whole, or it can be cut into neat pieces. It must be well cooked. Put it into a stewpan with the stock or water, the celery shredded, and the rice. Bring to the boil, then simmer gently for 1½ to 2 hours, until it is quite tender. Put on to a hot dish, arrange the rice round, and sprinkle a little chopped parsley over. If liked, the liquor may be reduced a little by boiling, and served as a sauce. If cooked whole, the pigeon may be served on a neat square of toast, and garnished with fresh parsley.

A savoury method of stewing pigeons is described on page 261, but the above is best for invalid cookery.

Partridge and Other Game

BOILED PARTRIDGE is described on page 263. The sauce should be omitted. If any is allowed, use a plain sauce.

GRILLED PARTRIDGE, described on page 264, is an appetising and digestible dish.

Other methods of cooking game are described on pages 253 to 269. Omit all spices, high flavourings, etc., which make the dish rich.

Plain Boiled Sweetbread

| 1 Heart Sweetbread. | Weak Stock, Milk, or Water. |

UTENSILS—Basin, saucepan, knife, toasting fork or toaster, kitchen spoon.

First blanch the sweetbread. To do this, soak it in slightly warm water for an hour, if possible, then put it on in fresh cold water to boil. Simmer for about 8 minutes, then put it into cold water to cool. This will make the sweetbread a good colour and firm. Remove all fat and any gristly part, but not the skin.

Put the trimmed sweetbread into a stewpan with stock, milk, or water, to cover. Bring to the boil, then simmer gently until tender. This will be in about 40 to 50 minutes. Dish it on a neat slice of toast and serve with white sauce, if allowed. Mushrooms can be cooked with the sweetbread, if they may be eaten. Sweetbread is very digestible, and usually proves appetising.

Stewed Sweetbread

1 Heart Sweetbread.	1 teaspoonful Arrowroot.
¼ pint White Stock or Milk.	1 Yolk of Egg (optional).
Pepper and Salt.	

UTENSILS—Basin, knife, stewpan, toasting fork or toaster, teaspoon, wooden spoon, pint measure.

Blanch the sweetbread as in the last recipe, then remove the skin. Break up the sweetbread into moderately small pieces of equal size. Put these into a stewpan with the stock or milk, cover closely, and simmer until tender. This will take about ¾ hour. When cooked, lift the pieces out and arrange them on squares of toast. Put these to keep warm while the sauce is being made.

Rub the arrowroot into a smooth paste with a little cold water, and add this to the liquor in the pan. Stir until the liquor boils again, then let it simmer, for 5 minutes, to cook the arrowroot, take the pan from the fire, and add the yolk of egg (or it may be omitted) and the seasoning, pour the sauce over the sweetbread, and serve at once as hot as possible.

Fried or Baked Sweetbread

| 1 Lamb's Throat Sweetbread. | Pepper and Salt. |
| ¼ oz. Butter. | Egg and Breadcrumbs. |

UTENSILS—Basin, saucepan, egg-beater, brush, grater, frying pan, plate.

Blanch the sweetbread as in previous recipes, but do not remove the skin nor break the flesh up. Beat the egg, and season it with pepper and salt. Brush the sweetbread over with this, then roll it in breadcrumbs so that it gets a good coat.

Put the butter in a frying pan, and fry the sweetbread until it is a nice golden colour. Drain as free from butter as possible, garnish with parsley, and serve. Or it can be put into the oven in a buttered pan, with a little oiled butter poured over, and baked for ½ hour. In frying, some prefer to cut the sweetbread into slices, and coat these well with egg and breadcrumbs.

Steamed Chop

| 1 Loin Chop.   Butter. | Pepper and Salt. |

UTENSILS—2 knives, kitchen plate, saucepan, basin.

This makes a nourishing and digestible meal, and does not resemble a boiled chop. Trim off most of the fat if necessary, then butter a plate, and put the chop on it. If a nice tin plate is available it is best. Sprinkle the chop lightly with pepper and salt, then place the plate on top of a saucepan or stewpan of boiling water, cover the chop with a basin, then let it cook for about 35 minutes, turning it once during the time. When cooked, serve the chop at once with the juice that has run from it.

Grilled or Broiled Chop

| 1 Loin Chop.   Butter. | Pepper and Salt. |

UTENSILS—Two knives, gridiron.

Trim the chop neatly, if it needs it, removing nearly all the fat. Get a clear fire ready, or light the gas grill. A small smoky blaze can be cleared in a coal fire by sprinkling a little salt on it Take a clean gridiron and butter the bars. Place the chop on, and, if possible, let it have a quick heat each side at first, then finish more slowly. This seals the pores in the meat, and makes the outer surface form an envelope for the juices.

Grill for 4 to 5 minutes on each side. It is best to turn it every 2 minutes or thereabouts. The amount of cooking depends on the thickness of the chop, and on whether it is wanted fully done or not. It is best lightly done, so that the outside is a nice brown and the inside red and juicy. In turning a chop, never insert a fork in the lean part. A fork may be used in the fat, but it is best to use tongs or two knives. Put the chop on a very hot plate, and serve at once. If allowed, a small pat of maître d'hôtel butter can be put on top of the hot chop (see Index).

Lamb or Mutton Cutlets

A small piece of best end of | Butter.
Neck of Mutton. |

UTENSILS—2 knives, gridiron, meat chopper or rolling pin.

There is no better way of cooking cutlets, to make them tempting to, and suited for, invalids, than grilling them. The meat should be prime, and the grilling carefully done, as in the last recipe. A juicy, properly cooked cutlet has a natural flavour that needs no varying or modifying. Get the butcher to saw off the chine-bone, and the cutlets can then be easily cut and divided. With a sharp knife cut down the centre between each bone. Flatten out the cutlets by gently " batting " them with the flat side of a wet meat chopper or a wet rolling pin.

With a very sharp knife trim off all skin and superfluous fat, leaving an edge of fat about a $\frac{1}{4}$ inch thick. Cut through from the edge of the cutlet to the bone just where the round piece of lean ends, then remove all meat from the thin end. Scrape the bone clean, and chop off any projecting bone there may be beyond the thick end. If on examining the meat the cutlets appear too thick, then cut one with and one without the bone. Grill as in the last recipe.

Mince of Fresh Meat

½ lb. lean Meat.	½ teaspoonful chopped Onion.
¼ pint Stock or Water.	1 teaspoonful Flour.
1 oz. Butter.	Pepper and Salt.

UTENSILS—Knife, teaspoon, pint measure, saucepan, kitchen spoon, toaster.

Mutton or chicken is best for this recipe, but any fresh meat may be treated in this way if desired. Neck of mutton will do for this, though any part may be used. It must be free from fat and skin. Cut the lean meat into very small dice. It need not be chopped or minced. Melt the butter in a saucepan, add the onion, and fry together without browning. Add the meat, and stir well, then shake in the flour and mix well again. Now add the stock or water, and let all just simmer until the meat is quite tender. This will be in about an hour. Season with pepper and salt, and serve with sippets of toasted bread.

Mutton Quenelles

¼ lb. lean Mutton.	Stock or Beef Tea.
1 Egg. Breadcrumbs.	Pepper and Salt.

UTENSILS—Knife, mincing machine, pestle and mortar, grater, tablespoon, 2 dessertspoons, sieve, plate, frying pan, egg-slice.

Chicken, beef or other meats may be used. Cut the meat into shreds, then pass it through a mincing machine. Put the minced meat into a mortar, with two tablespoonfuls of breadcrumbs, the egg, and seasoning. Add also a little stock or beef tea if necessary, but do not make the mixture too soft. Pound well, then rub through a sieve, scraping off the material underneath the sieve as it comes through, as this hastens the process. When all is through, take a dessertspoon wetted in warm water, and lift out a spoonful of the mixture. With a wet knife, smooth it over, rounded in the middle, so that the spoonful resembles an egg. Now, with another wet spoon, scoop the quenelle out of the first spoon and place it gently in a greased frying pan.

Do the rest of the mixture in this manner, then place the pan on the stove and gently pour in boiling water to reach half-way up the quenelles. Cover with a greased paper and poach (gently simmer) for about 12 minutes, when they should be firm and cooked. Lift out and drain on a cloth, then dish them on a square of toast. It is possible to make quenelles of almost any meat. Veal is excellent, also game, rabbit, chicken, etc. Quenelles are in reality forcemeat in a very appetising and nourishing form.

Stewed Ox-tail

1 Ox-tail.	1 Carrot.	A bunch of Herbs.
1 oz. Flour.	2 oz. Butter.	3 Cloves.
1 Turnip.	1 Onion.	A blade of Mace.

UTENSILS—Knife, stewpan, large spoon, piece of muslin, basin, toasting fork or toaster, strainer.

Divide the tail at the joints, and trim away as much fat as possible. Put the pieces into a stewpan, with cold water just to cover, and bring to the boil. When the water boils remove the scum. Now put in the vegetables (cut up) spices and herbs (tied in muslin), cover the pan closely, and bring to the boil again. Simmer gently until tender; this may take 3 hours.

Take out the pieces of tail, then make a thickening with the butter and flour, and add it to the liquor in the pan. Let this simmer again for 15 minutes, then remove from the fire, pick out the pieces of tail and the best pieces of vegetable, and put these on a hot dish. Strain the gravy, and pour this over, garnish with sippets of toast, and serve. If vegetables are not allowed they may be omitted.

VEGETABLES

Vegetables are a necessary food, and serve an excellent purpose when they can be taken. They are, however, somewhat indigestible and not always allowed. The small green vegetables are the most digestible, to which may be added tomatoes, celery and seakale. The green vegetables consist of spinach, boiled lettuce, cauliflower and Brussels sprouts.

Root vegetables are less digestible, these consisting of carrots, turnips, parsnips, etc. Potatoes are allowed, if properly cooked, dry and mealy. Vegetables for invalids should always be young, with the exception of potatoes.

Baked Tomatoes

Tomatoes.	Butter.		Pepper and Salt.

UTENSILS—Cloth, baking tin or fireproof dish, knife.

Wipe the tomatoes and remove the stalks. Butter a

baking tin or fireproof dish, put the tomatoes in side by side,
sprinkle them with a little pepper and salt, and put a greased
paper over. If liked, a small piece of butter can be put on
to each tomato. Bake in a moderate oven for about 12
minutes, until they are soft but not broken, then serve on a
hot dish. Some small pieces of fresh parsley make a pretty
garnish.

NOTE.—If allowed, baked tomatoes can be made savoury
by scooping a hole at the top of each and filling with breadcrumbs, chopped onion and a piece of butter.

Tomatoes au Gratin

Tomatoes.   Breadcrumbs. | Butter.   Pepper and Salt.

UTENSILS—Fireproof dish, knife, grater.

Butter a fireproof dish, slice the tomatoes, lay them in,
and sprinkle them with pepper and salt. Put some small
pieces of butter on top, and lastly, put a good layer of breadcrumbs, mixed with pieces of butter (or buttered breadcrumbs), on top of all. Bake in a moderate oven, for about
20 minutes, until the tomatoes are tender. Serve in the
dish in which they are cooked.

Boiled Lettuce

Lettuce.   Butter. | Pepper and Salt.

UTENSILS—Knife, basin, saucepan, colander.

Remove any discoloured or very coarse leaves. Strip off
all the other leaves, and let them be in cold water for a
little time. Drain them, then plunge all into a saucepan of
boiling water, slightly salted. Boil for about 20 minutes
with the lid off, and the leaves should then be tender. When
tender, drain well, then chop up the leaves. Return to the
dry saucepan with a little butter and seasoning. Shake
well as they re-heat, and, when hot, serve at once.

Mushrooms

There is considerable nourishment in the mushroom—
much more than the majority of people are aware. They are
also digestible, and, as a rule, will tempt a poor appetite
when served in a tempting manner. The baked mushroom is
perhaps the most appetising ; but other methods of cooking
this vegetable will be found from the Index. Tiny rolls of

bacon can accompany mushrooms, unless they are being served with other meat.

Potatoes

Various methods of preparing and cooking these can be found from the Index. Mashed potatoes are generally the most tempting to an invalid, and if prepared with cream are a nourishing dish. If cream or butter is not allowed, Potato Snow may be prepared by simply rubbing some well-cooked and dry floury potatoes through a wire sieve. If allowed to get cool, they may be re-heated in the oven, or in front of the fire, for a minute or two.

Potato Croquettes

½ lb. boiled Potatoes.	Egg and Breadcrumbs.
1 Yolk of Egg.	1 teaspoonful chopped Parsley.
½ oz. Butter. Frying Fat.	Pepper and Salt.

UTENSILS—Wire sieve or potato masher, 2 saucepans, wooden spoon, teaspoon, basin, egg-beater, grater, frying pan, sieve or rack, plate.

Well mash the cooked potatoes, or rub them through a wire sieve. Melt the butter in a saucepan. Add the potato, yolk of egg, parsley and seasoning. Stir until all are well mixed, and the mass binds, then turn out on to a plate, and make into ball or egg-shaped croquettes. Dip them in beaten-up egg, then roll in breadcrumbs. Fry in boiling fat until a nice golden brown, then take out and drain well.

The following vegetables may be used without ill results (if vegetables are allowed at all), and will be found by referring to the Vegetable section, pages 289 to 317, or to the Index :

Spinach   French beans
Celery   Vegetable marrow
Seakale   Rice and Macaroni can also be
Cauliflower   found from the Index.
Brussels sprouts

JELLIES

Jellies are usually the most tempting sweet dish to an invalid, but are not always nourishing. Those in which eggs or milk are used are the best in this respect, whilst those in which gelatine and isinglass are the chief ingredients afford little nourishment, though they are readily digested.

Calf's-foot jelly derives no nourishing qualities to speak of from the calf's foot, for this yields only gelatine ; and an equally good jelly can be made with prepared gelatine, if a good quality is used. Isinglass is the purest and most expensive form of gelatine. Calf's-foot jelly, and some others, are excellent as a means of administering nourishing foods, such as eggs, wine, etc., these being added in the making.

For invalids, it is best to set jelly in small dariole cups.

Milk Jelly

1 pint of Milk.   2 oz. Sugar. | 1 Calf's Foot (or ¾ oz. Gelatine.)
Rind of half a Lemon.

UTENSILS—Knife, saucepan, jar, cloth, meat chopper, basin, jelly moulds.

Cut the foot into four pieces, chopping the hoof-piece in two. Wash and cleanse them well in warm water, and trim off discoloured parts. Pick out the marrow from the bones, and remove any fat there is. Put the pieces into a saucepan, and bring to the boil quickly, then strain off the water, rinse the pieces in cold water, and rinse out the saucepan. This blanches the pieces of foot.

Put the pieces into a jar with all the other ingredients, place the jar in a vessel of boiling water and cook for 5 to 6 hours, until the meat almost drops off the bones. Now strain through a cloth, set aside to cool, remove every particle of grease, and it is ready for use.

If preferred, three-quarters of an ounce of good gelatine can be used instead of the calf's foot. The milk is boiled with the lemon rind, and this is poured over the gelatine and sugar in a basin. Stir until the gelatine is dissolved, and continue stirring until the jelly thickens like cream. This must be done or the jelly will not set in the moulds.

Egg Jelly

1 Egg.   Water. | 3 oz. Loaf Sugar.
¼ oz. Gelatine.   Juice of 1 Lemon.

UTENSILS—Lemon squeezer, 2 basins, pint measure, saucepan, egg-beater, cloth.

Rub the sugar on the rind of the lemon, then squeeze the juice out of the latter into a basin. Add water to the juice to make up half a pint. Put this into a saucepan with the sugar and gelatine, and add the egg well beaten, then

whisk the mixture until it is nearly boiling, and until the
gelatine is quite dissolved, but do not let it boil. Strain
through a cloth and it is ready for use.

Wine Jelly

¼ oz. Sheet Gelatine.	1 dessertspoonful Brandy.
¼ gill Lemon Juice.	2 oz. Loaf Sugar. 2 Cloves.
Rind of ¼ Lemon.	A small piece of Cinnamon.
¼ gill Sherry.	Half the White and Shell of an Egg.

1½ gills cold Water.

UTENSILS—Enamelled saucepan, knife, wire whisk, gill
measure, dessertspoon, lemon squeezer, cloth, basin.

If possible, use a clean enamelled saucepan of good size.
Let the rind of the lemon be pared very thinly, without any
white on it. Put all the ingredients into the saucepan except
the brandy. Whisk until the mixture is just about to boil,
then cease whisking. Let it boil up as high as it will, without
boiling over, then draw to one side, cover with a lid or plate,
then allow to stand for 10 minutes neither boiling nor
simmering. Strain through a cloth, passing it through more
than once if necessary to get it clear. Add the brandy, and
the jelly is ready for use.

Port Wine Jelly

½ pint Port Wine.	½ teaspoonful Red Currant Jelly.
½ oz. Gelatine. ¼ gill Water.	¼ oz. Loaf Sugar.

UTENSILS—Basin, kitchen spoon, teaspoon, gill measure,
strainer.

Dissolve the gelatine in the water slowly, add the sugar
and red currant jelly, and stir until all is dissolved. Add the
port wine, and, if liked, colour with a few drops of carmine.
Strain at once, and it is ready for use.

Farinaceous Jelly

½ oz. Small Sago.	½ oz. Pearl Barley.
½ oz. Whole Rice.	Rind and Juice of half a small
1 oz. Sugar. 1 pint Water.	Lemon.

UTENSILS—Two saucepans, colander or sieve, knife, cloth,
lemon squeezer.

The barley should be blanched. This is done by putting
it into a saucepan with cold water to cover, just bringing to
the boil, then straining it off and rinsing it. Well wash the
rice and sago. Put the barley, rice and sago into a clean

saucepan, with a pint of water and the thinly-pared rind of half a small lemon. Simmer gently for 3 hours, removing any scum that rises. Strain through a cloth, then add the lemon juice and sugar, and it is ready for use.

OTHER JELLIES will be found from the Index.

PUDDINGS

Of these there is great variety suited to the invalid. A few examples are given of light and nourishing puddings which do not appear in other parts of the book, and other suitable puddings which can be found from the Index.

Eggs and milk are the most nourishing ingredients, and these nearly always appear in sweet dishes. Next come the farinaceous materials ; and, when desired, a pudding can be made an agreeable means of administering wine. Starchy ingredients—arrowroot for instance—have less nutritious value, but they serve a good purpose when eggs and milk are used with them.

Flavourings must be simple. Essences can well be avoided, and only such materials as thinly-pared lemon rind, lemon juice, nutmeg and cinnamon should be used. If only a delicate flavour of lemon is required, this can be obtained by rubbing loaf-sugar on to the rind, then using this sugar.

Baked Arrowroot Pudding

1 pint Milk.   2 Eggs. | 1 oz. Arrowroot.
1 dessertspoonful Castor Sugar.

UTENSILS—Two basins, dessertspoon, saucepan, egg-beater, baking dish.

Mix the arrowroot into a cream with a little of the cold milk, then add the remaining milk to it. Put it to boil, stirring constantly, then let it boil for 5 minutes. Remove from the fire, add the sugar, and, when cooled a little, mix in the yolks of the eggs. Beat up the whites stiffly, with a pinch of salt, and stir lightly in. Pour into a greased baking dish, and bake until nicely browned and risen. Sprinkle sugar over, and serve at once, before it sinks.

Soufflé

½ pint Milk.   1 oz. Flour. | 1 dessertspoonful Castor Sugar.
3 Eggs.   1 oz. Butter. | A thin strip Lemon Rind.
1 teaspoonful Lemon Juice.

UTENSILS—Enamelled saucepan, wooden spoon, measuring spoons, basin, lemon squeezer, knife, egg-beater, 2 basins or moulds, large saucepan.

Melt the butter in an enamelled saucepan, stir in the flour, and mix together smoothly. Add the milk; bring to the boil, stirring all the time. Cook thoroughly, and when done it will draw away from the sides of the pan. Remove from the fire; add the sugar, lemon rind and juice, and the yolks of the eggs, beating the latter in one at a time. Beat the whites stiffly, with a pinch of salt, then stir them lightly in.

Well grease two basins, or plain moulds, and half-fill them with the mixture. Lay a buttered paper over, and put them in a saucepan, with boiling water reaching about half-way up the sides. Steam for 25 minutes, when the soufflés should be well risen. Turn out, and sprinkle with sugar.

A Delicate Bread Pudding

¼ lb. Breadcrumbs.	2 tablespoonfuls Castor Sugar.
2 Eggs.	The Rind and Juice of half a
1 pint Milk. 1 oz. Butter.	Lemon.

UTENSILS—Saucepan, grater, tablespoon, basin, lemon squeezer, pie-dish, egg-beater.

Put the milk into a saucepan, and add the butter, breadcrumbs and sugar, and bring slowly to the boil. Now remove from the fire, and add the yolks of the eggs and the lemon rind and juice. Pour the mixture into a buttered pie-dish, and bake in a moderate oven for 10 minutes.

Whip the whites of the eggs stiffly, with a pinch of salt, stir a tablespoonful of castor sugar in, then put on top of the pudding in rocky heaps. Put back into the oven for 3 or 4 minutes, and it is then done. Jam can be served with pudding, if allowed.

Custard Pie

½ pint Milk.   2 Eggs. | 1 dessertspoonful Castor Sugar.
Short Crust.

UTENSILS—Basin, wooden spoon, pie-dish, strainer, dessert-spoon, baking tin.

Break the eggs into a basin, add the sugar and beat well. Add the milk, and beat again. Line a small pie-dish thinly with short crust, and strain the mixture into it. Take a baking tin, put some water in it, and stand the dish in this.

Bake in a moderate oven, for about 15 to 20 minutes. Sprinkle with sugar, and serve.

Biscuit Puddings

2 oz. Ground Rice.	½ small teaspoonful Baking
2 oz. Castor Sugar.	Powder.
1 Egg.	Vanilla Flavouring.

UTENSILS—Basin, egg-beater, wooden spoon, teaspoon, small cups or dariole moulds.

Break the egg into a basin, add the sugar, and beat together to a thick froth. Stir in the ground rice, lightly, also the baking powder, and a few drops of vanilla. Butter some small cups, or dariole moulds, three-fourths fill them with the mixture, and bake in a moderate oven for about 15 minutes. Turn them out, and serve with a jam sauce.

Rusk Pudding

2 Rusks.	1 Egg.	¼ pint Milk.	Butter.
	1 teaspoonful Castor Sugar.		

UTENSILS—Pie-dish, basin, egg-beater, teaspoon.

Break up the rusks, and half-fill a small buttered pie-dish with them. Well beat the egg, add the milk and sugar to it, then beat again, and pour this over the rusks. Let the rusks soak for about 15 minutes, then put in a moderate oven, and bake from 10 to 12 minutes. Serve hot.

Sponge Pudding

2 penny Sponge Cakes.	1 teaspoonful Castor Sugar.
1½ gills Milk. 1 Egg.	Jam.

UTENSILS—Knife, glass dish, basin, wooden spoon, egg-beater, saucepan.

Slice the sponge cakes, spread a little jam on one half, then put the other on top again. Now cut them lengthwise, into three fingers each. Place these on a glass dish, moderately close together. Beat the egg and sugar together. Boil the milk, pour it on the egg, and mix well, then return to the saucepan, and stir until it thickens. Let it cool, then pour over the sponge cakes. The custard can be flavoured with lemon peel, vanilla or almond flavouring, if allowed.

COOKING FOR THE CHILDREN

IF you want your children to grow into strong, healthy men and women, if you want them to shine at school and at college, and if you want to send them well armed into the battle of life, you should teach them good food habits, and give them balanced meals from babyhood upwards.

Far too much attention is usually concentrated on the quantity of food to be given to children. It is not so much the quantity of food that matters, although this is also important, but the kind of food. Each child should have, not only food that will build and repair all parts of the body, and food that furnishes energy for the working of the muscles, but food that regulates the complicated chemical changes upon which growth and health depend. You cannot arrange this unless you are familiar with all the kinds of food that make up a menu, what each food is supposed to do, and in what proportion each food should appear in the daily diet. Let me give you a simple guide to balanced daily menus:

Guide to Balanced Daily Menus

FOODS THAT CHIEFLY BUILD MUSCLE (PROTEINS).—Milk, skimmed milk, cheese, eggs, fish, lamb, mutton, beef, veal, dried beans and peas, lentils, poultry, game, nuts, and all dishes containing a large quantity of any one or more of these foods, as bean soup, milk puddings, etc. Choose one for each meal.

FOODS THAT CHIEFLY SUPPLY RESERVE FORCE (FATS).—Butter, bacon, sausages, salt pork, fat ham, oily fish (herring, mackerel, sardines), cream, margarine, salad oil, mayonnaise, puddings and cakes made with fat and other ingredients, fried foods, etc. Choose two for each meal.

FOODS THAT CHIEFLY FURNISH FUEL (STARCHES).—All bread, buns, cakes, etc., all breakfast cereals, macaroni, rice, and puddings made with cereals, potatoes, beetroot, carrots, and other types of vegetables, bananas, puddings containing bread, cornflour, semolina, tapioca, etc. Choose two for each meal, or three if you give tiny portions.

FOODS THAT CHIEFLY FURNISH BULK (CLEANSERS).—Parsnips, spinach, and other coarse vegetables, green vegetables, berries and unpeeled fruit, coarse brown bread, gritty breakfast foods like bran and cornflakes, all salad plants, rhubarb, onions, all dried fruits and all fresh fruit except bananas, all cooked and tinned fruits, and drinks, jellies and ices containing fruit, etc. Choose at least one for each meal.

FOODS THAT CHIEFLY FURNISH CONDENSED ENERGY (SWEETS).—Honey, syrups, preserves, candies, cakes, iced cakes, sweet cooked fruit, sweet puddings, ice cream, biscuits. Choose one for each meal.

FOODS THAT CHIEFLY FURNISH LIQUID (DISSOLVENTS).—All non-alcholic drinks, including water, cocoa, coffee, tea and buttermilk, melons, cucumbers, tomatoes, berries, ices, etc. Choose two for each meal.

FOODS THAT CHIEFLY FURNISH ACIDS OR MINERALS, OR BOTH (TONICS).—All salads, all fresh green vegetables, all dried fruits and all fresh fruits except bananas, all drinks, jellies and ices made with fruit, tinned fruit, rhubarb, whole grain cereals, etc. Choose at least two for each meal.

FOODS THAT CHIEFLY FURNISH THE ELEMENTS NECESSARY TO LIFE AND GROWTH (VITAMINS).—Butter, cream, cheese, milk, carrots, cabbage, cauliflower, lettuce and other green salads, tomatoes, spinach, potatoes, parsnips, swede turnips, oranges, lemons, grapefruit, honey, apples, whole grain cereals, brown bread, brains, kidneys, liver, etc. Choose one or two for each meal.

Briefly, when planning your daily menus, you should see that they contain bread, cereals, potatoes ; butter, lard, fat meat and other fat ; one or more vegetables or fruit, especially green vegetables ; sugar, syrup or preserve, and other sweets. Several times a week add dried beans, lentils or peas ; tomatoes, raw lettuce or raw fruit ; eggs, fresh fish, lean meat, poultry or cheese, to the menus, and remember to give young children milk at every meal, orange or tomato juice every day, and two or three eggs a week.

Should children dislike porridge, you can sometimes overcome the distaste by serving with it stewed figs or prunes, or serving each portion on a thick slice of pared apple stewed in a little butter, but in this case the oatmeal should be sprinkled with sugar, mixed with an equal quantity of ground cinnamon, if liked ; or syrup can be served with the porridge.

No child can grow healthy and strong unless brought up on a balanced diet. A badly balanced diet results in rickets and many other evils. To bring up strong children, feed them on milk, small quantities of cod liver oil regularly, plenty of vegetables or vegetable juices, and fruit. They must also have a certain amount of bread, preferably wholemeal, cereals, sugars and fats in their diet, as well as eggs, fish and meat.

When you give a child only one vegetable daily, give preference to one that can be eaten raw, or which only needs a little cooking.

Every child should have at least a pint of milk a day, either to drink, or partly to drink and partly in the shape of a pudding, or in the form of cocoa made almost entirely of milk. Better still if one and a half pints or a quart is taken. If the child is less than two years old, give cod liver oil also daily, and make daily meals include one vegetable or fruit, though three or four in the day are better, and plenty of wholemeal bread, a good portion of cereal for breakfast and the midday meal, as well as other energy and body-building foods, without which no child can grow sturdy.

DIET FOR SCHOOL CHILDREN

HINTS ON PREPARING MEALS FOR SCHOOL CHILDREN

1. Try to allow $1\frac{1}{2}$ pints of milk for each child per day, either as a beverage or in a dish.

2. When the milk supply is limited for one reason or another, allow more butter, eggs and green vegetables than otherwise required.

3. When children are anæmic, see that they have plenty of iron in their food. This is best provided by eggs, meat, green vegetables, beetroot, dates, figs, raisins and other fruit.

4. See that all lunch boxes and dishes are scalded regularly, and teach children always to wash their hands and faces before meals, and never to use each other's forks, spoons, and drinking cups.

5. When children come home for the midday meal, be ready to serve them as soon as they arrive, to avoid gulping of food and a hurried departure afterwards.

6. If children buy part of their lunch themselves, impress on them how important it is to choose wholesome nutritious food, and not to waste their fruit money on cheap sweets.

7. Every meal should be well balanced. It is as wrong to give a large breakfast and a skimpy luncheon, as it is to give a large luncheon and a skimpy supper. Body waste goes on all day long and all night long, and should be replenished constantly and regularly.

A Week's Menus for School Children

SUNDAY

BREAKFAST.—Oranges; fried bacon, egg and bread; toasted brown bread, butter, and honey; weak tea, cocoa or milk.

DINNER.—Roast chicken, gravy, bread sauce, baked potatoes, cauliflower with melted butter sauce; baked custard and stewed gooseberries or tinned raspberries.

SUPPER.—Vegetable broth; fresh fruit; toast; gingerbread or biscuits, and warm milk. (Cheese, biscuits, watercress, and coffee for adults.)

MONDAY

BREAKFAST.—Pineapple slices; puffed rice; lightly boiled egg; toast and marmalade; cocoa or milk.

DINNER.—Chicken broth; cold salt beef; tomato and onion salad, scalloped potatoes; baked stuffed apples.

SUPPER.—Fish pie; green salad; stewed or tinned apricots and custard or junket; ginger snaps and milk.

TUESDAY

BREAKFAST.—Stewed figs; kedgeree, oatcakes; bread, butter and marmalade; weak tea or cocoa.

DINNER.—Minced steak stewed with sliced onions, mashed potatoes, mashed turnips; pancakes, or rhubarb tart and vanilla custard sauce.

SUPPER.—Cream of tomato soup; Yorkshire parkins and hot milk; oranges. (Sardines on toast for adults.)

WEDNESDAY

BREAKFAST.—Baked or stewed apples; shredded wheat; fried fresh herrings or kippers; toast, lemon marmalade; weak tea or hot milk.

DINNER.—Haricot mutton, new or boiled potatoes; tapioca cream, stewed prunes.

SUPPER.—Egg and tomato scramble on toast; lettuce salad; walnut jelly, sponge cake and hot milk. (Biscuits and cheese for adults.)

THURSDAY

BREAKFAST.—Glass of orange juice; post toasties; scrambled eggs on toast; bread and butter, honey; weak tea or cocoa.

DINNER.—Stewed beef olives, riced potatoes, buttered greens; pineapple fritters.

Supper.—Salmon loaf, lettuce and tomato salad; doughnuts, hot milk. (Coffee for adults.)

FRIDAY

BREAKFAST.—Stewed prunes; puffed wheat; fried fish cakes; toasted brown bread; orange marmalade; weak tea or coffee.

DINNER.—Boiled cod, egg sauce, boiled potatoes, green salad; baked rice pudding, stewed or tinned berries.

SUPPER.—Sliced cold ham and tongue; beetroot, potato and onion salad; Swiss roll and hot milk.

SATURDAY

BREAKFAST.—Sliced peaches; grape nuts; poached eggs on toast; bread and butter; gooseberry jelly; weak tea or coffee.

DINNER.—Baked liver or beef steak and kidney pie, steamed potatoes, buttered Brussels sprouts or greens; steamed fruit roll, hot pineapple sauce.

SUPPER.—Cup of bouillon, toast; banana jelly or fruit salad; queen cakes and hot milk. (Coffee for adults.)

DIET FOR YOUNG CHILDREN

Once a child has been weaned, and the milk diet gradually changed to a mixed diet, the sooner he is taught to taste different foods, the better. If children were taught to eat a variety of foods from the time they began to take solids, not only would there be every chance of their maintaining a balanced menu throughout life, but there would be fewer people with food prejudices to make matters difficult for those who have to cater for them. Solid foods should be gradually introduced through a semi-solid diet consisting of fruit juices, gruel made of cereals, and fruit and vegetable purées.

When planning the menus for children's breakfasts, dinners and suppers, you must remember that every child should start the day with a good breakfast, that the chief meal should be given in the middle of the day, and that simple suppers are best. You will probably have to allow for the younger members of the family demanding something in the form of lunch midway between breakfast and dinner. If so, keep the snack as light as possible. A glass of milk and a dry biscuit, or a sponge cake, should satisfy the pangs of hunger till dinner time comes round.

HINTS ON PLANNING MENUS FOR THE NURSERY

1. Allow 1½ pints to 1 quart of milk per day in one form or another. See that the milk is delivered in bottles, and is of a high grade.

2. Give an egg each day, or the equivalent weight of fish, meat or poultry—about 2 oz. when allowed.

3. If unable to provide wholemeal bread, and wholewheat grains served in other ways, provide plenty of fruit and vegetables, when allowed.

4. Both fruit and vegetables should appear at least once a day in a child's menu.

5. Give some kind of cereal or breakfast food every day, but it must not take the place of eggs, fruit, milk, meat or vegetables—that is to say, you cannot expect a child to live on cereals, such as oatmeal porridge, and keep his health. *The diet must be varied.*

6. Make children eat slowly and masticate their food well, and always give some crisp, dry foods that require thorough mastication, rather than a very sloppy diet.

Diet for 1 to 1½ Years

6 A.M.—Half a pint of warm milk.

8 A.M.—Two tablespoonfuls of orange or tomato juice, or sieved figs or prunes.

10 A.M.—Two to three tablespoonfuls of cooked cornflour,

or gruel made of barley or farina, with a tablespoonful or two of the top of the milk, and a very little honey ; one or two thin slices of stale brown bread and butter ; three-quarters of a cupful of warm milk.

11 A.M.—Drink of water.

12.30 P.M.—One cupful of cream of spinach or carrot soup or beef broth ; part of a baked potato ; wholemeal bread and butter ; or substitute a lightly boiled egg for the broth.

3.30 P.M.—Half a pint of warm milk.

5 P.M.—Drink of water.

6 A.M.—Two or three tablespoonfuls of cereal and the top of the milk, or, if there was no broth at midday, a cup of beef, chicken or mutton broth, containing a little cooked farina or cornflour thickening, or milk toast.

10 P.M.—If the child is awake about this time, give from half to one cupful of warm milk. A hard toast crust or a rusk can be given after the milk earlier in the day, to teach the child to chew and develop its jaws and teeth. Do not give anything with the water, or between meals.

You should have begun to give baby orange juice and the juice of stewed prunes at the age of six months, beginning with only one teaspoonful, and increasing the amount gradually until at a year old the child is taking all the juice of a medium-sized orange. *Do not either sweeten or add water to the juice*, and never give prepared fruit extracts, but obtain the fresh juice from the fruit yourself when required. Orange and prune juice can be given alternately, but the prune should be given in smaller quantity, and always administer it when there are signs of constipation. Apple can also be given after six months —stewed and sieved.

Do not start any new food in full quantity. Begin by giving only a teaspoonful of potato baked in its jacket, and continue until after a few weeks the whole of a medium potato is being given. As for an egg, start offering only a teaspoonful of mixed yolk and white, and increase the quantity by degrees, until at the end of a month or so a whole egg is being taken with relish. If for some reason you run out of the cereal for breakfast, give egg for this meal and substitute cereal for egg at dinner or supper.

TYPICAL BALANCED MENUS FOR ONE DAY

BREAKFAST.—Orange ; porridge and milk ; bread and

butter ; give only the *juice* of oranges to children under four years of age.

DINNER.—Barley broth ; poached egg on toast, spinach ; rice pudding.

SUPPER.—Bread and milk, or milk and rusks ; apple purée ; sponge cake.

Diet for 1½ to 2 Years

BREAKFAST.—Same as before, but serve the fruit as a first course instead of 2 hours earlier. Allow more milk, if wanted. Continue with *cooked* cereals, adding wheaten cereals to the list. No cereals with grits or husks should be given at this age.

10 A.M.—Drink of water.

DINNER, 12 NOON.—Small portion of brains, sweetbread, chicken, crisply fried bacon, or a small fresh meat ball or portion of boiled or steamed white fish. A little boiled potato or a potato baked in its jacket, mashed. A tablespoonful of sifted cooked carrots, peas, spinach, artichokes, celery, vegetable marrow, lettuce. Brown bread and butter. Blancmange, custard, rice, sago, semolina or tapioca pudding, or a piece of sponge cake, or one or two sponge fingers and a drink of milk.

3 P.M.—Drink of milk, and sponge biscuit, if wanted, or slice of brown bread and butter, rusk or toast.

5 P.M.—Drink of water.

SUPPER, 6 P.M.—Vary the following from day to day : Beef tea, clear soup, broth (chicken or mutton), cream of carrot or spinach, with a cooked cereal and milk, or a soft-boiled, poached or steamed egg, and milk toast. Serve with brown bread and butter, and follow with a drink of milk.

Remember when planning the meat course for a baby that you are *merely introducing him to meat.* The meat should be scraped down, raw, before making it into balls, and all the other meat dishes should be minced, and the fish finely flaked, and very great care taken to see that all bones are removed. The clear soup and broth can be thickened with a little barley or rice, and carrots, peas, beans, celery or tomatoes can be cooked in it, but these should be sieved when cooked. A tiny bit of crisply cooked bacon, finely minced, can be given once in a while in place of an egg, or in addition to a cereal. Brains and sweetbread should be boiled in slightly salted water, drained, and served minced and mixed with a pat of butter. Grill the meat balls, or fry them in a dry pan, and mince them. No dishes for small children should be highly seasoned ; use a little salt, when required, but no pepper or sharp sauces.

Keep on the same diet until THREE YEARS OF AGE, only allowing larger portions as the child grows. For supper, give an egg and a little vegetable purée occasionally, as well as soup or broth, but in this case omit the egg for breakfast or lunch.

Diet from 4 to 7 Years

Up to the age of four, no tea or coffee should be given, nor even cocoa, except as a flavouring after the age of three.

Generally speaking, the diet should follow on the lines prescribed for three-year-olds, but macaroni or spaghetti can be added to the dinner or supper menu, and either boiled, steamed or baked potato, or a green vegetable, no longer puréed, can be added to the broth and egg, or to the cereal and milk or milk pudding, for supper. The child can also have a little brown bread and butter, a slice of plain cake or gingerbread, or one or two biscuits, bread and jam or honey, with a cup of weak cocoa made with milk, or a glass of milk. Sometimes give a baked apple, some tinned pineapple or peaches or steamed rhubarb, or sliced banana and custard or junket, or jelly set with slices of banana, in place of the cake or biscuits.

TYPICAL BALANCED MENUS FOR ONE DAY

BREAKFAST, 8 A.M.—Apple, banana, two or three grapes, baked apple, or a few stewed figs or prunes. Whole grain cereal cooked in milk, served with certified milk, and honey or sugar. A soft-boiled, steamed, poached or scrambled egg, or a little crisp bacon. Bread or toast and butter. Milk or cocoa.

DINNER, 12.30.—Boiled, grilled or roast lamb or beef, roast, boiled or stewed chicken, or boiled or steamed white fish. Potatoes cooked any way but fried, and any vegetable except cucumber, beetroot, onion, sprouts, coarse cabbage, and cauliflower, which are indigestible and cause flatulence. Brown bread and butter. Puddings as given for two-year-olds.

SUPPER.—The same as for three-year-olds, but a little

simply cooked fish or chicken can sometimes be substituted for the egg.

It is no good, however, planning well balanced meals unless you serve them at regular intervals, see that there is no eating between meals, that food is well chewed, and that the child is kept quiet for at least half an hour after eating. Do not be afraid to give children pure sweets. Their body craves sugar. Many a child has been punished for taking sweets when the father and mother should have been punished for not providing him with an adequate amount of sugar. The best time to give sweets, however, is immediately after dinner or supper, not at any odd time between meals.

The main points a mother should remember in catering for her child are the necessity for punctuality, variety, and good cooking. Where there is a large family to cater for, her slogan should be " the same for all," but not when there is a child under the age of three. After three, the family must usually feed with the child, but on the lines just laid down. Only take care to measure the portions according to age.

FAMOUS OLD-FASHIONED DISHES

Aberdeen Roll

1 **lb.** minced Steak.	2 teaspoonfuls Spice.
1 breakfastcupful Breadcrumbs.	Small piece of finely-chopped
1 **lb.** Minced Bacon.	Onion.
2 Eggs.	Pepper and Salt, to taste.

UTENSILS—Wooden spoon, mincer, pudding cloth, pudding basin, saucepan, teaspoon, breakfast cup. *Enough for 4 or 5 persons.*

Mix all the ingredients together, tie them in a cloth, and boil for 3 hours. When cold, turn out and sprinkle with browned breadcrumbs, or glaze and decorate according to taste.

Abernethy Biscuits

½ **lb.** Flour. 1 Egg.	3 oz. Butter.
1½ tablespoonfuls Milk.	¼ teaspoonful Baking Powder.
1 teaspoonful Caraway Seeds.	3 oz. Castor Sugar.

UTENSILS—2 basins, wooden spoon, egg-beater, rolling pin, pastry board, baking sheet, measuring spoons, pastry cutter, sieve.

Sift the flour, then rub in the butter. Stir in the sugar, baking powder and seeds. Mix the beaten egg and milk together, and stir them into the dry ingredients. Turn the dough on to a lightly floured pastry board, roll it out thinly, cut it into small rounds, and bake 10 minutes on a buttered baking sheet in a moderate oven.

Athole Brose

1 **lb.** Heather Honey.	1½ pints Whisky.
1 cupful cold Water.	

UTENSILS—Basin, silver spoon, pint measure, cup.

Put the honey, which should be weighed free from comb, into a basin. Stir in the cold water, and keep stirring until the honey is dissolved, then gradually add the whisky. Stir quickly until the brose begins to froth, then bottle, cork tightly, and store in a cool, dry cupboard.

Athole Pudding

2 oz. Fresh Butter.	2 Eggs.
2 oz. Castor Sugar.	$\frac{1}{2}$ teaspoonful Baking Powder.
2$\frac{1}{2}$ oz. Flour.	1 Lemon.

UTENSILS—2 basins, wooden spoon, grater, sieve, buttered mould, saucepan, egg-beater, knife.

Beat the butter to a cream in a basin, and stir in the beaten eggs by degrees. Add the sugar, and flavour to taste with grated lemon rind. Lightly stir in the flour, sifted with the baking powder, and a tiny pinch of salt. Pour into a buttered mould and bake for 45 minutes in a steady oven.

Serve turned out onto a hot dish, and sprinkled with blanched and chopped almonds. Wine sauce can either be served separately, or poured round the pudding.

Ayrshire Shortbread

$\frac{1}{2}$ lb. Flour.	$\frac{1}{4}$ lb. Rice Flour.
$\frac{1}{4}$ lb. Butter.	$\frac{1}{4}$ lb. Castor Sugar.
1 Yolk of Egg.	2 tablespoonfuls Cream.

UTENSILS—Sieve, 2 basins, wooden spoon, pastry cutter, pastry board, rolling pin, baking sheet, fork, egg-beater, cake rack.

Sift the flour and rice flour into a basin, and lightly rub in the butter. Add the sugar, and mix the ingredients to a stiff paste with the beaten egg yolk and the cream. Roll out thinly, prick all over with a fork, and cut into rounds with a small cutter. Bake the cakes on a baking sheet lined with buttered paper, for about $\frac{1}{4}$ hour, till pale gold. Cool on a cake rack.

Bakewell Tart

Puff Pastry. 4 oz. Butter.	Apricot or Greengage Jam.
3 drops Almond Essence.	6 oz. Castor Sugar.
2 Egg Whites.	5 Egg Yolks.

UTENSILS—Pie-dish, saucepan, wooden spoon, 3 basins, metal spoon, egg-beater.

Line a pie-dish with puff pastry. Spread a layer of jam, about $\frac{1}{2}$ an inch thick, on the bottom. Melt the butter, and mix it in a basin with the sugar, almond essence, and the well-beaten yolks and whites of eggs. Mix well and pour over the jam, then bake first in a sharp oven, and then in reduced heat, till ready. The mixture can be flavoured with brandy before pouring over the jam.

Ballater Scones

2 teaspoonfuls Cream of Tartar.	1 small teaspoonful Baking Soda.
1 lb. Flour. ½ pint tepid Milk.	3 oz. Butter.

UTENSILS— Sieve, 2 basins, wooden spoon, saucepan, pastry brush, pastry board, rolling pin, pastry cutter.

Sift the flour and cream of tartar into a basin, and rub in the butter. Dissolve the soda in the milk, then add it to the other ingredients, and knead to a stiff paste with the hands. Turn it on to a pastry board and roll out to ½ an inch in thickness.

Cut into rounds and bake in a quick oven. When half-done, brush lightly with milk, and return to the oven to dry. Serve split open, and buttered hot.

Balmoral Tartlets

PASTRY

½ lb. Flour.	¼ lb. Butter.
1 teaspoon Lemon Juice.	Cold Water.

FILLING

¼ lb. Butter.	¼ lb. Castor Sugar.
2 beaten Eggs.	3 oz. stale Sponge-cake Crumbs.
½ oz. Cornflour.	2 oz. Glacé Cherries.

UTENSILS—Sieve, pastry board, rolling pin, 3 basins, wooden spoon, knife, patty-pans, egg-beater.

Sift the flour into a basin, stir in the salt, then cut in the butter in small walnuts. Squeeze in the lemon juice, and mix to a firm but light paste with water. Roll out on a floured board, fold in three, press the edges together along the fold, then turn the open edges till they are facing you and roll again. Repeat the rolling process three times, then fold and set in a cool place while you make the filling.

For the FILLING, cream the butter and sugar, then stir in the beaten eggs, cake crumbs, cornflour, and chopped cherries in the order given. Line patty-pans with the pastry, half-fill with the mixture, and bake in a hot oven for from 15 to 20 minutes.

Banbury Puffs

1 oz. Butter.	½ oz. Flour.
¼ lb. Currants.	1 tablespoonful Brandy.
½ oz. Mixed Peel.	2 oz. Moist Brown Sugar.
1 Yolk of Egg.	Flaky Pastry.

UTENSILS—Basin, saucepan, pastry board, rolling pin, pastry brush, pastry cutter, baking sheet, measuring spoons, wooden spoon.

Melt the butter in a saucepan, and stir in the flour. Cook till thick, cool, and add the other ingredients, then flavour to taste with ground allspice and cinnamon. Roll the pastry thinly, cut it into fairly large rounds, and cover half of each round with the mixture, leaving a tiny rim of pastry.

Fold pastry without the filling on top of the filling, after brushing the edges with cold water. Lightly press the edges together, then brush the tops with water and dust with castor sugar. Bake on a wet baking sheet, in a hot oven, for 25 minutes.

Bath Buns

¾ lb. Flour.　　　　　　　　2 oz. Castor Sugar.
½ oz. German Yeast.　　　 3 oz. mixed Candied Peel.
1 gill lukewarm Milk.　　　3 Eggs.　　¼ lb. Butter.
　　　　　　　 2 oz. Sultanas.

UTENSILS—3 basins, wooden spoon, strainer, gill measure, sieve, baking sheet.

Beat the yeast to a cream with a teaspoonful of castor sugar, add the milk, and strain it into half the sifted flour to make a sponge. Stand in a warm place for 1 hour, then rub the butter into the remainder of the flour. Add the cleaned sultanas, remainder of castor sugar, chopped mixed peel, and the sponge. Beat in the eggs, one at a time, with the hands, and put in a warm place to rise again.

When well risen, shape into twelve rocky buns, and sprinkle with a little crushed lump sugar. Stand again in a warm place to rise, then bake for about ¼ hour.

Bath Biscuits

1 quart warm Milk.　　　 1 lb. Butter.　　6½ lb. Flour.
2 oz. German Yeast.　　　½ lb. Castor Sugar.

UTENSILS—2 basins, rolling pin, pastry board, baking sheet, wooden spoon, cloth, fork, brush, round cutter.

Pour the milk into a basin, stir in the sugar, yeast, and a little of the flour to make a sponge. Cover with a cloth, and stand in a warm place till the dough rises—for 1½ hours. Rub the butter into the remainder of the flour, stir in the sponge and mix to a smooth dough.

Stand in a warm place again, covered, for 2 hours, then roll out thinly, and cut into rounds, three inches in diameter. Prick with a fork, place on a damp baking sheet, brush with milk, stand in a warm place for ½ an hour, then bake in a slow oven till crisp and brown.

Bristol Cake

3 tablespoonfuls Milk.	Grated Rind of 1 Lemon.
5 oz. Castor Sugar.	9 oz. Flour. 3 oz. Currants.
5 oz. Butter. 3 Eggs.	1 teaspoonful Baking Powder.

UTENSILS—Basins, wooden spoon, egg-beater, cake tin, sieve, brush, measuring spoons, grater, cake rack.

Beat the butter to a cream and add the sugar. Beat the eggs, then add eggs, and sifted flour alternately, to the butter and sugar. Beat the mixture well, stir in currants, lemon rind, milk, and baking powder. Pour into a round cake tin, greased, and lined with well-greased paper.

Bake about 1 hour in a moderate oven, and just before the cake is done, brush the top with white of egg, and dredge with castor sugar.

Chelsea Buns

1½ lb. Flour.	½ lb. Castor Sugar.
½ lb. Butter.	5 Eggs.
1¼ oz. Yeast.	Grated Rind of 1 Lemon.
¾ pint Sour Milk or Buttermilk.	

UTENSILS—Saucepan, wooden spoon, grater, sieve, 3 basins, rolling pin, pastry board, cloth, egg-beater, baking tin.

Warm the milk in a saucepan, and work the yeast and a teaspoonful of sugar together until they are liquid, then add heated milk. Sift the flour and salt into a basin, rub half the butter lightly into the flour, and add half the sugar and grated lemon rind. Add the beaten eggs to the milk and yeast, make a well in the centre of the flour, then mix well in. Beat the mixture thoroughly with a wooden spoon, cover the basin with a cloth, and put it in a warm place to rise for about 1½ hours, or until the dough has risen to twice its size.

Remove to a floured board, and roll out like a strip of pastry to about ¼ of an inch thick. Spread all over with the remainder of the butter and half the remaining sugar, fold in three and roll out thinly again. Dust with the remainder of the sugar and cut the strip in half, roll each strip up like a Swiss roll—not more than 1¼ inches in diameter—cut the rolls into pieces about 1¼ inches thick, and put these on a greased tin about one inch apart. Stand the pieces in the tin with the cut side uppermost, so that the coil shows. Put the tin in a warm place for about 25 minutes, or until each bun is almost as large again.

Shake a little coarsely crushed loaf sugar over them, and bake in a quick oven for about 25 minutes. If buttermilk is not available, curdle some sweet milk by squeezing a few drops of lemon juice into it.

Cornish Saffron Cake

1 lb. Dough.	½ teaspoonful Allspice.
¼ lb. Castor Sugar.	¼ lb. Currants.
¼ lb. Mixed Peel.	¼ lb. Butter.

½ pennyworth of Saffron.

UTENSILS—Basins, wooden spoon, pastry board, baking tin, measuring spoons, knife, cake rack.

Put the saffron in a basin, and cover it with 2 tablespoonfuls of boiling water. Stand it in a warm place till the water is yellow, then stir it into the dough. Wash and dry the currants, mince the peel, and stir them into the dough, together with the sugar, and, lastly, the melted butter. Be careful not to let the butter oil. Turn the dough on to a floured board and knead. Bake like bread in a buttered tin.

Cornish Splits

1 lb. Flour.	1 oz. Butter.
½ oz. Yeast.	½ pint Milk.
Pinch Salt.	1 teaspoon Castor Sugar.

UTENSILS—Sieve, 2 basins, wooden spoon, milk saucepan, pastry board, baking tin, brush, cloth, teaspoon.

Sift the salt and flour into a basin. Stir the yeast into the sugar. Melt the butter in the milk. When tepid, stir the butter and milk into the yeast, then with it mix the flour to a dough.

Stand the basin, covered, in a warm place till the dough is well risen. Knead and shape it into rounds half an inch thick. Brush them with milk, and bake them for 15 minutes, close together in a hot oven in a buttered baking tin. Serve hot or cold with butter or with clotted cream and strawberry jam.

Cullen Broth

1 lb. Neck of Mutton.	1 medium Carrot.
2 Leeks.	1 small Cabbage.
1 small Turnip.	2 Potatoes.
Salt and Pepper.	2½ quarts cold Water.

UTENSILS—Knife, saucepan, grater, pint measure.

Wash the mutton and cut it up into small pieces, jointing the bones. Put it into a saucepan with cold water, and boil for ½ hour. Cut the leeks into pieces, the turnip into dice. Dice half the carrot, and grate the other half. Chop the cabbage, pare the potatoes, and cut them up finely. Add all to the saucepan with the seasoning, and boil for 1 hour or longer. Add a teaspoonful of sugar just before serving.

Cumberland Currant Cake

Short Pastry.	Currants.	
Minced, Mixed Peel.	Sugar.	Spice.

UTENSILS—Pastry board, rolling pin, knife, pastry brush, fork, basin, baking tin.

Roll short pastry into an oblong strip 10 by 20 inches. Cut the strips into two 10-inch squares. Spread one square with washed currants, undried, and sprinkle with peel and mixed spice, then with sugar. Brush the edges with water and cover with the second piece of pastry. Lightly press with a rolling pin, prick with a fork, and bake on a buttered tin in a quick oven. Cut into four when cold.

Derby Savoury Pudding

2 cupfuls Breadcrumbs.	2 cupfuls Flour.
1 cupful fine Oatmeal.	¼ lb. minced Suet.
1 teaspoonful minced Sage.	1 lb. minced Onions.
Salt and Pepper, to taste.	2 Eggs.

1 pint hot Milk.

UTENSILS—2 basins, wooden spoon, grater, knife, baking tin, saucepan, cup, teaspoon.

Put the breadcrumbs and oatmeal in a basin. Pour over the milk, and stand 10 minutes. Beat in the eggs. Mix the flour, sage, and pepper and salt together, and beat them into the mixture, together with the onions. Bake 1 hour in a greased tin, like a Yorkshire pudding. Serve with roast goose, duck or pork.

Devonshire Junket

1 quart new Milk.	Powdered Sugar.
Nutmeg or Cinnamon.	1 dessertspoonful Rennet.
1 wineglassful Brandy or Rum.	Devonshire Cream.

UTENSILS—Double boiler, wooden spoon, junket or dessertspoon, wineglass, trifle dish.

Heat the milk till lukewarm, then pour it into a junke
or trifle dish. Stir in the rennet and brandy, and keep stirrin
for a few minutes, then place in a warm spot till set. Whe
cold, sift sugar over and a little powdered nutmeg or cinnamor
and cover with a layer of Devonshire cream. If the latter i
not procurable, substitute whipped cream, sweetened an
flavoured to taste.

Devonshire Pudding

2 large Apples.   2 oz. Sponge-cake Crumbs.
2 Eggs.   2 oz. Sugar.   1 pint Milk.
Apricot Jam.   Grated Rind of $\frac{1}{2}$ Lemon.

UTENSILS—Pie-dish, saucepan, spoon, egg-beater, grate
2 basins, knife, apple corer.

Put a layer of apricot jam in the bottom of a pie-dish
then the apples—peeled, cored and cut into rings. Boi
the milk with the sponge cake crumbs, add the sugar an
lemon rind, then beat up the yolks of the eggs and stir then
in. Pour over the apples and bake 25 minutes. Beat th
whites of eggs to a stiff froth, add $\frac{1}{2}$ oz. of sugar, pile on to
of pudding, and put in a moderate oven to set.

Devonshire Scallops

1 lb. cooked Potatoes.   1 teaspoonful chopped Parsley.
$\frac{1}{4}$ teaspoonful made Mustard.   Sprinkling of Cayenne Pepper.
4 oz. grated Cheese.   1 gill Milk.   1 oz. Butter.

UTENSILS—Sieve, wooden spoon, grater, scallop shells
basin, teaspoon, saucepan.

Rub the potatoes through a sieve. Melt the butter, ad
the sieved potatoes, parsley, grated cheese, leaving a littl
to sprinkle over the top, mustard, and cayenne, and bea
thoroughly. Put this mixture into sufficient buttered scallo
shells. Sprinkle with grated cheese and brown in a ho
oven or under a grill.

Dundee Cake

$\frac{1}{2}$ lb. Flour. $\frac{1}{4}$ lb. Currants. $\frac{3}{4}$ lb. Brown Sugar.
About 1 gill Milk.   3 Eggs.
6 oz. Butter.   1 teaspoonful Baking Powder.
$\frac{1}{2}$ lb. Rice Flour.   4 oz. candied Lemon Peel.

UTENSILS—Basins, wooden spoon, egg-beater, sieve, cake
tin, knife, teaspoon, cake rack.

Cream the butter and sugar, add the beaten eggs and

flour alternately, then stir in the rice flour and milk. Beat until the mixture is smooth, then add the baking powder, and, lastly, the currants, cleaned and picked, and the peel cut small. Pour into a greased and floured tin, and bake in moderate oven for about 2½ hours. This cake ought to be kept at least a week before cutting.

Dundee Pudding

3 oz. Sugar.	3 oz. Flour.
2 oz. Cake Crumbs.	½ lb. Muscatel Raisins.
½ teaspoonful Vanilla.	1½ teaspoonfuls Baking Powder.
3 oz. Butter. 2 Apples.	3 oz. Crumbs. 2 Eggs.
Pinch of Salt.	Milk to mix.

UTENSILS—3 basins, wooden spoon, knife, pudding mould, grater, egg-beater, teaspoon, saucepan.

Beat the butter and sugar to a cream. Mix the cake crumbs and flour together, and add flour and egg alternately to creamed butter and sugar, until well beaten in. Stone and chop the raisins, add them to the mixture, peel and shred the apples, and add all the other ingredients, using a little milk if necessary to make a soft mixture.

Butter a plain mould and decorate in star pattern with stoned raisins. Pour in the mixture, and steam for 2 hours. Serve with custard sauce.

Eccles Cakes

1 lb. Flaky Pastry.	2 oz. chopped Mixed Peel.
3 oz. cleaned Currants.	1½ oz. Butter.

Grated Nutmeg, to taste.

UTENSILS—Pastry board, rolling pin, knife, pastry brush, basin, teaspoon, baking sheet.

Roll the pastry to one-third of an inch thick. Cut it into rounds 4½ inches across, then turn the best side down on a floured board and wet the edges. Mix the melted butter, peel, currants, and nutmeg together. Put a heaped teaspoon of the mixture on the centre of each round, bunch up the edges of the pastry, and turn the bunched sides on the board. Roll out lightly till the currants show. Make a shallow cut down the middle of each. Brush with water, dredge with sugar, and bake in a quick oven for 20 minutes.

Everton Toffee

6 oz. Butter.	½ gill Milk.	1 lb. Sugar.

UTENSILS—Saucepan, baking tin or tin plate, knife.

Put the butter and sugar in a saucepan, add milk, and boil gently without stirring, until the mixture will set when tested in cold water. Allow it to stand until it ceases bubbling. Pour into hot buttered tin ; cut into squares when nearly cold.

Exeter Stew

1½ lb. Stewing Beef.
2 oz. Butter or Dripping.
2 Carrots and Turnips, if liked.
1 tablespoonful Vinegar.

3 Onions.
Salt and Pepper to taste.
1 tablespoonful Flour.
Dumplings.

UTENSILS—Saucepan, plate, fork, basin, knife, wooden spoon, measuring spoons. *Enough for 6 persons.*

Cut the beef into neat pieces, and fry in smoking-hot fat, for about 5 minutes. When brown all over, remove the meat to a plate, then brown the sliced onions lightly in the fat. Stir in the flour and season to taste, and thin down with the stock. When the mixture is boiling, return the meat to the saucepan, add the sliced carrots and turnips if wanted, cover, and simmer for 2 hours.

Add six or eight dumplings and cook another ½ hour. Serve the meat and vegetables garnished with dumplings.

THE DUMPLINGS

6 tablespoonfuls Flour.
3 oz. minced Suet.
1 dessertspoonful chopped Parsley.

¼ teaspoonful Baking Powder.
1 gill Water.
¼ teaspoonful powdered Sweet Herbs.

Pinch of Salt.

Mix all the dry ingredients together in a basin. Stir in enough water to make a smooth dough. When free from cracks, shape into small balls, and drop into the stew.

To vary the balls, use ½ cupful of crumbs with ¼ lb. flour, instead of the 6 tablespoonfuls of flour.

Felixstowe Tart

¼ lb. Cornflour.
3 oz. Butter.
1 tablespoonful Sugar.

1 cupful Milk.
¼ lb. Flour.   1 Egg.
1 teaspoonful Baking Powder.

UTENSILS—Egg-beater, sieve, 2 basins, cup, pastry board, rolling pin, fork, knife, plate, measuring spoons, wooden spoon.

Sift the dry ingredients into a basin, and rub in the butter. Beat the egg, mix it with milk, and use as much as is needed to moisten the ingredients. The dough should be soft. Turn on to a floured pastry board, roll out and place on an old buttered plate. Prick the centre with a fork and ornament the edges.

Bake till golden brown, then fill with jam and cover with stiffly frothed white of egg, mixed with 2 tablespoonfuls of fine sugar. Return to the oven and cook slowly till the meringue is set and a pale brown.

Forfar Bridies

| 1 lb. best Steak. | 3 oz. Beef Suet. |
| Flour. Salt to taste. | Water. 1 Onion. |

UTENSILS—Rolling pin, knife, basin, pastry board, pastry brush, spoon, baking sheet. *Enough for 3 or 4 persons.*

Beat the steak with a rolling pin, then cut it into narrow strips. Cut the strips into inch lengths, and season with salt and pepper, then divide them into three pieces. Add the minced suet, salt to taste, and minced onion.

Make a stiff pastry with flour, water and a pinch of salt, and roll it out. Cut it into oval shapes and cover the half of each oval with the meat. Sprinkle with suet, and brush the edges with cold water. Fold over and crimp the edges with finger and thumb, then cut a small hole in the centre of each. Bake about 30 minutes in a quick oven.

Forfarshire Barley Meal Scones

1 lb. Barley Meal.	¼ lb. Flour.
½ teaspoonful Salt.	3 cupfuls Buttermilk.
1 large teaspoonful Baking Soda.	

UTENSILS—Sieve, wooden spoon, 2 basins, teacup, teaspoon, pastry board, rolling pin, hot girdle, knife, plate.

Sift the flour and salt into a basin, and stir in the barley meal. Add the soda to the buttermilk, and when the milk fizzes, stir it into the dry ingredients. Make into a soft dough, turn quickly on to a floured board, and roll out to ½ an inch in thickness. Cut into rounds the size of a meat plate, and bake on a hot girdle till the underside is brown, when turn and brown on the other side.

Grasmere Ginger Cakes

½ lb. Flour.	3 oz. Castor Sugar.
6 oz. Butter.	2 Egg Yolks.
¼ oz. Ground Ginger.	2 oz. chopped Almonds.
2 teaspoonfuls Golden Syrup.	½ teaspoonful grated Lemon Rind.

UTENSILS—Sieve or flour sifter, 3 basins, wooden spoon, knife, pastry brush, egg-beater, grater, pastry board, rolling pin, teaspoon, baking tin.

Sift the flour, ginger, sugar, baking powder and a tiny pinch of salt into a basin. Beat the sugar and butter to a cream, and stir in flour alternately with beaten egg yolk. Add the syrup and lemon rind, and turn half of the mixture on to a floured pastry board. Roll out and brush with beaten egg and milk. Sprinkle with chopped peel, or chopped preserved ginger.

Roll out the remainder of the pastry, and place it on top. Brush it with egg and milk and sprinkle with almonds and sugar. Bake on a greased baking tin in a slow oven for ½ hour.

Helensburgh Toffee

3 lb. Granulated Sugar.	1 tin Swiss Milk.
1½ teacupfuls Water.	¼ lb. Butter.

Vanilla Essence.

UTENSILS—Saucepan, metal spoon, baking tin or tin plate, cup.

Melt the butter in a saucepan. Add the sugar, water and milk. Boil for 20 to 25 minutes, stirring continually in one direction. Add vanilla essence to taste just before pouring into a buttered tin.

Irish Barmbrack

8 oz. Flour.	1 oz. Butter.
1 oz. Castor Sugar. 1 oz. Peel.	3 oz. Sultanas.
½ teaspoonful Sugar.	1 gill tepid Milk.

UTENSILS—Saucepan, basin, wooden spoon, sieve, knife, cake tin.

Heat the milk and butter in a saucepan till lukewarm, and add, with the sugar, to the yeast. Sift the flour in a basin. Make a well in the centre, sprinkle salt round the edges, and pour the yeast mixture into the well. Mix to a loose paste, and beat with a wooden spoon for 5 minutes. Stir in the chopped peel and cleaned sultanas.

If liked, caraway seeds can be used instead of fruit. Pour at once into a buttered cake tin, and leave to rise in a warm place for $1\frac{1}{2}$ hours. When double its height, bake for about 20 minutes in a hot oven.

Irish Potato Cakes

8 boiled Potatoes. | Salt, Butter and Flour.

UTENSILS—Potato masher or fork, basin, pastry board, rolling pin, knife, girdle.

Mash the potatoes, then add salt and butter to taste, and enough flour to make a dry dough. Roll on a lightly floured board to half an inch in thickness. Cut into rectangular pieces and bake on a hot girdle. Serve split and buttered hot.

Kentish Flead Cakes

1 lb. Flour. 1 Egg. | 1 lb. Flead.
Pinch of Salt. | Cold Water.

UTENSILS—Sieve or flour sifter, basin, pastry board, rolling pin, knife, pastry brush, pastry cutter, patty-pans, egg-beater.

Sift the flour and salt into a basin. Rub lightly in a little scraped flead, then mix into a dough with cold water. Knead lightly and roll the dough out on a lightly floured board. Spread flakes of scraped flead over the paste, then fold the paste and beat it with a rolling pin.

Repeat the processes of spreading, folding, and beating until all the flead is used up. Roll to a quarter of an inch thickness and cut into small rounds. Brush with beaten egg and bake in buttered tins in a quick oven till golden. Serve hot for tea, or use the pastry for covering fruit or mince pies.

Kentish Oastcakes

1 teaspoonful Lemon Juice. | $\frac{1}{2}$ cupful Sugar.
1 lb. Flour. | 1 teaspoonful Baking Powder.
$\frac{1}{2}$ teaspoonful Salt. | $\frac{1}{4}$ lb. Lard. 7 oz. Currants.

UTENSILS—Sieve or flour sifter, basin, wooden spoon, pastry board, rolling pin, frying pan, cup, teaspoon.

Sift the dry ingredients into a basin, then rub in the lard. Stir in the currants, cleaned, and mix into a light dough with water mixed with lemon juice. Roll little pieces of dough out lightly and fry them till golden in a little hot lard. Serve hot for tea.

Lancashire Hot Pot

2 lb. best end Neck of Mutton.	3 Sheep's Kidneys.
2 lb. Potatoes.	12 Oysters. 1 lb. Onions.
½ pint Gravy or Stock.	1 oz. Butter.

UTENSILS—Knife, stewpan, fireproof baking dish. *Enough for 6 persons.*

Divide the meat into cutlets, and trim. Put the trimmings, short rib bones and onion into a stewpan, and make into a gravy with cold water. Put a layer of potato in the bottom of a fireproof baking dish. Arrange the cutlets slightly over-lapping on top. Cover with sliced kidney and one or two oysters. Season well and repeat layers, but the top layer must be halved potatoes.

Pour stock in down the side, dab with butter, and bake, covered, from 2 to 3 hours in a moderate oven. Brown before serving. The hot pot may require the addition of a little more gravy. Oysters can be omitted and ½ lb. of peeled mushrooms and 2 oz. of ham used instead.

Leicester Pudding

½ lb. Flour.	2 oz. Butter.
3 tablespoonfuls Sugar.	1 Egg. Jam.
¼ teaspoonful Baking Powder.	½ cup Milk.
Pinch of Salt.	

UTENSILS—2 basins, wooden spoon, measuring spoons, cup, pudding mould, saucepan.

Mix together the flour and baking powder, and cream the butter and sugar. Add the milk, flour, egg, sugar, and salt, beating all well together. Line a buttered mould with jam. Pour in the mixture, cover with buttered paper and steam for 2 hours.

Manchester Tart

½ pint Milk.	2 oz. Breadcrumbs.
1 oz. Castor Sugar.	2 oz. Butter.
2 Eggs.	1 tablespoonful Brandy.
Flaky Pastry.	Rind of 1 Lemon.

UTENSILS—Basins, saucepan, strainer, egg-beater, wooden spoon, tablespoon, knife, grater, pie-dish.

Put the crumbs in a basin, then add the rind of lemon to the milk, and bring to the boil. Strain the milk over the crumbs and stand for 5 minutes, or the peel can be left in and removed after the 5 minutes. Add the butter, beaten yolks of eggs, sugar and brandy. Put a layer of raspberry or

strawberry jam in a pie-dish lined with
in the mixture and bake gently for 45 n

Make a meringue with the whites of
sugar. Pile meringue on top, dredge wi
the oven. Serve cold with cream.

Northumberland Gridd

8 oz. Flour.	4 oz. Margarine o.
2 oz. Currants. **Milk.**	1 teaspoonful Baking Powder.

UTENSILS—Sieve or flour sifter, basin, pastry board,
rolling pin, knife, teaspoon, girdle.

Sift the flour, baking powder, and a good pinch of salt
into a basin. Rub in the fat, then add cleaned currants and
enough milk to make a soft dough. Roll out on a lightly
floured board and cut into small round cakes. Bake on a
hot girdle on both sides. Serve split, and buttered hot.

Norwich Cutlets

¼ lb. cooked Meat.	2 oz. Breadcrumbs.
¼ gill Stock or Gravy.	1 Egg.
1 teaspoonful Ketchup.	1 oz. cooked Rice.
¼ oz. Butter.	Pepper, Salt, Cayenne.

UTENSILS—Meat mincer, wooden spoon, frying pan, knife,
2 basins, egg-beater, grater, board, brush, teaspoon, gill
measure. *Enough for 1 or 2 persons.*

Mince the meat finely, remove fat and gristle, and mix
with the breadcrumbs and rice. Add the butter and seasonings,
and bind with the egg and stock. Turn on to a floured board,
shape into cutlets, brush with egg, toss in the crumbs, and
fry in hot fat. Dish in a circle, with a piece of macaroni in
the end of each cutlet, and garnish with parsley.

Oxford Sausages

½ lb. Pork.	½ lb. Veal. Herbs.
½ lb. Beef Suet.	4 oz. Breadcrumbs.
3 Sage Leaves.	¼ teaspoonful grated Lemon Rind.

UTENSILS—Meat mincer, basin, grater, knife, wooden
spoon, frying pan, egg-beater. *Enough for 4 or 5 persons.*

Put the pork, veal and suet through a mincer. Mix them
in a basin with pepper, salt, minced sage leaves, lemon rind,
and minced thyme and marjoram to taste. Stir in the
crumbs, and stock to moisten. Shape into sausages with

hands. Dip them in beaten egg and then in bread-
bs. Fry in smoking-hot fat till golden. Serve, garnished
th parsley, for luncheon.

Richmond Maids of Honour

Flaky Pastry.	Grated Rind and Juice ½ Lemon.
2 oz. Butter. 2 oz. Sugar.	1 Egg.
1 oz. Desiccated Cocoanut.	1 tablespoonful cooked Sago.

UTENSILS—Two basins, wooden spoon, grater, egg-beater,
patty-pans, lemon squeezer, pastry utensils.

Cream the butter and sugar in a basin, and stir in the
cocoanut and beaten egg. Add the lemon rind, juice and sago.
Half-fill patty-pans lined with flaky pastry, and bake in
a hot oven for about 15 minutes.

Scotch Currant Bun

CAKE CRUST

1½ lb. Flour.	6 oz. Butter.
1½ teaspoonfuls Baking Powder.	Beaten Egg to mix.

MIXTURE

1 lb. Flour.	¼ lb. Orange Peel.
½ oz. Jamaica Pepper.	2 lb. Raisins.
2½ lb. Currants.	6 oz. Sweet Almonds.
2 oz. Citron Peel.	½ lb. Demerara Sugar.
½ oz. Ground Ginger.	½ oz. Cinnamon.
1 teaspoonful Baking Soda.	2 oz. Lemon Peel.
1 tablespoonful Brandy.	Buttermilk, or Milk.
2 Eggs.	1 teaspoonful Cream of Tartar.

A little Black Pepper.

UTENSILS—Sieve or flour sifter, basins, knife, egg-beater,
cake tin, pastry board, rolling pin, skewer, fork, pastry brush,
egg-beater, measuring spoons, wooden spoon, cake rack.

Clean the fruits, and sift the soda and spices with the
flour. Add to the flour mixture, the stoned and chopped
raisins, washed, cleaned, and dried currants, minced peels,
chopped, blanched almonds, beaten eggs, brandy, and
buttermilk or ordinary milk. If preferred, use more eggs
and no milk. Grease the cake tin well, then make the crust.

THE CRUST.—Sift the flour with a pinch of salt, lightly
rub in the butter with tips of fingers, stir in the baking powder,
and make into a paste the consistency of good short crust,
with beaten egg.

Line a cake tin smoothly with paste, making sure that it
is evenly thin all over, and smooth out all wrinkles. Fill in

mixture—half of this quantity and two-thirds of the pastry makes a good-sized cake. Damp the top of the edge, flatten on a round top, and make four holes right down to the bottom of the cake with a skewer. Prick with a fork all over top, and brush with beaten egg. Bake till ready, then cool on a rack and keep at least a week before cutting.

Scotch Oatcakes

1 teacupful Oatmeal.	Pinch of Salt.
¼ teaspoonful Baking Soda.	1 teaspoonful Dripping or Fat.
¼ teacupful Water.	

UTENSILS—Basins, pastry board, rolling pin, knife, girdle, cup, teaspoon.

Heat a girdle. Mix the oatmeal and salt together. Mix the soda and fat with a little hot water (enough to melt the fat), then make up to required quantity (¼ cup) with cold water. Add this to the oatmeal, make into a soft paste, turn out on to a floured board and knead firmly.

When smooth, form into a round, press out with the hands, and then roll with a rolling pin to the thickness required. Rub firmly with oatmeal, cut into three or four, and turn and rub on other side with oatmeal. Cook on a hot girdle until the edges curl, then toast in front of the fire.

Shrewsbury Cakes

| ¾ lb. Flour. ½ an Egg. | ½ lb. Fresh Butter. |
| ½ lb. Castor Sugar. | ¼ gill Cream. |

UTENSILS—Basins, pastry board, rolling pin, knife, baking sheet, wooden spoon.

Rub the butter into the flour then stir in the sugar. Make into a paste with the cream and egg. Stand for ½ hour, roll out thinly on a lightly floured board, and cut into rounds three inches thick. Bake in a moderate oven till golden.

Windsor Cake

6 or 7 Eggs.	½ lb. Sugar.
½ lb. Butter.	1 lb. Flour.
½ lb. Muscatel Raisins.	¼ lb. Almonds.
1 teaspoonful Baking Powder.	2 oz. Orange Peel.
2 tablespoonfuls Rice Flour.	Vanilla to taste.
¼ lb. Currants. Salt.	¼ lb. Glacé Cherries.

UTENSILS—Knife, basins, egg-beater, wooden spoon, cake tin, cake rack, measuring spoons.

Blanch and shred the almonds, chop the peel, stone and

cut the raisins in halves, wash and dry the currants, dip the cherries in flour and quarter them. Mix the flour, rice flour and fruit together, and beat the eggs until creamy. Beat the butter and sugar to a cream, add the eggs by degrees, beating well, then the flour, and beat for 10 minutes. Add vanilla, salt and baking powder, and a little milk if necessary. Put the mixture into a well-buttered, papered cake tin, and bake in a moderate oven for 3 hours.

Yorkshire Parkins

1 lb. fine Oatmeal.
1 lb. medium Oatmeal.   Beer.
6 oz. Butter.   6 oz. Lard.

1 lb. Flour.   2½ lb. Treacle.
3 small teaspoonfuls Baking Soda.
½ oz. Ground Ginger.   2 Eggs.

UTENSILS—Sieve or flour sifter, basin, wooden spoon, saucepan, teaspoon, tumbler, cake tins, cake rack.

Sift the flour and ginger into a basin, then mix in the oatmeal. Rub in the butter and lard, then stir in the warmed treacle. Lastly, dissolve the soda in half a glass of beer, then mix into other ingredients. The dough should be dry enough to fall in drops. It must not run.

Turn into well-buttered cake tins, but only fill three-quarters full. Cook slowly till firm.

Yorkshire Pudding

3 heaped tablespoonfuls Flour.
1 small teaspoonful Salt.

1 Egg.   ½ gill Milk.
Water.   Dripping.

UTENSILS—Basin, wooden spoon, tablespoon, baking tin.
Enough for 2 persons.

Put the flour into the basin and make a well in the centre. Drop in the egg, sprinkle salt round the edge of the flour. Stir the egg and flour together, gradually adding milk, until a stiff batter. Thin with water to the consistency of thick cream. Beat well and leave it for 1½ hours. Thoroughly heat the dripping in the tin, pour in the beaten up batter and bake in a hot oven for 20 minutes. Serve immediately.

JEWISH COOKERY

To Fry Fish During Passover

Fish.   Egg.   Hot Oil. | Sieved Motsa Meal.

UTENSILS—Basin, plate, cloth, egg-beater, frying pan, fish-slice, sieve.

Wash the fish and lay them in salt and water for some time. Dry thoroughly, and dip in beaten egg. Toss in sieved meal, and fry in smoking-hot oil.

Grilled Fish

White Fish. | Salt and Pepper.
Oil. | Vinegar.

UTENSILS—Plate, cloth, wooden spoon, pastry brush, gridiron.

Wash and dry the fish. Mix equal quantities of oil and vinegar, seasoned with salt and pepper, on a plate. Dip the fish in the mixture and grill. When cooked, brush over with a little melted butter and serve.

Stewed Sheep's Heart with Celery

2 Sheep's Hearts. | 1 Onion.
2 heads Celery. | A few small Meat Balls.

UTENSILS—Basins, stewpan, knife, grater, chopping board, cup.

Wash the hearts well and soak in salt and water to take out the blood. Dry, slice, and lay them in a stewpan with the chopped onion, the celery washed and chopped, salt, pepper, nutmeg, a few meat balls, and a little lemon juice and browning. Stew slowly till tender, and serve with mashed potatoes.

THE MEAT BALLS

½ lb. Stewing Steak. | ¼ cup Breadcrumbs.
1 slice Onion. | ½ an Egg.
Parsley and Marjoram. | Salt.   Pepper.
Nutmeg. | A small piece chopped Lemon Peel.

Chop the meat very fine. Add the crumbs, minced onion, and herbs and seasonings to taste. Mix with the egg, form into balls and cook as directed.

Motsa Balls

2 Motsa Biscuits.	2 Eggs. Nutmeg.
1 piece Onion.	A little Parsley.
A little Marjoram.	2 tablespoonfuls sieved Matzos
1 tablespoonful shredded Suet.	Meal.

UTENSILS—Basin, knife, frying pan, tablespoon, sieve, saucepan.

Soak the biscuits and squeeze the water out. Shred the suet finely, and fry the onion in a little fat or oil. Mix all together, form into balls, and boil for 20 minutes.

Veal Soup

1 Knuckle of Veal.	6 Potatoes.
A piece of Carrot, Turnip and Celery.	A little Saffron.
	1 Leek.
1 clove of Garlic.	2 quarts Water.
Salt and Pepper.	1 blade of Mace.

UTENSILS—2 saucepans, knife, metal spoon, fork or potato masher, plate.

Bring the meat slowly to the boil in the water and skim very carefully. Cut up carrot, celery and turnip into small pieces and add ; then simmer till the veal leaves the bone.

Remove the meat from the pan, cut it up into little square pieces and return it to the saucepan. Stir in the boiled and mashed potatoes and seasoning. Serve in a hot soup tureen with a few Motsa balls.

Solomon Gundy

1 pickled Herring.	A little Vinegar. Oil.
Forcemeat Balls.	Parsley. Small Onion.
Seasoning.	Montpelier Butter.

UTENSILS—Knife, wooden spoon, basin, fork, chopping board.

Soak the herring, scald, and free it from skin and bone, then mince it finely. Chop and scald the onion, mince the parsley, and mix all together, adding a little oil, vinegar, black pepper and cayenne. Serve in a glass dish. This recipe should be made some time before wanted to allow the flavours to be well blended. Serve with cold potatoes.

THE MONTPELIER BUTTER

6 Anchovies.	1 teaspoonful Anchovy Paste.
2 Shallots.	1 tablespoonful Butter.
1 clove of Garlic.	Fennel to taste.
Yolks of 4 hard-boiled Eggs.	Salt. Cayenne.

UTENSILS—Pestle and mortar, knife, sieve, saucepan, teaspoon, tablespoon, plate.

Wash and bone the anchovies, then put them in a mortar with the paste and butter, and pound well. Chop the shallots and garlic, and keep them in boiling water for ½ hour, then add the other ingredients. Pound all well and rub through a sieve, and serve with Solomon Gundy.

Passover Rock Cakes

4 oz. Butter.	4 oz. Sugar.
1 tablespoonful Currants.	1 small teaspoonful sieved Meal.
2 Eggs.	A little chopped Lemon Rind.

1 dessertspoonful Ground Almonds.

UTENSILS—2 basins, egg-beater, wooden spoon, cake rack, baking tin, measuring spoons.

Cream the butter and sugar, in a basin. Add the other ingredients, and make into a paste with the beaten egg. Put in little rough heaps on a buttered baking tin. Sprinkle with castor sugar, and bake till golden. Cool on a cake rack. Time required—about 30 minutes.

Matzos Noddles

2 Eggs.	Salt to taste.
¼ cupful Potato Flour.	2 tablespoonfuls Matzos Meal.

UTENSILS—Basin, fork, spoon, palette knife, knife, frying pan, cup, tablespoon.

Add salt to the egg, beat it slightly and stir in the matzos meal and potato flour. Heat a little fat in a frying pan. Pour in the egg mixture and when cooked on one side, turn it out on to the other. Roll the pancake and cut it into noddles one-eighth of an inch wide. Drop into boiling soup before serving.

Matzos Kloese

1 tablespoonful Butter.	Matzos Meal. 3 Eggs.
½ cupful grated Almonds.	½ teaspoonful Sugar.
⅛ teaspoonful Salt.	⅛ teaspoonful grated Nutmeg.

UTENSILS—2 basins, wooden spoon, teaspoon, egg-beater, frying pan or saucepan, tablespoon, grater.

Beat the yolks very lightly, add seasoning, and the almonds, and enough matzos meal to make a stiff batter, then add the beaten egg whites. Drop by teaspoonfuls into deep, smoking-hot fat, and fry till light brown. Test one, and if it boils apart, add more meal. Place in the oven to keep warm, and put in the soup just when sending to table.

Marrow Balls

2 tablespoonfuls Marrow Fat.	A grating of Nutmeg.
¼ cupful sifted Matzos Meal.	2 Eggs.
¼ teaspoonful Salt.	

UTENSILS—2 basins, egg-beater, wooden spoon, knife, tablespoon, teaspoon, cup.

Split the bones and remove the marrow. Cream the marrow, and add the eggs, well beaten. Season, and add only enough meal to make a soft dough. Stand for several hours, then shape into balls the size of a marble. Try one in boiling water, and if it does not hold together, add more meal. Drop into boiling soup ¼ hour before serving

Hot Beet Relish

3 cupfuls cold, boiled, grated Beets.	½ cupful Horseradish.
¾ cupful Vinegar.	1 teaspoonful Salt.
	3 tablespoonfuls Castor Sugar.

UTENSILS—Grater, basin, wooden spoon, covered jars, cup, tablespoon, teaspoon.

Boil, peel and grate the beets, then mix them with the horseradish. Season with salt, pepper and sugar. Add all the vinegar that the horseradish and the beets will absorb. Store in covered jars and use as required. This relish will keep a long time.

Cholla

8 teacupfuls Flour.	Poppy Seeds.
2 Eggs.	2 teacupfuls hot Water.
1 tablespoonful Sugar.	1 tablespoonful Salt.
2 tablespoonfuls Vegetable Oil.	½ oz. Compressed Yeast.
¼ cupful tepid Water.	

UTENSILS—Flour sifter or sieve, 2 basins, wooden spoon, pastry board, knife, egg-beater, pastry brush, teacup, tablespoon, baking tin.

Sift the salt and sugar into a mixing basin, then add the oil, and cover with the hot water. Leave till tepid, then add the yeast, dissolved in the tepid water, then add beaten eggs and sifted flour alternately. Stir well, knead till smooth and elastic, then cover and stand in a warm place till twice its size.

Turn the dough on to a floured pastry board, divide it in

two, and shape with lightly floured hands into loaves or twisted rolls. If made into loaves, cut each loaf into three large and three small pieces, and roll each into long strips. Plait the small strips together and then plait the large strips together and place a large plait on the bottom of a floured tin with a small plait on top. Stand in a warm place till light, then brush with beaten egg and sprinkle with poppy seeds. Bake in a hot oven from 45 minutes to 1 hour, then cool in a draught so as to secure hard crusts.

Spiced Lebkuchen

4 Eggs.	2 cupfuls Flour.	1 teaspoonful Ground Cinnamon.
2 oz. Citron Peel.		¼ lb. blanched Almonds.
1 lb. Light Brown Sugar.		Icing Sugar.

UTENSILS—Wooden spoon, egg-beater, sieve or flour sifter, 3 baking or sandwich tins, knife, cup, measuring spoons, 3 basins.

Stir the sugar gradually into the well-beaten eggs, then beat again. Sift the flour and cinnamon together, then mix them with chopped almonds and chopped peel, and stir them into the egg and sugar.

Divide the mixture between three flat, buttered baking or sandwich tins, and bake in a hot oven for about ½ hour. When cool, cut into oblongs five inches long and half an inch wide. Spread with 1 cupful icing sugar, dissolved in 2 tablespoonfuls water and flavoured to taste, before removing from the tins.

Poppy Seed Biscuits

½ cupful Castor Sugar.	1 cupful Poppy Seeds.
½ cupful hot Milk.	1¼ cupfuls Flour.
1 cupful Currants.	¼ teaspoonful Cloves.
2 oz. Chocolate.	1 teaspoonful Baking Powder.
½ teaspoon Ground Cinnamon.	½ cupful Butter.

UTENSILS—Sieve or flour sifter, 3 basins, wooden spoon, grater, baking tins, cup, teaspoon, small saucepan, rack.

Turn the poppy seeds into a basin. Cover them with hot milk and leave them to soak. Beat the butter and sugar to a cream, and stir in the flour, sifted with the cloves and cinnamon, the cleaned currants, grated chocolate, and then the baking powder. Mix thoroughly together with the soaked poppy seeds, then drop the mixture in teaspoonfuls on to the buttered and floured baking tins. Bake for 20 minutes in a moderate oven, then cool on a rack.

Matzos Swiss Roll

4 Eggs. | ½ cupful Castor Sugar.
½ cupful Matzos Meal.

UTENSILS.—2 basins, wooden spoon, egg-beater, baking tin, pastry board, knife, cup, sieve.

Beat the yolks of eggs well in a basin, then stir in the sugar. Add the matzos meal, finely sifted, and fold in the stiffly frothed whites of eggs. Spread quickly in a baking tin, lined with oiled paper, and bake 10 minutes in a quick oven.

Turn onto a pastry board, sprinkled with castor sugar, and remove the paper. Spread quickly with lemon honey or jam, and roll up and sift with castor sugar.

Potato Pudding for Pesach

4 Eggs.	½ cupful Castor Sugar.
¼ teaspoonful Salt.	½ Lemon.
2 tablespoonfuls Almonds.	¼ lb. cold, boiled Potato.

UTENSILS—2 basins, egg-beater, wooden spoon, pie-dish, cup, tablespoon, teaspoon, baking tin, grater, saucepan, knife, lemon squeezer.

Beat the yolks of eggs well, then stir in the sugar. Add the almonds, lemon rind and juice, the grated potatoes, salt, and lastly the stiffly frothed whites of eggs. Turn into a well-greased pie-dish, place the dish in a baking-tin half-filled with boiling water, and bake ½ hour.

Serve with Chocolate Sauce, made with a cupful of boiling water, 1 ounce chocolate, ½ cupful of castor sugar and a pinch of salt, cooked to a syrup, then flavoured with vanilla to taste.

Matzos Apple Charlotte

1 Matzos. ¼ lb. Suet.	2 tablespoonfuls Raisins.
3 Eggs.	¼ cupful Castor Sugar.
1 tablespoonful Ground Almonds.	¼ teaspoonful Cinnamon.
2 cupfuls tart Apples.	Pinch of Ground Mace.

UTENSILS—2 basins, wooden spoon, knife, cup, tablespoon, teaspoon, egg-beater, pie-dish.

Put the matzos in a basin, cover with water, and when soft, squeeze it out of the water. Mix it in a basin with the finely shredded suet, minced apples, sugar, stoned and chopped raisins, almonds, spices and stiffly frothed whites of eggs. Bake about 1 hour in a moderate oven.

MENUS
FOR EVERYDAY

DO you find menu planning difficult ? You shouldn't if you remember that a perfect menu should not only appeal to the appetite but also nourish the body. The body requires certain food elements to keep it in health. When these elements are not included in the diet, anæmia, constipation, decayed teeth, blotched complexion, boils and other evidences of malnutrition are the penalty.

Before starting to plan a menu, you must consider for whom you are catering. If adults, in normal health, your work will be straightforward. If some members of your family are very old, bear this in mind when planning, for old people thrive best of all on the same diet as a young child. If you've to cater for both adults and children, the simplest way is to choose a fish or meat dish for adults which children can share, and make the adults take the same sweet that is suitable for children. Now let me give you some pointers on menu planning :—

1. If shorter menus for lunch, supper or dinner are wanted, omit fish if given, or sweet or savoury, according to taste. Substitute, when liked, biscuits and cheese for savoury. When dessert is not included in the menus which follow, it can always be added and, if liked, port can be served.

2. Arrange for fresh fruit at least once a day and, if possible, cooked fruit or tinned fruit as well.

3. Serve a green salad, tomatoes, celery, radishes or watercress once a day to people who live an active life, but if catering for any one who leads a sedentary life, include in two menus. For example, a green salad with lunch, and celery with cheese for dinner.

4. A cooked green vegetable should be served at one meal per day.

5. Don't start with a cream soup if a creamed fish, meat or sweet is to appear in the menu.

6. Avoid using the same flavouring twice in one menu.

7. Don't use the same food product twice in one menu, i.e. if serving a soup made with chicken stock, don't have chicken as the main course. Substitute meat, preferably dark.

8. Don't begin with fresh fruit, such as a fruit cocktail, grapefruit or melon if you mean to end with a fruit salad or dessert. Start with smoked salmon or oysters when giving a party, and sardines or soup, if catering for the family.

9. Unless you particularly wish to save electric current, gas, coal or oil depending on the fuel you use for cooking, use a different method for cooking each course. For example, follow grilled fish with a casserole of chicken, guinea fowl, game or meat, or with a roast bird or joint. If you have a roast, follow with a cold sweet or a steamed pudding.

NOTE.—Suggestions for wine to be served at dinner are included in the notes to menus, but their service is purely optional.

The menus which follow are suggestions for each meal in the week. They should be varied according to taste and with due regard to left-overs from the previous day.

Monday

Breakfast

Half Grapefruit

. . .

Scrambled Eggs and Grilled Bacon

. . .

Toast   Brown Bread
Orange Marmalade
Tea or Coffee

Lunch or Supper

Sliced Cold Ham
Baked Potatoes   Egg Mayonnaise
Green Tomato Chutney

. . .

Old-fashioned Apple Charlotte

. . .

Biscuits and Cheese

NOTE.—Serve radishes or celery with the biscuits and cheese, and cream or custard sauce with the Apple Charlotte.

Afternoon Tea

Brown Bread and Butter
Potted Salmon Sandwiches
Pikelets   Rock Cakes
Scotch Jam Sandwich

High Tea

Fried Fillets of Haddock

* * *

White Bread and Butter   Toast
Strawberry Jam

* * *

Eccles Cakes
Gingerbread

NOTE.—Serve fish with Piquante or Tomato sauce, and a green salad, if liked.

Dinner

Tomato Soup

* * *

Soufflé of Whiting

* * *

Roast Guinea Fowl
Buttered Green Peas   Chip Potatoes

* * *

Bakewell Tart

* * *

Scotch Nips

NOTE.—1. Serve tart with cream. If preferred, substitute biscuits and celery or watercress and cheese for savoury. Serve dry Graves or hock with fish, and claret with the bird.

NOTE.—2. Make Bakewell Tart and Tomato Soup, then prepare guinea fowl for oven. Prepare whiting for mixing with stock. Start roasting guinea fowl. Mix soufflé and start cooking. Put on fat for chips 15 minutes before required. Drain peas if using tinned and place in the top of a double boiler with lump of butter. If using fresh, shell as soon as bird is placed in oven, then put on to boil. Prepare Scotch Nip mixture and leave in saucepan. Cut bread into rounds, ready to fry. Mixture must be cooked and bread fried the moment the tart is taken in.

Tuesday

Breakfast

Pineapple

. . .

Grilled Pork Sausages
Grilled Tomatoes

. . .

Toast   **Sour Milk Griddle Scones**
Honey
Tea or Coffee

Lunch or Supper

Calf's Head Brawn
Bean Salad   **Cauliflower Cheese**
Pickled Red Cabbage

. . .

Loganberry Pudding

NOTE.—If string beans are not in season, substitute
Asparagus or Spanish Salad for Bean Salad.

Afternoon Tea

Hot Buttered Toast
Mustard and Cress Sandwiches
French Biscuits   Maids of Honour
Dundee Cake

NOTE.—If liked, spread hot toast with butter creamed
with caster sugar and ground cinnamon to taste.

High Tea

Sausage Rolls

. . .

White Bread and Butter   Tomatoes or Watercress
Apple Jelly

. . .

Shrewsbury Cakes
Cherry Cake

Dinner
Italian Cauliflower Soup
. . .
Baked Fillets with Tomato Sauce
. . .
Boiled Leg of Mutton
Mashed Potatoes   Carrots
Caper Sauce
. . .
Banana Mould
. . .
Cheese Straws

NOTE.—1. If preferred, substitute broad beans for the carrots. Serve Graves or hock with fish and sweet Sauterne with the sweet.

NOTE.—2. Make Banana Mould. About an hour before you begin to prepare dinner start boiling mutton. When ready to begin preparing dinner, prepare vegetables. Start cooking soup, fish and vegetables. Make Caper Sauce then measure out all ingredients for Cheese Straws, but don't bake them until ready to serve the sweet.

Wednesday

Breakfast
Oranges
. . .
Kedgeree
. . .
Toast   Buttermilk Loaf
Grapefruit Marmalade
Tea or Coffee

Lunch or Supper
Curried Eggs
Simple Salad   Pickled Cucumbers
. . .
Cornflour Blancmange
Stewed Dried Fruit

NOTE.—If cheese is wanted, serve with biscuits or toast, and spring onions.

Afternoon Tea

Milk Bread and Butter
Whitstable Sandwiches
Rice Buns **Ginger Snaps**
Caramel Layer Cake

High Tea

Grilled Kidneys

. . .

White Bread and Butter **Ballater Scones**
Damson Cheese

. . .

American Doughnuts
Chocolate Nougat Cake

NOTE.—Serve scones buttered hot, or split, buttered and spread with greengage jam.

Dinner

Shrimp Cocktail

. . .

Cream of Celery Soup

. . .

Roast Sirloin of Beef
Roast Potatoes **Scalloped Artichokes**

. . .

Orange Caramel

. . .

Stuffed Tomatoes

NOTE.—1. Serve cocktail with unsweetened biscuits, buttered, sprinkled with grated cheese and crisped under the grill. If fresh celery is not in season, use tinned celery or soup, or substitute Cream of Green Pea. Serve joint garnished with shredded horse-radish, when in season. Serve a glass of sherry with soup and claret or Burgundy with the joint.

NOTE.—2. Make Orange Caramel and Shrimp Cocktail first, and chill. Prepare and put joint in oven. If artichokes are not in season, substitute buttered greens or spinach. If horse-radish is not available, offer pickled beetroot. Bring potatoes to the boil and drain before putting in hot fat an hour before joint is ready.

Thursday

Breakfast

Grapefruit

. . .

Mushroom Omelet

. . .

Toast   Sour Milk Scones

Lemon Marmalade

Tea or Coffee

Lunch or Supper

Irish Stew

Buttered Greens

. . .

Stewed Pears and Cream

. . .

Oatcakes and Cheese

Afternoon Tea

Kentish Oatcakes

White Bread and Butter

Blackberry Jelly

Cornish Splits   Ginger Biscuits

Chocolate Cream Cake

High Tea

Fried Fresh Herrings

Toast and Watercress

. . .

Carievale Nut Bread and Butter

. . .

Balmoral Tartlets   Chelsea Buns

Raisin Slab Cake

NOTE.—If preferred, substitute potted meat sandwiches
and watercress for the herring.

Dinner

Hors d'Œuvres

. . .

Fish Soup

. . .

Mutton Cutlets with Tomatoes

Sauté Potatoes   Seakale or Brussels Sprouts

. . .

Sir Watkin Pudding

. . .

Dessert

NOTE.—1. Serve sardines, pickled beetroot, potato salad, and radishes or olives, and sliced Salami or liver sausage as hors d'œuvres with toast and butter. Offer claret with the cutlets and port with dessert.

NOTE.—2. Prepare and put pudding on to steam. Prepare and arrange hors d'œuvres in separate dishes, then prepare vegetables, fish and cutlets in this order.

Friday

Breakfast

Orange and Lemon Juice

. . .

Fried Kippers

. . .

Toast   Irish Potato Cakes

Red Currant Jelly

Tea or Coffee

Lunch or Supper

Aberdeen Roll

Salad of Cooked Vegetables   Apple and Tomato Chutney

. . .

Batter and Fruit Pudding

NOTE.—If a green salad is preferred, serve as well a vegetable charlotte or custard, Italian Risotto, or macaroni à la creme or Italienne.

Afternoon Tea

Bloater Cream Sandwiches
White Bread and Butter
Lemon Cheese
Rice Biscuits   Meringues
Canadian Layer Cake

High Tea

Fried Fish Cakes
Celery or Watercress

. . .

Toasted Brown Bread   White Bread and Butter
Potted Beef or Game
Quince Marmalade

. . .

Lemon Cheese Cakes
Coffee Cake

NOTE.—Make fish cakes of tinned salmon, haddock or codling. Garnish each, if liked, with a grilled roll of bacon. Serve with tomato ketchup.

Dinner

Potato Soup

. . .

Soles with White Wine

. . .

Roast Chicken
Roast or New Potatoes   Green Peas or French Beans

. . .

Harlequin Salad

. . .

Golden Cheese Marbles

NOTE.—1. Prepare and chill salad. Stuff, truss and roast chicken. Prepare vegetables then sole, and soup. Grate cheese for Marbles, but don't mix or cook until sweet has been served.

NOTE.—2. Serve Graves or hock with the fish and chicken and a glass of port after the savoury. If liked, a glass of sweet Sauterne can be served with the fruit salad.

Saturday

Breakfast

Pineapple

. . .

Rice Cakes and Bacon

. . .

Toast   Brown Bread
Orange Marmalade
Tea or Coffee

Lunch or Supper

Lancashire Hot Pot

. . .

Devonshire Junket
Stewed or Tinned Raspberries

. . .

Rolls   Cheese
Green Salad

Afternoon Tea

Egg and Anchovy Sandwiches
Northumberland Griddle Cakes
Ayrshire Shortbread   Bath Buns
Marshmallow Layer Cake

NOTE.—If hot griddle-cakes are not wanted, substitute
oven scones spread with greengage or strawberry jam.

High Tea

Boiled Salmon
Mayonnaise Sauce
Cucumber Sandwiches

. . .

Nut and Raisin Bread   Bread and Butter
Plum Jam

. . .

Ayrshire Shortbread
Spiced Raisin Cake

NOTE.—Serve salmon garnished with scalded, peeled,
sliced tomatoes, and lettuce leaves. If salmon is not in season,
substitute cold ham, and serve garnished like salmon, but with
brown bread and watercress sandwiches and chutney.

Dinner

Grapefruit

. . .

Kidney Soup

. . .

Roast Loin of Veal

Roast Potatoes   **Asparagus or Cauliflower**

. . .

Fleur of Cherries
Whipped Cream

. . .

Cheese Soufflé

NOTE.—1. If a fish course is wanted offer fried whitebait garnished with fried parsley and served with thin brown bread and butter. Serve sherry with the soup and hock with the veal.

NOTE.—2. Prepare and chill grapefruit, then prepare pastry case for the Fleur of Cherries. Prepare and start to cook veal, then prepare vegetables and fish if wanted. Finish off Fleur of Cherries and start preparations for soufflé, but don't cook until ready to start dinner.

Sunday

Breakfast

Oranges and Dates

. . .

Egg and Sausage Scramble

. . .

Toast   Brown Bread
Honey and Marmalade
Tea or Coffee

Dinner

Chicken Broth

. . .

Roast Forequarter of Lamb
Roast Potatoes   **Green Peas**
Mint Sauce

. . .

Gooseberry Fool

. . .

Biscuits, Green Salad and Cheese

NOTE.—1. If a more substantial menu is wanted, substitute Fruit Tart and cream for Gooseberry Fool. If fresh gooseberries are not in season, substitute tinned. Serve claret with the joint and port with the cheese.

NOTE.—2. Prepare and chill Gooseberry Fool. Prepare soup, and start joint cooking. Make mint sauce. Prepare vegetables. If having a tart, make pastry and prepare fruit. Wash and drain salad. Finish off vegetables and make gravy.

Afternoon Tea

Buttered Irish Barmbrack
Abernethy Biscuits   Windsor Cake
Fudge Layer Cake

NOTE.—If a savoury touch is wanted, serve toast or white bread and butter with Potted Cheese and spring onions.

High Tea

Galantine of Veal
Lettuce and Tomato Salad

. . .

White Bread and Butter   Brown Bread and Butter
Black Currant Jam

. . .

Sponge Sandwich with Whipped Fruit Filling
Scotch Lawn Tennis Cake

NOTE.—Offer mayonnaise sauce with the galantine.

Sunday Night Supper

Cold Boiled Fowl or Galantine of Sheep's Tongue
Salad Varsovienne

. . .

Bread and Butter: Toast
Radishes or Spring Onions

. . .

Orange Sponge
Raspberry Slices

. . .

Biscuits and Cheese

NOTE.—When making Salad Varsovienne, omit the $\frac{1}{2}$ cup diced veal given in recipe. If fresh berries are in season, substitute them for raspberry slices.

CARVING

FISH

Although fish may be easy to cut up, yet it is quite as possible to mangle and destroy its appearance as it is to destroy the look and flavour of a fowl. Fish requires in its way the same skill. There should be the same knowledge of the general anatomy, also of the choice and ordinary parts. Delicacies and tit-bits abound in all fish. A fish-slice should always be used, but the fork usually accompanying the fish-slice is not always considered a necessity. An ordinary dinner fork does just as well.

If a spoon or ladle has to be used, care must be taken never to spill, nor to heap up a great quantity of what is being helped upon a plate at a time. Avoid jerking, or the slipping of knife, fork, or slice, always keeping the elbows well into the sides, and letting the strength necessary to be exercised come from the hands and wrists. Do not grasp the carving implements too near the hilt. Hold them as much at the end of the handle as possible.

Cod

With regard to cod, the flaky method of dividing the fish should generally be adopted, the portion being served by inserting the slice between the flakes, not cutting through them ; though, under certain circumstances, the directions for the cutting up of salmon may be followed, with the addition that the liver and the sound of cod, playing as they do very important parts, must be dispensed in fair quantities with each helping of the solid. The carver must calculate the proportions which will allow a taste for each one that is served.

Cod's head and shoulders are looked upon by some as a vulgar dish. After delicately slicing, in one or two unbroken flakes, a small portion of the solid shoulder, a piece of the gelatinous flesh in and about the jowl should also be placed upon the plate, as this is particularly nutritious and succulent. It is impossible to do much more than to dig out this rather unmanageable substance, clearing away the jaw and other bones, and leaving them upon the dish.

Gurnet

The gurnet is treated with the fish-slice in precisely the same manner as haddock.

Haddock

The flakes should fall right and left upon the touch of the fish-knife's point as it is run down the spine. The thickest or shoulder end of the fish is the best.

John Dory

The John Dory is carved in the same manner as the turbot, whilst the skin is in itself a delicacy. The wart-like growths which mar to some extent the back of the turbot are absent in the John Dory, which may be said to be always the better the larger it is. The head, important as it looks, should be left untouched upon the dish.

Mackerel

Mackerel, though a simple dish to carve, must not be passed over without a word. When boiled, it should never be hacked by an attempt to divide it through and through; but the fish-slice should be inserted from the tail upwards to its gills—the tail part is considered a best part, also the roe if there is any. The head and backbone are easily disengaged from the remaining underneath side upon the dish without turning it over. A broiled mackerel, being split, should be cut through and through, bone and all.

Mullet

The red mullet makes very little demand upon dexterity, nothing being required beyond a fair division, lengthwise, into two parts, if the fish is too large for one. The so-called liver, usually just visible under the opening of the gill, is a choice morsel, and must be divided up fairly, whilst the head itself is worth picking. Small red mullet, however, besides being superior in quality to the large, have the advantage of being just sufficient for a single portion.

Salmon

Salmon is a fish which offers very little difficulty to the carver, and, so long as a due proportion of thick and thin (the back and flank) is neatly cut—in oblong squares—from the side lying uppermost, nothing remains to be attended to. It is best to begin cutting from the left, and also better, as in the case of the turbot, to raise the bone when the upper side is gone, than to attempt to turn the fish over to get at the remaining lower side. The head and tail, though usually despised, and rarely seen at table, have nevertheless some very succulent pickings on them, but do not offer very much scope for the carver to exercise his skill. He has but " to help " them as neatly as he can. This too is all he has to do when the fish is brought to the table in slices; he has but to make an equal division of the slice, taking care, of course, that each helping is made up of thick and thin together.

Sole and Small Flat Fish

The slice is first run down the centre, then a fillet is lifted off each side of this line. Next remove the bone (without turning the fish over), and, by running the slice down the centre, make two fillets or helpings of the lower half. This would be with a fair-sized sole; with a smaller one, two of the fillets might go to one helping, and, on the other hand, a very large sole might yield fillets that could each be divided into two.

Turbot

Laying the fish upon its back, run the slice in an imaginary line from the head to the tail; then divide the flesh into oblong squares, each terminating with a portion of the fin, for the fin of the turbot is a delicacy. When the white upper side is all served, it is better to lift off the bone (in doing which there is no difficulty, if the fish is well cooked) than to attempt to turn the fish over when the white front is all served.

Whiting

Is served in the same manner as haddock, if too large to serve whole as a portion.

MEAT

A very sharp knife is indispensable for good carving. For carving joints the handles of the knife and fork are short and the blades and prongs long. For game and poultry the very reverse of this is necessary, greater firmness of blade and point being requisite.

Beef

THE SIRLOIN

In the sirloin, the fillet or under-cut, being always better when eaten hot than cold, should have first attention. It must be cut across like a tongue, but in thick slices, as also should be the fat at the thinner end or flap, a portion of which should go with each slice of lean. The joint must be turned over, to enable the carver to get at the under-cut conveniently ; and, according to the number of persons to be helped, the slices should be cut at once, before setting the joint up in its proper position again. By this means, when helping from the main bulk of the joint, a portion of the fillet can be given to each, without having constantly to turn the joint from one side to the other.

Some people prefer that both upper and under side of a sirloin should be cut alike—that is, across—and, though generally considered an extravagant way, it is not without its advantages; the chief of these, of course, being that each slice has both brown and juicy meat—there being no outside cut. A piece of the fat from the flap or lower end of the joint must accompany every portion, as in the case of the fillet ; and it should be remembered that these two sorts of fat are very different in quality—the under, or fillet, being of a more juicy, delicate, and tender quality than the other, especially when hot.

The ordinary plan of carving the sirloin, however, is usually recommended, owing to the fact that lean and fat then go together with each slice. It is generally advised that, before slices are cut, the point of the knife should be inserted a short distance between the meat and the bone, both at the chine (or short upright bone) and the rib (or long bone). Then the knife has but to be passed down the face of the meat, and each slice comes away easily and clean from the edges. Only, of course, those who are helped first, in this instance, get the brown or well-done outside, and those later on the under-done or juicy. Therefore, it is always necessary for the carver to ask those whom he is helping whether they prefer well or under-done.

Slices of roast beef from the upper side cannot really be cut too thin, when carved in the ordinary fashion, excepting perhaps the first or outside slice, which, owing to its crispness, is better if cut a little thicker. The joint should be kept perfectly straight upon the dish, nothing looking worse or more awkward than for the meat to be twisted all awry. On no account may the carver stand up, set his arms akimbo, or bow his back; all the strength requisite can be exercised from his chair, by inclining the body sufficiently forward.

During all pauses in the carving, the knife and fork should be placed on the knife-rests, and never thrust and left under the joint; nor, while the carver adds the gravy to the plate of meat in front of him with the spoon in his right hand, must the knife and fork be in a bunch, as it were, in his left. The dish must not be tilted with the left hand, so as to fill the spoon more easily. If the meat dish has, as it should have, a well, there is no excuse for tilting it. A tiny crust of bread can be put under one end of the dish, to cant it a little, in the absence of a gravy well. If a portion of the garnish of horseradish is to go with each helping, it must be served with the points of the fork.

In carving the sirloin and similar ribbed joints, a too pliant blade is not desirable. When, however, dealing with a round of beef lying flat, or the boiled silverside, or a piece of roast boned beef, the knife cannot really be too yielding, nor can the slices be cut too thin. Never omit with this sort of joint, where one has to cut directly towards the fork, to raise its finger guard, for, if the knife slips, it will run straight up over the prongs, to the carver's hand.

AITCH-BONE AND ROUND OF BEEF

With the aitch-bone, as with the round of beef, it may be desirable to cut rather a thick slice from the outside before beginning to help; but the habit is wasteful, and should be adopted with judgment. These are not difficult joints to carve, if it is remembered that a knife with a thin pliant blade is absolutely necessary. A small piece of the fat must go with each helping.

Mutton

The rules laid down as to methods of using the carving knife and fork, etc., and the position of the carver—referred to when speaking of beef—are equally necessary with regard to haunch and saddle of mutton.

HAUNCH OF MUTTON

The first thing to be done in carving a haunch of mutton is to make a deep cut across at the knuckle end, down to the bone, with the point of the knife. This forms a basis for a well into which the gravy will run from every succeeding cut. The slices of meat are carved at right angles to the first incision—that is, all along, in continuous and thick (but not too thick) slices—the whole length of the joint. The moment room is obtained at the knuckle end, where the first cut was made, for the insertion of the spoon, the gravy which has accumulated in the hollow should be distributed with each helping, as it is the richest, being absolutely pure essence of meat. Care too must be taken never to forget to put a little extra fat upon each plate, as the haunch of mutton fat is very delicate ; and whoever is quick in helping the guests may be counted a good carver of mutton, for it should be as hot as possible.

SADDLE OF MUTTON

The saddle presents no great obstacles to the carver. If he has a preference for carving the slices obliquely instead of straight, the thin end of the saddle should then be on the right of the carver. Each side of the chine or backbone is to be dealt with alike, the first slice always taken from as close to the bone as possible. As the fat lying round the kidneys is usually much appreciated, a portion of it should go with every helping ; and therefore it is advisable for the carver, directly the cover is taken off the joint, to tilt the saddle a little on one side, and cut at once from underneath as much of this fat as will be required to go round.

LEG OF MUTTON

The leg of mutton owes some of its popularity to the ease with which it can be carved. Little has to be done, save to pass the knife straight down at right angles with the bone, then, according to the preference of the guests, fairly thick slices from either the knuckle or the upper end may be distributed, the knuckle end being always the better done, though not perhaps the choicest in flavour. When possible, the small end of the joint is placed to the left of the carver, but the joint will not always admit of this. It must be placed so that the thickest part of the meat can be cut into, and this has to be farthest from the carver (for it does not come quite on top). Many little fancies for certain titbits will be met with; two quaint pieces of brownish, crisply-roasted fat, like ears or little wings, protruding from the upper end of the joint, being, with the Pope's-eye, notable instances. Some are fond of having this joint dished with the under side uppermost, so as to get at the finely grained meat lying under the Pope's-eye; but this is an extravagant method of carving.

THE LOIN

On the butcher's proper attention to the process known as "jointing" depends mainly the facility with which a loin of mutton is carved. If it has been rightly attended to, the carving knife can be made easily to find its way between the chine-bone. The fat and lean go together with each bone, demanding little or no thought from the carver, except where an ugly or ragged bit of skin requires to be trimmed off neatly.

THE SHOULDER

With the shoulder of mutton, the knife has to be passed from the outer edge of the shoulder through the meat towards the carver, until the bone is reached. Take away slice after slice in this direction, then turn to the meat lying on either side of the blade-bone, and carve this lengthways. When no more can be obtained from the upper side of the joint, it must be turned, and there are many people who do not consider that they have had the best of a shoulder of mutton until this side is cut. It will now present almost the appearance of a new joint, being quite flat, offering several slices along its entire length, and which should be cut moderately thin. This under-side of the joint is known as the "oyster cut" and is often carved and served first.

LAMB is carved in the same way as mutton.

Venison

A haunch of venison is carved exactly like a haunch of mutton ; but, being somewhat larger, it is advised by some authorities that the broad end of the haunch, instead of the side, should be turned towards the carver to afford a greater command over the joint. A skilled carver should be independent of this except under great emergency. Epicures say that the slices cut close to the chine are better flavoured than those farther removed, and the carver must ask those whom he is helping which part they prefer. Neither must he omit to give some of the rich gravy always accumulating in the channel whence the slices are taken, nor an ample portion of fat with the lean. Expedition, but without hurry, is essential in carving venison, for, like mutton, it chills very rapidly. As the shoulder of venison is usually sent to table stewed and rolled, the bone having been removed, it presents no difficulty whatever to the carver.

Veal

ROAST BREAST

The roast breast of veal is composed of ribs and brisket. These are separated by one long incision down the length of the joint, and then the rib-bones are cut one by one, after the manner of chops. The gristly brisket may be cut in square portions—inquiring of the guests whether they prefer the brisket or the ribs. The brown, well-cooked parts in veal are usually most esteemed ; and if the sweetbread is sent to table with the joint it must be fairly distributed.

ROAST FILLET

The roast fillet of veal is carved like a round of beef, with the addition that a portion of the stuffing, which is inserted between the flap and the main bulk of the meat, is served with each helping, and that the brown outside, or first slice, is considered a very choice morsel.

The butcher is mainly responsible for the good carving of a loin of veal, for if the jointing is not properly done, it is hardly possible to carve it decently ; if he has done his work well, the carver has no difficulty in separating the bones, and the portions are cut much the same as with loin of mutton.

Portions of the kidney, and the kidney fat, lying on the under side of the joint, are served to each.

Calf's Head

When upon the dish, the nose should be to the left of the carver, and the first incision is made right down to the bone, and running all along from the nose to just beneath the ear, and slices are cut away in this direction. With each of these should go a piece of what is called the sweetbread of the throat, which is just under the ear. This is cut towards the carver. Calf's head has a quantity of succulent morsels, such as the ears, the flesh round the eyes, and the eyes themselves. Also the palate, which, lying under the head, is to be got at when the jaw-bone is removed; this likewise exposes some nice lean meat. On a separate dish the tongue and brains are served, of which every one is invited to partake.

Pork

SUCKING PIG

A sucking pig is served to table in four parts, the head being separated from the body and split in two, while the body itself is divided in two parts down the back. The carver, commencing on one side, makes a circular cut round the shoulder and removes this with the foreleg. The hind-leg is removed in the same way, and resembles a miniature ham. The ribs are next divided. The whole of a sucking pig is delicate, but the ribs mostly so.

THE LEG AND LOIN

Leg and loin of pork are carved like leg and loin of mutton. The loin must be well jointed, and the skin (which makes crackling) well scored. This is done by the butcher and cook before cooking. If the leg is stuffed, a portion of this must accompany each helping, if liked.

POULTRY

Once learn the anatomy and the best method of separating the limbs, and very little more knowledge is required to carve any bird properly.

Chicken

A chicken should lie upon its back with its tail end to
the left. The fork should be driven firmly, but delicately,
and almost perpendicularly into the breast a little to the
left of the centre, a prong on either side of the ridge of the
breast-bone.　Secure hold is thus obtained of the whole
carcase, and if it is intended to cut up the entire fowl at once,
it can be all but done without once removing the fork.

The next process is to separate the wing, or both wings,
and this is done by passing the knife sharply along the line
of the breast, as far outside the breast bone as will give a
fair share of meat to the wing, then cutting from left to right,
and downwards, letting the knife clear the merrythought and
strike the joint of the wing.　Unless it be an old bird the
joint is easily severed, and bone and flesh come away almost
with a touch.

Having removed both wings in this way, lower the fork
hand so as to turn the chicken a little on to its side, and
then pass the blade of the knife under the projecting elbow,
as we may call it, of the leg, and, forcing it outwards, disengage it too from the body by severing with the point of
the knife the joint by which it is still slightly held.　Then
turn the bird bodily over on to its other side, without removing
the fork, and dispose of the second leg in a similar fashion.
Now restore the chicken to its original position, pass the
knife across the breast a little to the right of the highest
point of the breast-bone.　Cut down gently, inclining the edge
of the blade to the right, press outwards and upwards slightly,
and the merrythought comes away.　The merrythought is
now disposed of by just separating the little joints by which
it is still attached when the upper end of its bone has been
separated from the breast.

Again turn the carcase on to its side, and by an action
with the knife, similar to that by which the legs were removed,
force away by an upward pressure the two side-bones one
after the other, that is the two bones which the removal of
the merrythought has revealed.　There is nothing now to
prevent the knife being swept clean through the ribs, and so
disengage breast and back.　At this stage the fork is withdrawn
from the breast, which has now become a trim, tempting,
and oblong portion ; the back only remains to be dealt with.
Turning it over, press the knife firmly down upon the right

end of it, and holding it so, steadily, lift the left extremity with the fork and the back is immediately dislocated near the centre; complete the separation by severing with the knife such portions of skin and flesh as may yet cause the two parts still to adhere one to the other. Arrange then all these various portions neatly on the dish, and, still assuming that the carving of the whole bird was necessary, it will be ready to serve, remembering that a piece of the liver should go with each wing. On some occasions—carving for a large number of children, for example—it may be necessary to divide each leg into two portions by severing the thigh bone from the drumstick, as it is called. Boiled or roast, such is the mode of cutting up a fowl.

If a fowl approach the proportions of a capon, the fork must not be driven into the breast at starting, because then the first thing to be done is to make the breast yield the utmost number of slices; these should be cut, to begin with, from as close to the wing as possible, working upwards on either side till the breast-bone is reached. Only when these, the choicest parts of the birds, are distributed, will it be necessary to go into the dissection of the carcase; and it must not be forgotten that under this method the wings are reduced to what may be called a mere picking.

Duck

The carving of a duck is done in the same manner as a chicken. It will, however, be found that the legs are set farther back on the body. When a very small and tender duckling is being carved, one wing and leg taken off together, without division, will be no more than enough for one portion.

The stuffing is got at by cutting open at its lower end, by a semicircular incision, the little apron of skin just below the breast. This should be done so neatly that it falls back into its place when the spoon is withdrawn, and must on no account be left jagged. The carver should never put any stuffing upon a plate without first asking whether it is liked. Some housekeepers, when a pair of ducks or ducklings are to be served, allow only one of them to be stuffed, and this is perhaps wise.

As with a large chicken, so with a large duck, the most must be made of its breast by cutting the utmost number of long and delicate slices that it will yield, commencing always as close to the wing as possible. Very marked will be the difference in the apparent amount of separate portions which will be got off a duck by a good and a bad carver; and it is only a little exaggeration to say that the good one will make the bird go twice as far as the bad. All sorts of odd out-of-the-way titbits can be got off the carcase by any one who has kept a watchful eye on a good carver—for practical carving is learned more thoroughly by watching an expert than by any other means.

Turkey

The turkey does not call for greater skill in carving than a fowl. The first thing to do is to cut neatly a succession of long slices from the breast, each with its nice little edge of untorn skin. The cutting of slices from the breast should begin as close to the wing as possible, and proceed upwards, on both sides, to the ridge of the breast-bone. This bird is stuffed at the neck end, and as the slices are carved from the breast it will be found that the stuffing is sliced also at the same time. The severing of the wings and legs is only on rare occasions necessary at table, as the breast of the bird usually yields an ample supply for an average number of guests. But in the event of the carver being called on to disjoint a leg or wing, it is done in just the same way as with a chicken. When, on the following day, the remains of a turkey appear in the form of a grill or a devil, the cook should have made any carving of the dish unnecessary.

Goose

Though the anatomy of this bird is similar to that of the chicken, the greater size and strength of the bird give toughness to the joints, and call for the exercise of more force in their separation. The point of the strong sharp blade must be made to find its way between the bones, as any attempt to cut through them will fail. Supposing the whole of the breast to be gone, and the leg and wing bones have to be operated on, proceed as with the chicken. Turn the bird on one side, and, after forcing the leg out with the blade of the knife, separate the thigh from its socket. The dissection of the remainder of the bird, upon its reappearance as a hash or casserole, will devolve upon the cook. Stuffing is an element of roast goose never to be overlooked; it is to be found and reached in the same way as in the duck. The skin of the apron and elsewhere is on no account to be torn off, particularly as with this bird it is considered very choice in flavour.

Guinea Fowl

Whether boiled or roast, is treated the same as turkey.

Pigeon

The bird is divided cleanly into two equal parts by a sharp strong cut, right through everything, as it were, from beak to tail. Each portion must be further manipulated by those before whom it is placed, the carver having no further concern with it. But should it be necessary to divide a pigeon into three portions, then a leg and wing from each side will make two and the breast a third.

GAME

Woodcock

When a woodcock is being carved it must be seen that all the trail is upon the toast, or, rather, that the liver, which is the essential element of the trail, is not still left within the body. To do this a slight touch of the knife, when the breast is secured with the fork, will force back the legs, and so, by disengaging the back, turn the bird, as it were, inside out ; the liver will then fall upon the toast, and should be spread upon it evenly, with the addition of a little pat of butter, pepper, and salt, and a squeeze of lemon. As to cutting up the woodcock, the task is very simple. The bird may be divided into two or three—the breast for one, and each leg and wing for the second and third portions, the same as with pigeon.

Snipe

The whole bird, with a piece of toast, does not usually form too large a portion for one good appetite ; but it may be made to do for two by splitting the bird exactly in halves as with a pigeon. This bird should be eaten hissing hot.

Plover and Quail

Are treated in the same manner as snipe. If the liver is spread on the toast, see that the little crop containing grit is removed, or it will make it uneatable.

Wild Duck

All wild fowl, including the teal and widgeon, offer to the carver the most tempting of breasts whence to cut away a succession of delicate slices. The breast alone is held to be the choice portion of the bird, though there is good picking elsewhere. Some consider that, before carving, the breast should be lightly scored, and in these scorings a little cayenne should be sprinkled (very sparingly), followed by a little lemon juice.

Rabbit

A rabbit for roasting is somewhat differently trussed from one that is intended for boiling. In the latter case the head is placed on the dish to the right of the carver; in the former to the left. In both cases, however, the back is the chief point to operate upon. If roast, separate the legs and shoulders on either side, then divide the back into equal parts. If boiled, a very similar process may be adopted ; the knife's point has but to be inserted where a joint appears, and it yields to the slightest pressure. Very seldom is the rabbit substantial enough to justify its treatment after the manner of the hare—that is, by taking slices out of the back down to the ribs, like saddle of mutton ; but, where the bulk of the animal is sufficient to allow of this, it is certainly the more attractive and easy method.

Hare

With the head on the left of the carver and the body lying at right angles to the line of sight, slices are cut out of the back all along its length from left to right, much as the breast of a turkey is carved ; and when all the meat has been cut away from both sides of the spine, both the legs must be disengaged by a sharp incision, much after the manner in which the wing of a chicken is removed. Then the shoulders, by a semicircular cut round the joint, are displaced, the point of the knife feeling for the junction at the socket of the bone. The stuffing, if any, must be served in moderation with each portion. Plenty of gravy should also be helped from the dish by the carver, in addition to that served separately ; otherwise the portions may look unattractively dry when first placed before the guests. All parts of a hare are full of flavour, and except that the back is usually the most tender, there is little superiority in it. The ears and brain are among the extra little titbits.

Partridge

In the old days roast partridges were served at the end of the dinner, and then only a small portion of the bird was served to each guest. In that case, the bird was cut up like a chicken, and the choicest morsels—the wings, the breast and the merrythought—were given to the guests of honour.

When the partridge appears as the chief feature at a meal, serve one bird on a hot plate to each guest, without carving. The birds can also be cut in half, from head to tail, as a pigeon, and half given to each guest ; or, for smaller portions, cut the bird into three, as directed with the pigeon.

Pheasant

If this bird is a good-sized one, and is served as one course of a dinner, it is sufficient to give a small helping, and in this case the breast will yield a sufficient number of slices, if carved in the manner described for a turkey ; otherwise the bird must be dissected entirely as if it were a chicken, remembering at the same time that, according to the position in the menu, so should the helping be proportioned. If a liberal portion is to be served, then give one or two slices from the breast with a piece from the less choice parts, but with a good picking on them. Bread sauce and gravy are served separately. Should there be a toast beneath the bird upon the dish, a piece of this must go with each portion.

Grouse

This can be served whole or divided into two or three portions, as described with pigeon. A piece of toast, too, usually served beneath the grouse, should find its way to everybody's plate.

HOUSEHOLD MANAGEMENT

ENTERTAINING WITHOUT A MAID

When entertaining at breakfast without a maid, have the table set with a bright breakfast cloth, a bread and butter plate and a knife and fork for bacon and eggs and a butter knife for each. If grapefruit be served, have it at each place with pointed spoon on the side before announcing breakfast. Set everything in place before you sit down so that you have not to rise in the middle of the meal and go to the kitchen. When boiled eggs are wanted, you can prepare them at table, or bring them in before you announce breakfast is ready. The host can serve the bacon and eggs, you can pour out coffee or tea, and have a tray wagon close beside you, so that you can move used dishes on to it, in order to keep the table tidy throughout the meal, without having to leave the room. Better still to keep to the old-fashioned English way of having whatever hot dish is served arranged on a hot plate on the sideboard along with plates, and let every one help themselves.

When it comes to lunch or supper, arrange the table so as to save trouble when the meal is in progress. If offering soup, have it placed ready in individual bouillon cups before you sit down. Eliminate carving and serving as much as possible by making individual fish or meat creams, or dishes en cocotte, the savoury course. When a fish mayonnaise is on the menu, arrange individual ones in the kitchen, and leave them in the refrigerator while the first course is being taken. You can make creams, custard, fruit fools, jellies, junket, salads, and steamed puddings also all individual. The point is that if the courses are served individually, it does away with serving dishes and so simplifies washing up. But it is absolutely necessary to have a tray wagon. For on it you can have the coffee tray, and underneath is space for all the used dishes, which can be placed there when the second course is arranged on the table. The side flaps can take the sweets or the biscuits and cheese.

Clear all soiled dishes on to the tray wagon between each course, and have whatever cold dishes are to be served ready there to place on the table afterwards. Between the main course and dessert you could rise and brush any crumbs off the table with the aid of a clean napkin and a plate.

When there are few to cater for it is a good idea to make the breakfast or luncheon omelet, the mushroom toasts and other savouries at a side table. But that means an electric toaster and a chafing dish. Only cooking at table saves your steps for then you do not have to run to the kitchen to stir on occasion and lift whatever is cooking.

Do not attempt at any time to entertain elaborately without the help of a maid. Give informal little parties like bridge and tennis parties, and make it the fashion for guests to help themselves or help each other. You will find your entertainments go well if they strike this informal note.

But before you try to do so *you must first learn to plan a menu easily prepared from dishes that require no last minute touches, and arrange the table and the food so that you do not need to run out to the kitchen between each course.*

Nothing is more disturbing to guests than to have a hostess always excusing herself in order to mix the salad dressing, whip the cream, or take the ice from the freezer.

Every meal should be leisurely, not one hustle from beginning to end, as it is if you entertain without a maid without first taking the trouble to learn how to do it in as charming a fashion as possible.

The first thing a hostess has to learn is *to make the most of a simple meal.* It is nonsense to imagine that you have to serve half a dozen courses to please your guests. Better three courses perfectly served than six offered anyhow. Then, make the shops help you all they can. See that any fowls come home cleaned and trussed as you want them, larded as required. Insist on any fish being cleaned and filleted, if you want fillets.

WHEN YOU GIVE INFORMAL PARTIES

Now, suppose you are keen on being known for your " teas "—well, before your guests arrive have your table all set, a long narrow table, if you are giving an afternoon crush. Provide plenty of little sandwiches, but remember it will be less trouble if you make half of them with bridge rolls instead of all with bread. Do not have large cakes. Provide a great variety of the tiniest you can find, ones that can be easily slipped into a saucer and so save the provision of plates which only add to the washing up. There are many attractive kinds of biscuits that you can choose as well. Remember to have plenty of crepe paper serviettes at hand. Though it is a tea, offer coffee as well, and let every one wait on themselves.

No matter what sort of party you give, whether afternoon or evening, the refreshments can always be about the same. Only in the summer time see that you have a plentiful supply of fruit punch or fruit lemonade. Have a glass jug of some fruit syrup handy with plenty of iced soda water, and a great bowl of cracked ice. Whatever you skimp on, do not skimp on ice.

When you ask friends in to bridge after dinner, or bring some one home from the pictures or a theatre for a bite to eat, have tray or table ready before you go out, or before the guests arrive. A good idea is to buy a long round sandwich loaf, with slices half the usual size sold. Butter thin slices lightly, cover some with cold tongue, some with slices of hard-boiled egg, sprinkled with paprika, some with a scraping of sardine butter, some with liver sausage, some with Gervais cheese, and some with chopped cooked ham, pepped up with tomato ketchup.

TO SAVE LABOUR IN THE HOME

Provide not only all the labour-saving appliances you can afford, but substitute fixtures and fittings that save labour.

CENTRAL HEATING, though it entails the handling of furnaces, saves attendance to room fires, and the carrying of fuel to every room. Where central heating is not available, substitute gas or electric fires for coal fires.

SOME SYSTEM OF DIRECT COMMUNICATION WITH THE KITCHEN, such as speaking tubes, or an internal system of telephones, saves maids running about.

A VACUUM CLEANER, creating no dust while in operation, is a good investment for a labour-saving home. But choose a first-class make, and use it for cleaning pictures, or soft furnishings, and upholstered furniture, as well as carpets, rugs and bedding.

AN ELECTRIC FLOOR POLISHER should be provided in every home where polished floors are the vogue. It saves maids getting down on their knees and wasting time and energy hand-polishing. Where electricity is not available, provide long-handled polishers, as well as long-handled mops with scrubbing brushes attached.

A GAS OR ELECTRIC COOKER can be substituted for a coal range if gas or electricity is laid on.

A CONSTANT SUPPLY OF HOT WATER guaranteed by a circulator, the central heat system, or an independent boiler saves the labour of boiling water, when required, in small quantities.

AN INCINERATOR run by gas, will save maids the trouble of disposing of garbage, and operates free from odour.

FIREPROOF GLASS AND CHINA, used for both cooking and serving, lessens the washing up.

A WATERLESS COOKER is not only a short-cut to delicious and economical meals, but it cooks a whole dinner on one small flame unattended, and so consumes little fuel.

A SELF-BASTING ROASTER, which can be used on a gas ring, or oil flame, or on top of an electric cooker, as well as in any oven, saves you the labour of basting.

A HIGH-PRESSURE COOKER is invaluable when a meal is wanted in a hurry. It may be used on any type of range, but saves more when you cook by gas, oil, or electricity.

STAINLESS AND RUSTLESS KNIVES save knife-cleaning.

STEP-SEATS in the kitchen do duty for steps and stools.

A MACHINE WHICH SLICES fruit for marmalade, as well as beans and other vegetables, does the work much quicker than chopping by hand.

A GAS POKER simplifies the lighting of fires, and with it neither wood nor paper is required.

Every season sees the introduction of some new labour savers. Most of them are good, such as the service wagon, which runs on rubber tyres and is invaluable for carrying plates, dishes and food from kitchen to dining-room, but you should study every labour saver very carefully before introducing it to your home. For some labour savers are more trouble to keep clean than they are worth.

THE KITCHEN AND ITS EQUIPMENT

There are kitchens *and* kitchens. A few of us have ideal kitchens. Some of us have given new life to ready-made kitchens. Most of us have to make the best of somebody else's kitchen. Given an ideal kitchen, it is easy to choose equipment to match. Given a ready-made kitchen, you have often to compromise with your ideas when selecting its equipment. Given somebody else's kitchen, you are usually torn between a desire to improve it, and a dislike of spending money on something that doesn't belong to you, and generally end in buying expensive equipment to make up for the deficiencies of the kitchen.

No matter what your kitchen is like, unless you have planned your own, when you have no one to blame but yourself if it is not right, you can usually make it more convenient and labour saving by careful choice of equipment. But before studying equipment, we will suggest the points to be remembered when building an ideal kitchen, when buying a house in which the kitchen is already complete with sink and range, perhaps also with a kitchen dresser and refrigerator, or when renting a flat or a house containing a kitchen that is far from your ideal.

TO BUILD AN IDEAL KITCHEN

1. Build the kitchen on the cool side of the house.
2. Allow sufficient space for two workers. If you plan to cook with electricity or gas, or oil, you can manage with a smaller kitchen than you would require if you used a coal range for cooking, because no space is required for the storage of fuel when cooking by electricity, gas, or oil.
3. Remember when planning to save steps, that if you arrange to have a number of doors opening into the kitchen, it may be convenient but it robs you of working space. You cannot place a refrigerator or a cooker against a door, for example, so that if you wish to have several doors, you must plan a kitchen large enough to allow for all the space required for your working equipment.
4. Always choose a square kitchen in preference to a long narrow one. No kitchen should be less than 8 ft. wide.
5. Arrange to have the windows put in as far apart as

possible so that you can have cross ventilation. The size of the windows should depend on the height of your rooms. Fix them so that the tops are about a foot from the ceiling. The bottoms should be so placed that you have at least 3 ft. beneath them for shelving, cupboard, or a table. The ideal window area should be a quarter that of the floor.

6. Plan all closets and cupboards to come on a level with the windows to avoid stooping unnecessarily, and have a closet with a rolling door placed above the sink to accommodate supplies required in dish washing. All closets should be built into the walls of the kitchen.

TO RECONSTRUCT A READY-BUILT KITCHEN

1. If there are too many cupboards with doors opening into the kitchen, and you want to get rid of one, close a cupboard 3 ft. up from the floor, and use only the top. This will give you space below for a drop zinc-shelf or table.

2. If space is limited, remove the old-fashioned dresser, and substitute an up-to-date kitchen cabinet.

3. Put in another window if necessary.

4. If the shelves in your cupboard are all the same size, and do not afford enough accommodation, have them removed and substitute graduated shelving.

5. Line your walls with linoleum 3 ft. up from the floor.

TO MAKE THE MOST OF A RENTED KITCHEN

1. Choose equipment, not fixtures, which will simplify work.

2. Cover a wooden floor with tiled linoleum.

3. Varnish your distempered or papered walls so that they can be washed down.

Furnish your kitchen before you furnish the rest of your home. For the kitchen is the workshop of the home, and if it is not well equipped, your home will not be well run.

Your Kitchen Range

Having decided whether you want a coal, electric, gas, or oil range, select one of the right height and the plainer the better, in order to simplify the cleaning. If the range must be depended upon to heat the kitchen in the winter, and if a tank for supplying hot water for the whole household has to be connected with it, your choice of range is limited. If your home has central heating, it is an easy matter to choose your cooking range. If you live in a town, you can have either an electric or a gas stove. That is, of course, if both electric light and gas are available. If you live in the country, you have usually to choose between a coal range and an oil stove. Sometimes you may find it is necessary to have both.

When selecting an electric, a gas, or an oil stove, you must consider the position of the oven. Never have anything to do with stoves fitted with ovens near the level of the floor. High ovens are much more convenient than those to which you have to stoop. Unfortunately, most stoves equipped with high ovens need a large amount of space, but if you take your time when selecting a stove you will find that there are some compact styles which do not take up more room than the old-fashioned range with its low oven.

TO CHOOSE A COAL RANGE

Select a model with a hot closet under the bath boiler. See that the oven is large enough to accommodate any joints or poultry you are likely to cook, and that the hot plate is large enough for your purpose. If you intend to heat water with your range fire, make sure that the fire space is large enough to do so. Have the range fitted with a lifting fire bottom and an opening hood, so that you can have an open fire when the range need not be closed for cooking.

If you only require a small range, try to select one with the parts wholly made of cast-iron. If you need a large range, give preference to one in w ich the oven door is lined with asbestos, and fitted with pedal-openers. The front bars of the fire should have some kind of door available for closing when the oven is in use, otherwise cold air will enter through the bars and chill the heat over the oven. See that a cinder sifter is fitted into the ashpan. If yours is a combined kitchen-dining-room or kitchen-living-room, select a convertible range which can be used equally well as a cooking stove and as an open sitting-room grate. There are various models to choose from, but select one in which there is no trace of a cooking stove when the range is converted into a sitting-room grate. Should you want a combination grate, which, while providing for every form of cooking and heating, includes a continuous hot water supply, select one which consumes the minimum of fuel. One model which is well recommended is equipped with an ingenious device by which it is forced to consume its smoke. Should you find that your kitchen fireplace backs against a wall which divides the kitchen from the living-room, hall or dining-room, in which an open fireplace is wanted, choose a double-sided range installation for the kitchen with fire bars showing the open fire in the living-room instead of in the kitchen. This is a very economical arrangement for a small house and should be taken into consideration when you are planning to build a home.

TO CHOOSE A GAS COOKER

Before buying a gas stove, you must consider the following points :

1. The number of persons for whom you have to cook. For you must not buy a stove with an oven that is either too large or too small for the needs of the family.

2. How much you can afford to spend on your stove.

3. If you want a simple up-to-date gas cooker, select one finished in plain or mottled enamel which is so easy to keep clean, equipped with a disc-bar hot plate which covers the top of the cooker for boiling, grilling, etc., and provides a firm rest for the smallest of pans, and a one-burner oven with a flue at the bottom, fitted with an automatic heat control. If you want a more elaborate gas range, choose a similar cooker with the addition of a spacious warming chamber with its own economy burner, and a one-level hot plate top.

4. Should you want a gas cooker in combination with a boiler, which heats the domestic water supply and one or two radiators, choose an all-enamel cooker with boiler to match, making certain that the boiler is one that burns up refuse, and is fitted with a front door which can be let down to show the cheerful rays of the coke fire when required.

5. If your gas cooker is large enough for everyday requirements, but you find it too small for any extra cooking that is needed, invest in a gas ring and an eye-level gas oven.

TO CHOOSE AN ELECTRIC COOKER

Give preference to an electric cooker with a removable oven and grill interiors, porcelain enamelled, with a thermometer fitted to the oven and a plate rack and splash guard.

When considering whether to have an electric or a gas cooker, remember that no matches are required to light an electric cooker. If you cook by electricity, your pots and pans, your ceilings, paint-work and wallpaper around the stove keep clean.

When you entertain without a maid, your work will be greatly simplified if you cook by electricity. Even though you use a gas cooker in the kitchen you will find an electric table stove a great labour saver. It is also invaluable to the thousands of busy workers who live in two rooms and in bed-sitting-rooms. In fact where homes are fitted with electricity, it is a great saving of labour to have electrically operated utensils such as the following :

Coffee percolator.	Water boiler.
Griller and toaster, or a separate grill and a separate toaster.	Milk steriliser. Saucepan with insulated handles.
Quick boiling plate.	Egg steamer.
Kettle.	Steam cooker.
Table stove.	Porringer.
Waffle iron.	

In place of the griller, toaster and boiling plate, you can have a breakfast cooker which combines all three.

TO CHOOSE AN OIL COOKER

Every home which is not fitted with electricity or gas, should have an oil cooker, which can be used in the summer when you wish to let out the coal range, in the winter, when you want the kettle boiling before the coal fire has burnt up, and all the year round when you need to do more cooking than can be done on a coal range.

Choose an oil cooking stove as you would a gas or an electric stove, with an oven large enough to accommodate joints or birds, not only for family use, but big enough to take the kind of joint or turkey you would have at Christmas time. Always choose the latest model of oil cooker. Every year sees some improvement in cookers. You can have them with or without wicks, as you prefer, small enough to boil only a kettle or one saucepan, or large enough to cook five-course dinners and do the family baking as well. Select the stove with the number of burners you would require when cooking a family dinner.

TO CHOOSE WATERLESS AND HIGH PRESSURE COOKERS

Select a HIGH PRESSURE COOKER with a cock for releasing the pressure, a safety valve which prevents accidents by automatically opening when the pressure becomes too great, and a steam gauge which registers the amount of pressure, and with containers so that more than one food can be cooked at one time. As no two pressure cookers are exactly alike, before using the particular make you have bought, study the directions given with it carefully. Pressure cookers are great savers of time and fuel and are more useful when used in combination with a gas or electric stove than with a coal range. Choose any make of high pressure cooker you fancy so long as it is very strong.

Select a WATERLESS COOKER furnished not only with two half-moon pans and a rack, but with a circular pan which can either take the place of the half-moon pans, or, when little space is wanted in the bottom of the cooker for cooking, can be used in addition to the half-moon pans. No kitchen is fully equipped that does not boast a waterless cooker, which is invaluable because of the following points :

1. All cooking can be done on top of one gas ring, coal fire, oil stove, or electric stove, so that fuel is greatly economised.

2. Cooked in this cooker, coarse vegetables and any inexpensive cuts of tough meat become tender.

3. You can bake, braise, fry, sauté, stew, and roast in the cooker.

4. All valuable nutritive elements, as well as flavours, are retained in food prepared in this cooker.

The Maintenance of Cooking Stoves

If your fire is too big for your requirements, you can lessen the quantity of coal consumed by adding cheeks, fire bricks, side bricks, backs, or a coal saver to your grate. Or you can give it a false bottom.

EQUIPMENT REQUIRED FOR A COAL RANGE

Coal hammer	Ash pan.
Coal shovel.	Fender.
Stove lifter.	Cinder shovel.
Steel kitchen poker	Kitchen guard.

CARE OF THE KITCHEN RANGE

Before starting to clean the range, close the kitchen door and window to prevent a draught from scattering the soot, and see that the oven door is closed. Open the flue doors, one at a time, and sweep down the soot with a flue brush, starting sweeping through the highest flue doors. Remove all soot, then sweep out and wash the oven thoroughly with hot soda water, to remove any grease. When the top of the stove is greasy, clean it in the same way. When thoroughly dry, apply black lead, moistened with turpentine, to the black parts. Clean steel mouldings with fine emery paper after moistening them with paraffin. If badly stained, rub first of all with moistened ashes, then finish off with emery paper.

CARE OF THE GAS COOKER

Rub the stove all over, inside and out, while still warm after using, with an oily cloth or a damp rag kept for the purpose. Poke a wire into the burner holes at least once a week to see that they are free from grime. If burners can be removed from the top, take them out once a month, together with all bars and movable parts. Boil for a few minutes in soda water, then scrub in hot water before drying. Wash the wire rack and dripping pan every time you grill or roast.

CARE OF THE ELECTRIC COOKER

Wipe the top of the boiling plate and wipe out the oven with a damp cloth immediately you have finished cooking. Then rub them vigorously with soft paper. On no account interfere with any heating elements, as they require no attention whatever. Do not use any sharp instrument when cleaning electric cookers. Wash any enamelled parts with hot, soapy water. If very grimy, clean with salt, but there is no excuse for allowing electric stoves to become dirty.

The Sink

It is not always possible to make fundamental alterations in the arrangement of your kitchen and scullery, for you may live in a rented house, or an old house which cannot be remodelled without considerable expenditure. If you are helping to plan a new house of your own, however, you can add much to its comfort and convenience by giving careful thought to the matter of the kitchen sink, and even in many ready-built houses something can be done to improve existing arrangements.

If there is room enough, it is a great convenience to have two sinks; one, in the scullery, for the washing of plates and dishes and for general kitchen use, the other, which may also be in the scullery, or in the kitchen or the china closet, should be reserved for silver, glass and special china.

Many small modern houses and flats are equipped only with a combined kitchen-scullery, and if you have to do your own household work this will prove a very handy arrangement, grouping, as it does, all the working centres together and saving many journeys to and fro. When, however, you have a maid or maids and there is no servants' sitting-room, it is better, if possible, to have a separate scullery where the washing-up can be done.

The sink itself is an item which requires careful consideration, and if the existing sink is unsuitable—in size, shape or fitting—it will be worth while to modify it to some extent, or even to replace it with a new design.

Except in a very big house where there is a great deal of washing-up, it is advisable to have a sink of only moderate size, fitted with a plug and a removable strainer over the vent pipe. Washing can then be done in the sink itself, if desired, without an additional basin. It is important also not to have the sink too shallow, or it cannot be used in this manner, and you will also find that when the taps are turned on, every one within reach will be splashed with water.

The height of the sink from the ground is also a matter which affects the comfort of the worker very considerably. A good average height is 3 ft. from the floor to the top edge of the sink. If you are possessed of a sink which is much too low, as is the case in many old houses, it is really worth while to have it refitted and raised to a suitable height. If this is impossible, you can simplify your tasks by placing the washing-up basin on a thick board or a wooden box. Similarly, if the sink is too high, increase your own height a little by standing on wooden slats or fibre matting. When you are having your sink fitted, make sure that sufficient space is left beneath the taps to stand a full-sized bucket comfortably. Do not, however, have the taps unnecessarily high, or splashing will occur. It is sometimes found convenient to place rubber fitments on the ends of the taps to concentrate the stream of water.

The most common materials for modern sinks are glazed fireclay and stoneware. These are easy to keep clean, and need only be washed down with hot soap and water after use, or with one of the special cleansing powders. It is not good to use abrasive cleansers too frequently, or the surface will gradually become impaired and stains and discoloration will result. In some old houses sinks of unglazed stone are still to be found ; but these are not healthy, since they absorb moisture, and if possible they should be replaced. Wooden sinks are also still in use, especially in large houses where there is a special sink for delicate china and glass—this, however, should be of teak, and not of any softer wood, or it will not be sufficiently proof against water and grease. An alternative method is to use wooden tubs or pulp bowls to prevent chipping and breakages.

The ideal surround for a sink is one of glazed tiles, which can be so easily cleaned, but if these are too expensive, a good substitute will be found in enamelled iron, painted in imitation of them. Washable paint or paper is also suitable but not so durable, and it is better to protect it in some way for a short distance above the sink.

Draining boards are also an important consideration. There should be one on each side of the sink, if you have room, so that dirty plates and dishes can be piled on one side and the washed utensils on the other. Clip-on boards can be used when space is limited, or a small folding table, hinged to the wall, will be found very useful. A plate rack is also a great convenience, and an iron saucepan stand will fit into some small corner and accommodate a dozen saucepans in a minimum of space.

COOKING UTENSILS

The materials employed for modern cookery utensils are so many and varied that when furnishing a new house it is quite difficult to decide which it shall be—aluminium or glazed fireclay, copper, iron or enamelware, or the newer fireproof glass. Usually one ends by assembling a mixed collection including a few examples of each kind.

Fireproof Glass

Fireproof glass has created quite a revolution in simple cookery ; it is so easy now to make an Irish stew, a soufflé, or a hot pot, and to leave it to cook slowly in the oven while the housework is done. An occasional glance in the oven is all that is necessary, for the contents can be seen through the glass, and at lunch time there is no dishing up, for the glass dishes look well on any table.

Not only casseroles, but baking dishes, divided vegetable dishes, tea and coffee pots, ramekins, round or square cake " tins," bouillon cups and scallop shells—in fact every kind of cooking utensil except those intended for use over the fire itself—can now be obtained in fireproof glass, and the well-known makes are guaranteed to withstand oven heat for two years.

Another advantage is ease of cleaning. Unfortunately, however, this glass does not as yet compare very favourably in price with such substances as earthenware and tin, but if care is taken, it will last for a long time and prove so much more convenient and attractive that it is worth the higher price.

Glazed Fireclay

This is another attractive material for oven cookery, and can be obtained either in brown earthenware, glazed inside, for casseroles, marmites, etc., or in white or other colours such as primrose, soft blue and green. These make very attractive entrée and gratin dishes, or individual dishes and shells for baking fish and eggs. Glazed fireclay has the advantage over glass that it can be used on the hot-plate of a stove as well as in the oven, though it must be protected by a sheet of asbestos from a naked flame.

Aluminium

Aluminium utensils are probably the most popular of all, owing to their cheapness, lightness, and bright, attractive appearance. Saucepans, kettles, frying pans and steamers are perhaps the most common, but aluminium is now used for every type of appliance from coffee percolators and tea-pots down to colanders, fish slices, liquid measures and sets of measuring spoons.

In ordinary use, aluminium saucepans require no special

cleaning, other than rubbing with a brush or mop, and rinsing with hot water and good soap. It is very important, however, not to use soda, or soap powders which might contain it, or minute particles will be dissolved and the surface will gradually deteriorate, while there is a danger that the solution may mix with the food that is next cooked in the saucepan.

There are three types of aluminium vessels—cast, stamped and spun. The latter are the cheapest, but are not very thick, and food cooked in them is liable to burn. Stamped aluminium is suitable for ordinary household wear, and if a specially strong utensil is required, the cast metal is very suitable. This is the most expensive of the three kinds, but is very durable and will withstand really hard wear.

Cast Iron and Enamelware

For an open grate or coal fire, cast iron kettles and pans are perhaps the most suitable of all. They are very strong and durable, and are suitable for cooking almost anything except milk, sauces, and other delicate foods. After use, they should be carefully dried or they are liable to rust, and kettles should be turned upside down to drain in a warm place before being put away for the night.

When buying enamelled saucepans for making sauces and boiling milk, etc., it is important to choose enamelled cast iron, and not the cheaper enamelled tin, which is too thin for the purpose. This can be used for boiling eggs or vegetables, or as the upper division of a double saucepan, but milk and egg mixtures will burn if placed over a naked flame, and before long the enamel will chip. The enamelled iron pans last so much longer than the tin, that the cost is no greater in the long run.

Copper

In old-fashioned kitchens, copper still occupies the place of honour, and certainly none of the modern labour-saving materials which have so largely superseded it, can compare in appearance with a gleaming row of polished copper pans. The initial outlay, and the work required to keep it bright and clean, are the chief disadvantages of this metal. Its strength and durability, however, and the fact that it is a very good conductor of heat and yet can stand extremely high temperatures, recommend it for use in large kitchens, or where time and the saving of labour are not the first considerations.

Stainless Steel

This is one of the newest materials for utensils and is more expensive than most others. It is, however, extremely durable, and keeps its bright appearance indefinitely without any special cleaning, so that it can be highly recommended to those who are prepared to make more than the minimum outlay in the equipment of their kitchen.

List of Kitchen Utensils

(*For family of 4 to 8 persons*)

1 Standard measuring cup.
1 Set measuring spoons.
1 Quart measure.
1 ½ pint measure.
1 Conical gravy strainer.
1 Stock pot with tap.
1 Fish trowel.
1 Fish-slice.
1 Egg poacher.
1 Egg steamer.
4 Stewpans, 2½, 3, 4, 6 pints.
2 Double boilers, 1 pint, 1 quart.
1 Yorkshire pudding tin.
1 Fish kettle—13 in.
1 Omelet pan.
3 Loaf tins.
1 Flour dredger.

1 Fish frying pan with frying basket.
1 Frying pan.
2 Kettles.
1 Set lipped shallow saucepans.
1 Cast-aluminium preserving pan.
1 Cast-aluminium lemon squeezer.
1 Steam cooker.
1 Set cake tins.
1 Self-basting roaster.
2 Baking dishes, 11 × 9 and 13 × 10.
12 patty-pans.
3 Assorted saucepans.
12 Tartlet pans.

CUTLERY

1 Bread knife.
2 Vegetable knives.
1 Chopping knife.
1 Soup ladle.
1 Pair steak tongs.
1 Egg-slice.
1 Basting ladle.
1 Pair of scissors.

1 Garnishing knife.
6 Iron spoons.
1 Corkscrew.
1 Tin-opener.
Set of grapefruit knives.
Set of skewers.
6 Forks.
6 Stainless knives.

1 Tomato slicer.
1 Palette knife.
1 Meat knife.
1 Toasting fork.
1 Steak beater.

6 Tablespoons.
6 Dessertspoons.
6 Teaspoons.
1 Mustard spoon.
1 Jam spoon.

ENAMELWARE

1 Colander.
1 Slop-pail and cover.
1 Set basins.
1 Set plates.
1 Sink drainer.
1 Soap dish.

1 Bread tin.
1 Flour tin.
1 Set weights and scales.
1 Toilet pail.
1 Set pie dishes.
2 Oval meat dishes.

1 Vegetable dresser.

GLASS AND CHINA

Glass jars for food supplies.
1 Butter jar.
2 Soufflé dishes.

1 Set mixing bowls.
1 Set milk jugs.
2 Jelly moulds.

FIREPROOF :

1 Set ramekins.
1 Set custard cups.
1 Round casserole.
1 Square casserole.
2 Pie-plates.

1 Oval-eared dish.
1 Round pudding dish.
1 Deep oval pie-dish.
1 Shallow oval pie-dish.
1 Oval entrée dish.

1 Fish or meat plate.

TINWARE

2 Funnels.
6 Dariole moulds, plain.
6 Dariole moulds, fluted.
1 Set biscuit cutters.
1 Set layer cake tins, square.
1 Set layer cake tins, round.
1 Set cutlet cutters.
1 Set plain vegetable cutters.
1 Set fluted pastry cutters.
2 Charlotte moulds.

1 Timbale mould.
1 Sponge cake tin.
1 Sponge finger tin.
1 Icing set.
2 Border moulds.
1 Raised pie mould.
1 Swiss roll tin.
1 Ice mould.
1 Set Cinderella moulds.
1 Egg whisk.

MISCELLANEOUS

1 Coarse sieve.
1 Hair sieve.
1 Salt dredger.
1 Pepper dredger.
1 Grater.
1 Spice box.
1 Set tea, coffee and sugar canisters.
1 Coffee percolator.
1 Flour scoop.
1 Pastry board.
1 Rolling pin.
1 Chopping board.
6 Wooden spoons.
1 Pastry brush.
1 Mincing machine.
1 Set of larding needles.
1 Paste jagger.
1 Ice pick.
1 Cake rack.
1 Flour sifter.
1 Pestle and mortar.
1 Pair butter pats.
1 Vegetable brush.
1 Sink brush.
1 Broom.
1 Mop and handle.
1 Dry mop.
1 Oil mop.
1 Bottle brush.
1 Saucepan scourer.
1 Set of stove brushes with flue brush.
1 Set of shoe brushes.
1 Dustpan and brush.
1 Furniture brush.
1 Feather brush.
2 Scrubbing brushes.
1 High pressure cooker.
1 Waterless cooker.
1 Pan lifter.
1 Trivet.
1 Dinner wagon.
1 Set of trays.
1 Vacuum sweeper.
1 Combined step-seat.
1 Oven thermometer.
1 Egg preserving pail.
1 Jelly-bag.
1 Refrigerator.

TO CHOOSE A REFRIGERATOR

Before selecting a refrigerator you must make certain how much storage space is available, for you should choose a refrigerator that fits into your wall and floor space. Some refrigerators are high and narrow, taking up very little floor space and not much of the wall horizontally. Others are broad and low. At the same time, when choosing, you must consider the needs of your family, for it is useless buying a refrigerator if it is not large enough to ensure fresh food for your family all the year round.

Every year sees some improvement in refrigerators. When you buy yours, be sure to choose the latest model, whether it be operated by gas, electricity, or oil. You cannot keep food pure without some kind of refrigeration, so a first-class refrigerator pays in the long run.

TABLE WARE

You must consider the needs of your family before choosing table ware. If yours is a ménage for two, and you intend to entertain only on a small scale, choose half breakfast, dinner, dessert, coffee, and tea services, half services of table glass, and, when possible, sets of six—as in the case of a lemonade set. Half a dozen each of the different knives and forks required will be sufficient, as well as of all other table ware which you can buy by the dozen or half-dozen. If you entertain on a large scale, select " a dozen of everything."

It is better to choose your glass and china from stock sets than to select exclusive designs which cannot be replaced. It is better to choose your silver also from stock designs, so that should any pieces be lost you can always replace them. Select a canteen, or cabinet of silver according to the needs of your ménage. Some cabinets and canteens are stocked with half a dozen of each different kind of fork, knife, and spoon, some with a dozen, and some with more. Choose according to the size of your family, and the entertaining you do.

To Lay the Table

No table can look attractive unless it looks symmetrical. To achieve a symmetrical effect, arrange china, glass, and silver in a geometrical fashion. Allow, if possible, twenty-four inches to each cover, though sixteen to twenty inches can be allowed when setting for a larger number than usual if your table will not extend.

When a table cloth is used, it should either go over a silence cloth of baize or flannel, laid carefully in place, or cork, raffia or other mats should be laid at each cover and where any hot dishes are placed, before laying the table cloth —but it is better to have a silence cloth because the effect is smoother. Lay your table cloth evenly, with the centre crease dividing the table exactly in half. If your table is oblong, choose a cloth with an oblong central design. If oval, with an oval central design. If round, with a round central design. That is, unless you have a table cloth with an all-over design. The ends of the table cloth should fall half-way to the floor.

To secure a geometrical effect, place a service plate, when you use it, otherwise the plate used for the first course, in position at each " cover," then arrange the cutlery and glass. Should mats be used, lay them in position before starting to arrange the cutlery and glass.

CUTLERY—Place the knives at the right of each place, starting from the outside in their order of use, with sharp edges turned towards the plate. Place the forks, tines up, in their order of use, from the outside of the left of the plate. Place the soup or bouillon spoons to the right of the knives. All silver should be placed half an inch from the edge of the table, and each piece should be equidistant from the other. If arranging silver for a family meal, place the dessert fork horizontally across the top of the " cover " with the handle to the left, and the spoon parallel above it, with the handle to the right. When entertaining, have the silver required for dessert arranged, if you like, in the same way, or if dessert happens to be a sundae, ice cream, or any individual sweet, the spoon should come in on the saucer or plate containing the dish—to the right of the latter.

GLASS—Place all glasses at the right of the plate at the tips of the knife blades, nearest to hand in the order of use. Lay napkins at the left of the cover, folded in squares for lunch or dinner. For tea, fold them triangularly, with the long side of the triangle parallel with the knife or pastry fork ; tea napkins should be about the size of a lady's pocket handker-chief. When a meal begins with grapefruit, the grapefruit spoon should be laid either on the outside of the knives where the soup spoon is usually put, or on the right of the plate containing grapefruit. Arrange spoons for fruit cocktails in the same way. Place peppers and salts at each corner of the table or between each " cover."

DESSERT—When giving a formal party, and dessert is to be served, place dessert plates, covered with a filmy d'oyley, with finger bowl arranged in the centre of each plate, and a fork to the left and a knife to the right of the bowl, on the serving table or sideboard, from where they can easily be removed to the table when required. Finger bowls should only be filled three-quarters full, and you can float in each either a slice of lemon or orange, or a few rose petals, or a sprig of mint or rose geranium. In hot weather, it is a good idea to put a little block of ice in each bowl.

To arrange a breakfast, tea, or after-lunch or after-dinner coffee tray, place all cups with their handles pointing to the right and lay the spoons on the saucers to the right of the cups, pointing the handles of the spoons in the same direction as the handles of the cups. The handles of tea and coffee cups as well as milk, cream and water jugs should also point to the right. When lemon is served with tea, arrange it in over-lapping slices in a flat, dainty glass dish, accompanied by a small fork, such as a butter fork. If there is no room on the table to put a coffee service at lunch, dinner, or Sunday night supper, arrange it on a dinner wagon, or stand a wagon on the left within reach of the hostess, or whoever is presiding at the table.

If you serve liqueurs with coffee, arrange liqueur glasses alternately with the coffee cups on the coffee tray, or stand them on a separate tray with the liqueurs. Some coffee services are sold with trays. If yours was chosen without a tray, select either an oblong, inlaid, Oriental brass tray, or a lacquered tray, or a beaten copper tray, for your coffee service.

When you cook your stews in a fireproof casserole, bake your flans on a fireproof glass flan plate, and your little savouries in fireproof glass ramekins, bring them to table in the silver-plated frames you can buy to fit them. You can also make your table more attractive still by serving cream, as it comes in the carton, in a silver-plated carton frame, and it is also possible to purchase similar frames for pots of jam, boxes of dates, tins of sardines, and the numerous varieties of cheese you can buy in round flat boxes.

Most people prefer to arrange their table centres before they lay the linen, glass and cutlery, but some leave the table centre to the last, for then they can see just how much space they can give to it. If dessert is to be served, at lunch or dinner, it is a good idea to place the dessert in the centre of the table, arranged either in a rustic or silver fruit basket, lined, when possible, with fruit foliage. In very hot weather, a block of ice placed in a deep frosted glass bowl makes an attractive centre if draped with fronds of asparagus or maiden-hair fern.

You must arrange your centre in harmony with the rest of your table. If your linen or your glass is coloured, then the same colour note should be repeated in the floral decorations.

But do not choose highly perfumed flowers. Always keep your floral decorations so low that people can see across the table. When fresh flowers are unavailable, the table centre can consist of a bowl of illuminated flowers or fruit, dessert, evergreens, a cactus plant, or an attractive dish or basket filled with ornamental gourds. Place a foliage or fruit centre on a d'oyley to match your other d'oyleys, unless a table cloth be used, when a d'oyley is not necessary.

The illumination of a dinner, tea, or supper table, is a matter of taste. If your home is lit by gas or electricity, you may prefer to eat at a table illuminated from above. Or the dining-room may be equipped with hidden lighting and candles on the table, or an illuminated flower or fruit bowl in the centre. If you wish to use electric candelabra, you can cover your table with an electrified table cloth. In the winter time, choose bright candles for table use, such as orange, yellow or red. In the summer, willow, white, and jade green candles are preferable, but again, the colour of your candles must harmonise with the rest of your table colour scheme. When you use table d'oyleys, honour them by giving them a very highly polished table surface to lie upon.

It is not necessary to have a complete dinner service. You can serve soup in fancy cups, and your sweet in fancy glass, but the fish and meat plates as well as bread and butter plates, when you use them, should be to match. Also have finger bowls to match other table glass. Serving spoons and forks should be arranged on a serving table or sideboard, except at a family meal, when they can be laid on the table in front of the servers. The mistress of the house usually serves the soup, vegetables and sweet, while the master serves the fish, and meat, poultry or game, unless these are handed round by the parlourmaid.

HOUSEHOLD LINEN

When buying your household linen, choose, as you choose your china, glass, and silver according to the size of your home, and the amount of entertaining you do. Generally speaking, allow for each single bed three pairs of sheets and six pillow slips, and for each double bed, three pairs of sheets and twelve pillow slips, unless bolster pillows are used, and covered by the top of the sheet, when only three slips would be required for the single bed and six slips for the double bed. Though blankets do not come under the linen, two pairs of top blankets, and two under blankets, as well as one eiderdown, should be allowed for each bed. Every bed should also have two day and two night covers, unless the day cover is made of some unwashable material, when one is sufficient. Oriental printed cotton covers make good night spreads. They are very durable and wash well. The following is a list for the remaining linen suitable for a household of four persons, and to allow for emergencies, such as illnesses, and for when guests come to stay.

LIST OF LINEN

12 Bath towels.
4 Bath mats.
24 Hand towels.
6 Guest towels.
6 Roller towels.
6 Bath sheets.
8 Kitchen table cloths.
8 Breakfast cloths with serviettes to match.
8 Luncheon or supper cloths.
2 Sets dinner mats with serviettes or 24 table napkins.
8 Sideboard cloths (if used).
6 Assorted tray cloths.
4 Afternoon tea cloths with serviettes.
12 Glass cloths.
12 Kitchen Cloths.
12 Housemaids' cloths. 6 Dust sheets.
6 Knife cloths. 6 Oven cloths.
8 Pudding cloths. 12 Dusters.
6 Dish cloths. 6 Floor cloths.

MARKETING
Fish

When fish are fresh, the flesh should be firm, gills red, and the smell should not be strong. All white fish, except plaice, should have creamy, bluish-tinted flesh. When choosing fish, look for the following signs in the different varieties :

COD.—Clear eyes, firm, white flesh, red gills.

CRABS.—Free from water, heavy and stiff.

CRAYFISH (Langouste).—Choose like lobster.

LOBSTERS.—Bright eyes, with tail drawn in under the body. When stale, the tail hangs limp, when fresh, it should spring back when you pull it out. Judge lobster, like crab, by its size. The heavier the better. Best in summer. Hen lobsters, which you can recognise by their coral spawn (used for garnishing and for certain sauces), are in good condition in winter.

OYSTERS.—When fresh, they close forcibly on the knife when opened. When dead, the shells remain open when forced, and then the oysters are unfit for eating.

SALMON.—Red flesh, silvery scales. When choosing whole salmon, select one with small head and tail and thick shoulders. Scotch salmon is best. Dutch and Canadian salmon is available when Scotch salmon is out of season.

SOLE.—Creamy in colour on under side. May be kept for 24 hours before cooking.

NOTE.—Sole and whiting are most suitable for invalids. Cod and turbot come next in the order of digestible fish. Herrings, mackerel and salmon are indigestible.

FISH MARKETING TABLE

JANUARY.—Bream, brill, cod, crabs, crawfish, crayfish, doreys, eels, flounders, gurnet, haddock, hake, halibut, lobster, mackerel, mullet, mussels, oysters, perch, plaice, prawns, Dutch salmon, scallops, skate, smelt, soles, sturgeon, trout, turbot, whitebait, whiting.

FEBRUARY.—Bream, brill, cod, crabs, crawfish, crayfish, doreys, eels, flounders, gurnet, haddock, hake, lobster, mackerel, red mullet, mussels, oysters, plaice, prawns, Scotch and Irish salmon, scallops, shrimps, skate, smelts, soles, sprats, sturgeon, turbot, whitebait, whiting.

MARCH.—Bream, brill, cod, crabs, doreys, eels, flounders, gurnet, haddock, hake, halibut, lobsters, mackerel, oysters, plaice, prawns, Scotch and Irish salmon, salmon trout, scallops, skate, slips, smelts, sprats, sturgeon, turbot, whitebait, whiting.

APRIL.—Bream, brill, salt and fresh cod, crabs, dabs, doreys, eels, gurnet, haddock, hake, herrings, halibut, lobsters, mackerel, oysters, plaice, prawns, Scotch and Irish salmon, scallops, smelts, soles, turbot, whitebait, whiting.

MAY.—Bream, brill, cod, conger-eels, crabs, crawfish, crayfish, eels, flounders, gurnet, haddock, hake, halibut, herrings, ling, lobsters, mackerel, mullet, perch, plaice, prawns, Scotch and Irish salmon, shrimps, skate, smelts, soles, trout, turbot, whitebait, whiting.

JUNE.—Bream, brill, crabs, crawfish, crayfish, eels, gurnet, haddock, hake, halibut, herrings, lobsters, mackerel, mullet, plaice, prawns, Scotch and Irish salmon, shrimps, skate, smelts, soles, trout, turbot, whitebait, whiting.

JULY.—Bream, brill, cod, crabs, crawfish, crayfish, eels, doreys, flounders, gurnet, haddock, hake, halibut, herrings, ling, lobsters, mackerel, mullet, perch, pike, plaice, prawns, Scotch and Irish salmon, shrimps, skate, soles, trout, turbot, whitebait, whiting.

AUGUST.—Bream, brill, cod, conger-eels, crabs, crawfish, crayfish, doreys, eels, flounders, gurnet, haddock, hake, halibut, herrings, lobsters, mackerel, mullet, mussels, oysters, pike.

SEPTEMBER.—Bream, brill, cod, crabs, doreys, eels, flounders, gurnet, haddock, hake, halibut, herrings, lobster, mackerel, mullet, oysters, plaice, prawns, Scotch and Irish salmon, shrimps, soles, sturgeon, turbot, whiting.

OCTOBER.—Bream, brill, cod, crabs, crawfish, crayfish, doreys, eels, flounders, gurnet, haddock, hake, halibut, herrings, lobsters, mackerel, mullet, mussels, oysters, salmon trout, scallops, smelts, turbot, whiting.

NOVEMBER.—Bream, brill, cod, crabs, crawfish, doreys, eels, gurnet, haddock, hake, halibut, herrings, lobsters, mackerel, oysters, plaice, prawns, Canadian chilled salmon, scallops, shrimps, soles, skate, sprats, turbot, whitebait, whiting.

DECEMBER.—Bream, brill, cod, crabs, crayfish, John Doreys, eels, flounders, gurnet, haddock, hake, halibut, herrings, lobsters, mackerel, oysters, plaice, prawns, scallops, skate, smelts, soles, sprats, turbot, whitebait, whiting.

Game

If you wish to include game in your menus, remember that birds are very expensive for the first week or so after they come into season, though old birds, which can be made tender if cooked in a casserole, are generally cheap, and usually cost less than poultry. When choosing any kind of game, avoid birds shattered by shot, or birds that are bruised and wet. Generally speaking, all game birds should have firm flesh. If, when examining the flesh, you see blue patches, this means the birds have hung too long.

To tell whether birds are young enough for roasting, or only fit for cooking in a casserole, feel the end of the breast-bone. It breaks easily when the bird is young. When old, it is difficult to break. All game should be plump and heavy. Hang birds by the neck in a current of air, undrawn and un-plucked. To test if a bird is ready for cooking, pluck a feather from the inside of a leg. If it comes away easily, have the bird prepared and cooked at once. If the feather is difficult to pluck, let the bird hang a little longer.

HINTS ON CHOOSING GAME

BLACK GAME.—Hang for a few days. Truss like a chicken. Lard with bacon before roasting. Good buy September and October. One bird is enough for 3 to 4 persons.

CAPERCAILZIE.—Bury in the ground for a few days before using. If unable to bury, *hang till really tender*. Good buy September to November. One bird is enough for 6 to 8 persons.

DUCKS (wild).—Pintail is best. Mallard comes next. Teal is third in excellence, and Widgeon fourth. The fresher they are eaten the better. Test for age and truss like a domestic duck. Good buy November and December. One pintail or mallard is enough for 3 or 4 persons. Teal—allow 1 per person, and one widgeon between 2 persons.

GROUSE.—*Young* birds for grilling, pies, puddings, roasting and salads. *Old* birds for making into puddings or soup, or cooking in a casserole. Young birds have short, round spurs. Good buy September. Allow one for 2 persons.

HARES.—When young the claws are smooth and ears easily torn. Rib bones should be well-fleshed. The hair on the belly of a young hare is whitish, on an old hare—fawn-coloured. Young hares should be roasted, after hanging, unpaunched, for about a week. Jug old hares or make them into soup, but they must be very fresh. Good buy October. Allow one for 5 or 6 persons.

HAZEL HENS.—Test for age, and lard well with bacon

before roasting. Cheap from February to August. Allow per person.

PARTRIDGES.—Hang from 10 to 14 days to obtain full flavour. Choose as for grouse. Good buy October and November. Allow one for 2 persons.

PHEASANTS.—The hen bird is plumper and more delicate in flavour than the cock. Choose with short or round spurs, downy feathers under the wing and pointed flight feathers. If flight feathers are rounded or the feathers under wings hard, the birds are unsuitable for roasting but can be cooked in a casserole or stewed. Good buy in winter. One bird is enough for 4 to 6 persons.

PLOVERS.—Only choose birds with short spurs. Only the crop and gizzard should be removed before roasting. Good buy from October to February. One bird is enough for 2 persons.

PTARMIGAN.—Pull a feather from the bird's tail. If it comes away easily, the bird has hung long enough. If the feather is hard to pull out, hang the bird a little longer in an airy larder by the head on a hook. Choose birds with short round spurs. Good buy from February to April. Allow one between 2 persons.

QUAIL.—Birds should have short round spurs and be prepared for roasting undrawn. Good buy September and October. One is enough for 1 person.

RABBITS.—Choose like hares. Good buy October to February. One rabbit is enough for 4 persons.

SNIPE.—Feet should be soft and spurs short. When feathers pull out easily they are ready for cooking. Best from November to February. One is enough for 1 person.

VENISON.—Fat should be bright and clear. If venison seems rather " high " when you buy it, wash it in warm water and dry well with a cloth before cooking. It should, however, have a slightly gamey flavour.

WOODCOCK.—When the feathers fall out at a gentle touch, the bird is ready to cook. Good buy October to November. One small bird is enough for 1 person.

GAME IN SEASON

JANUARY.—Black game (foreign), capercailzies, duck (wild), grouse, hares, partridges, pheasants, plovers, ptarmigan, rabbits, snipe, teal, widgeon, woodcock, doe venison.

FEBRUARY.—Black game (foreign), capercailzies, duck wild), hares, hazel hens, plovers, ptarmigan, rabbits, snipe, eal, widgeon, woodcock.

MARCH.—Black game (foreign), capercailzies, duck (wild), hares (foreign), hazel hens, pheasants (imported), plovers, ptarmigan (Norwegian), rabbits, snipe, teal (Dutch), widgeon, woodcock.

APRIL.—Black game (foreign), duck (Dutch wild), hares foreign), knots (Dutch), leverets, partridges (foreign), pheasants (foreign), plovers (golden), ptarmigan (foreign), rabbits, teal (Dutch), widgeon.

MAY.—Black cock, duck (wild), grey hens, hares, leverets, partridges, pheasants, plovers (golden), rabbits (English and Ostend), teal (Dutch), widgeon.

JUNE.—Black game (foreign), duck (foreign wild), hares (foreign), hazel hens (foreign), partridges (foreign), pheasants (foreign), plover (golden), rabbits, teal (Dutch), buck venison, widgeon.

JULY.—Black game (foreign), duck (wild), hares, hazel hens, partridges, plovers (golden), ptarmigan, rabbits, teal (Dutch), buck venison, widgeon.

AUGUST.—Black cock (Scotch), duck (wild), grey hen (Scotch), grouse, hares (Scotch), hazel hens (foreign), partridges, plovers, ptarmigan, rabbits, teal (foreign), buck venison, widgeon.

SEPTEMBER.—Black cock (Scotch), duck (wild), grouse, hares (Scotch and Norfolk), hazel hens (foreign), leverets (Norfolk), partridges, pintail ducks, plovers (golden), ptarmigan, rabbits, snipe, teal, buck venison, widgeon.

OCTOBER.—Black cock (Scotch), duck (wild), grouse, hares (Scotch), hazel hens (foreign), partridges (English and Scotch), pheasants (English and Scotch), pintail ducks, plovers (golden), rabbits, snipe, teal, widgeon, doe venison, woodcock.

NOVEMBER.—Black cock (Scotch), duck (wild), grey hen (Scotch), grouse, hares (Scotch and Norfolk), hazel hens (foreign), leverets (Norfolk), partridges (English and Scotch), pheasants (English and Scotch), pintail ducks, plovers (golden), ptarmigan (foreign), rabbits, snipe, teal, doe venison, widgeon, woodcock.

DECEMBER.—Same as NOVEMBER, with the addition of capercailzies.

Guide to Meat

TO CHOOSE BEEF

Prime beef should be bright carmine, marbled with yellow fat and with a thick outside layer of fat under a fine skin. The meat should be firm and elastic when touched. If flabby or sodden, avoid it. Best in winter, though seasonable all the year round.

CUTS FOR ROASTING.—The sirloin is the best joint. If liked, the undercut can be removed and laid aside for frying, grilling, or making up into entrées. If roasted with the sirloin, serve it while hot. Rump, buttock, aitchbone, fore-rib and middle ribs are also used for roasting. Rib, if boned and rolled, makes an economical joint. Top side and wing rib are both prime joints and economical.

CUTS FOR BOILING.—Brisket or buttock. Aitchbone can be salted and boiled. Brisket and thin flank also. Silverside is usually salted and boiled.

CUTS FOR STEWING.—Brisket, buttock, round, shin, or cheek.

CUTS FOR GRILLING OR FRYING.—Rump or fillet, or thick flank.

CUTS FOR BRAISING.—Rump steak.

CUTS FOR BEEF TEA, BROTH, OR STOCK.—Shin, skirt, tail, cheek, neck, or clod.

CUTS FOR PUDDINGS, PIES, CASSEROLES.—Round, thin flank, neck.

TO CHOOSE LAMB

Prime lamb should be firm fleshed with pearly white, hard fat. Look at the veins of the fore-quarter of the neck-end, and make sure they are a bluish tint before buying. If greenish, the lamb is stale.

CUTS FOR ROASTING.—Fore-quarter and hind-quarter when young. Saddle. Loin is a prime joint, but leg, also prime, is more economical. Shoulder, breast, " target," and best end of neck.

CUTS FOR STEWING OR CASSEROLES.—Scrag end of neck, breast, and " target."

CUTS FOR FRYING AND GRILLING.—Chops from loin, or cutlets from best end of neck.

CUTS FOR BOILING, BROTH, OR STOCK.—Breast, scrag end of neck and shank.

TO CHOOSE MUTTON

The flesh should be deep red and firmer than beef flesh and finely grained, with firm, white, waxen fat. Choose small boned and plump joints. The saddle, leg and loin are the prime joints for roasting and shoulder and neck are expensive joints.

CUTS FOR BONING, STUFFING AND ROASTING.—Loin, shoulder, and breast.

CUTS FOR BOILING.—Middle of neck and leg.

CUTS FOR STEWING, CASSEROLES, ETC.—Middle of neck. Buy scrag of mutton for BROTH or STOCK.

PORK

Flesh should be smooth, a pale red, and elastic, with rind thin, smooth and delicate, and fat white and firm. On no account allow yourself to be sold any pork with flesh that is clammy and flabby to the touch.

CUTS FOR ROASTING.—Fore-loin, hind-loin, leg, ribs, and neck.

CUTS FOR FRYING OR GRILLING.—Loin chops or neck cutlets.

CUTS FOR BOILING.—Leg, hand or spring. For SALTING AND BOILING, spring, hand, head and cheek.

VEAL

Flesh should be a pinkish white, with firm, very white, sweetly-smelling fat. On no account buy veal with soft fat and flabby flesh. The smaller the joint the better.

CUTS FOR ROASTING.—Breast, fillet, loin, leg, shoulder, neck.

CUTS FOR FRYING.—Fillet and cutlet.

CUTS FOR STEWING.—Breast, fillet, knuckle, shoulder and blade bone.

CUTS FOR STOCK.—Breast, neck or knuckle.

MEAT IN SEASON

JANUARY.—English and Scotch beef, English and Scotch lamb, New Zealand lamb, English and Scotch mutton, New Zealand mutton, English pork, English veal, Argentine chilled beef.

FEBRUARY.—English and Scotch beef, English and Scotch lamb, New Zealand lamb, English and Scotch mutton, New Zealand mutton, English pork, English veal, Argentine chilled beef.

MARCH.—English and Scotch beef, Devonshire, Somerset and Scotch lamb, New Zealand lamb, English and Scotch mutton, New Zealand mutton, English pork, English veal, Argentine chilled beef.

APRIL.—English and Scotch beef, Devonshire, Somerset and Scotch lamb, English and Scotch mutton, New Zealand mutton, English pork, English veal.

MAY.—English and Scotch beef, Devonshire, Somerset, and Scotch lamb, New Zealand lamb, English and Scotch mutton, English veal.

JUNE.—Same as MAY.

JULY.—Same as MAY.

AUGUST.—Same as MAY.

SEPTEMBER.—English and Scotch beef, English and Scotch lamb, New Zealand lamb, English and Scotch mutton, New Zealand mutton, English veal.

OCTOBER.—Same as SEPTEMBER.

NOVEMBER.—Same as SEPTEMBER.

DECEMBER.—Same as SEPTEMBER.

Poultry

Choose fresh birds, less then six months old if wanted for frying. Up to a year old for roasting. Breast should be plump, flesh firm, and though birds should be fat, their flesh must not look greasy. If free from smell and their feet are limp and moist, birds are fresh. If their flesh is discoloured, do not buy them.

To tell if birds are young, press end of breast-bone. It should be flabby and soft. If hard, birds are only fit for soup or stock. Young birds should also have short spurs and downy feathers.

TO CHOOSE POULTRY

CAPONS, CHICKENS AND FOWLS.—Black or yellow-legged birds for roasting, white-legged for boiling. Choose capons with short, pale-coloured combs and smooth legs, and fowls with smooth red combs and smooth legs.

DUCKS AND GEESE.—Should be plump with soft and pliable yellow feet, with fresh-coloured, brittle beaks, soft breast-bones, and yellow bills. Geese are best and cheapest in October and November. Goslings and ducklings from May till July, and ducks from September to October.

GUINEA FOWL.—Spurs should be short and feathers under the wings and on the breast soft and downy.

PIGEONS.—Should have small, pink legs and firm, fresh-coloured feet. If legs are large and very dark, birds are old and only fit for stewing.

TURKEYS.—Birds should be heavy, with fat breasts, short spurs, smooth, black legs and white flesh. Hang for three to four days before cooking. Good buy November to February.

POULTRY IN SEASON

JANUARY.—English capons, English chickens, English ducklings, fowl for soup, English geese, guinea fowls, Bordeaux pigeons, fat quails, Norfolk hen turkeys, English cock turkeys.

FEBRUARY.—Same as JANUARY.

MARCH.—Same as JANUARY, with the exception of Norfolk hen turkeys, and the addition of petits poussins.

APRIL.—Same as MARCH.

MAY.—English capons, English chickens, Aylesbury and Norfolk ducklings, English and Dutch petits poussins, English soup fowls, Bordeaux pigeons, fat quails.

JUNE.—Same as MAY, except for the addition of goslings.

JULY.—Same as JUNE, with the addition of imported turkeys.

AUGUST.—English capons, English chickens, English ducklings, English soup fowls, Bordeaux pigeons, guinea fowls, fat quails, geese.

SEPTEMBER.—Same as AUGUST.

OCTOBER.—Same as SEPTEMBER, with the addition of English and imported turkeys.

NOVEMBER.—Same as OCTOBER.

DECEMBER.—Same as NOVEMBER.

Vegetables

TO CHOOSE VEGETABLES

All green vegetables should be crisp and green. BRUSSELS SPROUTS—firm and fresh heads. CELERY—firm and compact with crisp stalks and fresh leaves. CELERIAC—firm, round roots. CHICORY—crisp and clean. CARROTS, CUCUMBERS, MARROWS, RADISHES, PARSNIPS, ONIONS and TURNIPS—firm and crisp and medium-sized. FRENCH BEANS—young and crisp. LETTUCE and ENDIVE—crisp. CAULIFLOWERS—full, white and compact, free from mildew, with crisp outer leaves. PEAS—pods should be crisp, plump and bright in colour. Also medium in size. POTATOES—even-sized. Choose waxy tubers for potato salad.

VEGETABLES IN SEASON

JANUARY.—Globe and Jerusalem artichokes, asparagus, Guernsey runner beans, beetroots, broccoli, Brussels sprouts, cabbages, carrots, celeriac, celery, cucumber, curly kale, endive, garlic, spring greens, leeks, lettuce, mint, mushrooms, mustard and cress, onions, parsley, parsnips, potatoes, Guernsey new potatoes, radishes, salsify, savoys, seakale, shallots, spinach, swedes, tomatoes, turnip tops.

FEBRUARY.—Globe and Jerusalem artichokes, asparagus, Jersey and Madeira beans, beetroot, broccoli, Brussels sprouts, cabbages, carrots, celery, cress, cucumbers, curly kale, endive, flageolets, leeks, lettuce, mushrooms, onions, parsley, parsnips, potatoes, radishes, salsify, savoys, seakale, spinach, spring greens, swedes, turnips, turnip tops.

MARCH.—Globe, Jerusalem, and Japanese artichokes, Guernsey runner beans, Madeira beans, beetroot, broccoli tops and purple or Cape broccoli, cabbages, carrots, cauliflower, celeriac, soup celery, chicory, cucumbers, curly kale, endive, flageolets, greens, leeks, lettuce, Madeira marrows, forced mushrooms, mushrooms, mustard and cress, onions, parsley, parsnips, Jersey peas, Guernsey potatoes, radishes, salsify, savoys, Scotch kale, seakale, spinach, swedes, tomatoes, turnips, turnip tops, watercress.

APRIL.—Globe artichokes, asparagus, Guernsey dwarf and runner beans, beetroot, broccoli, spring cabbage, carrots, cauliflower, soup celery, chicory, cucumbers, spring greens, leeks, lettuce, English marrows, mint, mushrooms (indoors), mustard and cress, spring onions, parsley, parsnips, Guernsey peas, Irish and Jersey potatoes, radishes, savoys, Scotch kale, seakale, spinach, swedes, turnips, turnip tops, watercress.

MAY.—Artichokes, asparagus (forced), beetroot, cabbage, carrots, cauliflowers, cucumbers, dandelions, endive, kidney beans, leeks, lettuce, mushrooms, onions, peas, new potatoes, radishes, rhubarb, corn salad, salads, seakale, sorrel, spinach, tomatoes, turnips, vegetable marrows.

JUNE.—Globe artichokes, asparagus, beans, beets, cabbages, carrots, cauliflowers, cresses, cucumbers, endive, horseradish, leeks, lettuce, mushrooms, onions, parsley, peas, potatoes, radishes, rhubarb, sorrel, spinach, tomatoes, turnips, vegetable marrows.

JULY.—Globe artichokes, aubergines, kidney and scarlet beans, broad beans, beetroot, cabbage, carrots, cauliflower, cucumbers, leeks, lettuce, mushrooms, green peas, potatoes, radishes, salad, spinach, tomatoes, turnips, vegetable marrows.

AUGUST.—Artichokes, aubergines, French, kidney and scarlet beans, beetroot, cabbage, carrots, cauliflower, soup celery, cucumbers, endive, leeks, lettuce, mushrooms, onions, parsnips, peas, potatoes, radishes, salads, salsify, shallots, spinach, turnips, vegetable marrows.

SEPTEMBER.—Artichokes, aubergines, dwarf and runner beans, beetroot, Brussels sprouts, cabbage, capsicum, carrots, cauliflower, celeriac, celery, chicory, cucumbers, endive, garlic, leeks, lettuce, mushrooms, mustard and cress, onions, parsley, parsnips, peas, salsify, potatoes, savoys, spinach, swedes, tomatoes, turnips, vegetable marrows.

OCTOBER.—Artichokes, aubergines, beans, beetroot, Brussels sprouts, cabbage, carrots, cauliflower, celeriac, celery, chicory, cucumbers, endive, garlic, leeks, mushrooms, onions, parsley, parsnips, peas, potatoes, salsify, savoys, scorzonera, shallots, spinach, tomatoes, turnips, vegetable marrows.

NOVEMBER.—Jerusalem and Japanese artichokes, Guernsey runner beans, flageolet beans, beetroot, Brussels sprouts, cabbages, carrots, cauliflower, celery, celeriac, chervil, chillies, corn salad, small cress, cucumbers, endive, horseradish, leeks, mint, mushrooms, onions, spring onions, parsley, parsnips, French peas, potatoes, sweet potatoes, radishes, salsify, savoys, Scotch kale, shallots, spinach, swedes, tomatoes, turnips, vegetable marrows.

DECEMBER.—Asparagus, Jersey and Madeira beans, flageolet beans, beetroot, Brussels sprouts, cabbage, carrots, cauliflower, celery, chicory, cucumbers, horseradish, leeks, forced mint, forced mushrooms, Spanish onions, parsley, parsnips, Canary new potatoes, forced rhubarb, salsify, savoys, Scotch kale, shallots, spinach, turnips.

Fruit

HOW TO CHOOSE FRUIT

All fruit should be fresh, ripe and perfectly sound. APPLES and PEARS should be free from bruises and specks. BANANAS, yellow, when wanted for use at once. BERRIES should be firm. CURRANTS, dry and ripe. GRAPES, sound. LEMONS, ORANGES and GRAPEFRUIT must be heavy in proportion to their size. PEACHES and APRICOTS should be firm and free from brown blotches. PINEAPPLES should be heavy and their pointed leaves easy to pull out. PLUMS, firm and sound.

FRUIT FOR PRESERVING is generally better under-ripe than over-ripe.

FRUIT AND NUTS IN SEASON

JANUARY.—English and Canadian apples, apricots, bananas, cranberries, dates, figs, granadillas, hot-house grapes, West Indian grapefruit, lemons, South African lychees, mandarins, melons, nectarines, Jaffa oranges, South African peaches, South African pears, pineapples, plums.

FEBRUARY.—English and Canadian apples, South African apricots, bananas, granadillas, hothouse and South African grapes, West Indian grapefruit, South African lychees, mandarins, mangoes, melons, nectarines, Jaffa oranges, South African peaches, Canadian and South African pears, Australian and South African pineapples, Australian and South African plums, rhubarb. NUTS.—Almonds, Barcelonas, Brazils, peanuts, walnuts.

MARCH.—English, Canadian, Australian, South African and New Zealand apples, Canary and Jamaica bananas, South African granadillas, hothouse, Australian and South African grapes, West Indian grapefruit, lemons, South African mangoes, melons, nectarines, Californian, Denia, Jaffa and Seville oranges, peaches, pears, pineapples, plums pomegranates. NUTS.—Almonds, Barcelonas, Brazils, cocoa-nuts, peanuts, pecans, sapucia, walnuts.

APRIL.—English, Canadian, Australian, South African and New Zealand apples, avocado pears, Jamaica bananas, South African granadillas, hothouse and white Haanepot grapes, grapefruit, limes, melons, Jaffa oranges, peaches, pears, persimmons, pineapples, plums, pomegranates, quinces, rhubarb, hothouse strawberries.

MAY.—Australian, New Zealand and South African apples, apricots, avocado pears, Jamaica bananas, cherries, currants, figs, gooseberries, grapes, limes, melons, nectarines, peaches, pears, Cape pineapples, pomegranates, quinces, hothouse strawberries.

JUNE.—Australian, New Zealand and South African apples, apricots, bananas, cherries, currants, figs, gooseberries, granadillas, grapes, Cape grapefruit, limes, melons, naatjes, nectarines, South African oranges, peaches, pears, pineapples, raspberries, rhubarb, strawberries.

JULY.—English, Australian and New Zealand apples, apricots, bananas, cantaloup, cherries, currants, figs, goose-berries, muscat grapes, grapefruit, greengages, lemons, loganberries, rock melons, South African naatjes, South African oranges, peaches, pears, pineapples, South African plums, raspberries, strawberries.

AUGUST.—English apples, bananas, blackberries, crab-apples, damsons, figs, gooseberries, grapes, grapefruit, green-gages, West Indian limes, loganberries, melons, mulberries, South African naatjes, nectarines, South African oranges, peaches, pears, pineapples, plums.

SEPTEMBER.—English and Canadian apples, bananas, bilberries, blackberries, damsons, figs, grapes, South African grapefruit, West Indian limes, medlars, melons, South African naatjes, nectarines, Australian and South African oranges, peaches, pears, pineapples, plums, quinces, sloes.

OCTOBER.—English and Canadian apples, Jamaica, bananas, blackberries, cranberries, damsons, grapes, South African and West Indian grapefruit, West Indian limes, medlars, melons, oranges, peaches, English and Canadian pears, pineapples, English and Canadian plums, pomegranates, quinces, sloes.

NOVEMBER.—English, Canadian and Nova Scotian apples

avocado pears, Jamaica bananas, Cape gooseberries, cranberries, custard apples, granadillas, Almerian, English and Muscat grapes, West Indian grapefruit, lemons, mangoes, melons, oranges, Canadian peaches, English and Canadian pears, persimmons, Cape pineapples, Canadian plums, pomegranates.

DECEMBER.—English and Canadian apples, South African apricots, avocado pears, Canary and Jamaica bananas, cranberries, custard apples, Almerian Muscat grapes, grapefruit, lemons, mandarins, mangoes, Denia and Jaffa oranges, South African peaches, English and Canadian pears, South African pineapples and plums, forced rhubarb.

Groceries

HINTS ON BUYING GROCERIES

Purchase groceries that will keep, in as large quantities as possible, taking advantage of cheap offers when they occur. Some groceries are cheap at certain seasons. Watch these seasons and buy in quantity groceries that keep.

BISCUITS.—Buy in small quantities unless for a large family.

CANDLES.—In large quantities.

CEREALS, such as rice, tapioca, etc., in large quantities. Choose *Patna rice* for curries, and *Carolina rice* for puddings. Choose *Genoa macaroni*.

CHEESE.—Buy in small quantities.

COFFEE.—Buy freshly roasted, preferably coffee beans or freshly ground beans, without chicory, unless preferred.

DRIED FRUITS.—Buy in small quantities, except when the new dried fruits come on to the market. *Currants* should be dry and soft. Have nothing to do with dirty-looking fruit. Choose *Valencia raisins* for puddings, and *Muscatel raisins* for dessert.

SALT.—Buy in small quantities.

SOAP.—Buy in large quantities.

SODA.—Buy in moderate quantities.

SPICES.—Buy in small quantities.

SUGAR.—Buy in large quantities. Choose *icing sugar*, free from lumps, for icing cakes. *Cane sugar* for preserving, *granulated sugar* for sweetening puddings, and *castor sugar* for fine cakes. *Loaf sugar* for tea, and *Demerara* or *centrifugal* for coffee. Use *Barbadoes* or *Demerara sugar* for spiced cakes and puddings.

TEA.—Buy in fairly large quantities. Some blends of tea are more suitable for use with the water in some localities, some for others.

TINNED FOODS.—Choose advertised brands, and have nothing to do with tinned foodstuffs that do not give the name of the canner. Reject any tin that bulges, as this is a sign that the contents are decomposing.

THE STORE ROOM

As a store cupboard or store room is primarily intended for storing dry goods, it must be dry and airy, and well equipped with shelves, hooks and nails. You can tack up on the back of the door a list of the months of the year, with special shopping notes written or typed against them. For example, in February and March, you would have listed Seville oranges, and preserving sugar for orange marmalade. You could include under each month vegetables or fruits to be pickled, herbs to be dried, and vinegar to be made. Under October, you might suggest buying ingredients for making plum puddings and mincemeat. In short, you should have each month's special programme, listed under each month, in the store room, so as to ensure shopping in season.

Choose, if possible, a store room facing the north. An ideal type of store room is a fairly large room, equipped with two ample cupboards, one for storing groceries and the other for storing cleaning materials, soap, etc. There should be a table in the centre, containing scales and weights, and a slate and pencil, so that all goods may be weighed out and checked on arrival. In the drawers should be a store book in which to enter the monthly purchases, price and quantity. By taking a note of the date of purchase, date of arrival, quantity bought, and prices paid, you can keep a strict watch on your household accounts. If you have a staff, arrange a fixed time for giving out stores, and adhere to it. When you notice certain stores are running low, make a note on a household indicator, so that goods will be remembered when next you order. The best way to give out stores is to pretend you are the grocer's shop, and measure or weigh out stores once or twice a week, just as the shopkeeper would do.

Air your store room every day, and see that the shelves of the cupboard are wiped down once a month, and the table dusted daily. Label all jars with the name of the contents, and arrange the large ones at the back of the shelves, and the small ones in front, so that all the labels can be seen. Now store your goods like this :

BISCUITS—in an airtight tin. BREAD and CAKE—in a ventilated earthenware crock. CANDLES—in their packets or boxes. CEREALS, such as barley, rice, sago, semolina tapioca, and all starchy foodstuffs such as macaroni and spaghetti, must be kept in covered jars. COFFEE—in an airtight tin. FLOUR—in an airtight bin or crock. JAMS, JELLIES, MARMALADES, PICKLES, PRESERVES and SAUCES—in the driest and coolest part of the room. MATCHES—in a tin box to protect from damp. SALT—in an earthenware jar or wooden box. SPICES—in closely corked small bottles, or tightly covered tin canisters. SUGAR—in earthenware or glass jars.

THE LARDER

Every larder should face due north, but if, owing to faulty planning, there is a possibility of the larder being contaminated by existing sanitary arrangements, either change the position of your larder, or have your sanitary arrangements corrected. Make certain that your larder is thoroughly ventilated, and insist on its being kept scrupulously clean. It should never be swept out. Wipe the shelves daily with a damp cloth to gather up the dust, and scrub the larder out weekly with water and carbolic soap. A meat safe should have the same treatment, and may need to be scrubbed even more frequently in hot weather.

Store all the semi-perishable foods, which include butter, eggs, lard, lemons, margarine, oranges, grapefruit and other tough-skinned fruit, in the larder. When food comes home from the shops, remove it from any paper wrappings, not only because certain foods deteriorate if stored in paper, but because paper attracts both beetles and mice.

As soon as meat and fish are delivered, remove paper wrappings, and place both under a perforated zinc cover if you have not a refrigerator in which to store them. The following hints should be followed :

1. Never store cooked meat on the dish in which it was served, as the remains of the gravy and congealed fat may turn it sour.
2. If meat is at all tainted, wash with vinegar and water, or with a weak solution of Condy's fluid—1 tablespoon to a quart of water.
3. Remove the spinal cord from lamb and veal as soon as meat arrives.
4. Leave all game undrawn until required for cooking.
5. Do not put anything away hot.
6. Turn all sauces, soups, and stocks out of pans before storing away.
7. Keep all sticky foods, such as jam, honey, syrup, treacle, etc., in tightly covered containers, to protect them from flies.

TO GET RID OF PESTS

To scare FLIES away from your larder, hang a small muslin bag of cloves up on a hook, unless you prefer to use fly papers. If you insist on windows and frames being washed frequently with disinfectant water, you should not be troubled with flies. The simplest way to get rid of RED ANTS is to leave a plate, smeared thickly with lard, overnight where the ants trouble you. In the morning, immerse the plate, which you will find covered with ants, in boiling water.

To get rid of MICE, buy a reliable trap and bait it with toasted cheese, raw meat, or any fat, then stop up mice holes with corks, dipped first in water then in cayenne. The same treatment will rid you of RATS.

To trap WASPS, leave a jam jar with a little jam in the bottom, uncovered, and when you have trapped a few, half-fill the jar with boiling water.

To exterminate BEETLES, fill jam jars to the depth of an inch with treacle and water, dip a brush in hot fat, and smear the inside of the jar with fat. Make one or two " staircases " of narrow strips of cardboard, and rub each strip with a cut onion, then prop one or two strips against each jar with the tops bent well inside, so that the beetles, once they get to the mouth of the jar, will topple over and be trapped.

WASHING UP

This is usually looked upon as one of the humblest and most irksome of household tasks, and is therefore performed without much thought or method. Actually, it is a job which, of all others, requires careful planning, so that it may be executed as satisfactorily as possible. Upon the careful washing of implements and utensils, the purity of the food supply largely depends, as well as the attractive appearance of the table. If the task is performed in a careless or slovenly manner, food receptacles become tainted, and silver, glass and china lose all their lustre.

Before preparing the washing-up water, all the dirty things should be collected and sorted into separate piles on a draining board or table at the right-hand side of the sink. Knives and silver should never be thrown together, either when clearing the table or when washing and drying, or the silver will soon become badly scratched. Cups and saucers and other delicate china should be placed in one pile, and greasy plates and dishes in another—the latter having been scraped free of scraps of food and grease with a flexible knife.

Washing-up water must be very hot, and if it is not sufficiently hot in the tap, a second kettle should be kept in readiness for the greasy utensils which will be washed at the end of the proceedings. A small quantity of soap is necessary, either in the form of soap flakes or powder, or part of a household bar. A good way of using up odd ends of soap is to place them in a tin, such as a small mustard tin, the bottom of which has been well perforated with a nail, and to which a string handle has been attached. The tin can then be dipped in the basin until sufficient lather is produced, and afterwards hung up till the next occasion. If your water supply is hard, a small quantity of washing soda must also be added, unless a soap powder containing a high percentage of soda is used. It is not necessary, however, to add more than a small lump or two of soda—a larger quantity is merely wasteful, and harmful to the hands.

When the hot water is ready, wash first all glasses, and dry them while they are steaming hot. Next wash the silver utensils, and give them an extra rub while drying the hot soapy water from them, and they will shine as though they had been specially polished. China should come next, the cleaner dishes first, then mixing utensils and knives. Lastly, saucepans, tins, frying pans, etc. Knives should never be completely immersed in the water, or their handles will be spoiled.

When the washing-up water becomes dirty, change it for a fresh supply, and if there are many plates and dishes to be washed, it is a good plan to have a second basin alongside in which to dip them, or to rinse them under the running tap.

If there is a plate rack above the sink, in which plates and dishes are left to drain, these should always be rinsed in fresh water after the preliminary washing. When they are thoroughly dry and ready to be packed away or ranged on the dresser, they should be wiped over with a clean dry cloth, or it can be made a habit to polish them before they are taken to the dining-room for the next meal.

If you have to do your washing-up alone, dry the glasses as soon as they are washed, and then the silver and special china, before washing the remainder of the utensils. The task is simplified considerably, however, if two workers can take part. A soft mop with a handle is the best implement, as your hands come less in contact with the water than when a dish-cloth is used. This should be thoroughly rinsed with hot water, squeezed out, and propped up to dry when finished with, or it will soon become sour.

There should be three drying up cloths, one for glass, one for silver, and a third for china and other ware, and these should always be rinsed out and hung up to dry after use, while all the drying-up cloths should be boiled once during the week.

Saucepans and baking dishes need more vigorous cleaning than mopping and rinsing, and a special stiff, narrow saucepan brush should be kept for this purpose. A steel-wool cleaner or an abrasive powder will be necessary for particularly burnt or coated vessels, but when using the former you should be careful to see that no particles of the metal are left behind to get into the food. Badly burnt saucepans can be easily cleaned by boiling in them a strong solution of washing soda— if necessary, for several hours. This method, however, is not suitable for aluminium vessels, as soda causes the surface of this metal to deteriorate. When aluminium saucepans become darkened and stained, they can be brightened by boiling in them something of an acid nature, such as lemon peel or apple parings.

Some very hot water should always be reserved for roasting tins, frying pans, etc., for the grease then comes away with little trouble, or they can be filled with water and brought to the boil, then rinsed and dried.

In houses where there are two sinks, it is usual for the parlourmaid or house-parlourmaid to wash the glass, silver and special china, as well as the tea things, in her own sink, which may be conveniently placed in the china pantry. In that case the cook-general or kitchen or scullery maid has the use of the scullery sink, where the plates, dishes and all cooking utensils are dealt with.

The Care of the Sink

When washing up is finished, the sink and washing-up utensils should always be carefully cleansed. If a dish-cloth has been used, place it in the basin with a little soap or soap powder, pour boiling water over, rinse thoroughly, squeeze out, and hang up—just as in the case of a mop. Next wash the basin, inside and out, with the soapy water and a sink brush, and use the same suds to wash down the sink.

Thoroughly rinse the sink afterwards with hot water, so as to clear the vent pipe and remove all grease from the gulley—which should also be brushed down regularly. If this is done, there will be no unpleasant smell from the sink, but in any case it is a wise precaution to pour a solution of some good carbolic disinfectant down the drain from time to time.

It is a good plan always to carry the water in which cauliflowers, cabbages, and other greens have been boiled, out into the garden or to throw it down the gulley outside the scullery. When poured down the sink, it leaves a very unpleasant smell.

HOUSEHOLD HINTS

By Florence Caulfield Hewlett

ALMONDS, To Salt:

Shell the almonds. Throw them into a pan of boiling water. Stand the pan on the back part of the stove for 5 minutes. Throw the almonds in cold water, then rub them between the hands or a cloth to remove the skins. Place them in a small wire basket in a frying pan with boiling salad oil, and fry till they become golden brown. Drain. Dredge them quickly with salt and toss occasionally till cool.

ALUMINIUM PLATE AND PANS, To clean:

Boil fruit peelings such as apple skins in the pan, and the discoloured marks will disappear. If aluminium gets burnt, water should be poured into the pot and a small onion added. If the pan is heated until the water boils, all the burnt matter will rise to the top. *Never* clean aluminium with *soda*, or *gritty* polishes, as the metal easily scratches.

ANTS, To get rid of:

Dissolve twopennyworth of tartar emetic in a tablespoonful of water and add a teaspoonful of sugar. Set the mixture in an open shallow dish where the ants are troublesome.

APPLE PARINGS, To use:

Stew them with a little sugar to provide good juice for your apple pies.

APPLES, To peel:

Have at hand a pan of cold water to which a few drops of lemon juice have been added. As you pare the apples drop them one by one into the water and they will keep a good colour.

APPLES, To preserve:

Choose sound apples. Wipe them dry and pack in a barrel or wooden box. Put a layer of bran between the apples so that they do not touch one another. Store the barrel in a cool place, but *not* where apples will freeze.

ASTRAKHAN COLLARS AND CUFFS, To repair :

Get an old stocking. hand-knitted, the colour of your collar and cuffs. Pull the knitting out and you will have a curly wool. Then with a large long needle, make a running stitch over the worn part, leaving loops after every stitch, and your collar and cuffs will be like new.

BABY, when he sits up in his pram :

Make a bag of strong warm material, large enough to put him in, and tie firmly with draw-string round his waist. Leave plenty of room for him to move his legs about inside. Put the strap of the safety harness of the pram round his waist over the bag and he will be snug and warm.

BABY'S BATH, To test the heat of :

Doctors recommend that the nurse should place her elbow in it. The skin of the hand is too coarse to gauge the heat of water accurately.

BABY'S FIRST KNITTED COAT :

When baby grows out of this, it can be made use of by sewing it part way up the front, then sewing on buttons and loops. Use it as a vest. This tip applies specially to the matinée shape.

BABY'S CHEAP COT MATTRESS, To make :

Take a strong piece of twill or strong piece of sheeting and fill evenly with fresh, sweet hay. To keep the hay in place, thread a sacking needle with fine white string and draw it through the mattress at regular intervals, knotting it firmly on either side and cutting close. Small leather tags, which can either be purchased or made at home from old kid gloves, may be used for tufting.

BABY'S FEEDERS or BIBS, To make :

Take a good-sized Turkish towel with either a fringed or bordered end and cut each end into three or four feeders, according to width. Allow about four inches of towelling besides the border, then cut across and hollow each one out in the centre, hem round and put two tapes on each, or one tape and a button.

BABY'S CAST-OFF LONG FLANNELS :

These can be used up by making each one into two pairs of warm stays for older children up to the age of four. Cut the flannels in half. Take the top half already pleated and the arm holes formed, and bind the remainder with Russian binding. Sew on the necessary buttons and make button holes where needed. Pleat the other half and make up like the first half.

BABY'S HAIR, To remove scurf from :

Well wash the hair and rub gently into the roots a little vaseline or olive oil. Leave it on for 24 hours. Then wash baby's head in lukewarm water. The scurf will come off easily. Use a very fine comb to lift it. Dry the hair with soft warm towels. Repeat this process if necessary two or three times. Perspiration causes scurf so do not let baby wear heavy bonnets.

BABY'S NAPKINS, Hints on use of :

Do not fold your baby's napkin from corner to corner, fold straight across. Put one end under baby, draw the other end between the legs and pin at both sides. If a girl, allow a thickness at the back, if a boy, turn a thickness in at the front ; this is easily done with the ordinary sized napkin. Do not fail to try this way as it prevents a lot of soreness, is neat, and prevents the soiling of clothes.

BABY'S PLAYBOX :

Take an old packing case. Line the bottom with a piece of waterproof, and then pad the bottom and sides with wadding and cover in some pretty bright material.

BABY'S SHAWL, To make :

Take one yard of double-width white cashmere and cut it into a square. Now " transfer " a border round and work it in silk. With the same kind of silk, fringe it all round or crochet a border if preferred.

BACON, To cook :

Take a slice of bacon, hold lightly under the cold water tap for a few seconds, wipe off the water, then lay the bacon in an earthenware or enamel dish, instead of in a frying pan, and cook in a hot oven for a few minutes. This method preserves the fat, and the flavour is improved.

BAGS, Use for old rubber hot-water :

Cut off the neck and thick rims, leaving two flat pieces of rubber about 12 in. by 8 in. One piece will make two soles for wearing inside thin walking shoes; the other half, if covered with black sateen, will make a useful kneeling mat.

BASIN, To mend when cracked :

When a large white basin is cracked, paint over the crack with white enamel. Then lay on a piece of white tape and give another coat of enamel. This will prevent the basin from breaking.

BASKETS, To preserve :

If baskets are occasionally scrubbed with hot soap-suds they will be found to last much longer.

BEADS OR PEARLS, To Thread :

When threading beads or pearls pass the thread through slightly warm candle wax, and let the melted wax from a burning candle drop on the end of your thread. Twist the end between the fingers, and when hardened you will have a very good substitute for a needle. Run on dental floss passed through wax.

BEANS AND PEAS, DRIED, To boil :

Soak overnight in water to which you have added a teaspoonful of sodium bicarbonate, and the beans will retain their colour and be beautifully soft.

BEANS, PEAS, etc., DRIED, To cook :

Put your dried beans, peas, or lentils into fast boiling water—or stock, if making soup. The result is excellent. In 20 to 30 minutes the peas or beans have become pulp. Beans take a little longer, perhaps, but a small piece of fat bacon boiled with them greatly hastens the cooking

BEANS, KIDNEY, To preserve :

Gather the beans when perfectly dry and lay them for one day in the hot sun. Have ready some earthenware or glass jars and common salt. First put in a layer of salt and then one of beans, taking care to cover each layer of beans with plenty of salt. When the jars are full, tie them down to keep the air from them. When cooking the beans, wash the strong brine from them and leave them in cold water overnight. In England, gather the beans before the frost catches them and when quite dry.

BED, DAMP, To detect :

Place a hand mirror for a few minutes between the sheets. If, when removed, the glass is misty, the bed is damp.

To Prevent Damp.—Leave a blanket on the top of the bed after it is made. Should you go away for two or three weeks you will find the bed quite dry on your return. The blanket, however, should be aired.

BED, SPRING, To clean :

Keep two dish mops just for this purpose. Get the dust out of the springs first with a dry mop, then take a damp mop and go over the springs. Wipe dry.

BED-SPREAD, To make :

Take wools of every imaginable colour, the brightest possible. Make a square in crochet of some 3 to 4 inches in a pretty open design, and for your model as to the mingled colours take a flower, say the forget-me-not of ardent blue and pink tones, with its yellow centre and dull-green leaves. When all the squares are done, sew them together and crochet a plain narrow black or dark-green border round the counterpane.

BEDSTEADS, To clean :

Sponge wooden bedsteads with a solution of hot alum and water, and iron ones with a cloth damped with paraffin. Cover the slats with fresh brown paper to prevent marking the mattress.

BEEKEEPERS, A hint to :

(For small bee keepers who keep for profit). I have four bee hives and I have had valuable hints given me by a most enthusiastic apiarist. In winter he tells me always to leave 30 lb. of honey in the hive. This should be there at the end of October.

It often happens that most of the surplus is stored in the supers, and there is not enough in the brood chamber when the supers are removed. If there are several hives, some may have more in the brood chamber than others, and those which have over 30 lb. can be relieved of a comb for the benefit of the needy. Even then it may be necessary to give extra food.

A popular custom with amateurs is to supply candy in cakes of 1 lb. or 2 lb. from time to time during the winter. This seems easy, and because the candy is an excellent food and is turned out commercially ready for use it appears to save trouble. It is, however, the worst method of feeding bees and should be done only as an emergency practice. The danger is that any disturbance in the winter may result in a draught through the hive, and the death of the bees from cold. To avoid disturbing the hive, during October the bees seal all cracks and crevices except the regular entrance, so that air cannot pass directly through. When candy is supplied, the seals are broken and the insects, being unable to go out for fresh gum, cannot renew them. It is *far better* to supply additional stores before the middle of October, so that the hive may be undisturbed through the winter months. Give them syrup, it is the most appropriate food. Make it from refined sugar. 12 lb. thoroughly dissolved in five pints or six pints of boiling water.

BICYCLE TYRES :

When a machine is not in use, the tyres should occasionally be rubbed over with a damp cloth. This will prevent them from cracking.

BLANKETS, To remove tea stains from :

Cover a deep basin with the stained parts. Sprinkle thickly with borax and pour water through the blanket. If the stains be of long standing soak them in glycerine for several hours and then wash the blanket when the stains are seen to have disappeared.

BLANKETS, NEW, To wash :

Dissolve 4 oz. of rock Fullers Earth in a quart of boiling water, adding enough cold water to cover the blankets. Soak them in this overnight, then squeeze out in the morning and rinse.

BLANKETS, To renew :

When a blanket becomes very thin in the middle cut it in two (cutting the thin part in the middle) and reverse the halves, putting the middle to the outside, and the outside to the middle. Run up the centre seam and hemstitch the sides. This will double the life of the blanket.

BLANKETS, To store :

Care should be taken when storing blankets. Powdered alum sprinkled over is an excellent moth preventative.

BLEACHING CLOTHES :

Garments or table linen which have become a bad colour may be bleached by spreading in the sun for several hours after being washed and boiled. On most of the farms in South Africa, clothes are washed by native women in the open in running streams. They are then beaten on stones or wooden boards and laid or hung out to bleach in the sun. This method, of course, does not apply to cities and towns where well-equipped modern laundries are to be found.

BLEACHING LIQUOR, To make :

Take ½ lb. chlorinated lime, ½ gallon boiling water and 2 tablespoonfuls of washing soda. Put the lime into a basin and pour the boiling water over, then add the soda and stir until it is dissolved. Strain through muslin and keep in a well-corked bottle. When using this liquor, hot water must be added in the proportion of four parts to one of the mixture.

A very weak solution of this may be used to restore the whiteness to discoloured cotton and linen. It is also used to remove old stains of tea and coffee, wine and fruit. A piece of soft linen is dipped into the diluted mixture and rubbed over the stain. Always rinse *very* thoroughly after use, for the chlorine, if left on, will *rot* the fabric.

This mixture can only be used for linen and cotton materials. It will completely destroy the fibres of silk and wool.

BLINDS, LINEN, To clean :

If your linen blinds have become soiled, remove them from the windows on the rollers and place them on the side of the bath. Make a lather of soap and warm water, and gently scrub the linen with a soft nail brush dipped in the suds. Be careful not to let the blinds get too wet. Wipe off the suds with a soft cloth, roll up the blinds tightly, and fix to the window again, then pull them down and leave to dry.

BLUE, To make liquid :

Dissolve 4 oz. of aniline blue in one gallon of boiling rain water. Keep closely covered till required. 12 drops only are required to a bucketful of water for ordinary laundry purposes.

BLUEING CLOTHES :

To prevent a patchy appearance, take 1 oz. china blue and 1 oz. oxalic acid. Add 1 quart boiling water. Stir until dissolved, and add two more quarts of boiling water, then strain through muslin and bottle. Use this mixture in the usual way in the rinsing water. It will be found better than the solid squares of blue, as it mixes evenly with the water and will never give the patchy appearance which sometimes occurs in the use of ordinary blue. A rather dark mixture of this will help to preserve the colour in light blue, mauve and green materials.

When mixing blue in hard water, add to the tub of water a cupful of milk. This prevents the linen from blueing unevenly or becoming streaky.

BOILER, To remove rust from :

Rub the boiler with unsalted fat of some kind, then put in some shavings and set fire to them. When the boiler is cold throw in a quantity of cabbage leaves and potato and turnip parings—in fact, all kinds of vegetable trimmings. Add enough water to cover, and boil for two hours. Empty carefully, rinse, and while the boiler is yet warm rub the sides and bottom of it with soft soap, leaving this on until the boiler is required. *Always empty and dry the boiler after use, and smear with soft soap.*

ANOTHER METHOD

Take 1 oz. of blue, powder it, and put it in a bottle with 1 quart clean water (rain water is preferable). Add ½ oz. of pulverised oxalic acid. A tablespoonful of the mixture is sufficient for a large washing.

BOOKS, To keep :

Damp affects books badly, and they should never be packed so tightly in their shelves that air cannot pass between them ; nor should they be kept where it is too warm, nor directly in the sunshine or the covers will fade and warp.

BOOKS, To remove stains from :

If grease of any kind be dropped on a page it can be removed quickly by placing a clean piece of blotting paper over the spot and passing a warm flat-iron carefully over it, so that the paper absorbs the grease. A little petrol carefully applied will remove stains. Ink stains will disappear if a mixture of salt and water (1 part of salt to 6 parts of water) be applied to them, and they be dried with clean white blotting paper and a warm iron. See that your iron is *warm, not hot.*

BOOKS, TORN, To repair :

The white of an egg can be used for repairing torn books, for glueing on small pieces of wood chipped off furniture, to clean and renovate a black straw hat, to clean and renovate leather chairs and sofas. These should be polished afterwards with a soft duster.

BOOTS AND SHOES, DAMP, To polish :

Add a few drops of paraffin to the blacking before applying to damp shoes or boots.

BOOTS AND SHOES, To soften :

Wash them in warm water, and afterwards well rub castor oil into the leather. They will not polish well until they have been in use, and the heat of the foot has caused the oil to be thoroughly absorbed by the leather.

BOOTS AND SHOES, Trees for :

Fill a pair of socks or stockings which fit the feet full of sawdust, and sew up the tops to keep the sawdust in. When the shoes are taken off put them on these uncommon trees. The shoes and boots will keep their shape as the sawdust absorbs the moisture.

BOOTS AND SHOES, BROWN, To blacken :

Apply the following mixture : Mix together equal parts of blue-black ink and ordinary blacking, and polish the boots with it. If well done, no one will believe that the boots or shoes were ever brown.

BOOTS, BROWN, Sea-water stains on :

To remove the stains, melt a small lump of washing soda in some hot milk. Take a clean piece of sponge, dip it in the mixture and rub it all over the shoes or boots. Put in the sun to dry. Then polish with a good brown shoe polish.

BOTTLES, To remove odours from :

If the bottle is of value, purchase some ground mustard seed and put a little into the bottle, fill it up with warm water and leave for a while. Shake well before pouring the liquid away, and rinse in cold water. No matter how strong the odour, it should have gone. If, however, there be the slightest trace of it, repeat the process.

BOTTLES, VINEGAR, To clean :

Put in some potato peelings, fill with water and allow to stand till the potato peel ferments. Then wash.

BOTTLES, WATER, STAINED, To clean :

Chop up very finely some raw potato. Add a little vinegar and put the potato and vinegar into the bottle. Shake it very well, add a little water, and again shake well. Then rinse out the bottle thoroughly. Tea leaves, salt and vinegar also clean discoloured and stained bottles.

BOTTLING FRUIT :

If your saucepan is not deep enough to take the usual fruit bottles, make a lid for it by turning another saucepan upside down, thus keeping in the steam. You then save buying the proper pans sold for the purpose, and the device answers splendidly.

BRASS, To brighten when tarnished :

Warm it, and then apply shellac melted in alcohol.

BRASS, To clean :

Mix emery powder to a paste with paraffin, then polish with a piece of old velvet.

" MALAY " BRASS :

Apply lemon and hot water, then cold water, and dry well and polish. Or use salt and wood ash, then rub the brass with **dry** tamarind. Polish **and dry** in the hot sun. No metal polish should be used.

BRASS, To renovate :

Fenders and fire irons of brass can be made **to look like** new by being re-lacquered at home. First clean them with metal polish. Obtain from a good ironmonger a bottle of cold lacquer, and apply it with a soft brush. It hardens immediately. This will keep bright if rubbed with a soft cloth and furniture polish occasionally, but do **not use** metal polish for it removes the lacquer.

BRASS BEDSTEAD or KERB, To clean :

Rub with furniture cream and afterwards polish with a soft duster.

BRASS DOOR KNOBS, When cleaning :

In order to protect the paint when cleaning brass door knobs, the following plan may be adopted. Take a piece of cardboard and cut in it a circular hole, pass this over the knob and there will be no fear of the surrounding woodwork becoming soiled.

BRASS POLISH, Indian :

Crush bathbrick to a fine powder and mix it with lubricating oil to a thin cream. Polish with a soft cloth.

BRASS WATER TAPS, Verdigris on :

When taps have been neglected and verdigris appears, clean them with an old toothbrush dipped in liquid ammonia. This will remove all stain without injury to the metal.

BREAD, To keep fresh :

Wash and dry a large potato, and put it in the bottom of your bread pan if you want bread to keep fresh for a considerable time.

BREAD, NEW, To cut :

You can cut new bread quite easily if you dip the **bread** knife into boiling water before each slice is cut.

BREAD, STALE, A use for :

Soak stale bread in water, then squeeze it as dry as possible and beat till smooth. To every pound of bread add

C.I.O.   **z**

3 oz. chopped suet, 1 teacupful flour, 1 small onion (chopped), 2 teaspoonfuls chopped parsley, $\frac{1}{4}$ teaspoonful dried mixed herbs, and pepper and salt. Mix all together, tie tightly in a cloth and boil 2 hours. When cold, cut into rounds, fry in bacon fat, and serve with bacon.

BREADCRUMBS, FRESH, To use :

If crumbled very fine, breadcrumbs may be used in puddings where flour is ordered, using four-fifths crumbs and one-fifth flour. Breadcrumbs can also be used for thickening gravy and soup.

BRICK, To use as an iron rest :

When ironing, an ordinary brick makes a far better rest for the iron than the usual metal stand. The latter is a good conductor of heat and consequently draws the heat from the iron quickly.

BROOM, WORN-OUT, A good use for :

When a sweeping broom becomes so worn in the middle that it is of no further use for sweeping, saw the head of the broom in half and insert handles into the two ends, thus making two useful hearth brushes.

BROOM-HOLDER, To make :

Put two large screws or nails into the wall about two inches apart. Drop the broom between them, handle downwards.

BRUSH, Use as clothes' sprinkler :

Clothes for ironing can be quickly sprinkled with water if a good-sized clothes brush be dipped into water and then shaken over them.

BRUSHES, BLACK-LEAD, To clean :

Wash occasionally in warm water to which soda has been added.

BRUSHES, EBONY, To wash :

Rub a little vaseline thoroughly into the wood and proceed to wash the brush in the usual way. After drying, polish with a dry duster. This prevents the wood from cracking and looking grey.

BRUSHES, SHAVING, A use for:

If you cannot get the dust out of cracks or ledges of woodwork with your duster, use an old shaving brush. These brushes can also come in for oiling a sewing machine or wringer. Also as black-lead brushes.

BUTTER, To choose:

When choosing butter put a knife into it. In salt butter, if there is anything rancid or unpleasant about its smell, it is bad. Fresh butter ought to smell like a nosegay, and be of the same colour all through. If sour in smell, it has not been sufficiently washed. If veiny and open it is probably not what it pretends to be.

BUTTER, To cream:

Butter will cream much more easily if placed in a basin which has just been rinsed with boiling hot water.

BUTTER, To salt for the winter:

Wash and well beat the butter to free it from any milky substance. Then to every pound of butter allow ¾ oz. salt and ¼ oz. of sugar. Mix thoroughly together. Pack in a stone jar. When the jar is nearly full put a piece of soft muslin over, and fill up the jar with salt. This can be removed when the butter is required for use. Tie paper over and store in a cool place.

BUTTONS, To fix on slippers:

Instead of using button fasteners, take a shoemaker's awl, bore a small hole and pass a boot lace up through the leather, then through the button, making another small hole in the leather, and passing the lace down through again, finishing off both ends of the lace with a knot.

BUTTONS, To preserve:

Cut some rounds of calico the size of the linen button required for the garment. Place three or four thicknesses together and button-hole stitch round the edge. The button is then ready to sew on. It will never *break* in the laundry, and seldom bends. It can easily be straightened, should it bend, when ironing the garment.

BUTTONS, FLAT, To sew on:

Place a pin over the holes (leaving room for the needle to pass through) and sew over the pin ; remove the pin and wind the shank of the button with thread. Secure the latter as usual. A flat button treated in this way will stay on longer than if sewn on without a shank.

BUTTONS, PEARL, To preserve when mangled:

Sew the buttons on to a tape the desired distance apart. Make button-holes on both sides of the plaquet holes instead of on one side only, then, with the tape on the inside of the garment, slot the buttons through the button-holes on the lower side of the plaquet. They can then be easily removed for ironing and washing.

CABBAGE, To make digestible:

When half-boiled, pour off the water and place in fresh boiling water.

CAKE, To keep moist:

Keep part of a loaf of bread with your cake in a tin with a close fitting lid, and the cake will not get dry.

CAKE, To remove from tin:

Place the baking tin and the cake for a few seconds in a basin of hot water. The heat loosens the cake and it can then be easily turned out. Or, stand the tin for a few moments on a damp tea-towel or dish-cloth, and the cake will then turn out easily without breaking.

CAKE, POTATO, To fry:

Put a tablespoonful of vinegar in the frying lard. This will prevent the cakes being *too greasy* when cooked.

CAKE, SPONGE, To make light:

Put a tablespoonful of tepid water in the cake mixture directly after pouring in the eggs. This gives you a beautifully light and spongy cake.

CAKE-MAKING HINTS:

To prevent the fruit from sinking, dredge a little flour over the raisins, etc., before adding them to the remainder of the ingredients. Also remember to shut the oven door very gently if it is opened while the cake is cooking. If the cake is inclined to burn at the bottom, place the tin containing it in a larger tin with two sticks across the bottom.

CANDLE ENDS, To make a polish of:
Melted and mixed with turpentine, candle ends make a good polish for stained floors.

CANDLES, To adapt to a large candlestick:
Put a piece of silver paper (tinfoil) round; the candle will burn itself out without igniting the silver paper.

CARAFES, To remove fur from:
Mix sufficient common salt, washing soda and vinegar together to make a damp mixture, to which add a few tea leaves and very small stones. Place this in the bottle and shake well. Afterwards rinse in clean cold water.

CARPETS, AXMINSTER, To sweep:
In sweeping these carpets, take care to brush them *the way of the pile*, otherwise the dust will be brushed *in* and not *out*.

CARPETS, Cleaner for:
Take sufficient Fuller's Earth and mix it to a paste with boiling water. Spread this thickly over the stain and allow it to remain for twenty-four hours. Brush the paste off with a whisk, and, in most cases, the stain will have disappeared. An *Old Carpet* that needs a thorough cleaning all over, can be rapidly treated on the floor it occupies. Thoroughly sweep it until no more dust can be brushed out, then make up a carpet soap of your own. Shred half an ounce of soap into half a pint of boiling water, add a teaspoonful of ammonia and a small lump of soda. A small brush should be lightly dipped into this and the carpet well scrubbed. Rinse this off by means of a cloth constantly wrung out almost dry in clean, warm water. Finally, rub with a perfectly dry cloth.

ANOTHER METHOD
If soot falls on your carpet, cover it with dry salt, and sweep it up carefully. If this is done quickly no trace of the soot will be left.

CARPETS, Moths in :

If carpets that have been put away or stored for some time show traces of moth, put a fine damp twill towel over the moth-eaten part, and with a very hot iron, press until the towel is dry. This will kill moth eggs and maggots.

CARPETS, To remove ink stains from :

Remove with a teaspoonful of oxalic acid, dissolved in a quarter of a pint of water.

CARPETS, SOOTY, To renew :

Rub the place marked by the soot on the carpet with a rag dipped in carbon tetrachloride. The mark must be rubbed *very well*, going round and round. Renew the rag as soon as it gets soiled. Carbon tetrachloride has slight anæsthetic properties so be careful not to inhale it.

CARPETS, WORN, To freshen :

When the treads are showing and the pile is worn off, get a small packet of dye, the colour that is most predominant in the carpet, and make a strong solution by mixing it in hot water. Apply to the worn parts with a small brush and let it dry.

CASSEROLE DISH, A makeshift :

Put your ingredients into an enamel pie-dish and cover over the top with a piece of white paper. Pleat this all round under the edge of the dish.

ANOTHER METHOD

Get a two-pound size jam jar, put a little saucer on top for a lid. Meat, milk puddings, vegetables and fish, can be cooked in this improvised casserole.

CEILINGS, PAPERED, To clean :

Mix 2 cupfuls of flour with a little cold water to make a ball of stiff paste. Roll the paste ball in dry flour and rub the paper with it. As the paste gets dirty keep dipping it in dry flour. After rubbing the paper all over with the paste, rub gently with a piece of old soft cloth.

CELLARS, To disinfect :

Sprinkle pulverised copperas, chloride of lime, or common lime, on the floors.

CELLARS, To dry :

If your cellar is damp, take two pounds of coarse kitchen salt, powder it and divide into four equal parts. Place salt in four empty tins and then put the tins in the cellar. The salt will absorb the moisture from the air. When the salt becomes saturated, stand the tins on a warm stove. The heat will cause the moisture to evaporate and make the tins of salt fit for use again.

CEMENT, Fireproof and Waterproof :

Pour enough vinegar into milk to make it curdle. Strain through a piece of muslin, and to a pint of what remains in the muslin add the whites of three eggs, and as much unslacked lime as is needed to form a suitable mash. The *oftener this cement comes into contact with fire, the harder* it becomes. It will withstand all kinds of boiling liquids. This cement *must be used as soon as it is made because it hardens* very quickly.

CHARCOAL, Value of :

Meat that has to be kept for a day or two before being cooked will remain fresh if sprinkled with charcoal. A piece of charcoal placed in the saucepan in which cabbage is boiled will prevent a disagreeable smell arising while cooking. Pieces of charcoal placed in flower vases will keep the water sweet, and if mixed with soil used for pot plants will keep it sweet.

CHEESE, To prevent drying and moulding :

Wrap it in a damp muslin cloth and sprinkle with vinegar. Keep in a cool, raised, covered dish.

CHIFFON, To wash :

Plunge white chiffon into warm soap suds, then lightly rub it between the palm of the hands. Rinse in clear warm water with a dash of ammonia in it. Squeeze out all water before putting it to dry in the sun. It will dry up into wrinkles, but smooth with a warm iron on some white flannel before it is quite dry.

CHILD'S DRESS, To let down :

Almost any material will do if you run in lines over the added piece. Use a colour to tone and run with short stitch under a longer stitch on outside. Several rows of this running is ornamental, and will hide a join or strengthen a weak part.

CHILDREN'S CLOTHING, To make nearly fireproof:

When washing put 2 oz. of alum or sal ammoniac in the rinsing water, or in the starch, and dissolve well. If they are treated in this way clothes will catch fire with difficulty.

CHIMNEYS, Care of:

Mix a pound of flowers of sulphur with $\frac{1}{2}$ lb. of powdered saltpetre, and occasionally when the fire is bright and clear, throw in an ounce or two of mixture. This removes without trouble or dust a great deal of the accumulated soot.

ANOTHER METHOD

Burn on a bright fire all kinds of tins, such as milk, salmon, fruit tins, etc., till they burn red, then lift off and throw away. They are excellent chimney cleaners.

CHIMNEY, To extinguish fire in:

Throw upon the fire the contents of the kitchen salt box and in a few seconds the flames will be extinguished.

CLOTHES BOILERS, To keep clean:

Scrub out the boiler to remove all traces of soap. Scour with a little turpentine, then wash with water and thoroughly dry.

CLOTHES LINE, To wash:

The best way to wash a clothes line is to wind it round a long board to prevent it from becoming tangled, and scrub it well with a brush.

COAL, To make last much longer:

Half a teaspoonful of saltpetre mixed with half a cup of water and poured over a scuttle of coals will not only induce a brighter fire but will make the coal last longer. A good handful of common washing soda dissolved in half a bucket of warm water if thrown over a hundredweight of coal and allowed to dry, will prolong the burning power by 25 per cent.

COAL BILL, To reduce:

Take old newspapers, paper bags, paste-board boxes and wrappings, lay them in the kitchen sink and soak in water until reduced to a pulp. Next morning squeeze and roll into balls the size of your fist. Roll in coal dust and use for stoking fires. Burn all orange and lemon skins, they give out great heat as well as a most delightful aroma. Coal dust moistened with hot dirty soda water and allowed to stand for an hour, can be used to bank up the fire when it is not needed for the time being.

COAT COLLAR, To remove grease from :

Rub with a cloth dipped in ammonia. Velvet collars may be treated in the same way, but must be held in front of a hot iron directly after to raise the pile.

COCOANUT FIBRE MATS, To clean :

Wash them with a strong, stiff brush, dipped in hot water and soda, then dip the brush in salt and water and brush them over once again. The salt helps to keep the fibre stiff. Before washing, they should be beaten right side downwards out of doors.

COD LIVER OIL STAINS, To remove :

Put the soiled garment over a soup plate and spread on the stain some carbon tetrachloride. Rub well in with a small sponge. Wash the garment in soapy water.

COFFEE, When short of milk :

Beat up an egg well, put a small portion into each cup and pour the coffee on to it.

COLLARS AND CUFFS, Glaze for :

First dip cuffs and collars in cold starch, then iron while damp. Take a piece of soft cloth or flannel, dip it into some French chalk and rub smoothly on the article on the right side. Finally, rub a piece of white curd soap over the chalk and iron the article on the right side only. The iron must not be too hot. When this treatment has been carried out the cuffs and collars will look like porcelain.

COLLARS, To iron :

When ironing collars, both stiff and soft, place a small round cake tin in the oven and put the collars in as they are ironed. This keeps them a round shape and stiffens them.

Keep the oven door open so that it does not get too hot. Leave the collars in only for a few minutes.

COPPER KETTLE, To clean :

Fill a grubby copper kettle with hot water and polish the outside with a rag dipped in buttermilk. If buttermilk cannot be obtained, sour milk may be used. If this is done once or twice it will keep the kettle in very good condition.

Before cleaning copper kettles fill them with boiling water. They will be found to polish more quickly.

COPPER WARE, To clean :

Take half a lemon, quarter it and use it for rubbing soiled copper. Let lemon juice remain on the copper for a few hours, then rub off with a soft rag. Finish re-polishing with furniture polish.

CORKS, To make air-tight :

Dip them into hot mutton fat and wax mixed in equal proportions. If the corks are treated like this, fruit and pickles will keep better, and retain their good colour.

CORNERS, To crochet easily :

The corners in squares of crochet are often puzzling as to turns. Place a hand mirror with a narrow frame upright on the lace. Adjust the mirror until the reflection forms a right angle with the lace. Crochet what you see on lace and mirror.

CORNERS, To wash before painting :

Take a fine wooden skewer and wrap a small piece of flannel round the point. Dip in soapy water and clean out the corners, then dip in clean water and use again.

CRACK IN IRON STOVE, To mend:

Make a mixture of equal quantities of wood ashes passed through a sieve, and of finely powdered clay, add a little common salt, and moisten with water. Apply to the stove when cold. The cement hardens when heated, and will neither split nor crack.

CRACK IN A ROOM, To plaster :

If you can secure no plaster, use a piece of calico a larger size than the hole and paste it well with any paste used for papering. Then stick the calico well over the hole, and when dry it stretches and allows you to paper over it.

CURTAIN FITTINGS, METAL :

To keep these in good condition, rub them periodically with a cloth slightly moistened with sweet oil. This will allow the rings, which may also be treated in similar manner, to run freely and prevents their jamming.

CURTAIN PINS AND RINGS, To clean :

Put them in a bowl with hot water and vinegar, two parts vinegar to one of water. Let them stand for a few hours and then rub on a coarse cloth and they will look like new.

CUSTARD POWDER, To make an excellent :

Take 7 drops of oil of nutmeg, 14 drops of oil of bitter almonds, 5 oz. cornflour, 6 oz. dried arrowroot. Mix all the ingredients *well together*.

DARNING, Hints on :

Huckaback towels showing holes, and all knitted garments, should be darned diagonally. In darning damask the pattern should be followed instead of making a square darn, and no loops must be left. For dresses, take a strand of ravelling from a straight seam, darn on the right side, but put in the needle at the place where it comes out and do not let the thread appear on the surface.

DOOR, Creaking :

A creaking door can be silenced by rubbing the hinges well with the lead of a pencil or a lump of dripping.

DRIPPING, To clarify :

Chop the dripping, and put it into a saucepan with enough water to cover well. Let it boil without a lid on the pan, till the liquid no longer looks milky, but is oily. Cool a little, then strain through a coarse piece of calico into a clean basin.

To clarify dripping which comes from meat. Put into a basin and pour over sufficient boiling water to cover it. Stir thoroughly and leave to cool, then the clear white dripping will form a solid lump on the top.

DUST-BIN, To make sanitary :

Burn a couple of newspapers, or two or three handfuls of straw in them each time they are emptied. This will remove every trace of grease or damp from the iron, and render the dust-bin quite free from any unpleasant smell. A little lime can be put at the bottom, if liked.

EGGS, To preserve :

Procure a tin of silicate of soda, or " water glass," as it is more commonly called. Dissolve this as directed, and when quite cold pour over the eggs, which have been placed in stone jars. Cover them closely. Eggs should keep fresh for months, but see that they are perfectly fresh before preserving.

EGGS, A substitute for :

One tablespoonful of tapioca, soaked for one or two hours in enough water to cover, is useful for binding rissoles or vegetable roasts in place of beaten eggs.

ANOTHER METHOD

If a tablespoonful of vinegar be put into a cake instead of an egg, the same result will be achieved at less cost.

EGG STAINS, To remove :

When table linen is stained with egg it should be soaked in cold water before being laundered.

EIDERDOWN QUILT, To wash :

Add a tablespoonful of household ammonia to a good lather of soap jelly and warm water. Soak the quilt in this for ten minutes, then squeeze and flop up and down for some time. If it still looks dirty, put in a fresh lather, then rinse twice in lukewarm water, to which has been added a small quantity of ammonia. Pass through the wringer and hang in the open air, taking it off the line repeatedly to shake well.

ENAMEL, HOME-MADE :

Finely crush a stick of sealing wax of the desired colour, place it in a bottle containing a small quantity of methylated spirits, shake thoroughly until completely dissolved, when the enamel will be ready for use.

ENAMEL BATH, To clean:

Moisten a tablespoonful of dry kitchen salt with a little spirits of turpentine, and scour the bath well with this, using an old leather or soft rag. Wash afterwards with warm soapy water and the result will astonish you.

ENAMELLED FURNITURE, To clean:

Remove all the dirty marks with a flannel dipped in methylated spirit, then wash at once with tepid water to which has been added a little fine oatmeal. Do not use soap or soda.

ENAMELLED FURNITURE, To polish:

Wash with soapy water, then rub well with flannel and a little paraffin oil. Polish with a clean soft duster.

ENAMELLED KITCHENWARE, White, To preserve:

This can be kept in first-class condition if occasionally it is put into a large vessel of cold water to which a tablespoonful of lye has been added. Put on the stove and allow to come to the boil, then wash in the usual way.

ENAMEL WARE, To stop leaks in:

If the holes are not very large, mix some bricklayer's cement to a thick paste and put it on the hole or holes, then allow to stand for two or three days to set. Rub over with emery cloth when dry.

FELT HATS, White, to clean:

Apply a paste of powdered calcined magnesia and water. When the paste has dried on the hat, brush it off with a clean brush.

FERNS AND GRASSES, To preserve:

Place them between sheets of blotting paper and leave them under a heavy weight for 48 hours.

FIRE BARS, To prevent turning red:

Rub with a raw onion or weak treacle and water, then apply the black lead with a rag or soft brush.

FISH-BONE, To remove:

The juice of half a lemon, slowly sucked, will often remove a fish-bone that has become lodged in the throat.

FISHY SMELL, To remove from saucepan :

Empty the tea leaves from the teapot into the pan, cover with water ; leave for few minutes, then rinse out and all taste or smell of fish will have gone.

FLANNEL, To remove scorch from :

Rub a lemon into the scorched part, and leave on it as much juice and pith as possible. Place the flannel in a strong light to dry, then wash, dry and iron.

FLANNELS, Coloured, To wash :

Do not rub with soap, but wash in tepid water in which soap jelly has been dissolved along with a little salt for pink and scarlet, and a teaspoonful of ammonia for blue. Wash quickly and rinse in salt and water, then shake and hang out immediately to dry in the open air, but not in the sun.

FLIES, To get rid of :

An excellent plan for trapping flies is to dip a sponge in boiling water and place it in a saucer. Pour on this half a teaspoonful of oil of lavender. This will give off a delicious perfume similar to violets, which for some reason, is not at all agreeable to flies. Moisten sponge with boiling water about twice a day, and with oil not more than once a week.

FLY MARKS, To remove from silk shades :

Dust stained shades or parts that are " fly soiled " with finely powdered French chalk. Mix together very well 1½ oz. of soft soap, ¼ pint methylated spirit, and ¼ pint of water. Rub this mixture carefully and lightly on the stains, both on the top of the shade and inside, using a soft rag or sponge. Wash the parts treated, with lukewarm water, and press gently with not too hot an iron.

FLOOR POLISH, Economical :

To mix. Melt 2 wax candles or oddments of candles, and ½ lb. shredded soap in 1 gill of boiling water, stir well. When cold add 2d. turpentine and 2d. linseed oil. Keep well covered.

FLOOR STAIN, A cheap :

Dissolve 1 oz. of permanganate of potash in 2 quarts of boiling water. Apply evenly to the floor with a good brush, and then polish with beeswax and turpentine.

FLOORS, Varnished, To wash:

Never wash varnished floors with hot water. Use a cloth wrung out in a little lukewarm water and dry each part as it is washed.

FOUNTAIN PEN, To clean:

Unscrew all the parts, soak them in vinegar for half an hour, and rinse in warm water.

FRENCH POLISH, The care of:

As a general rule French polished furniture should only be cleaned with a soft duster and a little water applied to remove any spots.

FRUIT PRESERVING HINTS:

1. Observe the strictest cleanliness.
2. Use fresh, ripe and *dry* fruit, and avoid damp over-ripe or under-ripe fruit.
3. Use best, pure, cane sugar only.
4. Allow from ¾ lb. of sugar to every pound of sweet fruit. Acid fruits require 1 lb. sugar to 1 lb. of fruit.
5. Have a steady but bright fire.
6. Boil continually, stir and skim frequently.
7. Do not fill the preserving pan too full.
8. Boil the fruit until it jellies or sets when cold.
9. Have the jars or pots perfectly clean and dry before filling.
10. Either cover the jars immediately or leave until the jars are quite cold, and cover with parchment paper.
11. Label the jars or pots with name of jam and date when made.
12. Store them in a cool but dry place, free from damp or draught.

FRUIT STAINS, To remove from linen:

Draw the stained part very tightly over a large round bowl or bucket. Stand on a chair and from as great a height as possible pour boiling water on to the stain until it disappears. Use a long-spouted gardener's can, or you may burn your arm. If the stains will not come out, try rubbing with salts of lemon, then rinse in boiling water, wash well out in blood-heat water.

FUR, To cut :

Damp the skin side and stretch the fur on a board with the fur side down. Fasten with small wire nails as fine as a pin. When the skin is thoroughly dry, measure and chalk. Cut it with a paring knife or any knife sharp enough. Sew carefully with fine stitches, using cotton thread. Never cut fur with scissors.

FUR, White, To keep in summer :

Beat and put in the sun for about 2 days, then sprinkle with magnesia and store.

FURNITURE CREAM, Home-made :

1 oz. beeswax, $\frac{1}{2}$ oz. white wax, $\frac{1}{2}$ oz. castile soap, $\frac{1}{2}$ pint turpentine, $\frac{1}{2}$ pint boiling water. Cut the soap up finely and boil it in the water. Pour it over the wax. Let it stand for 12 hours, then add the turpentine.

FURNITURE, To remove dents from .

Get a piece of brown paper and fold it five or six times, put it in hot water until it is completely saturated. Place on the dented part and then press it with a hot flat-iron until all the moisture is evaporated out of the paper. By that time the dent will have disappeared.

FURNITURE, To protect :

Place a thick sheet of white blotting paper under the covers of dressing tables, sideboards, etc. This will absorb any liquid which may be spilt before it can reach and harm the wood.

FURNITURE, To remove stains from :

Rub lightly with olive oil and methylated spirits.

FURNITURE, To kill worms in :

Apply paraffin to the parts affected. Insert it with a knitting needle into the largest holes daily for ten days.

FURNITURE, Upholstered, To clean :

Dust all the furniture well, and then with a vacuum cleaner continue removing the dust. Get some hot bran and rub well into the soiled parts. When all the dirt has been removed, brush off all trace of bran. Sponge with water or petrol and leave to dry.

FURNITURE, Velvet or Plush, To clean:

A piece of clean chamois leather wrung out in cold water is the best duster for velvet and plush.

FURNITURE REVIVER:

Take equal parts of turpentine, methylated spirits, vinegar and paraffin oil. Shake all together in a bottle, and the mixture is then ready for use. Put a little on a soft rag, and rub the furniture well, then polish with a soft duster Shake the bottle well before using.

GAME, To test if hung:

Pull a feather from the plumage at the lower part of the back near the tail. If it comes out quite easily the bird is " high " enough for the average consumer.

GARDEN FURNITURE, To preserve:

Rub with linseed oil periodically to prevent splitting and cracking.

GAS FIRES, Discoloured, To clean:

When a gas-fire is stained with smoke, sprinkle it liberally with salt when cold. When the gas is lit it will burn the salt away and leave the fire quite clean.

GAS TOASTER, To make:

Bore holes in a biscuit tin lid, then stretch wires over the lid from side to side. To toast, place on ring with the bread resting on the wires.

GLASS, CUT, Care of:

Wash the glass in warm soapy water made from soap flakes, using a small brush to get into the intricate parts. Dry with a fluffless linen cloth, and then rub with some soft tissue paper after rinsing in cold water containing a little vinegar. To induce a high polish, brush with a little French chalk. All methods that scratch the glass should be avoided, and for that reason ashes and sand, and all gritty or frictional scouring powders are taboo.

GLOVES, Light Kid or Suede, To clean :

Take a washing basin and throw in a little petrol. Throw in the gloves and wash well. Hang on a line (not in the sun) and let the wind dry them.

ANOTHER METHOD

Mix a little oatmeal and benzine to a paste. Rub on the gloves until it is quite dry, and the oatmeal falls off in flakes.

GLOVES, White Wash Leather, To wash :

Take some lukewarm water, add a little ammonia, and wash the gloves well in this water. Take them out and squeeze out well. Have ready another basin of warm soapy water. Wash the gloves in this. Do not squeeze the soap out. Fold between two towels and dry slowly.

GLUE, when dried in the bottle :

A little vinegar put into a bottle of dried-up glue will moisten and make it liquid again.

GREENS, To boil :

Add a piece of fat about the size of half a crown to the water in which greens are boiled, and the water will not boil over.

HANDBAGS, To clean :

Box calf and suede can be cleaned by brushing with powdered pumice, or, even better, by rubbing very gently with a small emery board. Finally, polish the bag (not suede) with colourless shoe cream. Rub off the cream well with a soft cloth. If this is not done the cream will stain your gloves.

HAM, An excellent way to boil :

Wrap your ham in greaseproof paper, and put a small Spanish onion in the water with the ham. When the ham is tender, leave it in the water until it is nearly cold to keep the flesh moist and improve the flavour.

INK STAINS, To remove :

Most ink stains on linen can be removed by rubbing with a slice of juicy lemon.

ANOTHER METHOD

Well rub any ink stains on linen with a ripe tomato cut in half, and the stains will then disappear in the wash. This remedy also proves satisfactory in removing ink from dark cloth ; the article should be sponged with cold rain water after the tomato is applied.

IRONING, To iron table napkins :

Put the damp napkins out flat, right side up, with hems, if any, at the side. Iron the hems first, then the selvedges, taking care to keep them straight. Then iron the centre. Turn over and press the wrong side. Fold in three equal parts lengthways, ironing the folds well. Then fold in three and press. Fold the strip in equal parts to form a square.

IRONMOULD, To prevent :

Before using a copper boiler, rub it well with a clean paraffin rag. Be sure always to fill the copper quite full of water. When finished never let the soapy water remain in with the idea of using it for cleaning purposes, as this is almost sure to cause ironmould. A capital idea is to empty the copper before the fire is quite out. This enables the copper to become absolutely dry.

JAM, BURNING OF, To prevent :

Drop a clean half-crown into the preserving pan when making jam. This prevents the jam sticking to the bottom.

JAM, To keep :

Store in a cool cupboard on shelves covered with white oil cloth. See that the cupboard is kept as dark as possible.

JAPANNED TRAYS, To remove marks from :

Use sweet oil. Rub it in well till all the marks disappear, then polish the tray with dry flour and a soft cloth. This method is especially good for removing hot water marks.

JELLY, To set quickly :

Stand the mould in a basin. Fill the basin with water to reach nearly to the top of the mould, then put a handful of kitchen salt into the water. The jelly will set in half the usual time.

JEWELLERY, To clean :

Apply camphorated chalk with a soft old toothbrush. Brush the chalk off again, and polish with a piece of plush or velvet. Gold and silver—any trinkets, in fact—may be treated in this way with excellent results.

KETTLE, To remove fur from :

Sal ammoniac will remove the fur from inside a kettle. Fill the kettle with cold water, add a little sal ammoniac to it, and boil. All the foreign matter collected round the sides will soon dissolve. Rinse the kettle well before using.

KNIFE HANDLES, To clean :

To clean and to keep the ivory from turning yellow, rub the handles well with a cut lemon. Afterwards wash them in soapy water, and dry immediately.

KNIFE HANDLES, To secure :

When a knife blade comes out of the handle, fix it in with a mixture of resin and brick dust, using equal quantities. Fill up the hole in the handle, and then heat the tang of the knife and press it into the resin-filled hole.

KNIVES, To store :

Rub the blades with mutton fat or vaseline and roll them in brown paper. This will prevent them from rusting.

KNIVES, RUSTY, To clean :

Stick the knives into the garden soil or a flower pot. Leave them there for an hour or two, then rub well with a damp cloth dipped in ashes, and clean in the usual way.

LACE, To iron :

Cover with clean white tissue paper. This prevents the shiny look seen on washed lace.

LACE, To mend simply :

Take a piece of American cloth of contrasting colour, place it underneath and tack it to the torn lace. It will be an easier job for the mender and she will notice the missing stitches quickly.

LACQUER-WARE, To renovate :

Place a sponge in warm soapy water, wring it out almost dry, then wash the lacquer-ware. Rinse with the sponge wrung out in clear rain water, and finally polish with a soft cloth. Lacquered furniture may be rubbed over with oil. This prevents the lacquer from cracking.

LAMPS, To prevent smoking :

To prevent a lamp from smoking, soak the wick in strong vinegar and dry well before use.

LEATHER, To renew :

Boil $\frac{1}{2}$ pint of linseed oil for 1 minute. Stand till it is nearly cold, then pour in $\frac{1}{2}$ pint of vinegar and stir till thoroughly mixed. Bottle and shake before using. Pour a little on a flannel and rub it well into the leather. Turn the flannel as it gets dirty, then rub with soft dusters till the polish is restored.

LEATHER UPHOLSTERY, To remove grease from :

Grease spots on leather upholstery are best treated with spirits of sal ammoniac. Dab the spots, allowing time for the liquid to act, then wash off with clean water. If the marks are of long standing the process may need to be repeated two or three times.

LEMONS, To keep fresh :

They can be kept quite fresh if they are placed in a jar of cold water and the water is changed every day.

LETTUCE, To crisp :

A few drops of lemon juice dropped into a basin of water in which you wash your lettuce will make it crisp, and remove all sand and slugs. Do not use salt ; salt makes lettuce flabby.

LINOLEUM, To lay :

Before laying linoleum, leave it in a room with a fairly warm temperature, or in a room that has the sun on it all day, so that the warmth may penetrate to the centre of the roll. Treated thus there is less risk of the floorcloth cracking during the process of laying. Then place the linoleum in position and cut to fit, but do not tack it until several days have elapsed. This allows the linoleum to " tread out " and so prevents the unsightly bulges which not infrequently occur.

LINOLEUM, To scrub :

Add a little paraffin to the water. It takes out dirt and grease, and gives a beautiful polish.

LOOKING GLASSES, To clean :

Rub with a rag dipped in methylated spirit and give a final polish with finely powdered blue.

MACKINTOSH, To renovate :

Boil half a pint of linseed oil and add to it 20 drops of trebene. Apply the mixture, while hot, to the mackintosh with a brush. After a couple of days, wash over the back, or wrong side, with an india-rubber solution reduced to a cream with methylated spirits. After two days the coat will be ready for use.

MACKINTOSH, RUBBER, To mend :

Apply a rubber solution to a piece of the material, and place it over the tear or rent. Then take a little French chalk and rub it over the patch. It will remove all traces of stickiness.

MATS, made from old army puttees :

Damp and iron the puttees well, then cut them into strips of equal length. Divide them in half and lay one half of the strips cross-ways over the other half, at the same time interlacing them to give a draught-board effect. Finish off the edges with binding.

MATS, TABLE, Labour saving :

Cut squares out of white oil baize, scallop round the edges, then ornament with painted flowers or stencils ; or leave plain. A damp cloth will soon remove stains. Valuable for nursery tables.

MEAT, Good pickle for :

To 4 gallons of water add 1 lb. brown sugar, 2 oz. salt-petre, and 6 oz. bay salt. Put the mixture in a pot to boil, skim carefully as scum rises. Take the liquor off and let it stand till quite cold before using.

MEDICINE CHEST, Handy, To make:

Take the top of an old grandfather's clock and remove all the worn out works. Glue neat little shelves inside and place it in a convenient place in your bedroom.

MICE HOLES, To stop up:

Corks dipped in turpentine are excellent to stop up mice holes.

MILDEW, ON LINEN, To remove:

Spots or large stains of mildew should be moistened and spread with finely powdered chalk, which must be well rubbed in. Then wash in the ordinary way. If the spots are of long standing it may be necessary to repeat the process.

ANOTHER METHOD

Dissolve 1½ oz. of chloride of lime in a quart of boiling water. Strain the liquid through a cloth and soak the mildewed articles (damping the articles well first), for several hours, and wash out well in cold water.

MILDEWED SILVER:

Try rubbing mildewed silver with paraffin and prepared chalk. If the mildew has really eaten into the silver, however, it will be impossible to remove the marks.

MILK, To keep fresh in hot weather:

Get an ordinary screw-stoppered bottle and a piece of blanket cut out to the size of the bottle, sew it round and cover the bottle. Dip it in cold water and hang it in the shade out of doors and you will find the milk keep icy cold. Only be sure to keep the blanket wet.

MOTHS, To remove from pianos:

Should moths get into a piano, make up a mixture of turpentine, benzoline and oil of lavender, and squirt this inside the instrument by means of a scent spray or small syringe. Use seven parts of benzoline to one of turpentine, adding a few drops of the oil.

MUSTARD, Value of:

In cases of poisoning, a tablespoonful of mustard stirred in ½ tumbler of warm water is a safe and quick-acting emetic.

Threatened colds and chills depart if the feet are given a hot water and mustard bath. For bad chest colds, a mustard poultice is excellent. To cure chilblains (unbroken) mix a teaspoonful of mustard with ½ pint of turpentine, leave one day, strain off, and rub the liquid on the chilblains and they will depart.

MUTTON, FROZEN, To improve flavour of:

Put the joint into a bowl, cover with boiling water in which you have dissolved a piece of soda the size of a hazel nut. After about 20 minutes take the joint out, wash with cold water, then dry on a cloth, and season before cooking. Treated thus, foreign mutton tastes equal to English. If the joint is too large to soak properly, turn it over when half the time has elapsed, and allow a few more minutes for drawing.

NAIL HOLES IN WOOD:

Can be filled up quite easily. Mix some sawdust with some glue, stirring until you get a stiff paste, then fill the holes with the paste. It will soon become hard, and the places can then be painted over with the necessary colour.

OIL PAINTING, To clean:

Rub the juice of a nice freshly cut potato over the painting, very gently, when the potato gets dirty cut off a slice and continue rubbing.

OMELET, if it sticks to pan:

Heat the pan well before using again, then scour it out with salt, using a greased soft paper. Always let the butter be smoking hot before putting your mixture in the pan.

ONION, To remove smell from hands:

A little mustard rubbed into the hands after peeling onions will remove the odour.

ORANGE AND LEMON PEEL, To use:

Get a thick-skinned orange or lemon, cut the rind very, very finely off and place it in bottles. Pour good brandy on the skins and let it stand for some months. It makes a delightful drink and flavouring for cakes, etc.

Another way to get just the pure orange and lemon oil is to cut the orange or lemon into quarters and squeeze the oil out of the skins into a wide-necked bottle.

Another use for the peels is to put them into a hot oven, and when perfectly dry, use them for lighting fires. Or dry them in the oven, and when perfectly dry, pound them up finely and store them in a bottle, to use for flavouring cakes and sweets.

PAINT, To clean :

Squeeze a clean cloth out of hot water. Dip it in whitening and with this rub the paint till all dirt is removed. Rinse well with clean water ; dry with a soft cloth and polish with a chamois leather. The whitening will not injure the most delicate colours.

PAINT, To remove smell of :

The smell of paint can easily be removed from a room by standing in it a pail of cold water containing a large handful of hay, or a cut-up onion or two. Leave the pail in the room for some hours and then if the paint smell still lingers throw away the water, fill up the pail with fresh water and hay or onions, and leave for 3 hours longer.

PAINT, VARNISHED, To polish :

Cedar oil applied with a soft duster will clean and polish varnished paint.

PANTRY, To keep dry :

Place a two-pound jar of lime in a small damp larder or pantry, the air can be kept dry, pure and sweet.

PAPIER MACHÉ, To clean :

Wash now and again in warm water and when quite dry rub over with sweet oil. If a high polish is desired, a good wax polish may be applied with a soft clean cloth, rubbed well in, and well polished.

PARSLEY, To dry for winter :

Take a bunch of parsley and, holding it by the stems, dip it in boiling water till it is a vivid green. Then put it in a quick oven to dry. Rub between the hands or through a coarse sieve.

PASTE FOR SCRAP BOOKS, To make :

Take the best laundry starch and add sufficient cold soft water to make a smooth paste. Pour on boiling water until it is clear and jelly-like. It is ready for use as soon as cool.

PASTE, To moisten :

Wet a rag and put it into your paste bottle. Cork tightly and your paste will never become too dry. In a week or two, when the cloth becomes dry, moisten again.

PASTRY, To keep crisp :

When making pastry that is to be served cold, use milk for moistening it. The pastry will keep short and crisp longer than if mixed with water.

PEEL, Lemon, dipped in salt :

Removes hot water marks on ivory. Rub afterwards with good furniture cream.

PEELING ONIONS, Hint on :

When peeling onions, begin at the root end and peel upwards, then the odour from the onions will scarcely affect your eyes at all.

PEPPER POTS, To prevent clogs in :

Place a dried pea in the pepper pot and it will prevent the holes in the lid from becoming clogged.

PEWTER, To clean :

Mix together 1 oz. each of rotten stone, ammonia and soft soap, and form it into a paste with boiling water. Mix well and keep the preparation in a covered jar. When it is to be used rub a little on the pewter, and then polish with a soft cloth dipped in powdered whitening.

PILLOWS, How to wash :

Empty out the down or feathers from the ticking case into a butter muslin bag, a bit larger than the ticking case. Sew the muslin bag up lightly and put it into a bathful of warm, soapy water. Squeeze the bag and contents under water. Use two or three waters if necessary, until no more dirt comes from the feathers. Then rinse thoroughly in warm water. Squeeze as much water as possible from the feathers and hang to dry in an airy position

PIPES AND TAPS, To thaw when frozen :
Heat a fire-brick in the oven, or several if you require them. When very hot, place them as near the frozen pipes or taps as possible. This will promote a slow thaw.

POTATOES, To bake :
Potatoes will bake more quickly if they are first allowed to stand in hot water for about 15 minutes.

POTATOES, MASHED :
Baking powder added to potatoes while mashing and beating, makes them much lighter—¼ teaspoonful is sufficient.

POTATO WATER, To make :
Dresses, carpets, rugs and all sorts of woollen garments can be cleaned with potato water without injury to their colour. Put a pint of water in a basin and grate into it two raw potatoes. Then strain through a sieve, allowing the liquid to run into another bowl containing another pint of water. Let this settle, then strain off the clear part into a bottle for future use. Dip a sponge into the liquid. With it rub the soiled garments carefully, and then wash them with clear cold water.

POT-POURRI, To make :
Scented rose petals should be gathered when they are dry and as they become available, and placed in the jar. Sprinkle salt on them as each fresh lot is put in. After they have stood for a week, a mixture prepared with the following ingredients is added : 40 drops of oil of lavender, 4 oz. orris root, 3 oz. oil of cloves, 10 drops of oil of cinnamon and 6 oz. angelica root. The petals of any fragrant roses are suitable. See also ROSE JAR.

POULTRY, To keep fresh :
Place a large peeled onion inside the birds that are not to be used or cooked for a day or two.

PRESERVING, Jam covers for :

Cut a piece of good white blotting paper the size of the top of the jam jar, put the blotting paper on the top of the thin paper which is covering the jam, then cover with parchment and fasten down with elastic bands. This will prevent any damp or air coming in contact with the jam.

PUDDING, SUET, To lighten :

Use the same quantity of stale bread, soaked in cold water and thoroughly squeezed, as of suet, and the pudding will be much lighter.

PUDDING, YORKSHIRE, To lighten .

Add a tablespoonful of hot water to the batter before putting it into the boiling fat.

PUTTY, To loosen :

When a new pane has to be inserted in a window, pass a red-hot poker slowly over the old putty, and it will then come out quite easily.

RAINSPOTS, To remove :

Hold the spotted parts over the steam coming from the spout of a kettle of boiling water. Shake the garment in the steam until moist, then continue to shake until it is dry.

RICE, To boil :

Add a little lemon juice to the water. This makes the rice white and grainy when cooked.

ROSE JAR, To make :

Gather lemon verbena, geranium, roses and lavender. Pull off all the petals and dry them slowly and thoroughly, *but not in the sun*. Put the rose leaves at the bottom of your jar, and sprinkle with salt. Add half the dried lavender and whatever other petals you have been able to find, and put in a few cracked cloves, some small pieces of cinnamon stick, and sprinkle with salt. Then some more rose leaves and a repetition of the first process. When the jar is full put in a few drops of eau de Cologne and 2 oz. of powdered orris root. Cover the jar for a few weeks. Be sure the leaves are perfectly dry, if not the mixture will not keep. Stir well from time to time.

RUGS, To keep flat at edges :

Take a piece of straight, boned petersham, from two to three inches in width, cut a piece the width of the rug, turn the rug on to the wrong side, place the petersham with its edge to the edge of the rug and oversew, taking care to turn it in at both ends to make it tidy. Oversew both edges of petersham. This will prevent the ends of the rug from curling up.

SAFETY STRAP for children :

Purchase a cheap pair of children's reins from a toy shop. Fasten the small straps round the child's waist, and slip the long reins round the table leg or the leg of a firm chair, and you can leave a little child in safety while you are out of the room.

SATIN, BLACK, To renovate :

Peel and slice two large raw potatoes into a basin. Cover with a pint of water, add a pinch of salt and stand all night. Sponge satin on the right side with this water, and wipe it slightly with a cloth. Iron on the wrong side.

SAUCEPAN, BURNT, To clean :

A burnt saucepan should be filled with cold water to which plenty of soda has been added. Let it stand for an hour or so, then heat the water slowly and allow it to simmer for a few minutes. The burnt particles will then come off quite easily.

SAUCEPANS AND BAKING TINS, To clean :

Take ½ lb. powdered whitening and 1 quart of water. Scrub the soiled inside with the mixture. Wash off with very hot water, and polish up the pans, etc., with a nice soft clean cloth.

SAUCEPANS, To keep boiling :

Three or four saucepans can be kept boiling over a gas ring if three or four builders' bricks are placed round it— the bricks, touching in the centre, over the gas ring.

SCENT BALLS, To make :

Buy a wax candle of good quality. If coloured, so much the better. Cut the wax into small pieces and put these in a tin. Then sprinkle some perfume freely over the lumps and finally melt the wax by placing the tin on a stove. Stir all the time so that the perfume is incorporated with the wax. When the wax is firm, but not hard, roll it into balls and put them aside to set.

SCENTED SOAP, To make :

Shred best yellow soap into an empty salt jar and put it into a saucepan of hot water on the fire. Slowly melt it down. When melted removed from the stove and add a few drops of oil of lavender, verbena or violet. Put in the oil drop by drop until the right strength of scent is obtained. When cooling, turn out and knead the soap, thus working the oil right through. Mould into shapes required and when cold wrap in grease paper and store. The longer new soap is kept before it is used, the less it will be wasted in use.

SCORCH MARKS, To remove :

Take $\frac{1}{4}$ lb. Fuller's earth, $\frac{1}{4}$ lb. washing soda, 1 pint vinegar, and two onions. Peel and slice the onions, then crush them in a basin. Add the vinegar and Fuller's earth. Mix well together. Put into a pan with the soda and simmer for 10 minutes. Strain through muslin and bottle. Apply with a piece of linen. Rinse well afterwards.

SERGE SKIRT, DARK, To clean :

Have a basin of very hot water. Take a nail brush. Place the skirt on a flat table, dip the brush in the hot water, and brush the skirt from waist to hem. Go over every inch and change the hot water as soon as it is dirty or cold. Hang the skirt up in the air until it is almost dry. Then iron on the wrong side until perfectly dry.

SEWING MACHINE, Care of :

Keep your machine covered when you are not using it. Oil once a week and well rub off all traces of the oil with a soft rag. Dust the machine well before using it and try the stitch on an old piece of rag before you sew the article you mean to stitch.

SHAWLS, WHITE WOOLLEN, To clean :

Spread a cloth over a table and on it stretch the shawl to be cleaned. Sprinkle it well with finely powdered starch and fold, sprinkling starch at each fold. Leave for a short time, then rub well together with both hands and shake off the starch.

SHOE POLISH, To soften :
Moisten with a little turpentine.

SHOES, BROWN LEATHER :
These can always look well polished. Each morning rub them well with the inside skin of a banana. Let them dry, then polish with a soft piece of rag. Afterwards they should be polished with a good brown shoe cream.

SHOES, LIGHT-COLOURED, To clean :
Rub with a paste of petrol and bran. Cover thickly with the paste, leave to dry for ten minutes, then shake off and dust with a clean damp cloth.

SHOES, PATENT LEATHER, Care of :
Take a soft rag and rub sweet oil into the leather twice a week.

SHOES, PATENT LEATHER, To clean :
Dip a rag in a little petrol. Rub the shoes well, then polish with a clean piece of soft rag.

SHOES, PATENT LEATHER, To renew :
Patent shoes should never be cleaned with ordinary shoe polish. Keep a small bottle of black spirit enamel handy, and when the shoes are cracked and shabby, apply a coating of enamel with a small paint brush.

SHOES, SMALL, Trees for :
Use whalebones or corset steels a little longer than the shoes. Wind them with narrow ribbon, then, bending them, slip one into each slipper. The ends of the steel will press gently against the toe and the back of the shoes, and keep them in shape.

SINK WASTE BASKET, Substitute for :
Place an ordinary flower pot in the sink for all waste pieces. The hole at the bottom allows for drainage. This

takes up less room than an ordinary sink basket and can be easily cleaned.

SLEEVES, To put in a dress or coat :

Take the tape measure and measure $2\frac{1}{2}$ inches from the under-arm seam, place a pin to mark the distance, then place the front seam of the sleeve to it.

SPATS, LIGHT COLOURED, To clean :

Peel a large potato and grate it in a basin. With this, sponge the gaiters or spats thoroughly all over, making them quite wet. Hang them up to dry and then brush well. The gaiters will then look quite new.

SPONGE, To clean :

Take a teaspoonful of permanganate of potash, dissolve it in a quart of warm water, and work the sponge in it for 10 minutes. Rinse in several clean waters.

SPOONS AND FORKS, To keep clean :

After washing allow them to stand for a few minutes in a jugful of soapy water containing a little ammonia.

STAINS, To treat :

The first essential is the treatment of any stains before washing.

Tea stains must be washed out in cold water, and then in boiling water ; they should be treated at once. A *coffee stain* must not be treated with cold water ; boiling water must be poured through several times until the mark disappears. A *cocoa stain* is treated like a tea stain. A *grass stain* should be wet with cold water, covered with cream of tartar and put in the sun. A *grease stain* on a light material can be removed by making a paste of Fuller's earth and cold water, covering the mark with it, allowing it to dry, then brushing off and renewing until the grease has been absorbed. This method does not affect the colour in any material. *Machine oil* stains should be covered with lard, washed with cold water, and then with hot soap and water. Or they can be simply rubbed with petrol or benzine on a clean cloth, if the stains are on material which will not wash.

STARCH GLOSS, To make:

Take ½ oz. powdered French chalk, 1 oz. powdered borax and ½ oz. spermaceti. Shake the spermaceti across the grain. Mix it with the other ingredients and rub to a powder. Add 1 teaspoonful to a pint of starch. This gives smooth ironing and lovely gloss.

STARCH, To save:

Place any left-over starch on one side, and when it settles drain off the clear water. Place the basin in the oven for 5 minutes, when the starch will form a hard cake.

STEEL, To keep bright:

Mix sweet oil and emery powder to a paste and apply it to the steel with a soft flannel. Then polish off with another piece of soft flannel.

STEEL, RUSTY, To clean:

Cut a large onion in half. Rub the cut halves on the *rust* marks. Leave the juice on for 2 days, then wash off and polish with turpentine and bathbrick.

STOCKINGS, BLACK, To wash:

Add a teaspoonful of pure malt vinegar to the rinsing water. This will preserve the colour and prevent stockings from turning a rusty black.

STRAW HATS, WHITE, To clean:

Brush all the dirt out, then apply salts of lemon. Dry the hats in the shade.

SUEDE BAG, To renovate:

Rub the bag with emery paper and brush very well afterwards with a soft brush.

SUEDE CUFFS AND COLLARS, To clean:

Take a new, soft, baby's hair-brush, dip it into petrol, and brush the collars and cuffs until all dirt is removed. Finish by using a good dry suede cleaner.

TAFFETA, To clean:

To clean taffeta, soak it in water in which 2 tablespoonfuls of salt have been dissolved, and then wash it in lukewarm water in which some ivory soap has been dissolved. To stiffen, add ½ teaspoonful of borax to the rinsing water. Do not wring. Hang the taffeta on the line and press before it is thoroughly dry.

TAR MARKS, To remove:

Soak a piece of white rag in eucalyptus oil and rub it on the affected part until the latter is quite clean. This method is suitable for the most delicate materials.

TEA LEAVES, Their use:

Never throw away tea leaves. When cleaning your tea-pot, squeeze the leaves very dry, throw them into a jar, and mix them with a little coarse kitchen salt. When turning out a room that has a thick carpet on the floor, before you start brushing your carpet, sprinkle the mixture over it, well in the corners, as it gathers up all dust.

If you pour boiling water on used tea leaves and leave for an hour in a bottle, the liquid can be used to clean mirrors, windows, glasses, varnished doors, furniture, linoleum and muddy black suede shoes, also black and navy blue skirts.

TEA POTS, METAL, To prevent mustiness in:

Dry inside of plated or silver teapots with a cloth, then put a lump of sugar inside. It will soak up any remaining moisture and prevent the pot from becoming musty.

TINS, KITCHEN, To clean:

Mix together equal proportions of pumice powder, whitening and soap powder. Wash the tins in boiling water first, well dry and then apply the mixture. Rinse and dry.

TINWARE, To prevent rusting:

Rub tinware with fresh lard and thoroughly heat in the oven before use.

TOBACCO, MILDEWED, To freshen:

If tobacco is slightly mildewed, lay it on gauze over boiling water and steam it. When dry it will be as good as ever.

TORTOISE-SHELL, To mend:

Bind the two parts together with a wet cloth, tape or linen. Heat a pair of tongs and press the joint with these until they unite.

UMBRELLA, MUD-STAINED, To clean:

Rub with a rag dipped in methylated spirits and the stains will disappear.

UMBRELLA, SILK, To renovate:

Put a tablespoonful of sugar into a basin and pour over it ½ pint boiling water. When the sugar has dissolved, open the umbrella and, starting from the ferrule, wash down the gores, drawing the sponge in a straight line to the edge. Hang the umbrella, still open, in the open air to dry.

UMBRELLA COVERS, BLACK, To mend:

Open the umbrella, dust and brush it well, then wipe all over with soft flannel dipped in petrol. When quite dry take a piece of black court plaster, a little bigger than the hole, attach it to the inner surface of the covering and the damage or rent will not be noticed.

UMBRELLA COVERS, To renew:

When black umbrellas look green, sponge them with cold tea. Take a cup of good strong tea, add about ten drops of liquid ammonia, and then use, rubbing the tea and ammonia in well. Dry in the shade where there is a good strong wind.

VACUUM FLASKS, To clean:

After use, wash out the flask with cold soapy water, rinse well and allow to drain. Avoid putting milk with tea or coffee that has to be kept in a vacuum flask. Never rinse the flask out in boiling water just before putting in cold drinks— always with cold water. If a hot drink is to be put in the flask, wash out in hot water.

VARNISHED PAINT, To clean:

When sufficient tea leaves have been laid aside, they should be placed in a tin basin full of water and soaked for ½ hour. The tea, when stirred, should be used instead of soap and water to clean the varnished surface.

VEGETABLE MATTER, To destroy when decayed:

Dissolve 1 lb. chlorate of lime in 2 quarts of water and apply. For an absorbent mixture, add 2 parts of powdered charcoal to one part of plaster of Paris, and sprinkle around freely.

VELVETEEN, To wash :

Add a little ammonia to a nice soapy lather. Plunge the velveteen garment into it, taking care the water is not too hot. Wash as quickly as possible without rubbing any soap on the material. Rinse well and thoroughly in two lots of warm water with a little ammonia added to each water. Hang at once in the open air to drip. Do not on any account squeeze or wring velvet on velveteen.

VINEGAR, Uses of :

A few drops of vinegar in a tumblerful of water is an excellent *mouth wash*. If you have a bad *headache* a handkerchief dipped in vinegar and placed on the forehead often cures the pain. Vinegar in *washing up water* removes the grease, brightens china and is a disinfectant. Vinegar and salt mixed together will take away *stains* on china, cleanse flower vases, water bottles and tumblers. Vinegar and linseed oil in equal parts make an excellent *furniture polish*. Vinegar *brightens glass*, brass and copper articles. Vinegar rubbed over *raw meat* makes it tender. Hot vinegar takes away *paint stains*, Vinegar and water in equal parts, clean *gilt frames*. Vinegar, diluted, applied to furniture before polishing, ensures a brilliant *polish*. Vinegar makes a new *gas mantle* last much longer—soak the mantle for 5 minutes in the vinegar, dry and burn off.

WALLS, To prevent dampness in :

Dry the walls thoroughly then varnish with the following : Mix 1 pint linseed oil with $1\frac{1}{2}$ oz. ground litharge and 2 oz. finely powdered resin. Apply this in successive coats, which, after the fifth, will form a hard and compact varnish that will exclude moisture.

WALLS, KITCHEN, To clean :

Add a little paraffin to a pail of warm soap suds, then wash the walls down. Do not use *hot* water as it will leave a mottled appearance.

WALLS, PAINTED, To clean :

Add 1 tablespoonful of bicarbonate of soda to 1 quart of warm water. Dip a soft cloth in liquid, wash down the walls, rinse with a cloth dipped in clean water and wipe dry.

WALLPAPER, VARNISHED, To clean:

Dust your walls well, then wipe over with paraffin and water, allowing 1 gill to a bucketful of hot water. Apply with a soft cloth when cold, and dry with a leather. Do not make the cloth too wet or you will have streams running down the walls.

WASHING POWDER, Home-made:

Take ¼ lb. powdered soap, 1 lb. soda crystals (dried in the oven), ¼ lb. powdered sal ammoniac. Mix well together.

WINDOWS, To clean:

Make a thin paste with a tablespoonful of whitening, a squeeze of laundry blue and methylated spirit. Apply with a rag and when dry polish off with a soft cloth.

WINDOWS, PAINTED, To clean:

Dip a piece of old flannel or woollen material into some paraffin oil and rub the windows lightly with this to remove the dirt. Afterwards polish with a dry soft duster. The oily pieces of flannel are most useful afterwards for lighting fires quickly.

WINDOWS, STEAMY, in cold weather:

Sometimes in cold weather windows are apt to steam when the rooms become hot. This can be obviated by applying a glycerine rag after polishing.

WINGS, WHITE, To clean:

Make a paste of French chalk and naphtha of the consistency of cream. Free the wings from dust and wipe them with a rag dipped in spirits of wine. Spread the cream over the wings and allow it to remain for 12 hours. Then brush off.

WOODWORK, To clean:

A few drops of turpentine in some warm suds is found to be an excellent thing for cleaning woodwork.

WOOLLENS, Shrinking of:

They can be restored to their original size and fluffiness by finishing off in clean soap suds instead of clear water. Never rub woollens. Squeeze them with the hands.

HINTS ON FIRST-AID, HEALTH AND BEAUTY

ANKLES, WEAK :

Salt, a teaspoonful to a pint of warm water, rubbed into weak ankles strengthens them.

ASTHMA, To relieve :

Soak some blotting paper in a strong solution of salt-petre, and then dry it. Take a piece about the size of your hand, set light to it and lay upon a plate beside the patient's bed.

BILIOUS ATTACK, To cure :

Take the juice of 1 lemon, ½ teaspoonful of carbonate of soda, and 2 or 3 tablespoonfuls of boiling water.

BLISTERS ON THE LIPS, Cure for :

Brush over with a little flexible collodion, and they will soon heal up. Tell your chemist when ordering the collodion what you need it for. The wrong kind would be most harmful.

BRUISES, To treat :

Take a little dry starch of arrowroot. Moisten it with cold water and lay it on the bruise. This should be done at once to prevent the action of the air on the skin.

BURN, SEVERE, To treat :

Give the patient a warm bath to which a handful of washing soda, or bath salts, has been added to render it alkaline. This is very comforting, and the clothes can be cut off under the water. Then put on any available oil, *except* camphorated, on strips of lint soaked in the oil. When the burn is dressed the strips of lint can be removed one at a time, so that the whole area of the burn is not exposed at once.

BURNS, Remedies for :

1. Put 1 pint linseed oil, ½ pint lime water and the yolks of 2 eggs in a bottle and shake well. Soak cotton wool with the preparation and apply. Bind on with a bandage.

2. Take some freshly gathered lavender buds and crush them well. Mix 1 lb. of pulp with 1½ lb. of unsalted lard. Boil slowly for a few minutes, stirring well. Pour into small pots and tie down. If applied at once when the burn occurs, no pain will be felt.

3. Use *carbonate of soda*, either in powder or made into a paste, applied to the raw surface, and then covered by compresses to exclude the air.

4. *Tincture of cantharis*, made in proportion of 1 drachm to a pint of hot water, is also an excellent application. It may be applied by simply putting wet cloths or compresses on the burnt surface and excluding the air. If the burn be a deep one, these compresses can be worn for a couple of days, kept saturated and then *calendula* (garden marigold) *ointment* may be applied on linen cloths. This can be continued until the parts are healed.

5. *The white of an egg* is very good for slight burns, in an emergency.

6. For small burns *cool water* is better in every way than these, and indeed for any but the most extensive burns it is one of the best remedies. An arm or a leg can be immersed in it and left there for a long while with great advantage.

7. Burns with alkalies, such as soap lye, should be treated with *vinegar* followed by applications of oil.

CHILBLAINS, To cure :

Bathe the affected part in water in which celery has been boiled, or rub the chilblain with plain lemon water.

COD LIVER OIL EMULSION, To make :

Take 10 oz. cod liver oil, 6 oz. glycerine, 1½ gills of lime water and a small tin of condensed milk. Stir over a pan, or pot of hot water, till melted. When melted add 2 more tablespoonfuls of condensed milk. Stir all well again, then pour into bottles.

COLD, To prevent :

A hot bath in which you have dissolved a handful of common salt relieves fatigue and often helps to break up or prevent a cold.

CORNS, To cure :

Soak some bread in vinegar for 2 days and put a piece as a cold poultice on the corn overnight, binding it on with a strip of rag. Every 3 days soak the feet in hot water and peel off a layer of the corn. Continue the treatment until the corn has entirely disappeared.

COUGH, Cure for :

Half a pound of common black treacle, ½ pint boiling water, 1d. laudanum, 1d. paregoric, 1d. essence of peppermint, 1d. essence of aniseed. Pour boiling water on the treacle and when nearly cold add the other liquids.

Dose.—For adults, 1 tablespoonful 3 or 4 times daily.
For children, 1 teaspoonful 3 or 4 times daily

COUGHS, WINTER, Remedy for :

Mix equal parts lemon juice, honey and cod liver oil together, and take a tablespoonful of the mixture whenever the cough is troublesome. It is better to make a small quantity at a time. Give a child a teaspoonful.

CROUP, Cure for :

Procure a piece of square camphor, and with a stone or hammer pound it well. Stir it into some melted lard. When quite set it is ready for use. Rub the throat and chest of the child at bedtime with the mixture. This treatment brings great relief to the child and by morning the croupy cough should have subsided.

CUTS, How to heal :

Bathe cuts with warm water and boracic and paint them with medicinal paraffin, using a clean paint brush. This treatment cleans the cuts and draws the edges together.

CUTS, To prevent becoming septic :

Drop iodine on a clean cut or scratch. Let it soak into the cut ; there will be no risk of the wound becoming poisoned if this is done *at once*.

DISINFECTANT, SIMPLE :

The following disinfectant is a refreshing one for a sick room, or any room that has an unpleasant odour pervading.

Put some freshly ground coffee into a saucer and in the centre place a small piece of camphor. Light it with a match. As it burns allow sufficient coffee to consume with it.

Powdered charcoal is another good disinfectant. So is common copperas, called sulphate of iron, which in its crude shape is quite cheap. It should be dissolved in water in the proportion of 1 lb. of copperas to 2 gallons of water, and thrown over evil-smelling places. It is one of the simplest and most convenient deodorisers and is very useful for flushing out sinks.

EARACHE, Cure for :

Make a bag of fine, very soft woollen material or flannel, large enough to cover the affected part. Stitch closely all round the bag leaving one side open. Put into the bag well-dried rock salt, enough to fill the bag three parts full, and stitch up. Or, better still, put the salt into a fine cotton bag and put that bag into the flannel one. Put the bag on a clean tart tin and into a good hot oven, until the salt has got very hot right through. Then place a piece of soft material on the bag and lay it on the affected spot. It is a splendid cure for earache.

EYES, RED AND INFLAMED, Cure for :

Bathe them night and morning in ice-cold water. Open the eyes in the water or gently throw the water up to the eyes. Also bathe them two or three times a day with a lotion of boracic powder mixed in lukewarm water to which add a few drops of rose water. If you find the lotion does not help, lie down for one hour in a dark room every afternoon after lunch and apply a light soft rag dipped in the rose water and boracic lotion to the eyes. Leave the rag on till all the moisture is evaporated. This treatment draws out inflammation and greatly relieves tired eyes.

FEET, TIRED, Remedy for :

Mix lemon juice and spirits of wine in equal quantities, and rub the mixture well into the skin night and morning.

FOMENTATION, BORACIC, To apply :

Cut boracic lint to the size required. Wrap it in an old clean handkerchief, fold lengthways, and place over a basin.

Pour boiling water through it. Wring out the handkerchief and unfold. Place the hot lint quickly over the wound. Cover with cotton wool and bandage.

FRECKLES, To remove :

Apply at night a mixture of equal parts of strained lemon juice, glycerine, olive oil and curdled milk.

GNAT AND MIDGE BITES, To prevent :

Sprinkle your stockings with violet powder mixed with a small amount of white pepper. A sprinkling of oil of lavender or oil of geranium is also an excellent cure.

HANDS, CHAPPED, Remedy for :

When your hands get rough and red, buy equal parts of soap liniment and glycerine, put them in a medicine bottle and fill up with water. Rub this on the hands and they will become soft and smooth in a short time.

HICCOUGHS, To cure :

Press the thumb of the right hand in the palm of the left, and hold the breath. If still bad, try a pinch of salt, or swallow one teaspoonful of vinegar.

LUMBAGO, Cure for :

Take a very soft piece of flannel, and sprinkle it with turpentine. Place on the part affected and lie on your back for $\frac{1}{2}$ hour. Do not leave the turpentine on too long or it may cause a blister.

A good medicinal cure for lumbago is 16 drops of oil of juniper in $\frac{1}{2}$ a wineglassful of gin, every 6 hours.

MOSQUITO BITES, Remedy for :

Dab the bite with solution of carbolic 1-20, to which a little eau de Cologne has been added. The solution can be made up quite cheaply by any chemist, and 4 to 5 oz. will last the whole summer, even if used by many people. Never go to Africa, or India, without a bottle of this mixture.

NAILS, BRITTLE :

Rub the nails well with cuticle cream every morning and evening, it serves to keep them in good condition. When manicuring, cut the nails into shape, file round and finish up by applying a good polishing paste or powder. Flannel polishes as well as any suede. To acquire the long French or Chinese appearance to nails, file the nails well away from the corners, bring them to a point. To keep them narrow and pointed squeeze them between your fingers night and morning, or buy a Chinese finger-nail cramp.

To keep long nails from splitting off and cracking, use lemon juice freely, three times a day, and brush them over at night with strong alum water.

The care of the *toe nails* is very much the same as of finger nails, some people treat them exactly in the same way. Never let the cuticle on your toe nails grow long or hard. If you cannot have a bath every day, wash your feet every night before going to rest, and if very tired and your feet ache underneath, add a good large lump of washing soda to water as hot as you can stand. The soda soon reduces inflammation of the foot and softens the cuticle and corns, if any. Then when you have dried your feet well, rub boracic powder well between each toe and on the joints.

NAILS, To clean:

Always keep on your washstand half a lemon, dig your nails into it before washing your hands. Should it harden the tips, rub in, after you have washed the lemon off, a simple softening lotion. 2 oz. oppodeldoc, 1 oz. glycerine, 2 drops peroxide, 4 oz. boiled lukewarm water. If your nails still remain stained, get some hot water and wash them well with pure white castile soap. The soap is a wonderful softener. Then take an orange stick and a small piece of cotton wool dipped in peroxide of hydrogen, and apply under the nails. By washing the hands in very hot water and soft soap you will find it much easier to push back the cuticle, and also to polish. A little oil of olives rubbed on the skin at the base of the nails at night keeps the cuticle soft and helps to prevent the formation of hang nails.

NEURALGIA, Cure for:

Heat witch hazel, dip a piece of wool in it, then wring out and hold to the place where the pain is. Repeat till the pain goes.

NURSING HINTS:

1. *To Freshen Air in a Sick Room.*—Place a teaspoonful of eau de Cologne in a coal shovel and set fire to it. Move the burning spirit about the room and a fragrant and refreshing scent will remain.

2. *Use for an old cracked Hot Water Bottle.*—Fill the bottle with salt and heat in a warm oven. Salt retains the heat for a long time, and by filling the bottle in this way it is very useful in case of illness.

3. *To make really good Barley Water.*—One teaspoonful of pearl barley and 1 quart cold water, bring to the boil and let it stand for 5 minutes, then strain. Add the juice of 2 lemons, and sugar to taste.

4. *To distinguish Poison Bottles.*—When medicines have all to be kept in one place, and on one shelf. Round the neck of bottle labelled " Poison " tie a wee toy bell ; the ringing of the bell will often prevent an accident.

5. *When Hot Flannels are constantly required.*—Put a saucepan with a steamer on the stove, keep the water in the saucepan boiling and lay the flannels in the steamer, then they can be changed easily and as often as necessary.

6. *A Bed Prop for a Sick Person.*—Take a square piece of strong material something like bed ticking. Make four holes, one at each corner, and put a thick cord through each hole. Then tie to each knob on the bed rail and either side of the bed through the spring or laths.

7. *If you have no Linseed Meal available for a Poultice.*—A most excellent one can be made by boiling a few good potatoes in their skins. When cooked, put them in a bag made of flannel, fasten the ends and roll them over with the rolling pin.

8. *To Make a Linseed Poultice.*—Put the linseed into a basin and pour over enough boiling water to make it into a stiff paste. Always mix with a warm spoon or knife. Spread the linseed on one half of a piece of muslin, and cover over with the other half of the muslin. Apply as hot as possible.

9. *To Keep the Weight of Bedclothes off an Injured Limb.*—Cut a child's wooden hoop in half, unite it in a cross with string or wire, and cover with strips of old soft rag. This makes a light and cheap cradle.

10. *In Case of Serious Illness.*—A bed of garden mould or

sand laid on the hearth in front of a fire will prevent the noise of falling coal cinders disturbing the patient.

11. *Advice in the Taking of Medicine.*—In the absence of specific instructions it is generally better to administer a dose of liquid medicine in, say one-fourth of a glassful of water. By diluting the dose it is rendered less irritating to the stomach, and if the medicine is bitter the taste is less noticeable.

NURSING BABY, Hints on :

1. *Ointment for Quite Young Babies when the parts become inflamed.*—Put some zinc ointment into a small pot or an egg cup, add sufficient castor oil to make it about the consistency of cream.

2. *To Prevent Scurf from Forming on Babies' Heads.*— Before bathing baby rub vaseline on his head.

3. *Prevent Baby Kicking off the Bedclothes at Night.*— Sew pieces of tape on the quilt and tie it to the sides of the cot underneath the bedding or mattress. Make baby's night-dress long enough to run a drawstring at the bottom.

4. *When Babies are Cutting their Teeth.*—At this time they often get colds in the head. To prevent the colds, rub the root and bridge of the nose with a little camphorated oil. Get your chemist to make up this paint: Menthol, 3 grains ; eucalyptus oil, 10 drops ; paroleine, 2 drachms. Gently apply this just inside the nostrils with a small camel hair brush every 2 hours. First put a little cold cream on the lip to prevent redness. This soon relieves " streaming of the nose and eyes." An occasional dose of fluid magnesia is helpful.

5. *When Baby is Run Down.*—Buy 4 oz. of the best fresh (rump) steak, cover with cold boiled water. Add ¼ teaspoonful salt, and leave it to draw for ½ hour. Strain liquor off and give a teaspoonful at a time, every 6 hours. For an older child give a wineglassful.

6. *When Baby is Weaned.*—Instead of giving him milk out of an ordinary teacup, try using a small feeding cup known in the pottery trade as a " pap cup." This will save endless wet feeders and waste of milk, and in a month or two baby will be able to drink out of a cup without disaster.

7. *Baby's Curly Hair.*—After baby's bath, warm a Turkish towel and gently rub all over the head, rubbing the hair upwards. When it is quite dry, damp all over with rose water

and with the tips of the fingers brush upwards. You will soon see tiny curls forming.

RHEUMATISM, A cure for :

Take 4 pennyworth of lump camphor and 3 pennyworth of methylated spirit. Break the camphor into small pieces and put it into a bottle. Pour on the methylated spirit and shake until dissolved. Rub the affected parts very well.

SCALDS, A cure for :

When you have had a bad scald, cover the scalded part immediately with white vaseline, and wrap in cotton wool to exclude the air. Few blisters will form and very little mark is left.

THROAT, INFLAMED :

Take drops of nitre on a lump of sugar, and for ulcerated throat, drops of brandy on lump sugar every 3 or 4 hours.

TOOTH, EXTRACTED, To remove pain after :

Apply olive oil to the outside of the face, rubbing it in well but very gently. When in bed, lie on something *soft and woolly.*

TOOTHACHE, Cure for :

Get your chemist to mix equal parts iodine and aconite. With a small brush paint the gums and put some in the tooth. *Do not swallow the mixture.*

TOOTH POWDER for children :

Mix together 4 oz. bicarbonate of soda and 3 oz. orris root. This prevents the teeth from decaying and preserves them. It also keeps them a good colour at a very small cost.

VARICOSE VEINS, To relieve :

Any pressure on the veins, such as is caused by garters, must be removed, and prolonged standing or walking should be avoided. If there is constipation or the liver is out of order, these matters should receive attention. A light, porous, elastic bandage is usually applied like a puttee before getting up in the morning, and only removed last thing at night.

VOMITING, In children :

After a child begins to walk, vomiting should be regarded seriously, as it may be the beginning of some illness, though it may also be due to indigestion, cold, fear or excitement. Give nothing but fluids until the child asks for food, and never press food upon him when unwell. If there is any rise in temperature, keep him in bed.

WARTS, Cure for :

Boil some potatoes, and with the water in which they are boiled, bathe the warts. At the end of a week they will have nearly, if not quite, gone. This remedy I have proved successful when all others had failed.

WASP STINGS, Cure for :

A piece of cut onion rubbed on a wasp sting will reduce the pain and swelling. To rub the sting with a " blue " bag slightly damp, or sweet oil, is also very excellent.

WHITLOW, To cure :

Cut a lemon in half, put your finger in the lemon. Then bandage both together with a soft bandage. Do not keep the lemon on the finger longer than 10 to 12 hours. At the end of that time take the piece of lemon off and put another piece on for 10 to 12 hours longer. This will remove all pain and at the end of 24 hours you will see a hole in your finger, the lemon having drawn the whitlow out.

WHOOPING COUGH, Remedy for :

Put one cupful of saltpetre in a saucepan with half a cupful of water. Let it stand on the side of the stove until the saltpetre is melted, then take some thick white blotting paper and cut it into four-inch squares and soak them in the saltpetre. Dry them in the sun, and burn one square in the bedroom at night on a tin or enamel or china plate. This is also a very good cure for ordinary colds.

GENERAL INDEX